CHRISTIAN HISTORY

have we had the array of resources we have today—

all designed to help us study and understand the Bible.

Take advantage of them!

When you get serious about daily Bible study,

you'll find that the Word of God will become

a lamp for your feet,

a light for your path,

and a map for your soul.

DR. DAVID JEREMIAH

I grew up with parents who centered our family's life around the Bible. My father was a pastor, a teacher of the Word. When he went to heaven, I was given all his sermon notes and Bibles. What an inheritance! My mother lived out God's Word in her parenting and hospitality, and in so many other ways. As a part of my legacy, I understood that the Bible was the key to a successful life.

Today, God's Word is still a focused priority of my life. And after preaching and teaching the Bible for more than 40 years, there's still so much that I want to study in greater detail. When I graduated from seminary, somebody told me, "David, you're going to fish out of this pond for the rest of your life." And they were right. After all this time, the Word is still teaching me about priorities and ministry, marriage and integrity, forgiveness and mercy, and the beauty of life with Christ.

Each week I spend hours preparing to teach the Word, and I am constantly discovering new insights that guide my life. The Bible is such a timeless book that, no matter your place or time in history, it always speaks to the important issues of life.

This is the only God-inspired book ever written; it is definitive and authoritative, and I have great confidence that as long as I am faithful to the text—honoring it as God's very Word—the result will be life transformation.

Despite these convictions, I struggled in my spirit about whether I should develop *The Jeremiah Study Bible*. I wasn't sure that my own study notes on God's Word were worthy of such an effort. Yet after a lifetime of teaching and preaching, I concluded that perhaps the insights God has given me, and the applications that have come to my heart, could be helpful to others as they live out their Christian faith each day.

The Bible has the greatest potential of all of life's influences to permanently transform lives. I am called to that work.

For those who use this study Bible,
my prayer is that you will
fall in love with Scripture in such a way
that His Word will be written on your heart.

This is a Bible for those I've come to love as a teacher—those who sit in the church I pastor and in churches around the world. I hope that it will also help those who are just now seeking God. I pray that because I have endeavored to make *The Jeremiah Study Bible* teachable and personal, it will find its place in your heart, encouraging you and growing you in your faith.

Welcome to *The Jeremiah Study Bible*,

Dr. David Jeremiah

THE PURPOSE OF
THE JEREMIAH STUDY BIBLE

There are a number of excellent Bible study resources available, each with its own purpose and approach. Let me cast a vision about what *The Jeremiah Study Bible* is designed to accomplish. My intent was not to create a technical resource for scholars or to develop a devotional Bible.

What you have in your hands has an ambitious yet simple threefold purpose: I want people to understand what the Bible says, what it means, and what it means specifically for them. These three things are central in my thinking when I prepare to teach, and they serve as the framework for the structure of this study Bible.

What It Says

First, I want to help people understand what the Bible says—and particularly what it says in its original context. For instance, if the text was written as a letter, how would the original recipients have understood its form and content? If it is history, where does the text reflect the events of that era?

I want to be true to Scripture. Our first priority should always be to read the Bible on its own terms, seeking to understand what the original authors were communicating to their audience, in their setting.

Sometimes people get fanciful with their interpretation of the Bible, and when they are finished, their interpretation has nothing to do with the actual content on the page. It is my desire to declare God's Word as it was originally meant to be understood.

What It Means

Second, it's important to talk about what Scripture means. How do I interpret what I am reading? Obviously, there is room for some differing opinions, but overall, the Bible is a self-interpreting book. We interpret one passage by other relevant passages, and each verse exists in a context that helps us understand what the verse really means.

What It Means for You

Third, I seek to explore what it means for you and me. When it comes to Bible study, information without application is stagnation. James compared the Bible to a mirror (James 1:22). As we gaze into the Word of God, we see ourselves reflected in it. We see our blemishes and stains. We see how we need to beautify our lives in God's sight. Perhaps we need to apply the salve of the Spirit, the highlighting graces of faith, or the corrective lines of obedience. Some people walk away from God's mirror without making the needed changes. "But," said James, "whoever looks intently into the perfect law that gives freedom, and continues in it—not forgetting what they have heard, but doing it—they will be blessed in what they do" (James 1:25).

You'll see that many of the notes and special features of this study Bible offer the vital component of practical application. Application is at the heart of my approach to ministry and to the Word, and it is what helps seal the Word in people's lives by the power of the Holy Spirit.

The purpose of *The Jeremiah Study Bible* can be boiled down to the three-step process I advocate for the study of God's Word:

> *Observation*—seeing what it says;
> *Interpretation*—understanding what it means; and
> *Application*—embracing what it means for me.

As you read the pages of this Bible, pray that God, through the Holy Spirit, will help you learn what His Word says, what it means, and what it means for you. It will change your life!

THE PURPOSE

The best illustration of how and why to study the Word of God is found in the following passage from the Book of Nehemiah: "[The priest] Ezra opened the book. All the people could see him . . . and as he opened it, the people all stood up. Ezra praised the LORD, the great God; and all the people lifted their hands and responded, 'Amen! Amen!' Then they bowed down and worshiped the LORD with their faces to the ground" (Neh. 8:5, 6).

Then Ezra and the other priests "read from the Book of the Law of God, making it clear and giving the meaning so that the people understood what was being read" (Neh. 8:8).

The Holy Spirit uses words of application to bring Bible study home to the heart.

In other words, Ezra and his fellow priests read the Word, they explained what it meant, and finally, they helped the people apply it to their lives.

It is important that people really understand the Word of God. This is first and foremost. And this is why we've released it in two major translations, the New King James Version and the New International Version. When I graduated from seminary, I was intent on making sure everybody understood the worthwhile investment I had made. But as I went along in the ministry, I realized that this did not matter to anyone. People simply wanted to hear and understand God's Word; they weren't interested in whether I could wow them with my understanding of Greek and Hebrew.

A diligent study of the Word

will bring us to a place of worship

in our hearts.

A diligent study of the Word will bring us to a place of worship in our hearts. The impact of the gospel, combined with the sheer grace of God, will cause us to bow before Him and celebrate His goodness. It will also compel us to confess how far we are from His standard.

You see, the Bible is grounded in real life, even as it opens up the far reaches of eternity to earth-weary travelers. It is filled with emotion and heartfelt experiences that we all can relate to. And as we study to understand it, occasionally it will drive us to our knees in repentance, or move us to fall on our faces before God in gratitude or adoration, penitence or grief.

In Nehemiah 8, when the people responded positively to the hearing of the Word, Ezra the priest told them: "Go and enjoy choice food and sweet drinks, and send some to those who have nothing prepared. This day is holy to our Lord. Do not grieve, for the joy of the LORD is your strength" (Neh. 8:10). Verse 12 concludes: "Then all the people went away to . . . celebrate with great joy, because they now understood the words that had been made known to them."

The two elements that are present at every revival are the study of God's Word and the mobilization of God's people. The Israelites went forth after hearing the words of Scripture, and they sought fellowship and started to minister—all because its truths had penetrated their hearts. When the people embraced the Word of God, they took action. Nehemiah 8 and 9 report that they reinstituted their feasts and did all the necessary work—and there was revival in the land.

It is a great thing when God's Word is set free in a person's life. No one ever stays the same.

PASSION

THE UNIQUE FEATURES OF
THE JEREMIAH STUDY BIBLE

The Jeremiah Study Bible is designed with your spiritual growth in mind, whether it is used purely for personal reading, for small-group study, for preparation to teach, or even to preach the Word of God. It contains what I intend as a rich treasure trove of resources to aid your own study.

BOOK INTRODUCTIONS

For each of the 66 books of the Bible, I have developed a brief yet highly informative introduction that summarizes the book's core message along with the historical and spiritual background out of which it was born. These introductions provide a wonderful starting point for discerning the context and content of the books. In addition, by going to www.JeremiahStudyBible.com, you can access my video introduction for each Bible book.

GALATIANS

BOOK INTRODUCTION

It would be difficult to imagine anyone ever making a change in life as dramatic, complete, and permanent as that of Saul of Tarsus.

As an ambitious, driven young Pharisee, Saul was rapidly gaining prestige within Judaism. The synagogue leaders in his hometown of Tarsus must have seen something in the youth and convinced his parents that he should be schooled in Jerusalem. There, Saul studied under Gamaliel, the most highly regarded rabbi of that era (Acts 5:34; 22:3), where, in his own words, he "was advancing in Judaism beyond many of my own age" (1:14).

Paul had more reason to be confident in his standing as a Jew than anyone in his circle. He was born a Jew (not a convert) who was circumcised according to the law on the eighth day. He was of the tribe of Benjamin, on whose territorial border sat the City of God, Jerusalem. He was a "Hebrew of Hebrews"—the best Jew of all Jews. Regarding obedience to the law, he was a Pharisee of the strictest order who could claim that he had obeyed every jot and tittle of the moral and ceremonial law . . . and no one would argue with him for saying so (Phil. 3:4–6).

When he was about 40, Saul decided he would not only teach his rigid brand of Judaism but would persecute and even kill people who believed in a heretical rabbi from Nazareth—Jesus (Acts 22:1–1; 26:1–3). With what he regarded as righteous fury, Saul tried to destroy this troubling new sect like a firefighter attacking small blazes in a forest. But as Saul's zeal reached its zenith, his self-made religious world came crashing down: he met the true and living Jesus—and absolutely nothing would ever be the same for him again.

Why is it important to consider the apostle Paul's pre-Christian commitment before reading the Book of Galatians? Because in this letter to the believers in Galatia, we find his same zealous intensity *only in reverse.* After his conversion, Paul was just as committed to the beauty and purity of Christianity as he had been to the strict legalism of his form of Judaism. Now he would battle heart and soul against any dilution or compromise in the gospel of Jesus Christ.

There were many times he had to defend the gospel. During the early expansion of Christianity, the first Christians were almost all Jews. Consequently, many tended to think that Christianity simply "added Jesus" to Judaism while retaining all the law's requirements. Although Paul made it clear that Jewish heritage might still be

To view Dr. Jeremiah's video introduction to Galatians, go to www.JeremiahStudyBible.com/ Galatians/Intro

GALATIANS

52

valued, he was zealous to declare that righteousness is obtained through faith in Jesus Christ, not self-effort.

Paul knew firsthand how difficult this transition could be—how radical it was to replace works with faith in Jesus, to rely on grace instead of merit. Scripture records that after his first missionary journey, the issue of Jewish influences on Gentile converts led to the first church conference in Jerusalem, which sorted out exactly what was and was not required as the spread of the faith produced burgeoning new Gentile congregations (Acts 15).

Possibly between his missionary trip to Galatia and the Jerusalem conference (c. AD 48), Paul wrote this letter, confronting this thorny problem in some of the churches he had founded with Barnabas on their first missionary journey. How fitting that God called the Jew of the Jews to draw a line in the sand, step over it, and refuse to allow any to follow except those willing to live by faith in Christ alone.

What It Says | From "Religion" to Relationship

In the message of Galatians, we see that the problem of legalism, which plagues so many modern believers, is as old as the first-century church. This epistle gives a realistic picture of the challenges of transitioning from a religion based on rules to one based on a relationship; from a life based on merit to one birthed by grace; from life empowered by human flesh to one experienced in the power of the Holy Spirit. Paul's letter to the Galatians has three parts, in which Paul addresses related sets of issues. First, he validates his own authority and shows that the apostles in Jerusalem proved his gospel. This was necessary because the Judaizers were saying that Paul had diluted the gospel by removing the religious requirements of Judaism in order to attract Gentile converts (1—2).

Second, because the heresy was coming from Jewish influencers, Paul explains why—in appealing to the experience of Abraham, the father of the Jews—the OT teaches the doctrine of justification by faith apart from the works of the law (3—4). Finally, Paul follows up by discussing the implications of sound doctrine for everyday life. He describes where freedom can be found (in Christ alone); how life can be lived in the power of the Spirit; and why circumcision of the flesh means nothing compared to being a new creation in Christ (5—6).

It Means | Justified by Faith

... examples in Galatians are drawn from the life and experience of Paul himself, as he recounts vignettes and hard-won truths from his early Christian life.

Paul: To defend the gospel he preached to the Galatians, Paul recounts his own calling by God, his confirmation by the apostles in Jerusalem, and an uncomfortable confrontation with the renowned apostle Peter over the purity of the faith (1—2).

The Law: Paul makes the point that trying to follow the law of Moses could never be a source of salvation for anyone, because no one has kept the law fully (3:10).

Abraham: Although the concept of faith was not new to Judaism, Paul reminds the Galatians that Abraham, the father of the Jews, was himself justified (declared righteous) before God by faith, not by works. Paul builds his case for justification by faith by appealing to what the Judaizers held most sacred: the OT and its law (... 9).

Flesh versus Spirit: Human flesh can produce only imperfect deeds by its own efforts (5:19–21), but men and women who have God's own indwelling Spirit can produce beautiful, fragrant fruit from the Life that flows through them (5:22, 23).

STUDY NOTES

At the bottom of each page of Bible text, you will find insightful study notes—more than 8,000 in all. Their purpose is not to simply paraphrase what you've already read in the passage but to enhance and deepen your understanding. My intent with these notes is to help you connect with the three elements of the study process: what it says, what it means, and what it means for you.

CROSS-REFERENCE SYSTEM

Many Bibles have elaborate center-column or in-text cross-reference systems. To make this one easier to use and read, *The Jeremiah Study Bible* has an extensive cross-reference system embedded in the study notes at the bottom of each page.

ONLINE RESOURCES

I pray that one of the most helpful resources will be the online material at www.JeremiahStudyBible.com. It can be accessed directly on your computer, tablet, or smartphone.

These online resources offer video introductions to every Bible book along with video clips, articles, and other materials that are not included in the study Bible. Because I don't intend to stop teaching anytime soon, our team will continue to enrich this website with new and helpful study aids.

THE FEATURES

SIDEBARS

Carefully positioned within the text throughout *The Jeremiah Study Bible* are hundreds of sidebars that offer additional insight and application, expanding far beyond the study notes. These sidebars are categorized under six general headings:

Picture This | The Houses of Israel • 4:11, 12

The references here to Rachel and Leah, the two who "built up the family of Israel" (see Gen. 35:23–26), and to the family "of Perez, whom

PICTURE THIS | Calls attention to dozens of enlightening and teachable word pictures and word studies.

Historically Speaking | James and Paul • 2:21–24

This passage led Martin Luther to question the value of the entire letter of James and call it "a right strawy epistle" without evangelical character. Today some believe the teaching of Paul contradicts the teaching of James, but this

HISTORICALLY SPEAKING | Highlights many interesting historical characters, customs, and places that make Scripture come alive.

 fyi | How to Love One Another • 3:11, 23

Christians are to love:

1. *Unconditionally.* God calls His sons and daughters to love people as they are and to pray that He will do a work in their lives

FYI | Adds surprising insights, color, and practical application to your exploration of the Bible.

Tough Questions | What were Esther's options? • 4:13-16

Mordecai candidly reminded Esther that she faced three options:

1. She might perish. According to the law that had just been passed, once it was

TOUGH QUESTIONS | Tackles difficult personal and doctrinal questions with wisdom and fresh perspective.

For Reflection | Overcoming Worry • 6:25–34

Three times in this text, Jesus says, "Do not worry" (6:25, 31, 34). Jesus gives five reasons why we should not worry:

1. *Worry is inconsistent* (6:25). If we can

FOR REFLECTION | Asks you to pause and reflect on biblical truths and thought-provoking expressions that will pique your interest and touch your heart.

Teaching Points | Follow the Compass of Truth • 4:1

Paul warns us that false teachers will come. How do we know when teaching departs from the faith of the Bible? Use these truths as a

TEACHING POINTS | Shares numerous practical, teachable moments from my 40 years as a Bible teacher.

The doctrine of the virgin birth of Christ teaches that Jesus was divinely conceived in the virgin Mary's womb by the Holy Spirit, thus bringing together His two natures: deity and humanity.

The virgin birth of Jesus is foretold in the OT. The prophet Isaiah writes, "Therefore the Lord himself will give you a sign: The virgin will conceive and give birth to a son, and will call him Immanuel" (Isa. 7:14). The Hebrew word for *virgin* here is *almah*, which means a woman who is pure and virtuous, who has not been intimate with a man. The word appears only seven times in the Hebrew Scriptures, and in every appearance it refers to a chaste, unmarried woman, not just a "girl," as some critics suggest. In the Greek, the word *parthenos* means exactly the same thing: a woman who has not known a man—a virgin.

ESSENTIALS OF THE CHRISTIAN FAITH ARTICLES

Placed strategically throughout *The Jeremiah Study Bible* are more than 60 full-page articles that bear unique importance to a Christian's understanding of faith. I've chosen subjects that demand more treatment than a note or sidebar could contain on topics that are critical to the spiritual vitality of the reader.

TEACHER'S TOPICAL INDEX

There's an old adage that says, "If you want to learn the Scriptures, be a teacher." So a specially created topical index for Bible teachers is included, listing the primary themes covered within the content of this Bible as well as key biblical references from both the Old and New Testaments on each respective topic.

GENERAL CONCORDANCE

An extensive Bible concordance is included to aid you in finding key words, particularly in the *New International Version*.

OTHER VALUABLE RESOURCES

The Jeremiah Study Bible contains a variety of charts and maps keyed to particular Bible passages to bring even greater relevance and understanding to your reading of Scripture.

THE REWARDS OF CONSISTENT BIBLE STUDY

After 40 years in ministry, this little concept came alive for me just within the past few months: people who study the Bible consistently find themselves continually being surprised by God. He includes so much in His Word that if we just keep digging for it, those riches will be found. This is life-changing.

The Bible, according to its own testimony, is the nourishment people need for their spiritual life. Apart from the Scriptures, there is no food. If you want to grow spiritually, if you want to build a strong foundation for your life, if you want to have a marriage that has some strength to it, the principles for all these things and more are found in one place and one place only— the Word of God.

So, if you want to know what I consider to be the most exciting thing about studying the Bible, it is the constant newness of it. The Bible is new every morning. And no matter how many times I study it—even when I've studied a passage before—I make fresh discoveries that enhance my life and faith as I return to study it again. I don't know of any other book like that in the history of books.

I tell people all the time, "I don't worry so much about the things in the Bible that I don't understand. My challenges are the things I really do understand and the demands they make on my life."

The challenge for me is to live life at a higher level than I could ever hope to aspire to without the guidance of Scripture. And I trust that *The Jeremiah Study Bible* will help you attain that higher level as God speaks to you through His Word.

WAYS TO STUDY
THE BIBLE EFFECTIVELY

Read It! Find time every day to read the Bible. Build this into your routine each morning or evening. Pray as you read, asking God for insight.

Look for a New Verse Every Day. As you read, ask God for a special verse to meet that day's need. Read until you arrive at that verse, and then write it down and carry it with you. You'll discover new strength!

Study Book-to-Verse-to-Word. One of the best methods for Bible study is book-to-verse-to-word, sometimes called inductive Bible study. Choose the book you want to study, then read through the book introduction and the Bible text several times for a sweep of its contents. Then read all you can about the background of that book. Next…

Look for the Outline and Theme of the Book. After that, you're ready to study chapter by chapter. Read through each chapter, making notes, underlining verses, and looking for key thoughts. When you have a good idea of what each chapter says, study the individual verses themselves, down to the various words that are used. Then…

Read the Bible with Pen in Hand. Underline, circle, and draw lines from verse to verse. Thoroughly read *The Jeremiah Study Bible* notes and their cross-references. Scribble comments and insights in the margins, and post dates beside verses that God gives you on particular days. Someone once said, "A well-marked Bible means a well-fed soul." You can also use a journal to analyze sentences, paraphrase verses, and condense passages, list points, and record observations.

Memorize Scripture and Meditate on It. Memorized Scripture is the fodder of meditation, and meditating on God's Word opens the door of our hearts to the real riches of Scripture. When we memorize God's Word, we can think about it all the time, mulling it over as we eat breakfast, as we drive to work, as we fall asleep at night. We digest its meaning, and it becomes part of us.

Join a Bible Study Group. One of the most exciting developments in many churches has been the proliferation of Bible study groups. Find a good group and sign up. The right small group can make a big difference in your appreciation of Scripture.

INTRODUCING
DR. DAVID JEREMIAH

A man with a passionate commitment to teach the Word of God, Dr. David Jeremiah has an extraordinary ability to communicate and a dedicated worldwide audience. Since 1981, he has been senior pastor of the 8,000-member Shadow Mountain Community Church in El Cajon, a suburb of San Diego, California.

For more than 30 years, Dr. Jeremiah has led a global ministry anchored by his nationwide television broadcast seen in approximately 200 million homes each week.

Including the *Turning Point* weekly radio program, now heard on more than 1,800 stations and outlets worldwide, he has a weekly audience of more than 10 million.

He is the author of more than 40 books, including multiple *New York Times, USA Today,* and *Wall Street Journal* bestsellers such as *Captured by Grace; What in the World Is Going On?;* and *God Loves You: He Always Has—He Always Will.*

Drawing on more than 40 years of in-depth Bible study, Dr. Jeremiah has produced *The Jeremiah Study Bible,* a deeply personal and comprehensive study of God's Word with one clear goal in mind—to help you understand what God is saying to you today.

THE
JEREMIAH
STUDY BIBLE

THE
JEREMIAH
STUDY BIBLE

DR. DAVID JEREMIAH

The Jeremiah Study Bible
Copyright © 2016 by David Jeremiah, Inc.

Published by Worthy Publishing, a division of Worthy Media, Inc. Worthy is a registered trademark of Worthy Media, Inc.

HELPING PEOPLE EXPERIENCE THE HEART OF GOD

Library of Congress Control Number: 2016020844

For foreign and subsidiary rights, contact the Rights Department at Worthy Publishing; www.worthypublishing.com

Published in association with Yates & Yates; www.yates2.com

The features "Parables of Jesus," "Harmony of the Gospels," "Miracles of Jesus," "Prophecies of the Messiah," and "Table of Weights and Measurements" are courtesy of Thomas Nelson Publishers (see www.thomasnelson.com/bibles).

Cover Design: FaceOut Studio
Interior Design: Koechel Peterson & Associates; Melissa Reagan; Bart Dawson
Author Photo: Alan Weissman Photography, 2011

Printed in the United States of America

16 17 18 19 20 RRD 10 9 8 7 6 5 4 3 2 1

THE OLD TESTAMENT (OT)

THE NEW TESTAMENT (NT)

ACKNOWLEDGMENTS

AUTHOR OF STUDY NOTES, SIDEBARS & ARTICLES
Dr. David Jeremiah

PUBLISHER & DESIGNER
Byron D. Williamson

EXECUTIVE EDITOR
Kris Bearss

PROJECT DIRECTOR
Jeana Ledbetter

ASSOCIATE EXECUTIVE EDITOR
Wayne Hastings

ASSOCIATE EDITOR & RESEARCH ASSISTANT
Beau Sager

DIRECTOR OF PRODUCTION & PROJECT MANAGER
Kimberly Shell

CONTRIBUTING WRITERS
The Barton-Veerman Group:
David Veerman
Bruce Barton (Consultant)
Nancy Ryken Taylor
Vincent Bacote
Brian Dennert
Rick Ezell
Afton Rorvik
Linda Chaffee Taylor
Neil Wilson

Steve Halliday
Larry Libby
Heather McMurray
Scott Stocking

SPECIAL FEATURES
William Kruidenier

CONTRIBUTING EDITORS & RESEARCHERS
Adept Content Solutions
Christine M. Anderson
Timothy J. Beals/Credo Communications
Jean Bloom
Teasi Cannon
Jennifer Day
Ruth DeJager
Kate Etue
Jennifer Hesse
Christa Kinde
Wayne R. Kinde
Ryan Lewelling
Ed Longabaugh
Kyle L. Olund
Sherman Shell
Jean Syswerda

THEOLOGICAL ADVISORS & CONTENT COLLABORATORS

Ronald B. Allen, PhD
Senior Professor of Bible Exposition
Dallas Theological Seminary

Sten-Erik Armitage, ThM
Director of Spiritual Formation & Leadership
Dallas Theological Seminary

Robert B. Chisholm Jr., PhD
Chair, Department of Old Testament; Professor of Old Testament
Dallas Theological Seminary

Gary F. Coombs, PhD
President
Southern California Seminary

Chuck Emert, PhD
Professor of Bible and Theology
Southern California Seminary

Lance Higginbotham, ThM
Adjunct Professor of Theological Studies
Trinity Evangelical Divinity School

Dennis R. Magary, PhD
Chair, Department of Old Testament and Semitic Languages
Associate Professor of Old Testament and Semitic Languages
Trinity Evangelical Divinity School

David Mathewson, PhD
Associate Professor of New Testament
Denver Theological Seminary

Steven D. Mathewson, PhD
Adjunct Professor of Preaching, Trinity Evangelical Divinity School
Adjunct Professor of Pastoral Studies, Moody Bible Institute

Nicholas Perrin, PhD
Professor of Biblical Studies
Wheaton College Graduate School

Joshua E. Williams, PhD
Associate Professor of Old Testament
Southwestern Baptist Theological Seminary

Gary Yates, PhD
Associate Professor of Old Testament
Liberty Baptist Theological Seminary

TYPESETTING & GRAPHIC DESIGN

Koechel Peterson & Associates
Hudson Bible
Bart Dawson
Melissa Reagan

PROOFREADING

Adept Content Solutions
Peachtree Editorial Services
The Bates Corporation

The Bible is the Word of God in the words of man. The Bible is one book—it has one ultimate author (God) and one story line with a beginning and an end—but it can also be viewed as a collection of individual books with different authors, settings, and themes.

Theme. While there are many subthemes in the Bible such as sin, forgiveness, salvation, love, eternity, and the Trinity, the overall theme is redemption. Including Creation, the Fall, Redemption, and Restoration—the story begins in Genesis and ends in Revelation. Closely aligned to the theme of redemption is that of the kingdom of God breaking in—with God invading the kingdom of sin and darkness in order to rescue humanity and bring individuals into the kingdom of light (Col. 1:12–14).

Structure. There are 39 Old Testament (OT) books and 27 New Testament (NT) books. Books written at the same time as the biblical books, called the Apocrypha, are only considered to be authoritative by the Roman Catholic Church. Protestant Bibles contain the 66 books that were canonized by the end of the fourth century AD by the Council of Laodicea.

The 39 books of the OT are collected into five subgroups:

- *Pentateuch* (Genesis–Deuteronomy)—Also called the "five books of Moses," these span the period from creation to Israel's preparation to enter the Promised Land.

- *Historical Books* (Joshua–Esther)—These 12 books cover Israel's entry into the Promised Land, the monarchy, the destruction of Israel by Assyria and Babylon, and the Jews' return from exile in Babylon.

- *Poetic Books* (Job–Song of Songs)—Also known as Wisdom Literature, these five books contain the collected poetry (songs) and wisdom from the psalmists and (primarily) King Solomon.

- *Major Prophets* (Isaiah–Daniel)—These are called the "major" prophets because of their length, not because their content is more important.

- *Minor Prophets* (Hosea–Malachi)—These 12 prophets delivered shorter oracles in Israel prior to the northern kingdom's destruction in 722 BC and the southern kingdom's in 586 BC, as well as to the Jews who returned from exile in Babylon.

Literature. Consistent with the literature during the time its books were written, the Bible contains many different styles of writing:

- *Poetry*—While some books are all poetry (Psalms, Song of Songs, and Lamentations), many other OT prophetic books contain poetry. The NT contains only a few examples of poetry (see Luke 1:46–55, 68–79).

- *Law*—The Mosaic laws were the civil, ceremonial, and moral guide for the nation of Israel, summarized in the Ten Commandments (Ex. 20:1–17; Deut. 5:6–21).

- *History*—The 12 historical books of the OT are the best examples, but Acts in the NT is also a historical book.

- *Prophecy*—The major and minor prophets make up the bulk of this genre, but prophetic utterances are also found throughout the four Gospels and the NT epistles.

- *Apocalyptic*—This category contains writings about the coming Day of the Lord and the end of the present age. Apocalyptic writing is found primarily in Isaiah, Daniel, Ezekiel, Zechariah, and Revelation.

- *Wisdom*—Job, Ecclesiastes, and Proverbs (and possibly James in the NT) are the best examples of books that focus on grappling with life in a skillful manner that pleases God.

- *Gospel*—The four Gospels that open the NT chronicle the life of Jesus and His message of the good news of the kingdom of God.

- *Epistles*—There are 21 letters in the NT written by the apostles to new Christian churches. The author of Hebrews is unknown.

Authorship. Spirit-enabled men captured God's divine thoughts and words to produce an authoritative record of the story of redemption. The Bible was written over a span of 1,500 years by more than 40 authors from all walks of life—from kings to farmers, historians to fishermen, prophets to apostles. It was written in three languages (Hebrew, Aramaic, Greek) in four different geopolitical regions: the Middle East, Mesopotamia, Asia Minor, and southern Europe. Some books were written and lightly edited (like Moses' books and certain historical books), some were dictated to a scribe (Paul's epistles), and some were the result of scholarly research (Luke and Acts). The authors, inspired by God, withheld none of the failures of mankind, even their own.

The Bible has been the most influential book in world history because its message originated with God and resolves the most pressing human need: reconciliation with Him.

The Teacher's Topical Index is a resource tool to help you study and teach the Bible by major biblical topics. The index references Articles (A), Sidebars (S), Maps (M), and Charts (C) from *The Jeremiah Study Bible*, plus other important Scripture references.

The goal of the New International Version (NIV) is to enable English-speaking people from around the world to read and hear God's eternal Word in their own language. Our work as translators is motivated by our conviction that the Bible is God's Word in written form. We believe that the Bible contains the divine answer to the deepest needs of humanity, sheds unique light on our path in a dark world and sets forth the way to our eternal well-being. Out of these deep convictions, we have sought to recreate as far as possible the experience of the original audience—blending transparency to the original text with accessibility for the millions of English speakers around the world. We have prioritized accuracy, clarity and literary quality with the goal of creating a translation suitable for public and private reading, evangelism, teaching, preaching, memorizing and liturgical use. We have also sought to preserve a measure of continuity with the long tradition of translating the Scriptures into English.

The complete NIV Bible was first published in 1978. It was a completely new translation made by over a hundred scholars working directly from the best available Hebrew, Aramaic and Greek texts. The translators came from the United States, Great Britain, Canada, Australia and New Zealand, giving the translation an international scope. They were from many denominations and churches—including Anglican, Assemblies of God, Baptist, Brethren, Christian Reformed, Church of Christ, Evangelical Covenant, Evangelical Free, Lutheran, Mennonite, Methodist, Nazarene, Presbyterian, Wesleyan and others. This breadth of denominational and theological perspective helped to safeguard the translation from sectarian bias. For these reasons, and by the grace of God, the NIV has gained a wide readership in all parts of the English-speaking world.

The work of translating the Bible is never finished. As good as they are, English translations must be regularly updated so that they will continue to communicate accurately the meaning of God's Word. Updates are needed in order to reflect the latest developments in our understanding of the biblical world and its languages and to keep pace with changes in English usage. Recognizing, then, that the NIV would retain its ability to communicate God's Word accurately only if it were regularly updated, the original translators established the Committee on Bible Translation (CBT). The Committee is a self-perpetuating group of biblical scholars charged with keeping abreast of advances in biblical scholarship and changes in English and issuing periodic updates to the NIV. The CBT is an independent, self-governing body and has sole responsibility for the NIV text. The Committee mirrors the original group of translators in its diverse international and denominational makeup and in its unifying commitment to the Bible as God's inspired Word.

In obedience to its mandate, the Committee has issued periodic updates to the NIV. An initial revision was released in 1984. A more thorough revision process was completed in 2005, resulting in the separately published TNIV. The updated NIV you now have in your hands builds on both the original NIV and the TNIV and represents the latest effort of the Committee to articulate God's unchanging Word in the way the original authors might have said it had they been speaking in English to the global English-speaking audience today.

TRANSLATION PHILOSOPHY

The Committee's translating work has been governed by three widely accepted principles about the way people use words and about the way we understand them.

First, the meaning of words is determined by the way that users of the language actually use them at any given time. For the biblical languages, therefore, the Committee utilizes the best and most recent scholarship on the way Hebrew, Aramaic and Greek words were being used in biblical times. At the same time, the Committee carefully studies the state of modern English. Good translation is like good communication: one must know the target audience so that the appropriate choices can be made about which English words to use to represent the original words of Scripture. From its inception, the NIV has had as its target the general English-speaking population all over the world, the "International" in its title reflecting this concern. The aim of the Committee is to put the Scriptures into natural English that will communicate effectively with the broadest possible audience of English speakers.

Modern technology has enhanced the Committee's ability to choose the right English words to convey the meaning of the original text. The field of computational linguistics harnesses the power of computers to provide broadly applicable and current data about the state of the language. Translators can now access huge databases of modern English to better understand the current meaning and usage of key words. The Committee utilized this resource in preparing the 2011 edition of the NIV. An area of especially rapid and significant change in English is the way certain nouns and pronouns are used to refer to human beings. The Committee therefore requested experts in computational linguistics at Collins Dictionaries to pose some key questions about this usage to its database of English—the largest in the world, with over 4.4 billion words, gathered from several English-speaking countries and including both spoken and written English. (The Collins Study, called "The Development and Use of Gender Language in Contemporary English," can be accessed at *http://www.thenivbible.com/about-the-niv/about-the-2011-edition/*.) The study revealed that the most popular words to describe the human race in modern U.S. English were "humanity," "man" and "mankind." The Committee then used this data in the updated NIV, choosing from among these three words (and occasionally others also) depending on the context.

A related issue creates a larger problem for modern translations: the move away from using the third-person masculine singular pronouns—"he/him/his"—to refer to men and women equally. This usage does persist in some forms of English, and this revision therefore occasionally uses these pronouns in a generic sense. But the tendency, recognized in day-to-day usage and confirmed by the Collins study, is away from the generic use of "he," "him" and "his." In recognition of this shift in language and in an effort to translate into the natural English that people are actually using, this revision of the NIV generally uses other constructions when the biblical text is plainly addressed to men and women equally. The reader will encounter especially frequently a "they," "their" or "them" to express a generic singular idea. Thus, for instance, Mark 8:36 reads: "What good is it for someone to gain the whole world, yet forfeit their soul?" This generic use of the "distributive" or "singular" "they/them/their" has been used for many centuries by respected writers of English and has now become established as standard English, spoken and written, all over the world.

A second linguistic principle that feeds into the Committee's translation work is that meaning is found not in individual words, as vital as they are, but in larger clusters: phrases, clauses, sentences, discourses. Translation is not, as many people think, a matter of word substitution: English word x in place of Hebrew word y. Translators must first determine the meaning of the words of the biblical languages in the context of the passage and then select English words that accurately communicate that meaning to modern listeners and readers. This means that accurate translation will not always reflect the exact structure of the original language. To be sure, there is debate over the degree to which translators should try to preserve the "form" of the original text in English. From the beginning, the NIV has taken a mediating position on this issue. The manual produced when the translation that became the NIV was first being planned states: "If the Greek or Hebrew syntax has a good parallel in modern English, it should be used. But if there is no good parallel, the English syntax appropriate to the meaning of the original is to be chosen." It is fine, in other words, to carry over the form of the biblical languages into English—but not at the expense of natural expression. The principle that meaning resides in larger clusters of words means that the Committee has not insisted on a "word-for-word" approach to translation. We certainly believe that every word of Scripture is inspired by God and therefore to be carefully studied to determine what God is saying to us. It is for this reason that the Committee labors over every single word of the original texts, working hard to determine how each of those words contributes to what the text is saying. Ultimately, however, it is how these individual words function in combination with other words that determines meaning.

A third linguistic principle guiding the Committee in its translation work is the recognition that words have a spectrum of meaning. It is popular to define a word by using another word, or "gloss," to substitute for it. This substitute word is then sometimes called the "literal" meaning of a word. In fact, however, words have a range of possible meanings. Those meanings will vary depending on the context, and words in one language will usually not occupy the same semantic range as words in another language. The Committee therefore studies each original word of Scripture in its context to identify its meaning in a particular verse and then chooses an appropriate English word (or phrase) to represent it. It is impossible, then, to translate any given Hebrew, Aramaic or Greek word with the same English word all the time. The Committee does try to translate related occurrences of a word in the original languages with the same English word in order to preserve the connection for the English reader. But the Committee generally privileges clear natural meaning over a concern with consistency in rendering particular words.

TEXTUAL BASIS

For the Old Testament the standard Hebrew text, the Masoretic Text as published in the latest edition of *Biblia Hebraica*, has been used throughout. The Masoretic Text tradition contains marginal notations that offer variant readings. These have sometimes been followed instead of the text itself. Because such instances involve variants within the Masoretic tradition, they have not been indicated in the textual notes. In a few cases, words in the basic consonantal text have been divided differently than in the Masoretic Text. Such cases are usually indicated in the textual footnotes. The Dead Sea Scrolls contain biblical texts that represent an earlier stage of the transmission of the Hebrew text. They have been consulted, as have been the Samaritan Pentateuch and the ancient scribal traditions concerning deliberate textual changes. The translators also consulted the more important early versions. Readings from these versions, the Dead Sea Scrolls and the scribal traditions were occasionally followed where the Masoretic Text seemed doubtful and where accepted principles of textual criticism showed that one or more of these textual witnesses appeared to provide the correct reading. In rare cases, the translators have emended the Hebrew text where it appears to have become corrupted at an even earlier stage of its transmission. These departures from the Masoretic Text are also indicated in the textual footnotes. Sometimes the vowel indicators (which are later additions to the basic consonantal text) found in the Masoretic Text did not, in the judgment of the translators, represent the correct vowels for the original text. Accordingly, some words have been read with a different set of vowels. These instances are usually not indicated in the footnotes.

The Greek text used in translating the New Testament has been an eclectic one, based on the latest editions of the Nestle-Aland/United Bible Societies' Greek New Testament. The translators have made their choices among the variant readings in accordance with widely accepted principles of New Testament textual criticism. Footnotes call attention to places where uncertainty remains.

The New Testament authors, writing in Greek, often quote the Old Testament from its ancient Greek version, the Septuagint. This is one reason why some of the Old Testament quotations in the NIV New Testament are not identical to the corresponding passages in the NIV Old Testament. Such quotations in the New Testament are indicated with the footnote "(see Septuagint)."

FOOTNOTES AND FORMATTING

Footnotes in this version are of several kinds, most of which need no explanation. Those giving alternative translations begin with "Or" and generally introduce the alternative with the last word preceding it in the text, except when it is a single-word alternative. When poetry is quoted in a footnote a slash mark indicates a line division.

It should be noted that references to diseases, minerals, flora and fauna, architectural details, clothing, jewelry, musical instruments and other articles cannot always be identified with precision. Also, linear measurements and measures of capacity can only be approximated (see the Table of Weights and Measures). Although *Selah*, used mainly in the Psalms, is probably a musical term, its meaning is uncertain. Since it may interrupt reading and distract the reader, this word has not been kept in the English text, but every occurrence has been signaled by a footnote.

As an aid to the reader, sectional headings have been inserted. They are not to be regarded as part of the biblical text and are not intended for oral reading. It is the Committee's hope that these headings may prove more helpful to the reader than the traditional chapter divisions, which were introduced long after the Bible was written.

Sometimes the chapter and/or verse numbering in English translations of the Old Testament differs from that found in published Hebrew texts. This is particularly the case in the Psalms, where the traditional titles are included in the Hebrew verse numbering. Such differences are indicated in the footnotes at the bottom of the page. In the New Testament, verse numbers that marked off portions of the traditional English text not supported by the best Greek manuscripts now appear in brackets, with a footnote indicating the text that has been omitted (see, for example, Matthew 17:[21]).

Mark 16:9–20 and John 7:53—8:11, although long accorded virtually equal status with the rest of the Gospels in which they stand, have a questionable standing in the textual history of the New Testament, as noted in the bracketed annotations with which they are set off. A different typeface has been chosen for these passages to indicate their uncertain status.

Basic formatting of the text, such as lining the poetry, paragraphing (both prose and poetry), setting up of (administrative-like) lists, indenting letters and lengthy prayers within narratives and the insertion of sectional headings, has been the work of the Committee. However, the choice between single-column and double-column formats has been left to the publishers. Also the issuing of "red-letter" editions is a publisher's choice—one that the Committee does not endorse.

The Committee has again been reminded that every human effort is flawed— including this revision of the NIV. We trust, however, that many will find in it an improved representation of the Word of God, through which they hear his call to faith in our Lord Jesus Christ and to service in his kingdom. We offer this version of the Bible to him in whose name and for whose glory it has been made.

The Committee on Bible Translation

OLD TESTAMENT

הַוְּדֵל רוּמְזִמ חַצֵנְמַל

עִיקְרָה דִיגֵּם וְרְדִי הָשֶׁאֲמוּ לָא דוּבְכ סִירְפֵסְמ סַיַמְשַׁה

תַעַד־הֵוֲחִי הָלְַיְלֵל הָלְַיְלֵל רִמֵא עִיבִּי סְרַל סְנֵי

סְלֹוק עָמֶשְׁנ יִלֵּב סִירְבַד וְיֵאֹר רֵמֵא־נְיֵא

סֵדְב לְהֵא־בָּשׂ שֶׂמֶשַׁל סֶהֵילְמ לְבֵּת הָצְקְבּוּ בַּק אֲלֵּי וְזְרָאֵה־לְכַב

הַרֵא זִוְּהַל רוֹבְנָכ שִׁישִׁי וְתְפַחֵמ אֲצֵי נָתְּהַכ אוֹהַו

GENESIS

YOU INTENDED TO HARM ME

YOU INTENDED TO HARM ME,

but God intended it for good

to accomplish what is now being done,

the saving of many lives.

So then, don't be afraid.

GENESIS 50:20, 21

As God's Spirit hovered over the face of the primeval waters (1:2), so God's Spirit hovered over the hand of Moses as he discerned what to include in this crucial "book of beginnings." Moses was not on hand to witness the events of Genesis personally. In fact, he was not born until approximately 300 years after Joseph died. But he very possibly had the oral histories—and perhaps some written accounts—of those events from the people who were there. And most importantly, God's Spirit was there as time began and earth was born, as Adam and Eve were confronted by the tempter in the Garden, as Abram and Sarai sojourned into a foreign land and became Abraham and Sarah, the father and mother of many nations, and as God delivered Joseph first from a pit and then from a prison cell to the right hand of Egypt's throne.

The divine "breath" of God directed Moses to produce a book of beginnings that contained the precise parts of the story that would accomplish God's purpose (2 Tim. 3:16; 2 Pet. 1:21). Moses' account recorded the story of redemption from perfect creation to sin, salvation, sanctification, and then security with God forever.

WHAT IT SAYS | *The First Sin, the First Promise of a Savior*
Moses authored not only the Book of Genesis but the next four books of the Bible as well. Together they are referred to as the Pentateuch (a five-part book) or Torah ("Instruction") by Jewish people.

Genesis can be summarized in more than one way, each capsulation providing a different, and helpful, perspective:

- Genesis 1—11 is primeval history; 12—50 is patriarchal history.
- Genesis 1—11 tells the story of the human race (the peoples); 12—50 tells the story of the Hebrews (one people).
- Genesis 1—11 is the story of four great events (Creation, the Fall, the Flood, Babel); 12—50 is the story of four great persons (Abraham, Isaac, Jacob, Joseph, and descendants).
- Genesis 1—11 focuses on the beginning of sin; 12—50 focuses on the beginning of salvation.

No matter how we summarize it, Genesis chronicles not just the creation of the first earth and the first humans but also the beginning of the sky and sea, the botanical kingdom, the sun and moon, and the animal kingdom. It also presents the beginnings of worship, marriage, society, nations, and the founding of false religions. But its most important moment, told in the book's early chapters, sets the

To view Dr. Jeremiah's video introduction to Genesis, go to www.JeremiahStudyBible.com/Genesis/Intro

stage for the entire biblical story: the moment when sin enters in and redemption responds.

When Adam and Eve chose to yield to Satan and their own desires instead of God's will, sin began. Through them, humanity's eyes were opened to the knowledge of good and evil. Not only was the serpent cursed, the ground was cursed as well. Instead of the ground being a place that volunteered its bounty for the benefit of man, woman, and beast, it became something of an opponent, yielding in part to the sweat of the human brow (3:19).

But another plan was initiated then too—a plan to reverse the effects of humanity's sin. To the tempter who had led Adam and Eve into sin, Yahweh said, "And I will put enmity between you and the woman, and between your offspring and hers; he will crush your head, and you will strike his heel" (3:15). This is the first statement of "good news" from God after Satan introduced sin into the world: One will come to make things right. There will be a struggle—both will be bruised. But the serpent will suffer a permanent bruise to the head and the offspring of the woman only a temporary bruise to the heel.

In short, the entire Bible is the working out of this promise. The first few chapters of Genesis make a prophetic promise—the fulfillment of which is recorded in the last few chapters of Revelation. In between is the telling of the story begun in Genesis 1:1.

What It Means | *One Beginning Begets Another*
Genesis tells of the beginning of the world and everything in it. More importantly, it launches the story of redemption—God's plan to reveal His glory through unswerving loyalty to the descendants of Abraham and unconditional love for a planet full of people who have turned their backs on Him (1—3).

- Sovereignty: God's sovereignty is revealed throughout Genesis. In spite of humans disobeying God and introducing sin into God's perfect creation, Yahweh remains in control. In reflecting on his own troubles, Joseph tells his brothers in Egypt that what they meant for evil, God meant for good (50:20). That theme begins in Genesis 3 and runs throughout the Bible. God is sovereign over all, including the enemy's attempts to destroy what He has declared "good."
- Redemption: The scarlet thread of redemption that runs through the Bible begins with the hides of animals used to cover sinful Adam and Eve (3:21) and ends with the blood of Christ, the Lamb of God (John 1:29), on Calvary's cross washing away the sins of the world.
- Humanity: Genesis introduces the mercy and grace God displays toward a sinful and self-directed people, the human race. God's grace in the lives of the patriarchs (Abraham, Isaac, Jacob) and Jacob's 12 sons demonstrates that God not only has a plan for redemption but intends to see it through to completion.

What It Means for You | *God's Good Plan Will Prevail*
No matter what life brings, no matter how evil intrudes, God has a plan, and His ultimate plan cannot be frustrated. Many of the events recorded in Genesis permanently affected life on earth—the fall of Adam and Eve, the destruction of the world by the great flood, the folly at the tower of Babel. Yet in spite of those epic events, God's plan to send a Redeemer and gather a people for Himself was right on schedule and still is. We can trust God's ability to make sense of our lives when our world is upside down. Moreover we can trust His goodness. He will weave our failures and the evil designs of others into a covering that blesses us and accomplishes His every purpose (50:20; Rom. 8:28).

GENESIS

The Beginning

1 In the beginning God created the heavens and the earth. ²Now the earth was formless and empty, darkness was over the surface of the deep, and the Spirit of God was hovering over the waters.

³And God said, "Let there be light," and there was light. ⁴God saw that the light was good, and he separated the light from the darkness. ⁵God called the light "day," and the darkness he called "night." And there was evening, and there was morning—the first day.

⁶And God said, "Let there be a vault between the waters to separate water from water." ⁷So God made the vault and separated the water under the vault from the water above it. And it was so. ⁸God called the vault "sky." And there was evening, and there was morning—the second day.

⁹And God said, "Let the water under the sky be gathered to one place, and let dry ground appear." And it was so. ¹⁰God called the dry ground "land," and the gathered waters he called "seas." And God saw that it was good.

¹¹Then God said, "Let the land produce vegetation: seed-bearing plants and trees on the land that bear fruit with seed in it, according to their various kinds." And it was so. ¹²The land produced vegetation: plants bearing seed according to their kinds and trees bearing fruit with seed in it according to their kinds. And God saw that it was good. ¹³And there was evening, and there was morning—the third day.

¹⁴And God said, "Let there be lights in the vault of the sky to separate the day from the night, and let them serve as signs to mark sacred times, and days and years, ¹⁵and let them be lights in the vault of the sky to give light on the earth." And it was so. ¹⁶God made two great lights—the greater light to govern the day and the lesser light to govern the night. He also made the stars. ¹⁷God set them in the vault of the sky to give light on the earth, ¹⁸to govern the day and the night, and to separate light from darkness. And God saw that it was

---

 Hints of the Trinity • 1:1, 2, 26

Many people read "God created the heavens and the earth" (1:1) and assume that only God the Father is responsible for creating everything that exists. But all three members of the Trinity were active in Creation. The Word—Jesus Christ—is the Creator God and was there at the beginning (John 1:1-3; Col. 1:15, 16; Heb. 1:2). The Spirit of God was present as well, hovering like a mother bird over the earth (1:2). In addition, 1:26 and 11:7 quote the Lord as saying, "Let us," introducing a forthcoming action. What's more, God's name in the Hebrew of Genesis 1, *Elohim*, is in the plural. So from the opening words of Scripture, God not only exists but exists in three Persons.

Those three Persons work in tandem and also glorify one another. A close study of the Gospel of John clearly shows the triune relationship. Jesus, for example, answers our prayers to bring glory to the Father. He said, "And I will do whatever you ask in my name, so that the Father may be glorified in the Son" (John 14:13). John 17:1 in particular shows the power of this mutual glorification: "Father, the hour has come. Glorify your Son, that your Son may glorify you."

1:1 | This opening verse is a topic sentence summarizing the entire chapter. The Hebrew verb **created**—a word associated only with God in the Bible—speaks of that which only God can do. It also signifies something new or remarkable being established out of nothing (1:3; Isa. 40:26; Rev. 4:11). **In the beginning**, God was already there (Ps. 90:2). He existed before time began. *See the article "God the Creator" on page 8.*

1:2 | The earth was **formless and empty**. On the first three days of creation God gave the earth form (light, water, sky, land), and on days four through six He filled the emptiness with life (Jer. 4:23).

1:3 | The enshrouding darkness and enveloping waters in 1:2 are now about to be reversed. The calling for **light** is, in a sense, symbolic of the grace and presence of God in the world. The rest of the Bible may be viewed as an extension of God bringing light into darkness (2 Cor. 4:6).

1:5 | The word **day** (Heb. *yom*) always means a 24-hour, solar day when it is accompanied by a numerical adjective like "one" or "two." God sovereignly labeled His creation with the elements of time clearly delineated so it would be understood that the days of Creation week were established on a strict pattern of time. God created the heavens and the earth in six, 24-hour, solar days.

1:11, 12 | Two points here refute evolutionary order: (1) plants were created before animals, and (2) the **land produced vegetation** immediately. The latter suggests that the earth was created "mature" rather than evolving over eons.

1:14 | Moses may have avoided calling the sun and the moon by name because the Egyptians believed them to be gods (Deut. 4:19). Seasons (**sacred times**) occur and tides do not consume entire continents because of the precise 23-degree tilt of the earth's axis. God left out no detail in His design (Ps. 74:16; 136:5-9).

Except for the divinity of Jesus Christ, no issue polarizes believers and skeptics as much as the question of the origin of planet Earth. Is the world the result of divine creation or evolution?

As to "who," the Genesis creation account, along with all of Scripture, leaves no doubt about earth's origin: "In the beginning God created the heavens and the earth" (1:1). This one statement speaks to time and space ("in the beginning") as well as all matter ("the heavens and the earth") being established out of nothing, with the tacit assumption that God always was and always is.

As to "how" and "when" God created the heavens and the earth, the Bible is no less clear. The Genesis account speaks in plain language, and when Scripture speaks in this way, the plain meaning is to be preferred in all biblical interpretation: God spent six days creating and on the seventh day He rested. There is no reason to doubt whether "day" was used in the manner normally understood then and now—a 24-hour period of time. Those periods were divided by the same markers we presently use: evening and morning (1:5, 8, 13, 19, 23, 31).

Perhaps the strongest evidence that "day" in Genesis refers to a normal day comes from the person who wrote the Creation narrative—Moses. The fourth of the Ten Commandments given by God to Moses concerns the normal seven-day workweek in Israel: "Six days you shall labor and do all your work, but the seventh day is a sabbath to the LORD your God. On it you shall not do any work . . . For in six days the LORD made the heavens and the earth, . . . but he rested on the seventh day" (Ex. 20:8–11). Moses uses the creation week as a model for how the Israelites were to live their own lives during a seven-day cycle: work six days and rest on the seventh day.

We have to ask: how would the Israelites who received this commandment have understood it? The parallel between their workweek and God's "work" week, written by the same person, is ample proof for taking the days of Creation as normal days.

God's purposeful creation of the heavens and the earth extends also to those He created in His image. Our lives have purpose and meaning because we are the handiwork of the Creator-God who "fearfully and wonderfully" created us and fashioned our days "before one of them came to be" (Ps. 139:14–16). Not only are we physically created in God's image to represent Him on the earth (1:26, 27), we are spiritually created in Christ when we are born again (John 3:3–8). "Therefore, if anyone is in Christ, the new creation has come: The old has gone, the new is here!" (2 Cor. 5:17).

God's role as Creator will not be complete until He has fashioned "a new heaven and a new earth" (Rev. 21:1) as the dwelling place for the redeemed.

For Further Reading: Job 38:4–38; Ps. 102:25; 104:1–26; Isa. 40:2; 45:18; Matt. 19:4, 5; John 1:1–3; Col. 1:16; Heb. 1:10

good. ¹⁹And there was evening, and there was morning—the fourth day. ²⁰And God said, "Let the water teem with living creatures, and let birds fly above the earth across the vault of the sky." ²¹So God created the great creatures of the sea and every living thing with which the water teems and that moves about in it, according to their kinds, and every winged bird according to its kind. And God saw that it was good. ²²God blessed them and said, "Be fruitful and increase in number and fill the water in the seas, and let the birds increase on the earth." ²³And there was evening, and there was morning—the fifth day. ²⁴And God said, "Let the land produce living creatures according to their kinds: the livestock, the creatures that move along the ground, and the wild animals, each according to its kind." And it was so. ²⁵God made the wild animals according to their kinds, the livestock according to their kinds, and all the creatures that move along the ground according to their kinds. And God saw that it was good.

²⁶Then God said, "Let us make mankind in our image, in our likeness, so that they may rule over the fish in the sea and the birds in the sky, over the livestock and all the wild animals,ᵃ and over all the creatures that move along the ground."

²⁷So God created mankind in his own image,
    in the image of God he created them;
    male and female he created them.

²⁸God blessed them and said to them, "Be fruitful and increase in number; fill the earth and subdue it. Rule over the fish in the sea and the birds in the sky and over every living creature that moves on the ground."

²⁹Then God said, "I give you every seed-bearing plant on the face of the whole earth and every tree that has fruit with seed in it. They will be yours for food. ³⁰And to all the beasts of the earth and all the birds in the sky and all the creatures that move along the ground—everything that has the breath of life in it—I give every green plant for food." And it was so.

³¹God saw all that he had made, and it was very good. And there was evening, and there was morning—the sixth day.

2 Thus the heavens and the earth were completed in all their vast array.

²By the seventh day God had finished the work he had been doing; so on the seventh day he rested from all his work. ³Then God blessed the seventh day and made it holy, because on it he rested from all the work of creating that he had done.

Adam and Eve

⁴This is the account of the heavens and the earth when they were created, when the LORD God made the earth and the heavens.

ᵃ 26 Probable reading of the original Hebrew text (see Syriac); Masoretic Text *the earth*

1:20–23 | The most notable of God's creations on the fifth day are the **great creatures of the sea**, a term used elsewhere in the Bible for monsters of the deep called Leviathan and Rahab (e.g., Isa. 27:1; Job 26:12). For **birds** and marine life to be created at the same time contradicts the sequence proposed by evolutionists.
1:26–28 | The creation of humans as **male and female** forms the high point of the chapter. Unlike the rest of creation, women and men are made in God's **image** and are thus able to reason, to create, and to commune with their Creator (Ps. 100:3). The Incarnation was necessitated because God desired to rescue that which He values most highly—the human race!
1:26, 27 | **Us** reveals that the Father, Son, and Holy Spirit exist in relationship. Because humans are made in the **image** of the triune God, they too are relational beings. **Likeness** indicates physical similarity, not just spiritual resemblance.
1:26 | As God's image-bearers, humans are symbols of Himself in the world. This is evidenced when people put their faith in Jesus: their spiritual nature changes so that it mirrors His (2 Cor. 3:18; Col. 3:10). The Lord also affirms it here by allowing humans to **rule over** nature and delegating them as earth's stewards (9:2; Ps. 8:6–8).
1:27 | Both **male and female** are made in God's image, proving that neither gender is superior to the other—they each equally reflect His character as God's masterpieces!

1:28 | The divine command to **be fruitful and increase in number** is repeated at the "second beginning" of humanity following the great Flood (9:1). Marriage is the only human institution that God created before the Fall. Thus we know that marriage, and sex within marriage, are holy in His eyes. Procreation is part of God's mandate for creation and His blessing on the human race.
1:29, 30 | In earth's perfect state, neither man nor beast was carnivorous; they were given **every seed-bearing plant** as well as **fruit . . . for food**.
1:31 | As God completed every part of creation, He called it "good" (1:4 10, 12, 18, 21, 25). After the **sixth day**, He declared all His work **very good**—and He has never changed His mind (Ps. 104:24; 1 Tim. 4:4). Even when humans introduced sin into the world, He did not abandon His creation but worked to restore it instead.
2:1, 2 | An argument against evolutionary theory is the fact that the act of creation was **completed** after the sixth day. This accords with the First Law of Thermodynamics, which states that the universe is now closed and no longer expanding.
2:3 | God **blessed** and made the Sabbath day **holy**, setting it apart for a special purpose that would meet humanity's spiritual and physical needs (Ex. 20:8–11; 31:17; Mark 2:27). *Holy* means to be completely devoted to God.

[5]Now no shrub had yet appeared on the earth[a] and no plant had yet sprung up, for the LORD God had not sent rain on the earth and there was no one to work the ground, [6]but streams[b] came up from the earth and watered the whole surface of the ground. [7]Then the LORD God formed a man[c] from the dust of the ground and breathed into his nostrils the breath of life, and the man became a living being.

[8]Now the LORD God had planted a garden in the east, in Eden; and there he put the man he had formed. [9]The LORD God made all kinds of trees grow out of the ground— trees that were pleasing to the eye and good for food. In the middle of the garden were the tree of life and the tree of the knowledge of good and evil.

[10]A river watering the garden flowed from Eden; from there it was separated into four headwaters. [11]The name of the first is the Pishon; it winds through the entire land of Havilah, where there is gold. [12](The gold of that land is good; aromatic resin[d] and onyx are also there.) [13]The name of the second river is the Gihon; it winds through the entire land of Cush.[e] [14]The name of the third river is the Tigris; it runs along the east side of Ashur. And the fourth river is the Euphrates.

[15]The LORD God took the man and put him in the Garden of Eden to work it and take care of it. [16]And the LORD God commanded the man, "You are free to eat from any tree in the garden; [17]but you must not eat from the tree of the knowledge of good and evil, for when you eat from it you will certainly die."

[18]The LORD God said, "It is not good for the man to be alone. I will make a helper suitable for him."

[19]Now the LORD God had formed out of the ground all the wild animals and all the birds in the sky. He brought them to the man to see what he would name them; and whatever the man called each living creature, that was its name. [20]So the man gave names to all the livestock, the birds in the sky and all the wild animals.

But for Adam[f] no suitable helper was found. [21]So the LORD God caused the man to fall into a deep sleep; and while he was sleeping, he took one of the man's ribs[g] and then closed up the place with flesh. [22]Then the LORD God made a woman from the rib[h] he had taken out of the man, and he brought her to the man.

[23]The man said,

"This is now bone of my bones
    and flesh of my flesh;
she shall be called 'woman,'
    for she was taken out of man."

---

[a] 5 Or *land*; also in verse 6   [b] 6 Or *mist*   [c] 7 The Hebrew for *man (adam)* sounds like and may be related to the Hebrew for *ground (adamah)*; it is also the name *Adam* (see verse 20).   [d] 12 Or *good; pearls*   [e] 13 Possibly southeast Mesopotamia   [f] 20 Or *the man*   [g] 21 Or *took part of the man's side*   [h] 22 Or *part*

2:4–7 | Since Adam and Eve did not exist and Moses was not alive as this **account** of Creation unfolded, only God—through the inspiration of the Holy Spirit—could have provided this part of the Genesis record to Moses.

2:4 | **The LORD God** is a new name. All through chapter 1, God's name is *'elohim*, a Hebrew term speaking of power, majesty, and transcendence. Beginning with this verse, the name God is joined with the name Yahweh (conventionally rendered as "LORD" in English translations), indicating that He is immediate and involved rather than remote. Both views of God are necessary!

2:7 | Here, the Hebrew term for creation (**formed**) is pictorial in nature, describing the work of a potter; thus the **dust of the ground** should be understood as clay. The image of God at a potter's wheel, fashioning the body of the **man**, is a wondrous image of His love and grace (Lam. 4:2; Rom. 9:21). God **breathed** the **breath of life** directly into humans rather than simply giving them life—distinguishing them from the animals.

2:8 | When Yahweh God planted a **garden**, it was not a flower or vegetable garden; the word and all the descriptors that follow signify an orchard.

2:9 | The **tree of life** reappears in the description of the New Jerusalem (Rev. 2:7; 22:2, 14). The other **tree** specifically mentioned here contained the power of full **knowledge**, emphasized by the opposite extremes, **good and evil**. The punishment for eating of this tree was certain death (2:17).

2:10–14 | **Eden** was a real place, but only its pre-Flood geographical location is recorded here. The present tense in use signals that Moses probably referenced Adam's own account in this section.

2:15 | Some people claim that **work** is the result of the Fall, but this verse confirms that meaningful labor existed before sin entered in. (See also the stewardship component of God's blessing on men and women in 1:28.) What changed as a result of sin was that work became toil.

2:16 | Obedience is at the core of all that God wants for and from His children. In Eden, God does not ask the first man and woman for love or faithfulness, only for obedience to one fundamental command: "If you want to walk with Me, do what I say."

2:17 | As soon as Adam and Eve sinned against God by eating of the tree, the process of death began. They became susceptible to the physical degeneration of old age and disease, and they faced a more serious form of death: spiritual death and eternal separation from God (Rom. 5:5; 6:23; James 1:15).

2:18–22 | As Adam named the animals, he became aware that none resembled him. So the Lord created someone *like* Adam yet *different*. The woman was his **helper** (or "help meet," with the sense of corresponding precisely to him)—one who supplied strengths that Adam lacked. The Hebrew term does not imply that the helper is weaker or less valuable than the one who is helped. In fact, in Hebrew, *help* is a word of power. The woman is a "power" matching the man!

2:18 | One reason God created Eve was because Adam's aloneness was **not good**—a contrast to the rest of creation, which God declared "good." Relationships are part of humanity's basic design. Marriage in particular is ideally a relationship in which each spouse brings true companionship to the other.

2:22 | The Hebrew word for **man** is *yish*; the word for **woman** is *yishshah*, the feminine form of the same word. What he is, she is— with gender distinctions. Rather than diminishing the woman, this title should lift her up.

Teaching Points — God's Design for Marriage • 2:23–25

Marriage is one man and one woman united spiritually, emotionally, physically, publicly, and legally in a lifetime bond of loyal love. God designed marriage:

1. To be a partnership between one man and one woman.
2. To be a permanent union.
3. To produce spiritual unity between husband and wife.
4. To provide for the procreation of children.
5. To positively channel sexual and emotional energy.
6. To serve as a principal building block of society.
7. To be a picture of His relationship with Israel and of Christ's relationship with the church.

²⁴That is why a man leaves his father and mother and is united to his wife, and they become one flesh.

²⁵Adam and his wife were both naked, and they felt no shame.

The Fall

3 Now the serpent was more crafty than any of the wild animals the LORD God had made. He said to the woman, "Did God really say, 'You must not eat from any tree in the garden'?"

²The woman said to the serpent, "We may eat fruit from the trees in the garden, ³but God did say, 'You must not eat fruit from the tree that is in the middle of the garden, and you must not touch it, or you will die.'"

⁴"You will not certainly die," the serpent said to the woman. ⁵"For God knows that when you eat from it your eyes will be opened, and you will be like God, knowing good and evil."

⁶When the woman saw that the fruit of the tree was good for food and pleasing to the eye, and also desirable for gaining wisdom, she took some and ate it. She also gave some to her husband, who was with her, and he ate it. ⁷Then the eyes of both of them were opened, and they realized they were naked; so they sewed fig leaves together and made coverings for themselves.

⁸Then the man and his wife heard the sound of the LORD God as he was walking in the garden in the cool of the day, and they hid from the LORD God among the trees of the garden. ⁹But the LORD God called to the man, "Where are you?"

¹⁰He answered, "I heard you in the garden, and I was afraid because I was naked; so I hid."

¹¹And he said, "Who told you that you were naked? Have you eaten from the tree that I commanded you not to eat from?"

¹²The man said, "The woman you put here with me—she gave me some fruit from the tree, and I ate it."

¹³Then the LORD God said to the woman, "What is this you have done?"

The woman said, "The serpent deceived me, and I ate."

¹⁴So the LORD God said to the serpent, "Because you have done this,

"Cursed are you above all livestock
    and all wild animals!
You will crawl on your belly
    and you will eat dust
    all the days of your life.
¹⁵And I will put enmity
    between you and the woman,

2:24 | Here are the life-changing, foundational principles of Christian marriage: that a man break from the emotional ties to his parents and be permanently **united** (lit., glued together) **to his wife**, and that man and woman become **one flesh** (Matt. 19:5; Eph. 5:31). Without these operating principles, there can be no real unity. With them, God can bring two people together into a singular, beautiful wholeness that is deeply blessed.

2:25 | Minus sin, the first married couple **felt no shame**. There was no self-consciousness or anxiety about what the other person thought; husband and wife were perfectly secure with one another. God designed marriage for this.

3:1–5 | Satan attacked God's character in three ways: (1) by creating doubt about God's love—misquoting God's instructions to Adam and Eve; (2) by denying the truth of God's word—telling Eve she would **not certainly die** if she disregarded the Lord's command; (3) by accusing God of jealousy—suggesting that God was worried Adam and Eve would become **like** Him if they ate from this tree. In this exchange, Eve shifted from heeding God's will to obeying her own. It is the struggle that will plague all of humanity from this point forward.

3:1 | By manifesting himself in another form as a means to deceive someone into doubting and disobeying God, Satan establishes himself as a force to be reckoned with (2 Cor. 11:3; Rev. 12:9; 20:10).

3:2, 3 | Eve did what so many people do even now: she revised and then rejected what God said. This sin always produces the same result—separation from God and, ultimately, death—unless sin is atoned for.

3:5, 6 | Satan's words contained partial truth (**your eyes will be opened**), a common tactic of his when tempting humans. He appealed to Eve's desires, just as he did with Christ in the wilderness, and as he does with all Christians (Luke 4:1–12; 1 John 2:16). When Adam **ate** of the fruit, sin and death became earth's realities (Rom. 5:12).

3:8–10 | When humans do wrong, their impulse is to hide (if they are still sensitive to sin). Sin disrupts a person's relationship with others and with God (Isa. 59:2). Still, God seeks a relationship (Luke 19:10; Rom. 5:7, 8).

3:12, 13 | Adam tried to place the blame for his sin onto Eve (**the woman**) and even God Himself (**you put** [her] **with me**). Eve, in turn, blamed **the serpent**. Human nature is to point to someone else when caught in sin, but God is never fooled; He sees and knows everything.

Before and After the Fall • 3:4–7

Before Adam and Eve sinned, they enjoyed three very special privileges:

1. They were in communion with God; they walked and talked with Him.
2. They knew God as He is. Their minds were not clouded by falsehoods or half-truths.
3. They possessed spiritual life. They were alive not just physically, but in every sense of the word their souls were alive.

The Effects of Sin. When Adam and Eve disobeyed God's command and fell into rebellion, they lost all three of their God-given privileges:

1. Their intimate communion was broken; Adam and Eve hid from God.
2. When they believed Satan's lie, their knowledge was corrupted and their understanding of God damaged. What God had said became twisted in their minds.
3. Perhaps most important, instead of knowing life as they once had known it with God, they began to know death.

Our Present Condition. Apart from God, our present condition mirrors what Adam and Eve knew after the Fall:

1. We are alienated from God.
2. We are ignorant of the truth of God.
3. We are condemned to physical and spiritual death.

Everything that Adam lost in the Fall is exactly what people lack today without Jesus Christ.

---

and between your offspring[a] and
   hers;
he will crush[b] your head,
   and you will strike his heel."

¹⁶To the woman he said,

"I will make your pains in childbearing
   very severe;
with painful labor you will give birth
   to children.
Your desire will be for your husband,
   and he will rule over you."

¹⁷To Adam he said, "Because you listened to your wife and ate fruit from the tree about which I commanded you, 'You must not eat from it,'

"Cursed is the ground because of you;

through painful toil you will eat food
   from it
   all the days of your life.
¹⁸It will produce thorns and thistles for
   you,
   and you will eat the plants of the field.
¹⁹By the sweat of your brow
   you will eat your food
until you return to the ground,
   since from it you were taken;
for dust you are
   and to dust you will return."

²⁰Adam[c] named his wife Eve,[d] because she would become the mother of all the living.
²¹The LORD God made garments of skin for Adam and his wife and clothed them.

ᵃ 15 Or seed   ᵇ 15 Or strike   ᶜ 20 Or The man   ᵈ 20 Eve probably means living.

3:14–19 | Two curses followed man's sin: the curse on **the serpent** (Satan) and the curse on **the ground**. These curses will not be resolved until the events described in Revelation 20–22. Notice that man and woman are not cursed. God blessed them in 1:28; once God blesses, He cannot curse (Num. 23:7, 8).
3:15 | Some scholars call this verse the *protoevangelium* (*proto* means "first"; *evangelium* means "gospel") because the words **he will crush your head, and you will strike his heel** contain the seed form of the earliest statement of the "first gospel"–the good news of salvation. The coming of the woman's offspring was fulfilled in Jesus' birth (Matt. 1–2; Luke 2; Gal. 4:4). On the cross, Jesus' body was bruised and broken; at the second coming of Christ, Satan's head will be crushed (Rom. 16:20).
3:16–19 | With the curse on humanity came five tragic realities: sorrow, pain, relational discord, sweat, and death (Job 14:1; Rom. 8:20–22). This movement toward breakdown anticipated science's Second Law of Thermodynamics. It also counters evolution, which claims that systems improve over time.

3:17 | **Adam** bore the weight of the curse of the ground because he was the head–not only of his **wife** but also of all humankind. With Adam's sin, humanity's paradise became a hostile wilderness: the roses grew thorns and the tigers became meat eaters. The entire world groans for Eden to be re-created. When Christ returns to rule and reign on this earth during the Millennium, life will resume as it was before the curse (Ps. 65). The full resolution will be in the eternal state (Rev. 21–22).
3:21 | With sin comes self-consciousness and shame. God made Adam and Eve **garments of skin** from animals; thus blood was shed as a result of their sin. This event foreshadows the necessity of blood sacrifices–first of animals and then of Christ–to bridge humanity's sin-separation from God (Heb. 9:22). What God does to fully clothe the couple demonstrates the inadequacy of the fig-leaf coverings that Adam and Eve made for themselves (3:7). Human attempts at self-sufficiency will always fall short of God's abundant provision.

²²And the LORD God said, "The man has now become like one of us, knowing good and evil. He must not be allowed to reach out his hand and take also from the tree of life and eat, and live forever." ²³So the LORD God banished him from the Garden of Eden to work the ground from which he had been taken. ²⁴After he drove the man out, he placed on the east side*ᵃ* of the Garden of Eden cherubim and a flaming sword flashing back and forth to guard the way to the tree of life.

Cain and Abel

4 Adam*ᵇ* made love to his wife Eve, and she became pregnant and gave birth to Cain.*ᶜ* She said, "With the help of the LORD I have brought forth*ᵈ* a man." ²Later she gave birth to his brother Abel.

Now Abel kept flocks, and Cain worked the soil. ³In the course of time Cain brought some of the fruits of the soil as an offering to the LORD. ⁴And Abel also brought an offering—fat portions from some of the firstborn of his flock. The LORD looked with favor on Abel and his offering, ⁵but on Cain and his offering he did not look with favor. So Cain was very angry, and his face was downcast.

⁶Then the LORD said to Cain, "Why are you angry? Why is your face downcast? ⁷If you do what is right, will you not be accepted? But if you do not do what is right, sin is crouching at your door; it desires to have you, but you must rule over it."

⁸Now Cain said to his brother Abel, "Let's go out to the field."*ᵉ* While they were in the field, Cain attacked his brother Abel and killed him.

⁹Then the LORD said to Cain, "Where is your brother Abel?"

"I don't know," he replied. "Am I my brother's keeper?"

¹⁰The LORD said, "What have you done? Listen! Your brother's blood cries out to me from the ground. ¹¹Now you are under a curse and driven from the ground, which opened its mouth to receive your brother's blood from your hand. ¹²When you work the ground, it will no longer yield its crops for you. You will be a restless wanderer on the earth."

¹³Cain said to the LORD, "My punishment is more than I can bear. ¹⁴Today you are driving me from the land, and I will be hidden from your presence; I will be a restless wanderer on the earth, and whoever finds me will kill me."

¹⁵But the LORD said to him, "Not so*ᶠ*; anyone who kills Cain will suffer vengeance seven times over." Then the LORD put a mark on Cain so that no one who found him would kill him. ¹⁶So Cain went out from the LORD's presence and lived in the land of Nod,*ᵍ* east of Eden.

¹⁷Cain made love to his wife, and she became pregnant and gave birth to Enoch. Cain was then building a city, and he named it after his son Enoch. ¹⁸To Enoch was born Irad, and Irad was the father of Mehujael, and Mehujael was the father of Methushael, and Methushael was the father of Lamech.

¹⁹Lamech married two women, one named Adah and the other Zillah. ²⁰Adah gave birth to Jabal; he was the father of those who live in tents and raise livestock. ²¹His brother's name was Jubal; he was the father of all who play stringed instruments and pipes. ²²Zillah also had a son, Tubal-Cain, who forged all kinds of tools out of*ʰ* bronze and iron. Tubal-Cain's sister was Naamah.

²³Lamech said to his wives,

"Adah and Zillah, listen to me;
    wives of Lamech, hear my words.
I have killed a man for wounding me,
    a young man for injuring me.

ᵃ 24 Or placed in front.   ᵇ 1 Or The man   ᶜ 1 Cain sounds like the Hebrew for brought forth or acquired.   ᵈ 1 Or have acquired   ᵉ 8 Samaritan Pentateuch, Septuagint, Vulgate and Syriac; Masoretic Text does not have "Let's go out to the field."   ᶠ 15 Septuagint, Vulgate and Syriac; Hebrew Very well   ᵍ 16 Nod means wandering (see verses 12 and 14).   ʰ 22 Or who instructed all who work in

---

4:1–8 | Genesis is the book of firsts. This chapter features the first mother, the first birth, the first family, the first murder, the first martyrdom, and the first conflict between the two seeds of Adam.

4:1 | In Hebrew, the name **Cain** sounds like the verb translated **I have brought forth**. Eve believed she had received the promise of 3:15 and that her son would conquer Satan and reverse the effects of the Fall. This first birth affirms the truth that all children are a gift from the Lord.

4:3, 4 | **Cain** and **Abel** reflect every person's choice regarding how to approach Almighty God. The shepherd Abel was careful to give on God's terms: he offered his finest, the **fat portions from some of the firstborn of his flock**. In contrast, farmer Cain's sacrifice was merely a token, offered on his own casual terms. Cain's gift was not given from a heart devoted to God (Num. 18:12; Heb. 11:4).

4:5–7 | Cain's response to God hints at why God **did not look**

with favor on Cain and his offering. Those who become **angry** when someone in authority legitimately corrects them reveal selfish hearts. Cain further rejected God's authority by ignoring God's invitation to make the right choice.

4:10 | Abel's **blood cries out to** [Almighty God] **from the ground** for judgment against the one who killed him. God gives life to all things, and He alone possesses the right to take it away.

4:16 | **Cain** is mentioned three times in the NT, each time as a negative example (Heb. 11:4; 1 John 3:12; Jude 11). His is a sad tale of the effects of sin in the world.

4:23, 24 | Before the law was given, no restraints were placed on vengeance. If someone injured a person, that person or his relatives could destroy the perpetrator. **Lamech** demonstrates this world of unrestrained vengeance. Limited retaliation will come with the giving of the law (Ex. 21:24; Deut. 19:19–21).

For Reflection   The Power of an Obituary Column • 5:1–32

A pastor friend told me that a woman in his congregation had been trying to get a neighbor to come to church. On the Sunday that the neighbor finally did attend, the pastor happened to be preaching the fifth chapter of Genesis. In perusing the chapter, the woman was mortified that her friend would have to sit through an exposition of what is essentially an obituary column. But her guest was already there, and it was too late to turn him away.

She had no cause for worry: her neighbor was saved by hearing that sermon. He realized that if all those people had died, he was going to die too, and he needed to prepare for death by getting right with God. From beginning to end, in every chapter and verse, God's Word is living and powerful (Heb. 4:12).

24 If Cain is avenged seven times,
    then Lamech seventy-seven times."

25 Adam made love to his wife again, and she gave birth to a son and named him Seth,ᵃ saying, "God has granted me another child in place of Abel, since Cain killed him." 26 Seth also had a son, and he named him Enosh.

At that time people began to call onᵇ the name of the LORD.

From Adam to Noah

5 This is the written account of Adam's family line.

When God created mankind, he made them in the likeness of God. 2 He created them male and female and blessed them. And he named them "Mankind"ᶜ when they were created.

3 When Adam had lived 130 years, he had a son in his own likeness, in his own image; and he named him Seth. 4 After Seth was born, Adam lived 800 years and had other sons and daughters. 5 Altogether, Adam lived a total of 930 years, and then he died.

6 When Seth had lived 105 years, he became the fatherᵈ of Enosh. 7 After he became the father of Enosh, Seth lived 807 years and had other sons and daughters. 8 Altogether, Seth lived a total of 912 years, and then he died.

9 When Enosh had lived 90 years, he became the father of Kenan. 10 After he became the father of Kenan, Enosh lived 815 years and had other sons and daughters. 11 Altogether, Enosh lived a total of 905 years, and then he died.

12 When Kenan had lived 70 years, he became the father of Mahalalel. 13 After he became the father of Mahalalel, Kenan lived

840 years and had other sons and daughters. 14 Altogether, Kenan lived a total of 910 years, and then he died.

15 When Mahalalel had lived 65 years, he became the father of Jared. 16 After he became the father of Jared, Mahalalel lived 830 years and had other sons and daughters. 17 Altogether, Mahalalel lived a total of 895 years, and then he died.

18 When Jared had lived 162 years, he became the father of Enoch. 19 After he became the father of Enoch, Jared lived 800 years and had other sons and daughters. 20 Altogether, Jared lived a total of 962 years, and then he died.

21 When Enoch had lived 65 years, he became the father of Methuselah. 22 After he became the father of Methuselah, Enoch walked faithfully with God 300 years and had other sons and daughters. 23 Altogether, Enoch lived a total of 365 years. 24 Enoch walked faithfully with God; then he was no more, because God took him away.

25 When Methuselah had lived 187 years, he became the father of Lamech. 26 After he became the father of Lamech, Methuselah lived 782 years and had other sons and daughters. 27 Altogether, Methuselah lived a total of 969 years, and then he died.

28 When Lamech had lived 182 years, he had a son. 29 He named him Noahᵉ and said, "He will comfort us in the labor and painful toil of our hands caused by the ground the LORD has cursed." 30 After Noah was born, Lamech lived 595 years and had other sons and daughters. 31 Altogether, Lamech lived a total of 777 years, and then he died.

32 After Noah was 500 years old, he became the father of Shem, Ham and Japheth.

ᵃ 25 Seth probably means granted.   ᵇ 26 Or to proclaim   ᶜ 2 Hebrew adam   ᵈ 6 Father may mean ancestor; also in verses 7-26.   ᵉ 29 Noah sounds like the Hebrew for comfort.

5:3–31 | The refrain **and then he died** is used throughout this chapter—until **Enoch** (5:24). He did not die; he walked with God right out of his earthly home and into his heavenly home.
5:21-24 | **Enoch** was an ordinary man who did one extraordinary

thing: he **walked faithfully with God** (the first person of whom this is said, and one of only several men whom the Bible describes in this way). Enoch was so close to God that God took Enoch into His confidence and gave him information about the coming judgment (Heb. 11:5; Jude 14).

Wickedness in the World

6 When human beings began to increase in number on the earth and daughters were born to them, [2]the sons of God saw that the daughters of humans were beautiful, and they married any of them they chose. [3]Then the LORD said, "My Spirit will not contend with[a] humans forever, for they are mortal[b]; their days will be a hundred and twenty years."

[4]The Nephilim were on the earth in those days—and also afterward—when the sons of God went to the daughters of humans and had children by them. They were the heroes of old, men of renown.

[5]The LORD saw how great the wickedness of the human race had become on the earth, and that every inclination of the thoughts of the human heart was only evil all the time. [6]The LORD regretted that he had made human beings on the earth, and his heart was deeply troubled. [7]So the LORD said, "I will wipe from the face of the earth the human race I have created—and with them the animals, the birds and the creatures that move along the ground—for I regret that I have made them." [8]But Noah found favor in the eyes of the LORD.

Noah and the Flood

[9]This is the account of Noah and his family.

Noah was a righteous man, blameless among the people of his time, and he walked faithfully with God. [10]Noah had three sons: Shem, Ham and Japheth.

Who are the sons of God? • 6:2

There are three primary theories about the *sons of God*. In Job (1:6; 2:1; 38:7), the term sons of God describes angels. In this theory, fallen angels saw the daughters of men, were filled with lust, and cohabited with them, producing giants called "Nephilim" (6:4), who were half angelic and half human. A second possibility is that the sons of God were the descendants of Seth who married Cain's female descendants. A third view is that the sons of God were powerful kings who collected wives, leading to the beginning of royal polygamy. In any case, the relationships seem to have involved sexual perversion, with men taking any women they wanted.

[11]Now the earth was corrupt in God's sight and was full of violence. [12]God saw how corrupt the earth had become, for all the people on earth had corrupted their ways. [13]So God said to Noah, "I am going to put an end to all people, for the earth is filled with violence because of them. I am surely going to destroy both them and the earth. [14]So make yourself an ark of cypress[c] wood; make rooms in it and coat it with pitch inside and out. [15]This is how you are to build it: The ark is to be three hundred cubits long, fifty cubits wide and thirty cubits high.[d] [16]Make a roof for it, leaving below the roof an opening one cubit[e] high all around.[f] Put a door in the side of the ark and make lower, middle and upper

[a] *3* Or *My spirit will not remain in*   [b] *3* Or *corrupt*   [c] *14* The meaning of the Hebrew for this word is uncertain.   [d] *15* That is, about 450 feet long, 75 feet wide and 45 feet high or about 135 meters long, 23 meters long and 14 meters high   [e] *16* That is, about 18 inches or about 45 centimeters   [f] *16* The meaning of the Hebrew for this clause is uncertain.

6:1-4 | This is a difficult passage, but the likely meaning of **the sons of God . . . the daughters of humans** is that fallen angels took on the human form of men and married human women (lit., "the daughters of Adam"). This illicit marriage of spirit beings and human beings was an affront to the divine order of reproducing according to one's kind (1:24).
6:3 | This is the second outright mention of the Spirit in Genesis. The first is in connection with Creation (1:2), while this one—**My Spirit will not contend . . . forever**—speaks of destruction. Like the people of Noah's day, those who do not respond to God's Spirit have no guarantee that He will continue to prod, convict, and remind them of the importance of fellowship with Him. That humanity's **days will be a hundred and twenty years** can mean either that the Flood would come after 120 years or, less likely, that the average human lifespan would be 120 years.
6:5 | In the Bible's most definitive statement about human depravity, such emphatic words are used that there is no room for misinterpretation: **every inclination** of every person's **heart** was **only evil all the time.** (There is no word in the Hebrew Bible for the mind, so *heart* represents a person's thinking as well as his or her emotions and will.) Although the people of Noah's day were exceedingly wicked—in essence, evil all the time in every thought and deed—no part of any individual's life to this day has escaped the consequent corruption of original sin (Ps. 14:1-3; Rom. 6:5). Only the blood of Christ removes sin's stain.

6:6 | That God's **heart was deeply troubled** by humanity's wickedness shows that He has emotions (1 Sam. 15:11, 29; 2 Sam. 24:16; Isa. 63:10; Eph. 4:30). He sorrows over the sin of His children in the way a human parent grieves over a rebellious or estranged son or daughter.
6:8, 9 | Why was **Noah** chosen? For the same reason anyone is chosen: because he **found favor**—the undeserved grace of God. It is God's grace that saves depraved humans from the flood of sin, not a person's works (Eph. 2:8, 9). In the OT, to be **righteous** means to be genuine and sincere. In the NT, it means to be right with God. In both cases, Noah qualified!
6:9 | Virtually nothing is known about the first 500 years of Noah's life except that he was a **righteous** man—the only **blameless** person then living **among the people of his time** on earth. And like Enoch, he **walked faithfully with God** (5:21, 22).
6:13 | Noah labored unremarkably for the first two-thirds of his life and was approaching "retirement age" when the call of God came. Throughout history, God has often raised up a champion for the cause of righteousness in a time of widespread immorality.
6:14-16 | The **ark** God commanded Noah to build was huge: three stories high (45 feet) and 450 feet long. However, most contemporary depictions of the ark are too boatlike. The ark was not a ship designed to travel from one port to another but a floating box intended to keep living things from drowning. This massive construction project took Noah and his three sons about 100 years to complete (5:32; 7:6, 11).

decks. [17]I am going to bring floodwaters on the earth to destroy all life under the heavens, every creature that has the breath of life in it. Everything on earth will perish. [18]But I will establish my covenant with you, and you will enter the ark—you and your sons and your wife and your sons' wives with you. [19]You are to bring into the ark two of all living creatures, male and female, to keep them alive with you. [20]Two of every kind of bird, of every kind of animal and of every kind of creature that moves along the ground will come to you to be kept alive. [21]You are to take every kind of food that is to be eaten and store it away as food for you and for them."

[22]Noah did everything just as God commanded him.

7 The LORD then said to Noah, "Go into the ark, you and your whole family, because I have found you righteous in this generation. [2]Take with you seven pairs of every kind of clean animal, a male and its mate, and one pair of every kind of unclean animal, a male and its mate, [3]and also seven pairs of every kind of bird, male and female, to keep their various kinds alive throughout the earth. [4]Seven days from now I will send rain on the earth for forty days and forty nights, and I will wipe from the face of the earth every living creature I have made."

[5]And Noah did all that the LORD commanded him.

[6]Noah was six hundred years old when the floodwaters came on the earth. [7]And Noah and his sons and his wife and his sons' wives entered the ark to escape the waters of the flood. [8]Pairs of clean and unclean animals, of birds and of all creatures that move along the ground, [9]male and female, came to Noah and entered the ark, as God had commanded Noah. [10]And after the seven days the floodwaters came on the earth.

[11]In the six hundredth year of Noah's life, on the seventeenth day of the second month—on that day all the springs of the great deep burst forth, and the floodgates of the heavens were opened. [12]And rain fell on the earth forty days and forty nights.

[13]On that very day Noah and his sons, Shem, Ham and Japheth, together with his wife and the wives of his three sons, entered the ark. [14]They had with them every wild animal according to its kind, all livestock according to their kinds, every creature that moves along the ground according to its kind and every bird according to its kind, everything with wings. [15]Pairs of all creatures that have the breath of life in them came to Noah and entered the ark. [16]The animals going in were male and female of every living thing, as God had commanded Noah. Then the LORD shut him in.

FLOOD CHRONOLOGY • 7:1–8:17	
Day 1	Noah and his family board the ark. Seven pairs of all clean and one pair of all unclean animals board the ark.
Day 7	Floodwaters come on the earth.
Day 40	Last day of rain.
Day 150	After all things outside the ark die, the flood recedes.
Day 224	Tops of the mountains dry.
Day 264	Noah sends out a raven.
Day 271	Noah releases a dove that returns because there is no dry land.
Day 278	Noah releases the dove again, and it returns with an olive leaf.
Day 285	Noah releases the dove, but it does not return.
Day 314	Noah removes the covering of the ark, so he can see the dry land.
Day 370	God tells Noah to leave the ark with his family and all the animals.

6:17 | When God approached Noah to build an ark because **floodwaters** would come **on the earth**, the earth had received only moisture from the ground, never any rain (2:5, 6). So Noah's obedience was truly "by faith" (Heb. 11:7). He could not anticipate what was coming based on past experience; still, he believed God, and that was enough reason for him to build.

6:18 | This is the first mention of a **covenant**. In it, God promises to redeem a people for Himself (9:9–17).

6:22 | God gave Noah exact proportions, and Noah **did everything just as God commanded him.** People want to pick and choose what to believe, but Noah believed and obeyed *everything* God said—and that obedience saved him and his family as well as all the generations after him. Present obedience to the whole truth of God's Word can impact future generations as well.

7:2 | Because the **clean** animals would be used for sacrifices after the Flood, Noah brought **seven** of each—both male and

female—onto the ark (8:20; 9:3; Lev. 11:1–47).

7:7 | Noah's entire family believed God—**his sons and his wife and his sons' wives.** In fact, they were the only true believers in that violent and corrupt era (1 Pet. 2:5; 3:20). Faith is not transferable within a family, but it can be contagious.

7:11, 12 | Water, now unrestrained by God, comes from everywhere—not just from below the ground (**all the springs of the great deep**), but for the first time ever, from **the floodgates of the heavens**.

7:16 | Noah obeyed God's instructions for boarding the ark, but God Himself **shut him in** when all the preparations were complete. The closed door symbolized God's protection. According to Pastor R. Kent Hughes, the message of the Flood is not the Flood itself or even God's judgment; rather, "the story focuses on Noah as the kind of man who is saved out of a lost world. The message is salvific"—the faithful God rescues and safely delivers His righteous ones.

[17] For forty days the flood kept coming on the earth, and as the waters increased they lifted the ark high above the earth. [18] The waters rose and increased greatly on the earth, and the ark floated on the surface of the water. [19] They rose greatly on the earth, and all the high mountains under the entire heavens were covered. [20] The waters rose and covered the mountains to a depth of more than fifteen cubits. [a,b] [21] Every living thing that moved on land perished—birds, livestock, wild animals, all the creatures that swarm over the earth, and all mankind. [22] Everything on dry land that had the breath of life in its nostrils died. [23] Every living thing on the face of the earth was wiped out; people and animals and the creatures that move along the ground and the birds were wiped from the earth. Only Noah was left, and those with him in the ark.

[24] The waters flooded the earth for a hundred and fifty days.

8 But God remembered Noah and all the wild animals and the livestock that were with him in the ark, and he sent a wind over the earth, and the waters receded. [2] Now the springs of the deep and the floodgates of the heavens had been closed, and the rain had stopped falling from the sky. [3] The water receded steadily from the earth. At the end of the hundred and fifty days the water had gone down, [4] and on the seventeenth day of the seventh month the ark came to rest on the mountains of Ararat. [5] The waters continued to recede until the tenth month, and on the first day of the tenth month the tops of the mountains became visible.

[6] After forty days Noah opened a window he had made in the ark [7] and sent out a raven, and it kept flying back and forth until the water had dried up from the earth. [8] Then he sent out a dove to see if the water had receded from the surface of the ground. [9] But the dove could find nowhere to perch because there was water over all the surface of the earth; so it returned to Noah in the ark. He reached out his hand and took the dove and brought it back to himself in the ark. [10] He waited seven more days and again sent out the dove from the ark. [11] When the dove returned to him in the evening, there in its beak was a freshly plucked olive leaf! Then Noah knew that the water had receded from the earth. [12] He waited seven more days and sent the dove out again, but this time it did not return to him.

[13] By the first day of the first month of Noah's six hundred and first year, the water had dried up from the earth. Noah then removed the covering from the ark and saw that the surface of the ground was dry. [14] By the twenty-seventh day of the second month the earth was completely dry.

[15] Then God said to Noah, [16] "Come out of the ark, you and your wife and your sons and their wives. [17] Bring out every kind of living creature that is with you—the birds, the animals, and all the creatures that move along the ground—so they can multiply on the earth and be fruitful and increase in number on it."

[18] So Noah came out, together with his sons and his wife and his sons' wives. [19] All the animals and all the creatures that move along the ground and all the birds—everything that moves on land—came out of the ark, one kind after another.

[20] Then Noah built an altar to the LORD and, taking some of all the clean animals and clean birds, he sacrificed burnt offerings on it. [21] The LORD smelled the pleasing

---

[a] 20 That is, about 23 feet or about 6.8 meters   [b] 20 Or rose more than fifteen cubits, and the mountains were covered

---

7:19–23 | The use of emphatic words communicates how complete and catastrophic the Flood was: the waters **rose greatly**, covering everything **under the entire heavens . . . every living thing . . . perished**, including **all** human beings and animals; all living things were **wiped from the earth**. The biblical record makes it clear that every creature outside the ark perished, without exception.
8:1–3 | Because of Noah's righteousness, **God remembered** him and all that were in the ark, and the Lord moved nature on behalf of this remnant to bring them out of the boat. They would be the means by which God would restore and repopulate the earth (9:1, 19).

8:1 | **Remembered** does not mean that God forgot but that He took action to fulfill His promise (Ps. 106:4).
8:6–12 | Noah's faith, obedience, and righteousness have been commended throughout this account. As careful as he was to obey God's commands before the Flood, he was equally patient and purposeful while waiting for the waters to recede.
8:20 | Noah's first act upon exiting the ark was to build an **altar** commemorating the Lord's deliverance. This set an important example for his sons, who would be the "Adams" of the post-Flood earth.

aroma and said in his heart: "Never again will I curse the ground because of humans, even though[a] every inclination of the human heart is evil from childhood. And never again will I destroy all living creatures, as I have done.

²² "As long as the earth endures,
    seedtime and harvest,
    cold and heat,
    summer and winter,
    day and night
    will never cease."

God's Covenant With Noah

9 Then God blessed Noah and his sons, saying to them, "Be fruitful and increase in number and fill the earth. ²The fear and dread of you will fall on all the beasts of the earth, and on all the birds in the sky, on every creature that moves along the ground, and on all the fish in the sea; they are given into your hands. ³Everything that lives and moves about will be food for you. Just as I gave you the green plants, I now give you everything.

⁴ "But you must not eat meat that has its lifeblood still in it. ⁵And for your lifeblood I will surely demand an accounting. I will demand an accounting from every animal. And from each human being, too, I will demand an accounting for the life of another human being.

⁶ "Whoever sheds human blood,
    by humans shall their blood be shed;
    for in the image of God
    has God made mankind.

⁷ As for you, be fruitful and increase in number; multiply on the earth and increase upon it."

⁸Then God said to Noah and to his sons with him: ⁹ "I now establish my covenant with you and with your descendants after you ¹⁰and with every living creature that was with you—the birds, the livestock and all the wild animals, all those that came out of the ark with you—every living creature on earth. ¹¹I establish my covenant with

---

you: Never again will all life be destroyed by the waters of a flood; never again will there be a flood to destroy the earth."

¹²And God said, "This is the sign of the covenant I am making between me and you and every living creature with you, a covenant for all generations to come: ¹³I have set my rainbow in the clouds, and it will be the sign of the covenant between me and the earth. ¹⁴Whenever I bring clouds over the earth and the rainbow appears in the clouds, ¹⁵I will remember my covenant between me and you and all living creatures of every kind. Never again will the waters become a flood to destroy all life. ¹⁶Whenever the rainbow appears in the clouds, I will see it and remember the everlasting covenant between God and all living creatures of every kind on the earth."

¹⁷So God said to Noah, "This is the sign of the covenant I have established between me and all life on the earth."

The Sons of Noah

¹⁸The sons of Noah who came out of the ark were Shem, Ham and Japheth. (Ham was the father of Canaan.) ¹⁹These were the three sons of Noah, and from them came the people who were scattered over the whole earth.

²⁰Noah, a man of the soil, proceeded[b] to plant a vineyard. ²¹When he drank some

---

[a] 21 Or humans, for   [b] 20 Or soil, was the first

9:1–17 | God established the institution of the family in 2:18–25; He establishes the institution of government here. God also makes a dietary concession from the original created order (1:29), allowing humans to eat **everything that lives and moves** (9:3) instead of just plants (Acts 10:9–16).

9:5, 6 | The phrase **whoever sheds human blood, by humans shall their blood be shed** invokes capital punishment as just retribution for murder under certain conditions—a mandate that has not been rescinded.

9:9–17 | God's **covenant** with Noah—the first of four covenants that God initiates in the OT—includes all animals and Noah's descendants.

9:12, 13 | A **rainbow** is associated with God's glory in both the Old and New Testaments (Ezek. 1:28; Rev. 4:3). Here, it will be a perpetual **sign** of His faithful promise to every future generation and every living creature.

9:18, 19 | Noah had only three sons: **Shem, Ham,** and **Japheth.** But from these three young men, the **whole earth** was populated once more.

of its wine, he became drunk and lay un-covered inside his tent. ²²Ham, the fa-ther of Canaan, saw his father naked and told his two brothers outside. ²³But Shem and Japheth took a garment and laid it across their shoulders; then they walked in backward and covered their father's na-ked body. Their faces were turned the other way so that they would not see their father naked.

²⁴When Noah awoke from his wine and found out what his youngest son had done to him, ²⁵he said,

"Cursed be Canaan!
   The lowest of slaves
   will he be to his brothers."

²⁶He also said,

"Praise be to the Lord, the God of
   Shem!
May Canaan be the slave of Shem.
²⁷May God extend Japheth's^a territory;
   may Japheth live in the tents of
   Shem,
   and may Canaan be the slave of
   Japheth."

²⁸After the flood Noah lived 350 years. ²⁹Noah lived a total of 950 years, and then he died.

The Table of Nations

10 This is the account of Shem, Ham and Japheth, Noah's sons, who them-selves had sons after the flood.

The Japhethites
²The sons^b of Japheth:
   Gomer, Magog, Madai, Javan, Tubal,
   Meshek and Tiras.
³The sons of Gomer:
   Ashkenaz, Riphath and Togarmah.
⁴The sons of Javan:
   Elishah, Tarshish, the Kittites
   and the Rodanites.^c ⁵(From these
   the maritime peoples spread out
   into their territories by their clans

within their nations, each with its own language.)

The Hamites
⁶The sons of Ham:
   Cush, Egypt, Put and Canaan.
⁷The sons of Cush:
   Seba, Havilah, Sabtah, Raamah and
   Sabteka.
The sons of Raamah:
   Sheba and Dedan.

⁸Cush was the father^d of Nimrod, who became a mighty warrior on the earth. ⁹He was a mighty hunter before the Lord; that is why it is said, "Like Nimrod, a mighty hunt-er before the Lord." ¹⁰The first centers of his kingdom were Babylon, Uruk, Akkad and Kalneh, in^e Shinar.^f ¹¹From that land he went to Assyria, where he built Nineveh, Rehoboth Ir,^g Calah ¹²and Resen, which is between Nineveh and Calah—which is the great city.

¹³Egypt was the father of
   the Ludites, Anamites, Lehabites,
   Naphtuhites, ¹⁴Pathrusites, Kas-
   luhites (from whom the Philistines
   came) and Caphtorites.
¹⁵Canaan was the father of
   Sidon his firstborn,^h and of the Hittites, ¹⁶Jebusites, Amorites, Girgashites, ¹⁷Hivites, Arkites, Si-
   nites, ¹⁸Arvadites, Zemarites and
   Hamathites.

Later the Canaanite clans scattered ¹⁹and the borders of Canaan reached from Sidon toward Gerar as far as Gaza, and then to-ward Sodom, Gomorrah, Admah and Ze-boyim, as far as Lasha.
²⁰These are the sons of Ham by their clans and languages, in their territories and nations.

---

^a *27 Japheth sounds like the Hebrew for extend.*   ^b *2 Sons may mean descendants or successors or nations; also in verses 3, 4, 6, 7, 20-23, 29 and 31.*   ^c *4 Some manuscripts of the Masoretic Text and Samaritan Pentateuch (see also Septuagint and 1 Chron. 1:7); most manuscripts of the Masoretic Text Dodanites*   ^d *8 Father may mean ancestor or predecessor or founder; also in verses 13, 15, 24 and 26.*   ^e *10 Or Uruk and Akkad—all of them in*   ^f *10 That is, Babylonia*   ^g *11 Or Nineveh with its city squares*   ^h *15 Or of the Sidonians, the foremost*

9:20, 21 | The Bible's candid portrayal of the heroes of the faith gives a complete picture of God's redemptive plan and His ability to use flawed humans. Noah's plunge from exemplary faithfulness to a drunken, disgraceful stupor is a reminder that no one ever stops needing grace, even in old age. Every Christian is prone to sin; there is no riding on the coattails of past obedience.
9:24–27 | The descendants of Ham's cursed son **Canaan** eventu-ally became Israel's primary enemy, the Canaanites. From the sons of Ham, additional enemy nations would be born in succeeding generations, including Babylon (10:6–10).

10:6 | **Cush** is sometimes called Ethiopia, and **Put**, Libya (Ezek. 38:5). The Cushites, a major people group in the southern part of modern-day Sudan, have significant connections with Egypt, and through Egypt, connections with the Hebrew people. Moses' second wife was a Cushite (Num. 12:1).
10:8–10 | **Nimrod** was the first world dictator, and he founded **Babylon**. Babylon is second only to Jerusalem as the most-mentioned city in the Bible (over 280 times), but every reference is negative. Babylon represents the false systems of religion on the earth.

The Two Idols of Babel • 11:4

God's intent for the nations was for people to spread across the earth, not to congregate in one place. In the beginning He told mankind to "be fruitful and increase in number; fill the earth" (1:28; 9:1), because He wanted the whole earth populated with His image-bearers (1:26, 27). This command was a foreshadowing of the Great Commission in which Jesus told His disciples to repopulate the earth with a new "race" of spiritual people (Matt. 28:16–20), born again in "the image of his Son" (Rom. 8:29).

As Paul explained, God scattered men and set "the boundaries of their lands" (Acts 17:26) so they would seek after God. Humankind, settling in smaller communities throughout the world, would not be tempted toward the self-importance and self-reliance that massive centralization would foster—and did indeed foster at Shinar.

Nimrod's new world order was an act of rebellion against God because it was motivated by pride. The presumption of utter independence forced God out of the people's hearts and deposed Him as the rightful King of their lives, replacing Him with self. In 11:4 we discover that the two idols of the tower builders' hearts were security and significance—the security of controlling their circumstances and the significance of creating a city and a tower that would magnify their name.

The Semites

²¹ Sons were also born to Shem, whose older brother was[a] Japheth; Shem was the ancestor of all the sons of Eber.

²² The sons of Shem:

Elam, Ashur, Arphaxad, Lud and Aram.

²³ The sons of Aram:

Uz, Hul, Gether and Meshek.[b]

²⁴ Arphaxad was the father of[c] Shelah,

and Shelah the father of Eber.

²⁵ Two sons were born to Eber:

One was named Peleg,[d] because in his time the earth was divided; his brother was named Joktan.

²⁶ Joktan was the father of

Almodad, Sheleph, Hazarmaveth, Jerah, ²⁷ Hadoram, Uzal, Diklah, ²⁸ Obal, Abimael, Sheba, ²⁹ Ophir, Havilah and Jobab. All these were sons of Joktan.

³⁰ The region where they lived stretched from Mesha toward Sephar, in the eastern hill country.

³¹ These are the sons of Shem by their clans and languages, in their territories and nations.

³² These are the clans of Noah's sons, according to their lines of descent, within their nations. From these the nations spread out over the earth after the flood.

The Tower of Babel

11 Now the whole world had one language and a common speech. ² As people moved eastward,[e] they found a plain in Shinar[f] and settled there.

³ They said to each other, "Come, let's make bricks and bake them thoroughly." They used brick instead of stone, and tar for mortar. ⁴ Then they said, "Come, let us build ourselves a city, with a tower that reaches to the heavens, so that we may make a name for ourselves; otherwise we will be scattered over the face of the whole earth."

⁵ But the LORD came down to see the city and the tower the people were building. ⁶ The LORD said, "If as one people speaking the same language they have begun to do this, then nothing they plan to do will be impossible for them. ⁷ Come, let us go down and confuse their language so they will not understand each other."

---

[a] 21 Or Shem, the older brother of   [b] 23 See Septuagint and 1 Chron. 1:17; Hebrew Mash.   [c] 24 Hebrew; Septuagint father of Cainan, and Cainan was the father of   [d] 25 Peleg means division.   [e] 2 Or from the east; or in the east   [f] 2 That is, Babylonia

---

10:21-25 | Shem's great-grandson **Eber** is mentioned before his own sons, which reveals his importance to the Jewish people. Eber was an ancestor of Abraham, and the word *Hebrew* is likely derived from his name.

11:2 | **Shinar**, in the region now known as Iraq, was the location of the ancient kingdom of Babylon. The mighty leader Nimrod (see note on 10:8–10) was the one who decided to draw all peoples together to form a powerful society and secure their unified might by constructing a massive tower—a symbol of human pride.

11:3, 4 | Here the tower builders refer to themselves repeatedly (**us, we, ourselves**), yet they never mention God. Their attitude resoundingly echoed Satan's unholy ambition as expressed in the words of the Babylonian king: "I will ascend to the heavens; I will raise my throne above the stars of God; . . . I will make myself like

the Most High" (Isa. 14:13, 14). The people were driven not only by rebellious pride (**make a name**) and self-sufficiency but also by fear (**otherwise we will be scattered**).

11:5 | Of course God could see the Tower of Babel from the moment of its inception, but for the writer to mention that **the LORD came down to see the city** humorously emphasizes how far above their tower the Lord was. The people could never reach the heavens or attain God's greatness no matter how high they might build.

11:8, 9 | Nimrod's attempt to move all people to Shinar directly opposed God's command to multiply and fill the earth (1:28; 9:1), so God **scattered** the people. From this point on, humans diversified into distinct linguistic, ethnic, and societal groupings—all in need of the message of God's grace.

⁸So the LORD scattered them from there over all the earth, and they stopped building the city. ⁹That is why it was called Babel[a]—because there the LORD confused the language of the whole world. From there the LORD scattered them over the face of the whole earth.

From Shem to Abram

¹⁰This is the account of Shem's family line.

Two years after the flood, when Shem was 100 years old, he became the father[b] of Arphaxad. ¹¹And after he became the father of Arphaxad, Shem lived 500 years and had other sons and daughters.

¹²When Arphaxad had lived 35 years, he became the father of Shelah. ¹³And after he became the father of Shelah, Arphaxad lived 403 years and had other sons and daughters.[c]

¹⁴When Shelah had lived 30 years, he became the father of Eber. ¹⁵And after he became the father of Eber, Shelah lived 403 years and had other sons and daughters.

¹⁶When Eber had lived 34 years, he became the father of Peleg. ¹⁷And after he became the father of Peleg, Eber lived 430 years and had other sons and daughters.

¹⁸When Peleg had lived 30 years, he became the father of Reu. ¹⁹And after he became the father of Reu, Peleg lived 209 years and had other sons and daughters.

²⁰When Reu had lived 32 years, he became the father of Serug. ²¹And after he became the father of Serug, Reu lived 207 years and had other sons and daughters.

²²When Serug had lived 30 years, he became the father of Nahor. ²³And after he became the father of Nahor, Serug lived 200 years and had other sons and daughters.

²⁴When Nahor had lived 29 years, he became the father of Terah. ²⁵And after he became the father of Terah, Nahor lived 119 years and had other sons and daughters.

²⁶After Terah had lived 70 years, he became the father of Abram, Nahor and Haran.

Abram's Family

²⁷This is the account of Terah's family line.

Terah became the father of Abram, Nahor and Haran. And Haran became the father of Lot. ²⁸While his father Terah was still alive, Haran died in Ur of the Chaldeans, in the land of his birth. ²⁹Abram and Nahor both married. The name of Abram's wife was Sarai, and the name of Nahor's wife was Milkah; she was the daughter of Haran, the father of both Milkah and Iskah. ³⁰Now Sarai was childless because she was not able to conceive.

³¹Terah took his son Abram, his grandson Lot son of Haran, and his daughter-in-law Sarai, the wife of his son Abram, and together they set out from Ur of the Chaldeans to go to Canaan. But when they came to Harran, they settled there.

³²Terah lived 205 years, and he died in Harran.

The Call of Abram

12 The LORD had said to Abram, "Go from your country, your people and your father's household to the land I will show you.

²"I will make you into a great nation,
    and I will bless you;
I will make your name great,
    and you will be a blessing.[d]
³I will bless those who bless you,
    and whoever curses you I will curse;
and all peoples on earth
    will be blessed through you."[e]

---

[a] 9 That is, Babylon; *Babel* sounds like the Hebrew for *confused.*   [b] 10 *Father* may mean *ancestor*; also in verses 11-25.   [c] 12,13 Hebrew; Septuagint (see also Luke 3:35, 36 and note at Gen. 10:24) *35 years, he became the father of Cainan. ¹³And after he became the father of Cainan, Arphaxad lived 430 years and had other sons and daughters, and then he died. When Cainan had lived 130 years, he became the father of Shelah. And after he became the father of Shelah, Cainan lived 330 years and had other sons and daughters*   [d] 2 Or *be seen as blessed*   [e] 3 Or *earth / will use your name in blessings* (see 48:20)

11:26–28 | Abram was from **Ur of the Chaldeans**, long thought to be the major city by the same name near the Persian Gulf on the west side of the Euphrates River. It is now believed that the phrase *of the Chaldeans* was added to distinguish Abraham's Ur—east of Harran in far North Aram—from its more famous counterpart. Like the rest of the world at the time of Abram, Ur was probably a polytheistic city. This is where God would first appear to Abram.
11:26, 27 | Joshua 24:2 says of **Terah**—Abram's father—that he and his fathers "long ago . . . lived beyond the Euphrates River and worshiped other gods." So **Abram** (who becomes Abraham; 17:5) grew up in a family of idolaters as well as an idolatrous nation. Yet the one true God would call him out of that environment into a relationship with Himself.
11:29 | Sarai's name will later be changed to Sarah (17:15).

11:31 | Terah moved his family—including his son **Abram**, his grandson **Lot**, and his daughter-in-law **Sarai**—from their native land for reasons that the text does not state. **Harran** was a city of idolatry, just like the city they had left.
12:1–3 | These difficult commands from **the LORD . . . to Abram** (later called Abraham; 17:5, 6) were connected to extraordinary blessing. God's blessing of Abram would be both material and spiritual; Abraham's blessing of others would be spiritual (Gal. 3:14).
12:3–5 | As part of this covenant, God promised that those who treated Abram poorly would be cursed. History shows this to be true—those who abuse the Jewish people pay a price. The ultimate blessing, however, would be realized in the coming of the Messiah, in whom **all peoples on earth will be blessed** (Gal. 3:8). Abram's obedience was evident: he departed just as **the LORD had told him.**

> **Picture This** **Abraham's Tents and Altars • 12:8**
>
> It has been said that for Abram (who would be renamed Abraham), the symbol of his life was a tent, but the secret of his life was an altar. The tent spoke of his pilgrimage, of the fact that he never owned the land. There were times in Abram's life that he moved from place to place. There were also long periods where he lived in tents in the regions of Hebron or Beersheba. But only rarely do we read of Abraham living for a time in a city (20:1).
>
> The altar speaks of his fellowship with God, for it was the focal point of his worship. As God confirmed His commands, Abram confirmed his faith by worshiping and building an altar. In addition to Abram's worship was his witness. Refusing to worship on pagan altars, Abram built his own—a clear testimony of his commitment to the one true God. This is remarkable because he had been an idolater (Josh. 24:2). And when he "called on the name of the LORD," it was more than prayer; he proclaimed those promises in the Lord's name, testifying of his faith in the living God to the people who observed his worship.
>
> A tent and an altar are also the picture of the Christian life. According to God's Word, we are pilgrims and strangers here—the tent. But we are also to be in fellowship with the Lord by way of worship—the altar. And we, like Abram and Sarai, are to be witnesses of the reality of God in our lives.

⁴So Abram went, as the LORD had told him; and Lot went with him. Abram was seventy-five years old when he set out from Harran. ⁵He took his wife Sarai, his nephew Lot, all the possessions they had accumulated and the people they had acquired in Harran, and they set out for the land of Canaan, and they arrived there.

⁶Abram traveled through the land as far as the site of the great tree of Moreh at Shechem. At that time the Canaanites were in the land. ⁷The LORD appeared to Abram and said, "To your offspring*ᵃ* I will give this land." So he built an altar there to the LORD, who had appeared to him.

⁸From there he went on toward the hills east of Bethel and pitched his tent, with Bethel on the west and Ai on the east. There he built an altar to the LORD and called on the name of the LORD.

⁹Then Abram set out and continued toward the Negev.

Abram in Egypt

¹⁰Now there was a famine in the land, and Abram went down to Egypt to live there for a while because the famine was severe. ¹¹As he was about to enter Egypt, he said to his wife Sarai, "I know what a beautiful woman you are. ¹²When the Egyptians see you, they will say, 'This is his wife.' Then they will kill me but will let you live. ¹³Say you are my sister,

so that I will be treated well for your sake and my life will be spared because of you."

¹⁴When Abram came to Egypt, the Egyptians saw that Sarai was a very beautiful woman. ¹⁵And when Pharaoh's officials saw her, they praised her to Pharaoh, and she was taken into his palace. ¹⁶He treated Abram well for her sake, and Abram acquired sheep and cattle, male and female donkeys, male and female servants, and camels.

¹⁷But the LORD inflicted serious diseases on Pharaoh and his household because of Abram's wife Sarai. ¹⁸So Pharaoh summoned Abram. "What have you done to me?" he said. "Why didn't you tell me she was your wife? ¹⁹Why did you say, 'She is my sister,' so that I took her to be my wife? Now then, here is your wife. Take her and go!" ²⁰Then Pharaoh gave orders about Abram to his men, and they sent him on his way, with his wife and everything he had.

Abram and Lot Separate

13 So Abram went up from Egypt to the Negev, with his wife and everything he had, and Lot went with him. ²Abram had become very wealthy in livestock and in silver and gold.

³From the Negev he went from place to place until he came to Bethel, to the place

ᵃ 7 Or seed

12:7-9 | The words **the LORD appeared** suggest a pre-incarnate appearance of Christ. Here in Canaan God first promised Abram **this land** (Ps. 105:9–12).

12:10–16 | Sarah, or **Sarai** as she is called here, was 65 years old and still **a beautiful woman**. She was also Abram's half sister (20:12). In **Egypt**, Abram's decision to conceal this fact and disclose only part of the truth endangered her: she was **taken into** [Pharaoh's] **palace** as a potential addition to the royal harem. Perhaps Abram forgot that God's people can always trust in His provision.

12:17-20 | God intended for Abram to be a blessing; instead, he became a curse (**the LORD inflicted serious diseases on Pharaoh and his household**). Even though Abram's sin was the primary offense, Pharaoh was implicated and consequently suffered.

13:2 | The Bible indicates that being **wealthy** is no sin, but wealth seriously increases a believer's responsibility. God's people should view wealth with a sense of stewardship rather than ownership (1 Tim. 6:9–11; 1 John 3:17). In Abram's case, the riches were in **livestock and in silver and gold**. There was no currency; coinage was not devised until the Persian period.

between Bethel and Ai where his tent had been earlier [4]and where he had first built an altar. There Abram called on the name of the LORD.

[5]Now Lot, who was moving about with Abram, also had flocks and herds and tents. [6]But the land could not support them while they stayed together, for their possessions were so great that they were not able to stay together. [7]And quarreling arose between Abram's herders and Lot's. The Canaanites and Perizzites were also living in the land at that time.

[8]So Abram said to Lot, "Let's not have any quarreling between you and me, or between your herders and mine, for we are close relatives. [9]Is not the whole land before you? Let's part company. If you go to the left, I'll go to the right; if you go to the right, I'll go to the left."

[10]Lot looked around and saw that the whole plain of the Jordan toward Zoar was well watered, like the garden of the LORD, like the land of Egypt. (This was before the LORD destroyed Sodom and Gomorrah.) [11]So Lot chose for himself the whole plain of the Jordan and set out toward the east. The two men parted company: [12]Abram lived in the land of Canaan, while Lot lived among the cities of the plain and pitched his tents near Sodom. [13]Now the people of Sodom were wicked and were sinning greatly against the LORD.

[14]The LORD said to Abram after Lot had parted from him, "Look around from where you are, to the north and south, to the east and west. [15]All the land that you see I will give to you and your offspring[a] forever. [16]I will make your offspring like the dust of the earth, so that if anyone could count the dust, then your offspring could be counted. [17]Go, walk through the length and breadth of the land, for I am giving it to you."

[18]So Abram went to live near the great trees of Mamre at Hebron, where he pitched his tents. There he built an altar to the LORD.

fyi Recovering from Detours in Faith • 13:4

Abram's journey to Egypt was prompted by "a famine in the land" (12:10). In this journey, we have something that foreshadows the coming of Israel to Egypt (47:1), the eventual deliverance of the people (Ex. 14), and the journey and return of Jesus and his family to Egypt (Matt. 2:14, 15, 21). In all three cases, danger brought them to Egypt and God brought them back (Hosea 11:1).

After Abram's misadventures in Egypt, he returned to Bethel. *Beth* ("house") and *El* ("God") combine to form *Bethel*, the "House of God." Abram built an altar there before he went to Egypt (12:9). When he returned, it was to the sacred place outside the ancient city—the location of the altar where he had met God. When we find ourselves in difficulty, seeming to be adrift in our lives, we need to do what Abram did: return to our "Bethel," the house of God, and call "on the name of the LORD."

Abram Rescues Lot

14 At the time when Amraphel was king of Shinar,[b] Arioch king of Ellasar, Kedorlaomer king of Elam and Tidal king of Goyim, [2]these kings went to war against Bera king of Sodom, Birsha king of Gomorrah, Shinab king of Admah, Shemeber king of Zeboyim, and the king of Bela (that is, Zoar). [3]All these latter kings joined forces in the Valley of Siddim (that is, the Dead Sea Valley). [4]For twelve years they had been subject to Kedorlaomer, but in the thirteenth year they rebelled.

[5]In the fourteenth year, Kedorlaomer and the kings allied with him went out and defeated the Rephaites in Ashteroth Karnaim, the Zuzites in Ham, the Emites in Shaveh Kiriathaim [6]and the Horites in the hill country of Seir, as far as El Paran near the desert. [7]Then they turned back and went to En Mishpat (that is, Kadesh), and they conquered the whole territory of the

---

[a] 15 Or seed; also in verse 16   [b] 1 That is, Babylonia; also in verse 9

13:7 | Abram and Lot had so much livestock that their herdsmen were at odds. The **Canaanites and Perizzites** also used the grazing lands. Christians are supposed to live in such a way that unbelievers see them showing love to one another. Christian unity is their witness to a watching world (John 13:35; 1 Pet. 3:8).
13:8, 9 | Abram had the rights in this matter, but he gave **Lot** first choice because they were **close relatives** (Ps. 133:1). Abram was not greedy and did not grasp for the best; he could allow Lot to choose first because he entrusted his future to God—the definition of walking by faith (Phil. 2:14, 15; Rom. 13:9).
13:10–17 | The Hebrew verb translated to **looked around** means "seek out, look with care" (22:4). Lot chose for himself what he believed to be the best land, yet this was the territory of **Sodom** and **Gomorrah**—two of the most perverse and **wicked** cities at that time

(2 Pet. 2:7, 8; Jude 7). Lot's selfish choice would prove disastrous, because over time it would draw him into Sodom's ways. All decisions have implications beyond the moment.
13:14, 15 | Abram waited until God spoke, and then he looked at the land before him. Despite Lot's choice, Yahweh (the principal personal name of God in the OT; Ex. 3:14, 15) blessed Abram with far more land—the whole of Canaan, **north . . . south . . . east and west**—and then vowed to give the land to Abram's **offspring forever**, a heightening of the promise in 12:7.
14:1–12 | Lot suffered great material loss and was taken captive in this conflict between Eastern and local powers—further consequences of his decision to live in **Sodom**. Because Abram was dwelling near Hebron at the time (13:18), he was spared any trouble. **Shinar** is Babylon (10:10).

Historically Speaking

Melchizedek • 14:18–20

Melchizedek is a picture (a type) of Jesus Christ in the OT—one who illustrates Christ's eternal priesthood (and kingship). He is *not* Christ Himself (Heb. 7:1–9), in an appearance before His incarnation, as some Bible teachers believe.

The account of Melchizedek and Bera (14:2) is a tale of two kings and two cities. Unlike King Bera of Sodom—the epitome of Canaanite idolatry and godlessness (13:13)—King Melchizedek of (Jeru) Salem was the embodiment of true belief in the God who is over all, the Creator and Sustainer of heaven and earth.

The presence of Melchizedek within Scripture demonstrates the unity of the Bible as well as the significance of Christ. In Genesis 14, he is introduced as a king and Scripture's first priest. About a thousand years later, David is given a stunning prophecy of Messiah as a priest akin to Melchizedek (Ps. 110:4). More than a thousand years after that, the writer of Hebrews explains that Melchizedek foreshadows Jesus Christ, the King of kings, and His priestly ministry.

It is remarkable that King Melchizedek is also called "priest of God Most High." Obviously, Melchizedek had no connection with Levi, the father of the priesthood in Israel. Further, Melchizedek was not the founder of a line of priests, as was Aaron. So how was he a priest? Because God said so. As we see throughout the Book of Hebrews and elsewhere, this is exactly how Jesus is priest. The words "in the order of Melchizedek" (Ps. 110:4) don't describe a lineage of priests; they mean "in the same manner as Melchizedek"—because God said so. There are only two biblical figures in this category: Melchizedek (the type) and Christ (the antitype, or fulfillment of the foreshadowed person). And the priesthood of Jesus is eternal!

Amalekites, as well as the Amorites who were living in Hazezon Tamar.

⁸Then the king of Sodom, the king of Gomorrah, the king of Admah, the king of Zeboyim and the king of Bela (that is, Zoar) marched out and drew up their battle lines in the Valley of Siddim ⁹against Kedorlaomer king of Elam, Tidal king of Goyim, Amraphel king of Shinar and Arioch king of Ellasar—four kings against five. ¹⁰Now the Valley of Siddim was full of tar pits, and when the kings of Sodom and Gomorrah fled, some of the men fell into them and the rest fled to the hills. ¹¹The four kings seized all the goods of Sodom and Gomorrah and all their food; then they went away. ¹²They also carried off Abram's nephew Lot and his possessions, since he was living in Sodom.

¹³A man who had escaped came and reported this to Abram the Hebrew. Now Abram was living near the great trees of Mamre the Amorite, a brother[a] of Eshkol and Aner, all of whom were allied with Abram. ¹⁴When Abram heard that his relative had been taken captive, he called out the 318 trained men born in his household and went in pursuit as far as Dan. ¹⁵During the night Abram divided his men to attack them and he routed them, pursuing them

as far as Hobah, north of Damascus. ¹⁶He recovered all the goods and brought back his relative Lot and his possessions, together with the women and the other people.

¹⁷After Abram returned from defeating Kedorlaomer and the kings allied with him, the king of Sodom came out to meet him in the Valley of Shaveh (that is, the King's Valley).

¹⁸Then Melchizedek king of Salem brought out bread and wine. He was priest of God Most High, ¹⁹and he blessed Abram, saying,

"Blessed be Abram by God Most High,
    Creator of heaven and earth.
²⁰And praise be to God Most High,
    who delivered your enemies into
        your hand."

Then Abram gave him a tenth of everything. ²¹The king of Sodom said to Abram, "Give me the people and keep the goods for yourself."

²²But Abram said to the king of Sodom, "With raised hand I have sworn an oath to the LORD, God Most High, Creator of

---

ᵃ 13 Or *a relative; or an ally*

14:10 | The **Valley of Siddim** had many **tar pits**, sometimes called slime pits. These became traps for some of the soldiers as they fled for the hills.

14:14–16 | When Abram heard that his nephew **(relative)** was captured, he risked his own life to bring **Lot** and the family's goods **back** to Sodom. Still, Lot would not leave Sodom (see note on 14:1–12). People are often inclined to return to their old sins

and habits, even if God has given them a means of escape.
14:18–20 | **Melchizedek** was a true **priest** (Ps. 110:4; Heb. 7:1). As such, Abram gave him a **tenth** of all he owned, even before tithing (giving God a tenth) was instituted in God's law. Melchizedek was also **king of Salem**, the early name for Jerusalem. Here, **God Most High** describes His sovereignty over all things (Ps. 50:14) and distinguishes the one true God from pagan gods.

Tough Questions

How were people saved in the OT? • 15:6

Many Jewish people at the time of Jesus believed that salvation was a "reward" for keeping the law of God. In this view, salvation is something earned, not a gift of grace. Orthodox Jews in our own day speak of works of righteousness such as public reading of Torah, reciting prayers, and giving to the poor as ways to placate God instead of offering sacrifices since there is no temple today. If the keeping of rules were a possible means of achieving salvation from sin and death, then Jesus' sacrifice and resurrection—His atonement for our sins—would be unnecessary.

Others argue that since all people who are saved are ultimately saved on the basis of the shed blood of Christ, people in the days of the OT were saved because of their sure hope in the coming of the Messiah as someone who would suffer and die on their behalf (Isa. 53:6). But what we may see as a wondrous line of prophetic passages describing the coming of the Savior today is something that people in OT times could not possibly have put together. This was certainly true of Abraham. He had no Scripture at all—he lived long before the prophetic passages were written. Not even Genesis 3:15, the "first gospel" was available to him, for Genesis (which includes Abraham's story) was not written until hundreds of years after he died.

The few words of Genesis 15:6 (only five words in Hebrew) are of inestimable importance, however. If we replace the pronouns, this reads: "Abram believed the LORD, and [the LORD] credited [his faith] to [Abram] as righteousness." Many Jewish people in Paul's day argued that a man had to be circumcised and had to keep the law in its fullness to be saved (Acts 15:5). Paul, however, shows in Romans 4 that Abraham was justified by his faith, quoting Genesis 15:6, and that his acceptance of the rite of circumcision (17:26) was an act of obedience by a person who was already saved. What grace we find in the living God!

heaven and earth, ²³that I will accept nothing belonging to you, not even a thread or the strap of a sandal, so that you will never be able to say, 'I made Abram rich.' ²⁴I will accept nothing but what my men have eaten and the share that belongs to the men who went with me—to Aner, Eshkol and Mamre. Let them have their share."

The LORD's Covenant With Abram

15 After this, the word of the LORD came to Abram in a vision:

"Do not be afraid, Abram.
    I am your shield,ᵃ
    your very great reward.ᵇ"

²But Abram said, "Sovereign LORD, what can you give me since I remain childless and the one who will inheritᶜ my estate is Eliezer of Damascus?" ³And Abram said, "You

have given me no children; so a servant in my household will be my heir."

⁴Then the word of the LORD came to him: "This man will not be your heir, but a son who is your own flesh and blood will be your heir." ⁵He took him outside and said, "Look up at the sky and count the stars—if indeed you can count them." Then he said to him, "So shall your offspringᵈ be."

⁶Abram believed the LORD, and he credited it to him as righteousness.

⁷He also said to him, "I am the LORD, who brought you out of Ur of the Chaldeans to give you this land to take possession of it."

⁸But Abram said, "Sovereign LORD, how can I know that I will gain possession of it?"

⁹So the LORD said to him, "Bring me a heifer, a goat and a ram, each three years old, along with a dove and a young pigeon."

ᵃ 1 Or sovereign   ᵇ 1 Or shield; / your reward will be very great   ᶜ 2 The meaning of the Hebrew for this phrase is uncertain.   ᵈ 5 Or seed

---

14:22, 23 | Abram resisted the offer to keep the goods of the **king of Sodom**, unwilling to be in his debt. Abram, **with raised hand**, a dramatic gesture, reinforced his oath to refuse any item from King Bera (14:2)—**not even a thread or the strap of a sandal**. Those who are allied with **the LORD, God Most High, Creator of heaven and earth** do not need what any earthly king has to offer.

15:1 | This is the first time **Do not be afraid** is recorded in the Bible. Fear comes when God's people take their eyes off the One who promises and begin to worry about the promise (Isa. 41:10). Because he had just refused great wealth (14:21–23) and did not yet have an heir, Abram needed to know that God was his **shield** and **very great reward**—his Protector and Provider (Ps. 7:10; 84:9).

15:2, 3 | Abram was **childless**, but for a man of extraordinary wealth, it was important to avoid dying without a plan for inheritance—ancient culture's mark of irresponsibility. So he did what

others in his situation would do: he adopted a servant, **Eliezer**, as his **heir**. This "quest for a son" motif underlies Abram's entire story.

15:6 | This verse sets the clear pattern traced throughout the Scriptures: a person is saved only and always by grace through faith—nothing more (Rom. 4:3; Gal. 3:6; James 2:23). In other words, God applied the results of the atonement (**righteousness**) to those who **believed the LORD** in OT times. Those people were, in essence, saved on credit, waiting for that payment for sin to be made. Now that Jesus has made the payment, citizens on this side of Calvary need only look back and trust what He did on the cross. *See the article "Salvation by Faith" on page 26.*

15:7, 8 | God was not only the provider of the covenant with Abram, but also His character and unchanging presence (**I am the LORD**) were its promise. Still, Abram wanted a sign. More important than a sign, however, is an obedient will.

ESSENTIALS
of the Christian Faith

Salvation by Faith
Genesis 15:6

There is only one way to enter into right standing with God, and that is by faith. This is not a new revelation in the NT. Believing in God and acting on that belief as a demonstration of faith have always been the way to "get right" with God.

The first act of faith recorded in Scripture is seen in Eve's response to God at the birth of her first son, Cain: "With the help of the LORD I have brought forth a man" (4:1). In a lovely wordplay (in Hebrew, the words "I have brought forth" sound very much like the boy's name), she directly associates her son with Yahweh's actions. Here, Eve is described as a woman of deep faith in the Lord. This is remarkable, since this is the first thing we read following the expulsion from the Garden (3:24).

Another remarkable act of faith described early in the Bible is Noah's decision to build the ark and preserve the seed of the human race in obedience to God's instruction. As strange as the request may have seemed, Noah believed (obeyed) God—and proved it. Hebrews 11:7 communicates the significance of this: "By faith Noah, when warned about things not yet seen, in holy fear built an ark to save his family. By his faith he . . . became heir of the righteousness that is in keeping with faith."

Righteousness is the fundamental need of the human race. Noah was declared righteous by God because he believed, not because he built. Building the ark was a manifestation of Noah's righteousness, not the means to his righteousness.

Later, Abraham (Abram) was declared righteous by God in the same way. God had called him to be the father of a new nation when he was 75 years old, but well into his eighties Abraham and his wife were still childless. One night, God took Abraham outside and said: "Look up at the sky and count the stars—if indeed you can count them. . . . So shall your offspring be" (15:5).

Something happened to Abraham's faltering faith when God showed him the countless stars in the sky. Something settled in Abraham's heart—faith that Yahweh's words would come true—"Abram believed the LORD." When that happened, God recognized it as saving faith and "credited it to [Abram] as righteousness" (15:6).

Credited and reckoned are accounting and legal terms. Ledgers are credited and debts are erased. In the cases of Noah and Abraham, they were credited with righteousness on the basis of their faith. The only way that could have happened outside of God's "accounting" transfer would have been to live a perfect life—a life with no deficits of any kind. Such a person would be listed in the "credit" column of the ledger on the basis of their own perfection.

But no human being except Jesus Christ has lived such a life. The only way we can be viewed as righteous in God's sight is for God to give us credit for the life Christ lived. The one thing He asks from us in return is faith—that we believe His word to us concerning what He has done to make us right with Him.

In the later period of OT times, obedience to the laws God gave through Moses was no more a means of salvation than it is in NT times. However, compliance with God's laws was a witness to one's faith in God. As Jesus said, "Why do you call me, 'Lord, Lord,' and do not do what I say?" (Luke 6:46). True faith is always expressed by actions that please God.

Faith is the same for us as for Noah, Abraham, and anyone else who has ever believed: it "is confidence in what we hope for and assurance about what we do not see" (Heb. 11:1). "And without faith it is impossible to please God, because anyone who comes to him must believe that he exists and that he rewards those who earnestly seek him" (Heb. 11:6).

For Further Reading: 1 Chron. 5:20; Prov. 16:20; 28:25; Isa. 33:6; Matt. 17:20; Gal. 3:11, 12; Heb. 11.

¹⁰Abram brought all these to him, cut them in two and arranged the halves opposite each other; the birds, however, he did not cut in half. ¹¹Then birds of prey came down on the carcasses, but Abram drove them away.

¹²As the sun was setting, Abram fell into a deep sleep, and a thick and dreadful darkness came over him. ¹³Then the LORD said to him, "Know for certain that for four hundred years your descendants will be strangers in a country not their own and that they will be enslaved and mistreated there. ¹⁴But I will punish the nation they serve as slaves, and afterward they will come out with great possessions. ¹⁵You, however, will go to your ancestors in peace and be buried at a good old age. ¹⁶In the fourth generation your descendants will come back here, for the sin of the Amorites has not yet reached its full measure."

¹⁷When the sun had set and darkness had fallen, a smoking firepot with a blazing torch appeared and passed between the pieces. ¹⁸On that day the LORD made a covenant with Abram and said, "To your descendants I give this land, from the Wadi*a* of Egypt to the great river, the Euphrates— ¹⁹the land of the Kenites, Kenizzites, Kadmonites, ²⁰Hittites, Perizzites, Rephaites, ²¹Amorites, Canaanites, Girgashites and Jebusites."

Hagar and Ishmael

16 Now Sarai, Abram's wife, had borne him no children. But she had an Egyptian slave named Hagar; ²so she said to Abram, "The LORD has kept me from having children. Go, sleep with my slave; perhaps I can build a family through her."

Abram agreed to what Sarai said. ³So after Abram had been living in Canaan ten years, Sarai his wife took her Egyptian slave Hagar and gave her to her husband to be his wife. ⁴He slept with Hagar, and she conceived.

When she knew she was pregnant, she began to despise her mistress. ⁵Then Sarai

---

Picture This | To Cut a Covenant • 15:8–17

To establish and confirm a covenant in Abram's day, usually the two parties would walk between the pieces of the sacrificial animals, saying, in effect, "May what has happened to these creatures happen to me if I break the covenant." The Hebrew expression "to cut a covenant" pertains to the act of cutting the sacrificial animals in two (15:10).

Because this was Yahweh's sovereign covenant with Abram, not an agreement between equals, symbols of God ("a smoking firepot with a blazing torch") passed between those pieces; Abram did not. The Lord made the covenant with no conditions—independent of Abram—and He would fulfill it in His time.

---

said to Abram, "You are responsible for the wrong I am suffering. I put my slave in your arms, and now that she knows she is pregnant, she despises me. May the LORD judge between you and me."

⁶"Your slave is in your hands," Abram said. "Do with her whatever you think best." Then Sarai mistreated Hagar; so she fled from her.

⁷The angel of the LORD found Hagar near a spring in the desert; it was the spring that is beside the road to Shur. ⁸And he said, "Hagar, slave of Sarai, where have you come from, and where are you going?"

"I'm running away from my mistress Sarai," she answered.

⁹Then the angel of the LORD told her, "Go back to your mistress and submit to her." ¹⁰The angel added, "I will increase your descendants so much that they will be too numerous to count."

¹¹The angel of the LORD also said to her:

"You are now pregnant
　and you will give birth to a son.
You shall name him Ishmael,*b*

---

a 18 Or river   *b* 11 Ishmael means God hears.

15:9-18 | God used a familiar ancient custom—a **covenant**—to solemnly ratify His agreement with Abram.
15:18-21 | These verses offer new details about the covenant God promised Abram earlier (12:2, 3, 7): the Lord gave **this land** to Abram's **descendants**. The specific territory—about 300,000 square miles—covered far more area than the nation of Israel has ever occupied. But in the future kingdom, it will all be theirs.
16:1-3 | Ten years had passed since the Lord's first promise to Abram in 12:2, and Sarai knew the Lord Himself had **kept** her from having **children**. So in a selfless (though impatient) act on behalf of her husband, she proposed using her servant as a surrogate—and Abram **agreed**. Like Adam with Eve in the Garden, Abram's temptation came from the person closest to him (3:17). And in spite of the great visions God had given Abram, the realities of the couple's age

and Sarai's barrenness seemed greater at that moment.
16:4-6 | After Hagar **conceived** and her contempt robbed Sarai of her happiness, Sarai blamed her husband (**You are responsible**). The Hebrew word speaks of wrong brought on her by Hagar, yet Sarai **mistreated** Hagar in spite of cultural codes that demanded dignified treatment of surrogate mothers. Hagar, Abram, and Sarai all sinned.
16:7-12 | God's commands are often accompanied by assurances and compassion. In Hagar's moment of hopelessness, God sent the **angel of the LORD**—a phrase strongly suggesting a pre-incarnate appearance of Christ (22:11, 15; Judg. 2:4; 6:11; 13:3; 1 Kgs. 19:7)—to ease her despair. This promise to **increase** her **descendants** would be fulfilled with the birth of Ishmael, from whom the Arabic people would descend.

Historically Speaking   Circumcision • 17:1–14

Circumcision is the surgical removal of the foreskin of the male reproductive organ. Other cultures in biblical times practiced circumcision. For example, there is evidence of the practice in ancient Egypt. Young men were usually circumcised at puberty, to prepare them for marriage and as an entrance into adult responsibilities.

God told Abraham to circumcise his baby son Isaac as a sign and seal of God's covenant with him. In addition, Abraham circumcised his son Ishmael and was circumcised himself (17:23–27). The Hebrew people were instructed to continue the practice, marking them as God's covenant people.

The Hebrews were the only ancients to circumcise babies, which freed the practice from any association with fertility rituals. Circumcision was an outward, physical sign of that which God wanted to be true inwardly (Deut. 10:16). In the NT, Paul used circumcision to represent all of the law and those who thought they could be right with God by obeying the law. He then went on to teach that inward circumcision—allowing God to cut sin out of our hearts—would forevermore be the mark of devotion to the Lord. Thus, Christians today are not under the command to be circumcised (Gal. 5:6).

for the LORD has heard of your
  misery.
¹²He will be a wild donkey of a man;
  his hand will be against everyone
  and everyone's hand against him,
  and he will live in hostility
  toward[a] all his brothers."

¹³She gave this name to the LORD who spoke to her: "You are the God who sees me," for she said, "I have now seen[b] the One who sees me." ¹⁴That is why the well was called Beer Lahai Roi[c]; it is still there, between Kadesh and Bered.

¹⁵So Hagar bore Abram a son, and Abram gave the name Ishmael to the son she had borne. ¹⁶Abram was eighty-six years old when Hagar bore him Ishmael.

The Covenant of Circumcision

17 When Abram was ninety-nine years old, the LORD appeared to him and said, "I am God Almighty[d]; walk before me faithfully and be blameless. ²Then I will make my covenant between me and you and will greatly increase your numbers."

³Abram fell facedown, and God said to him, ⁴"As for me, this is my covenant with you: You will be the father of many nations. ⁵No longer will you be called Abram[e]; your name will be Abraham,[f] for I have made you a father of many nations. ⁶I will make you very fruitful; I will make nations of you, and kings will come from you. ⁷I will establish my covenant as an everlasting covenant between me and you and your descendants after you for the generations to come, to be your God and the God of your descendants after you. ⁸The whole land of Canaan, where you now reside as a foreigner, I will give as an everlasting possession to you and your descendants after you; and I will be their God."

⁹Then God said to Abraham, "As for you, you must keep my covenant, you and your descendants after you for the generations to come. ¹⁰This is my covenant with you and your descendants after you, the covenant you are to keep: Every male among you shall be circumcised. ¹¹You are to undergo circumcision, and it will be the sign of the covenant between me and you. ¹²For the generations to come every male among you who is eight days old must be circumcised, including those born in your household or bought with money from a foreigner—those who are not your offspring. ¹³Whether born in your

[a] 12 Or live to the east / of   [b] 13 Or seen the back of   [c] 14 Beer Lahai Roi means well of the Living One who sees me.   [d] 1 Hebrew El-Shaddai   [e] 5 Abram means exalted father.   [f] 5 Abraham probably means father of many.

16:13–16 | Hagar was totally alone in the wilderness, yet God sought her out. Hagar gave the well the memorial name **Beer Lahai Roi** ("well of the Living One who sees me") to indicate that God finds His children when they are forgotten. **Ishmael** means "God hears."
17:1 | In telling Abram to **walk** before Him, God asked for Abram's submission and silence—his wholehearted obedience. Abram could not become the person he should be until he stopped trusting in himself and his schemes and strategies. In the Hebrew, **God Almighty** (Heb. *El Shaddai*) suggests a majestic mountain, lofty and lasting—in which there is a crevasse for protection.
17:4–16 | Abram and Sarai's original names honored pagan deities. Now that God had promised they would be **father** and **mother of nations** (17:4, 16), including the Hebrew people, He gave them new names that signified their relationship with the one true God.

The Lord changed the name of **Abram** ("exalted father") to **Abraham** ("father of many") and changed Sarai's name to **Sarah**. Both Sarai and Sarah mean "princess," but the new name has a new dimension: she would henceforth be a "princess [of God]."
17:7, 8 | This was an **everlasting covenant**—so even if Abraham's descendants proved faithless, God would remain faithful in fulfilling His promises (Gal. 3:17; Rev. 21:7).
17:10–12 | **Circumcision** was the symbol of the Lord's gracious covenant with Abraham, just as the Sabbath symbolized His gracious covenant with Moses (Ex. 20:8–11; Deut. 5:12–15). Every Jewish male child was to be circumcised **eight days** after birth (Lev. 12:3)—just the right time biologically speaking. The eighth day presents fewer concerns of infection, and some also suggest that an infant's blood coagulates better at this time.

household or bought with your money, they must be circumcised. My covenant in your flesh is to be an everlasting covenant. ¹⁴Any uncircumcised male, who has not been circumcised in the flesh, will be cut off from his people; he has broken my covenant."

¹⁵God also said to Abraham, "As for Sarai your wife, you are no longer to call her Sarai; her name will be Sarah. ¹⁶I will bless her and will surely give you a son by her. I will bless her so that she will be the mother of nations; kings of peoples will come from her."

¹⁷Abraham fell facedown; he laughed and said to himself, "Will a son be born to a man a hundred years old? Will Sarah bear a child at the age of ninety?" ¹⁸And Abraham said to God, "If only Ishmael might live under your blessing!"

¹⁹Then God said, "Yes, but your wife Sarah will bear you a son, and you will call him Isaac.ᵃ I will establish my covenant with him as an everlasting covenant for his descendants after him. ²⁰And as for Ishmael, I have heard you: I will surely bless him; I will make him fruitful and will greatly increase his numbers. He will be the father of twelve rulers, and I will make him into a great nation. ²¹But my covenant I will establish with Isaac, whom Sarah will bear to you by this time next year." ²²When he had finished speaking with Abraham, God went up from him.

²³On that very day Abraham took his son Ishmael and all those born in his household or bought with his money, every male in his household, and circumcised them, as God told him. ²⁴Abraham was ninety-nine years old when he was circumcised, ²⁵and his son Ishmael was thirteen; ²⁶Abraham and his son Ishmael were both circumcised on that very day. ²⁷And every male in Abraham's household, including those born in his household or bought from a foreigner, was circumcised with him.

The Three Visitors

18 The Lord appeared to Abraham near the great trees of Mamre while he was sitting at the entrance to his tent in the heat of the day. ²Abraham looked up and saw three men standing nearby. When he saw them, he hurried from the entrance of his tent to meet them and bowed low to the ground.

³He said, "If I have found favor in your eyes, my lord,ᵇ do not pass your servant by. ⁴Let a little water be brought, and then you may all wash your feet and rest under this tree. ⁵Let me get you something to eat, so you can be refreshed and then go on your way—now that you have come to your servant."

"Very well," they answered, "do as you say."

⁶So Abraham hurried into the tent to Sarah. "Quick," he said, "get three seahsᶜ of the finest flour and knead it and bake some bread."

⁷Then he ran to the herd and selected a choice, tender calf and gave it to a servant, who hurried to prepare it. ⁸He then brought some curds and milk and the calf that had been prepared, and set these before them. While they ate, he stood near them under a tree.

⁹"Where is your wife Sarah?" they asked him.

"There, in the tent," he said.

¹⁰Then one of them said, "I will surely return to you about this time next year, and Sarah your wife will have a son."

Now Sarah was listening at the entrance to the tent, which was behind him. ¹¹Abraham and Sarah were already very old, and Sarah was past the age of childbearing. ¹²So Sarah laughed to herself as she thought, "After I am worn out and my lord is old, will I now have this pleasure?"

¹³Then the Lord said to Abraham, "Why did Sarah laugh and say, 'Will I really have a child, now that I am old?' ¹⁴Is anything too hard for the Lord? I will return to you at the appointed time next year, and Sarah will have a son."

¹⁵Sarah was afraid, so she lied and said, "I did not laugh."

But he said, "Yes, you did laugh."

ᵃ 19 *Isaac means he laughs.*   ᵇ 3 *Or eyes, Lord*   ᶜ 6 *That is, probably about 36 pounds or about 16 kilograms*

17:17 | Both Abraham's laughter here and Sarah's in 18:12 anticipate the wonderful conclusion to the story in 21:1–7; the Lord would ultimately laugh with them in indescribable joy!

17:18–21 | For the first time, God revealed the identity of the **son** of the **covenant: Isaac**. The Lord also clarified that **Sarah will bear** him. Although Ishmael was not the promised son, God kept His word to **make him fruitful**: his descendants are citizens of some of the wealthiest nations in the world today. See note on 16:7–12.

17:23–27 | Abraham obeyed precisely, both as a parent and personally.

18:1–8 | One of these **three men** was the Lord (18:22); the other two were angels. This is one of the mysterious manifestations of Jesus in the OT before His incarnation (see note on 16:7–12). God's people demonstrate the reality of their faith when they humbly, hospitably, and responsively serve one another, as Abraham did his guests (Heb. 13:2).

18:10–15 | God reaffirmed in Sarah's hearing that Abraham would have a **son** and that the child would be born of **Sarah** (see note on 17:18–21), an announcement that so challenged even her strong faith that she **laughed to herself**. The text indicates that she denied her laughter even as it lingered in her voice.

Abraham Pleads for Sodom

16 When the men got up to leave, they looked down toward Sodom, and Abraham walked along with them to see them on their way. 17 Then the LORD said, "Shall I hide from Abraham what I am about to do? 18 Abraham will surely become a great and powerful nation, and all nations on earth will be blessed through him.*a* 19 For I have chosen him, so that he will direct his children and his household after him to keep the way of the LORD by doing what is right and just, so that the LORD will bring about for Abraham what he has promised him."

20 Then the LORD said, "The outcry against Sodom and Gomorrah is so great and their sin so grievous 21 that I will go down and see if what they have done is as bad as the outcry that has reached me. If not, I will know."

22 The men turned away and went toward Sodom, but Abraham remained standing before the LORD.*b* 23 Then Abraham approached him and said: "Will you sweep away the righteous with the wicked? 24 What if there are fifty righteous people in the city? Will you really sweep it away and not spare*c* the place for the sake of the fifty righteous people in it? 25 Far be it from you to do such a thing—to kill the righteous with the wicked, treating the righteous and the wicked alike. Far be it from you! Will not the Judge of all the earth do right?"

26 The LORD said, "If I find fifty righteous people in the city of Sodom, I will spare the whole place for their sake."

27 Then Abraham spoke up again: "Now that I have been so bold as to speak to the Lord, though I am nothing but dust and ashes, 28 what if the number of the righteous is five less than fifty? Will you destroy the whole city for lack of five people?"

"If I find forty-five there," he said, "I will not destroy it."

29 Once again he spoke to him, "What if only forty are found there?"

He said, "For the sake of forty, I will not do it."

30 Then he said, "May the Lord not be angry, but let me speak. What if only thirty can be found there?"

He answered, "I will not do it if I find thirty there."

31 Abraham said, "Now that I have been so bold as to speak to the Lord, what if only twenty can be found there?"

He said, "For the sake of twenty, I will not destroy it."

32 Then he said, "May the Lord not be angry, but let me speak just once more. What if only ten can be found there?"

He answered, "For the sake of ten, I will not destroy it."

33 When the LORD had finished speaking with Abraham, he left, and Abraham returned home.

Sodom and Gomorrah Destroyed

19 The two angels arrived at Sodom in the evening, and Lot was sitting in the gateway of the city. When he saw them, he got up to meet them and bowed down with his face to the ground. 2 "My lords," he said, "please turn aside to your servant's house. You can wash your feet and spend the night and then go on your way early in the morning."

"No," they answered, "we will spend the night in the square."

3 But he insisted so strongly that they did go with him and entered his house. He prepared a meal for them, baking bread without yeast, and they ate. 4 Before they had gone to bed, all the men from every part of the city of Sodom—both young and old—surrounded the house. 5 They called to Lot, "Where are the men who came to you tonight? Bring them out to us so that we can have sex with them."

---

a 18 Or will use his name in blessings (see 48:20)   *b* 22 Masoretic Text; an ancient Hebrew scribal tradition *but the LORD remained standing before Abraham*   *c* 24 Or forgive; also in verse 26

18:17–19 | That the Lord did not **hide** His plans or the secrets of His heart **from Abraham** demonstrates that this servant of God was indeed a friend of God (2 Chron. 20:7; James 2:23). The phrase **I have chosen him** reinforces this. The Lord knew that Abraham would **direct his children and his household** to follow Him.
18:20–32 | The Lord fully understood what was happening in Sodom; He did not need to **go down and see**. But as in other times in Scripture, He graciously accommodates His language here for human understanding.
18:23–32 | Abraham's opening question should not be misunderstood; he knew God cared about the righteous. As the "negotiations" went from **fifty** to **ten**, Abraham was possibly thinking of Lot and his family—his wife and their two daughters and their husbands—and assuming that at least a few others besides them must be **righteous**.

18:32 | According to the deal that Abraham negotiated with God, Lot and his family members should have died, because not even **ten** righteous people could be found. Yet God showed mercy on Lot (19:12–25) because of Abraham's intercession. God hears the prayers of His people when they passionately and persistently come to Him (Heb. 10:22; James 5:16). What incredible things would happen if the Lord heard a steady stream of intercessory prayer from Christians everywhere?
19:1–11 | Vile sinfulness had so captured the heart of **all the men from every part of the city** that when anyone entered the city, the inhabitants thought only, *This is fresh flesh.* The intention of the men of Sodom toward these visitors was clear: they wanted to **have sex with them** (Lev. 18:22, 29; 20:13; Judg. 19:22; Rom. 1:26, 27; 1 Cor. 6:9; Jude 7).

Moving toward Wickedness • 19:1

In the Genesis account of Lot's movements, we see that Lot first gained the grasslands near Sodom (13:10). Then he settled outside Sodom (13:12), only to eventually move into the city itself (14:12). Chapter 19 opens with him "sitting in the gateway of the city"—the place where the city elders held court. Lot was part of Sodom's council of elders, which means that he knew what was going on there, even if he could do little to stem the tide of pervasive sin. Although a NT passage states that he was "tormented" by the wickedness of the city (2 Pet. 2:7, 8), still, he stayed.

This greatly contrasts with Abraham. Abraham lived in a tent, while Lot had a house. Abraham was a pilgrim and a stranger in the land; Lot settled down in corrupt Sodom. When judgment fell on Sodom and Gomorrah, God extended mercy to Lot, only because of Abraham ("remembered Abraham"; 19:29). Our moves toward wickedness in any regard subject us to not only compromise but danger, and often, even destruction. No good can come from a believer's failure to flee from sin and temptation.

⁶Lot went outside to meet them and shut the door behind him ⁷and said, "No, my friends. Don't do this wicked thing. ⁸Look, I have two daughters who have never slept with a man. Let me bring them out to you, and you can do what you like with them. But don't do anything to these men, for they have come under the protection of my roof."

⁹"Get out of our way," they replied. "This fellow came here as a foreigner, and now he wants to play the judge! We'll treat you worse than them." They kept bringing pressure on Lot and moved forward to break down the door.

¹⁰But the men inside reached out and pulled Lot back into the house and shut the door. ¹¹Then they struck the men who were at the door of the house, young and old, with blindness so that they could not find the door.

¹²The two men said to Lot, "Do you have anyone else here — sons-in-law, sons or daughters, or anyone else in the city who belongs to you? Get them out of here, ¹³because we are going to destroy this place. The outcry to the LORD against its people is so great that he has sent us to destroy it."

¹⁴So Lot went out and spoke to his sons-in-law, who were pledged to marry[a] his daughters. He said, "Hurry and get out of this place, because the LORD is about to destroy the city!" But his sons-in-law thought he was joking.

¹⁵With the coming of dawn, the angels urged Lot, saying, "Hurry! Take your wife and your two daughters who are here, or you will be swept away when the city is punished."

¹⁶When he hesitated, the men grasped his hand and the hands of his wife and of his two daughters and led them safely out of the city, for the LORD was merciful to them. ¹⁷As soon as they had brought them out, one of them said, "Flee for your lives! Don't look back, and don't stop anywhere in the plain! Flee to the mountains or you will be swept away!"

¹⁸But Lot said to them, "No, my lords,[b] please! ¹⁹Your[c] servant has found favor in your[c] eyes, and you[c] have shown great kindness to me in sparing my life. But I can't flee to the mountains; this disaster will overtake me, and I'll die. ²⁰Look, here is a town near enough to run to, and it is small. Let me flee to it—it is very small, isn't it? Then my life will be spared."

²¹He said to him, "Very well, I will grant this request too; I will not overthrow the town you speak of. ²²But flee there quickly, because I cannot do anything until you reach it." (That is why the town was called Zoar.[d])

²³By the time Lot reached Zoar, the sun had risen over the land. ²⁴Then the LORD rained down burning sulfur on Sodom and Gomorrah—from the LORD out of the heavens. ²⁵Thus he overthrew those cities and the entire plain, destroying all those living in the cities—and also the vegetation in the

[a] 14 Or were married to   [b] 18 Or No, Lord; or No, my lord   [c] 19 The Hebrew is singular.   [d] 22 Zoar means small.

19:6–9 | Lot's words (calling the wicked men of Sodom **my friends**) and his offer to give up his **two daughters** to the mob revealed how desperate he was for the men to relent. The ancient code of hospitality required a person to protect guests, but Lot went too far, and his angelic visitors had to rescue him (2 Pet. 2:7, 8).

19:12–14 | When the Lord decided to judge Sodom and Gomorrah, he warned Lot through the **two men**, who were actually angels (19:1). The reaction of his **sons-in-law** shows that he had lost influence within his own family. Because the sons-in-law are never mentioned again, they must have died in the destruction.

19:15, 16 | Those who quit walking in the will of God stop listening to Him. Even on the day when God promised to judge Sodom, Lot was reluctant to leave. His insensitivity to God's truth, a consequence of his years in Sodom, caused him to resist God's rescue—twice! (See note on 19:17–23.) Ultimately, the angels were forced to lead him out physically, along with his **wife** and **daughters**.

19:17–23 | Lot was urged to **flee to the mountains**, but he begged God to let him flee to a nearby **town** instead. In another act of mercy, the Lord granted his request.

land. ²⁶But Lot's wife looked back, and she became a pillar of salt.

²⁷Early the next morning Abraham got up and returned to the place where he had stood before the LORD. ²⁸He looked down toward Sodom and Gomorrah, toward all the land of the plain, and he saw dense smoke rising from the land, like smoke from a furnace.

²⁹So when God destroyed the cities of the plain, he remembered Abraham, and he brought Lot out of the catastrophe that overthrew the cities where Lot had lived.

Lot and His Daughters

³⁰Lot and his two daughters left Zoar and settled in the mountains, for he was afraid to stay in Zoar. He and his two daughters lived in a cave. ³¹One day the older daughter said to the younger, "Our father is old, and there is no man around here to give us children — as is the custom all over the earth. ³²Let's get our father to drink wine and then sleep with him and preserve our family line through our father."

³³That night they got their father to drink wine, and the older daughter went in and slept with him. He was not aware of it when she lay down or when she got up.

³⁴The next day the older daughter said to the younger, "Last night I slept with my father. Let's get him to drink wine again tonight, and you go in and sleep with him so we can preserve our family line through our father." ³⁵So they got their father to drink wine that night also, and the younger daughter went in and slept with him. Again he was not aware of it when she lay down or when she got up.

³⁶So both of Lot's daughters became pregnant by their father. ³⁷The older daughter had a son, and she named him Moabᵃ; he is the father of the Moabites of today. ³⁸The younger daughter also had a son, and she named him Ben-Ammiᵇ; he is the father of the Ammonitesᶜ of today.

Abraham and Abimelek

20 Now Abraham moved on from there into the region of the Negev and lived between Kadesh and Shur. For a while he stayed in Gerar, ²and there Abraham said of his wife Sarah, "She is my sister." Then Abimelek king of Gerar sent for Sarah and took her.

³But God came to Abimelek in a dream one night and said to him, "You are as good as dead because of the woman you have taken; she is a married woman."

⁴Now Abimelek had not gone near her, so he said, "Lord, will you destroy an innocent nation? ⁵Did he not say to me, 'She is my sister,' and didn't she also say, 'He is my brother'? I have done this with a clear conscience and clean hands."

⁶Then God said to him in the dream, "Yes, I know you did this with a clear conscience, and so I have kept you from sinning against me. That is why I did not let you touch her. ⁷Now return the man's wife, for he is a prophet, and he will pray for you and you will live. But if you do not return her, you may be sure that you and all who belong to you will die."

⁸Early the next morning Abimelek summoned all his officials, and when he told them all that had happened, they were very much afraid. ⁹Then Abimelek called Abraham in and said, "What have you done to us? How have I wronged you that you have brought such great guilt upon me and my kingdom? You have done things to me that should never be done." ¹⁰And Abimelek asked Abraham, "What was your reason for doing this?"

¹¹Abraham replied, "I said to myself, 'There is surely no fear of God in this place, and they will kill me because of my wife.' ¹²Besides, she really is my sister, the daughter of my father though not of my mother; and she became my wife. ¹³And when God

ᵃ 37 Moab sounds like the Hebrew for from father.　ᵇ 38 Ben-Ammi means son of my father's people.　ᶜ 38 Hebrew Bene-Ammon

---

19:24-26 | The names **Sodom and Gomorrah** are used throughout Scripture as examples of human depravity and God's resulting judgment (Deut. 29:23; Isa. 1:9; 13:19; Jer. 49:18; Amos 4:11; Matt. 10:15; 2 Pet. 2:6; Jude 7), and as a cautionary tale. The disobedience of Lot's **wife** is also a lesson to stop longing for the past and to start looking toward the future to which God is calling. When Lot's wife looked back, she turned into a monument to the divided heart. **19:30-38** | While Lot's life teaches much about the persistence of God's mercy, it also reveals the price a person pays for a lifetime of wrong choices. Lot went wrong when he began to seek what God did not want him to have. All his small concessions landed him in a **cave**, drunken and defeated. The descendants of his daughters' incest—the **Moabites** and the **Ammonites**—were historic enemies of Israel. Lot is not mentioned again in the Book of Genesis after this sordid incident. **20:1-17** | Some critical scholars claim the stories in chapters 12

and 20 must be two accounts of the same event (called "doublets"), but these are two separate events detailing the same sin. Abraham's failures to trust God for protection could have jeopardized his wife and the covenant had God not intervened each time. **20:7** | Abraham is called a **prophet**—the first use of the word in the Bible (Ps. 105:12-15). Here, though, it implies a person who has a close relationship with God rather than one speaking for God. **20:9-11** | Sometimes the people of God see right conduct among individuals who are themselves far from God. Abimelek's words rebuked Abraham's sinful deceit. **20:11** | **No fear of God in this place** means that Abraham did not expect just dealings from others (Ps. 36:11). Still, this does not excuse Abraham's action. Fear of God produces a reverence that shows itself in thought, word, and deed (Prov. 16:6). Surprisingly, Abraham feared other humans more than God in this instance.

had me wander from my father's household, I said to her, 'This is how you can show your love to me: Everywhere we go, say of me, "He is my brother." ' "

14 Then Abimelek brought sheep and cattle and male and female slaves and gave them to Abraham, and he returned Sarah his wife to him. 15 And Abimelek said, "My land is before you; live wherever you like."

16 To Sarah he said, "I am giving your brother a thousand shekels[a] of silver. This is to cover the offense against you before all who are with you; you are completely vindicated."

17 Then Abraham prayed to God, and God healed Abimelek, his wife and his female slaves so they could have children again, 18 for the LORD had kept all the women in Abimelek's household from conceiving because of Abraham's wife Sarah.

The Birth of Isaac

21 Now the LORD was gracious to Sarah as he had said, and the LORD did for Sarah what he had promised. 2 Sarah became pregnant and bore a son to Abraham in his old age, at the very time God had promised him. 3 Abraham gave the name Isaac[b] to the son Sarah bore him. 4 When his son Isaac was eight days old, Abraham circumcised him, as God commanded him. 5 Abraham was a hundred years old when his son Isaac was born to him.

6 Sarah said, "God has brought me laughter, and everyone who hears about this will laugh with me." 7 And she added, "Who would have said to Abraham that Sarah would nurse children? Yet I have borne him a son in his old age."

Hagar and Ishmael Sent Away

8 The child grew and was weaned, and on the day Isaac was weaned Abraham held a great feast. 9 But Sarah saw that the son whom Hagar the Egyptian had borne

---

When Sarah says, "God has brought me laughter, and everyone who hears about this will laugh with me," she summarizes a wonderful series of events. Abraham had fallen on his face and laughed when he finally heard that he would father a child by his very aged wife Sarah (17:17). It is as though he had come to a point where the idea of fatherhood at his age and motherhood at Sarah's age were just too much to take in. When Sarah heard the same message, she also laughed in disbelief (18:12). Her laughter was understandable because of her greatly advanced age (89 years).

In both cases, the Hebrew word for *laugh* is the verb *sahaq*. But it is God who has the last laugh! When the child of promise is born, all of heaven laughs. The child is named *yishaq* ("Isaac") from *sahaq*. Now God is laughing and the child, Isaac, is the embodiment of this wondrous divine laughter. As God said to Abraham, "Is anything too hard for the LORD?" (18:14; Matt. 19:26).

to Abraham was mocking, 10 and she said to Abraham, "Get rid of that slave woman and her son, for that woman's son will never share in the inheritance with my son Isaac."

11 The matter distressed Abraham greatly because it concerned his son. 12 But God said to him, "Do not be so distressed about the boy and your slave woman. Listen to whatever Sarah tells you, because it is through Isaac that your offspring[c] will be reckoned. 13 I will make the son of the slave into a nation also, because he is your offspring."

14 Early the next morning Abraham took some food and a skin of water and gave them to Hagar. He set them on her shoulders and then sent her off with the boy. She went on her way and wandered in the Desert of Beersheba.

---

a 16 That is, about 25 pounds or about 12 kilograms   b 3 Isaac means he laughs.   c 12 Or seed

---

20:14–18 | Abimelek showed Abraham the kind of grace and generosity that Abraham—who knew God—should have shown to him. When the king returned **Sarah** and the gifts to Abraham and the Lord reopened the wombs of the women in Abimelek's household, it publicly affirmed Sarah's honor. God prevented anything that might discredit the birth of Isaac.

21:1, 2 | These verses mention the Lord's promise three times to illustrate that everything happens exactly as God says it will (18:14; 1 Sam. 2:21; Gal 4:23).

21:4 | Abraham celebrated his son's birth by doing **as God commanded:** When **Isaac was eight days old,** he **circumcised him** (17:10). Obeying God from the beginning is a great start for any father.

21:6, 7 | Sarah's joy was beyond description: **God has brought me laughter** (Ps. 126:2; Isa. 54:1). Isaac's name means "Yahweh laughs." Her faith is celebrated in Hebrews 11:11 "because

she considered him faithful who had made the promise."

21:9 | Ishmael, who was a teenager when Isaac was born, had to know that this birth was nothing but a miracle of God's grace. Nevertheless, when Isaac became the center of attention, Ishmael began to scoff at him, and perhaps even his parents (Gal. 4:28, 29).

21:11–13 | Sarah's demand **distressed Abraham greatly**, because he loved Ishmael. To banish a surrogate mother went against cultural norms as well. Ultimately, this was such a personal and painful decision for Abraham that the Lord had to tell him to **listen** to Sarah. Obeying God can be heart-wrenching, but it must be done. In the end, both sons were greatly blessed.

21:14–21 | Sometimes God brings believers to a difficult place in the wilderness to discipline them so they can realize their need for Him. In the **desert**, people can see themselves as they really are (Ps. 119:67, 75). There they learn that He hears and will never leave or forsake His children (Deut. 31:6).

¹⁵ When the water in the skin was gone, she put the boy under one of the bushes. ¹⁶ Then she went off and sat down about a bowshot away, for she thought, "I cannot watch the boy die." And as she sat there, she^a began to sob.

¹⁷ God heard the boy crying, and the angel of God called to Hagar from heaven and said to her, "What is the matter, Hagar? Do not be afraid; God has heard the boy crying as he lies there. ¹⁸ Lift the boy up and take him by the hand, for I will make him into a great nation."

¹⁹ Then God opened her eyes and she saw a well of water. So she went and filled the skin with water and gave the boy a drink. ²⁰ God was with the boy as he grew up. He lived in the desert and became an archer. ²¹ While he was living in the Desert of Paran, his mother got a wife for him from Egypt.

The Treaty at Beersheba

²² At that time Abimelek and Phicol the commander of his forces said to Abraham, "God is with you in everything you do. ²³ Now swear to me here before God that you will not deal falsely with me or my children or my descendants. Show to me and the country where you now reside as a foreigner the same kindness I have shown to you."

²⁴ Abraham said, "I swear it."

²⁵ Then Abraham complained to Abimelek about a well of water that Abimelek's servants had seized. ²⁶ But Abimelek said, "I don't know who has done this. You did not tell me, and I heard about it only today."

²⁷ So Abraham brought sheep and cattle and gave them to Abimelek, and the two men made a treaty. ²⁸ Abraham set apart seven ewe lambs from the flock, ²⁹ and Abimelek asked Abraham, "What is the meaning of these seven ewe lambs you have set apart by themselves?"

³⁰ He replied, "Accept these seven lambs from my hand as a witness that I dug this well."

³¹ So that place was called Beersheba,^b because the two men swore an oath there.

For Reflection
His Only Son • 22:1, 2

From our perspective, God's command to Abraham is horribly cruel. One scholar has written that in this chapter, Abraham begins a "journey into God-forsakenness." It begins with God calling Abraham's name. God then uses words of increasing emotional significance to issue His instruction: "Take *your son*, your *only son* whom *you love*—Isaac." Each phrase pierces closer to Abraham's heart.

The Hebrew word used here for "only" son is *yahid*, an unusual term for something that is unique and irreplaceable. It is translated in the Greek version of the Hebrew Bible by *monogenes*, rendered sometimes as "the one and only," the very word that is used of Jesus in the NT (John 1:14). Ishmael was a beloved and honored son of Abraham (17:18), but Isaac was *yahid*—the uniquely born son of Abraham and Sarah—and was so named *monogenes* in Hebrews 11:17. And Jesus? He is *monogenes*! He is the One whose conception is an even greater miracle than that of Isaac! Two sons. One of Abraham, one of God. Each was the one and only; each was priceless.

---

³² After the treaty had been made at Beersheba, Abimelek and Phicol the commander of his forces returned to the land of the Philistines. ³³ Abraham planted a tamarisk tree in Beersheba, and there he called on the name of the LORD, the Eternal God. ³⁴ And Abraham stayed in the land of the Philistines for a long time.

Abraham Tested

22 Some time later God tested Abraham. He said to him, "Abraham!"

"Here I am," he replied.

² Then God said, "Take your son, your only son, whom you love — Isaac — and go to the region of Moriah. Sacrifice him there as a burnt offering on a mountain I will show you."

³ Early the next morning Abraham got up and loaded his donkey. He took with him

---

^a 16 Hebrew; Septuagint *the child*   ^b 31 *Beersheba* can mean *well of seven* and *well of the oath.*

21:22–34 | Abraham's interactions with the Philistine king (**Abimelek**) and the army commander (**Phicol**) over wells and water rights were one way he was a blessing to the nations (12:2, 3).
22:1–19 | Satan tempts people to bring out their worst; God may test His beloved ones to bring out their best (1 Cor. 10:13; James 1:12–14). The people closest to God often find themselves in the midst of the biggest tests. But Christians must remember: God will only ask them to do what He will enable them to do.
22:2–4 | All people have three parts to their personality: intellect, emotions, and will. Each was included in this test as God sought to refine Abraham to a purer faith (James 1:1–5). When God

commanded Abraham to **sacrifice** his promised son as a **burnt offering**, Isaac was approximately 15. In this defining moment, God asked Abraham to take all his future hopes—all that Abraham expected from the Lord according to His covenant—and surrender them on an altar. Although this instruction made no human sense, he did not argue or plead; he simply obeyed (Ps. 119:60).
22:2 | **Moriah** and Calvary (the place of Jesus' crucifixion) are other names for the same place: the threshing floor that David purchased from Araunah (2 Sam. 24:21–25), north of the city of Jerusalem. This particular hill (not a mountain) was also the site of both Hebrew temples.

two of his servants and his son Isaac. When he had cut enough wood for the burnt offering, he set out for the place God had told him about. [4]On the third day Abraham looked up and saw the place in the distance. [5]He said to his servants, "Stay here with the donkey while I and the boy go over there. We will worship and then we will come back to you."

[6]Abraham took the wood for the burnt offering and placed it on his son Isaac, and he himself carried the fire and the knife. As the two of them went on together, [7]Isaac spoke up and said to his father Abraham, "Father?"

"Yes, my son?" Abraham replied.

"The fire and wood are here," Isaac said, "but where is the lamb for the burnt offering?"

[8]Abraham answered, "God himself will provide the lamb for the burnt offering, my son." And the two of them went on together.

[9]When they reached the place God had told him about, Abraham built an altar there and arranged the wood on it. He bound his son Isaac and laid him on the altar, on top of the wood. [10]Then he reached out his hand and took the knife to slay his son. [11]But the angel of the LORD called out to him from heaven, "Abraham! Abraham!"

"Here I am," he replied.

[12]"Do not lay a hand on the boy," he said. "Do not do anything to him. Now I know that you fear God, because you have not withheld from me your son, your only son."

[13]Abraham looked up and there in a thicket he saw a ram[a] caught by its horns. He went over and took the ram and sacrificed it as a burnt offering instead of his son. [14]So Abraham called that place The LORD Will Provide. And to this day it is said, "On the mountain of the LORD it will be provided."

[15]The angel of the LORD called to Abraham from heaven a second time [16]and said, "I swear by myself, declares the LORD, that because you have done this and have not withheld your son, your only son, [17]I will surely bless you and make your descendants as numerous as the stars in the sky and as the sand on the seashore. Your descendants will take possession of the cities of their enemies, [18]and through your offspring[b] all nations on earth will be blessed,[c] because you have obeyed me."

[19]Then Abraham returned to his servants, and they set off together for Beersheba. And Abraham stayed in Beersheba.

Nahor's Sons

[20]Some time later Abraham was told, "Milkah is also a mother; she has borne sons to your brother Nahor: [21]Uz the firstborn, Buz his brother, Kemuel (the father of Aram), [22]Kesed, Hazo, Pildash, Jidlaph and Bethuel." [23]Bethuel became the father of Rebekah. Milkah bore these eight sons to Abraham's brother Nahor. [24]His concubine, whose name was Reumah, also had sons: Tebah, Gaham, Tahash and Maakah.

The Death of Sarah

23 Sarah lived to be a hundred and twenty-seven years old. [2]She died at Kiriath Arba (that is, Hebron) in the land of Canaan, and Abraham went to mourn for Sarah and to weep over her.

[3]Then Abraham rose from beside his dead wife and spoke to the Hittites.[d] He said, [4]"I am a foreigner and stranger among you. Sell me some property for a burial site here so I can bury my dead."

[5]The Hittites replied to Abraham, [6]"Sir, listen to us. You are a mighty prince among us. Bury your dead in the choicest of our tombs. None of us will refuse you his tomb for burying your dead."

---

[a] 13 Many manuscripts of the Masoretic Text, Samaritan Pentateuch, Septuagint and Syriac; most manuscripts of the Masoretic Text *a ram behind him*   [b] 18 Or *seed*   [c] 18 Or *and all nations on earth will use the name of your offspring in blessings* (see 48:20)   [d] 3 Or *the descendants of Heth*; also in verses 5, 7, 10, 16, 18 and 20

22:3, 4 | The phrase **early the next morning**, which was also used when God told Abraham to send Ishmael away (21:14), anticipates actions that were particularly difficult to accomplish. Abraham's obedience was so complete that **he had cut enough wood for the burnt offering** in advance, realizing that wood at the altar site might be scarce. Moriah was about 45 miles north of Beersheba, a three days' journey at that time.

22:5 | The Hebrew term translated **worship** describes the specific act of a person bowing all the way to the ground. More important is the force of the verbs here: *worship* and **will come back to you** express great determination and faith. Abraham in effect told his servants: once these acts of worship are complete, Isaac and I *will* return. Abraham had no precedent for believing God would somehow bring his son back to life after the offering (Heb. 11:17–19), for no one had ever seen a resurrection. Nevertheless, he trusted God to do the impossible, maybe because he had already seen God deliver the impossible through Isaac's birth.

22:10–12 | Just as with Hagar and Ishmael in the wilderness (21:16, 17), God spoke at the very moment Abraham needed to hear from Him: just as he **took the knife to slay** Isaac. God did not want Abraham's son to die; He wanted Abraham's submission to Himself. When God said, **Now I know that you fear God**, He validated Abraham's deep faith.

22:12 | In Hebrew, to **fear God** describes saving faith; it also indicates one who values God, in awe, wonder, and worship. In Scripture, fearing God takes priority over every other response to Him (Deut. 10:12, 20; Eccl. 12:13). This may be one reason God tests the faith of His servants (James 2:21, 22).

22:13–18 | Abraham's confidence that God would provide ("God himself will provide") in 22:8 is rewarded here, for God honors those who honor Him. God reaffirmed His covenant to Abraham with the most steadfast of oaths (**I swear by myself**). **The LORD Will Provide** is a fitting name for Moriah (**the mountain of the LORD**), because here God provided not only a ram in Isaac's place but also a Savior in humanity's place (see note on 22:2).

⁷Then Abraham rose and bowed down before the people of the land, the Hittites. ⁸He said to them, "If you are willing to let me bury my dead, then listen to me and intercede with Ephron son of Zohar on my behalf ⁹so he will sell me the cave of Machpelah, which belongs to him and is at the end of his field. Ask him to sell it to me for the full price as a burial site among you."

¹⁰Ephron the Hittite was sitting among his people and he replied to Abraham in the hearing of all the Hittites who had come to the gate of his city. ¹¹"No, my lord," he said. "Listen to me; I giveᵃ you the field, and I giveᵃ you the cave that is in it. I giveᵃ it to you in the presence of my people. Bury your dead."

¹²Again Abraham bowed down before the people of the land ¹³and he said to Ephron in their hearing, "Listen to me, if you will. I will pay the price of the field. Accept it from me so I can bury my dead there."

¹⁴Ephron answered Abraham, ¹⁵"Listen to me, my lord; the land is worth four hundred shekelsᵇ of silver, but what is that between you and me? Bury your dead."

¹⁶Abraham agreed to Ephron's terms and weighed out for him the price he had named in the hearing of the Hittites: four hundred shekels of silver, according to the weight current among the merchants.

¹⁷So Ephron's field in Machpelah near Mamre—both the field and the cave in it, and all the trees within the borders of the field—was deeded ¹⁸to Abraham as his property in the presence of all the Hittites who had come to the gate of the city. ¹⁹Afterward Abraham buried his wife Sarah in the cave in the field of Machpelah near Mamre (which is at Hebron) in the land of Canaan. ²⁰So the field and the cave in it were deeded to Abraham by the Hittites as a burial site.

Isaac and Rebekah

24 Abraham was now very old, and the LORD had blessed him in every way. ²He said to the senior servant in his household, the one in charge of all that he had, "Put your hand under my thigh. ³I want you to swear by the LORD, the God of heaven and the God of earth, that you will not get a wife for my son from the daughters of the Canaanites, among whom I am living, ⁴but will go to my country and my own relatives and get a wife for my son Isaac."

⁵The servant asked him, "What if the woman is unwilling to come back with me to this land? Shall I then take your son back to the country you came from?"

⁶"Make sure that you do not take my son back there," Abraham said. ⁷"The LORD, the God of heaven, who brought me out of my father's household and my native land and who spoke to me and promised me on oath, saying, 'To your offspringᶜ I will give this land'—he will send his angel before you so that you can get a wife for my son from there. ⁸If the woman is unwilling to come back with you, then you will be released from this oath of mine. Only do not take my son back there." ⁹So the servant put his hand under the thigh of his master Abraham and swore an oath to him concerning this matter.

¹⁰Then the servant left, taking with him ten of his master's camels loaded with all kinds of good things from his master. He set out for Aram Naharaimᵈ and made his way to the town of Nahor. ¹¹He had the camels kneel down near the well outside the town; it was toward evening, the time the women go out to draw water.

¹²Then he prayed, "LORD, God of my master Abraham, make me successful today, and show kindness to my master Abraham. ¹³See, I am standing beside this spring, and the daughters of the townspeople are coming out to draw water. ¹⁴May it be that when I say to a young woman, 'Please let down your jar that I may have a drink,' and she says, 'Drink, and I'll water your camels too'—let her be the one you have chosen for

---

ᵃ 11 Or sell   ᵇ 15 That is, about 10 pounds or about 4.6 kilograms   ᶜ 7 Or seed
ᵈ 10 That is, Northwest Mesopotamia

23:1–18 | Abraham managed two camps—one in Hebron, one in Beersheba. Presumably, he was in Beersheba when **Sarah** died in **Hebron**. Abraham considered himself **a foreigner and stranger** in the land, and Sarah's death may have reinforced this: he had been promised all this territory but had to buy **property for a burial site**. While his neighbors never understood him, they deeply respected him, calling him **a mighty prince** and offering to give him the cave. Every believer is a stranger in this world (Eph. 2:19). Those who make a real impact realize that their ultimate home and meaning is in heaven (1 Chron. 29:15; Heb. 11:9, 13–16).

23:20 | When Abraham died, this **field** became his **burial site** (25:7–11) too, as it would be for Isaac (35:27–29), Rebekah, Jacob, and Leah (49:31; 50:13). Only Rachel was not buried here (35:16–20).

24:1–3 | To place a **hand under** someone's **thigh** symbolized a binding oath. To **swear by the LORD**, or to vow by His authority, verbally affirmed this commitment. Although the **senior servant** is not named here, some Bible teachers identify him as Eliezer (15:2).

24:3–9 | In faithfulness to the one true God, Abraham made his servant vow that he would **not get a wife for** Isaac from among the idolatrous **Canaanites**. Like Abraham with this servant, the Lord is not offended when His people request clarity so that they can know His will and do it well.

24:10–14 | To discern God's will, a person must first be determined to do it. More frequently, Christians try to determine it before doing it. Prayers like this—for wisdom, grace, and clarity regarding the Lord's will—are ones the Lord honors. God has a wonderful way of affirming His plans after His servants step out in faith (Ps. 37:5).

your servant Isaac. By this I will know that you have shown kindness to my master."

¹⁵ Before he had finished praying, Rebekah came out with her jar on her shoulder. She was the daughter of Bethuel son of Milkah, who was the wife of Abraham's brother Nahor. ¹⁶ The woman was very beautiful, a virgin; no man had ever slept with her. She went down to the spring, filled her jar and came up again.

¹⁷ The servant hurried to meet her and said, "Please give me a little water from your jar."

¹⁸ "Drink, my lord," she said, and quickly lowered the jar to her hands and gave him a drink.

¹⁹ After she had given him a drink, she said, "I'll draw water for your camels too, until they have had enough to drink." ²⁰ So she quickly emptied her jar into the trough, ran back to the well to draw more water, and drew enough for all his camels. ²¹ Without saying a word, the man watched her closely to learn whether or not the LORD had made his journey successful.

²² When the camels had finished drinking, the man took out a gold nose ring weighing a beka*ᵃ* and two gold bracelets weighing ten shekels.*ᵇ* ²³ Then he asked, "Whose daughter are you? Please tell me, is there room in your father's house for us to spend the night?"

²⁴ She answered him, "I am the daughter of Bethuel, the son that Milkah bore to Nahor." ²⁵ And she added, "We have plenty of straw and fodder, as well as room for you to spend the night."

²⁶ Then the man bowed down and worshiped the LORD, ²⁷ saying, "Praise be to the LORD, the God of my master Abraham, who has not abandoned his kindness and faithfulness to my master. As for me, the LORD has led me on the journey to the house of my master's relatives."

²⁸ The young woman ran and told her mother's household about these things. ²⁹ Now Rebekah had a brother named Laban, and he hurried out to the man at the spring. ³⁰ As soon as he had seen the nose ring, and the bracelets on his sister's arms, and had heard Rebekah tell what the man said to her, he went out to the man and found him standing by the camels near the

Picture This — A Good Steward • 24:10–14

A steward is somebody who administrates another person's affairs and does it with the deep desire to reflect that person's will in the carrying out of the duties. Abraham's servant wonderfully illustrates that ideal, not only in his obedience, but also in his prayers and faithful follow-through. Abraham's steward was accountable for "all kinds of good things from his master." Considering Abraham's extraordinary wealth, this was a significant responsibility that required great trustworthiness and integrity. Every Christian should view themselves likewise—as God's stewards—and strive to faithfully and carefully oversee His resources and work here on earth.

spring. ³¹ "Come, you who are blessed by the LORD," he said. "Why are you standing out here? I have prepared the house and a place for the camels."

³² So the man went to the house, and the camels were unloaded. Straw and fodder were brought for the camels, and water for him and his men to wash their feet. ³³ Then food was set before him, but he said, "I will not eat until I have told you what I have to say."

"Then tell us," Laban said.

³⁴ So he said, "I am Abraham's servant. ³⁵ The LORD has blessed my master abundantly, and he has become wealthy. He has given him sheep and cattle, silver and gold, male and female servants, and camels and donkeys. ³⁶ My master's wife Sarah has borne him a son in her old age, and he has given him everything he owns. ³⁷ And my master made me swear an oath, and said, 'You must not get a wife for my son from the daughters of the Canaanites, in whose land I live, ³⁸ but go to my father's family and to my own clan, and get a wife for my son.'

³⁹ "Then I asked my master, 'What if the woman will not come back with me?'

⁴⁰ "He replied, 'The LORD, before whom I have walked faithfully, will send his angel with you and make your journey a success, so that you can get a wife for my son from my own clan and from my father's family. ⁴¹ You

---

ᵃ 22 That is, about 1/5 ounce or about 5.7 grams   ᵇ 22 That is, about 4 ounces or about 115 grams

---

24:14–20 | This was answered prayer! The servant asked God to do something so significant that he would not miss the woman God had **chosen for . . . Isaac**. And **before he had finished praying**, **Rebekah** arrived. It was common courtesy to offer water to another person at a well, but offering to draw water for animals was not. And to do so for all 10 **camels** was extraordinary.
24:29–31 | Rebekah's brother **Laban** was impressed by the objects of wealth this servant had brought with him—from the jewelry to the

camels. (In antiquity, only the very affluent owned camels.) Seeing an opportunity to improve his own situation, he invited the servant to stay at his house. Laban's materialism and opportunism resurfaced later.
24:34–49 | The servant recounted the events that had brought him before Laban and **Bethuel**, Rebekah's father. Readers today may chafe at the repetition in these stories, but the text was originally written to be read aloud. The repetition made the storytelling more memorable and also wrote these scriptural lessons and histories on people's hearts.

will be released from my oath if, when you go to my clan, they refuse to give her to you—then you will be released from my oath.'

⁴²"When I came to the spring today, I said, 'LORD, God of my master Abraham, if you will, please grant success to the journey on which I have come. ⁴³See, I am standing beside this spring. If a young woman comes out to draw water and I say to her, "Please let me drink a little water from your jar," ⁴⁴and if she says to me, "Drink, and I'll draw water for your camels too," let her be the one the LORD has chosen for my master's son.'

⁴⁵"Before I finished praying in my heart, Rebekah came out, with her jar on her shoulder. She went down to the spring and drew water, and I said to her, 'Please give me a drink.'

⁴⁶"She quickly lowered her jar from her shoulder and said, 'Drink, and I'll water your camels too.' So I drank, and she watered the camels also.

⁴⁷"I asked her, 'Whose daughter are you?'

"She said, 'The daughter of Bethuel son of Nahor, whom Milkah bore to him.'

"Then I put the ring in her nose and the bracelets on her arms, ⁴⁸and I bowed down and worshiped the LORD. I praised the LORD, the God of my master Abraham, who had led me on the right road to get the granddaughter of my master's brother for his son. ⁴⁹Now if you will show kindness and faithfulness to my master, tell me; and if not, tell me, so I may know which way to turn."

⁵⁰Laban and Bethuel answered, "This is from the LORD; we can say nothing to you one way or the other. ⁵¹Here is Rebekah; take her and go, and let her become the wife of your master's son, as the LORD has directed."

⁵²When Abraham's servant heard what they said, he bowed down to the ground before the LORD. ⁵³Then the servant brought out gold and silver jewelry and articles of clothing and gave them to Rebekah; he also gave costly gifts to her brother and to her mother. ⁵⁴Then he and the men who were with him ate and drank and spent the night there.

When they got up the next morning, he said, "Send me on my way to my master."

⁵⁵But her brother and her mother replied, "Let the young woman remain with us ten days or so; then you*ᵃ* may go."

⁵⁶But he said to them, "Do not detain me, now that the LORD has granted success to my journey. Send me on my way so I may go to my master."

⁵⁷Then they said, "Let's call the young woman and ask her about it." ⁵⁸So they called Rebekah and asked her, "Will you go with this man?"

"I will go," she said.

⁵⁹So they sent their sister Rebekah on her way, along with her nurse and Abraham's servant and his men. ⁶⁰And they blessed Rebekah and said to her,

"Our sister, may you increase
    to thousands upon thousands;
may your offspring possess
    the cities of their enemies."

⁶¹Then Rebekah and her attendants got ready and mounted the camels and went back with the man. So the servant took Rebekah and left.

⁶²Now Isaac had come from Beer Lahai Roi, for he was living in the Negev. ⁶³He went out to the field one evening to meditate,*ᵇ* and as he looked up, he saw camels approaching. ⁶⁴Rebekah also looked up and saw Isaac. She got down from her camel ⁶⁵and asked the servant, "Who is that man in the field coming to meet us?"

"He is my master," the servant answered. So she took her veil and covered herself.

⁶⁶Then the servant told Isaac all he had done. ⁶⁷Isaac brought her into the tent of his mother Sarah, and he married Rebekah. So she became his wife, and he loved her; and Isaac was comforted after his mother's death.

The Death of Abraham

25 Abraham had taken another wife, whose name was Keturah. ²She bore him Zimran, Jokshan, Medan, Midian, Ishbak and Shuah. ³Jokshan was the father of Sheba and Dedan; the descendants of Dedan were the Ashurites, the Letushites and the Leummites. ⁴The sons of Midian were Ephah, Epher, Hanok, Abida and Eldaah. All these were descendants of Keturah.

ᵃ 55 Or *she*   *ᵇ* 63 The meaning of the Hebrew for this word is uncertain.

24:50–59 | With the family's approval secured, the servant gave them valuable gifts of betrothal, which served as a dowry. Although Rebekah knew nothing about Isaac, she knew that God had led the servant of Abraham to her, so according to custom, she agreed to **go.** By faith she left everything that was familiar to venture to an unknown place, much as Abraham and Sarah had (12:1–4). **24:60** | This brief blessing echoes the words of the covenant given

to Abraham in 22:17: "I will surely bless you and make your descendants as numerous as the stars in the sky and as the sand on the seashore. Your descendants will take possession of the cities of their enemies."

25:1–6 | The importance of the paragraph lies in the disposition of **gifts.** Abraham made sure there would be no dispute over his goods after he died. He showed great responsibility here (2 Cor. 12:14).

[5] Abraham left everything he owned to Isaac. [6] But while he was still living, he gave gifts to the sons of his concubines and sent them away from his son Isaac to the land of the east.

[7] Abraham lived a hundred and seventy-five years. [8] Then Abraham breathed his last and died at a good old age, an old man and full of years; and he was gathered to his people. [9] His sons Isaac and Ishmael buried him in the cave of Machpelah near Mamre, in the field of Ephron son of Zohar the Hittite, [10] the field Abraham had bought from the Hittites.[a] There Abraham was buried with his wife Sarah. [11] After Abraham's death, God blessed his son Isaac, who then lived near Beer Lahai Roi.

Ishmael's Sons

[12] This is the account of the family line of Abraham's son Ishmael, whom Sarah's slave, Hagar the Egyptian, bore to Abraham.

[13] These are the names of the sons of Ishmael, listed in the order of their birth: Nebaioth the firstborn of Ishmael, Kedar, Adbeel, Mibsam, [14] Mishma, Dumah, Massa, [15] Hadad, Tema, Jetur, Naphish and Kedemah. [16] These were the sons of Ishmael, and these are the names of the twelve tribal rulers according to their settlements and camps. [17] Ishmael lived a hundred and thirty-seven years. He breathed his last and died, and he was gathered to his people. [18] His descendants settled in the area from Havilah to Shur, near the eastern border of Egypt, as you go toward Ashur. And they lived in hostility toward[b] all the tribes related to them.

Jacob and Esau

[19] This is the account of the family line of Abraham's son Isaac.

Abraham became the father of Isaac, [20] and Isaac was forty years old when he married Rebekah daughter of Bethuel the Aramean from Paddan Aram[c] and sister of Laban the Aramean.

[21] Isaac prayed to the LORD on behalf of his wife, because she was childless. The LORD answered his prayer, and his wife Rebekah became pregnant. [22] The babies jostled each other within her, and she said, "Why is this happening to me?" So she went to inquire of the LORD.

[23] The LORD said to her,

"Two nations are in your womb,
  and two peoples from within you will
    be separated;
  one people will be stronger than the
    other,
  and the older will serve the younger."

[24] When the time came for her to give birth, there were twin boys in her womb. [25] The first to come out was red, and his whole body was like a hairy garment; so they named him Esau.[d] [26] After this, his brother came out, with his hand grasping Esau's heel; so he was named Jacob.[e] Isaac was sixty years old when Rebekah gave birth to them.

[27] The boys grew up, and Esau became a skillful hunter, a man of the open country, while Jacob was content to stay at home among the tents. [28] Isaac, who had a taste for wild game, loved Esau, but Rebekah loved Jacob.

---

[a] 10 Or the descendants of Heth   [b] 18 Or lived to the east of   [c] 20 That is, Northwest Mesopotamia   [d] 25 Esau may mean hairy.   [e] 26 Jacob means he grasps the heel, a Hebrew idiom for he deceives.

25:7–9 | This is a legacy for any Christian: Abraham walked with God for a hundred years. When he died at age 175, Isaac was 75, while Jacob and Esau were 15. Despite a history of bad feelings, **his sons Isaac and Ishmael buried** their father together, as brothers.
25:8 | **Full of years** can also be rendered "satisfied," meaning Abraham not only lived long but also well and was ready to die. This was a fulfillment of the Lord's covenant with him (15:15). **Was gathered to his people** speaks of blessed reunions in the life to come (Num. 20:24; Deut. 32:50).
25:12–18 | The inclusion of Ishmael's **family line** demonstrates that the Lord continued to love and care for Abraham's first son,
even though Isaac was the son of the covenant.
25:19–28 | The **family line** of **Isaac** is the focus of the narrative, so the story follows the lives of Isaac and Rebekah's two sons, **Esau** and **Jacob**. This is the family of promise.
25:22–26 | This divine word to Rebekah—that **the older will serve the younger**—not only explained the unusual movements she felt in her womb but also foretold a reversal of patriarchal custom (Rom. 9:10–13). **Esau**, the firstborn, would have expected to receive both the birthright and the blessing and have the younger serving him. **Jacob** means "he grasps the heel." His name also foreshadows the discord that these brothers would bring to the family.

[29] Once when Jacob was cooking some stew, Esau came in from the open country, famished. [30] He said to Jacob, "Quick, let me have some of that red stew! I'm famished!" (That is why he was also called Edom.[a])

[31] Jacob replied, "First sell me your birthright."

[32] "Look, I am about to die," Esau said. "What good is the birthright to me?"

[33] But Jacob said, "Swear to me first." So he swore an oath to him, selling his birthright to Jacob.

[34] Then Jacob gave Esau some bread and some lentil stew. He ate and drank, and then got up and left.

So Esau despised his birthright.

Isaac and Abimelek

26 Now there was a famine in the land— besides the previous famine in Abraham's time—and Isaac went to Abimelek king of the Philistines in Gerar. [2] The LORD appeared to Isaac and said, "Do not go down to Egypt; live in the land where I tell you to live. [3] Stay in this land for a while, and I will be with you and will bless you. For to you and your descendants I will give all these lands and will confirm the oath I swore to your father Abraham. [4] I will make your descendants as numerous as the stars in the sky and will give them all these lands, and through your offspring[b] all nations on earth will be blessed,[c] [5] because Abraham obeyed me and did everything I required of him, keeping my commands, my decrees and my instructions." [6] So Isaac stayed in Gerar.

[7] When the men of that place asked him about his wife, he said, "She is my sister," because he was afraid to say, "She is my wife." He thought, "The men of this place might kill me on account of Rebekah, because she is beautiful."

[8] When Isaac had been there a long time, Abimelek king of the Philistines looked down from a window and saw Isaac caressing his wife Rebekah. [9] So Abimelek summoned Isaac and said, "She is really your wife! Why did you say, 'She is my sister'?"

Isaac answered him, "Because I thought I might lose my life on account of her."

[10] Then Abimelek said, "What is this you have done to us? One of the men might well have slept with your wife, and you would have brought guilt upon us."

[11] So Abimelek gave orders to all the people: "Anyone who harms this man or his wife shall surely be put to death."

[12] Isaac planted crops in that land and the same year reaped a hundredfold, because the LORD blessed him. [13] The man became rich, and his wealth continued to grow until he became very wealthy. [14] He had so many flocks and herds and servants that the Philistines envied him. [15] So all the wells that his father's servants had dug in the time of his father Abraham, the Philistines stopped up, filling them with earth.

[16] Then Abimelek said to Isaac, "Move away from us; you have become too powerful for us."

[17] So Isaac moved away from there and encamped in the Valley of Gerar, where he settled. [18] Isaac reopened the wells that had been dug in the time of his father Abraham, which the Philistines had stopped up after Abraham died, and he gave them the same names his father had given them.

[19] Isaac's servants dug in the valley and discovered a well of fresh water there. [20] But the herders of Gerar quarreled with those of Isaac and said, "The water is ours!" So he named the well Esek,[d] because they disputed with him. [21] Then they dug another well, but they quarreled over that one also; so he named it Sitnah.[e] [22] He moved on from there and dug another well, and no one quarreled over it. He named it Rehoboth,[f] saying, "Now the LORD has given us room and we will flourish in the land."

[23] From there he went up to Beersheba. [24] That night the LORD appeared to him and said, "I am the God of your father Abraham. Do not be afraid, for I am with you; I will

---

[a] 30 *Edom* means red.   [b] 4 Or *seed*   [c] 4 Or *and all nations on earth will use the name of your offspring in blessings* (see 48:20)   [d] 20 *Esek* means dispute.   [e] 21 *Sitnah* means opposition.   [f] 22 *Rehoboth* means room.

25:29-34 | The **birthright** included several privileges: (1) recognition as the oldest son, (2) a double portion of the inheritance upon the father's death, and (3) regard as the leader of the family. The birthright could be given away or sold, but the older son would then lose the latter two aspects of the birthright. Esau's choice showed how little he valued these spiritual blessings (Matt. 16:26; Heb. 12:16).
26:2-22 | Isaac's circumstances—and sins—were similar to his father's. So was God's covenant with him. Isaac's personal blessings were dependent on his obedience to God and were therefore conditional; but the covenant itself was dependent on God's

character and was therefore unconditional (15:17-21).
26:6-11 | Unfortunately sons sometimes take on the sins of the fathers (20:1-7). Only through heaven's healing can families break generational sin.
26:23-25 | The LORD **appeared to him**, demonstrating that Isaac was blessed in the same manner as his father (12:7, 8). Like Abraham, Isaac built an **altar** (13:4; 22:9).
26:24 | In the OT, men of God were called servants of the Lord (Josh. 14:7; 24:29; Ps. 89:3; Isa. 20:3). Here, God calls Abraham **my servant**. Nothing is more desirable than to be a servant of the Living God (Mark 10:42-45; Gal. 5:13).

bless you and will increase the number of your descendants for the sake of my servant Abraham."

²⁵Isaac built an altar there and called on the name of the LORD. There he pitched his tent, and there his servants dug a well.

²⁶Meanwhile, Abimelek had come to him from Gerar, with Ahuzzath his personal adviser and Phicol the commander of his forces. ²⁷Isaac asked them, "Why have you come to me, since you were hostile to me and sent me away?"

²⁸They answered, "We saw clearly that the LORD was with you; so we said, 'There ought to be a sworn agreement between us' — between us and you. Let us make a treaty with you ²⁹that you will do us no harm, just as we did not harm you but always treated you well and sent you away peacefully. And now you are blessed by the LORD."

³⁰Isaac then made a feast for them, and they ate and drank. ³¹Early the next morning the men swore an oath to each other. Then Isaac sent them on their way, and they went away peacefully.

³²That day Isaac's servants came and told him about the well they had dug. They said, "We've found water!" ³³He called it Shibah,ᵃ and to this day the name of the town has been Beersheba.ᵇ

Jacob Takes Esau's Blessing

³⁴When Esau was forty years old, he married Judith daughter of Beeri the Hittite, and also Basemath daughter of Elon the Hittite. ³⁵They were a source of grief to Isaac and Rebekah.

27 When Isaac was old and his eyes were so weak that he could no longer see, he called for Esau his older son and said to him, "My son."

"Here I am," he answered.

²Isaac said, "I am now an old man and don't know the day of my death. ³Now then, get your equipment — your quiver and bow — and go out to the open country to hunt some wild game for me. ⁴Prepare me the kind of tasty food I like and bring it to me to eat, so that I may give you my blessing before I die."

⁵Now Rebekah was listening as Isaac spoke to his son Esau. When Esau left for the open country to hunt game and bring it back, ⁶Rebekah said to her son Jacob, "Look, I overheard your father say to your brother Esau, ⁷'Bring me some game and prepare me some tasty food to eat, so that I may give you my blessing in the presence of the LORD before I die.' ⁸Now, my son, listen carefully and do what I tell you: ⁹Go out to the flock and bring me two choice young goats, so I can prepare some tasty food for your father, just the way he likes it. ¹⁰Then take it to your father to eat, so that he may give you his blessing before he dies."

¹¹Jacob said to Rebekah his mother, "But my brother Esau is a hairy man while I have smooth skin. ¹²What if my father touches me? I would appear to be tricking him and would bring down a curse on myself rather than a blessing."

¹³His mother said to him, "My son, let the curse fall on me. Just do what I say; go and get them for me."

¹⁴So he went and got them and brought them to his mother, and she prepared some tasty food, just the way his father liked it. ¹⁵Then Rebekah took the best clothes of Esau her older son, which she had in the house, and put them on her younger son Jacob. ¹⁶She also covered his hands and the smooth part of his neck with the goatskins. ¹⁷Then she handed to her son Jacob the tasty food and the bread she had made.

¹⁸He went to his father and said, "My father."

"Yes, my son," he answered. "Who is it?"

¹⁹Jacob said to his father, "I am Esau your firstborn. I have done as you told me. Please sit up and eat some of my game, so that you may give me your blessing."

²⁰Isaac asked his son, "How did you find it so quickly, my son?"

ᵃ 33 *Shibah* can mean *oath* or *seven*.   ᵇ 33 *Beersheba* can mean *well of the oath* and *well of seven*.

26:26-33 | Isaac's dealings with **Abimelek** resembled his father's (21:22-34), with much the same result. When the Philistines observed that Isaac was **blessed by the LORD**, it was a remarkable testimony, since they hated God. If God's people keep pressing forward, doing His will, their lives may impact even their enemies (Matt. 5:44).

27:1-17 | Jacob's concern that he might bring a **curse** on himself suggests he may not have known about the Lord's word to his mother (25:23). Rebekah was the real instigator (note the verb phrases in 27:14-17), willfully helping to deceive her own husband and son. Her failure to wait on God created great strife within the family and years of negative consequences for her favorite son.

27:1-4 | Although Jacob may not have known about the Lord's word to Rebekah, **Isaac** did (25:23). By trying to reverse God's expressed order for the blessing and confer it on **Esau**, Isaac rebelled. But God's will cannot be thwarted. Rebekah and Isaac did what people often do: they failed to work in God's way in spite of knowing God's word. His work must be done His way.

27:13-29 | Rebekah's conduct had a sad impact on Jacob: he became a deceiver, just like his mother. Jacob carried off the deception too well; his aged father was tricked by **food**, **touch**, **voice**, and **smell**. He also spoke lie upon lie. Deception rarely produces only sinful actions; lying words are almost always close behind. Isaac's final words to Jacob on cursing and blessing echo God's original promise to Abram (12:3).

"The LORD your God gave me success," he replied.

²¹Then Isaac said to Jacob, "Come near so I can touch you, my son, to know whether you really are my son Esau or not."

²²Jacob went close to his father Isaac, who touched him and said, "The voice is the voice of Jacob, but the hands are the hands of Esau." ²³He did not recognize him, for his hands were hairy like those of his brother Esau; so he proceeded to bless him. ²⁴"Are you really my son Esau?" he asked.

"I am," he replied.

²⁵Then he said, "My son, bring me some of your game to eat, so that I may give you my blessing."

Jacob brought it to him and he ate; and he brought some wine and he drank. ²⁶Then his father Isaac said to him, "Come here, my son, and kiss me."

²⁷So he went to him and kissed him. When Isaac caught the smell of his clothes, he blessed him and said,

"Ah, the smell of my son
  is like the smell of a field
  that the LORD has blessed.
²⁸May God give you heaven's dew
  and earth's richness—
  an abundance of grain and new wine.
²⁹May nations serve you
  and peoples bow down to you.
Be lord over your brothers,
  and may the sons of your mother
    bow down to you.
May those who curse you be cursed
  and those who bless you be blessed."

³⁰After Isaac finished blessing him, and Jacob had scarcely left his father's presence, his brother Esau came in from hunting. ³¹He too prepared some tasty food and brought it to his father. Then he said to him, "My father, please sit up and eat some of my game, so that you may give me your blessing."

³²His father Isaac asked him, "Who are you?"

"I am your son," he answered, "your firstborn, Esau."

³³Isaac trembled violently and said, "Who was it, then, that hunted game and brought it to me? I ate it just before you came and I blessed him—and indeed he will be blessed!"

³⁴When Esau heard his father's words, he burst out with a loud and bitter cry and said to his father, "Bless me—me too, my father!"

³⁵But he said, "Your brother came deceitfully and took your blessing."

³⁶Esau said, "Isn't he rightly named Jacob*ᵃ? This is the second time he has taken advantage of me: He took my birthright, and now he's taken my blessing!" Then he asked, "Haven't you reserved any blessing for me?"

³⁷Isaac answered Esau, "I have made him lord over you and have made all his relatives his servants, and I have sustained him with grain and new wine. So what can I possibly do for you, my son?"

³⁸Esau said to his father, "Do you have only one blessing, my father? Bless me too, my father!" Then Esau wept aloud.

³⁹His father Isaac answered him,

"Your dwelling will be
  away from the earth's richness,
  away from the dew of heaven above.
⁴⁰You will live by the sword
  and you will serve your brother.
But when you grow restless,
  you will throw his yoke
  from off your neck."

⁴¹Esau held a grudge against Jacob because of the blessing his father had given him. He said to himself, "The days of mourning for my father are near; then I will kill my brother Jacob."

⁴²When Rebekah was told what her older son Esau had said, she sent for her younger son Jacob and said to him, "Your brother Esau is planning to avenge himself by killing you. ⁴³Now then, my son, do what I say: Flee at once to my brother Laban in Harran. ⁴⁴Stay with him for a while until your brother's fury subsides. ⁴⁵When your brother is no longer angry with you and forgets what you did to him, I'll send word for you to come back from there. Why should I lose both of you in one day?"

ᵃ *36* Jacob means *he grasps the heel*, a Hebrew idiom for *he takes advantage of* or *he deceives*.

27:30–38 | Esau's words after realizing he had lost the blessing—**Isn't he rightly named Jacob?**—demonstrate the significance of biblical names (see note on 25:22–26). Deathbed declarations could not be reversed or challenged. Once spoken, these blessings "lived," so there was nothing the deceived Isaac could do. Esau's desperation and bitterness is evident in statements such as **Bless me—me too, my father!** and **Haven't you reserved any blessing for me? 27:36** | All too often people blame others for their actions. Even

though Esau had voluntarily sold his birthright to Jacob, the older brother claimed Jacob **took** his **birthright** and now his **blessing**. Esau did receive a blessing; it was just not the principal blessing. **27:41–45** | **Esau held a grudge against Jacob.** These words indicate a possible fratricide, like that of Cain and Abel (4:8). Rebekah told Jacob to **flee** to her **brother Laban in Harran** for protection; however, it cost her a future with him, for he lived with Laban for more than two decades.

[46]Then Rebekah said to Isaac, "I'm disgusted with living because of these Hittite women. If Jacob takes a wife from among the women of this land, from Hittite women like these, my life will not be worth living."

28 So Isaac called for Jacob and blessed him. Then he commanded him: "Do not marry a Canaanite woman. [2]Go at once to Paddan Aram,[a] to the house of your mother's father Bethuel. Take a wife for yourself there, from among the daughters of Laban, your mother's brother. [3]May God Almighty[b] bless you and make you fruitful and increase your numbers until you become a community of peoples. [4]May he give you and your descendants the blessing given to Abraham, so that you may take possession of the land where you now reside as a foreigner, the land God gave to Abraham." [5]Then Isaac sent Jacob on his way, and he went to Paddan Aram, to Laban son of Bethuel the Aramean, the brother of Rebekah, who was the mother of Jacob and Esau.

[6]Now Esau learned that Isaac had blessed Jacob and had sent him to Paddan Aram to take a wife from there, and that when he blessed him he commanded him, "Do not marry a Canaanite woman," [7]and that Jacob had obeyed his father and mother and had gone to Paddan Aram. [8]Esau then realized how displeasing the Canaanite women were to his father Isaac; [9]so he went to Ishmael and married Mahalath, the sister of Nebaioth and daughter of Ishmael son of Abraham, in addition to the wives he already had.

Jacob's Dream at Bethel

[10]Jacob left Beersheba and set out for Harran. [11]When he reached a certain place, he stopped for the night because the sun had set. Taking one of the stones there, he put it under his head and lay down to sleep. [12]He had a dream in which he saw a stairway resting on the earth, with its top reaching to heaven, and the angels of God were ascending and descending on it. [13]There

IN HIS FATHER'S FOOTSTEPS

Harran
Aleppo
Ebla
Qatna
Mediterranean Sea
Damascus
Asheroth
Hazor
Shechem
Beersheba

above it[c] stood the LORD, and he said: "I am the LORD, the God of your father Abraham and the God of Isaac. I will give you and your descendants the land on which you are lying. [14]Your descendants will be like the dust of the earth, and you will spread out to the west and to the east, to the north and to the south. All peoples on earth will be blessed through you and your offspring.[d] [15]I am with you and will watch over you wherever you go, and I will bring you back to this land. I will not leave you until I have done what I have promised you."

---

[a] 2 That is, Northwest Mesopotamia; also in verses 5, 6 and 7   [b] 3 Hebrew *El-Shaddai*   [c] 13 Or *There beside him*   [d] 14 Or *will use your name and the name of your offspring in blessings* (see 48:20)

27:46—28:6 | Esau's marriage to the **Hittite women** distressed both his parents (26:34, 35). Isaac's charge to his son about intermarriage (**Canaanite woman**) repeated Abraham's charge to his servant in 24:3—a journey that found Rebekah for Isaac. Isaac then issued **the blessing given to Abraham**, which centered him fully in the Abrahamic Covenant.
28:5 | Jacob's journey to Harran in the region of **Paddan Aram** was remarkable in two respects. First, it was a journey of perhaps 850 miles that was done *on foot*. Second, Jacob retraced most of the journey of his grandparents Abraham and Sarah—but in the opposite direction.
28:6-9 | Esau attempted to return to his parents' good graces by marrying a daughter of **Ishmael son of Abraham**. However, he did not separate himself from his pagan wives.

28:10-22 | This was the first of two meetings between God and Jacob at **Bethel** (35:15). On this occasion, Jacob dreamed of a **stairway** spanning **earth . . . to heaven** with **angels of God** traversing it. The stairway is a splendid metaphor of the eternal God's desire to communicate with mere humans. Spectacularly, the Lord appeared **above** the stairway and declared that His promises to Abraham and Isaac extended to Jacob as well. Jacob's stone pillow became the crown or a memorial **pillar** where he vowed fidelity to the Lord.
28:13-15 | Bethel ("the house of God") was instantly a sacred place for Jacob. It was there God met with him, dealt with him, and took a special interest in his needs. The words **I am with you and will watch over you wherever you go** must have reassured Jacob when he was alone and on the run (Num. 6:24; Deut. 31:6-8; Ps. 121:5, 7, 8).

[16] When Jacob awoke from his sleep, he thought, "Surely the LORD is in this place, and I was not aware of it." [17] He was afraid and said, "How awesome is this place! This is none other than the house of God; this is the gate of heaven."

[18] Early the next morning Jacob took the stone he had placed under his head and set it up as a pillar and poured oil on top of it. [19] He called that place Bethel,[a] though the city used to be called Luz.

[20] Then Jacob made a vow, saying, "If God will be with me and will watch over me on this journey I am taking and will give me food to eat and clothes to wear [21] so that I return safely to my father's household, then the LORD[b] will be my God [22] and[c] this stone that I have set up as a pillar will be God's house, and of all that you give me I will give you a tenth."

Jacob Arrives in Paddan Aram

29 Then Jacob continued on his journey and came to the land of the eastern peoples. [2] There he saw a well in the open country, with three flocks of sheep lying near it because the flocks were watered from that well. The stone over the mouth of the well was large. [3] When all the flocks were gathered there, the shepherds would roll the stone away from the well's mouth and water the sheep. Then they would return the stone to its place over the mouth of the well.

[4] Jacob asked the shepherds, "My brothers, where are you from?"

"We're from Harran," they replied.

[5] He said to them, "Do you know Laban, Nahor's grandson?"

"Yes, we know him," they answered.

[6] Then Jacob asked them, "Is he well?"

"Yes, he is," they said, "and here comes his daughter Rachel with the sheep."

[7] "Look," he said, "the sun is still high; it is not time for the flocks to be gathered. Water the sheep and take them back to pasture."

[8] "We can't," they replied, "until all the flocks are gathered and the stone has been rolled away from the mouth of the well. Then we will water the sheep."

[9] While he was still talking with them, Rachel came with her father's sheep, for she was a shepherd. [10] When Jacob saw Rachel daughter of his uncle Laban, and Laban's sheep, he went over and rolled the stone away from the mouth of the well and watered his uncle's sheep. [11] Then Jacob kissed Rachel and began to weep aloud. [12] He had told Rachel that he was a relative of her father and a son of Rebekah. So she ran and told her father.

[13] As soon as Laban heard the news about Jacob, his sister's son, he hurried to meet him. He embraced him and kissed him and brought him to his home, and there Jacob told him all these things. [14] Then Laban said to him, "You are my own flesh and blood."

Jacob Marries Leah and Rachel

After Jacob had stayed with him for a whole month, [15] Laban said to him, "Just because you are a relative of mine, should you work for me for nothing? Tell me what your wages should be."

[16] Now Laban had two daughters; the name of the older was Leah, and the name of the younger was Rachel. [17] Leah had weak[d] eyes, but Rachel had a lovely figure and was beautiful. [18] Jacob was in love with Rachel and said, "I'll work for you seven years in return for your younger daughter Rachel."

[19] Laban said, "It's better that I give her to you than to some other man. Stay here with me." [20] So Jacob served seven years to get Rachel, but they seemed like only a few days to him because of his love for her.

[21] Then Jacob said to Laban, "Give me my wife. My time is completed, and I want to make love to her."

[22] So Laban brought together all the people of the place and gave a feast. [23] But when evening came, he took his daughter Leah and brought her to Jacob, and Jacob made love to her. [24] And Laban gave his servant Zilpah to his daughter as her attendant.

[25] When morning came, there was Leah! So Jacob said to Laban, "What is this you have done to me? I served you for Rachel, didn't I? Why have you deceived me?"

[26] Laban replied, "It is not our custom here to give the younger daughter in marriage

---

[a] 19 Bethel means house of God.   [b] 20,21 Or Since God . . . father's household, the LORD   [c] 21,22 Or household, and the LORD will be my God, [22] then   [d] 17 Or delicate

---

29:1–20 | Jacob met **Rachel** at a **well** and **was in love with** her, but he had arrived in Paddan Aram without possessions or lavish gifts— a great disadvantage in securing a wife in those times. So he **served seven years** for Rachel in place of a dowry.
29:21–23 | Weddings in biblical times featured a huge **feast**.

Afterward, the bridegroom was escorted to the tent of the bride where the marriage was consummated. Jacob probably drank too much at the feast and did not realize Laban gave him **Leah** rather than Rachel. Laban deceived Jacob, just as Jacob had deceived both Esau and Isaac.

before the older one. ²⁷Finish this daughter's bridal week; then we will give you the younger one also, in return for another seven years of work."

²⁸And Jacob did so. He finished the week with Leah, and then Laban gave him his daughter Rachel to be his wife. ²⁹Laban gave his servant Bilhah to his daughter Rachel as her attendant. ³⁰Jacob made love to Rachel also, and his love for Rachel was greater than his love for Leah. And he worked for Laban another seven years.

Jacob's Children

³¹When the LORD saw that Leah was not loved, he enabled her to conceive, but Rachel remained childless. ³²Leah became pregnant and gave birth to a son. She named him Reuben,ᵃ for she said, "It is because the LORD has seen my misery. Surely my husband will love me now."

³³She conceived again, and when she gave birth to a son she said, "Because the LORD heard that I am not loved, he gave me this one too." So she named him Simeon.ᵇ

³⁴Again she conceived, and when she gave birth to a son she said, "Now at last my husband will become attached to me, because I have borne him three sons." So he was named Levi.ᶜ

³⁵She conceived again, and when she gave birth to a son she said, "This time I will praise the LORD." So she named him Judah.ᵈ Then she stopped having children.

30 When Rachel saw that she was not bearing Jacob any children, she became jealous of her sister. So she said to Jacob, "Give me children, or I'll die!"

²Jacob became angry with her and said, "Am I in the place of God, who has kept you from having children?"

³Then she said, "Here is Bilhah, my servant. Sleep with her so that she can bear children for me and I too can build a family through her."

⁴So she gave him her servant Bilhah as a wife. Jacob slept with her, ⁵and she became pregnant and bore him a son. ⁶Then Rachel said, "God has vindicated me; he has listened to my plea and given me a son." Because of this she named him Dan.ᵉ

⁷Rachel's servant Bilhah conceived again and bore Jacob a second son. ⁸Then Rachel said, "I have had a great struggle with my sister, and I have won." So she named him Naphtali.ᶠ

⁹When Leah saw that she had stopped having children, she took her servant Zilpah and gave her to Jacob as a wife. ¹⁰Leah's servant Zilpah bore Jacob a son. ¹¹Then Leah said, "What good fortune!"ᵍ So she named him Gad.ʰ

¹²Leah's servant Zilpah bore Jacob a second son. ¹³Then Leah said, "How happy I am! The women will call me happy." So she named him Asher.ⁱ

¹⁴During wheat harvest, Reuben went out into the fields and found some mandrake plants, which he brought to his mother Leah. Rachel said to Leah, "Please give me some of your son's mandrakes."

¹⁵But she said to her, "Wasn't it enough that you took away my husband? Will you take my son's mandrakes too?"

"Very well," Rachel said, "he can sleep with you tonight in return for your son's mandrakes."

¹⁶So when Jacob came in from the fields that evening, Leah went out to meet him. "You must sleep with me," she said. "I have hired you with my son's mandrakes." So he slept with her that night.

¹⁷God listened to Leah, and she became pregnant and bore Jacob a fifth son. ¹⁸Then Leah said, "God has rewarded me for giving my servant to my husband." So she named him Issachar.ʲ

¹⁹Leah conceived again and bore Jacob a sixth son. ²⁰Then Leah said, "God has

---

ᵃ 32 Reuben sounds like the Hebrew for he has seen my misery; the name means see, a son.   ᵇ 33 Simeon probably means one who hears.   ᶜ 34 Levi sounds like and may be derived from the Hebrew for attached.   ᵈ 35 Judah sounds like and may be derived from the Hebrew for praise.   ᵉ 6 Dan here means he has vindicated. ᶠ 8 Naphtali means my struggle.   ᵍ 11 Or "A troop is coming!"   ʰ 11 Gad can mean good fortune or a troop.   ⁱ 13 Asher means happy.   ʲ 18 Issachar sounds like the Hebrew for reward.

29:28 | Polygamy was practiced in ancient times but often produced family struggles. That Jacob **finished the week with Leah** probably refers to the expectation that a newly married couple would "honeymoon" for a week. With his obligation to **Leah** complete, Jacob finally married **Rachel**.

29:31–30:24 | The births of Jacob's first 11 sons were met with joy, but there was also a backdrop of sadness because of the rivalry between **Leah** and **Rachel**. Each of Leah's four sons was given a name that represented her happiness as a mother and her continued pain at being the less-loved wife: **Reuben** ("see, a son"), **Simeon** ("one who hears"), **Levi** ("attached"), and **Judah** ("praise"). **30:3–13** | **Bilhah**, Rachel's servant, became a surrogate for Rachel as Hagar was for Sarah (16:1–4). Two sons were born in this manner for

Rachel: **Dan** ("he has vindicated") and **Naphtali** ("my struggle"). **Zilpah**, Leah's servant, also became a surrogate. She gave birth to two sons for her mistress: **Gad** ("good fortune" or "a troop") and **Asher** ("happy"). **30:14–17** | **Mandrake plants** were considered an aphrodisiac and a stimulant for conception in some cultures (Song 7:13). Rachel schemed to get the mandrakes—but Leah got pregnant. So often people scheme and plan, only to see the opposite of what they want. This happens when people seek to do their own will instead of God's. **30:18–21** | **Leah** gave birth to three more children: sons **Issachar** ("reward") and **Zebulun** ("honor"), and a daughter, **Dinah** ("judgment"). Leah recognized **God** as the one who **presented** her with children. From Eve (4:1) onward, Scripture always attributes the conception of a child to the grace of the Lord.

presented me with a precious gift. This time my husband will treat me with honor, because I have borne him six sons." So she named him Zebulun.[a]

21 Some time later she gave birth to a daughter and named her Dinah.

22 Then God remembered Rachel; he listened to her and enabled her to conceive. 23 She became pregnant and gave birth to a son and said, "God has taken away my disgrace." 24 She named him Joseph,[b] and said, "May the LORD add to me another son."

Jacob's Flocks Increase

25 After Rachel gave birth to Joseph, Jacob said to Laban, "Send me on my way so I can go back to my own homeland. 26 Give me my wives and children, for whom I have served you, and I will be on my way. You know how much work I've done for you."

27 But Laban said to him, "If I have found favor in your eyes, please stay. I have learned by divination that the LORD has blessed me because of you." 28 He added, "Name your wages, and I will pay them."

29 Jacob said to him, "You know how I have worked for you and how your livestock has fared under my care. 30 The little you had before I came has increased greatly, and the LORD has blessed you wherever I have been. But now, when may I do something for my own household?"

31 "What shall I give you?" he asked.

"Don't give me anything," Jacob replied. "But if you will do this one thing for me, I will go on tending your flocks and watching over them: 32 Let me go through all your flocks today and remove from them every speckled or spotted sheep, every dark-colored lamb and every spotted or speckled goat. They will be my wages. 33 And my honesty will testify for me in the future, whenever you check on the wages you have paid me. Any goat in my possession that is not speckled or spotted, or any lamb that is not dark-colored, will be considered stolen."

34 "Agreed," said Laban. "Let it be as you have said." 35 That same day he removed all the male goats that were streaked or spotted, and all the speckled or spotted female goats (all that had white on them) and all the dark-colored lambs, and he placed them in the care of his sons. 36 Then he put a three-day journey between himself and Jacob, while Jacob continued to tend the rest of Laban's flocks.

37 Jacob, however, took fresh-cut branches from poplar, almond and plane trees and made white stripes on them by peeling the bark and exposing the white inner wood of the branches. 38 Then he placed the peeled branches in all the watering troughs, so that they would be directly in front of the flocks when they came to drink. When the flocks were in heat and came to drink, 39 they mated in front of the branches. And they bore young that were streaked or speckled or spotted. 40 Jacob set apart the young of the flock by themselves, but made the rest face the streaked and dark-colored animals that belonged to Laban. Thus he made separate flocks for himself and did not put them with Laban's animals. 41 Whenever the stronger females were in heat, Jacob would place the branches in the troughs in front of the animals so they would mate near the branches, 42 but if the animals were weak, he would not place them there. So the weak animals went to Laban and the strong ones to Jacob. 43 In this way the man grew exceedingly prosperous and came to own large flocks, and female and male servants, and camels and donkeys.

Jacob Flees From Laban

31 Jacob heard that Laban's sons were saying, "Jacob has taken everything our father owned and has gained all this wealth from what belonged to our father." 2 And Jacob noticed that Laban's attitude toward him was not what it had been.

3 Then the LORD said to Jacob, "Go back to the land of your fathers and to your relatives, and I will be with you."

30:22–24 | Years of barrenness so deeply affected **Rachel** that she felt as if **God remembered** and **listened to her** when she finally conceived. When Scripture says God "remembers" someone, it means He will soon act on behalf of that person. An all-knowing God cannot forget anyone.

30:25, 26 | Jacob's agreement with Laban and his position as an adopted son meant he could not be sent on his **way** to live independently unless Laban allowed it. Moses' circumstances with Reuel (also called Jethro) in Midian were similar (Ex. 2:18, 20-21; 4:18).

30:27–33 | Jacob's clever plan for his **wages**—choosing the atypical animals—made the animals easy to distinguish and meant Laban could not cheat on the deal.

30:34–43 | Using colored **branches** might seem like magic, but they are symbols of Jacob's use of selective breeding—all within the context of trusting in God's provision (31:3, 10–13).

31:1–4 | The mention of **Laban's sons** demonstrates new family dynamics. When Jacob first arrived, Laban had two daughters but no sons (29:15–17). Once he had natural-born sons, Jacob's status was at risk, because that culture gave biological sons precedence over adopted ones, no matter their age. Yet the Lord assured Jacob with blessing and direction: **Go back . . . I will be with you**.

Rachel was not an idolater. In fact, Joseph's godly life was, in part, a product of the faith of his mother, Rachel.

That she stole these household idols ("gods") to take with her must be understood within the greater context of this passage (31:14–21). In ancient Near Eastern culture, which was polytheistic (Josh. 24:2), possession of the household idols was a sign of the right of inheritance. Rachel wanted these small objects (clay figurines about 8 to 10 inches high) in her possession, probably as a hedge, just in case anyone questioned Jacob's position as the family's next-in-line after Laban. She did not need these symbols of inheritance, however, because God had appointed Jacob an heir to His covenant, which would far surpass any earthly heritage.

⁴So Jacob sent word to Rachel and Leah to come out to the fields where his flocks were. ⁵He said to them, "I see that your father's attitude toward me is not what it was before, but the God of my father has been with me. ⁶You know that I've worked for your father with all my strength, ⁷yet your father has cheated me by changing my wages ten times. However, God has not allowed him to harm me. ⁸If he said, 'The speckled ones will be your wages,' then all the flocks gave birth to speckled young; and if he said, 'The streaked ones will be your wages,' then all the flocks bore streaked young. ⁹So God has taken away your father's livestock and has given them to me.

¹⁰"In breeding season I once had a dream in which I looked up and saw that the male goats mating with the flock were streaked, speckled or spotted. ¹¹The angel of God said to me in the dream, 'Jacob.' I answered, 'Here I am.' ¹²And he said, 'Look up and see that all the male goats mating with the flock are streaked, speckled or spotted, for I have seen all that Laban has been doing to you. ¹³I am the God of Bethel, where you anointed a pillar and where you made a vow to me. Now leave this land at once and go back to your native land.'"

¹⁴Then Rachel and Leah replied, "Do we still have any share in the inheritance of our father's estate? ¹⁵Does he not regard us as foreigners? Not only has he sold us, but he has used up what was paid for us. ¹⁶Surely all the wealth that God took away from our father belongs to us and our children. So do whatever God has told you."

¹⁷Then Jacob put his children and his wives on camels, ¹⁸and he drove all his livestock ahead of him, along with all the goods he had accumulated in Paddan Aram,ᵃ to go to his father Isaac in the land of Canaan.

¹⁹When Laban had gone to shear his sheep, Rachel stole her father's household gods. ²⁰Moreover, Jacob deceived Laban the Aramean by not telling him he was running away. ²¹So he fled with all he had, crossed the Euphrates River, and headed for the hill country of Gilead.

Laban Pursues Jacob

²²On the third day Laban was told that Jacob had fled. ²³Taking his relatives with him, he pursued Jacob for seven days and caught up with him in the hill country of Gilead. ²⁴Then God came to Laban the Aramean in a dream at night and said to him, "Be careful not to say anything to Jacob, either good or bad."

²⁵Jacob had pitched his tent in the hill country of Gilead when Laban overtook him, and Laban and his relatives camped there too. ²⁶Then Laban said to Jacob, "What have you done? You've deceived me, and you've carried off my daughters like captives in war. ²⁷Why did you run off secretly and deceive me? Why didn't you tell me, so I could send you away with joy and

---

ᵃ 18 That is, Northwest Mesopotamia

31:7 | Often the flaws someone criticizes in others are the flaws that person has as well. For 20 years (31:38, 41), Laban **cheated** Jacob **by changing** his **wages ten times**. God permitted Jacob to see in Laban what was once true of himself. If believers ask God to help them see themselves clearly, He can replace their critical spirits with gracious hearts and instill a fresh love and mercy so they desire to grow in Him (1 Cor. 13:5).

31:10–13 | **The angel of God** spoke to Jacob in a **dream** and confirmed God's role in the success of Jacob's selective breeding program. When the Lord described Himself as **the God of Bethel**, it reminded Jacob of God's covenant with him in that place years earlier (28:15).

31:11 | When God puts a **dream** in a Christian's heart, that person

must be sure to respond as Jacob did: **Here I am**. The Lord wants His children to exercise faith and participate in His plan, but in His time and on His terms.

31:14–21 | Jacob's wives were concerned about the status of the family **inheritance**: when they departed, would they lose what they otherwise would have received? **Rachel and Leah** eventually learned that their blessings came from the Lord through Jacob, not through their father.

31:22–35 | **Laban** decided to pursue Jacob and his family until God warned him **in a dream** to heed His words. Laban seemed overly concerned with retrieving the **gods** (idols)—further evidence that Laban was more concerned about his possessions than anything else.

singing to the music of timbrels and harps? [28] You didn't even let me kiss my grandchildren and my daughters goodbye. You have done a foolish thing. [29] I have the power to harm you; but last night the God of your father said to me, 'Be careful not to say anything to Jacob, either good or bad.' [30] Now you have gone off because you longed to return to your father's household. But why did you steal my gods?"

[31] Jacob answered Laban, "I was afraid, because I thought you would take your daughters away from me by force. [32] But if you find anyone who has your gods, that person shall not live. In the presence of our relatives, see for yourself whether there is anything of yours here with me; and if so, take it." Now Jacob did not know that Rachel had stolen the gods.

[33] So Laban went into Jacob's tent and into Leah's tent and into the tent of the two female servants, but he found nothing. After he came out of Leah's tent, he entered Rachel's tent. [34] Now Rachel had taken the household gods and put them inside her camel's saddle and was sitting on them. Laban searched through everything in the tent but found nothing.

[35] Rachel said to her father, "Don't be angry, my lord, that I cannot stand up in your presence; I'm having my period." So he searched but could not find the household gods.

[36] Jacob was angry and took Laban to task. "What is my crime?" he asked Laban. "How have I wronged you that you hunt me down? [37] Now that you have searched through all my goods, what have you found that belongs to your household? Put it here in front of your relatives and mine, and let them judge between the two of us.

[38] "I have been with you for twenty years now. Your sheep and goats have not miscarried, nor have I eaten rams from your flocks. [39] I did not bring you animals torn by wild beasts; I bore the loss myself. And you demanded payment from me for whatever was stolen by day or night. [40] This was my situation: The heat consumed me in the daytime and the cold at night, and sleep fled from my eyes. [41] It was like this for the twenty years I was in your household. I worked for you fourteen years for your two daughters and six years for your flocks, and you changed my wages ten times. [42] If the God of my father, the God of Abraham and the Fear of Isaac, had not been with me, you would surely have sent me away empty-handed. But God has seen my hardship and the toil of my hands, and last night he rebuked you."

[43] Laban answered Jacob, "The women are my daughters, the children are my children, and the flocks are my flocks. All you see is mine. Yet what can I do today about these daughters of mine, or about the children they have borne? [44] Come now, let's make a covenant, you and I, and let it serve as a witness between us."

[45] So Jacob took a stone and set it up as a pillar. [46] He said to his relatives, "Gather some stones." So they took stones and piled them in a heap, and they ate there by the heap. [47] Laban called it Jegar Sahadutha, and Jacob called it Galeed.[a]

[48] Laban said, "This heap is a witness between you and me today." That is why it was called Galeed. [49] It was also called Mizpah,[b] because he said, "May the LORD keep watch between you and me when we are away from each other. [50] If you mistreat my daughters or if you take any wives besides my daughters, even though no one is with us, remember that God is a witness between you and me."

[51] Laban also said to Jacob, "Here is this heap, and here is this pillar I have set up between you and me. [52] This heap is a witness, and this pillar is a witness, that I will not go past this heap to your side to harm you and that you will not go past this heap and pillar to my side to harm me. [53] May the God of Abraham and the God of Nahor, the God of their father, judge between us."

So Jacob took an oath in the name of the Fear of his father Isaac. [54] He offered a sacrifice there in the hill country and invited his relatives to a meal. After they had eaten, they spent the night there.

---

[a] 47 The Aramaic *Jegar Sahadutha* and the Hebrew *Galeed* both mean *witness heap.*
[b] 49 *Mizpah* means *watchtower.*

31:36–42 | As Jacob rebuked Laban for 20 years of unjust treatment, he also credited God for protecting and prospering his life. If not for God's provision, Jacob would have been **empty-handed**. **The Fear of Isaac** is another reference to the Lord.
31:43–55 | **Laban** refused to cede anything to Jacob easily. He first asserted that the **daughters . . . children . . . and the flocks** were his. Finally, he suggested they make a pact. This was a parity **covenant**, one made between parties who did not trust each other. Consequently, the statement **May the LORD keep**

watch between you and me when we are away from each other was not a sign of affection. Each man was saying that because they could not trust each other, the Lord would judge any breach of their covenant.
31:46–50 | Two names were assigned to the place of this human covenant. The name is given in Aramaic (the language of Laban) and in Hebrew (the language of Jacob), with both names meaning **this heap is a witness**. It is also known as **Mizpah**, meaning "watchtower."

[55]Early the next morning Laban kissed his grandchildren and his daughters and blessed them. Then he left and returned home.[a]

Jacob Prepares to Meet Esau

32[b] Jacob also went on his way, and the angels of God met him. [2]When Jacob saw them, he said, "This is the camp of God!" So he named that place Mahanaim.[c]

[3]Jacob sent messengers ahead of him to his brother Esau in the land of Seir, the country of Edom. [4]He instructed them: "This is what you are to say to my lord Esau: 'Your servant Jacob says, I have been staying with Laban and have remained there till now. [5]I have cattle and donkeys, sheep and goats, male and female servants. Now I am sending this message to my lord, that I may find favor in your eyes.' "

[6]When the messengers returned to Jacob, they said, "We went to your brother Esau, and now he is coming to meet you, and four hundred men are with him."

[7]In great fear and distress Jacob divided the people who were with him into two groups,[d] and the flocks and herds and camels as well. [8]He thought, "If Esau comes and attacks one group,[e] the group[e] that is left may escape."

[9]Then Jacob prayed, "O God of my father Abraham, God of my father Isaac, LORD, you who said to me, 'Go back to your country and your relatives, and I will make you prosper,' [10]I am unworthy of all the kindness and faithfulness you have shown your servant. I had only my staff when I crossed this Jordan, but now I have become two camps. [11]Save me, I pray, from the hand of my brother Esau, for I am afraid he will come and attack me, and also the mothers with their children. [12]But you have said, 'I will surely make you prosper and will make your descendants like the sand of the sea, which cannot be counted.' "

[13]He spent the night there, and from what he had with him he selected a gift for his brother Esau: [14]two hundred female goats and twenty male goats, two hundred ewes and twenty rams, [15]thirty female camels with their young, forty cows and ten bulls, and twenty female donkeys and ten male donkeys. [16]He put them in the care of his servants, each herd by itself, and said to his servants, "Go ahead of me, and keep some space between the herds."

[17]He instructed the one in the lead: "When my brother Esau meets you and asks, 'Who do you belong to, and where are you going, and who owns all these animals in front of you?' [18]then you are to say, 'They belong to your servant Jacob. They are a gift sent to my lord Esau, and he is coming behind us.' "

[19]He also instructed the second, the third and all the others who followed the herds: "You are to say the same thing to Esau when you meet him. [20]And be sure to say, 'Your servant Jacob is coming behind us.' " For he thought, "I will pacify him with these gifts I am sending on ahead; later, when I see him, perhaps he will receive me." [21]So Jacob's gifts went on ahead of him, but he himself spent the night in the camp.

Jacob Wrestles With God

[22]That night Jacob got up and took his two wives, his two female servants and his eleven sons and crossed the ford of the Jabbok. [23]After he had sent them across the stream, he sent over all his possessions. [24]So Jacob was left alone, and a man wrestled with him till daybreak. [25]When the man saw that he could not overpower him, he touched the socket of Jacob's hip so that his hip was wrenched as he wrestled with the man. [26]Then the man said, "Let me go, for it is daybreak."

But Jacob replied, "I will not let you go unless you bless me."

[27]The man asked him, "What is your name?"

---

[a] 55 In Hebrew texts this verse (31:55) is numbered 32:1.   [b] In Hebrew texts 32:1-32 is numbered 32:2-33.   [c] 2 Mahanaim means two camps.   [d] 7 Or camps   [e] 8 Or camp

---

32:1–21 | **The angels of God met** Jacob on his way back to Canaan—a powerful symbol of God's favor. Because he feared being overtaken by Esau, Jacob **divided the people who were with him** to protect them and then prayed powerfully in his moment of trouble. He also arranged magnificent gifts of choice animals in three **herds**, with instructions to his servants to tell Esau that Jacob was giving the gifts. Jacob hoped this gesture would persuade Esau to **receive** him.

32:24–29 | The **man** refers to a *theophany*, an OT appearance of Christ. Jacob did not initiate the contest. God wanted to separate the self-willed Jacob from all supports until he was **left alone** before Him (Hosea 12:3, 4)—something the Lord still does with some of His followers.

32:25 | The Hebrew word for **touched** may indicate any type of touch, from a gentle caress to an afflicting strike. Apparently Jacob experienced the latter. Jacob proved strong (**the man . . . could not overpower him**) as the pair **wrestled** through the night. One outcome was a lifelong weakness in Jacob's **hip** (32:31; 2 Cor. 12:7). **The man** was apparently the Lord Himself.

32:27–30 | **Your name will no longer be Jacob** is evidence of a remarkable transformation. Jacob's birth name described him grasping the heel of his brother, Esau (25:24–26). The nightlong wrestling match, however, made him **Israel**, a positive name meaning "he struggles with God" (Num. 24:5). Going forward, Scripture uses the names interchangeably. Jacob named the place **Peniel**, meaning "the face of God."

"Jacob," he answered.

[28] Then the man said, "Your name will no longer be Jacob, but Israel,[a] because you have struggled with God and with humans and have overcome."

[29] Jacob said, "Please tell me your name."

But he replied, "Why do you ask my name?" Then he blessed him there.

[30] So Jacob called the place Peniel,[b] saying, "It is because I saw God face to face, and yet my life was spared."

[31] The sun rose above him as he passed Peniel,[c] and he was limping because of his hip. [32] Therefore to this day the Israelites do not eat the tendon attached to the socket of the hip, because the socket of Jacob's hip was touched near the tendon.

Jacob Meets Esau

33 Jacob looked up and there was Esau, coming with his four hundred men; so he divided the children among Leah, Rachel and the two female servants. [2] He put the female servants and their children in front, Leah and her children next, and Rachel and Joseph in the rear. [3] He himself went on ahead and bowed down to the ground seven times as he approached his brother.

[4] But Esau ran to meet Jacob and embraced him; he threw his arms around his neck and kissed him. And they wept. [5] Then Esau looked up and saw the women and children. "Who are these with you?" he asked.

Jacob answered, "They are the children God has graciously given your servant."

[6] Then the female servants and their children approached and bowed down. [7] Next, Leah and her children came and bowed down. Last of all came Joseph and Rachel, and they too bowed down.

[8] Esau asked, "What's the meaning of all these flocks and herds I met?"

"To find favor in your eyes, my lord," he said.

[9] But Esau said, "I already have plenty, my brother. Keep what you have for yourself."

[10] "No, please!" said Jacob. "If I have found favor in your eyes, accept this gift from me. For to see your face is like seeing the face of God, now that you have received me favorably. [11] Please accept the present that was brought to you, for God has been gracious to me and I have all I need." And because Jacob insisted, Esau accepted it.

[12] Then Esau said, "Let us be on our way; I'll accompany you."

[13] But Jacob said to him, "My lord knows that the children are tender and that I must care for the ewes and cows that are nursing their young. If they are driven hard just one day, all the animals will die. [14] So let my lord go on ahead of his servant, while I move along slowly at the pace of the flocks and herds before me and the pace of the children, until I come to my lord in Seir."

[15] Esau said, "Then let me leave some of my men with you."

"But why do that?" Jacob asked. "Just let me find favor in the eyes of my lord."

[16] So that day Esau started on his way back to Seir. [17] Jacob, however, went to Sukkoth, where he built a place for himself and made shelters for his livestock. That is why the place is called Sukkoth.[d]

[18] After Jacob came from Paddan Aram,[e] he arrived safely at the city of Shechem in Canaan and camped within sight of the city. [19] For a hundred pieces of silver,[f] he bought from the sons of Hamor, the father of Shechem, the plot of ground where he pitched his tent. [20] There he set up an altar and called it El Elohe Israel.[g]

Dinah and the Shechemites

34 Now Dinah, the daughter Leah had borne to Jacob, went out to visit the women of the land. [2] When Shechem son of Hamor the Hivite, the ruler of that area, saw her, he took her and raped her. [3] His heart was drawn to Dinah daughter of Jacob; he loved the young woman and spoke tenderly to her. [4] And Shechem said to his father Hamor, "Get me this girl as my wife."

---

[a] 28 *Israel* probably means *he struggles with God.*   [b] 30 *Peniel* means *face of God.*   [c] 31 Hebrew *Penuel,* a variant of *Peniel*   [d] 17 *Sukkoth* means *shelters.*   [e] 18 That is, Northwest Mesopotamia   [f] 19 Hebrew *hundred kesitahs;* a *kesitah* was a unit of money of unknown weight and value.   [g] 20 *El Elohe Israel* can mean *El is the God of Israel* or *mighty is the God of Israel.*

32:31 | After the encounter, Jacob **was limping because of his hip,** each step reminding him that he no longer operated in his own strength but in God's. Jacob was changed for the better—from cunning to clinging, from resisting to resting, from the crafty one to the conquered one.

33:1–15 | Although **Jacob** and **Esau** were reconciled in this touching moment, their descendants rarely lived peacefully together (see the Book of Obadiah).

33:20 | The **altar** Jacob built, or perhaps rebuilt from the one Abraham had built on the same site (12:6–8), signaled his strong intentions to worship God. **El Elohe Israel** means "El [God] is the God of Israel."

34:1–31 | The rape of **Dinah** is sad in itself, but its aftermath is shameful. In Dinah's innocent desire to meet other women (34:1), she became a victim of **Shechem son of Hamor,** who went from rapist to suitor.

34:5–29 | Despite his son's wretched behavior, **Shechem's father** sought peaceful alliances between his people and Jacob's family, including intermarriage. To take vengeance against Shechem, Dinah's brothers—**Jacob's sons**—led by **Simeon and Levi**—convinced Hamor, Shechem, and the men of their city to be **circumcised,** only to murder them when they were weakened afterward.

⁵When Jacob heard that his daughter Dinah had been defiled, his sons were in the fields with his livestock; so he did nothing about it until they came home.

⁶Then Shechem's father Hamor went out to talk with Jacob. ⁷Meanwhile, Jacob's sons had come in from the fields as soon as they heard what had happened. They were shocked and furious, because Shechem had done an outrageous thing in*a* Israel by sleeping with Jacob's daughter—a thing that should not be done.

⁸But Hamor said to them, "My son Shechem has his heart set on your daughter. Please give her to him as his wife. ⁹Intermarry with us; give us your daughters and take our daughters for yourselves. ¹⁰You can settle among us; the land is open to you. Live in it, trade*b* in it, and acquire property in it."

¹¹Then Shechem said to Dinah's father and brothers, "Let me find favor in your eyes, and I will give you whatever you ask. ¹²Make the price for the bride and the gift I am to bring as great as you like, and I'll pay whatever you ask me. Only give me the young woman as my wife."

¹³Because their sister Dinah had been defiled, Jacob's sons replied deceitfully as they spoke to Shechem and his father Hamor. ¹⁴They said to them, "We can't do such a thing; we can't give our sister to a man who is not circumcised. That would be a disgrace to us. ¹⁵We will enter into an agreement with you on one condition only: that you become like us by circumcising all your males. ¹⁶Then we will give you our daughters and take your daughters for ourselves. We'll settle among you and become one people with you. ¹⁷But if you will not agree to be circumcised, we'll take our sister and go."

¹⁸Their proposal seemed good to Hamor and his son Shechem. ¹⁹The young man, who was the most honored of all his father's family, lost no time in doing what they said, because he was delighted with Jacob's daughter. ²⁰So Hamor and his son Shechem went to the gate of their city to speak to the men of their city. ²¹"These men are friendly toward us," they said. "Let them live in our land and trade in it; the land has plenty of room for them. We can marry their daughters and they can marry ours. ²²But the men will agree to live with us as one people only on the condition that our males be circumcised, as they themselves are. ²³Won't their livestock, their property and all their other animals become ours? So let us agree to their terms, and they will settle among us."

²⁴All the men who went out of the city gate agreed with Hamor and his son Shechem, and every male in the city was circumcised.

²⁵Three days later, while all of them were still in pain, two of Jacob's sons, Simeon and Levi, Dinah's brothers, took their swords and attacked the unsuspecting city, killing every male. ²⁶They put Hamor and his son Shechem to the sword and took Dinah from Shechem's house and left. ²⁷The sons of Jacob came upon the dead bodies and looted the city where*c* their sister had been defiled. ²⁸They seized their flocks and herds and donkeys and everything else of theirs in the city and out in the fields. ²⁹They carried off all their wealth and all their women and children, taking as plunder everything in the houses.

³⁰Then Jacob said to Simeon and Levi, "You have brought trouble on me by making me obnoxious to the Canaanites and Perizzites, the people living in this land. We are few in number, and if they join forces against me and attack me, I and my household will be destroyed."

³¹But they replied, "Should he have treated our sister like a prostitute?"

Jacob Returns to Bethel

35 Then God said to Jacob, "Go up to Bethel and settle there, and build an altar there to God, who appeared to you when you were fleeing from your brother Esau."

²So Jacob said to his household and to all who were with him, "Get rid of the foreign gods you have with you, and purify yourselves and change your clothes. ³Then come, let us go up to Bethel, where I will build an altar to God, who answered me in the day of my distress and who has been with me wherever I have gone." ⁴So they gave Jacob all the foreign gods they had and the rings in their ears, and Jacob buried them under the oak at Shechem. ⁵Then they set out, and the terror of God fell on the towns all around them so that no one pursued them.

---

a 7 Or against   *b* 10 Or move about freely; also in verse 21   *c* 27 Or because

---

34:30, 31 | Using the holy rite of circumcision as a tool of conquest and murder violated God's purposes, offended Jacob, and **brought trouble on** him with a fear of reprisals from the **people living in this land.** But the brothers remained unrepentant and justified their actions by saying, **Should he have treated our sister like a prostitute?**

35:1–4 | Before Jacob could return to his homeland, he had to **get rid of the foreign gods** that were in his household—the ones Rachel stole (31:22–35) and the ones that might be among the possessions of **all who were with him.**

fyi **Joseph's Background • 35:22**

A little background on the family dynamics in which Joseph grew up provides context for the rest of his story.

Among Joseph's brothers, Reuben was the firstborn—the presumed heir of his father—but he forfeited this right because he slept with his father's concubine. The birthright then passed in part to Joseph, the firstborn of Jacob's other wife, Rachel (1 Chron. 5:1–2). Although Judah, the fourth son, would father the line of promise that led to David and ultimately to Jesus, Joseph was given the "double share" (with two sons founding tribes on their own; 48:1–20).

It is well known that "Israel [Jacob] loved Joseph more than any of his other sons" (Gen. 37:3). This is because he was the first son of Jacob's favorite wife, Rachel, and because Joseph was the son of Jacob's "old age." In family systems such as these, aging fathers prized younger sons as marks of their masculinity. The special robe that Jacob made for Joseph became a symbol of favoritism that caused the brothers to hate Joseph beyond words. The competitive disdain between Rachel and Leah probably contributed to this as well.

⁶Jacob and all the people with him came to Luz (that is, Bethel) in the land of Canaan. ⁷There he built an altar, and he called the place El Bethel,ᵃ because it was there that God revealed himself to him when he was fleeing from his brother.

⁸Now Deborah, Rebekah's nurse, died and was buried under the oak outside Bethel. So it was named Allon Bakuth.ᵇ

⁹After Jacob returned from Paddan Aram,ᶜ God appeared to him again and blessed him. ¹⁰God said to him, "Your name is Jacob,ᵈ but you will no longer be called Jacob; your name will be Israel.ᵉ" So he named him Israel.

¹¹And God said to him, "I am God Almighty;ᶠ be fruitful and increase in number. A nation and a community of nations will come from you, and kings will be among your descendants. ¹²The land I gave to Abraham and Isaac I also give to you, and I will give this land to your descendants after you." ¹³Then God went up from him at the place where he had talked with him.

¹⁴Jacob set up a stone pillar at the place where God had talked with him, and he poured out a drink offering on it; he also poured oil on it. ¹⁵Jacob called the place where God had talked with him Bethel.ᵍ

The Deaths of Rachel and Isaac

¹⁶Then they moved on from Bethel. While they were still some distance from Ephrath, Rachel began to give birth and had great difficulty. ¹⁷And as she was having great difficulty in childbirth, the midwife said to her, "Don't despair, for you have another son." ¹⁸As she breathed her last—for she was dying—she named her son Ben-Oni.ʰ But his father named him Benjamin.ⁱ

¹⁹So Rachel died and was buried on the way to Ephrath (that is, Bethlehem). ²⁰Over her tomb Jacob set up a pillar, and to this day that pillar marks Rachel's tomb.

²¹Israel moved on again and pitched his tent beyond Migdal Eder. ²²While Israel was living in that region, Reuben went in and slept with his father's concubine Bilhah, and Israel heard of it.

Jacob had twelve sons:
²³The sons of Leah:
  Reuben the firstborn of Jacob,
  Simeon, Levi, Judah, Issachar and Zebulun.
²⁴The sons of Rachel:
  Joseph and Benjamin.
²⁵The sons of Rachel's servant Bilhah:
  Dan and Naphtali.
²⁶The sons of Leah's servant Zilpah:
  Gad and Asher.

These were the sons of Jacob, who were born to him in Paddan Aram.

²⁷Jacob came home to his father Isaac in Mamre, near Kiriath Arba (that is, Hebron), where Abraham and Isaac had stayed. ²⁸Isaac lived a hundred and eighty years. ²⁹Then he breathed his last and died and was gathered to his people, old and full of years. And his sons Esau and Jacob buried him.

ᵃ 7 El Bethel means God of Bethel.   ᵇ 8 Allon Bakuth means oak of weeping.
ᶜ 9 That is, Northwest Mesopotamia; also in verse 26   ᵈ 10 Jacob means he grasps
the heel, a Hebrew idiom for he deceives.   ᵉ 10 Israel probably means he struggles
with God.   ᶠ 11 Hebrew El-Shaddai   ᵍ 15 Bethel means house of God.
ʰ 18 Ben-Oni means son of my trouble.   ⁱ 18 Benjamin means son of my right hand.

35:6, 7 | Previously, the place where Jacob had met God (28:10–22) was named "house of God" (**Bethel**); its new name was more powerful: "God of the house of God (**El Bethel**)," suggesting Jacob's personal relationship with God Himself. It was no longer just a place but represented a Person! These historical accounts make it clear that even though God's men

and women may stumble, they get up with God's help and keep growing in grace.
35:16–20 | As **Rachel** was dying in childbirth, she named her baby Ben-Oni ("son of my trouble"). Her bereaved husband renamed him **Benjamin** ("son of my right hand"). Rachel was buried near **Bethlehem**, the only matriarch not buried in Hebron (see note on 23:20).

Esau's Descendants

36 This is the account of the family line of Esau (that is, Edom).

²Esau took his wives from the women of Canaan: Adah daughter of Elon the Hittite, and Oholibamah daughter of Anah and granddaughter of Zibeon the Hivite— ³also Basemath daughter of Ishmael and sister of Nebaioth.

⁴Adah bore Eliphaz to Esau, Basemath bore Reuel, ⁵and Oholibamah bore Jeush, Jalam and Korah. These were the sons of Esau, who were born to him in Canaan.

⁶Esau took his wives and sons and daughters and all the members of his household, as well as his livestock and all his other animals and all the goods he had acquired in Canaan, and moved to a land some distance from his brother Jacob. ⁷Their possessions were too great for them to remain together; the land where they were staying could not support them both because of their livestock. ⁸So Esau (that is, Edom) settled in the hill country of Seir.

⁹This is the account of the family line of Esau the father of the Edomites in the hill country of Seir.

¹⁰These are the names of Esau's sons:
  Eliphaz, the son of Esau's wife Adah, and Reuel, the son of Esau's wife Basemath.
¹¹The sons of Eliphaz:
  Teman, Omar, Zepho, Gatam and Kenaz.
¹²Esau's son Eliphaz also had a concubine named Timna, who bore him Amalek. These were grandsons of Esau's wife Adah.
¹³The sons of Reuel:
  Nahath, Zerah, Shammah and Mizzah. These were grandsons of Esau's wife Basemath.
¹⁴The sons of Esau's wife Oholibamah daughter of Anah and granddaughter of Zibeon, whom she bore to Esau:
  Jeush, Jalam and Korah.

¹⁵These were the chiefs among Esau's descendants:
  The sons of Eliphaz the firstborn of Esau:

Historically Speaking

Esau's Descendants • 36:1–43

The Edomites, Esau's descendants, are mentioned almost 150 times in the Bible—and the division between them and the descendants of Jacob never went away. During the Exodus, God told Israel to leave the Edomites alone (Deut. 2:4–8) because they were "relatives." But Edom refused to let the Israelites enter the land (Num. 20:14–21). Later, they became bitter enemies of King David (2 Sam. 8:13). The Book of Obadiah is a pronouncement of God's judgment on Edom for its oppression and cruelty toward the Israelites. How sad that the people of Esau became an enemy to the heritage of Jacob: the people of Israel.

  Chiefs Teman, Omar, Zepho, Kenaz, ¹⁶Korah,ᵃ Gatam and Amalek. These were the chiefs descended from Eliphaz in Edom; they were grandsons of Adah.
¹⁷The sons of Esau's son Reuel:
  Chiefs Nahath, Zerah, Shammah and Mizzah. These were the chiefs descended from Reuel in Edom; they were grandsons of Esau's wife Basemath.
¹⁸The sons of Esau's wife Oholibamah:
  Chiefs Jeush, Jalam and Korah. These were the chiefs descended from Esau's wife Oholibamah daughter of Anah.
¹⁹These were the sons of Esau (that is, Edom), and these were their chiefs.

²⁰These were the sons of Seir the Horite, who were living in the region:
  Lotan, Shobal, Zibeon, Anah, ²¹Dishon, Ezer and Dishan. These sons of Seir in Edom were Horite chiefs.
²²The sons of Lotan:
  Hori and Homam.ᵇ Timna was Lotan's sister.
²³The sons of Shobal:
  Alvan, Manahath, Ebal, Shepho and Onam.
²⁴The sons of Zibeon:
  Aiah and Anah. This is the Anah who discovered the hot springsᶜ in the desert while he was grazing the donkeys of his father Zibeon.
²⁵The children of Anah:

ᵃ 16 Masoretic Text; Samaritan Pentateuch (also verse 11 and 1 Chron. 1:36) does not have *Korah.*   ᵇ 22 Hebrew *Hemam,* a variant of *Homam* (see 1 Chron. 1:39)   ᶜ 24 Vulgate; Syriac *discovered water;* the meaning of the Hebrew for this word is uncertain.

36:1–43 | This chapter ends Esau's story. Including the **family line of Esau** (otherwise known as **Edom**) it demonstrates the Lord's continuing love for Isaac's other son, even though Jacob is the son of the covenant.

Dishon and Oholibamah daughter of Anah.

26 The sons of Dishon[a]:

Hemdan, Eshban, Ithran and Keran.

27 The sons of Ezer:

Bilhan, Zaavan and Akan.

28 The sons of Dishan:

Uz and Aran.

29 These were the Horite chiefs:

Lotan, Shobal, Zibeon, Anah, 30 Dishon, Ezer and Dishan. These were the Horite chiefs, according to their divisions, in the land of Seir.

The Rulers of Edom

31 These were the kings who reigned in Edom before any Israelite king reigned:

32 Bela son of Beor became king of Edom. His city was named Dinhabah.

33 When Bela died, Jobab son of Zerah from Bozrah succeeded him as king.

34 When Jobab died, Husham from the land of the Temanites succeeded him as king.

35 When Husham died, Hadad son of Bedad, who defeated Midian in the country of Moab, succeeded him as king. His city was named Avith.

36 When Hadad died, Samlah from Masrekah succeeded him as king.

37 When Samlah died, Shaul from Rehoboth on the river succeeded him as king.

38 When Shaul died, Baal-Hanan son of Akbor succeeded him as king.

39 When Baal-Hanan son of Akbor died, Hadad[b] succeeded him as king. His city was named Pau, and his wife's name was Mehetabel daughter of Matred, the daughter of Me-Zahab.

40 These were the chiefs descended from Esau, by name, according to their clans and regions:

Timna, Alvah, Jetheth, 41 Oholibamah, Elah, Pinon, 42 Kenaz, Teman, Mibzar, 43 Magdiel and Iram. These were the chiefs of Edom, according to their settlements in the land they occupied.

This is the family line of Esau, the father of the Edomites.

Joseph's Dreams

37 Jacob lived in the land where his father had stayed, the land of Canaan.

2 This is the account of Jacob's family line.

Joseph, a young man of seventeen, was tending the flocks with his brothers, the sons of Bilhah and the sons of Zilpah, his father's wives, and he brought their father a bad report about them.

3 Now Israel loved Joseph more than any of his other sons, because he had been born to him in his old age; and he made an ornate[c] robe for him. 4 When his brothers saw that their father loved him more than any of them, they hated him and could not speak a kind word to him.

5 Joseph had a dream, and when he told it to his brothers, they hated him all the more. 6 He said to them, "Listen to this dream I had: 7 We were binding sheaves of grain out in the field when suddenly my sheaf rose and stood upright, while your sheaves gathered around mine and bowed down to it."

8 His brothers said to him, "Do you intend to reign over us? Will you actually rule us?" And they hated him all the more because of his dream and what he had said.

9 Then he had another dream, and he told it to his brothers. "Listen," he said, "I had another dream, and this time the sun and moon and eleven stars were bowing down to me."

10 When he told his father as well as his brothers, his father rebuked him and said, "What is this dream you had? Will your mother and I and your brothers actually come and bow down to the ground before you?" 11 His brothers were jealous of him, but his father kept the matter in mind.

Joseph Sold by His Brothers

12 Now his brothers had gone to graze their father's flocks near Shechem, 13 and Israel said to Joseph, "As you know, your brothers are grazing the flocks near Shechem. Come, I am going to send you to them."

"Very well," he replied.

---

[a] 26 Hebrew Dishan, a variant of Dishon   [b] 39 Many manuscripts of the Masoretic Text, Samaritan Pentateuch and Syriac (see also 1 Chron. 1:50); most manuscripts of the Masoretic Text Hadar   [c] 3 The meaning of the Hebrew for this word is uncertain; also in verses 23 and 32.

37:3 | The Hebrew phrase for **an ornate robe** describes a robe with "long sleeves and skirts" rather than varied hues. Although Joseph's coat was definitely an ornamental, distinctive garment, the coat was significant for its symbolism, not its beauty: Joseph would be the heir of his father. Joseph's 11 brothers had coats too. Their tunics were short-sleeved and short-waisted, making it easier for them to do their work.

37:12–17 | Because it was the dry season, Jacob's 10 older sons traveled from Hebron to find grasslands and water for their flocks. Joseph's obedience to his father was courageous (considering the hostility of his siblings) and complete. When he did not find his brothers near **Shechem** as expected, he continued to **Dothan**, about 12 miles away by the roads of the day.

¹⁴So he said to him, "Go and see if all is well with your brothers and with the flocks, and bring word back to me." Then he sent him off from the Valley of Hebron.

When Joseph arrived at Shechem, ¹⁵a man found him wandering around in the fields and asked him, "What are you looking for?"

¹⁶He replied, "I'm looking for my brothers. Can you tell me where they are grazing their flocks?"

¹⁷"They have moved on from here," the man answered. "I heard them say, 'Let's go to Dothan.'"

So Joseph went after his brothers and found them near Dothan. ¹⁸But they saw him in the distance, and before he reached them, they plotted to kill him.

¹⁹"Here comes that dreamer!" they said to each other. ²⁰"Come now, let's kill him and throw him into one of these cisterns and say that a ferocious animal devoured him. Then we'll see what comes of his dreams."

²¹When Reuben heard this, he tried to rescue him from their hands. "Let's not take his life," he said. ²²"Don't shed any blood. Throw him into this cistern here in the wilderness, but don't lay a hand on him." Reuben said this to rescue him from them and take him back to his father.

²³So when Joseph came to his brothers, they stripped him of his robe—the ornate robe he was wearing— ²⁴and they took him and threw him into the cistern. The cistern was empty; there was no water in it.

²⁵As they sat down to eat their meal, they looked up and saw a caravan of Ishmaelites coming from Gilead. Their camels were loaded with spices, balm and myrrh, and they were on their way to take them down to Egypt.

²⁶Judah said to his brothers, "What will we gain if we kill our brother and cover up his blood? ²⁷Come, let's sell him to the Ishmaelites and not lay our hands on him; after all, he is our brother, our own flesh and blood." His brothers agreed.

²⁸So when the Midianite merchants came by, his brothers pulled Joseph up out of the cistern and sold him for twenty shekels[a] of silver to the Ishmaelites, who took him to Egypt.

²⁹When Reuben returned to the cistern and saw that Joseph was not there, he tore his clothes. ³⁰He went back to his brothers and said, "The boy isn't there! Where can I turn now?"

³¹Then they got Joseph's robe, slaughtered a goat and dipped the robe in the blood. ³²They took the ornate robe back to their father and said, "We found this. Examine it to see whether it is your son's robe."

³³He recognized it and said, "It is my son's robe! Some ferocious animal has devoured him. Joseph has surely been torn to pieces."

³⁴Then Jacob tore his clothes, put on sackcloth and mourned for his son many days. ³⁵All his sons and daughters came to comfort him, but he refused to be comforted. "No," he said, "I will continue to mourn until I join my son in the grave." So his father wept for him.

³⁶Meanwhile, the Midianites[b] sold Joseph in Egypt to Potiphar, one of Pharaoh's officials, the captain of the guard.

Judah and Tamar

38 At that time, Judah left his brothers and went down to stay with a man of Adullam named Hirah. ²There Judah met the daughter of a Canaanite man named Shua. He married her and made love to her; ³she became pregnant and gave birth to a son, who was named Er. ⁴She conceived again and gave birth to a son and named him Onan. ⁵She gave birth to still another son and named him Shelah. It was at Kezib that she gave birth to him.

⁶Judah got a wife for Er, his firstborn, and her name was Tamar. ⁷But Er, Judah's firstborn, was wicked in the LORD's sight; so the LORD put him to death.

⁸Then Judah said to Onan, "Sleep with your brother's wife and fulfill your duty to her as a brother-in-law to raise up offspring

---

[a] 28 That is, about 8 ounces or about 230 grams   [b] 36 Samaritan Pentateuch, Septuagint, Vulgate and Syriac (see also verse 28); Masoretic Text *Medanites*

37:18–22 | The brothers plotted to **kill** Joseph and throw him into a **cistern** (pit). **Reuben**, the oldest brother, convinced them to throw Joseph into a cistern alive instead, with the secret hope that he might rescue Joseph later. This move saved Joseph's life. Cisterns were dug as reservoirs for water, sloping downward and outward with a narrow opening at the top. A person thrown into one would be unable to escape because there were no handholds or footholds.
37:25–28 | **Judah**, seeing a way to **gain** from their crime, recommended they **sell** Joseph as a slave. The sale was tantamount to death (42:21), but the brothers believed it would relieve them of direct responsibility. The price of **twenty shekels of silver** marks the integrity of this account; later in Israel's history, a slave would

be sold for 30 shekels of silver. Ironically, the traveling merchants were **Ishmaelites**, descendants of Ishmael, the first son of Abraham (25:12–18).
37:29–35 | **Reuben** was distressed when he **returned** and found the cistern empty. As the firstborn, he bore a great responsibility for his younger brothers. **Where can I turn now?** describes his feelings of turmoil for both Joseph and himself. **Jacob**—a deceiver in earlier times—was deceived by his sons into thinking that **Joseph** was dead.
38:1–30 | The story of **Judah** serves as a foil for the story of Joseph. When he **left his brothers** and married a **Canaanite** woman, he put the Lord's plans for salvation in jeopardy. This happened while Joseph was in slavery.

Historically Speaking | **Widows and Heirs •** 38:7–14

Because an heir was so important to families in these times, cultural demands required the next of kin to marry the bereaved widow in hopes of producing a son so that her deceased husband would have an heir. This tradition, called levirate marriage, later became part of the Lord's gracious provisions for Israel (Deut. 25:5–10) and served to preserve the line of David in the Book of Ruth. Onan, Judah's second son, strategically avoided his duty for his brother, so the Lord killed him also (46:12; Num. 26:19). And Judah's third son, Shelah, never was given Tamar as a wife, perhaps because Judah somehow blamed her for the deaths of his other two sons.

for your brother." ⁹But Onan knew that the child would not be his; so whenever he slept with his brother's wife, he spilled his semen on the ground to keep from providing offspring for his brother. ¹⁰What he did was wicked in the LORD's sight; so the LORD put him to death also.

¹¹Judah then said to his daughter-in-law Tamar, "Live as a widow in your father's household until my son Shelah grows up." For he thought, "He may die too, just like his brothers." So Tamar went to live in her father's household.

¹²After a long time Judah's wife, the daughter of Shua, died. When Judah had recovered from his grief, he went up to Timnah, to the men who were shearing his sheep, and his friend Hirah the Adullamite went with him. ¹³When Tamar was told, "Your father-in-law is on his way to Timnah to shear his sheep," ¹⁴she took off her widow's clothes, covered herself with a veil to disguise herself, and then sat down at the entrance to Enaim, which is on the road to Timnah. For she saw that, though Shelah had now grown up, she had not been given to him as his wife.

¹⁵When Judah saw her, he thought she was a prostitute, for she had covered her face. ¹⁶Not realizing that she was his daughter-in-law, he went over to her by the

roadside and said, "Come now, let me sleep with you."

"And what will you give me to sleep with you?" she asked.

¹⁷"I'll send you a young goat from my flock," he said.

"Will you give me something as a pledge until you send it?" she asked.

¹⁸He said, "What pledge should I give you?"

"Your seal and its cord, and the staff in your hand," she answered. So he gave them to her and slept with her, and she became pregnant by him. ¹⁹After she left, she took off her veil and put on her widow's clothes again.

²⁰Meanwhile Judah sent the young goat by his friend the Adullamite in order to get his pledge back from the woman, but he did not find her. ²¹He asked the men who lived there, "Where is the shrine prostitute who was beside the road at Enaim?"

"There hasn't been any shrine prostitute here," they said.

²²So he went back to Judah and said, "I didn't find her. Besides, the men who lived there said, 'There hasn't been any shrine prostitute here.'"

²³Then Judah said, "Let her keep what she has, or we will become a laughingstock. After all, I did send her this young goat, but you didn't find her."

²⁴About three months later Judah was told, "Your daughter-in-law Tamar is guilty of prostitution, and as a result she is now pregnant."

Judah said, "Bring her out and have her burned to death!"

²⁵As she was being brought out, she sent a message to her father-in-law. "I am pregnant by the man who owns these," she said. And she added, "See if you recognize whose seal and cord and staff these are."

²⁶Judah recognized them and said, "She is more righteous than I, since I wouldn't give her to my son Shelah." And he did not sleep with her again.

²⁷When the time came for her to give birth, there were twin boys in her womb.

38:7–24 | The text does not say what sin Judah's oldest son, Er, committed; just that he was so wicked **the LORD put him to death** (1 Chron. 2:3). In Tamar's desperation to produce an heir, she contrived a plan to deceive her **father-in-law** into having sexual relations with her. **Judah** found her—a woman he believed to be a prostitute—**by the roadside**, unaware that his daughter-in-law was impersonating a cultic prostitute. The Hebrew word translated **prostitute** in 38:21 describes a person whose identity is hidden. Tamar was able to fool Judah because she had **covered her face** and was sitting where prostitutes often sat.

38:18 | The **seal** was a cylinder with distinctive markings carried around the neck on a **cord** that was specifically associated with its owner. The seal was pressed in moist clay as a signature. It is implied that the **staff** had distinctive identifying marks as well.
38:26 | Judah's words are astonishing: **She is more righteous than I.** Tamar was motivated by a desperate desire to complete her obligations according to the traditions of her time (which later became part of the Law; Deut. 25:5–10). Judah withheld his son **Shelah** from Tamar, forcing her to take drastic action.

28 As she was giving birth, one of them put out his hand; so the midwife took a scarlet thread and tied it on his wrist and said, "This one came out first." 29 But when he drew back his hand, his brother came out, and she said, "So this is how you have broken out!" And he was named Perez.*a* 30 Then his brother, who had the scarlet thread on his wrist, came out. And he was named Zerah.*b*

Joseph and Potiphar's Wife

39 Now Joseph had been taken down to Egypt. Potiphar, an Egyptian who was one of Pharaoh's officials, the captain of the guard, bought him from the Ishmaelites who had taken him there. 2 The LORD was with Joseph so that he prospered, and he lived in the house of his Egyptian master. 3 When his master saw that the LORD was with him and that the LORD gave him success in everything he did, 4 Joseph found favor in his eyes and became his attendant. Potiphar put him in charge of his household, and he entrusted to his care everything he owned. 5 From the time he put him in charge of his household and of all that he owned, the LORD blessed the household of the Egyptian because of Joseph. The blessing of the LORD was on everything Potiphar had, both in the house and in the field. 6 So Potiphar left everything he had in Joseph's care; with Joseph in charge, he did not concern himself with anything except the food he ate.

Now Joseph was well-built and handsome, 7 and after a while his master's wife took notice of Joseph and said, "Come to bed with me!"

8 But he refused. "With me in charge," he told her, "my master does not concern himself with anything in the house; everything he owns he has entrusted to my care. 9 No one is greater in this house than I am.

In the first verses of Genesis 39, we read a rich description of Joseph's successes: "the LORD gave him success in everything he did." These accomplishments are the result of four things:

1. Joseph's industry and stewardship of his abilities
2. His devotion to his master and to God
3. God's active presence
4. God's sovereign help in Joseph's life and work

Great tests often come to those who are experiencing great prosperity and success. Most people seem to handle one set of circumstances better than another, although in some ways, it is probably harder to deal with prosperity. Joseph was rare: he remained steadfast and strong in both adversity and prosperity.

My master has withheld nothing from me except you, because you are his wife. How then could I do such a wicked thing and sin against God?" 10 And though she spoke to Joseph day after day, he refused to go to bed with her or even be with her.

11 One day he went into the house to attend to his duties, and none of the household servants was inside. 12 She caught him by his cloak and said, "Come to bed with me!" But he left his cloak in her hand and ran out of the house.

13 When she saw that he had left his cloak in her hand and had run out of the house, 14 she called her household servants. "Look," she said to them, "this Hebrew has been brought to us to make sport of us! He came in here to sleep with me, but I screamed. 15 When he heard me scream for help, he left his cloak beside me and ran out of the house."

---

a 29 *Perez means breaking out.*   *b* 30 *Zerah can mean scarlet or brightness.*

38:29 | Jesse—the father of David—was a descendant of **Perez**, one of the twin sons of Judah and Tamar (Ruth 4:18; Matt. 1:3). Only a God of grace could make a Canaanite woman like Tamar and a prodigal man like Judah members of His royal line and ancestors of the Messiah.
39:1 | This verse frames Judah's story in the previous chapter and picks up the account of **Joseph** from 37:36. While Judah, a free man, betrayed his family and disobeyed the Lord, his younger brother Joseph, a slave in a foreign nation (**Egypt**), showed great faith and righteousness.
39:2 | Although Joseph was physically alone, **the LORD was with Joseph**—a statement repeated twice in this chapter (39:21, 23). Because of this support, Joseph not only endured but also prospered. The same is true for all of God's servants, no matter their circumstances. Fellowship with the Lord means freedom from fear and loneliness (Isa. 43:1, 2; Matt. 28:20).

39:3, 4 | When Joseph's **master saw that the LORD was with him**, it revealed that Joseph both glorified God and pleased Potiphar—fulfilling the divine promise that Abraham's descendants would bless others (12:2; 39:5). Consequently, Potiphar put Joseph **in charge of his household**, an enormous honor.
39:6–10 | Joseph apparently had his mother's attractive features, being **well-built and handsome** (29:17). Unfortunately, his handsomeness was a scourge in this situation. Even though Potiphar's **wife** pressured Joseph **day after day**, he did not give in because he knew how much he owed his master and that all sin is ultimately **against God** (Ps. 51:4).
39:10–20 | Joseph's rejection angered Potiphar's wife so much that she conspired to destroy him. Death, rather than imprisonment, was more in keeping with the (false) charge of attempted rape against Joseph. Because Potiphar was captain of the guard, he could have demanded Joseph's execution. Instead, he **put him in prison**.

[16] She kept his cloak beside her until his master came home. [17] Then she told him this story: "That Hebrew slave you brought us came to me to make sport of me. [18] But as soon as I screamed for help, he left his cloak beside me and ran out of the house."

[19] When his master heard the story his wife told him, saying, "This is how your slave treated me," he burned with anger. [20] Joseph's master took him and put him in prison, the place where the king's prisoners were confined.

But while Joseph was there in the prison, [21] the LORD was with him; he showed him kindness and granted him favor in the eyes of the prison warden. [22] So the warden put Joseph in charge of all those held in the prison, and he was made responsible for all that was done there. [23] The warden paid no attention to anything under Joseph's care, because the LORD was with Joseph and gave him success in whatever he did.

The Cupbearer and the Baker

40 Some time later, the cupbearer and the baker of the king of Egypt offended their master, the king of Egypt. [2] Pharaoh was angry with his two officials, the chief cupbearer and the chief baker, [3] and put them in custody in the house of the captain of the guard, in the same prison where Joseph was confined. [4] The captain of the guard assigned them to Joseph, and he attended them.

After they had been in custody for some time, [5] each of the two men — the cupbearer and the baker of the king of Egypt, who were being held in prison — had a dream the same night, and each dream had a meaning of its own.

[6] When Joseph came to them the next morning, he saw that they were dejected. [7] So he asked Pharaoh's officials who were in custody with him in his master's house, "Why do you look so sad today?"

[8] "We both had dreams," they answered, "but there is no one to interpret them."

Then Joseph said to them, "Do not interpretations belong to God? Tell me your dreams."

[9] So the chief cupbearer told Joseph his dream. He said to him, "In my dream I saw a vine in front of me, [10] and on the vine were three branches. As soon as it budded, it blossomed, and its clusters ripened into grapes. [11] Pharaoh's cup was in my hand, and I took the grapes, squeezed them into Pharaoh's cup and put the cup in his hand."

[12] "This is what it means," Joseph said to him. "The three branches are three days. [13] Within three days Pharaoh will lift up your head and restore you to your position, and you will put Pharaoh's cup in his hand, just as you used to do when you were his cupbearer. [14] But when all goes well with you, remember me and show me kindness; mention me to Pharaoh and get me out of this prison. [15] I was forcibly carried off from the land of the Hebrews, and even here I have done nothing to deserve being put in a dungeon."

[16] When the chief baker saw that Joseph had given a favorable interpretation, he said to Joseph, "I too had a dream: On my head were three baskets of bread.[a] [17] In the top basket were all kinds of baked goods for Pharaoh, but the birds were eating them out of the basket on my head."

[18] "This is what it means," Joseph said. "The three baskets are three days. [19] Within three days Pharaoh will lift off your head and impale your body on a pole. And the birds will eat away your flesh."

[20] Now the third day was Pharaoh's birthday, and he gave a feast for all his officials. He lifted up the heads of the chief cupbearer and the chief baker in the presence of his officials: [21] He restored the chief cupbearer to his position, so that he once again put the cup into Pharaoh's hand— [22] but he impaled the chief baker, just as Joseph had said to them in his interpretation.

[23] The chief cupbearer, however, did not remember Joseph; he forgot him.

---

[a] 16 Or *three wicker baskets*

39:21-23 | God's support of Joseph did not cease even in prison (Ps. 139:7–12); even there he was given a trusted position of oversight. Yet Joseph understood he was not the architect of his success. He worked hard and obeyed the Lord, but God did all the rest (Ex. 11:3; Ps. 1:3; Rom. 8:38, 39): **the LORD was with** Joseph. **He showed him kindness and granted him favor**, and **gave him success in whatever he did**. **40:2, 3** | The offenses of the **cupbearer** and **baker** are not revealed, but the chief cupbearer was expected to taste all the king's food to ensure it had not been poisoned. The baker was expected to make the food. The Hebrew phrase translated **prison** reveals Joseph's location: it literally means "the round house" (39:20), a place of confinement where royal prisoners were kept apart from common criminals.

40:6, 7 | Joseph was in prison for a crime he did not commit. Yet rather than pitying himself, he noticed that the butler and baker were **dejected** and asked **why**. Helping others is often a good antidote when one's own circumstances are difficult.
40:8-22 | In the ancient Near East, dreams were considered a source of divine revelation, so people asked magicians or wise men to interpret their dreams. Joseph recognized that dreams and their interpretations **belong to God**. Notice how the slightly different wording of the two interpretations revealed each man's future: Pharaoh would **lift up** the head of one and **lift off** the head of the other. Only days later, Pharaoh **impaled the chief baker**.
40:23 | The cupbearer **forgot** Joseph, but God did not.

fyi Behind the Scenes • 41:1–16

God works behind the scenes to make His work go forward. Consider what had to happen for Joseph to be brought before Pharaoh to interpret his dreams:

1. Potiphar's wife had to wrongly accuse Joseph.
2. Joseph had to be imprisoned.
3. The keeper of the prison had to favor Joseph.
4. Joseph had to be given free range in the prison.
5. Pharaoh's cupbearer and baker had to be thrown into the same prison as Joseph.
6. Joseph had to meet them and be present the day both were disconcerted about their dreams.
7. The cupbearer had to remember his dream for nearly two years.
8. The cupbearer had to be present the day Pharaoh's dreams went uninterpreted.
9. Pharaoh had to be willing to bring a prisoner into his court to try to interpret his dreams.
10. Joseph had to receive the interpretation of Pharaoh's dreams from God.

God orchestrated all of this, just so His perfect will would be done.

Pharaoh's Dreams

41 When two full years had passed, Pharaoh had a dream: He was standing by the Nile, [2] when out of the river there came up seven cows, sleek and fat, and they grazed among the reeds. [3] After them, seven other cows, ugly and gaunt, came up out of the Nile and stood beside those on the riverbank. [4] And the cows that were ugly and gaunt ate up the seven sleek, fat cows. Then Pharaoh woke up.

[5] He fell asleep again and had a second dream: Seven heads of grain, healthy and good, were growing on a single stalk. [6] After them, seven other heads of grain sprouted — thin and scorched by the east wind. [7] The thin heads of grain swallowed up the seven healthy, full heads. Then Pharaoh woke up; it had been a dream.

[8] In the morning his mind was troubled, so he sent for all the magicians and wise men of Egypt. Pharaoh told them his dreams, but no one could interpret them for him.

[9] Then the chief cupbearer said to Pharaoh, "Today I am reminded of my shortcomings. [10] Pharaoh was once angry with his servants, and he imprisoned me and the chief baker in the house of the captain of the guard. [11] Each of us had a dream the same night, and each dream had a meaning of its own. [12] Now a young Hebrew was there with us, a servant of the captain of the guard. We told him our dreams, and he interpreted them for us, giving each man the interpretation of his dream. [13] And things turned out exactly as he interpreted them to us: I was restored to my position, and the other man was impaled."

[14] So Pharaoh sent for Joseph, and he was quickly brought from the dungeon. When he had shaved and changed his clothes, he came before Pharaoh.

[15] Pharaoh said to Joseph, "I had a dream, and no one can interpret it. But I have heard it said of you that when you hear a dream you can interpret it."

[16] "I cannot do it," Joseph replied to Pharaoh, "but God will give Pharaoh the answer he desires."

[17] Then Pharaoh said to Joseph, "In my dream I was standing on the bank of the Nile, [18] when out of the river there came up seven cows, fat and sleek, and they grazed among the reeds. [19] After them, seven other cows came up — scrawny and very ugly and lean. I had never seen such ugly cows in all the land of Egypt. [20] The lean, ugly cows ate up the seven fat cows that came up first. [21] But even after they ate them, no one could tell that they had done so; they looked just as ugly as before. Then I woke up.

[22] "In my dream I saw seven heads of grain, full and good, growing on a single stalk. [23] After them, seven other heads sprouted — withered and thin and scorched by the east wind. [24] The thin heads of grain

---

41:1–8 | Important messages in Scripture are often given twice. The repetition in Pharaoh's **dream**, properly understood, would have great bearing on Egypt's future as well as Joseph's. That it was repeated to Pharaoh twice suggests it dare not be missed (41:32).
41:9–16 | God's timing is always perfect.
41:15, 16 | Most people would have given themselves the credit

for the dream's successful interpretation simply to gain the favor of Pharaoh. But Joseph promptly replied, **I cannot do it, . . . but God will give Pharaoh the answer**, and then repeatedly affirmed this (41:25, 28, 32). Whether interpreting publicly or privately (40:8), Joseph's response and message never changed, signs of integrity and faithfulness.

swallowed up the seven good heads. I told this to the magicians, but none of them could explain it to me."

25 Then Joseph said to Pharaoh, "The dreams of Pharaoh are one and the same. God has revealed to Pharaoh what he is about to do. 26 The seven good cows are seven years, and the seven good heads of grain are seven years; it is one and the same dream. 27 The seven lean, ugly cows that came up afterward are seven years, and so are the seven worthless heads of grain scorched by the east wind: They are seven years of famine.

28 "It is just as I said to Pharaoh: God has shown Pharaoh what he is about to do. 29 Seven years of great abundance are coming throughout the land of Egypt, 30 but seven years of famine will follow them. Then all the abundance in Egypt will be forgotten, and the famine will ravage the land. 31 The abundance in the land will not be remembered, because the famine that follows it will be so severe. 32 The reason the dream was given to Pharaoh in two forms is that the matter has been firmly decided by God, and God will do it soon.

33 "And now let Pharaoh look for a discerning and wise man and put him in charge of the land of Egypt. 34 Let Pharaoh appoint commissioners over the land to take a fifth of the harvest of Egypt during the seven years of abundance. 35 They should collect all the food of these good years that are coming and store up the grain under the authority of Pharaoh, to be kept in the cities for food. 36 This food should be held in reserve for the country, to be used during the seven years of famine that will come upon Egypt, so that the country may not be ruined by the famine."

37 The plan seemed good to Pharaoh and to all his officials. 38 So Pharaoh asked them, "Can we find anyone like this man, one in whom is the spirit of God*a*?"

39 Then Pharaoh said to Joseph, "Since God has made all this known to you, there is no one so discerning and wise as you.

40 You shall be in charge of my palace, and all my people are to submit to your orders. Only with respect to the throne will I be greater than you."

Joseph in Charge of Egypt

41 So Pharaoh said to Joseph, "I hereby put you in charge of the whole land of Egypt." 42 Then Pharaoh took his signet ring from his finger and put it on Joseph's finger. He dressed him in robes of fine linen and put a gold chain around his neck. 43 He had him ride in a chariot as his second-in-command,*b* and people shouted before him, "Make way*c*!" Thus he put him in charge of the whole land of Egypt.

44 Then Pharaoh said to Joseph, "I am Pharaoh, but without your word no one will lift hand or foot in all Egypt." 45 Pharaoh gave Joseph the name Zaphenath-Paneah and gave him Asenath daughter of Potiphera, priest of On,*d* to be his wife. And Joseph went throughout the land of Egypt.

46 Joseph was thirty years old when he entered the service of Pharaoh king of Egypt. And Joseph went out from Pharaoh's presence and traveled throughout Egypt. 47 During the seven years of abundance the land produced plentifully. 48 Joseph collected all the food produced in those seven years of abundance in Egypt and stored it in the cities. In each city he put the food grown in the fields surrounding it. 49 Joseph stored up huge quantities of grain, like the sand of the sea; it was so much that he stopped keeping records because it was beyond measure.

50 Before the years of famine came, two sons were born to Joseph by Asenath daughter of Potiphera, priest of On. 51 Joseph named his firstborn Manasseh*e* and said, "It is because God has made me forget all my trouble and all my father's household." 52 The second son he named Ephraim*f* and said, "It is because God has made me fruitful in the land of my suffering."

a 38 Or of the gods   b 43 Or in the chariot of his second-in-command; or in his second chariot   c 43 Or Bow down   d 45 That is, Heliopolis; also in verse 50   e 51 Manasseh sounds like and may be derived from the Hebrew for forget.   f 52 Ephraim sounds like the Hebrew for twice fruitful.

41:33–37 | Joseph recommended this solution not to get a job; it was highly improbable that a prisoner would be chosen for the role he described. Pharaoh did not worship or understand Joseph's God, but he recognized something special in this man—a divine empowerment beyond good leadership (Job 32:8; Isa. 46:9–11).

41:41 | God does not measure a steward by success, reputation, or fame. God treasures and requires faithfulness, and God prepares and promotes on that basis alone.

41:42–45 | In the sudden onrush of honor, Joseph gained the symbol of the king's power (**his signet ring**), a wardrobe of privilege,

royal jewelry, a **chariot**, a position as **second-in-command**, an Egyptian **name** (which means "God speaks and lives"), and a **wife** from a prominent family.

41:51, 52 | Amid Egypt's pervasive paganism, Joseph never deserted his spiritual heritage, shown by the Hebrew names he gave his sons: **Manasseh** ("forgetfulness") and **Ephraim** ("fruitfulness"). Joseph's first son symbolized putting the **trouble** and mistreatment by his family (**father's household**) behind him. His second son was a tangible reminder of God's faithfulness even in a foreign land. Wise Christians surround themselves with reminders of God's goodness as a way to move beyond their pasts.

[53] The seven years of abundance in Egypt came to an end, [54] and the seven years of famine began, just as Joseph had said. There was famine in all the other lands, but in the whole land of Egypt there was food. [55] When all Egypt began to feel the famine, the people cried to Pharaoh for food. Then Pharaoh told all the Egyptians, "Go to Joseph and do what he tells you."

[56] When the famine had spread over the whole country, Joseph opened all the storehouses and sold grain to the Egyptians, for the famine was severe throughout Egypt. [57] And all the world came to Egypt to buy grain from Joseph, because the famine was severe everywhere.

Joseph's Brothers Go to Egypt

42 When Jacob learned that there was grain in Egypt, he said to his sons, "Why do you just keep looking at each other?" [2] He continued, "I have heard that there is grain in Egypt. Go down there and buy some for us, so that we may live and not die."

[3] Then ten of Joseph's brothers went down to buy grain from Egypt. [4] But Jacob did not send Benjamin, Joseph's brother, with the others, because he was afraid that harm might come to him. [5] So Israel's sons were among those who went to buy grain, for there was famine in the land of Canaan also.

[6] Now Joseph was the governor of the land, the person who sold grain to all its people. So when Joseph's brothers arrived, they bowed down to him with their faces to the ground. [7] As soon as Joseph saw his brothers, he recognized them, but he pretended to be a stranger and spoke harshly to them. "Where do you come from?" he asked.

"From the land of Canaan," they replied, "to buy food."

[8] Although Joseph recognized his brothers, they did not recognize him. [9] Then he remembered his dreams about them and said to them, "You are spies! You have come to see where our land is unprotected."

[10] "No, my lord," they answered. "Your servants have come to buy food. [11] We are all the sons of one man. Your servants are honest men, not spies."

[12] "No!" he said to them. "You have come to see where our land is unprotected."

[13] But they replied, "Your servants were twelve brothers, the sons of one man, who lives in the land of Canaan. The youngest is now with our father, and one is no more."

[14] Joseph said to them, "It is just as I told you: You are spies! [15] And this is how you will be tested: As surely as Pharaoh lives, you will not leave this place unless your youngest brother comes here. [16] Send one of your number to get your brother; the rest of you will be kept in prison, so that your words may be tested to see if you are telling the truth. If you are not, then as surely as Pharaoh lives, you are spies!" [17] And he put them all in custody for three days.

[18] On the third day, Joseph said to them, "Do this and you will live, for I fear God: [19] If you are honest men, let one of your brothers stay here in prison, while the rest of you go and take grain back for your starving households. [20] But you must bring your youngest brother to me, so that your words may be verified and that you may not die." This they proceeded to do.

[21] They said to one another, "Surely we are being punished because of our brother. We saw how distressed he was when he pleaded with us for his life, but we would not listen; that's why this distress has come on us."

[22] Reuben replied, "Didn't I tell you not to sin against the boy? But you wouldn't listen! Now we must give an accounting for his blood." [23] They did not realize that Joseph could understand them, since he was using an interpreter.

[24] He turned away from them and began to weep, but then came back and spoke

---

For Reflection — **Regret versus Repentance • 42:22**

Joseph's brothers give us a picture of the difference between regret and repentance. Often people are filled with regret because they have been found out in their sin. Their sorrow is not a godly sorrow that leads to repentance; it is an expression of the pain of being exposed.

Undoubtedly, the brothers regretted the deeds done to Joseph, but their regret had not yet turned into repentance. Joseph, through the providence of God, would bring these brothers from a plateau of regret to the pinnacle of repentance and true sorrow for doing wrong. And God would use them in the founding of His great nation, Israel.

to them again. He had Simeon taken from them and bound before their eyes.

²⁵ Joseph gave orders to fill their bags with grain, to put each man's silver back in his sack, and to give them provisions for their journey. After this was done for them, ²⁶ they loaded their grain on their donkeys and left.

²⁷ At the place where they stopped for the night one of them opened his sack to get feed for his donkey, and he saw his silver in the mouth of his sack. ²⁸ "My silver has been returned," he said to his brothers. "Here it is in my sack."

Their hearts sank and they turned to each other trembling and said, "What is this that God has done to us?"

²⁹ When they came to their father Jacob in the land of Canaan, they told him all that had happened to them. They said, ³⁰ "The man who is lord over the land spoke harshly to us and treated us as though we were spying on the land. ³¹ But we said to him, 'We are honest men; we are not spies. ³² We were twelve brothers, sons of one father. One is no more, and the youngest is now with our father in Canaan.'

³³ "Then the man who is lord over the land said to us, 'This is how I will know whether you are honest men: Leave one of your brothers here with me, and take food for your starving households and go. ³⁴ But bring your youngest brother to me so I will know that you are not spies but honest men. Then I will give your brother back to you, and you can trade[a] in the land.'"

³⁵ As they were emptying their sacks, there in each man's sack was his pouch of silver! When they and their father saw the money pouches, they were frightened. ³⁶ Their father Jacob said to them, "You have deprived me of my children. Joseph is no more and Simeon is no more, and now you want to take Benjamin. Everything is against me!"

³⁷ Then Reuben said to his father, "You may put both of my sons to death if I do not bring him back to you. Entrust him to my care, and I will bring him back."

³⁸ But Jacob said, "My son will not go down there with you; his brother is dead and he is the only one left. If harm comes to him on the journey you are taking, you will bring my gray head down to the grave in sorrow."

The Second Journey to Egypt

43 Now the famine was still severe in the land. ² So when they had eaten all the grain they had brought from Egypt, their father said to them, "Go back and buy us a little more food."

³ But Judah said to him, "The man warned us solemnly, 'You will not see my face again unless your brother is with you.' ⁴ If you will send our brother along with us, we will go down and buy food for you. ⁵ But if you will not send him, we will not go down, because the man said to us, 'You will not see my face again unless your brother is with you.'"

⁶ Israel asked, "Why did you bring this trouble on me by telling the man you had another brother?"

⁷ They replied, "The man questioned us closely about ourselves and our family. 'Is your father still living?' he asked us. 'Do you have another brother?' We simply answered his questions. How were we to know he would say, 'Bring your brother down here'?"

---

[a] 34 Or move about freely

42:24 | Reuben was absent when Joseph was sold into slavery; he also attempted to save the boy. This made Simeon, the second oldest, responsible for what the brothers did; thus Joseph **had Simeon taken from them and bound before their eyes.** Jacob's harsh words about Simeon in his deathbed blessing suggest that Simeon showed a lifelong pattern of cruelty (49:5–7).

42:25–28 | Joseph showed kindness when he had the **silver** put back in the sacks of his brothers. Yet the brothers were **trembling**, afraid that they might be accused of theft when they returned to Egypt.

42:29–34 | The additional details in the account the **brothers** gave of their experiences reveal some spiritual progress. They had problems to confess to Jacob; refreshingly, they told the truth.

42:35–38 | **Reuben** distinguished himself by selflessly vowing (**put both of my sons to death**) to rescue Simeon from Egypt and safely return **Benjamin**. The depth of Jacob's grief was evident—he felt he could not endure one more loss.

43:3–14 | From this moment on, leadership among the brothers shifts from Reuben to **Judah**. Judah, eloquent and persuasive, soon stood before Joseph with Benjamin present, pleading for all their lives with Jacob's approval.

[8]Then Judah said to Israel his father, "Send the boy along with me and we will go at once, so that we and you and our children may live and not die. [9]I myself will guarantee his safety; you can hold me personally responsible for him. If I do not bring him back to you and set him here before you, I will bear the blame before you all my life. [10]As it is, if we had not delayed, we could have gone and returned twice."

[11]Then their father Israel said to them, "If it must be, then do this: Put some of the best products of the land in your bags and take them down to the man as a gift—a little balm and a little honey, some spices and myrrh, some pistachio nuts and almonds. [12]Take double the amount of silver with you, for you must return the silver that was put back into the mouths of your sacks. Perhaps it was a mistake. [13]Take your brother also and go back to the man at once. [14]And may God Almighty[a] grant you mercy before the man so that he will let your other brother and Benjamin come back with you. As for me, if I am bereaved, I am bereaved."

[15]So the men took the gifts and double the amount of silver, and Benjamin also. They hurried down to Egypt and presented themselves to Joseph. [16]When Joseph saw Benjamin with them, he said to the steward of his house, "Take these men to my house, slaughter an animal and prepare a meal; they are to eat with me at noon."

[17]The man did as Joseph told him and took the men to Joseph's house. [18]Now the men were frightened when they were taken to his house. They thought, "We were brought here because of the silver that was put back into our sacks the first time. He wants to attack us and overpower us and seize us as slaves and take our donkeys."

[19]So they went up to Joseph's steward and spoke to him at the entrance to the house. [20]"We beg your pardon, our lord," they said, "we came down here the first time to buy food. [21]But at the place where we stopped for the night we opened our sacks and each of us found his silver—the exact weight—in the mouth of his sack. So

we have brought it back with us. [22]We have also brought additional silver with us to buy food. We don't know who put our silver in our sacks."

[23]"It's all right," he said. "Don't be afraid. Your God, the God of your father, has given you treasure in your sacks; I received your silver." Then he brought Simeon out to them.

[24]The steward took the men into Joseph's house, gave them water to wash their feet and provided fodder for their donkeys. [25]They prepared their gifts for Joseph's arrival at noon, because they had heard that they were to eat there.

[26]When Joseph came home, they presented to him the gifts they had brought into the house, and they bowed down before him to the ground. [27]He asked them how they were, and then he said, "How is your aged father you told me about? Is he still living?"

[28]They replied, "Your servant our father is still alive and well." And they bowed down, prostrating themselves before him.

[29]As he looked about and saw his brother Benjamin, his own mother's son, he asked, "Is this your youngest brother, the one you told me about?" And he said, "God be gracious to you, my son." [30]Deeply moved at the sight of his brother, Joseph hurried out and looked for a place to weep. He went into his private room and wept there.

[31]After he had washed his face, he came out and, controlling himself, said, "Serve the food."

[32]They served him by himself, the brothers by themselves, and the Egyptians who ate with him by themselves, because Egyptians could not eat with Hebrews, for that is detestable to Egyptians. [33]The men had been seated before him in the order of their ages, from the firstborn to the youngest; and they looked at each other in astonishment. [34]When portions were served to them from Joseph's table, Benjamin's portion was five times as much as anyone else's. So they feasted and drank freely with him.

[a] 14 Hebrew El-Shaddai

43:16, 17 | Joseph, a type of Christ, was breaking down the hard hearts of his brothers by this outstanding exhibition of grace. Grace is what God gives to undeserving people.

43:32 | Joseph sat **by himself** because the **Egyptians** considered the Semitic herdsmen unfit to be at the same table with them. In antiquity, Egyptians shaved all body hair to control lice, took baths regularly, and wore little clothing. The Hebrews were hairy, unbathed, and wore robes. Sitting and eating with them was **detestable** to them. Yet in this case, the "Egyptian" Joseph

wanted nothing more than to sit and dine with his brothers!

43:33, 34 | When Joseph seated his brothers by birth order, they **looked at each other in astonishment**, with a growing sense of mystery about what this Egyptian official knew about them. Joseph gradually revealed himself to his siblings. He also continued to test their hearts. This time, Joseph gave Benjamin a serving **five times** larger than the others to discover if the brothers still had a problem with jealousy. But no one said a word. That which was a stumbling block to them years before was gone.

fyi   Safer Pastures • 43:32

When God sent Jacob's family into seclusion in Egypt, the question could be asked, "Why would they be any safer among the pagan Egyptians than they would have been among the pagan Canaanites?" There is one answer, but it is supported by two verses in Genesis. First, when Joseph served his brothers a meal, the Egyptians ate separately: "Egyptians could not eat with Hebrews, for that is detestable to Egyptians." Second, the Hebrews, because of their vocation, were sent to the region of Goshen to live, "for all shepherds are detestable to the Egyptians" (46:34). In other words, the Egyptians considered the Hebrews so socially inferior to themselves that there was little danger of co-mingling or intermarriage. With the Canaanites, as Israel's future would show, intermarriage—and the idolatry that came with the Canaanite culture—was always a pervasive concern.

A Silver Cup in a Sack

44 Now Joseph gave these instructions to the steward of his house: "Fill the men's sacks with as much food as they can carry, and put each man's silver in the mouth of his sack. ²Then put my cup, the silver one, in the mouth of the youngest one's sack, along with the silver for his grain." And he did as Joseph said.

³As morning dawned, the men were sent on their way with their donkeys. ⁴They had not gone far from the city when Joseph said to his steward, "Go after those men at once, and when you catch up with them, say to them, 'Why have you repaid good with evil? ⁵Isn't this the cup my master drinks from and also uses for divination? This is a wicked thing you have done.'"

⁶When he caught up with them, he repeated these words to them. ⁷But they said to him, "Why does my lord say such things? Far be it from your servants to do anything like that! ⁸We even brought back to you from the land of Canaan the silver we found inside the mouths of our sacks. So why would we steal silver or gold from your master's house? ⁹If any of your servants is found to have it, he will die; and the rest of us will become my lord's slaves."

¹⁰"Very well, then," he said, "let it be as you say. Whoever is found to have it will become my slave; the rest of you will be free from blame."

¹¹Each of them quickly lowered his sack to the ground and opened it. ¹²Then the steward proceeded to search, beginning with the oldest and ending with the youngest. And the cup was found in Benjamin's sack. ¹³At this, they tore their clothes. Then they all loaded their donkeys and returned to the city.

¹⁴Joseph was still in the house when Judah and his brothers came in, and they threw themselves to the ground before him. ¹⁵Joseph said to them, "What is this you have done? Don't you know that a man like me can find things out by divination?"

¹⁶"What can we say to my lord?" Judah replied. "What can we say? How can we prove our innocence? God has uncovered your servants' guilt. We are now my lord's slaves—we ourselves and the one who was found to have the cup."

¹⁷But Joseph said, "Far be it from me to do such a thing! Only the man who was found to have the cup will become my slave. The rest of you, go back to your father in peace."

¹⁸Then Judah went up to him and said: "Pardon your servant, my lord, let me speak a word to my lord. Do not be angry with your servant, though you are equal to Pharaoh himself. ¹⁹My lord asked his servants, 'Do you have a father or a brother?' ²⁰And we answered, 'We have an aged father, and there is a young son born to him in his old age. His brother is dead, and he is the only one of his mother's sons left, and his father loves him.'

²¹"Then you said to your servants, 'Bring him down to me so I can see him for myself.' ²²And we said to my lord, 'The boy cannot leave his father; if he leaves him, his father

---

44:1–17 | Joseph's brothers had conspired against Joseph out of hate. Here, Scripture shows Joseph conspiring against them out of love. Joseph, God's servant, arranged the coming events in the brothers' lives for the express purpose of bringing them face-to-face with their sin.

44:2–5 | Egyptians used the **cup** of **divination** in rites intended to reveal the future. Presumably, Joseph did not engage in this pagan practice, but as a ruler in Egypt he would have such an instrument in his house. Joseph had this special cup placed in Benjamin's sack (**the youngest**) to discern whether his brothers considered Benjamin a threat, as Joseph had been years before. Would they stand with Benjamin or sell him out?

44:12–16 | The brothers passed the test; as soon as the **cup was**

found in Benjamin's sack, they **returned** to Egypt, accompanying Benjamin to his trial. Joseph had waited for someone to stand up on behalf of the family and confess sin. **Judah** did so here. Judah was certain Benjamin had not stolen the cup, so what **guilt** was he confessing? It could be only the sin that he and the others committed 20 years before when they sold Joseph into slavery.

44:16–34 | Because Joseph had declared that the one who had the cup would **become** his **slave**, Benjamin's freedom was at risk. **Judah** stepped forward and recounted the entire story, including himself in every aspect. He also explained the effect it would have on their father if their youngest brother was kept in Egypt. His magnanimous suggestion—**let your servant remain here . . . in place of the boy**—showed a true change of heart.

will die.' ^{23}But you told your servants, 'Unless your youngest brother comes down with you, you will not see my face again.' ^{24}When we went back to your servant my father, we told him what my lord had said.

^{25} "Then our father said, 'Go back and buy a little more food.' ^{26}But we said, 'We cannot go down. Only if our youngest brother is with us will we go. We cannot see the man's face unless our youngest brother is with us.'

^{27} "Your servant my father said to us, 'You know that my wife bore me two sons. ^{28}One of them went away from me, and I said, "He has surely been torn to pieces." And I have not seen him since. ^{29}If you take this one from me too and harm comes to him, you will bring my gray head down to the grave in misery.'

^{30} "So now, if the boy is not with us when I go back to your servant my father, and if my father, whose life is closely bound up with the boy's life, ^{31}sees that the boy isn't there, he will die. Your servants will bring the gray head of our father down to the grave in sorrow. ^{32}Your servant guaranteed the boy's safety to my father. I said, 'If I do not bring him back to you, I will bear the blame before you, my father, all my life!'

^{33} "Now then, please let your servant remain here as my lord's slave in place of the boy, and let the boy return with his brothers. ^{34}How can I go back to my father if the boy is not with me? No! Do not let me see the misery that would come on my father."

Joseph Makes Himself Known

45 Then Joseph could no longer control himself before all his attendants, and he cried out, "Have everyone leave my presence!" So there was no one with Joseph when he made himself known to his brothers. ^{2}And he wept so loudly that the Egyptians heard him, and Pharaoh's household heard about it.

^{3}Joseph said to his brothers, "I am Joseph! Is my father still living?" But his brothers were not able to answer him, because they were terrified at his presence.

^{4}Then Joseph said to his brothers, "Come close to me." When they had done so, he said, "I am your brother Joseph, the one you sold into Egypt! ^{5}And now, do not be distressed and do not be angry with yourselves for selling me here, because it was to save lives that God sent me ahead of you. ^{6}For two years now there has been famine in the land, and for the next five years there will be no plowing and reaping. ^{7}But God sent me ahead of you to preserve for you a remnant on earth and to save your lives by a great deliverance.^{a}

^{8} "So then, it was not you who sent me here, but God. He made me father to Pharaoh, lord of his entire household and ruler of all Egypt. ^{9}Now hurry back to my father and say to him, 'This is what your son Joseph says: God has made me lord of all Egypt. Come down to me; don't delay. ^{10}You shall live in the region of Goshen and be near me—you, your children and grandchildren, your flocks and herds, and all you have. ^{11}I will provide for you there, because five years of famine are still to come. Otherwise you and your household and all who belong to you will become destitute.'

^{12} "You can see for yourselves, and so can my brother Benjamin, that it is really I who am speaking to you. ^{13}Tell my father about all the honor accorded me in Egypt and about everything you have seen. And bring my father down here quickly."

^{14}Then he threw his arms around his brother Benjamin and wept, and Benjamin embraced him, weeping. ^{15}And he kissed all his brothers and wept over them. Afterward his brothers talked with him.

^{16}When the news reached Pharaoh's palace that Joseph's brothers had come, Pharaoh and all his officials were pleased. ^{17}Pharaoh said to Joseph, "Tell your brothers, 'Do this: Load your animals and return to the land of Canaan, ^{18}and bring your father and your families back to me. I will give you the best of the land of Egypt and you can enjoy the fat of the land.'

^{19} "You are also directed to tell them, 'Do this: Take some carts from Egypt for your children and your wives, and get your father and come. ^{20}Never mind about your

---

^{a} 7 Or *save you as a great band of survivors*

45:3–8 | Silence followed the words **I am Joseph!** Previously, Joseph spoke only in Egyptian through an interpreter, but now he spoke in Hebrew to his brothers. The object of their hatred and the evidence of their sin stood before them, and they were **terrified** in his presence. Joseph's statement that **to save lives . . . God sent me ahead of you** showed his ability to see God at work, turning the tragedies of life into triumphs.
45:14, 15 | Most touching is Joseph's reunion with his younger

brother, **Benjamin**. Joseph **kissed all his brothers** to demonstrate forgiveness: Reuben, unstable as water; Simeon and Levi, who brought trouble; and Judah, who saved Joseph's life by suggesting that he be sold. Reconciliation brings peace, protection, provision, and proximity (nearness).
45:16–21 | At Pharaoh's bidding and Joseph's instruction, **the sons of Israel** did exactly what they were supposed to do. This is the step of faith that people take to accomplish God's will.

belongings, because the best of all Egypt will be yours.' "

21 So the sons of Israel did this. Joseph gave them carts, as Pharaoh had commanded, and he also gave them provisions for their journey. 22 To each of them he gave new clothing, but to Benjamin he gave three hundred shekels[a] of silver and five sets of clothes. 23 And this is what he sent to his father: ten donkeys loaded with the best things of Egypt, and ten female donkeys loaded with grain and bread and other provisions for his journey. 24 Then he sent his brothers away, and as they were leaving he said to them, "Don't quarrel on the way!"

25 So they went up out of Egypt and came to their father Jacob in the land of Canaan. 26 They told him, "Joseph is still alive! In fact, he is ruler of all Egypt." Jacob was stunned; he did not believe them. 27 But when they told him everything Joseph had said to them, and when he saw the carts Joseph had sent to carry him back, the spirit of their father Jacob revived. 28 And Israel said, "I'm convinced! My son Joseph is still alive. I will go and see him before I die."

Jacob Goes to Egypt

46 So Israel set out with all that was his, and when he reached Beersheba, he offered sacrifices to the God of his father Isaac.

2 And God spoke to Israel in a vision at night and said, "Jacob! Jacob!"

"Here I am," he replied.

3 "I am God, the God of your father," he said. "Do not be afraid to go down to Egypt, for I will make you into a great nation there. 4 I will go down to Egypt with you, and I will surely bring you back again. And Joseph's own hand will close your eyes."

5 Then Jacob left Beersheba, and Israel's sons took their father Jacob and their children and their wives in the carts that Pharaoh had sent to transport him. 6 So Jacob and all his offspring went to Egypt, taking with them their livestock and the possessions they had acquired in Canaan. 7 Jacob brought with him to Egypt his sons and

grandsons and his daughters and granddaughters—all his offspring.

8 These are the names of the sons of Israel (Jacob and his descendants) who went to Egypt:

Reuben the firstborn of Jacob.
9 The sons of Reuben:
    Hanok, Pallu, Hezron and Karmi.
10 The sons of Simeon:
    Jemuel, Jamin, Ohad, Jakin, Zohar and Shaul the son of a Canaanite woman.
11 The sons of Levi:
    Gershon, Kohath and Merari.
12 The sons of Judah:
    Er, Onan, Shelah, Perez and Zerah (but Er and Onan had died in the land of Canaan).
    The sons of Perez:
        Hezron and Hamul.
13 The sons of Issachar:
    Tola, Puah,[b] Jashub[c] and Shimron.
14 The sons of Zebulun:
    Sered, Elon and Jahleel.
15 These were the sons Leah bore to Jacob in Paddan Aram,[d] besides his daughter Dinah. These sons and daughters of his were thirty-three in all.

16 The sons of Gad:
    Zephon,[e] Haggi, Shuni, Ezbon, Eri, Arodi and Areli.
17 The sons of Asher:
    Imnah, Ishvah, Ishvi and Beriah.
    Their sister was Serah.
    The sons of Beriah:
        Heber and Malkiel.
18 These were the children born to Jacob by Zilpah, whom Laban had given to his daughter Leah—sixteen in all.

19 The sons of Jacob's wife Rachel:
    Joseph and Benjamin. 20 In Egypt, Manasseh and Ephraim were born to

---

[a] 22 That is, about 7 1/2 pounds or about 3.5 kilograms   [b] 13 Samaritan Pentateuch and Syriac (see also 1 Chron. 7:1); Masoretic Text *Puvah*
[c] 13 Samaritan Pentateuch and some Septuagint manuscripts (see also Num. 26:24 and 1 Chron. 7:1); Masoretic Text *Iob*   [d] 15 That is, Northwest Mesopotamia
[e] 16 Samaritan Pentateuch and Septuagint (see also Num. 26:15); Masoretic Text *Ziphion*

45:26—46:4 | When Jacob heard that Joseph was **still alive**, he was **stunned**. On his journey to Egypt to see his long-lost son, Israel arrived at **Beersheba** and offered **sacrifices to the God of his father Isaac**. These words signify a continuity of faith, from one generation to the next. God then graciously spoke to him in a dream (**a vision at night**), assuring Jacob that all would be well in the journey to Egypt and promising a peaceful death with his favored son at his side (**Joseph's own hand will close your eyes**).

46:8–26 | After listing Simeon's first five sons, Scripture adds: **and Shaul the son of a Canaanite woman**. It is uncertain whether this marriage indicated a hardness of heart on Simeon's part, or if Simeon's Canaanite wife was a believer. **The sons of Judah** include the three that were born to his Canaanite wife, the daughter of Shuah, as well as the two children of Tamar. Judah was now a forgiven man, and his tribe would be a leader within the family.

Tough Questions
Why do Genesis and Acts reveal a discrepancy in the size of Jacob's family? • 46:27

There appears to be a biblical discrepancy in the descriptions of the size of Jacob's family that left Canaan and sought refuge in Egypt. Moses says the number was 70 (46:27; Ex. 1:5; Deut. 10:22); in Stephen's speech to the Sanhedrin in Acts, he says the number was 75 (Acts 7:14). The extra five arise from Stephen's use of the Septuagint, the Greek version of the OT. There, Genesis 46:20 adds to the list the names of five of Joseph's sons and grandsons born to him in Egypt, taking the total from 70 to 75.

Joseph by Asenath daughter of Potiphera, priest of On.ᵃ

²¹ The sons of Benjamin:

Bela, Beker, Ashbel, Gera, Naaman, Ehi, Rosh, Muppim, Huppim and Ard.

²² These were the sons of Rachel who were born to Jacob—fourteen in all.

²³ The son of Dan:

Hushim.

²⁴ The sons of Naphtali:

Jahziel, Guni, Jezer and Shillem.

²⁵ These were the sons born to Jacob by Bilhah, whom Laban had given to his daughter Rachel—seven in all.

²⁶ All those who went to Egypt with Jacob—those who were his direct descendants, not counting his sons' wives—numbered sixty-six persons. ²⁷ With the two sonsᵇ who had been born to Joseph in Egypt, the members of Jacob's family, which went to Egypt, were seventyᶜ in all.

²⁸ Now Jacob sent Judah ahead of him to Joseph to get directions to Goshen. When they arrived in the region of Goshen, ²⁹ Joseph had his chariot made ready and went to Goshen to meet his father Israel. As soon as Joseph appeared before him, he threw his arms around his fatherᵈ and wept for a long time.

³⁰ Israel said to Joseph, "Now I am ready to die, since I have seen for myself that you are still alive."

³¹ Then Joseph said to his brothers and to his father's household, "I will go up and speak to Pharaoh and will say to him, 'My brothers and my father's household, who were living in the land of Canaan, have come to me. ³² The men are shepherds; they tend livestock, and they have brought along

their flocks and herds and everything they own.' ³³ When Pharaoh calls you in and asks, 'What is your occupation?' ³⁴ you should answer, 'Your servants have tended livestock from our boyhood on, just as our fathers did.' Then you will be allowed to settle in the region of Goshen, for all shepherds are detestable to the Egyptians."

47 Joseph went and told Pharaoh, "My father and brothers, with their flocks and herds and everything they own, have come from the land of Canaan and are now in Goshen." ² He chose five of his brothers and presented them before Pharaoh.

³ Pharaoh asked the brothers, "What is your occupation?"

"Your servants are shepherds," they replied to Pharaoh, "just as our fathers were." ⁴ They also said to him, "We have come to live here for a while, because the famine is severe in Canaan and your servants' flocks have no pasture. So now, please let your servants settle in Goshen."

⁵ Pharaoh said to Joseph, "Your father and your brothers have come to you, ⁶ and the land of Egypt is before you; settle your father and your brothers in the best part of the land. Let them live in Goshen. And if you know of any among them with special ability, put them in charge of my own livestock."

⁷ Then Joseph brought his father Jacob in and presented him before Pharaoh. After Jacob blessedᵉ Pharaoh, ⁸ Pharaoh asked him, "How old are you?"

⁹ And Jacob said to Pharaoh, "The years of my pilgrimage are a hundred and thirty. My years have been few and difficult, and they do not equal the years of the pilgrimage of

ᵃ 20 That is, Heliopolis　ᵇ 27 Hebrew; Septuagint the nine children　ᶜ 27 Hebrew (see also Exodus 1:5 and note); Septuagint (see also Acts 7:14) seventy-five　ᵈ 29 Hebrew around him　ᵉ 7 Or greeted

46:29, 30 | Upon the tender reunion of father and son, **Israel** (Jacob) was **ready to die**. Yet God blessed him in **Goshen**, and Jacob lived for 17 more years. When God fulfills a longing, people often gain a new zest for life and have a renewed vision for their future.

47:1-6 | **Goshen** was a choice location for the families of Jacob as **shepherds**. The Egyptians were experts in farming, but this land was more suitable for flocks.

47:7-10 | Not only did **Joseph** love his father, he was also proud of him. Many Egyptian hieroglyphics depict shepherds as uncouth, lowly people. Yet Joseph, the servant of Pharaoh, brought his aged shepherd father to **Pharaoh**, where Jacob met and **blessed** him. Pharaoh was lord among men and had power on the earth, but Jacob was a prince of God and had power in heaven.

my fathers." [10]Then Jacob blessed[a] Pharaoh and went out from his presence.

[11]So Joseph settled his father and his brothers in Egypt and gave them property in the best part of the land, the district of Rameses, as Pharaoh directed. [12]Joseph also provided his father and his brothers and all his father's household with food, according to the number of their children.

Joseph and the Famine

[13]There was no food, however, in the whole region because the famine was severe; both Egypt and Canaan wasted away because of the famine. [14]Joseph collected all the money that was to be found in Egypt and Canaan in payment for the grain they were buying, and he brought it to Pharaoh's palace. [15]When the money of the people of Egypt and Canaan was gone, all Egypt came to Joseph and said, "Give us food. Why should we die before your eyes? Our money is all gone."

[16]"Then bring your livestock," said Joseph. "I will sell you food in exchange for your livestock, since your money is gone." [17]So they brought their livestock to Joseph, and he gave them food in exchange for their horses, their sheep and goats, their cattle and donkeys. And he brought them through that year with food in exchange for all their livestock.

[18]When that year was over, they came to him the following year and said, "We cannot hide from our lord the fact that since our money is gone and our livestock belongs to you, there is nothing left for our lord except our bodies and our land. [19]Why should we perish before your eyes—we and our land as well? Buy us and our land in exchange for food, and we with our land will be in bondage to Pharaoh. Give us seed so that we may live and not die, and that the land may not become desolate."

[20]So Joseph bought all the land in Egypt for Pharaoh. The Egyptians, one and all, sold their fields, because the famine was too severe for them. The land became Pharaoh's, [21]and Joseph reduced the people to servitude,[b] from one end of Egypt to the other.

[22]However, he did not buy the land of the priests, because they received a regular allotment from Pharaoh and had food enough from the allotment Pharaoh gave them. That is why they did not sell their land.

[23]Joseph said to the people, "Now that I have bought you and your land today for Pharaoh, here is seed for you so you can plant the ground. [24]But when the crop comes in, give a fifth of it to Pharaoh. The other four-fifths you may keep as seed for the fields and as food for yourselves and your households and your children."

[25]"You have saved our lives," they said. "May we find favor in the eyes of our lord; we will be in bondage to Pharaoh."

[26]So Joseph established it as a law concerning land in Egypt—still in force today—that a fifth of the produce belongs to Pharaoh. It was only the land of the priests that did not become Pharaoh's.

[27]Now the Israelites settled in Egypt in the region of Goshen. They acquired property there and were fruitful and increased greatly in number.

[28]Jacob lived in Egypt seventeen years, and the years of his life were a hundred and forty-seven. [29]When the time drew near for Israel to die, he called for his son Joseph and said to him, "If I have found favor in your eyes, put your hand under my thigh and promise that you will show me kindness and faithfulness. Do not bury me in Egypt, [30]but when I rest with my fathers, carry me out of Egypt and bury me where they are buried."

"I will do as you say," he said.

[31]"Swear to me," he said. Then Joseph swore to him, and Israel worshiped as he leaned on the top of his staff.[c]

Manasseh and Ephraim

48 Some time later Joseph was told, "Your father is ill." So he took his two sons Manasseh and Ephraim along with him. [2]When Jacob was told, "Your son Joseph has come to you," Israel rallied his strength and sat up on the bed.

---

[a] 10 Or said farewell to   [b] 21 Samaritan Pentateuch and Septuagint (see also Vulgate); Masoretic Text and he moved the people into the cities   [c] 31 Or Israel bowed down at the head of his bed

---

47:13–26 | The verses from 42:1–47:12 form a parentheses explaining what happens when Joseph's family comes to Egypt. This passage, which resumes the story about the **famine** and the manner in which Joseph handled it, summarizes 41:53–57. While administering a government in crisis, Joseph was also orchestrating the reconciliation of his family.

47:27 | Israel **increased greatly in number** so that the 70 persons who moved to be near Joseph (46:27) grew to an astonishing number within a few generations. This was part of God's work to fulfill His covenant promises and make Abraham, Isaac, and Jacob "as numerous as the stars" (22:17; 26:4). The number of Israelites would eventually frighten the Egyptians (Ex. 1:9; Deut. 10:22).

48:1–11 | Knowing **Jacob** was near death, Joseph brought his two sons, **Manasseh and Ephraim**, to their grandfather so he could bless them. Jacob told them his story: **God Almighty appeared to me at Luz in the land of Canaan, and there he blessed me**. As Jacob looked back at the end of his life, he vividly remembered God's involvement and provision.

Picture This

Seven Great Illustrations of Faith in Genesis • 48:15

Jacob began his blessing on Joseph with the words "May the God before whom my fathers Abraham and Isaac walked faithfully."

After Adam, seven great men walk across the pages of Genesis to illustrate the principles of faith.

- Abel brought a more excellent sacrifice to God and, in doing so, illustrated the simplicity of faith (4:2–5).
- Enoch was translated to heaven because of his godliness and his consistent walk. He illustrated the stability of faith (5:24).
- Noah built an ark in obedience to the Lord and preached salvation through that ark to all who would listen. As a result of his preaching, his whole family was saved from destruction. He illustrated the significance of faith, for "without faith it is impossible to please God" (6—9; Heb. 11:6).
- Abraham trusted God in the face of insurmountable objections and obstacles and was willing to fly in the face of God's great promise to him in sacrificing his own son. He illustrated the sacrifice of faith (22).
- Isaac submitted to his earthly father and unresistingly yielded to his heavenly Father. He illustrated the submission of faith (22).
- Jacob was the most up-and-down man in the Bible: from victory to defeat and from triumph to tragedy. Jacob illustrated the steps of faith or the school of faith (25—49).
- Joseph was victorious and triumphant at every place where we find him. He illustrated the success of faith (37—50).

³Jacob said to Joseph, "God Almighty*ᵃ* appeared to me at Luz in the land of Canaan, and there he blessed me ⁴and said to me, 'I am going to make you fruitful and increase your numbers. I will make you a community of peoples, and I will give this land as an everlasting possession to your descendants after you.'

⁵"Now then, your two sons born to you in Egypt before I came to you here will be reckoned as mine; Ephraim and Manasseh will be mine, just as Reuben and Simeon are mine. ⁶Any children born to you after them will be yours; in the territory they inherit they will be reckoned under the names of their brothers. ⁷As I was returning from Paddan,*ᵇ* to my sorrow Rachel died in the land of Canaan while we were still on the way, a little distance from Ephrath. So I buried her there beside the road to Ephrath" (that is, Bethlehem).

⁸When Israel saw the sons of Joseph, he asked, "Who are these?"

⁹"They are the sons God has given me here," Joseph said to his father.

Then Israel said, "Bring them to me so I may bless them."

¹⁰Now Israel's eyes were failing because of old age, and he could hardly see. So

Joseph brought his sons close to him, and his father kissed them and embraced them.

¹¹Israel said to Joseph, "I never expected to see your face again, and now God has allowed me to see your children too."

¹²Then Joseph removed them from Israel's knees and bowed down with his face to the ground. ¹³And Joseph took both of them, Ephraim on his right toward Israel's left hand and Manasseh on his left toward Israel's right hand, and brought them close to him. ¹⁴But Israel reached out his right hand and put it on Ephraim's head, though he was the younger, and crossing his arms, he put his left hand on Manasseh's head, even though Manasseh was the firstborn.

¹⁵Then he blessed Joseph and said,

"May the God before whom my fathers
    Abraham and Isaac walked
        faithfully,
the God who has been my shepherd
    all my life to this day,
¹⁶the Angel who has delivered me from
        all harm
    —may he bless these boys.

ᵃ 3 Hebrew El-Shaddai   ᵇ 7 That is, Northwest Mesopotamia

48:13, 14 | The blessing of the older son was to be given with the **right hand**, and the younger son's blessing with the **left hand**. Joseph positioned **Manasseh** (the older) and **Ephraim** (the younger) so Jacob could simply reach out his hands and bless them respectively. But Jacob crossed his hands, so once again the younger was blessed above the older (25:23; 27:28–40).

48:15–22 | Throughout the history of Israel, **Ephraim** was indeed blessed among the tribes. In fact, this tribe was so blessed that

when the northern kingdom separated from the southern kingdom, the name of Ephraim, its principal tribe, was sometimes a synonym for Israel. As a son of Joseph, **Manasseh** was also greatly blessed, and Ephraim and Manasseh together were the two most populous among the 12 tribes of Israel.

48:16 | The word **Angel** is capitalized to signal the short form of the full phrase, the Angel of the Lord. It likely refers to Jesus and the night that Jacob wrestled with the man (32:22–32).

May they be called by my name
and the names of my fathers
Abraham and Isaac,
and may they increase greatly
on the earth."

[17] When Joseph saw his father placing his right hand on Ephraim's head he was displeased; so he took hold of his father's hand to move it from Ephraim's head to Manasseh's head. [18] Joseph said to him, "No, my father, this one is the firstborn; put your right hand on his head."

[19] But his father refused and said, "I know, my son, I know. He too will become a people, and he too will become great. Nevertheless, his younger brother will be greater than he, and his descendants will become a group of nations." [20] He blessed them that day and said,

"In your[a] name will Israel pronounce
this blessing:
'May God make you like Ephraim
and Manasseh.' "

So he put Ephraim ahead of Manasseh. [21] Then Israel said to Joseph, "I am about to die, but God will be with you[b] and take you[b] back to the land of your[b] fathers. [22] And to you I give one more ridge of land[c] than to your brothers, the ridge I took from the Amorites with my sword and my bow."

Jacob Blesses His Sons

49 Then Jacob called for his sons and said: "Gather around so I can tell you what will happen to you in days to come.

[2] "Assemble and listen, sons of Jacob;
listen to your father Israel.

[3] "Reuben, you are my firstborn,
my might, the first sign of my
strength,
excelling in honor, excelling in
power.
[4] Turbulent as the waters, you will no
longer excel,

for you went up onto your father's
bed,
onto my couch and defiled it.

[5] "Simeon and Levi are brothers—
their swords[d] are weapons of
violence.
[6] Let me not enter their council,
let me not join their assembly,
for they have killed men in their anger
and hamstrung oxen as they
pleased.
[7] Cursed be their anger, so fierce,
and their fury, so cruel!
I will scatter them in Jacob
and disperse them in Israel.

[8] "Judah,[e] your brothers will praise you;
your hand will be on the neck of
your enemies;
your father's sons will bow down to
you.
[9] You are a lion's cub, Judah;
you return from the prey, my son.
Like a lion he crouches and lies down,
like a lioness—who dares to rouse
him?
[10] The scepter will not depart from
Judah,
nor the ruler's staff from between his
feet,[f]
until he to whom it belongs[g] shall come
and the obedience of the nations
shall be his.
[11] He will tether his donkey to a vine,
his colt to the choicest branch;
he will wash his garments in wine,
his robes in the blood of grapes.
[12] His eyes will be darker than wine,
his teeth whiter than milk.[h]

[13] "Zebulun will live by the seashore
and become a haven for ships;
his border will extend toward Sidon.

---

[a] 20 The Hebrew is singular.   [b] 21 The Hebrew is plural.   [c] 22 The Hebrew for ridge of land is identical with the place name Shechem.   [d] 5 The meaning of the Hebrew for this word is uncertain.   [e] 8 Judah sounds like and may be derived from the Hebrew for praise.   [f] 10 Or from his descendants   [g] 10 Or to whom tribute belongs; the meaning of the Hebrew for this phrase is uncertain.   [h] 12 Or will be dull from wine, / his teeth white from milk

---

49:1 | Because God knows the end from the beginning (Isa. 46:8–11), the aged **Jacob** could poetically and prophetically describe each son's setting, character, and future prospects as well as that of his progeny. These blessings would extend to them **in days to come**.
49:3, 4 | **Reuben** lost his birthright because he sinned against his father (35:22). So Jacob said Reuben was **turbulent as the waters** and that his tribe would **no longer excel**. No one from Reuben's tribe is ever mentioned in Scripture as prophet, military leader, or judge (cf. Deut. 27:20; 1 Chron. 5:1, 2).
49:5–7 | Jacob was so angry at the conduct of **Simeon and Levi**

in Shechem (34) that he said, **I will scatter them in Jacob and disperse them in Israel**. This happened in different ways. Simeon's allotment was in the southern region of Canaan, where cities could not be built; Levi was not given a tribal allotment at all but became the priestly tribe, with special cities throughout the land (Num. 35:6–8).
49:8–12 | Jacob's blessing on the tribe of **Judah** has references to the coming of Jesus through the line of this tribe (Num. 24:17; Luke 1:32, 33). The tribe of Judah ultimately became the leader of all the tribes of Israel. That is why the **lion** is such a powerful symbol for it.

^{14} "Issachar is a rawboned^a donkey
  lying down among the sheep pens.^{b}
^{15} When he sees how good is his resting
    place
  and how pleasant is his land,
he will bend his shoulder to the burden
  and submit to forced labor.

^{16} "Dan^c will provide justice for his
    people
  as one of the tribes of Israel.
^{17} Dan will be a snake by the roadside,
  a viper along the path,
that bites the horse's heels
  so that its rider tumbles backward.

^{18} "I look for your deliverance, LORD.

^{19} "Gad^d will be attacked by a band of
    raiders,
  but he will attack them at their heels.

^{20} "Asher's food will be rich;
  he will provide delicacies fit for a
    king.

^{21} "Naphtali is a doe set free
  that bears beautiful fawns.^{e}

^{22} "Joseph is a fruitful vine,
  a fruitful vine near a spring,
  whose branches climb over a wall.^{f}
^{23} With bitterness archers attacked him;
  they shot at him with hostility.
^{24} But his bow remained steady,
  his strong arms stayed^g limber,
because of the hand of the Mighty One
    of Jacob,
  because of the Shepherd, the Rock
    of Israel,
^{25} because of your father's God, who
    helps you,
  because of the Almighty,^{h} who
    blesses you
with blessings of the skies above,
  blessings of the deep springs below,
  blessings of the breast and womb.
^{26} Your father's blessings are greater
    than the blessings of the ancient
      mountains,
  than^i the bounty of the age-old hills.
Let all these rest on the head of Joseph,
  on the brow of the prince among^j his
    brothers.

^{27} "Benjamin is a ravenous wolf;
  in the morning he devours the prey,
  in the evening he divides the
    plunder."

^{28} All these are the twelve tribes of Israel, and this is what their father said to them when he blessed them, giving each the blessing appropriate to him.

The Death of Jacob

^{29} Then he gave them these instructions: "I am about to be gathered to my people. Bury me with my fathers in the cave in the field of Ephron the Hittite, ^{30} the cave in the field of Machpelah, near Mamre in Canaan, which Abraham bought along with the field as a burial place from Ephron the Hittite. ^{31} There Abraham and his wife Sarah were buried, there Isaac and his wife Rebekah were buried, and there I buried Leah. ^{32} The field and the cave in it were bought from the Hittites.^{k} "

^{33} When Jacob had finished giving instructions to his sons, he drew his feet up into the bed, breathed his last and was gathered to his people.

50 Joseph threw himself on his father and wept over him and kissed him. ^{2} Then Joseph directed the physicians in his service to embalm his father Israel. So the physicians embalmed him, ^{3} taking a full forty days, for that was the time required for embalming. And the Egyptians mourned for him seventy days.

^{4} When the days of mourning had passed, Joseph said to Pharaoh's court, "If I have found favor in your eyes, speak to Pharaoh for me. Tell him, ^{5} 'My father made me swear an oath and said, "I am about to die; bury me in the tomb I dug for myself in the land of Canaan." Now let me go up and bury my father; then I will return.' "

^{6} Pharaoh said, "Go up and bury your father, as he made you swear to do."

^{7} So Joseph went up to bury his father. All Pharaoh's officials accompanied him — the dignitaries of his court and all the dignitaries of Egypt— ^{8} besides all the members of

---

^{a} 14 Or strong ^{b} 14 Or the campfires; or the saddlebags ^{c} 16 Dan here means he provides justice. ^{d} 19 Gad sounds like the Hebrew for attack and also for band of raiders. ^{e} 21 Or free; / he utters beautiful words ^{f} 22 Or Joseph is a wild colt, / a wild colt near a spring, / a wild donkey on a terraced hill ^{g} 23,24 Or archers will attack . . . will shoot . . . will remain . . . will stay ^{h} 25 Hebrew Shaddai ^{i} 26 Or of my progenitors, / as great as ^{j} 26 Or of the one separated from ^{k} 32 Or the descendants of Heth

---

49:20 | Jacob's statement that **Asher's food will be rich** was fulfilled; the tribe's fertile land was good for growing olive trees (Deut. 33:24, 25). That oil was even more valuable in antiquity than it is today.
50:1–11 | Jacob's last request was to be buried in Canaan (47:29,

30). When Joseph shared this with Pharaoh, Egypt's monarch gave Jacob a funeral worthy of a king out of respect for Joseph, sending **all Pharaoh's officials** and **chariots and horsemen** in the funeral procession.

Joseph's household and his brothers and those belonging to his father's household. Only their children and their flocks and herds were left in Goshen. [9]Chariots and horsemen[a] also went up with him. It was a very large company.

[10]When they reached the threshing floor of Atad, near the Jordan, they lamented loudly and bitterly; and there Joseph observed a seven-day period of mourning for his father. [11]When the Canaanites who lived there saw the mourning at the threshing floor of Atad, they said, "The Egyptians are holding a solemn ceremony of mourning." That is why that place near the Jordan is called Abel Mizraim.[b]

[12]So Jacob's sons did as he had commanded them: [13]They carried him to the land of Canaan and buried him in the cave in the field of Machpelah, near Mamre, which Abraham had bought along with the field as a burial place from Ephron the Hittite. [14]After burying his father, Joseph returned to Egypt, together with his brothers and all the others who had gone with him to bury his father.

Joseph Reassures His Brothers

[15]When Joseph's brothers saw that their father was dead, they said, "What if Joseph holds a grudge against us and pays us back for all the wrongs we did to him?" [16]So they sent word to Joseph, saying, "Your father left these instructions before he died: [17]'This is what you are to say to Joseph: I ask you to forgive your brothers the sins and the wrongs they committed in treating you

so badly.' Now please forgive the sins of the servants of the God of your father." When their message came to him, Joseph wept.

[18]His brothers then came and threw themselves down before him. "We are your slaves," they said.

[19]But Joseph said to them, "Don't be afraid. Am I in the place of God? [20]You intended to harm me, but God intended it for good to accomplish what is now being done, the saving of many lives. [21]So then, don't be afraid. I will provide for you and your children." And he reassured them and spoke kindly to them.

The Death of Joseph

[22]Joseph stayed in Egypt, along with all his father's family. He lived a hundred and ten years [23]and saw the third generation of Ephraim's children. Also the children of Makir son of Manasseh were placed at birth on Joseph's knees.[c]

[24]Then Joseph said to his brothers, "I am about to die. But God will surely come to your aid and take you up out of this land to the land he promised on oath to Abraham, Isaac and Jacob." [25]And Joseph made the Israelites swear an oath and said, "God will surely come to your aid, and then you must carry my bones up from this place."

[26]So Joseph died at the age of a hundred and ten. And after they embalmed him, he was placed in a coffin in Egypt.

---

[a] 9 Or charioteers   [b] 11 Abel Mizraim means mourning of the Egyptians.
[c] 23 That is, were counted as his

50:19–21 | Joseph's brothers had nothing to fear—even at Jacob's passing—because their brother, recognizing the sovereignty of God (**God intended it for good**), would not take God's role as judge (**Am I in the place of God?**). This is a lesson for every person who has ever been wronged.
50:22–25 | Even though **Joseph** lived most of his life as an Egyptian, he did not want his remains to stay in Egypt. He belonged with

the Hebrew people in the Land of Promise (**carry my bones up from this place**). In his dying moments, Joseph offered a testimony of faith in God's promise (13:14–15).
50:26 | At Joseph's death, he was placed in a **coffin** in the fashion of the Egyptians. Moses had Joseph's remains carried from Egypt during the Exodus (Ex. 13:19); Joshua buried them at Shechem (Josh. 24:32).

EXODUS

DO NOT BE AFRAID.

Stand firm and you will see

the deliverance the LORD

will bring you today.

EXODUS 14:13

EXODUS

BOOK INTRODUCTION

The Book of Exodus is Israel's birth certificate, detailing the first moments of a nation. Their temporary sojourn in Egypt to escape a famine in Canaan turned out to be 400 years of enslavement and suffering for Abraham's descendants—400 years that were part of God's plan (Gen. 15:13). Egypt had once been a fruitful place to live under the protection of Jacob's son Joseph, who was Pharaoh's second-in-command. But when a new ruler with no allegiance to Joseph or his family grew wary of the increasing number of Hebrews in the nation, he made the descendants of Abraham his slaves to quash any potential rebellion (1:8–11).

At a time when many Hebrew baby boys were being killed in Egypt, one male infant survived, thanks to his mother's smart thinking. That child, Moses, was raised in the royal courts of Egypt, where he received the finest education available in the world. He would no doubt have risen in the royal hierarchy of Egypt as his forefather Joseph had done—except that he could not escape the mistreatment of his Hebrew relatives as they suffered under the yoke of slavery: "By faith Moses, when he had grown up, refused to be known as the son of Pharaoh's daughter. He chose to be mistreated along with the people of God" (Heb. 11:24, 25).

After murdering an Egyptian who was beating a Hebrew, Moses was forced to flee the land of his birth and take refuge for 40 years in the land of Midian, where he had a surprise encounter with the God of his forefathers (3:1–15). The Lord commissioned Moses to return to Egypt and to demand the release of his relatives from slavery. After first resisting the call, Moses ultimately returned to Egypt to begin the next chapter in God's redemption and recovery project.

Moses and his brother, Aaron, confronted the ruling monarch who was oppressing Israel, bringing God's demand that Pharaoh release the slaves. Rejecting the request out of hand, the king revealed a hard, cynical heart: "Who is the LORD . . . ? I do not know the LORD and I will not let Israel go" (5:2). What followed was a dramatic series of judgments, in the form of plagues, which would teach Pharaoh and his people who the Lord is, showing them the extent of His power over nature, over Pharaoh, and over all the gods of Egypt.

Once they were free, it fell to Moses to instruct his people concerning their God and to begin the journey toward their new home.

To view Dr. Jeremiah's video introduction to Exodus, go to www.JeremiahStudyBible.com/Exodus/Intro

What It Says | *Rescue, Journey, and Revelation*

The Book of Exodus falls into three natural divisions: the deliverance of Israel from Egypt (1:1—13:16), the journey to Mount Sinai (13:17—18:27), and the revelation of the Law (19:1—40:38). Israel had arrived in Egypt as a family of 70 with not only personal belongings but also a solemn promise from the Lord to Abraham. They came out as a nation of perhaps more than two million with Yahweh's own instruction on true worship and holy living, a land to inhabit, and a leader to guide them to the Promised Land. What is more, they had the Lord Himself to love, teach, and lead them.

In Genesis, God revealed Himself as Elohim, the transcendent God of creation (Gen. 1:1), as El Shaddai, the majestic God of protection (Gen. 17:1), and as Yahweh, God in personal relationship with His people (Gen. 2:4). In Exodus, God revealed Himself much more fully (6:2, 3)—as God with a name by which Israel will know Him: Yahweh, the One who says "I AM WHO I AM" (3:14). This revelation of God to His people was the first step in forming a theocracy—a God-King who would rule over His people.

What It Means | *Pictures of the Lamb to Come*

The Exodus from Egypt is the foundational act in the history of Judaism, replayed centuries later as Jewish sojourners from all over the world streamed into the Middle East to reestablish the Jewish state in the twentieth century. The Exodus also foreshadows the redemption from slavery to sin through Christ. The Passover lamb in Egypt became "the Lamb of God, who takes away the sin of the world!" (John 1:29; 1 Cor. 5:7). Other major themes in the book include:

The Law: The Lord's gracious gift of the Law begins with the celebrated Ten Commandments (20:1–17) and is followed by statutes that together form the covenant between God the King and Israel His subjects. Israel was established with the Lord as its Sovereign and with law being the balance scale that tilted toward blessing or punishment, depending on whether it was obeyed or rejected.

Worship: After the Law was received at Sinai, the people needed a means of continual relationship with God through worship. God would dwell in the midst of His people in the tabernacle—a portable temple and dwelling place for His presence—to be carried with the Israelites as they traveled to the Promised Land (25—31).

The Tabernacle: The tabernacle, its furnishings, and its use prefigure the time when God would come to dwell ("tabernacle") among His people in human form in Jesus Christ (John 1:14). Every major form and function of the tabernacle, and later the temple in Jerusalem, pointed to the coming of Israel's Messiah and His roles of Prophet, Priest, King, Sage, and Suffering Servant (35—40).

What It Means for You | *Checking the Cloud*

As the Israelite journey into that vast wilderness began, the Lord reassured His people with the cloud of His presence, showing them where and when to camp (13:21). But that meant they had to watch the cloud every day. When it stayed, they stayed. When it moved, they loaded up and followed.

Knowing that God goes ahead of us removes much of the fear from the dramatic changes in life. In such seasons, however, it is easy for us to become preoccupied with our situation and take our eyes off "the cloud." Our all-knowing Leader has promised to guide our steps and give us the wisdom we need (Prov. 16:9; James 1:5–7), but we must first set aside our anxiety, quiet our hearts, and set our minds on seeking His will and His timing (Phil. 4:6, 7). That way, when the cloud moves, we will be ready.

To access Dr. Jeremiah's digital library on Exodus, go to
www.JeremiahStudyBible.com/Exodus/library

THE WILDERNESS WANDERINGS

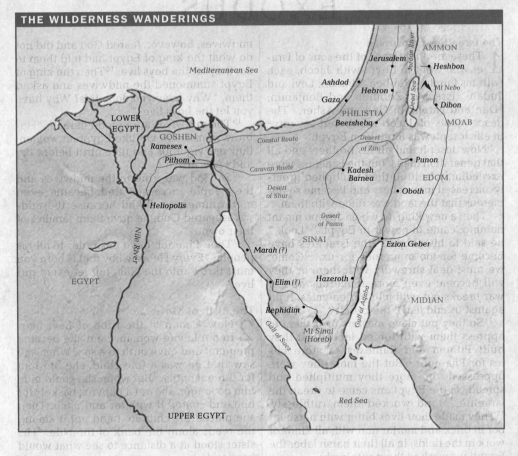

The Israelites Oppressed

1 These are the names of the sons of Israel who went to Egypt with Jacob, each with his family: [2]Reuben, Simeon, Levi and Judah; [3]Issachar, Zebulun and Benjamin; [4]Dan and Naphtali; Gad and Asher. [5]The descendants of Jacob numbered seventy[a] in all; Joseph was already in Egypt.

[6]Now Joseph and all his brothers and all that generation died, [7]but the Israelites were exceedingly fruitful; they multiplied greatly, increased in numbers and became so numerous that the land was filled with them.

[8]Then a new king, to whom Joseph meant nothing, came to power in Egypt. [9]"Look," he said to his people, "the Israelites have become far too numerous for us. [10]Come, we must deal shrewdly with them or they will become even more numerous and, if war breaks out, will join our enemies, fight against us and leave the country."

[11]So they put slave masters over them to oppress them with forced labor, and they built Pithom and Rameses as store cities for Pharaoh. [12]But the more they were oppressed, the more they multiplied and spread; so the Egyptians came to dread the Israelites [13]and worked them ruthlessly. [14]They made their lives bitter with harsh labor in brick and mortar and with all kinds of work in the fields; in all their harsh labor the Egyptians worked them ruthlessly.

[15]The king of Egypt said to the Hebrew midwives, whose names were Shiphrah and Puah, [16]"When you are helping the Hebrew women during childbirth on the delivery stool, if you see that the baby is a boy, kill him; but if it is a girl, let her live." [17]The midwives, however, feared God and did not do what the king of Egypt had told them to do; they let the boys live. [18]Then the king of Egypt summoned the midwives and asked them, "Why have you done this? Why have you let the boys live?"

[19]The midwives answered Pharaoh, "Hebrew women are not like Egyptian women; they are vigorous and give birth before the midwives arrive."

[20]So God was kind to the midwives and the people increased and became even more numerous. [21]And because the midwives feared God, he gave them families of their own.

[22]Then Pharaoh gave this order to all his people: "Every Hebrew boy that is born you must throw into the Nile, but let every girl live."

The Birth of Moses

2 Now a man of the tribe of Levi married a Levite woman, [2]and she became pregnant and gave birth to a son. When she saw that he was a fine child, she hid him for three months. [3]But when she could hide him no longer, she got a papyrus basket[b] for him and coated it with tar and pitch. Then she placed the child in it and put it among the reeds along the bank of the Nile. [4]His sister stood at a distance to see what would happen to him.

[5]Then Pharaoh's daughter went down to the Nile to bathe, and her attendants were walking along the riverbank. She saw the

---

[a] 5 Masoretic Text (see also Gen. 46:27); Dead Sea Scrolls and Septuagint (see also Acts 7:14 and note at Gen. 46:27) *seventy-five*   [b] 3 The Hebrew can also mean *ark*, as in Gen. 6:14.

1:1–6 | The opening verses of Exodus provide context for Moses' life: **the sons of Israel** were **in Egypt** because the family of **Jacob** had been led there by the providence of God (Gen. 37–50).

1:7 | About 600,000 men of fighting age left Egypt (12:37). Factoring in older men, women, children, and the infirm, the total number of Hebrew people was probably about 2.5 million by this time. **The Israelites** had **multiplied greatly** in the 370 years or so since Jacob and his family of 70 had arrived in the land.

1:8–11 | Nearly 400 years of history are summarized in these verses, representing a line of pharaohs, not just one. The **new king, to whom Joseph meant nothing . . . in Egypt**, was likely one of the pharaohs during the Hyksos takeover (beginning c. 1720 BC). Even after Egypt's native rulers returned to power (c. 1550 BC), the Hebrew people were no longer honored in memory of Joseph.

1:11–22 | Three unsuccessful methods were used to limit the exploding population growth of the Hebrews: (1) working the Hebrews to exhaustion, and even to death; (2) commanding **the Hebrew midwives** to commit infanticide; (3) selective annihilation, with baby boys being cast into the River Nile while baby girls were spared.

1:15–22 | **Shiphrah and Puah**—possibly leaders of the guild of midwives—refused to commit infanticide, fearing the real King more than their earthly ruler (Luke 12:4, 5; Acts 5:29). These women were likely Egyptians who came to faith in Yahweh and were included in Israel (**he gave them families of their own**).

2:1–10 | **Fine** means "favored." For Moses' parents to hide **him for three months** until he was in safe hands was an act of faith lauded in Hebrews 11:23.

2:3 | The Hebrew word for **papyrus basket** can also mean "ark," which alludes to Noah. As in his day, the ark (or floating basket) served here as a vessel of divine deliverance. The basket was placed securely **among the reeds along the bank of the Nile** where the current was slight, so it would not wash out to sea. It was also placed where the women of the palace would see it when they came to dip in the waters of the Nile as part of their religious ritual.

2:5–10 | The **Pharaoh's daughter** (probably Hatshepsut) knew immediately that this child was a Hebrew because he was circumcised (Gen. 17:9–14). Her adoption of Moses as her son along with the selection of Moses' own **mother** as his wet **nurse** are two ways that God preserved the infant. **Moses** in Egyptian most likely means "born," but the Hebrew equivalent means "to be drawn out." God would later use him to draw His people **out of the water** (14).

The Moses Mystique • 2:11, 12

Moses murdered a man (2:11, 12), argued with God about helping to rescue the Hebrew slaves (3—4), lost his temper with the Israelites when they sinned (32:19), and was prohibited from entering the Promised Land because he disobeyed God in the wilderness (Num. 20:6–12). But Moses died full of grace and favor with God because he got up more times than he fell down (Deut. 34).

When we consider heroes revered by Judaism, Islam, and Christianity, no individual other than Jesus shines more brightly than Moses. The NT mentions Moses—the deliverer of the Hebrews from Egypt—more times than any other OT figure, and he is the most prominent prophetic figure in the Muslim Koran. What is it about Moses that makes him a hero to so many?

The juxtaposition of failure and faith is probably at the heart of Moses' mystique. We can identify with Moses' failure as a young man guilty of manslaughter. We can also identify with his fears and doubts when God called him to be the deliverer of his Hebrew countrymen. But beyond identifying with Moses' humanity, we revere his faith—he was brave, faithful, outspoken, compassionate, and loyal. And he kept his eye on the eternal prize. Moses was all we know we are and all we know we want to be. He was a failure, but he was also faithful. And God honored his faithfulness instead of rejecting him for his failure.

If you have failed, do not give up. God used Moses, and He wants to use you.

---

basket among the reeds and sent her female slave to get it. ⁶She opened it and saw the baby. He was crying, and she felt sorry for him. "This is one of the Hebrew babies," she said.

⁷Then his sister asked Pharaoh's daughter, "Shall I go and get one of the Hebrew women to nurse the baby for you?"

⁸"Yes, go," she answered. So the girl went and got the baby's mother. ⁹Pharaoh's daughter said to her, "Take this baby and nurse him for me, and I will pay you." So the woman took the baby and nursed him. ¹⁰When the child grew older, she took him to Pharaoh's daughter and he became her son. She named him Moses,ᵃ saying, "I drew him out of the water."

Moses Flees to Midian

¹¹One day, after Moses had grown up, he went out to where his own people were and watched them at their hard labor. He saw an Egyptian beating a Hebrew, one of his own people. ¹²Looking this way and that and seeing no one, he killed the Egyptian and hid him in the sand. ¹³The next day he went out and saw two Hebrews fighting. He asked the one in the wrong, "Why are you hitting your fellow Hebrew?"

¹⁴The man said, "Who made you ruler and judge over us? Are you thinking of killing me as you killed the Egyptian?" Then Moses was afraid and thought, "What I did must have become known."

¹⁵When Pharaoh heard of this, he tried to kill Moses, but Moses fled from Pharaoh and went to live in Midian, where he sat down by a well. ¹⁶Now a priest of Midian had seven daughters, and they came to draw water and fill the troughs to water their father's flock. ¹⁷Some shepherds came along and drove them away, but Moses got up and came to their rescue and watered their flock.

¹⁸When the girls returned to Reuel their father, he asked them, "Why have you returned so early today?"

¹⁹They answered, "An Egyptian rescued us from the shepherds. He even drew water for us and watered the flock."

²⁰"And where is he?" Reuel asked his daughters. "Why did you leave him? Invite him to have something to eat."

²¹Moses agreed to stay with the man, who gave his daughter Zipporah to Moses in marriage. ²²Zipporah gave birth to a son, and Moses named him Gershom,ᵇ saying, "I have become a foreigner in a foreign land."

²³During that long period, the king of Egypt died. The Israelites groaned in their slavery and cried out, and their cry for help

---

ᵃ 10 Moses sounds like the Hebrew for draw out.   ᵇ 22 Gershom sounds like the Hebrew for a foreigner there.

2:11–15 | This Pharaoh (likely Thutmose III) had been raised with Moses. The murder of a slave master by a privileged member of the royal family would not have warranted a death sentence, so Pharaoh's desire **to kill Moses** was about removing him as a potential successor to the throne. The land of **Midian** is in present-day Saudi Arabia, the land east of the Gulf of Aqaba.

2:16–22 | Moses spent most of his first 40 years in Pharaoh's palace, learning to be a student, a statesman, and a soldier. He then spent the next 40 years of his life in the desert, taking care of his father-in-law's sheep. From prince to shepherd was a demotion, yet

Moses learned the qualities he would need as Israel's future emancipator, including humility and patience. In the desert, God teaches people who He really is. It is only when we are totally yielded to Him that our giftings become graces.

2:21 | Much like Jacob with Laban (see Gen. 29 and notes), the runaway Moses was not financially able to enter into an independent marriage, so he became Jethro's adopted son. He then became his son-in-law upon marrying **Zipporah** (4:18). After 40 years of service, the flocks he tended would still belong to Jethro (3:1).

because of their slavery went up to God. [24]God heard their groaning and he remembered his covenant with Abraham, with Isaac and with Jacob. [25]So God looked on the Israelites and was concerned about them.

Moses and the Burning Bush

3 Now Moses was tending the flock of Jethro his father-in-law, the priest of Midian, and he led the flock to the far side of the wilderness and came to Horeb, the mountain of God. [2]There the angel of the LORD appeared to him in flames of fire from within a bush. Moses saw that though the bush was on fire it did not burn up. [3]So Moses thought, "I will go over and see this strange sight—why the bush does not burn up."

[4]When the LORD saw that he had gone over to look, God called to him from within the bush, "Moses! Moses!"

And Moses said, "Here I am."

[5]"Do not come any closer," God said. "Take off your sandals, for the place where you are standing is holy ground." [6]Then he said, "I am the God of your father,[a] the God of Abraham, the God of Isaac and the God of Jacob." At this, Moses hid his face, because he was afraid to look at God.

[7]The LORD said, "I have indeed seen the misery of my people in Egypt. I have heard them crying out because of their slave drivers, and I am concerned about their suffering. [8]So I have come down to rescue them from the hand of the Egyptians and to bring them up out of that land into a good and spacious land, a land flowing with milk and honey—the home of the Canaanites, Hittites, Amorites, Perizzites, Hivites and Jebusites. [9]And now the cry of the Israelites has reached me, and I have seen the way the Egyptians are oppressing them. [10]So now, go. I am sending you to Pharaoh to bring my people the Israelites out of Egypt."

[11]But Moses said to God, "Who am I that I should go to Pharaoh and bring the Israelites out of Egypt?"

[12]And God said, "I will be with you. And this will be the sign to you that it is I who have sent you: When you have brought the people out of Egypt, you[b] will worship God on this mountain."

[13]Moses said to God, "Suppose I go to the Israelites and say to them, 'The God of your fathers has sent me to you,' and they ask me, 'What is his name?' Then what shall I tell them?"

[14]God said to Moses, "I AM WHO I AM.[c] This is what you are to say to the Israelites: 'I am has sent me to you.'"

[15]God also said to Moses, "Say to the Israelites, 'The LORD,[d] the God of your fathers—the God of Abraham, the God of Isaac and the God of Jacob—has sent me to you.'

"This is my name forever,
    the name you shall call me
    from generation to generation.

[16]"Go, assemble the elders of Israel and say to them, 'The LORD, the God of your fathers—the God of Abraham, Isaac and Jacob—appeared to me and said: I have watched over you and have seen what has been done to you in Egypt. [17]And I have promised to bring you up out of your misery in Egypt into the land of the Canaanites, Hittites, Amorites, Perizzites, Hivites

<hr>

[a] 6 Masoretic Text; Samaritan Pentateuch (see Acts 7:32) *fathers*   [b] 12 The Hebrew is plural.   [c] 14 Or *I WILL BE WHAT I WILL BE*   [d] 15 The Hebrew for LORD sounds like and may be related to the Hebrew for *I AM* in verse 14.

<hr>

2:23–25 | **Heard** and **remembered** indicate that the Lord's time had come: He would return Moses to Egypt and send Him as the answer to the people's prayers (3:7–10). God always has someone ready when His people cry out to Him in their need. More importantly, Yahweh revealed Himself as the One who hears, remembers, sees (**looked on**), and knows (**concerned about**) His children.

3:1–9 | This appearance of **the angel of the LORD** is the first instance of direct revelation to Moses. After 80 years, Moses was now ready to fulfill the Lord's calling. No other leader in biblical times had such a lengthy training period. Times of preparation are never wasted; God knows that, properly prepared, His servants can do more in 40 years than they could do in 120 unprepared.

3:1–6 | Mount **Horeb** (Sinai) is not only where Moses received his divine commission at the burning **bush**, but it is also the place where Yahweh would give Israel His gracious gift of the Law (19–20).

3:5–10 | For these divine moments, the area near the bush was the Lord's house because of the Lord's presence (**holy ground**). The resulting command to **take off your sandals** reflects this. In Afro-Asian culture, people do not wear shoes inside a home. **I have come**

down to rescue them were words for Israel, but they also point to the future incarnation of Jesus (John 1:14).

3:11, 12 | Moses typified human response when God calls someone to do what seems beyond them (**Who am I . . . ?**), yet the success of any divine mission is never dependent on human abilities. The Lord's words—**I will be with you**—were intended to focus Moses on the true Source of his future success.

3:13–15 | When God said, **I AM WHO I AM**, He declared His eternal, unchanging, uncreated self-existence. The identification of the Lord as **the God of your fathers** is enormously important. Moses and the Hebrew people needed to know that this was no "new god"—the Deliverer of Israel ever is and ever will be (6:2, 3; 34:5–7; Gen. 12:1; John 8:58).

3:15–22 | The Lord's plan was to rescue His children from bondage so they could worship Him and be established as His chosen people. Because the Hebrews were slaves with no resources, the **articles of silver and gold** were necessary to finance the building of a tabernacle. God also equipped Moses with the words for the **elders of Israel** as well as Pharaoh (**the king of Egypt**). God provides all that is needed to serve Him (2 Pet. 1:3).

Teaching Points   The Excuses • 3:11-15

1. *Moses hid behind incorrect theology.* We are often burdened by what God asks us to do because we think He wants us to be the deliverer. In response to Moses' first excuse, God essentially said: "Moses, I do not want to help you do this through Me; I want to do it through you!"

2. *Moses hid behind insufficient knowledge.* God countered Moses' second excuse with this truth: It is not what you know that counts; it is who you know.

3. *Moses hid behind an inferior self-concept.* But the Lord confirmed: it is not who you are that matters; it is who I am.

4. *Moses hid behind inadequate ability (speech).* When God calls us to a task, He will enable us to do that which He commands. The Lord's response to this excuse? It's not your ability that counts, but Mine.

5. *Moses hid behind incomplete trust (send someone else).* God always has a man or woman ready when He needs one.

We should not be too hard on Moses, for we have been in that same position.

• We say, "I can't do this for You." And God says, "Then let *Me* do it through *you.*"
• We say, "I don't know enough." God says, "You know Me. That's enough."
• We say, "No one will respect me." God says, "That's not important. What is important is that they respect Me."
• We say, "I don't have the ability." God says, "My grace is sufficient; it's My ability that counts."
• We say, "God, send someone else." And God says, "This is not a request."

When we feel inadequate to do the things God desires, we can be encouraged by the ways God met Moses' needs, questions, and fears. We never know what God might do through us.

and Jebusites—a land flowing with milk and honey.'

18 "The elders of Israel will listen to you. Then you and the elders are to go to the king of Egypt and say to him, 'The LORD, the God of the Hebrews, has met with us. Let us take a three-day journey into the wilderness to offer sacrifices to the LORD our God.' 19But I know that the king of Egypt will not let you go unless a mighty hand compels him. 20So I will stretch out my hand and strike the Egyptians with all the wonders that I will perform among them. After that, he will let you go.

21 "And I will make the Egyptians favorably disposed toward this people, so that when you leave you will not go empty-handed. 22Every woman is to ask her neighbor and any woman living in her house for articles of silver and gold and for clothing, which you will put on your sons and daughters. And so you will plunder the Egyptians."

Signs for Moses

4 Moses answered, "What if they do not believe me or listen to me and say, 'The LORD did not appear to you'?"

2Then the LORD said to him, "What is that in your hand?"

"A staff," he replied.

3The LORD said, "Throw it on the ground." Moses threw it on the ground and it became a snake, and he ran from it. 4Then the LORD said to him, "Reach out your hand and take it by the tail." So Moses reached out and took hold of the snake and it turned back into a staff in his hand. 5"This," said the LORD, "is so that they may believe that the LORD, the God of their fathers—the God of Abraham, the God of Isaac and the God of Jacob—has appeared to you."

6Then the LORD said, "Put your hand inside your cloak." So Moses put his hand into his cloak, and when he took it out, the skin was leprous[a]—it had become as white as snow.

7"Now put it back into your cloak," he said. So Moses put his hand back into his cloak, and when he took it out, it was restored, like the rest of his flesh.

8Then the LORD said, "If they do not believe you or pay attention to the first sign, they may believe the second. 9But if they do not believe these two signs or listen to you, take some water from the Nile and pour it on the dry ground. The water you take from the river will become blood on the ground."

a 6 The Hebrew word for *leprous* was used for various diseases affecting the skin.

4:2 | Moses' **staff** was probably nothing more than a long walking stick. Although it had no supernatural properties, the Lord would include it in the many miracles pertaining to the delivery of His people.

4:3-9 | The last of the **signs** God gave Moses foreshadowed the first plague: **water . . . will become blood**.

For Reflection — Confirming God's Will • 4:18–26

When it comes to the will of God:

Commitment comes first, confirmation second. Our human nature wants to reverse this order. But God's people have to step out into the water before they see the Lord part it. Waiting for the confirmation means you will never make the commitment. God confirms it after we say yes. It was not until Moses said, "I will go" and actually started the journey that God showed him, "This is the way; walk in it" (Isa. 30:21).

Obedience first, new instruction second. With the will of God, new instruction is given only after old instruction is obeyed. The Lord was intent on killing Moses if his son was not circumcised according to the demands of the covenant. If God were to speak to us in this regard, He might say, "If you walk in the light I've given you, I will give you more." One of the reasons we do not have more divine guidance is that we have not followed the instruction God has already given us in His Word.

Routine requirements first, great responsibilities second. Within God's will, great responsibilities do not cancel out routine requirements. Moses should have been more concerned about his son's circumcision, a basic requirement of the Abrahamic covenant. Perhaps it seemed too mundane and insignificant to him compared to something as big as the emancipation of the Israelites from Egypt. But with God, both routines and responsibilities are essential.

As you commit your heart to trust and obey God in the small things, He will move you from confusion to confidence concerning His will for your life!

[10] Moses said to the LORD, "Pardon your servant, Lord. I have never been eloquent, neither in the past nor since you have spoken to your servant. I am slow of speech and tongue."

[11] The LORD said to him, "Who gave human beings their mouths? Who makes them deaf or mute? Who gives them sight or makes them blind? Is it not I, the LORD? [12] Now go; I will help you speak and will teach you what to say."

[13] But Moses said, "Pardon your servant, Lord. Please send someone else."

[14] Then the LORD's anger burned against Moses and he said, "What about your brother, Aaron the Levite? I know he can speak well. He is already on his way to meet you, and he will be glad to see you. [15] You shall speak to him and put words in his mouth; I will help both of you speak and will teach you what to do. [16] He will speak to the people for you, and it will be as if he were your mouth and as if you were God to him. [17] But take this staff in your hand so you can perform the signs with it."

Moses Returns to Egypt

[18] Then Moses went back to Jethro his father-in-law and said to him, "Let me return to my own people in Egypt to see if any of them are still alive."

Jethro said, "Go, and I wish you well."

[19] Now the LORD had said to Moses in Midian, "Go back to Egypt, for all those who wanted to kill you are dead." [20] So Moses took his wife and sons, put them on a donkey and started back to Egypt. And he took the staff of God in his hand.

[21] The LORD said to Moses, "When you return to Egypt, see that you perform before Pharaoh all the wonders I have given you the power to do. But I will harden his heart so that he will not let the people go. [22] Then say to Pharaoh, 'This is what the LORD says: Israel is my firstborn son, [23] and I told you, "Let my son go, so he may worship me." But you refused to let him go; so I will kill your firstborn son.' "

[24] At a lodging place on the way, the LORD met Moses[a] and was about to kill him. [25] But Zipporah took a flint knife, cut off her son's foreskin and touched Moses' feet with it.[b] "Surely you are a bridegroom of blood to me," she said. [26] So the LORD let him alone. (At that time she said "bridegroom of blood," referring to circumcision.)

---

[a] 24 Hebrew *him*   [b] 25 The meaning of the Hebrew for this clause is uncertain.

4:10 | Moses' excuse to God was similar to the prophet Jeremiah's (Jer. 1:6): **I have never been eloquent.** Because Moses was trained in the elocution of the Egyptians (Acts 7:22), he did not need an oratory refresher course; he needed to trust the Lord. If God could speak from a burning bush, He could speak through Moses in front of Pharaoh.
4:11–17 | Moses' reticence led to the Lord's anger and a change of direction. Moses would continue to be the leader of the people, but Aaron would be Moses' **mouth**. In this section we learn the biblical meaning of the word *prophet:* a spokesman (**he will speak to the people for you**) for the Lord (6:28—7:6).

4:18–23 | After 40 years, Moses was still bound to **his father-in-law** and adoptive father, **Jethro** (3:1). So for Moses to **go back to Egypt** and freely accomplish God's purpose, he needed to be released from his familial responsibilities. Jethro's kindness was seen in the words **Go, and I wish you well.** This was also a confirmation of the Lord's will to Moses.
4:20 | Moses' shepherding stick became the **staff of God.** When we serve God, whatever is ours may become His to use for His glory.
4:22, 23 | For the Lord to call **Israel . . . my firstborn son** (Jer. 31:9; Hosea 11:1) would have offended Pharaoh (likely Amenhotep II), who viewed himself as the favored son of the Egyptian gods.

²⁷The LORD said to Aaron, "Go into the wilderness to meet Moses." So he met Moses at the mountain of God and kissed him. ²⁸Then Moses told Aaron everything the LORD had sent him to say, and also about all the signs he had commanded him to perform.

²⁹Moses and Aaron brought together all the elders of the Israelites, ³⁰and Aaron told them everything the LORD had said to Moses. He also performed the signs before the people, ³¹and they believed. And when they heard that the LORD was concerned about them and had seen their misery, they bowed down and worshiped.

Bricks Without Straw

5 Afterward Moses and Aaron went to Pharaoh and said, "This is what the LORD, the God of Israel, says: 'Let my people go, so that they may hold a festival to me in the wilderness.'"

²Pharaoh said, "Who is the LORD, that I should obey him and let Israel go? I do not know the LORD and I will not let Israel go."

³Then they said, "The God of the Hebrews has met with us. Now let us take a three-day journey into the wilderness to offer sacrifices to the LORD our God, or he may strike us with plagues or with the sword."

⁴But the king of Egypt said, "Moses and Aaron, why are you taking the people away from their labor? Get back to your work!" ⁵Then Pharaoh said, "Look, the people of the land are now numerous, and you are stopping them from working."

⁶That same day Pharaoh gave this order to the slave drivers and overseers in charge of the people: ⁷"You are no longer to supply the people with straw for making bricks; let them go and gather their own straw. ⁸But require them to make the same number of bricks as before; don't reduce the quota. They are lazy; that is why they are crying out, 'Let us go and sacrifice to our God.'

⁹Make the work harder for the people so that they keep working and pay no attention to lies."

¹⁰Then the slave drivers and the overseers went out and said to the people, "This is what Pharaoh says: 'I will not give you any more straw. ¹¹Go and get your own straw wherever you can find it, but your work will not be reduced at all.'" ¹²So the people scattered all over Egypt to gather stubble to use for straw. ¹³The slave drivers kept pressing them, saying, "Complete the work required of you for each day, just as when you had straw." ¹⁴And Pharaoh's slave drivers beat the Israelite overseers they had appointed, demanding, "Why haven't you met your quota of bricks yesterday or today, as before?"

¹⁵Then the Israelite overseers went and appealed to Pharaoh: "Why have you treated your servants this way? ¹⁶Your servants are given no straw, yet we are told, 'Make bricks!' Your servants are being beaten, but the fault is with your own people."

¹⁷Pharaoh said, "Lazy, that's what you are—lazy! That is why you keep saying, 'Let us go and sacrifice to the LORD.' ¹⁸Now get to work. You will not be given any straw, yet you must produce your full quota of bricks."

¹⁹The Israelite overseers realized they were in trouble when they were told, "You are not to reduce the number of bricks required of you for each day." ²⁰When they left Pharaoh, they found Moses and Aaron waiting to meet them, ²¹and they said, "May the LORD look on you and judge you! You have made us obnoxious to Pharaoh and his officials and have put a sword in their hand to kill us."

God Promises Deliverance

²²Moses returned to the LORD and said, "Why, Lord, why have you brought trouble on this people? Is this why you sent me?

4:24–26 | When a person says yes to God's service, the Lord will often begin to reveal neglected areas of obedience. Moses' failure to circumcise his second son Eliezer according to the Lord's covenant with Abraham forced a disgusted **Zipporah** to save her husband's life by circumcising the baby herself.
4:27–31 | During their reunion **at the mountain of God** (Mount Horeb), the same location where the Lord first called Moses to deliver Israel from Egypt, the biological brothers became brothers in the ministry.
5:1–5 | Pharaoh's response to Moses and Aaron's entreaty (**Who is the LORD, that I should obey him?**) should be read as contempt, not ignorance. In the ruler's disregard for the Lord's commands, the Lord would **strike . . . with plagues** and death (**the sword**) on the Egyptians so that there would be no doubt regarding the answer.
5:6–14 | Pharaoh's decree meant the Hebrews had to **gather their own straw** to make brick during the evening and early-morning hours and then still put in a full day's work—oppressive conditions.

In ancient times, straw was added to the clay-and-mud mixture to give greater strength and cohesion to the sun-dried brick. Because straw was not readily available, the Hebrew slaves had **to gather stubble**, small pieces of straw, and their production of bricks slowed while their **quota** remained.
5:15–21 | The **Israelite overseers** were their own work foremen. **Obnoxious to Pharaoh** literally means, "You have made us a stench in his presence." Moses was accused of making the people's situation worse.
5:22—6:9 | Four times here, the Lord reminds Moses of His sovereignty, identity, and promises: **I am the LORD.** This is the same Yahweh of the patriarchs—the same Lord of the Abrahamic covenant—but in the events of the Exodus, His name would be **fully known.** With successive **I will** statements, God promised to: (1) rescue and redeem His people from Egypt; (2) make them His people; (3) be their God; and (4) bring them to the Promised Land.

For Reflection · Why? • 5:22

This three-letter word expresses our deepest questions.

- Moses prayed, "Why, Lord, why have you brought trouble on this people? Is this why you sent me?" (5:22).
- Joshua cried, "Alas, Sovereign Lord, why did you ever bring this people across the Jordan to deliver us into the hands of the Amorites to destroy us?" (Josh. 7:7).
- Gideon cried, "Why has all this happened to us?" (Judg. 6:13).
- Nehemiah asked, "Why is the house of God neglected?" (Neh. 13:11).
- Job cried, "Why did I not perish at birth?" (Job 3:11).
- A psalmist wrote, "Why, Lord, do you stand far off? Why do you hide yourself in times of trouble?" (Ps. 10:1).
- David prayed, "Why are you so far from saving me, so far from my cries of anguish?" (Ps. 22:1).
- Asaph asked, "O God, why have you rejected us forever?" (Ps. 74:1).
- Isaiah asked, "Why, Lord, do you make us wander from your ways?" (Isa. 63:17).
- Jeremiah mourned, "Why have you afflicted us so that we cannot be healed?" (Jer. 14:19).
- And Jesus cried out on the cross, saying, "My God, my God, why have you forsaken me?" (Matt. 27:46).

Anne Graham Lotz put it well: "If we don't figure out how to process the whys of life, we'll end up cynical, resulting in a catastrophic loss of faith. If we don't answer correctly, we'll grow bitter, resulting in a darkened personality. In Christ are hidden all the mysteries of wisdom and knowledge. We believe He has the capacity of working all things for the good to those who love Him. We know He works all things according to the ultimate purposes of His counsel. We consider 'all is right that seems most wrong if it be His sweet will.'"

Not a sparrow falls to the ground without His seeing it. Not a problem arises without His knowing it. Even when we do not understand, we can trust. And when we trust, joy breaks through the clouds like rays of sunshine. We can also reassure ourselves that someday we will understand it all better.

---

²³Ever since I went to Pharaoh to speak in your name, he has brought trouble on this people, and you have not rescued your people at all."

6 Then the Lord said to Moses, "Now you will see what I will do to Pharaoh: Because of my mighty hand he will let them go; because of my mighty hand he will drive them out of his country."

²God also said to Moses, "I am the Lord. ³I appeared to Abraham, to Isaac and to Jacob as God Almighty,ᵃ but by my name the Lordᵇ I did not make myself fully known to them. ⁴I also established my covenant with them to give them the land of Canaan, where they resided as foreigners. ⁵Moreover, I have heard the groaning of the Israelites, whom the Egyptians are enslaving, and I have remembered my covenant.

⁶"Therefore, say to the Israelites: 'I am the Lord, and I will bring you out from under the yoke of the Egyptians. I will free you from being slaves to them, and I will redeem you with an outstretched arm and with mighty acts of judgment. ⁷I will take you as my own people, and I will be your God. Then you will know that I am the Lord your God, who brought you out from under the yoke of the Egyptians. ⁸And I will bring you to the land

I swore with uplifted hand to give to Abraham, to Isaac and to Jacob. I will give it to you as a possession. I am the Lord.'"

⁹Moses reported this to the Israelites, but they did not listen to him because of their discouragement and harsh labor.

¹⁰Then the Lord said to Moses, ¹¹"Go, tell Pharaoh king of Egypt to let the Israelites go out of his country."

¹²But Moses said to the Lord, "If the Israelites will not listen to me, why would Pharaoh listen to me, since I speak with faltering lipsᶜ?"

Family Record of Moses and Aaron

¹³Now the Lord spoke to Moses and Aaron about the Israelites and Pharaoh king of Egypt, and he commanded them to bring the Israelites out of Egypt.

¹⁴These were the heads of their familiesᵈ:

The sons of Reuben the firstborn son of Israel were Hanok and Pallu, Hezron and Karmi. These were the clans of Reuben.

ᵃ 3 Hebrew El-Shaddai   ᵇ 3 See note at 3:15.   ᶜ 12 Hebrew I am uncircumcised of lips; also in verse 30   ᵈ 14 The Hebrew for families here and in verse 25 refers to units larger than clans.

6:14–27 | The genealogy presented here (which is probably a shortened one) follows that of Genesis 46:8–15 and lists **Aaron** **and Moses** in the line of **Levi**. Levi's descendants were especially important, because from them came the true priests in Israel.

¹⁵The sons of Simeon were Jemuel, Jamin, Ohad, Jakin, Zohar and Shaul the son of a Canaanite woman. These were the clans of Simeon.

¹⁶These were the names of the sons of Levi according to their records: Gershon, Kohath and Merari. Levi lived 137 years.

¹⁷The sons of Gershon, by clans, were Libni and Shimei.

¹⁸The sons of Kohath were Amram, Izhar, Hebron and Uzziel. Kohath lived 133 years.

¹⁹The sons of Merari were Mahli and Mushi.

These were the clans of Levi according to their records.

²⁰Amram married his father's sister Jochebed, who bore him Aaron and Moses. Amram lived 137 years.

²¹The sons of Izhar were Korah, Nepheg and Zikri.

²²The sons of Uzziel were Mishael, Elzaphan and Sithri.

²³Aaron married Elisheba, daughter of Amminadab and sister of Nahshon, and she bore him Nadab and Abihu, Eleazar and Ithamar.

²⁴The sons of Korah were Assir, Elkanah and Abiasaph. These were the Korahite clans.

²⁵Eleazar son of Aaron married one of the daughters of Putiel, and she bore him Phinehas.

These were the heads of the Levite families, clan by clan.

²⁶It was this Aaron and Moses to whom the LORD said, "Bring the Israelites out of Egypt by their divisions." ²⁷They were the ones who spoke to Pharaoh king of Egypt about bringing the Israelites out of Egypt—this same Moses and Aaron.

Aaron to Speak for Moses

²⁸Now when the LORD spoke to Moses in Egypt, ²⁹he said to him, "I am the LORD. Tell Pharaoh king of Egypt everything I tell you."

³⁰But Moses said to the LORD, "Since I speak with faltering lips, why would Pharaoh listen to me?"

7 Then the LORD said to Moses, "See, I have made you like God to Pharaoh, and your brother Aaron will be your prophet. ²You are to say everything I command you, and your brother Aaron is to tell Pharaoh to let the Israelites go out of his country. ³But I will harden Pharaoh's heart, and though I multiply my signs and wonders in Egypt, ⁴he will not listen to you. Then I will lay my hand on Egypt and with mighty acts of judgment I will bring out my divisions, my people the Israelites. ⁵And the Egyptians will know that I am the LORD when I stretch out my hand against Egypt and bring the Israelites out of it."

⁶Moses and Aaron did just as the LORD commanded them. ⁷Moses was eighty years old and Aaron eighty-three when they spoke to Pharaoh.

Aaron's Staff Becomes a Snake

⁸The LORD said to Moses and Aaron, ⁹"When Pharaoh says to you, 'Perform a miracle,' then say to Aaron, 'Take your staff and throw it down before Pharaoh,' and it will become a snake."

¹⁰So Moses and Aaron went to Pharaoh and did just as the LORD commanded. Aaron threw his staff down in front of Pharaoh and his officials, and it became a snake. ¹¹Pharaoh then summoned wise men and sorcerers, and the Egyptian magicians also did the same things by their secret arts: ¹²Each one threw down his staff and it became a snake. But Aaron's staff swallowed up their staffs. ¹³Yet Pharaoh's heart became hard and he would not listen to them, just as the LORD had said.

The Plague of Blood

¹⁴Then the LORD said to Moses, "Pharaoh's heart is unyielding; he refuses to let the people go. ¹⁵Go to Pharaoh in the morning as he goes out to the river. Confront him on the bank of the Nile, and take in your hand the staff that was changed into a snake. ¹⁶Then say to him, 'The LORD, the God of the Hebrews, has sent me to say to you: Let my people go, so that they may worship me in the wilderness. But until now you have not listened. ¹⁷This is what the LORD says: By this you will know that I am the LORD: With the staff that is in my hand I will strike

7:1–7 | Like God to Pharaoh means simply that Moses would represent the One who sent him to Pharaoh, not that Moses would be God to him.

7:8–13 | This is the first time we read of the Lord speaking to both brothers. When the Lord defied the gods of Egypt and the power of Pharaoh, it was a message to Egypt's ruler and to the Hebrew people that the Egyptian gods were incomparable to Him.

7:14—12:30 | A pharaoh's principal governing function was to ensure stability. The 10 plagues—which would each include natural phenomena out of natural order—would destroy the emotional and economic stability of Egypt and devastate the land, ultimately pointing to Israel's God as the true Sustainer and Lord of creation. The plagues were marked by: (1) exquisite timing—they were subject to the word of Yahweh and the acts of Moses; (2) overwhelming intensity; and (3) occasional selectivity (the Egyptians would experience trouble while Israel would not).

Was the water turned to real blood? • 7:19

This plague polluted all the waters of Egypt, including the Nile's tributaries, rivers, ponds, and pools. Some commentators claim the blood was not human sera but an annual inundation of the Nile River in which tons of red soil particles coupled with innumerable amounts of algae pollute the waters with a resultant red tide—a red tide that is both repulsive and deadly. But two facts point to this as an act of God alone: (1) The plague began and ended as soon as Aaron stretched out his hand in obedience to the Lord. (2) Even the water that had already been drawn ("in vessels") turned to blood. So it was that Yahweh revealed His power and demonstrated the impotence of the supposed god, Nile.

the water of the Nile, and it will be changed into blood. [18]The fish in the Nile will die, and the river will stink; the Egyptians will not be able to drink its water.' "

[19]The LORD said to Moses, "Tell Aaron, 'Take your staff and stretch out your hand over the waters of Egypt—over the streams and canals, over the ponds and all the reservoirs—and they will turn to blood.' Blood will be everywhere in Egypt, even in vessels[a] of wood and stone."

[20]Moses and Aaron did just as the LORD had commanded. He raised his staff in the presence of Pharaoh and his officials and struck the water of the Nile, and all the water was changed into blood. [21]The fish in the Nile died, and the river smelled so bad that the Egyptians could not drink its water. Blood was everywhere in Egypt.

[22]But the Egyptian magicians did the same things by their secret arts, and Pharaoh's heart became hard; he would not listen to Moses and Aaron, just as the LORD had said. [23]Instead, he turned and went into his palace, and did not take even this to heart. [24]And all the Egyptians dug along the Nile to get drinking water, because they could not drink the water of the river.

The Plague of Frogs

[25]Seven days passed after the LORD struck the Nile. 8[b] [1]Then the LORD said to Moses, "Go to Pharaoh and say to him, 'This is what the LORD says: Let my people go, so

that they may worship me. [2]If you refuse to let them go, I will send a plague of frogs on your whole country. [3]The Nile will teem with frogs. They will come up into your palace and your bedroom and onto your bed, into the houses of your officials and on your people, and into your ovens and kneading troughs. [4]The frogs will come up on you and your people and all your officials.' "

[5]Then the LORD said to Moses, "Tell Aaron, 'Stretch out your hand with your staff over the streams and canals and ponds, and make frogs come up on the land of Egypt.' "

[6]So Aaron stretched out his hand over the waters of Egypt, and the frogs came up and covered the land. [7]But the magicians did the same things by their secret arts; they also made frogs come up on the land of Egypt.

[8]Pharaoh summoned Moses and Aaron and said, "Pray to the LORD to take the frogs away from me and my people, and I will let your people go to offer sacrifices to the LORD."

[9]Moses said to Pharaoh, "I leave to you the honor of setting the time for me to pray for you and your officials and your people that you and your houses may be rid of the frogs, except for those that remain in the Nile."

[10]"Tomorrow," Pharaoh said.

Moses replied, "It will be as you say, so that you may know there is no one like the LORD our God. [11]The frogs will leave you and your houses, your officials and your people; they will remain only in the Nile."

[12]After Moses and Aaron left Pharaoh, Moses cried out to the LORD about the frogs he had brought on Pharaoh. [13]And the LORD did what Moses asked. The frogs died in the houses, in the courtyards and in the fields. [14]They were piled into heaps, and the land reeked of them. [15]But when Pharaoh saw that there was relief, he hardened his heart and would not listen to Moses and Aaron, just as the LORD had said.

The Plague of Gnats

[16]Then the LORD said to Moses, "Tell Aaron, 'Stretch out your staff and strike the dust of the ground,' and throughout the land of

---

[a] 19 Or even on their idols   [b] In Hebrew texts 8:1-4 is numbered 7:26-29, and 8:5-32 is numbered 8:1-28.

7:15-25 | Pharaoh would go to **the bank of the Nile** (8:20) not to drink but to pay homage, for the Nile River was worshiped as a god. So it is no coincidence that the first plague on the Egyptians was directed against the false god of the Nile.
8:1-7 | An Egyptian frog goddess, Heqet, was associated with childbirth and connected with the Nile. But now **frogs** became symbols of death. Although Pharaoh's magicians were able to duplicate

the first three signs, it is significant that in no case were they able to stop or prevent the plagues.
8:8-15 | Here, a common pattern begins: the pestilence comes; the pain is felt; Pharaoh seeks **relief** and promises to **let** God's **people go**; the plague is dismissed; and Pharaoh resists God's grace once again (see 3:19; 4:21; 5:2; 7:3, 13, 14).

Egypt the dust will become gnats." [17]They did this, and when Aaron stretched out his hand with the staff and struck the dust of the ground, gnats came on people and animals. All the dust throughout the land of Egypt became gnats. [18]But when the magicians tried to produce gnats by their secret arts, they could not.

Since the gnats were on people and animals everywhere, [19]the magicians said to Pharaoh, "This is the finger of God." But Pharaoh's heart was hard and he would not listen, just as the LORD had said.

The Plague of Flies

[20]Then the LORD said to Moses, "Get up early in the morning and confront Pharaoh as he goes to the river and say to him, 'This is what the LORD says: Let my people go, so that they may worship me. [21]If you do not let my people go, I will send swarms of flies on you and your officials, on your people and into your houses. The houses of the Egyptians will be full of flies; even the ground will be covered with them.

[22]"'But on that day I will deal differently with the land of Goshen, where my people live; no swarms of flies will be there, so that you will know that I, the LORD, am in this land. [23]I will make a distinction[a] between my people and your people. This sign will occur tomorrow.'"

[24]And the LORD did this. Dense swarms of flies poured into Pharaoh's palace and into the houses of his officials; throughout Egypt the land was ruined by the flies.

[25]Then Pharaoh summoned Moses and Aaron and said, "Go, sacrifice to your God here in the land."

[26]But Moses said, "That would not be right. The sacrifices we offer the LORD our God would be detestable to the Egyptians. And if we offer sacrifices that are detestable in their eyes, will they not stone us? [27]We must take a three-day journey into the wilderness to offer sacrifices to the LORD our God, as he commands us."

Historically Speaking   **So Many Gods • 8:8**

The Egyptians were an exceedingly polytheistic people, with as many as 80 different gods. They had gods everywhere. In fact, almost every living creature we can name was in some sense a god: lion, ox, ram, wolf, dog, cat, vulture, falcon, hippopotamus, crocodile, cobra, dolphin, different kinds of fish and trees, small animals including the frog, and even some insects such as the locust and the scarab beetle. It is a mistake to say that each plague was an attack on an Egyptian deity (e.g., the Egyptians did not worship lice/gnats or flies). However, all the plagues did attack the role of Pharaoh, who was considered a son of the gods.

[28]Pharaoh said, "I will let you go to offer sacrifices to the LORD your God in the wilderness, but you must not go very far. Now pray for me."

[29]Moses answered, "As soon as I leave you, I will pray to the LORD, and tomorrow the flies will leave Pharaoh and his officials and his people. Only let Pharaoh be sure that he does not act deceitfully again by not letting the people go to offer sacrifices to the LORD."

[30]Then Moses left Pharaoh and prayed to the LORD, [31]and the LORD did what Moses asked. The flies left Pharaoh and his officials and his people; not a fly remained. [32]But this time also Pharaoh hardened his heart and would not let the people go.

The Plague on Livestock

9 Then the LORD said to Moses, "Go to Pharaoh and say to him, 'This is what the LORD, the God of the Hebrews, says: "Let my people go, so that they may worship me." [2]If you refuse to let them go and continue to hold them back, [3]the hand of the LORD will bring a terrible plague on your livestock in the field—on your horses, donkeys and camels and on your cattle, sheep

[a] 23 Septuagint and Vulgate; Hebrew will put a deliverance

8:16–19 | For **dust** to be turned to **gnats** or lice (the Hebrew word describes either one) was particularly awful for the scrupulously clean Egyptians. With this plague, Pharaoh's magicians could no longer duplicate the Lord's signs, and finally they acknowledged what Pharaoh would not: **This is the finger of God**.
8:21–24 | **Flies** were common pests in arid Egypt, but now they were an affliction of unprecedented magnitude (Ps. 78:45)—except where God's people lived (**Goshen**). This is the first plague in which God singled out the Egyptians and protected the Hebrew people (see note on 7:14).
8:25–28 | Moses rejected the ploy to let the Hebrew people make sacrifices **here in the land** (Egypt), citing that Israel's sacrificial sheep **would be detestable to the Egyptians**. Because the Egyptians

considered these animals unclean, such sacrifices came with the risk of the Hebrews being stoned (Gen. 43:32; 46:34). Pharaoh's offer of a short trek **into the wilderness** was similarly refused. God will not accept compromise when He has issued a command.
9:3–7 | Agriculture was, and remains, Egypt's premier economic resource, with wealth measured in cattle and other **livestock** that the Egyptians possessed for work and for war. When God struck their animals with **a terrible plague**, He was beginning to single out the Egyptians and destroy their economy. Earlier plagues caused irritation and pain but not the widespread loss of personal property. As in the case of the flies (8:22), all of Israel's livestock was spared.
9:3 | **Cattle** were often worshiped in Egypt as representatives of various deities.

Tough Questions

Did God cause Pharaoh to sin? • 9:12; 10:1, 2

The Bible never says God instills evil in people's hearts. Some try to refute this by pointing out the verses that say "the LORD hardened Pharaoh's heart." However, these statements speak about the nature of Pharaoh's heart, not about God overriding someone's free will.

That Pharaoh hardened his own heart numerous times in this account reveals that he was not a good man whom the Lord caused to do evil; he was an evil man whom the Lord would not allow to do good (Rom. 9:14–23). Some hearts are like clay—the sun's heat will harden them. Others are like wax—the sun will cause them to melt. The sun is not at fault for hardening one substance and melting the other; the result depends on the nature of the material. Pharaoh's heart was the sort that would harden when exposed to God's light.

As the sovereign Ruler over all, God will bring rebellious individuals and nations to the doom their wickedness inevitably demands (Ezek. 14:17). Yet in His mercy, just as He did here, He first gives them full opportunity to turn from their ways and obey Him.

and goats. ⁴But the LORD will make a distinction between the livestock of Israel and that of Egypt, so that no animal belonging to the Israelites will die.'"

⁵The LORD set a time and said, "Tomorrow the LORD will do this in the land." ⁶And the next day the LORD did it: All the livestock of the Egyptians died, but not one animal belonging to the Israelites died. ⁷Pharaoh investigated and found that not even one of the animals of the Israelites had died. Yet his heart was unyielding and he would not let the people go.

The Plague of Boils

⁸Then the LORD said to Moses and Aaron, "Take handfuls of soot from a furnace and have Moses toss it into the air in the presence of Pharaoh. ⁹It will become fine dust over the whole land of Egypt, and festering boils will break out on people and animals throughout the land."

¹⁰So they took soot from a furnace and stood before Pharaoh. Moses tossed it into the air, and festering boils broke out on people and animals. ¹¹The magicians could not stand before Moses because of the boils that were on them and on all the Egyptians. ¹²But the LORD hardened Pharaoh's heart and he would not listen to Moses and Aaron, just as the LORD had said to Moses.

The Plague of Hail

¹³Then the LORD said to Moses, "Get up early in the morning, confront Pharaoh and say to him, 'This is what the LORD, the God of the Hebrews, says: Let my people go, so that they may worship me, ¹⁴or this time I will send the full force of my plagues against you and against your officials and your people, so you may know that there is no one like me in all the earth. ¹⁵For by now I could have stretched out my hand and struck you and your people with a plague that would have wiped you off the earth. ¹⁶But I have raised you up*a* for this very purpose, that I might show you my power and that my name might be proclaimed in all the earth. ¹⁷You still set yourself against my people and will not let them go. ¹⁸Therefore, at this time tomorrow I will send the worst hailstorm that has ever fallen on Egypt, from the day it was founded till now. ¹⁹Give an order now to bring your livestock and everything you have in the field to a place of shelter, because the hail will fall on every person and animal that has not been brought in and is still out in the field, and they will die.'"

²⁰Those officials of Pharaoh who feared the word of the LORD hurried to bring their slaves and their livestock inside. ²¹But those who ignored the word of the LORD left their slaves and livestock in the field.

²²Then the LORD said to Moses, "Stretch out your hand toward the sky so that hail will fall all over Egypt—on people and animals and on everything growing in the fields of Egypt." ²³When Moses stretched out his

---

a 16 Or have spared you

9:8–11 | The **boils** came with no warning on **people and animals**. This is similar to the affliction suffered by Job (Job 2:7).
9:12 | After this sixth plague, **the LORD hardened Pharaoh's heart**. Previously, either Pharaoh had hardened his own heart (8:15, 32) or his heart grew hard (7:22; 8:19; 9:7). This wording means only that Pharaoh was given over to his own will, just as the Lord had spoken to Moses (4:21; 7:3). God is never one to coerce someone to do evil.
9:13–35 | The **worst hailstorm that has ever fallen on Egypt** would destroy agriculture as well as harm people and livestock. That

these plagues were sent **against** Pharaoh personally means they were intended to have a deep impact.
9:16 | Even with his hardened heart, Pharaoh served the Lord's greater **purpose**. Everyone accomplishes God's will in the end. Those who conform to His will accomplish it willingly; those who do not conform accomplish it inadvertently, as an unwitting tool in His hands.
9:19–25 | After six plagues, some of Pharaoh's servants believed the message about the coming hail and had their **slaves** and livestock brought **inside** for cover. Others, however, **ignored the word of the LORD**—and the consequences were devastating.

staff toward the sky, the LORD sent thunder and hail, and lightning flashed down to the ground. So the LORD rained hail on the land of Egypt; ²⁴ hail fell and lightning flashed back and forth. It was the worst storm in all the land of Egypt since it had become a nation. ²⁵ Throughout Egypt hail struck everything in the fields—both people and animals; it beat down everything growing in the fields and stripped every tree. ²⁶ The only place it did not hail was the land of Goshen, where the Israelites were.

²⁷ Then Pharaoh summoned Moses and Aaron. "This time I have sinned," he said to them. "The LORD is in the right, and I and my people are in the wrong. ²⁸ Pray to the LORD, for we have had enough thunder and hail. I will let you go; you don't have to stay any longer."

²⁹ Moses replied, "When I have gone out of the city, I will spread out my hands in prayer to the LORD. The thunder will stop and there will be no more hail, so you may know that the earth is the LORD's. ³⁰ But I know that you and your officials still do not fear the LORD God."

³¹ (The flax and barley were destroyed, since the barley had headed and the flax was in bloom. ³² The wheat and spelt, however, were not destroyed, because they ripen later.)

³³ Then Moses left Pharaoh and went out of the city. He spread out his hands toward the LORD; the thunder and hail stopped, and the rain no longer poured down on the land. ³⁴ When Pharaoh saw that the rain and hail and thunder had stopped, he sinned again: He and his officials hardened their hearts. ³⁵ So Pharaoh's heart was hard and he would not let the Israelites go, just as the LORD had said through Moses.

The Plague of Locusts

10 Then the LORD said to Moses, "Go to Pharaoh, for I have hardened his heart and the hearts of his officials so that I may perform these signs of mine among them ² that you may tell your children and grandchildren how I dealt harshly with the Egyptians and how I performed my signs among them, and that you may know that I am the LORD."

³ So Moses and Aaron went to Pharaoh and said to him, "This is what the LORD, the God of the Hebrews, says: 'How long will you refuse to humble yourself before me? Let my people go, so that they may worship me. ⁴ If you refuse to let them go, I will bring locusts into your country tomorrow. ⁵ They will cover the face of the ground so that it cannot be seen. They will devour what little you have left after the hail, including every tree that is growing in your fields. ⁶ They will fill your houses and those of all your officials and all the Egyptians—something neither your parents nor your ancestors have ever seen from the day they settled in this land till now.' " Then Moses turned and left Pharaoh.

⁷ Pharaoh's officials said to him, "How long will this man be a snare to us? Let the people go, so that they may worship the LORD their God. Do you not yet realize that Egypt is ruined?"

⁸ Then Moses and Aaron were brought back to Pharaoh. "Go, worship the LORD your God," he said. "But tell me who will be going."

⁹ Moses answered, "We will go with our young and our old, with our sons and our daughters, and with our flocks and herds, because we are to celebrate a festival to the LORD."

¹⁰ Pharaoh said, "The LORD be with you— if I let you go, along with your women and children! Clearly you are bent on evil.^a ¹¹ No! Have only the men go and worship the LORD, since that's what you have been asking for." Then Moses and Aaron were driven out of Pharaoh's presence.

¹² And the LORD said to Moses, "Stretch out your hand over Egypt so that locusts swarm over the land and devour everything growing in the fields, everything left by the hail." ¹³ So Moses stretched out his staff over Egypt, and the LORD made an east wind blow across the land all that day and all that night. By morning the wind had brought the locusts; ¹⁴ they invaded all Egypt and settled down in every area of the country in great numbers. Never before had there been such a plague of locusts, nor will there ever be

---

^a 10 Or Be careful, trouble is in store for you!

9:27-30 | Pharaoh's confession was accurate but insincere, as he admitted only what he thought he must in order to relieve the pressure. He had not yet come to **fear the LORD God.**

10:3-6 | The hail-locust combo was an unprecedented and utterly catastrophic attack on Egypt's famed agriculture, with the **locusts** devouring the **little** that was **left after the hail** damage.

Yahweh resists the proud (Ps. 18:27; 31:23; 101:5; 119:21; Prov. 6:12-19; 16:5; 1 Pet. 5:5); therefore, He denounced the pride of Pharaoh.

10:8-11 | Pharaoh was shrewd enough to understand that if **only the men** went to worship, they surely would return to their families and he would not risk losing his slave labor.

Teaching Points

The Purpose of Plagues • 11:1-10

- To demonstrate God's power publicly (8:19; 11:9; Rom. 9:17)
- To denounce the sin of Pharaoh and his people (9:27, 34)
- To defy the gods of Egypt (12:12)
- To distinguish Israel from all other nations (11:7)
- To develop the faith of His own people (Deut. 4:33, 34)

God was not just judging the people of Egypt; He was preparing the people of Israel to leave that land and have the courage and the power to go out and be His people, freed from dependence on another nation.

again. ¹⁵They covered all the ground until it was black. They devoured all that was left after the hail—everything growing in the fields and the fruit on the trees. Nothing green remained on tree or plant in all the land of Egypt.

¹⁶Pharaoh quickly summoned Moses and Aaron and said, "I have sinned against the LORD your God and against you. ¹⁷Now forgive my sin once more and pray to the LORD your God to take this deadly plague away from me."

¹⁸Moses then left Pharaoh and prayed to the LORD. ¹⁹And the LORD changed the wind to a very strong west wind, which caught up the locusts and carried them into the Red Sea.ᵃ Not a locust was left anywhere in Egypt. ²⁰But the LORD hardened Pharaoh's heart, and he would not let the Israelites go.

The Plague of Darkness

²¹Then the LORD said to Moses, "Stretch out your hand toward the sky so that darkness spreads over Egypt—darkness that can be felt." ²²So Moses stretched out his hand toward the sky, and total darkness covered all Egypt for three days. ²³No one could see anyone else or move about for three days. Yet all the Israelites had light in the places where they lived.

²⁴Then Pharaoh summoned Moses and said, "Go, worship the LORD. Even your women and children may go with you; only leave your flocks and herds behind."

²⁵But Moses said, "You must allow us to have sacrifices and burnt offerings to present to the LORD our God. ²⁶Our livestock too must go with us; not a hoof is to be left behind. We have to use some of them in worshiping the LORD our God, and until we get there we will not know what we are to use to worship the LORD."

²⁷But the LORD hardened Pharaoh's heart, and he was not willing to let them go. ²⁸Pharaoh said to Moses, "Get out of my sight! Make sure you do not appear before me again! The day you see my face you will die."

²⁹"Just as you say," Moses replied. "I will never appear before you again."

The Plague on the Firstborn

11 Now the LORD had said to Moses, "I will bring one more plague on Pharaoh and on Egypt. After that, he will let you go from here, and when he does, he will drive you out completely. ²Tell the people that men and women alike are to ask their neighbors for articles of silver and gold." ³(The LORD made the Egyptians favorably disposed toward the people, and Moses himself was highly regarded in Egypt by Pharaoh's officials and by the people.)

⁴So Moses said, "This is what the LORD says: 'About midnight I will go throughout Egypt. ⁵Every firstborn son in Egypt will die, from the firstborn son of Pharaoh, who sits on the throne, to the firstborn son of the female slave, who is at her hand mill, and all the firstborn of the cattle as well. ⁶There will be loud wailing throughout Egypt—worse than there has ever been or ever will be again. ⁷But among the Israelites not a dog will bark at any person or animal.' Then you will know that the LORD makes a distinction between Egypt and Israel. ⁸All these

ᵃ 19 Or the Sea of Reeds

10:16–20 | Despite Pharaoh's insincere confession, the Lord in His mercy blew the locusts away with **a very strong west wind**. Still, Pharaoh would not let the people of Israel go.

10:21–23 | The ninth plague brought a darkness so thick it could **be felt**. Even a normal eclipse was often considered an omen, but this one lasted **for three days**. The people of Israel, in the land of Goshen, were again exempt from this plague.

10:24–26 | Pharaoh proposed yet another compromise: allowing the **women and children** to **go** with the adults into the wilderness if they left the **flocks and herds behind**. Most likely Pharaoh planned to confiscate all of Israel's livestock to replace what his people had lost through the earlier plagues; then he would send his army

to retrieve the Hebrew people. Moses and Aaron rejected the offer because they knew they must obey God completely, and that meant leaving **not a hoof . . . behind**.

11:2, 3 | This is the second announcement that the Lord would make **the Egyptians favorably disposed toward the people** of Israel (3:21, 22). Moses even found favor (**was highly regarded**) among **Pharaoh's officials**.

11:5 | In Egypt, **the firstborn son of Pharaoh** was the presumed heir to the throne; thus, the death of Pharaoh's son would be both a personal and a national tragedy. Thutmose IV was likely the one who gained the throne as a result of the death of his older brother.

Picture This

The Symbolism of Passover • 12:6–14

God commanded the Hebrew people to keep the Passover Festival as "a lasting ordinance," and Jewish people still do. They commemorate this night when God miraculously protected their ancestors from the plague of death; most, however, do not understand that the Passover ultimately points to the redemption brought by Christ.

The roasted flesh of the lamb was to be accompanied with bitter herbs, reminding the children of Israel of their bitter bondage in Egypt. Their haste in eating, combined with their clothing, represented their readiness to travel. So did the bread made without yeast.

Some Bible teachers claim that yeast (or leaven) was prohibited because it was a symbol of sin. If that were the case, then leavening would have always been prohibited. The reason for commanding unleavened bread is given in 12:34–39, with the description of the actual Passover. The first Passover meal was prepared with urgency because the people had no idea when they were to leave. Properly prepared, raised bread is a time-consuming task. Unleavened bread could be made much more quickly.

The Passover lamb itself prefigured Jesus (John 1:29, 36; 1 Cor. 5:7)—the perfect and sinless Lamb of God (2 Cor. 5:21; 1 Pet. 2:21, 22; 1 John 3:5). The sacrificial blood, painted on the doorframes of the houses, not only saved the Hebrew people from the curse of death but also pointed to the shed blood of Jesus and His defeat over eternal death (Rom. 6:9).

officials of yours will come to me, bowing down before me and saying, 'Go, you and all the people who follow you!' After that I will leave." Then Moses, hot with anger, left Pharaoh.

⁹The LORD had said to Moses, "Pharaoh will refuse to listen to you—so that my wonders may be multiplied in Egypt." ¹⁰Moses and Aaron performed all these wonders before Pharaoh, but the LORD hardened Pharaoh's heart, and he would not let the Israelites go out of his country.

The Passover and the Festival of Unleavened Bread

12 The LORD said to Moses and Aaron in Egypt, ²"This month is to be for you the first month, the first month of your year. ³Tell the whole community of Israel that on the tenth day of this month each man is to take a lamb*a* for his family, one for each household. ⁴If any household is too small for a whole lamb, they must share one with their nearest neighbor, having taken into account the number of people there are. You are to determine the amount of lamb needed in accordance with what each person will eat. ⁵The animals you choose must be year-old males without defect, and you may take them from the sheep or the goats. ⁶Take care of them until the fourteenth day

of the month, when all the members of the community of Israel must slaughter them at twilight. ⁷Then they are to take some of the blood and put it on the sides and tops of the doorframes of the houses where they eat the lambs. ⁸That same night they are to eat the meat roasted over the fire, along with bitter herbs, and bread made without yeast. ⁹Do not eat the meat raw or boiled in water, but roast it over a fire—with the head, legs and internal organs. ¹⁰Do not leave any of it till morning; if some is left till morning, you must burn it. ¹¹This is how you are to eat it: with your cloak tucked into your belt, your sandals on your feet and your staff in your hand. Eat it in haste; it is the LORD's Passover.

¹²"On that same night I will pass through Egypt and strike down every firstborn of both people and animals, and I will bring judgment on all the gods of Egypt. I am the LORD. ¹³The blood will be a sign for you on the houses where you are, and when I see the blood, I will pass over you. No destructive plague will touch you when I strike Egypt.

¹⁴"This is a day you are to commemorate; for the generations to come you shall celebrate it as a festival to the LORD—a lasting ordinance. ¹⁵For seven days you are to eat

---

a 3 The Hebrew word can mean *lamb* or *kid*; also in verse 4.

12:2 | Yahweh began the calendar of Israel with the Exodus. **The first month of** the Hebrew **year**, called Abib (or Aviv), literally means "the ear" month because at this time—about April for us—the ears of grain have developed.

12:3–6 | God's specific instructions about the Passover **lamb** (a goat's kid was also acceptable) would ensure that in every way, it was fit for sacred sacrifice.

12:12, 13 | The one who would **pass through** the land of **Egypt** was not some angel of death as is commonly assumed. According to the

repeated pronoun **I**, it was the Lord Himself, bringing **judgment on all the gods of Egypt**.

12:14–28 | This lengthy section describes the ordinances for the Passover. The Passover is preceded by **the Festival of Unleavened Bread**, a period of **seven days** in which no leaven is permitted in meals or in the people's homes. To commemorate that first Passover, all succeeding Passovers were to be marked by the eating of unleavened bread (called *matzo* today).

bread made without yeast. On the first day remove the yeast from your houses, for whoever eats anything with yeast in it from the first day through the seventh must be cut off from Israel. ¹⁶On the first day hold a sacred assembly, and another one on the seventh day. Do no work at all on these days, except to prepare food for everyone to eat; that is all you may do.

¹⁷ "Celebrate the Festival of Unleavened Bread, because it was on this very day that I brought your divisions out of Egypt. Celebrate this day as a lasting ordinance for the generations to come. ¹⁸In the first month you are to eat bread made without yeast, from the evening of the fourteenth day until the evening of the twenty-first day. ¹⁹For seven days no yeast is to be found in your houses. And anyone, whether foreigner or native-born, who eats anything with yeast in it must be cut off from the community of Israel. ²⁰Eat nothing made with yeast. Wherever you live, you must eat unleavened bread."

²¹Then Moses summoned all the elders of Israel and said to them, "Go at once and select the animals for your families and slaughter the Passover lamb. ²²Take a bunch of hyssop, dip it into the blood in the basin and put some of the blood on the top and on both sides of the doorframe. None of you shall go out of the door of your house until morning. ²³When the LORD goes through the land to strike down the Egyptians, he will see the blood on the top and sides of the doorframe and will pass over that doorway, and he will not permit the destroyer to enter your houses and strike you down.

²⁴ "Obey these instructions as a lasting ordinance for you and your descendants. ²⁵When you enter the land that the LORD will give you as he promised, observe this ceremony. ²⁶And when your children ask you, 'What does this ceremony mean to you?' ²⁷then tell them, 'It is the Passover sacrifice to the LORD, who passed over the houses of the Israelites in Egypt and spared our homes when he struck down the Egyptians.' " Then the people bowed down and worshiped.

²⁸The Israelites did just what the LORD commanded Moses and Aaron.

²⁹At midnight the LORD struck down all the firstborn in Egypt, from the firstborn of Pharaoh, who sat on the throne, to the firstborn of the prisoner, who was in the dungeon, and the firstborn of all the livestock as well. ³⁰Pharaoh and all his officials and all the Egyptians got up during the night, and there was loud wailing in Egypt, for there was not a house without someone dead.

The Exodus

³¹During the night Pharaoh summoned Moses and Aaron and said, "Up! Leave my people, you and the Israelites! Go, worship the LORD as you have requested. ³²Take your flocks and herds, as you have said, and go. And also bless me."

³³The Egyptians urged the people to hurry and leave the country. "For otherwise," they said, "we will all die!" ³⁴So the people took their dough before the yeast was added, and carried it on their shoulders in kneading troughs wrapped in clothing. ³⁵The Israelites did as Moses instructed and asked the Egyptians for articles of silver and gold and for clothing. ³⁶The LORD had made the Egyptians favorably disposed toward the people, and they gave them what they asked for; so they plundered the Egyptians.

³⁷The Israelites journeyed from Rameses to Sukkoth. There were about six hundred thousand men on foot, besides women and children. ³⁸Many other people went up with them, and also large droves of livestock, both flocks and herds. ³⁹With the dough the Israelites had brought from Egypt, they baked loaves of unleavened bread. The dough was without yeast because they had been driven out of Egypt and did not have time to prepare food for themselves.

⁴⁰Now the length of time the Israelite people lived in Egypt^a was 430 years. ⁴¹At the end of the 430 years, to the very day, all the LORD's divisions left Egypt. ⁴²Because the

---

^a 40 Masoretic Text; Samaritan Pentateuch and Septuagint Egypt and Canaan

---

12:21–28 | The continued use of the word **strike** in this context indicates the Lord's severe and intentional judgment.
12:29–32 | Just as God had promised, a night of judgment came to pass on **Egypt** and Pharaoh (Ps. 105:26–45), with not one household spared. At this, Pharaoh relented, allowing all the people to **go** with their **flocks and herds**.
12:32 | Only the one with true authority may **bless** another. Moses represented the supreme authority: the Lord.
12:35 | In gaining **articles of silver and gold and . . . clothing** from the Egyptians, the Hebrew people, who had worked 400 years as slaves, were finally rewarded for their work. God's people left Egypt

with the wealth of the Egyptian people (3:21, 22; 11:2, 3; Ps. 105:37).
12:37, 38 | Numbers 1:45, 46 reports that the nation had more than 603,000 men 20 years and older mustered into the citizen army (see note on 1:7). **Many other people went up with** the Hebrew people, including some Egyptians and people from Kush. Those who journeyed with Israel must have had different motives, but some would come to faith in Yahweh and become part of the people of God (Num. 12:1).
12:40, 41 | For nearly four centuries, the people had prayed as they languished under slavery (Gen. 15:13; Acts 7:6; Gal. 3:17). Now they walked out with freedom as promised. Many believe the date of the Exodus to be 1446 BC.

LORD kept vigil that night to bring them out of Egypt, on this night all the Israelites are to keep vigil to honor the LORD for the generations to come.

Passover Restrictions

⁴³The LORD said to Moses and Aaron, "These are the regulations for the Passover meal:

"No foreigner may eat it. ⁴⁴Any slave you have bought may eat it after you have circumcised him, ⁴⁵but a temporary resident or a hired worker may not eat it.

⁴⁶"It must be eaten inside the house; take none of the meat outside the house. Do not break any of the bones. ⁴⁷The whole community of Israel must celebrate it.

⁴⁸"A foreigner residing among you who wants to celebrate the LORD's Passover must have all the males in his household circumcised; then he may take part like one born in the land. No uncircumcised male may eat it. ⁴⁹The same law applies both to the native-born and to the foreigner residing among you."

⁵⁰All the Israelites did just what the LORD had commanded Moses and Aaron. ⁵¹And on that very day the LORD brought the Israelites out of Egypt by their divisions.

Consecration of the Firstborn

13 The LORD said to Moses, ² "Consecrate to me every firstborn male. The first offspring of every womb among the Israelites belongs to me, whether human or animal."

³Then Moses said to the people, "Commemorate this day, the day you came out of Egypt, out of the land of slavery, because the LORD brought you out of it with a mighty hand. Eat nothing containing yeast. ⁴Today, in the month of Aviv, you are leaving. ⁵When the LORD brings you into the land of the Canaanites, Hittites, Amorites, Hivites and Jebusites—the land he swore to your ancestors to give you, a land flowing with milk and honey—you are to observe this ceremony in this month: ⁶For seven days eat

bread made without yeast and on the seventh day hold a festival to the LORD. ⁷Eat unleavened bread during those seven days; nothing with yeast in it is to be seen among you, nor shall any yeast be seen anywhere within your borders. ⁸On that day tell your son, 'I do this because of what the LORD did for me when I came out of Egypt.' ⁹This observance will be for you like a sign on your hand and a reminder on your forehead that this law of the LORD is to be on your lips. For the LORD brought you out of Egypt with his mighty hand. ¹⁰You must keep this ordinance at the appointed time year after year.

¹¹"After the LORD brings you into the land of the Canaanites and gives it to you, as he promised on oath to you and your ancestors, ¹²you are to give over to the LORD the first offspring of every womb. All the firstborn males of your livestock belong to the LORD. ¹³Redeem with a lamb every firstborn donkey, but if you do not redeem it, break its neck. Redeem every firstborn among your sons.

¹⁴"In days to come, when your son asks you, 'What does this mean?' say to him, 'With a mighty hand the LORD brought us out of Egypt, out of the land of slavery. ¹⁵When Pharaoh stubbornly refused to let us go, the LORD killed the firstborn of both people and animals in Egypt. This is why I sacrifice to the LORD the first male offspring of every womb and redeem each of my firstborn sons.' ¹⁶And it will be like a sign on your hand and a symbol on your forehead that the LORD brought us out of Egypt with his mighty hand."

Crossing the Sea

¹⁷When Pharaoh let the people go, God did not lead them on the road through the Philistine country, though that was shorter. For God said, "If they face war, they might change their minds and return to Egypt." ¹⁸So God led the people around by the desert road toward the Red Sea.ᵃ The Israelites went up out of Egypt ready for battle.

ᵃ 18 Or the Sea of Reeds

13:2 | **Consecrate** means to separate from sin and devote wholly to God. At Creation, God set apart the Sabbath (Gen. 2:3) for Himself and His own purposes. Here, the Lord consecrated **the first offspring . . . whether human or animal** (13:11-16). Later, the tabernacle would be designated as the set-apart place of God (25). **13:8, 9** | In each successive generation, Passover would be a teaching opportunity within the family (**I do this because of what the LORD did for me**), with all members considering themselves present with their ancestors at the Exodus (**when I came out of Egypt**).
13:11-16 | In remembrance of the Lord's preservation of Israel's first sons, **the firstborn** were to **belong to the LORD**, yet only

firstborn sons were to be redeemed. Most firstborn male animals were to be sacrificed, except those that were considered ritually unclean (such as donkeys). Later, the Jewish people tied phylacteries—prayer boxes—as **a sign** of this on the **hand** and a **symbol** on the **forehead**.
13:17, 18 | The **shorter** route to the Promised Land involved heading east around the curve of the Mediterranean Sea, then north **through . . . Philistine country**. The longer **desert** route that **God led** them on may have seemed strange, but the Hebrew people needed time to become an organized nation fit for war. God's way is always best, even when it takes His people through the wilderness.

¹⁹Moses took the bones of Joseph with him because Joseph had made the Israelites swear an oath. He had said, "God will surely come to your aid, and then you must carry my bones up with you from this place."[a]

²⁰After leaving Sukkoth they camped at Etham on the edge of the desert. ²¹By day the LORD went ahead of them in a pillar of cloud to guide them on their way and by night in a pillar of fire to give them light, so that they could travel by day or night. ²²Neither the pillar of cloud by day nor the pillar of fire by night left its place in front of the people.

14 Then the LORD said to Moses, ²"Tell the Israelites to turn back and encamp near Pi Hahiroth, between Migdol and the sea. They are to encamp by the sea, directly opposite Baal Zephon. ³Pharaoh will think, 'The Israelites are wandering around the land in confusion, hemmed in by the desert.' ⁴And I will harden Pharaoh's heart, and he will pursue them. But I will gain glory for myself through Pharaoh and all his army, and the Egyptians will know that I am the LORD." So the Israelites did this.

⁵When the king of Egypt was told that the people had fled, Pharaoh and his officials changed their minds about them and said, "What have we done? We have let the Israelites go and have lost their services!" ⁶So he had his chariot made ready and took his army with him. ⁷He took six hundred of the best chariots, along with all the other chariots of Egypt, with officers over all of them. ⁸The LORD hardened the heart of Pharaoh king of Egypt, so that he pursued the Israelites, who were marching out boldly. ⁹The Egyptians—all Pharaoh's horses and chariots, horsemen[b] and troops—pursued the Israelites and overtook them as they camped by the sea near Pi Hahiroth, opposite Baal Zephon.

¹⁰As Pharaoh approached, the Israelites looked up, and there were the Egyptians, marching after them. They were terrified and cried out to the LORD. ¹¹They said to Moses, "Was it because there were no graves in Egypt that you brought us to the desert to die? What have you done to us by bringing us out of Egypt? ¹²Didn't we say to you in Egypt, 'Leave us alone; let us serve the Egyptians'? It would have been better for us to serve the Egyptians than to die in the desert!"

¹³Moses answered the people, "Do not be afraid. Stand firm and you will see the deliverance the LORD will bring you today. The Egyptians you see today you will never see again. ¹⁴The LORD will fight for you; you need only to be still."

¹⁵Then the LORD said to Moses, "Why are you crying out to me? Tell the Israelites to move on. ¹⁶Raise your staff and stretch out your hand over the sea to divide the water so that the Israelites can go through the sea on dry ground. ¹⁷I will harden the hearts of the Egyptians so that they will go in after them. And I will gain glory through Pharaoh and all his army, through his chariots and his horsemen. ¹⁸The Egyptians will know that I am the LORD when I gain glory through Pharaoh, his chariots and his horsemen."

¹⁹Then the angel of God, who had been traveling in front of Israel's army, withdrew and went behind them. The pillar of cloud also moved from in front and stood behind them, ²⁰coming between the armies of Egypt and Israel. Throughout the night the

---

[a] *19* See Gen. 50:25.   [b] *9* Or *charioteers;* also in verses 17, 18, 23, 26 and 28

13:18, 19 | That God's people **went up out of Egypt ready for battle** suggests that they had a plan in place—presumably backed by much earnest prayer—for the time when Pharaoh would actually let them go. Joseph's last words—that he wanted his **bones** taken to the Promised Land—were a proclamation of his faith in God's promise to bring the people back there (Gen. 50:24–26). The ancestral **oath** to honor Joseph was now kept by Moses.

13:21, 22 | The guiding pillars of **cloud by day . . . fire by night** were the Lord Himself leading Israel, illuminating the people's path, protecting them, providing reassurance, and directing their movements. Christians today have the Word of God, which provides guidance (Ps. 119:105) and assurance of His presence (Matt. 28:18–20).

14:2–4 | Rather than moving in a straight path, the Lord told Moses to have the people **turn back and encamp** near the Red Sea. Such movements convinced Pharaoh that the Hebrew people were full of **confusion** and wandering like lost sheep in **the desert**. God, however, was drawing the Egyptian army into His trap.

14:5–9 | Pharaoh pursued the Hebrew people with a large army: 600 **of the best chariots** that each carried two people—one to drive and one to fight. A frightening sight!

14:10–14 | What a sharp change from the people's perspective on the night their children were spared and they left Egypt with their heads held high! Moses responded to their fear and grumbling with a most remarkable inspirational speech. Israel wanted to run, but Yahweh was about to **fight for** His people. He still defends His children today.

14:15–18 | Next, the Lord ordered the people of Israel **to move on** (forward in direction). The fact that Israel was facing the Red Sea posed no problem for God. When things seem impossible, the people of God need to obediently follow Him in faith, leaving the outcome to Him.

14:19 | Here, **the angel of God** (see note on 12:12, 13; Gen. 21:17; 31:11)—an appearance of the Lord—**withdrew and went behind** the camp of Israel, joined by a second appearance, the **pillar of cloud** (13:21; 33:9–11) to shield the people from their enemies.

14:20 | Beyond the miracle of the pillar of cloud itself is the fact that the **cloud brought darkness** to the Egyptians but **light** to the people of Israel. The same event can secure victory for one army and defeat another. This was true of the Exodus and will be true of the second coming of Christ (Rev. 19).

cloud brought darkness to the one side and light to the other side; so neither went near the other all night long.

²¹ Then Moses stretched out his hand over the sea, and all that night the LORD drove the sea back with a strong east wind and turned it into dry land. The waters were divided, ²² and the Israelites went through the sea on dry ground, with a wall of water on their right and on their left.

²³ The Egyptians pursued them, and all Pharaoh's horses and chariots and horsemen followed them into the sea. ²⁴ During the last watch of the night the LORD looked down from the pillar of fire and cloud at the Egyptian army and threw it into confusion. ²⁵ He jammed*ᵃ* the wheels of their chariots so that they had difficulty driving. And the Egyptians said, "Let's get away from the Israelites! The LORD is fighting for them against Egypt."

²⁶ Then the LORD said to Moses, "Stretch out your hand over the sea so that the waters may flow back over the Egyptians and their chariots and horsemen." ²⁷ Moses stretched out his hand over the sea, and at daybreak the sea went back to its place. The Egyptians were fleeing toward*ᵇ* it, and the LORD swept them into the sea. ²⁸ The water flowed back and covered the chariots and horsemen—the entire army of Pharaoh that had followed the Israelites into the sea. Not one of them survived.

²⁹ But the Israelites went through the sea on dry ground, with a wall of water on their right and on their left. ³⁰ That day the LORD saved Israel from the hands of the Egyptians, and Israel saw the Egyptians lying dead on the shore. ³¹ And when the Israelites saw the mighty hand of the LORD displayed against the Egyptians, the people feared the LORD and put their trust in him and in Moses his servant.

The Song of Moses and Miriam

15 Then Moses and the Israelites sang this song to the LORD:

"I will sing to the LORD,
  for he is highly exalted.
Both horse and driver
  he has hurled into the sea.

² "The LORD is my strength and my
    defense*ᶜ*;
  he has become my salvation.
He is my God, and I will praise him,
  my father's God, and I will exalt him.
³ The LORD is a warrior;
  the LORD is his name.
⁴ Pharaoh's chariots and his army
  he has hurled into the sea.
The best of Pharaoh's officers
  are drowned in the Red Sea.*ᵈ*
⁵ The deep waters have covered them;
  they sank to the depths like a
    stone.
⁶ Your right hand, LORD,
  was majestic in power.
Your right hand, LORD,
  shattered the enemy.

⁷ "In the greatness of your majesty
  you threw down those who opposed
    you.
You unleashed your burning anger;
  it consumed them like stubble.
⁸ By the blast of your nostrils
  the waters piled up.
The surging waters stood up like a
    wall;
  the deep waters congealed in the
    heart of the sea.
⁹ The enemy boasted,
  'I will pursue, I will overtake them.
I will divide the spoils;
  I will gorge myself on them.
I will draw my sword
  and my hand will destroy them.'
¹⁰ But you blew with your breath,
  and the sea covered them.
They sank like lead
  in the mighty waters.

ᵃ 25 See Samaritan Pentateuch, Septuagint and Syriac; Masoretic Text removed   ᵇ 27 Or from   ᶜ 2 Or song   ᵈ 4 Or the Sea of Reeds; also in verse 22

14:21, 22 | A strong east wind was again used in a supernatural act of the Lord (see note on 10:16-20), this time to divide the waters into two walls and create a passageway for the people. The crossing of the Red Sea was for the people of Israel what the death and resurrection of Christ are for the believer today (Rom. 6:4).

14:25-27 | Jammed means "bound" or "took off." The Lord made the chariot wheels hard to turn so that these fearsome carriages were made ineffective (see Judg. 4:14-16; 5:4, 5). For the Lord to cause **the sea** to return **back to its place** just as the Egyptians were entering it is also a miracle (Ps. 77:10-20).

14:31 | Here is the definitive statement of the Hebrew people coming to true faith at the time of the Exodus. The language **put their trust in him** (or "believed" in Him) also describes Abram's faith

in Genesis 15:6—with the same result: the people were declared righteous (Rom. 4:9-12).

15:1-18 | The Song of the Sea (composed by **Moses**) is the first psalm in the Bible. At key moments in their history, the Hebrew people created songs like this to commemorate God's great works. **The LORD is my strength and my defense** means "He is my strong song; He is my reason for singing" (Ps. 118:14; Isa. 12:2).

15:3 | In the conflict between the Hebrew people and the Egyptians, God reveals Himself as **a warrior** for His people! There was no battle between defenseless Israel and Egypt; Yahweh fought (and still does fight) for His children (14:25).

15:6 | The Lord's **right hand** is a symbol of His authority and direct involvement with His people (15:12, 16; Ps. 17:7; 118:15).

[11] Who among the gods
    is like you, LORD?
Who is like you—
    majestic in holiness,
awesome in glory,
    working wonders?

[12] "You stretch out your right hand,
    and the earth swallows your
      enemies.
[13] In your unfailing love you will lead
    the people you have redeemed.
In your strength you will guide them
    to your holy dwelling.
[14] The nations will hear and tremble;
    anguish will grip the people of
      Philistia.
[15] The chiefs of Edom will be terrified,
    the leaders of Moab will be seized
      with trembling,
the people[a] of Canaan will melt away;
[16]   terror and dread will fall on them.
By the power of your arm
    they will be as still as a stone—
until your people pass by, LORD,
    until the people you bought[b] pass by.
[17] You will bring them in and plant them
    on the mountain of your inheritance—
the place, LORD, you made for your
      dwelling,
    the sanctuary, LORD, your hands
      established.

[18] "The LORD reigns
    for ever and ever."

[19] When Pharaoh's horses, chariots and horsemen[c] went into the sea, the LORD brought the waters of the sea back over them, but the Israelites walked through the sea on dry ground. [20] Then Miriam the prophet, Aaron's sister, took a timbrel in her hand, and all the women followed her, with timbrels and dancing. [21] Miriam sang to them:

"Sing to the LORD,
    for he is highly exalted.
Both horse and driver
    he has hurled into the sea."

The Waters of Marah and Elim

[22] Then Moses led Israel from the Red Sea and they went into the Desert of Shur. For three days they traveled in the desert without finding water. [23] When they came to Marah, they could not drink its water because it was bitter. (That is why the place is called Marah.[d]) [24] So the people grumbled against Moses, saying, "What are we to drink?"

[25] Then Moses cried out to the LORD, and the LORD showed him a piece of wood. He threw it into the water, and the water became fit to drink.

There the LORD issued a ruling and instruction for them and put them to the test. [26] He said, "If you listen carefully to the LORD your God and do what is right in his eyes, if you pay attention to his commands and keep all his decrees, I will not bring on you any of the diseases I brought on the Egyptians, for I am the LORD, who heals you."

[27] Then they came to Elim, where there were twelve springs and seventy palm trees, and they camped there near the water.

Manna and Quail

16 The whole Israelite community set out from Elim and came to the Desert of Sin, which is between Elim and Sinai, on the fifteenth day of the second month after they had come out of Egypt. [2] In the desert the whole community grumbled against Moses and Aaron. [3] The Israelites said to them, "If only we had died by the LORD's hand in Egypt! There we sat around pots of meat and ate all the food we wanted, but you have brought us out into this desert to starve this entire assembly to death."

[4] Then the LORD said to Moses, "I will rain down bread from heaven for you. The people are to go out each day and gather enough for that day. In this way I will test them and see whether they will follow my instructions. [5] On the sixth day they are to prepare what they bring in, and that is to be twice as much as they gather on the other days."

---

[a] 15 Or rulers   [b] 16 Or created   [c] 19 Or charioteers   [d] 23 Marah means bitter.

15:14, 15 | The dramatic way in which the Lord delivered the Hebrew people from Pharaoh's army at the Red Sea caused Yahweh's name to be feared among neighboring nations (Josh. 2:9). Yet even the nations' fears did not hearten the Hebrew people to take the land the Lord had promised them (Num. 13–14).
15:20, 21 | **Miriam** was Moses' sister, too, but perhaps she is referred to as **Aaron's sister** because of his priestly role and her role here in leading Israel's worship. She was the first female **prophet** in Scripture but not the only one. Others include Deborah (Judg. 4:4), Anna (Luke 2:36), and Philip's daughters (Acts 21:9).

15:22–26 | People can change from praise to complaint so easily: Israel's elation lasted just **three days**, until they encountered **bitter**, brackish water at **Marah**. Moses cried out to God, and the Lord revealed Himself as Yahweh Rophe (**the LORD, who heals**). The Healer of the water promised to protect the people if they would obey Him.
16:1–3 | **The Desert of Sin** may have been in the southwestern region of the Sinai Peninsula, along the shore of the Red Sea. Gone from Egypt for only a month, **the whole community** accused **Moses and Aaron** of deliberately leading them into the **desert to starve** them **to death**.

⁶So Moses and Aaron said to all the Israelites, "In the evening you will know that it was the LORD who brought you out of Egypt, ⁷and in the morning you will see the glory of the LORD, because he has heard your grumbling against him. Who are we, that you should grumble against us?" ⁸Moses also said, "You will know that it was the LORD when he gives you meat to eat in the evening and all the bread you want in the morning, because he has heard your grumbling against him. Who are we? You are not grumbling against us, but against the LORD."

⁹Then Moses told Aaron, "Say to the entire Israelite community, 'Come before the LORD, for he has heard your grumbling.'"

¹⁰While Aaron was speaking to the whole Israelite community, they looked toward the desert, and there was the glory of the LORD appearing in the cloud.

¹¹The LORD said to Moses, ¹²"I have heard the grumbling of the Israelites. Tell them, 'At twilight you will eat meat, and in the morning you will be filled with bread. Then you will know that I am the LORD your God.'"

¹³That evening quail came and covered the camp, and in the morning there was a layer of dew around the camp. ¹⁴When the dew was gone, thin flakes like frost on the ground appeared on the desert floor. ¹⁵When the Israelites saw it, they said to each other, "What is it?" For they did not know what it was.

Moses said to them, "It is the bread the LORD has given you to eat. ¹⁶This is what the LORD has commanded: 'Everyone is to gather as much as they need. Take an omer⁽ᵃ⁾ for each person you have in your tent.'"

¹⁷The Israelites did as they were told; some gathered much, some little. ¹⁸And when they measured it by the omer, the one who gathered much did not have too much, and the one who gathered little did not have too little. Everyone had gathered just as much as they needed.

¹⁹Then Moses said to them, "No one is to keep any of it until morning."

²⁰However, some of them paid no attention to Moses; they kept part of it until morning, but it was full of maggots and began to smell. So Moses was angry with them.

²¹Each morning everyone gathered as much as they needed, and when the sun grew hot, it melted away. ²²On the sixth day, they gathered twice as much — two omers⁽ᵇ⁾ for each person — and the leaders of the community came and reported this to Moses. ²³He said to them, "This is what the LORD commanded: 'Tomorrow is to be a day of sabbath rest, a holy sabbath to the LORD. So bake what you want to bake and boil what you want to boil. Save whatever is left and keep it until morning.'"

²⁴So they saved it until morning, as Moses commanded, and it did not stink or get maggots in it. ²⁵"Eat it today," Moses said, "because today is a sabbath to the LORD. You will not find any of it on the ground today. ²⁶Six days you are to gather it, but on the seventh day, the Sabbath, there will not be any."

²⁷Nevertheless, some of the people went out on the seventh day to gather it, but they found none. ²⁸Then the LORD said to Moses, "How long will you⁽ᶜ⁾ refuse to keep my commands and my instructions? ²⁹Bear in mind that the LORD has given you the Sabbath; that is why on the sixth day he gives you bread for two days. Everyone is to stay where they are on the seventh day; no one is to go out." ³⁰So the people rested on the seventh day.

³¹The people of Israel called the bread manna.⁽ᵈ⁾ It was white like coriander seed and tasted like wafers made with honey. ³²Moses said, "This is what the LORD has commanded: 'Take an omer of manna and keep it for the generations to come, so they can see the bread I gave you to eat in the wilderness when I brought you out of Egypt.'"

ᵃ 16 That is, possibly about 3 pounds or about 1.4 kilograms; also in verses 18, 32, 33 and 36   ᵇ 22 That is, possibly about 6 pounds or about 2.8 kilograms   ᶜ 28 The Hebrew is plural.   ᵈ 31 Manna sounds like the Hebrew for What is it? (see verse 15).

16:4, 5 | For them to survive without food from any natural source required the Lord to do what only He could do: for five days each week, He delivered daily portions of **bread from heaven** for each individual; on the sixth day, there was a double provision; and on the seventh, there was none at all. What anyone needs to get through the "desert" is not available except from God Himself.
16:7, 8 | Moses showed that the people's **grumbling**, leveled at their human leaders, was actually **against the LORD**. This is true anytime a child of God grumbles.
16:9, 10 | The people had experienced the work of the Lord and had been under the word of the Lord; now they were to experience the wonder of the Lord. The revelation of His **glory . . . in the cloud** was designed to instill confidence and to compel faithfulness.

16:13–16 | The meal of **quail** was a miracle (Num. 11:31–35), but the **thin flakes** was the greater surprise. The word *manna* comes from the question the Hebrew people asked that first morning: **What is it?** (Heb., *man hu*). Manna would be their food for the next 40 years, until the new generation entered the Promised Land (16:35; Josh. 5:11, 12). The amount of food the Lord provided was staggering: one day's "delivery" for more than 2 million people for nearly 40 years!
16:22–26 | Not only did the Lord miraculously provide manna for the people, but He also miraculously preserved manna from **the sixth day** for use on the Sabbath (called "the seventh day" in Gen. 2:1–3)—the first mention of the term in Scripture. In this, Israel learned to observe this **day of . . . rest** even before the Ten Commandments were issued (20:8–11).

[33] So Moses said to Aaron, "Take a jar and put an omer of manna in it. Then place it before the Lord to be kept for the generations to come."

[34] As the Lord commanded Moses, Aaron put the manna with the tablets of the covenant law, so that it might be preserved. [35] The Israelites ate manna forty years, until they came to a land that was settled; they ate manna until they reached the border of Canaan.

[36] (An omer is one-tenth of an ephah.)

Water From the Rock

17 The whole Israelite community set out from the Desert of Sin, traveling from place to place as the Lord commanded. They camped at Rephidim, but there was no water for the people to drink. [2] So they quarreled with Moses and said, "Give us water to drink."

Moses replied, "Why do you quarrel with me? Why do you put the Lord to the test?"

[3] But the people were thirsty for water there, and they grumbled against Moses. They said, "Why did you bring us up out of Egypt to make us and our children and livestock die of thirst?"

[4] Then Moses cried out to the Lord, "What am I to do with these people? They are almost ready to stone me."

[5] The Lord answered Moses, "Go out in front of the people. Take with you some of the elders of Israel and take in your hand the staff with which you struck the Nile, and go. [6] I will stand there before you by the rock at Horeb. Strike the rock, and water will come out of it for the people to drink." So Moses did this in the sight of the elders of Israel. [7] And he called the place Massah[a] and Meribah[b] because the Israelites quarreled and

because they tested the Lord saying, "Is the Lord among us or not?"

The Amalekites Defeated

[8] The Amalekites came and attacked the Israelites at Rephidim. [9] Moses said to Joshua, "Choose some of our men and go out to fight the Amalekites. Tomorrow I will stand on top of the hill with the staff of God in my hands."

[10] So Joshua fought the Amalekites as Moses had ordered, and Moses, Aaron and Hur went to the top of the hill. [11] As long as Moses held up his hands, the Israelites were winning, but whenever he lowered his hands, the Amalekites were winning. [12] When Moses' hands grew tired, they took a stone and put it under him and he sat on it. Aaron and Hur held his hands up — one on one side, one on the other — so that his hands remained steady till sunset. [13] So Joshua overcame the Amalekite army with the sword.

[14] Then the Lord said to Moses, "Write this on a scroll as something to be remembered and make sure that Joshua hears it, because I will completely blot out the name of Amalek from under heaven."

[15] Moses built an altar and called it The Lord is my Banner. [16] He said, "Because hands were lifted up against[c] the throne of the Lord,[d] the Lord will be at war against the Amalekites from generation to generation."

Jethro Visits Moses

18 Now Jethro, the priest of Midian and father-in-law of Moses, heard of everything God had done for Moses and for his people Israel, and how the Lord had brought Israel out of Egypt.

---

[a] 7 *Massah* means *testing*.   [b] 7 *Meribah* means *quarreling*.   [c] 16 Or *to*
[d] 16 The meaning of the Hebrew for this clause is uncertain.

16:31, 35 | Although the **manna** tasted sweet on their tongues (**like wafers made with honey**), its true sweetness was in its sufficiency to sustain the people from the land of slavery to the land of promise. God's provisions are sweet for those who are willing to "taste and see that the Lord is good" (Ps. 34:8).

17:1–8 | The people complained again, forgetting that if God could part the Red Sea, He could provide **water . . . to drink**. The Lord's assurance of His presence with Moses—**I will stand there before you**—recalls the first time Moses heard these words, at the burning bush (3:12).

17:5, 6 | Paul writes about this event: "They drank from the spiritual rock that accompanied them, and that rock was Christ" (1 Cor. 10:4). The smitten stone of this chapter pictures Christ who, when He was smitten upon the cross, became the fountainhead of blessing, the Redeemer of the world.

17:8 | The Hebrew people had not been trained for war in their years of servitude in Egypt, but Moses had been given a royal course in leadership and warfare during his "palace years." This was an unprovoked attack from a brother nation—the Amalekites were descendants of Esau, the brother of Jacob (Gen. 36:12, 16).

17:9, 10 | **Joshua** would be Moses' personal minister for the next 40 years. He was also put in charge of the military, beginning with the conflict with the **Amalekites**. By holding the **staff of God**, Moses physically demonstrated total dependence on God's authority and power.

17:10-16 | **As long as Moses held up his hands** in a gesture of dependence on Yahweh, the battle went Israel's way. When he wearied and lowered his hand, the battle went the Amalekites' way. Neither Moses nor the staff was empowering Joshua and his army; the God of Abraham, Isaac, and Jacob was ensuring the victory. After the battle, **Moses built an altar** and named it as a memorial to the Lord in the manner of the patriarchs (e.g., Gen. 12:7–9).

17:16 | Because the Amalekites attacked the Hebrew people as they journeyed from Egypt to the Promised Land, Yahweh announced through Moses a most solemn oath: **the Lord will be at war against the Amalekites from generation to generation**. Later, Moses told the generation of Hebrew people entering the Promised Land to blot out the enemy nation (Deut. 25:19). A final encounter between Israel and the Amalekites served as a victory for Israel and a failure for King Saul (1 Sam. 15).

[2] After Moses had sent away his wife Zipporah, his father-in-law Jethro received her [3] and her two sons. One son was named Gershom,[a] for Moses said, "I have become a foreigner in a foreign land"; [4] and the other was named Eliezer,[b] for he said, "My father's God was my helper; he saved me from the sword of Pharaoh."

[5] Jethro, Moses' father-in-law, together with Moses' sons and wife, came to him in the wilderness, where he was camped near the mountain of God. [6] Jethro had sent word to him, "I, your father-in-law Jethro, am coming to you with your wife and her two sons."

[7] So Moses went out to meet his father-in-law and bowed down and kissed him. They greeted each other and then went into the tent. [8] Moses told his father-in-law about everything the LORD had done to Pharaoh and the Egyptians for Israel's sake and about all the hardships they had met along the way and how the LORD had saved them.

[9] Jethro was delighted to hear about all the good things the LORD had done for Israel in rescuing them from the hand of the Egyptians. [10] He said, "Praise be to the LORD, who rescued you from the hand of the Egyptians and of Pharaoh, and who rescued the people from the hand of the Egyptians. [11] Now I know that the LORD is greater than all other gods, for he did this to those who had treated Israel arrogantly." [12] Then Jethro, Moses' father-in-law, brought a burnt offering and other sacrifices to God, and Aaron came with all the elders of Israel to eat a meal with Moses' father-in-law in the presence of God.

[13] The next day Moses took his seat to serve as judge for the people, and they stood around him from morning till evening. [14] When his father-in-law saw all that Moses was doing for the people, he said, "What is this you are doing for the people? Why do you alone sit as judge, while all these people stand around you from morning till evening?"

[15] Moses answered him, "Because the people come to me to seek God's will. [16] Whenever they have a dispute, it is brought to me, and I decide between the parties and inform them of God's decrees and instructions."

[17] Moses' father-in-law replied, "What you are doing is not good. [18] You and these people who come to you will only wear yourselves out. The work is too heavy for you; you cannot handle it alone. [19] Listen now to me and I will give you some advice, and may God be with you. You must be the people's representative before God and bring their disputes to him. [20] Teach them his decrees and instructions, and show them the way they are to live and how they are to behave. [21] But select capable men from all the people—men who fear God, trustworthy men who hate dishonest gain—and appoint them as officials over thousands, hundreds, fifties and tens. [22] Have them serve as judges for the people at all times, but have them bring every difficult case to you; the simple cases they can decide themselves. That will make your load lighter, because they will share it with you. [23] If you do this and God so commands, you will be able to stand the strain, and all these people will go home satisfied."

[24] Moses listened to his father-in-law and did everything he said. [25] He chose capable men from all Israel and made them leaders of the people, officials over thousands, hundreds, fifties and tens. [26] They served as judges for the people at all times. The difficult cases they brought to Moses, but the simple ones they decided themselves.

[27] Then Moses sent his father-in-law on his way, and Jethro returned to his own country.

At Mount Sinai

19 On the first day of the third month after the Israelites left Egypt—on that very day—they came to the Desert of Sinai. [2] After they set out from Rephidim, they entered the Desert of Sinai, and Israel camped there in the desert in front of the mountain.

[3] Then Moses went up to God, and the LORD called to him from the mountain and said, "This is what you are to say to the descendants of Jacob and what you are to tell

---

[a] 3 *Gershom* sounds like the Hebrew for *a foreigner there.*   [b] 4 *Eliezer* means *my God is helper.*

18:1-27 | The respect and mutual regard seen in the reunion of **Jethro** and Moses demonstrates family dynamics in the ancient Near East in the Late Bronze Age (see notes on 2:21; 4:18, 24–26). Moses constantly deferred to Jethro as **his father-in-law**, even though he had been released from familial duties.
18:17, 18 | Jethro identified two problems. First, judging Israel by himself—with no help from the nation's elders in such day-to-day affairs—was wearing Moses out. Second, the people were frustrated because they could not get prompt relief.

18:19-26 | Leaders who delegate properly not only are **able to stand the strain** and continue their work far longer, but they bring peace to their people. By selecting **men** of ability (**capable**), spirituality (**who fear God**), honesty (**trustworthy**), and integrity (**who hate dishonest gain**) to help judge the people (Deut. 1:9–18), Moses could reestablish his own priorities: praying (**bring their disputes to** God), teaching (God's **decrees and instructions**), and leading (**show them the way . . . to live and . . . behave**) (Acts 6:2–4).

God's purposes in giving His Law to Israel have been misunderstood through the centuries—most notably by the Jewish people themselves. By the time of Jesus, most Jewish people believed that keeping the Law was the means of salvation. Adhering to the rite of circumcision (first commanded by God in Genesis 17) and keeping the Law (first given by God in Exodus 20) was said, even by some Jewish believers in Jesus, to be necessary for Gentiles (Acts 15:5). But salvation was, and is, God's gift by grace, through faith (Eph. 2:4–9) in the substitutionary death of Christ (Acts 15:11); it can never be earned.

These basic facts need to be understood.

First, the Lord gave His Law to a redeemed community. Just as Abraham was justified—that is, declared righteous (Gen. 15:6; Rom. 4)—before he was circumcised (Gen. 17:23–27), so Israel came to saving faith (11–12; 14:30, 31) before God delivered the Law (beginning at 20:1). This chronology alone rules out any plan of salvation based on the keeping of the Law.

Second, while we often speak of "the Law of Moses," Moses was the faithful servant who transmitted God's word and will to the Hebrew people. The Law is the Law of Yahweh!

Third, the Law as it was given in the Pentateuch was given distinctly to Israel, for their life in a specific locality (the land of Canaan) in a specific historical setting (from the late Bronze Age into the early Roman era).

Fourth, the translation "law" is seared into the biblical mindset, but the basic meaning of the Hebrew word (*torah*) is "instruction" and is best seen pictorially as God's outstretched hand pointing to the road His people should walk.

In the giving of the Law, God makes clear His purposes.

First, the Lord meant for Torah to be the principal means whereby His people would maintain righteous living in relationship with Him and others (Matt. 22:37–40). Knowing God and loving God (Deut. 6:4, 5) were the essential elements of the people's relationship with God. Treating others with equity (Lev. 19:17, 18) was to be the hallmark of the King's people.

Second, the laws of distinction such as the dietary laws of Leviticus 11 were intended to develop in Israel a sense of being God's chosen people, a nation set apart from other nations of the day. This was especially necessary in Canaan, where idolatry and immorality were promoted. Everyone else would eat what was available; the Hebrew people had a list of permitted foods to make them distinct and holy. The same is true for the Sabbath (20:8–11). The Hebrew people had a workweek that was unique in the ancient world. Other agrarian cultures did the work of plowing, planting, and harvesting as needed; only Israel rested on the seventh day—no matter what work needed to be done.

Third, the blessings of the covenant were not just for the enjoyment of the Hebrew people; they were also to be an attractive force for bringing others to faith in the Lord (Ps. 34:8). Evangelism in Hebrew Scripture was basically a "drawing in" of people as they witnessed the blessings of God in the lives of the Hebrew people. Torah revealed His goodness and protection in a compelling way.

Fourth, the Lord purposed His Torah to be the principal source of knowledge concerning true worship. In no other area were Canaanite beliefs and practices as wrong as in that of worship. Thus, more "space" is given in Torah to the concept of worship than any other topic—from the design and construction of the tabernacle (25—40) to the system of sacrifices (Lev. 1—7) and the feasts and festivals (Lev. 16; 23). Worship "in the Spirit and in truth" (John 4:21–24) is critically important to God.

By the time of Jesus, the gracious nature of God's gift of the Law for the good of the people (Deut. 6:1–3) had been lost. Instead of grace on grace, the Jewish people added laws on laws, making the Law a most heavy burden and its accomplishment an impossible task. But Jesus came to provide a better way for all who would believe in Him.

For Further Reading: Deut. 6:1–9; Neh. 9:13, 14; Ps. 1; 19; 119; Matt. 23:1–36; Luke 16:16, 17; Acts 15:1–29; Rom. 2:17–29; 3:21–31; 4:1–23; Gal. 2:16; 5:18

the people of Israel: [4]'You yourselves have seen what I did to Egypt, and how I carried you on eagles' wings and brought you to myself. [5]Now if you obey me fully and keep my covenant, then out of all nations you will be my treasured possession. Although the whole earth is mine, [6]you[a] will be for me a kingdom of priests and a holy nation.' These are the words you are to speak to the Israelites."

[7]So Moses went back and summoned the elders of the people and set before them all the words the LORD had commanded him to speak. [8]The people all responded together, "We will do everything the LORD has said." So Moses brought their answer back to the LORD.

[9]The LORD said to Moses, "I am going to come to you in a dense cloud, so that the people will hear me speaking with you and will always put their trust in you." Then Moses told the LORD what the people had said.

[10]And the LORD said to Moses, "Go to the people and consecrate them today and tomorrow. Have them wash their clothes [11]and be ready by the third day, because on that day the LORD will come down on Mount Sinai in the sight of all the people. [12]Put limits for the people around the mountain and tell them, 'Be careful that you do not approach the mountain or touch the foot of it. Whoever touches the mountain is to be put to death. [13]They are to be stoned or shot with arrows; not a hand is to be laid on them. No person or animal shall be permitted to live.' Only when the ram's horn sounds a long blast may they approach the mountain."

[14]After Moses had gone down the mountain to the people, he consecrated them, and they washed their clothes. [15]Then he said to the people, "Prepare yourselves for the third day. Abstain from sexual relations."

[16]On the morning of the third day there was thunder and lightning, with a thick cloud over the mountain, and a very loud trumpet blast. Everyone in the camp trembled. [17]Then Moses led the people out of the camp to meet with God, and they stood at the foot of the mountain. [18]Mount Sinai was covered with smoke, because the LORD descended on it in fire. The smoke billowed up from it like smoke from a furnace, and the whole mountain[b] trembled violently. [19]As the sound of the trumpet grew louder and louder, Moses spoke and the voice of God answered him.[c]

[20]The LORD descended to the top of Mount Sinai and called Moses to the top of the mountain. So Moses went up [21]and the LORD said to him, "Go down and warn the people so they do not force their way through to see the LORD and many of them perish. [22]Even the priests, who approach the LORD, must consecrate themselves, or the LORD will break out against them."

[23]Moses said to the LORD, "The people cannot come up Mount Sinai, because you yourself warned us, 'Put limits around the mountain and set it apart as holy.'"

[24]The LORD replied, "Go down and bring Aaron up with you. But the priests and the people must not force their way through to come up to the LORD, or he will break out against them."

[25]So Moses went down to the people and told them.

The Ten Commandments

20 And God spoke all these words:

[2]"I am the LORD your God, who brought you out of Egypt, out of the land of slavery.

[3]"You shall have no other gods before[d] me.

[4]"You shall not make for yourself an image in the form of anything in heaven above or on the earth beneath or in the waters below. [5]You

---

[a] 5,6 Or possession, for the whole earth is mine. [6] You   [b] 18 Most Hebrew manuscripts; a few Hebrew manuscripts and Septuagint and all the people   [c] 19 Or and God answered him with thunder   [d] 3 Or besides

---

19:1–14 | God fulfilled His promise to bring the people to **Mount Sinai** to worship Him (3:12). As was ancient wedding custom, Israel was to purify themselves for three days prior to the Lord's visitation, preparing their bodies, minds, and hearts for their covenantal marriage to the Lord. To ready oneself to meet with the Lord involves a person's undivided attention.

19:5, 6 | Because **the whole earth is** the Lord's, He can do with it as He pleases (Ps. 24:1)—and in His **covenant** with Moses and Abraham, He designated a **treasured** people for Himself and a land for His people (Gen. 15:12–21). As **a kingdom of priests and a holy nation** (see 1 Pet. 2:5, 9), God planned to bless all the families of the earth through Israel (Gen. 12:2, 3; John 4:22; Rom. 9:4, 5).

19:16–20 | This appearance of the Lord was marked by extraordinary phenomena as He **descended on** Sinai **in fire**. That He

physically spoke to Moses (by **voice**) in the people's hearing was important so that they would "put their trust in [Moses]" (19:9). Trumpets are sometimes associated with great pronouncements of God; the volume and intensity of this **trumpet blast** were unprecedented.

19:21–25 | To be in the presence of a holy God required boundaries. It was God's mercy that had Moses **warn the people** so they would not die.

20:1–17 | The Ten Commandments, also referred to as the Decalogue (Deut. 5:6–22), were written in the form of great king-vassal treaties from the second millennium BC, complete with preamble, prologue, and a statement of responsibilities and conditions. Earlier (19:5, 6), the Lord had stipulated how He would bless the people if they honored this covenant.

Tough Questions

How can God be jealous? • 20:5

When we come to the words "For I, the LORD your God, am a jealous God," it sounds alarms in our heads: Is not jealousy a bad thing? How can a good God be jealous? Of what can the Incomparable One be jealous? Does God's jealousy give a basis for our jealousy?

The solutions may be found in two ideas. First, while our own feelings of jealousy are likely based on issues such as envy of others and insecurities in ourselves, nothing of the sort is possible of God! He has none to envy! It is the fact that He is incomparable—totally beyond compare with anything or anyone—that leads to divine jealousy. Whenever someone attempts to substitute anything else for God (an idol), this is an affront to God. He will defend His uniqueness and majesty—for that is at the core of His being. "I am the LORD" means, among other things, that He and He alone is God.

Second, the Hebrew verb translated "to be jealous" describes deep emotions that involve both jealousy and zeal. When this word and related nouns are used to describe God, the idea is not one of pettiness or vindictiveness. It describes the zeal of Yahweh as the one and only God among His people. This makes all human "jealousies" immaterial. This passage is all about God and the truth of who He is. If there is anything about which we may rightly be jealous, it is to protect the reputation of the one true God.

shall not bow down to them or worship them; for I, the LORD your God, am a jealous God, punishing the children for the sin of the parents to the third and fourth generation of those who hate me, [6] but showing love to a thousand generations of those who love me and keep my commandments.

[7] "You shall not misuse the name of the LORD your God, for the LORD will not hold anyone guiltless who misuses his name.

[8] "Remember the Sabbath day by keeping it holy. [9] Six days you shall labor and do all your work, [10] but the seventh day is a sabbath to the LORD your God. On it you shall not do any work, neither you, nor your son or daughter, nor your male or female servant, nor your animals, nor any foreigner residing in your towns. [11] For in six days the LORD made the heavens and the earth, the sea, and all that is in them, but he rested on the seventh day. Therefore the LORD blessed the Sabbath day and made it holy.

[12] "Honor your father and your mother, so that you may live long in the land the LORD your God is giving you.

[13] "You shall not murder.

[14] "You shall not commit adultery.

[15] "You shall not steal.

[16] "You shall not give false testimony against your neighbor.

[17] "You shall not covet your neighbor's house. You shall not covet your neighbor's wife, or his male or female servant, his ox or donkey, or anything that belongs to your neighbor."

[18] When the people saw the thunder and lightning and heard the trumpet and saw the mountain in smoke, they trembled with fear. They stayed at a distance [19] and said to Moses, "Speak to us yourself and we will

---

20:1–12 | The phrase **the LORD your God** is repeated five times here to emphasize the authority behind these commandments as well as His personal relationship with His people.

20:3, 4 | The people of Israel were constantly beset with the idea of many gods. Yet only one true God exists, and He insists on **no other gods before** or besides Him. In ancient times, true monotheism (belief in one god) was unique to Israel.

20:4–6 | The second commandment banned all idolatrous images in Israel. The Lord is **jealous** for His singularity in the lives of His people and will not tolerate any rivals for their affection (Zech. 1:14; 8:2; James 4:5). This is an expression of His love; He wants the very best for His people.

20:5, 6 | Every person is, in part, a product of certain choices by parents, grandparents, and other ancestors. But God lavishes His mercy on **those who love** Him, emphasizing not decades of generational curses but centuries of blessings.

20:7 | This third commandment is based on the sacredness of God's holy name, Yahweh. **Misuses** means to regard as having no worth. **The name of the LORD** should never be used manipulatively (Num. 22:18), caustically, crudely, or casually, because it trivializes the character and work of God.

20:8–11 | Rooted in the Creation account (Gen. 2:1–3), the fourth commandment provides a weekly reminder of God's holiness. For the people of Israel, the requirement of **Sabbath** meant no member of one's household—not even one's **animals**—should do any **work** at all on "Rest-Day." It also served as a special sign between the Lord and Israel (31:12–17; Neh. 9:13–15; Ezek. 20:12, 20), for no other nations officially observed this.

20:12 | The fifth commandment means to treat one's **father and . . . mother** with dignity and respect. The idea is the opposite of the term *misuses* in 20:7. Paul notes that this commandment is the first one with a promise (Eph. 6:2): **so that you may live long in the land**. As such, it ought to inform and encourage God's people today to respect age and care for the elderly, whether or not they are relatives (21:15, 17; e.g., Lev. 19:3, 32; Deut. 27:16; Prov. 1:8; 16:31; 20:20; 23:22; 30:17).

20:13 | The sixth commandment not only prohibits the unlawful taking of human life but honors the sacredness of all innocent life including that of unborn children. The Law made provisions for self-protection (22:2), military service (Num. 1:3), public executions (21:12), and accidental death (21:13, 14).

The Law Regarding Voluntary Servanthood • 21:1–6

Among Hebrew servants, servitude was limited to six years, and family considerations were involved. So if a Hebrew servant had married while a servant, he had two options at the time of his release: he could be released and be separated from his family, or he could remain a servant and thereby remain with his wife and children. If he chose lifelong bondage, legal action and a physical sign ("pierce his ear") were required. This voluntary servitude for reasons of love may be the image behind Paul's use of "servant" (slave) in places such as Romans 1:1.

listen. But do not have God speak to us or we will die."

20 Moses said to the people, "Do not be afraid. God has come to test you, so that the fear of God will be with you to keep you from sinning."

21 The people remained at a distance, while Moses approached the thick darkness where God was.

Idols and Altars

22 Then the LORD said to Moses, "Tell the Israelites this: 'You have seen for yourselves that I have spoken to you from heaven: 23 Do not make any gods to be alongside me; do not make for yourselves gods of silver or gods of gold.

24 " 'Make an altar of earth for me and sacrifice on it your burnt offerings and fellowship offerings, your sheep and goats and your cattle. Wherever I cause my name to be honored, I will come to you and bless you. 25 If you make an altar of stones for me, do not build it with dressed stones, for you will defile it if you use a tool on it. 26 And do not go up to my altar on steps, or your private parts may be exposed.'

21 "These are the laws you are to set before them:

Hebrew Servants

2 "If you buy a Hebrew servant, he is to serve you for six years. But in the seventh

year, he shall go free, without paying anything. 3 If he comes alone, he is to go free alone; but if he has a wife when he comes, she is to go with him. 4 If his master gives him a wife and she bears him sons or daughters, the woman and her children shall belong to her master, and only the man shall go free.

5 "But if the servant declares, 'I love my master and my wife and children and do not want to go free,' 6 then his master must take him before the judges.[a] He shall take him to the door or the doorpost and pierce his ear with an awl. Then he will be his servant for life.

7 "If a man sells his daughter as a servant, she is not to go free as male servants do. 8 If she does not please the master who has selected her for himself,[b] he must let her be redeemed. He has no right to sell her to foreigners, because he has broken faith with her. 9 If he selects her for his son, he must grant her the rights of a daughter. 10 If he marries another woman, he must not deprive the first one of her food, clothing and marital rights. 11 If he does not provide her with these three things, she is to go free, without any payment of money.

Personal Injuries

12 "Anyone who strikes a person with a fatal blow is to be put to death. 13 However, if it is not done intentionally, but God lets

---

[a] 6 Or before God   [b] 8 Or master so that he does not choose her

---

20:14 | The seventh commandment honors marriage. **Adultery** is such a serious transgression that it was a capital crime according to the Law (Lev. 20:10; Deut. 22:22). Jesus taught that even lustful looks may constitute betrayal (Matt. 5:27–30).

20:15 | The eighth commandment respects and validates the sanctity of owning personal property. **You shall not steal** safeguards individuals as well as entire societies.

20:16 | The ninth commandment honors truth-telling, even to the point of prohibiting slander (23:1; Prov. 10:18; 12:17; 19:9; 24:28; Titus 3:1, 2; James 4:11; 1 Pet. 2:1). The best opportunity for justice rests on the assumption of truthfulness in a sworn **testimony**.

20:17 | The tenth commandment is about controlling the desires of the heart. Sinful thoughts beget sinful actions (Matt. 15:19; James 1:14, 15), so it is no surprise that covetous people often break the commandments in order to satisfy their greed.

20:18–21 | **The fear of God** motivates a desire to both obey and honor Him. Tragically, Israel would soon lose their reverence for the Lord.

20:22–26 | These instructions about the fashioning of any **altar**

were not only to ensure proper worship but to prevent anything being built to look like an alluring idol.

21:1–35 | The Ten Commandments were given without a preceding cause, making them unique in the law codes of the ancient Near East. Most laws, like the ones in this chapter and following, were established in answer to specific cases. People were to be treated justly (especially slaves and victims), personal property was to be protected, and moral and ceremonial principles were to be observed (Lev. 25:39–43; Deut. 15:12–18).

21:12–17 | The case laws in the Mosaic Law distinguished between two kinds of killing: premeditated murder and involuntary manslaughter, or accidental death. Following the great Flood, God said premeditated murder should be punished by death (Gen. 9:6), but the person who accidentally killed someone could seek refuge at the tabernacle **altar** during the wilderness years or in the cities of refuge after Israel was in the land (Num. 35:6–34; Deut. 19:1–13; Josh. 20:1–9). Mistreatment of one's **father or mother** was worthy of death as well (Lev. 20:9; Matt. 15:4).

it happen, they are to flee to a place I will designate. [14] But if anyone schemes and kills someone deliberately, that person is to be taken from my altar and put to death.

[15] "Anyone who attacks[a] their father or mother is to be put to death.

[16] "Anyone who kidnaps someone is to be put to death, whether the victim has been sold or is still in the kidnapper's possession.

[17] "Anyone who curses their father or mother is to be put to death.

[18] "If people quarrel and one person hits another with a stone or with their fist[b] and the victim does not die but is confined to bed, [19] the one who struck the blow will not be held liable if the other can get up and walk around outside with a staff; however, the guilty party must pay the injured person for any loss of time and see that the victim is completely healed.

[20] "Anyone who beats their male or female slave with a rod must be punished if the slave dies as a direct result, [21] but they are not to be punished if the slave recovers after a day or two, since the slave is their property.

[22] "If people are fighting and hit a pregnant woman and she gives birth prematurely[c] but there is no serious injury, the offender must be fined whatever the woman's husband demands and the court allows. [23] But if there is serious injury, you are to take life for life, [24] eye for eye, tooth for tooth, hand for hand, foot for foot, [25] burn for burn, wound for wound, bruise for bruise.

[26] "An owner who hits a male or female slave in the eye and destroys it must let the slave go free to compensate for the eye. [27] And an owner who knocks out the tooth of a male or female slave must let the slave go free to compensate for the tooth.

[28] "If a bull gores a man or woman to death, the bull is to be stoned to death, and its meat must not be eaten. But the owner of the bull will not be held responsible. [29] If, however, the bull has had the habit of goring and the owner has been warned but has not kept it penned up and it kills a man or woman, the bull is to be stoned and its owner also is to be put to death. [30] However, if payment is demanded, the owner may redeem his life by the payment of whatever is demanded. [31] This law also applies if the bull gores a son or daughter. [32] If the bull gores a male or female slave, the owner must pay thirty shekels[d] of silver to the master of the slave, and the bull is to be stoned to death.

[33] "If anyone uncovers a pit or digs one and fails to cover it and an ox or a donkey falls into it, [34] the one who opened the pit must pay the owner for the loss and take the dead animal in exchange.

[35] "If anyone's bull injures someone else's bull and it dies, the two parties are to sell the live one and divide both the money and the dead animal equally. [36] However, if it was known that the bull had the habit of goring, yet the owner did not keep it penned up, the owner must pay, animal for animal, and take the dead animal in exchange.

Protection of Property

22 [e] "Whoever steals an ox or a sheep and slaughters it or sells it must pay back five head of cattle for the ox and four sheep for the sheep.

[2] "If a thief is caught breaking in at night and is struck a fatal blow, the defender is not guilty of bloodshed; [3] but if it happens after sunrise, the defender is guilty of bloodshed.

"Anyone who steals must certainly make restitution, but if they have nothing, they must be sold to pay for their theft. [4] If the stolen animal is found alive in their possession—whether ox or donkey or sheep—they must pay back double.

[5] "If anyone grazes their livestock in a field or vineyard and lets them stray and they graze in someone else's field, the offender must make restitution from the best of their own field or vineyard.

[6] "If a fire breaks out and spreads into thornbushes so that it burns shocks of grain or standing grain or the whole field, the one who started the fire must make restitution.

[7] "If anyone gives a neighbor silver or goods for safekeeping and they are stolen from the neighbor's house, the thief, if caught, must pay back double. [8] But if the

---

[a] 15 Or kills   [b] 18 Or with a tool   [c] 22 Or she has a miscarriage   [d] 32 That is, about 12 ounces or about 345 grams   [e] In Hebrew texts 22:1 is numbered 21:37, and 22:2-31 is numbered 22:1-30.

21:22, 23 | An unborn child has the same value before God as any other human being. And if that unborn one is killed through the premeditated action of another, God considers that equivalent to taking the life of the mother.
21:23, 24 | Life for life, eye for eye . . . bruise for bruise served as guidelines for judges, not as permission for individuals seeking revenge in personal relationships. This law restricted the exacting of punishment—it must fit the crime (Lev. 24:19, 20; Deut. 19:21)—thereby preventing the cruel and barbaric punishments that characterized many ancient cultures. Jesus used this principle as a starting point in teaching His followers not to retaliate (Matt. 5:38-48).
22:7-13 | Honesty and integrity hold a healthy and productive society together; neighbors need to be able to trust each other. These laws protected loans of personal property.

thief is not found, the owner of the house must appear before the judges, and they must[a] determine whether the owner of the house has laid hands on the other person's property. [9]In all cases of illegal possession of an ox, a donkey, a sheep, a garment, or any other lost property about which somebody says, 'This is mine,' both parties are to bring their cases before the judges.[b] The one whom the judges declare[c] guilty must pay back double to the other.

[10] "If anyone gives a donkey, an ox, a sheep or any other animal to their neighbor for safekeeping and it dies or is injured or is taken away while no one is looking, [11]the issue between them will be settled by the taking of an oath before the LORD that the neighbor did not lay hands on the other person's property. The owner is to accept this, and no restitution is required. [12]But if the animal was stolen from the neighbor, restitution must be made to the owner. [13]If it was torn to pieces by a wild animal, the neighbor shall bring in the remains as evidence and shall not be required to pay for the torn animal.

[14] "If anyone borrows an animal from their neighbor and it is injured or dies while the owner is not present, they must make restitution. [15]But if the owner is with the animal, the borrower will not have to pay. If the animal was hired, the money paid for the hire covers the loss.

Social Responsibility

[16] "If a man seduces a virgin who is not pledged to be married and sleeps with her, he must pay the bride-price, and she shall be his wife. [17]If her father absolutely refuses to give her to him, he must still pay the bride-price for virgins.

[18] "Do not allow a sorceress to live.

[19] "Anyone who has sexual relations with an animal is to be put to death.

[20] "Whoever sacrifices to any god other than the LORD must be destroyed.[d]

[21] "Do not mistreat or oppress a foreigner, for you were foreigners in Egypt.

[22] "Do not take advantage of the widow or the fatherless. [23]If you do and they cry out to

me, I will certainly hear their cry. [24]My anger will be aroused, and I will kill you with the sword; your wives will become widows and your children fatherless.

[25] "If you lend money to one of my people among you who is needy, do not treat it like a business deal; charge no interest. [26]If you take your neighbor's cloak as a pledge, return it by sunset, [27]because that cloak is the only covering your neighbor has. What else can they sleep in? When they cry out to me, I will hear, for I am compassionate.

[28] "Do not blaspheme God[e] or curse the ruler of your people.

[29] "Do not hold back offerings from your granaries or your vats.[f]

"You must give me the firstborn of your sons. [30]Do the same with your cattle and your sheep. Let them stay with their mothers for seven days, but give them to me on the eighth day.

[31] "You are to be my holy people. So do not eat the meat of an animal torn by wild beasts; throw it to the dogs.

Laws of Justice and Mercy

23 "Do not spread false reports. Do not help a guilty person by being a malicious witness.

[2] "Do not follow the crowd in doing wrong. When you give testimony in a lawsuit, do not pervert justice by siding with the crowd, [3]and do not show favoritism to a poor person in a lawsuit.

[4] "If you come across your enemy's ox or donkey wandering off, be sure to return it. [5]If you see the donkey of someone who hates you fallen down under its load, do not leave it there; be sure you help them with it.

[6] "Do not deny justice to your poor people in their lawsuits. [7]Have nothing to do with a false charge and do not put an innocent or honest person to death, for I will not acquit the guilty.

[8] "Do not accept a bribe, for a bribe blinds those who see and twists the words of the innocent.

---

[a] 8 Or before God, and he will   [b] 9 Or before God   [c] 9 Or whom God declares
[d] 20 The Hebrew term refers to the irrevocable giving over of things or persons to the LORD, often by totally destroying them.   [e] 28 Or Do not revile the judges
[f] 29 The meaning of the Hebrew for this phrase is uncertain.

22:18 | Sorcery was considered a dangerous demonic practice, thus the Hebrew people were commanded to stay away from everything associated with the occult (Lev. 20:6; Deut. 18:9–14; 1 Sam. 28; 2 Chron. 33:6; Isa. 47:12–15). Paul calls sorcery one of "the acts of the flesh" (Gal. 5:19, 20).
22:21–27 | God's laws protect the underprivileged because He cares for them (**I am compassionate**). Strangers were to be treated benevolently because the Hebrew people had been **foreigners in Egypt** (23:9); likewise, those without protection—**the widow** and **the**

fatherless and the **needy**—were not to be exploited (Deut. 24:17, 18; Jer. 7:6, 7).
22:26, 27 | Under the law, a creditor had the right to seize a debtor's coat. Here, however, God said the garment should be returned **by sunset** so the impoverished person would not get cold. Compassion was always a part of the Law.
23:1–8 | To act with integrity and to show mercy and humanity—even to one's enemy—was essential to the Law. These verses anticipate the "Golden Rule" (Matt. 7:12; Rom. 12:20).

9 "Do not oppress a foreigner; you yourselves know how it feels to be foreigners, because you were foreigners in Egypt.

Sabbath Laws

10 "For six years you are to sow your fields and harvest the crops, 11 but during the seventh year let the land lie unplowed and unused. Then the poor among your people may get food from it, and the wild animals may eat what is left. Do the same with your vineyard and your olive grove.

12 "Six days do your work, but on the seventh day do not work, so that your ox and your donkey may rest, and so that the slave born in your household and the foreigner living among you may be refreshed.

13 "Be careful to do everything I have said to you. Do not invoke the names of other gods; do not let them be heard on your lips.

The Three Annual Festivals

14 "Three times a year you are to celebrate a festival to me.

15 "Celebrate the Festival of Unleavened Bread; for seven days eat bread made without yeast, as I commanded you. Do this at the appointed time in the month of Aviv, for in that month you came out of Egypt.

"No one is to appear before me empty-handed.

16 "Celebrate the Festival of Harvest with the firstfruits of the crops you sow in your field.

"Celebrate the Festival of Ingathering at the end of the year, when you gather in your crops from the field.

17 "Three times a year all the men are to appear before the Sovereign LORD.

18 "Do not offer the blood of a sacrifice to me along with anything containing yeast.

"The fat of my festival offerings must not be kept until morning.

19 "Bring the best of the firstfruits of your soil to the house of the LORD your God.

"Do not cook a young goat in its mother's milk.

God's Angel to Prepare the Way

20 "See, I am sending an angel ahead of you to guard you along the way and to bring you to the place I have prepared. 21 Pay attention to him and listen to what he says. Do not rebel against him; he will not forgive your rebellion, since my Name is in him. 22 If you listen carefully to what he says and do all that I say, I will be an enemy to your enemies and will oppose those who oppose you. 23 My angel will go ahead of you and bring you into the land of the Amorites, Hittites, Perizzites, Canaanites, Hivites and Jebusites, and I will wipe them out. 24 Do not bow down before their gods or worship them or follow their practices. You must demolish them and break their sacred stones to pieces. 25 Worship the LORD your God, and his blessing will be on your food and water. I will take away sickness from among you, 26 and none will miscarry or be barren in your land. I will give you a full life span.

27 "I will send my terror ahead of you and throw into confusion every nation you encounter. I will make all your enemies turn their backs and run. 28 I will send the hornet ahead of you to drive the Hivites, Canaanites and Hittites out of your way. 29 But I will not drive them out in a single year, because the land would become desolate and the wild animals too numerous for you. 30 Little by little I will drive them out before you, until you have increased enough to take possession of the land.

31 "I will establish your borders from the Red Sea[a] to the Mediterranean Sea,[b] and from the desert to the Euphrates River. I will give into your hands the people who live in the land, and you will drive them out before you. 32 Do not make a covenant with them or with their gods. 33 Do not let them live in your land or they will cause you to sin against me, because the worship of their gods will certainly be a snare to you."

---

[a] 31 Or the Sea of Reeds   [b] 31 Hebrew to the Sea of the Philistines

---

23:10-12 | The command to let **the poor . . . get food** from the resting land in **the seventh year** is one of many passages in the Law that charged the wealthy to make provision for the impoverished (Lev. 19:9, 10; 23:22; 25:25, 35–38).

23:14-19 | **Three** annual festivals were appointed for Israel (Lev. 23), **the Festival of:** (1) **Unleavened Bread**, which includes Passover; (2) **Harvest**, also known as the Feast of Weeks, or Pentecost; (3) **Ingathering**, or the Feast of Tabernacles (Sukkoth). **Do not cook a young goat in its mother's milk** (Deut. 14:21) prohibited the types of cruelty committed in ancient Canaanite sacrifices. Jewish authorities later interpreted this verse to mean that one must not eat dairy products with meat products—a standard law among observant Jewish people today.

23:20-23 | This **angel** that the Lord sent to keep Israel on the right path may have been a special guardian angel (perhaps Michael; see Dan. 12:1), but more likely, it was the Lord Himself or the preincarnate Christ (Gen. 24:7).

23:23-33 | The Lord had already announced the ban on the peoples of Canaan in His covenant with Abram (Gen. 15:16, 19–21). The reasons for His judgment are given as well: **their gods . . . their practices**. The Canaanites had polluted the Promised Land with their debased practices and would corrupt the people of Israel if allowed to remain in the land (see Judah's experience in Gen. 38; Deut. 20:16–18). God promised to not only **give** the enemy into Israel's **hands** but also bless Israel's obedience.

The Covenant Confirmed

24 Then the LORD said to Moses, "Come up to the LORD, you and Aaron, Nadab and Abihu, and seventy of the elders of Israel. You are to worship at a distance, [2]but Moses alone is to approach the LORD; the others must not come near. And the people may not come up with him."

[3]When Moses went and told the people all the LORD's words and laws, they responded with one voice, "Everything the LORD has said we will do." [4]Moses then wrote down everything the LORD had said.

He got up early the next morning and built an altar at the foot of the mountain and set up twelve stone pillars representing the twelve tribes of Israel. [5]Then he sent young Israelite men, and they offered burnt offerings and sacrificed young bulls as fellowship offerings to the LORD. [6]Moses took half of the blood and put it in bowls, and the other half he splashed against the altar. [7]Then he took the Book of the Covenant and read it to the people. They responded, "We will do everything the LORD has said; we will obey."

[8]Moses then took the blood, sprinkled it on the people and said, "This is the blood of the covenant that the LORD has made with you in accordance with all these words."

[9]Moses and Aaron, Nadab and Abihu, and the seventy elders of Israel went up [10]and saw the God of Israel. Under his feet was something like a pavement made of lapis lazuli, as bright blue as the sky. [11]But God did not raise his hand against these leaders of the Israelites; they saw God, and they ate and drank.

[12]The LORD said to Moses, "Come up to me on the mountain and stay here, and I will give you the tablets of stone with the law and commandments I have written for their instruction."

[13]Then Moses set out with Joshua his aide, and Moses went up on the mountain of God. [14]He said to the elders, "Wait here for us until we come back to you. Aaron and Hur are with you, and anyone involved in a dispute can go to them."

[15]When Moses went up on the mountain, the cloud covered it, [16]and the glory of the LORD settled on Mount Sinai. For six days the cloud covered the mountain, and on the seventh day the LORD called to Moses from within the cloud. [17]To the Israelites the glory of the LORD looked like a consuming fire on top of the mountain. [18]Then Moses entered the cloud as he went on up the mountain. And he stayed on the mountain forty days and forty nights.

Offerings for the Tabernacle

25 The LORD said to Moses, [2]"Tell the Israelites to bring me an offering. You are to receive the offering for me from everyone whose heart prompts them to give. [3]These are the offerings you are to receive from them: gold, silver and bronze; [4]blue, purple and scarlet yarn and fine linen; goat hair; [5]ram skins dyed red and another type of durable leather[a]; acacia wood; [6]olive oil for the light; spices for the anointing oil and for the fragrant incense; [7]and onyx stones and other gems to be mounted on the ephod and breastpiece.

[8]"Then have them make a sanctuary for me, and I will dwell among them. [9]Make this tabernacle and all its furnishings exactly like the pattern I will show you.

The Ark

[10]"Have them make an ark[b] of acacia wood—two and a half cubits long, a cubit and a half wide, and a cubit and a half high.[c] [11]Overlay it with pure gold, both inside and out, and make a gold molding around it.

---

[a] 5 Possibly the hides of large aquatic mammals   [b] 10 That is, a chest   [c] 10 That is, about 3 3/4 feet long and 2 1/4 feet wide and high or about 1.1 meters long and 68 centimeters wide and high; similarly in verse 17

24:1–8 | Moses confirmed the covenant—the **words and laws** of the Lord (**the Book of the Covenant**)—with the people. This occasion was accompanied by magnificent pageantry and sacrificial worship, as well as Israel's collective pledge of obedience (Heb. 9:19, 20). The 12 **stone pillars** represented the 12 **tribes**.

24:12–15 | God Himself had **written** the Ten Commandments on **tablets of stone** (31:18; Deut. 9:9). **Joshua**, Moses' future successor, accompanied Moses up the mountain.

24:16–18 | **The glory of the Lord** was first manifested in the form of a covering **cloud** and then a **consuming**, purifying **fire** that symbolized His holiness (Deut. 4:36). Into that cloud went Moses for 40 days and nights, where he received the plans for the tabernacle and the priesthood. That same divine glory would soon fill the tabernacle (40:34–38).

25:1–40:38 | Most of the remaining chapters specify the construction, care, and coordination of the tabernacle—everything from building materials to decorations, instruments, regulations,

offerings, furniture arrangement, wardrobe, and personnel. The details of this ornate place of worship—symbolizing the presence of a holy God and typifying Christ's future redemption of humanity—are so important that two complete records of them are given (25–31; 35–40). The tabernacle was not just a place of worship; it was a structure where Yahweh would **meet** (commune) with His people.

25:1–9 | **The pattern** (design and specifications) and all the regulations for the tabernacle came from **the Lord** Himself; Moses was simply His spokesperson and foreman.

25:2 | This instruction about **the offering** reflects the type of giving commanded in 2 Corinthians 9:7. Joyful, willing offerings have ever been God's desire.

25:10–22 | The most prominent furnishing in the tabernacle was a small wooden chest (**the ark of the covenant**) that would contain the two **tablets of the covenant law**. The ark was placed in the Most Holy Place (40:17–21) and was to be transported on a frame with **rings** and **poles** (25:13–15). No human was to touch it.

> **Picture This**   **Cherubim • 25:17–20**
>
> The word *cherub* describes a well-established image in the ancient Near East. These were composite creatures portrayed with the head of a man, the body of a bull and lion, and the wings of an eagle. (See the four living creatures in Ezek. 1:5–9 for a permutation of these ideas.) The cherubim (plural of *cherub*) that faced each other on the atonement cover represented angels in the presence of the Lord's glory. Some scholars say they pictured the ideal future state of redeemed humankind as they gazed at the merciful God on His throne.
>
> The extensive use of cherubim in the tabernacle is remarkable. In addition to the golden images resting on the atonement cover, artistic designs of cherubim were woven into the beautiful fine linen used both for the 10 curtains inside the building as well as the curtain that separated the Holy Place from the Most Holy Place (26:31–35). Elsewhere, Scripture describes them as surrounding the Lord Almighty (1 Sam. 4:4; Isa. 37:16), so their symbolic presence throughout the tabernacle—the earthly dwelling of God at that time—is fitting.

¹²Cast four gold rings for it and fasten them to its four feet, with two rings on one side and two rings on the other. ¹³Then make poles of acacia wood and overlay them with gold. ¹⁴Insert the poles into the rings on the sides of the ark to carry it. ¹⁵The poles are to remain in the rings of this ark; they are not to be removed. ¹⁶Then put in the ark the tablets of the covenant law, which I will give you.

¹⁷ "Make an atonement cover of pure gold—two and a half cubits long and a cubit and a half wide. ¹⁸And make two cherubim out of hammered gold at the ends of the cover. ¹⁹Make one cherub on one end and the second cherub on the other; make the cherubim of one piece with the cover, at the two ends. ²⁰The cherubim are to have their wings spread upward, overshadowing the cover with them. The cherubim are to face each other, looking toward the cover. ²¹Place the cover on top of the ark and put in the ark the tablets of the covenant law that I will give you. ²²There, above the cover between the two cherubim that are over the ark of the covenant law, I will meet with you and give you all my commands for the Israelites.

The Table

²³ "Make a table of acacia wood—two cubits long, a cubit wide and a cubit and a half high.ᵃ ²⁴Overlay it with pure gold and make a gold molding around it. ²⁵Also make around it a rim a handbreadthᵇ wide and put a gold molding on the rim. ²⁶Make four gold rings for the table and fasten them to the four corners, where the four legs are. ²⁷The rings are to be close to the rim to hold the poles used in carrying the table. ²⁸Make the poles of acacia wood, overlay them with gold and carry the table with them. ²⁹And make its plates and dishes of pure gold, as well as its pitchers and bowls for the pouring out of offerings. ³⁰Put the bread of the Presence on this table to be before me at all times.

The Lampstand

³¹ "Make a lampstand of pure gold. Hammer out its base and shaft, and make its flowerlike cups, buds and blossoms of one piece with them. ³²Six branches are to extend from the sides of the lampstand—three on one side and three on the other. ³³Three cups shaped like almond flowers with buds and blossoms are to be on one branch, three on the next branch, and the same for all six branches extending from the lampstand. ³⁴And on the lampstand there are to be four cups shaped like almond flowers with buds and blossoms. ³⁵One bud shall be under the first pair of branches extending from the lampstand, a second bud under the second pair, and a third bud under the third pair—six branches in all. ³⁶The buds and branches shall all be of one piece with the lampstand, hammered out of pure gold.

³⁷ "Then make its seven lamps and set them up on it so that they light the space

---

ᵃ 23 That is, about 3 feet long, 1 1/2 feet wide and 2 1/4 feet high or about 90 centimeters long, 45 centimeters wide and 68 centimeters high   ᵇ 25 That is, about 3 inches or about 7.5 centimeters

---

25:17–22 | The **atonement cover** (Heb., "to cover over, to make propitiation") was the ark's lid, made of **pure gold**. Here—within the Most Holy Place, between the cloud of the Lord's glory and the stone tablets of the Law—was the place of atonement where the Lord also promised to **meet with** Moses and reveal His will for the people through Moses (29:42; 30:6, 36; Num. 7:89; Ps. 91:1). Today, God's people have access to God's presence through Jesus Christ (Heb. 10:19–25), our "atonement cover" (Rom. 3:25; 1 John 2:2). Because of Christ's shed blood, the throne of God is the believer's throne of grace.

25:23–30 | Like the ark of the covenant, the **table** was made of **acacia wood**—a hardwood resistant to insects—and overlaid with gold. Twelve loaves of **the bread of the Presence** (lit., "bread of faces") represented each of the tribes of Israel (Lev. 24:5–9) and served to remind the Lord of His people. The bread also symbolized Christ as the "bread of life" (John 6:35, 48).

25:31–40 | The menorah, a most exquisite **lampstand of pure gold**, was the only source of man-made light within the tabernacle. It pointed to Christ as the "light of the world" (John 1:9; 3:19; 9:5; 12:46).

in front of it. [38]Its wick trimmers and trays are to be of pure gold. [39]A talent[a] of pure gold is to be used for the lampstand and all these accessories. [40]See that you make them according to the pattern shown you on the mountain.

The Tabernacle

26 "Make the tabernacle with ten curtains of finely twisted linen and blue, purple and scarlet yarn, with cherubim woven into them by a skilled worker. [2]All the curtains are to be the same size—twenty-eight cubits long and four cubits wide.[b] [3]Join five of the curtains together, and do the same with the other five. [4]Make loops of blue material along the edge of the end curtain in one set, and do the same with the end curtain in the other set. [5]Make fifty loops on one curtain and fifty loops on the end curtain of the other set, with the loops opposite each other. [6]Then make fifty gold clasps and use them to fasten the curtains together so that the tabernacle is a unit.

[7]"Make curtains of goat hair for the tent over the tabernacle—eleven altogether. [8]All eleven curtains are to be the same size—thirty cubits long and four cubits wide.[c] [9]Join five of the curtains together into one set and the other six into another set. Fold the sixth curtain double at the front of the tent. [10]Make fifty loops along the edge of the end curtain in one set and also along the edge of the end curtain in the other set. [11]Then make fifty bronze clasps and put them in the loops to fasten the tent together as a unit. [12]As for the additional length of the tent curtains, the half curtain that is left over is to hang down at the rear of the tabernacle. [13]The tent curtains will be a cubit[d] longer on both sides; what is left will hang over the sides of the tabernacle so as to cover it. [14]Make for the tent a covering of ram skins dyed red, and over that a covering of the other durable leather.[e]

[15]"Make upright frames of acacia wood for the tabernacle. [16]Each frame is to be ten cubits long and a cubit and a half wide,[f] [17]with two projections set parallel to each other. Make all the frames of the tabernacle in this way. [18]Make twenty frames for the south side of the tabernacle [19]and make forty silver bases to go under them—two bases for each frame, one under each projection.

[20]For the other side, the north side of the tabernacle, make twenty frames [21]and forty silver bases—two under each frame. [22]Make six frames for the far end, that is, the west end of the tabernacle, [23]and make two frames for the corners at the far end. [24]At these two corners they must be double from the bottom all the way to the top and fitted into a single ring; both shall be like that. [25]So there will be eight frames and sixteen silver bases—two under each frame.

[26]"Also make crossbars of acacia wood: five for the frames on one side of the tabernacle, [27]five for those on the other side, and five for the frames on the west, at the far end of the tabernacle. [28]The center crossbar is to extend from end to end at the middle of the frames. [29]Overlay the frames with gold and make gold rings to hold the crossbars. Also overlay the crossbars with gold.

[30]"Set up the tabernacle according to the plan shown you on the mountain.

[31]"Make a curtain of blue, purple and scarlet yarn and finely twisted linen, with cherubim woven into it by a skilled worker. [32]Hang it with gold hooks on four posts of acacia wood overlaid with gold and standing on four silver bases. [33]Hang the curtain from the clasps and place the ark of the covenant law behind the curtain. The curtain will separate the Holy Place from the Most Holy Place. [34]Put the atonement cover on the ark of the covenant law in the Most Holy Place. [35]Place the table outside the curtain on the north side of the tabernacle and put the lampstand opposite it on the south side.

[36]"For the entrance to the tent make a curtain of blue, purple and scarlet yarn and finely twisted linen—the work of an embroiderer. [37]Make gold hooks for this curtain and five posts of acacia wood overlaid with gold. And cast five bronze bases for them.

The Altar of Burnt Offering

27 "Build an altar of acacia wood, three cubits[g] high; it is to be square, five cubits long and five cubits wide.[h] [2]Make a

---

[a] 39 That is, about 75 pounds or about 34 kilograms   [b] 2 That is, about 42 feet long and 6 feet wide or about 13 meters long and 1.8 meters wide   [c] 8 That is, about 45 feet long and 6 feet wide or about 13.5 meters long and 1.8 meters wide   [d] 13 That is, about 18 inches or about 45 centimeters   [e] 14 Possibly the hides of large aquatic mammals (see 25:5)   [f] 16 That is, about 15 feet long and 2 1/4 feet wide or about 4.5 meters long and 68 centimeters wide   [g] 1 That is, about 4 1/2 feet or about 1.4 meters   [h] 1 That is, about 7 1/2 feet or about 2.3 meters long and wide

---

26:1-37 | The detailed instructions of the **tabernacle** produced a place of strength and beauty. Each shape and shade and material had significance and meaning, some of which is unknown to us today. When the Hebrew people came to worship the Lord there, they were surrounded by symbols of His holiness and grace (Ps. 27:4; 84:1, 2, 4). **Cherubim** were everywhere in the tabernacle as reminders that God's angelic host stand ever ready to help (Heb. 9:5).

The tabernacle was a portable worship center that was always placed at the geographical center of the nation of Israel, with all the tribes camped around it in a designated formation. Those approaching the tabernacle would first see the white linen walls of the court of the tabernacle, which formed an enclosure 150 feet long and 75 feet wide. The linen fence that surrounded this area was suspended on posts of bronze; the whiteness of the fence announced to all who approached that this was a holy place. Access to the courtyard of the tabernacle was gained through one entrance (27:16) that was 30 feet wide and seven feet high. The entire nation of Israel had only one way to God (John 14:6; Acts 4:12)!

Located inside the courtyard was the tabernacle itself. The word *tabernacle* means "tent." The tabernacle was a flat-roofed, oblong tent 15 feet in height and width and 45 feet long. The tabernacle was made of gorgeous woven curtains of blue, purple, and scarlet yarns and linen. It was covered in three layers. The first consisted of curtains made of goat hair. That layer was covered with two layers of animal skins—dyed-red ram hides (perhaps hinting at the sacrifices done at the tabernacle) and the "durable" hides of an aquatic animal, such as the dolphin (a protection from the elements). The tent itself was constructed with frames overlaid with gold and was entered by a doorway made of curtains. The lovely woven curtains emphasized the beauty of true worship.

Inside the tabernacle were two compartments divided by an ornate curtain woven of the same colors as the outer covering and embroidered with gold and inlaid with cherubim. The curtain was supported by four golden posts set on silver bases. The first compartment was called the Holy Place, and the second compartment was the inner chamber known as the Most Holy Place. The floor was the desert sand, a significant reminder that the priests were still on earth and that nothing was permanent about their position (26:31–35).

horn at each of the four corners, so that the horns and the altar are of one piece, and overlay the altar with bronze. ³Make all its utensils of bronze—its pots to remove the ashes, and its shovels, sprinkling bowls, meat forks and firepans. ⁴Make a grating for it, a bronze network, and make a bronze ring at each of the four corners of the network. ⁵Put it under the ledge of the altar so that it is halfway up the altar. ⁶Make poles of acacia wood for the altar and overlay them with bronze. ⁷The poles are to be inserted into the rings so they will be on two sides of the altar when it is carried. ⁸Make the altar hollow, out of boards. It is to be made just as you were shown on the mountain.

The Courtyard

⁹ "Make a courtyard for the tabernacle. The south side shall be a hundred cubitsᵃ long and is to have curtains of finely twisted linen, ¹⁰with twenty posts and twenty bronze bases and with silver hooks and bands on the posts. ¹¹The north side shall also be a hundred cubits long and is to have curtains, with twenty posts and twenty bronze bases and with silver hooks and bands on the posts.

¹² "The west end of the courtyard shall be fifty cubitsᵇ wide and have curtains, with ten posts and ten bases. ¹³On the east end, toward the sunrise, the courtyard shall also be fifty cubits wide. ¹⁴Curtains fifteen cubitsᶜ long are to be on one side of the entrance, with three posts and three bases, ¹⁵and curtains fifteen cubits long are to be on the other side, with three posts and three bases.

¹⁶ "For the entrance to the courtyard, provide a curtain twenty cubitsᵈ long, of blue, purple and scarlet yarn and finely twisted linen—the work of an embroiderer—with four posts and four bases. ¹⁷All the posts around the courtyard are to have silver bands and hooks, and bronze bases. ¹⁸The courtyard shall be a hundred cubits long and fifty cubits wide,ᵉ with curtains of finely twisted linen five cubitsᶠ high, and with bronze bases. ¹⁹All the other articles used in the service of the tabernacle, whatever their function, including all the tent pegs for it and those for the courtyard, are to be of bronze.

ᵃ 9 That is, about 150 feet or about 45 meters; also in verse 11   ᵇ 12 That is, about 75 feet or about 23 meters; also in verse 13   ᶜ 14 That is, about 23 feet or about 6.8 meters; also in verse 15   ᵈ 16 That is, about 30 feet or about 9 meters   ᵉ 18 That is, about 150 feet long and 75 feet wide or about 45 meters long and 23 meters wide   ᶠ 18 That is, about 7 1/2 feet or about 2.3 meters

27:1-18 | Here are instructions for the outer **courtyard** of the **tabernacle**. Because this is where animal sacrifices were offered, only the pieces that the priests needed for this duty were placed here: **the altar** of burnt offering (30:28; Lev. 4:7)—also known as the bronze altar (38:30)—and the bronze bowl (40:6, 7) for washing. The altar was quite large (about 7 1/2 feet square and 4 1/2 feet high), despite the fact it had to be portable.

27:9-19 | The **courtyard for the tabernacle** was a rectangle outlined by a wall of **curtains** and **posts** (20 on the south side, 20 on the north, and 10 on the west end). These curtains, which were nearly 8 feet tall, blocked public view into the courtyard.

Oil for the Lampstand

[20]"Command the Israelites to bring you clear oil of pressed olives for the light so that the lamps may be kept burning. [21]In the tent of meeting, outside the curtain that shields the ark of the covenant law, Aaron and his sons are to keep the lamps burning before the LORD from evening till morning. This is to be a lasting ordinance among the Israelites for the generations to come.

The Priestly Garments

28 "Have Aaron your brother brought to you from among the Israelites, along with his sons Nadab and Abihu, Eleazar and Ithamar, so they may serve me as priests. [2]Make sacred garments for your brother Aaron to give him dignity and honor. [3]Tell all the skilled workers to whom I have given wisdom in such matters that they are to make garments for Aaron, for his consecration, so he may serve me as priest. [4]These are the garments they are to make: a breastpiece, an ephod, a robe, a woven tunic, a turban and a sash. They are to make these sacred garments for your brother Aaron and his sons, so they may serve me as priests. [5]Have them use gold, and blue, purple and scarlet yarn, and fine linen.

The Ephod

[6]"Make the ephod of gold, and of blue, purple and scarlet yarn, and of finely twisted linen—the work of skilled hands. [7]It is to have two shoulder pieces attached to two of its corners, so it can be fastened. [8]Its skillfully woven waistband is to be like it—of one piece with the ephod and made with gold, and with blue, purple and scarlet yarn, and with finely twisted linen.

[9]"Take two onyx stones and engrave on them the names of the sons of Israel [10]in the order of their birth—six names on one stone and the remaining six on the other. [11]Engrave the names of the sons of Israel on the two stones the way a gem cutter engraves a seal. Then mount the stones in gold filigree settings [12]and fasten them on the shoulder pieces of the ephod as memorial stones for the sons of Israel. Aaron is to bear the names on his shoulders as a memorial before the LORD. [13]Make gold filigree settings [14]and two braided chains of pure gold, like a rope, and attach the chains to the settings.

The Breastpiece

[15]"Fashion a breastpiece for making decisions—the work of skilled hands. Make it like the ephod: of gold, and of blue, purple and scarlet yarn, and of finely twisted linen. [16]It is to be square—a span[a] long and a span wide—and folded double. [17]Then mount four rows of precious stones on it. The first row shall be carnelian, chrysolite and beryl; [18]the second row shall be turquoise, lapis lazuli and emerald; [19]the third row shall be jacinth, agate and amethyst; [20]the fourth row shall be topaz, onyx and jasper.[b] Mount them in gold filigree settings. [21]There are to be twelve stones, one for each of the names of the sons of Israel, each engraved like a seal with the name of one of the twelve tribes.

[22]"For the breastpiece make braided chains of pure gold, like a rope. [23]Make two gold rings for it and fasten them to two corners of the breastpiece. [24]Fasten the two gold chains to the rings at the corners of the breastpiece, [25]and the other ends of the chains to the two settings, attaching them to the shoulder pieces of the ephod at the front. [26]Make two gold rings and attach them to the other two corners of the breastpiece on the inside edge next to the ephod. [27]Make two more gold rings and attach them to the bottom of the shoulder pieces on the front of the ephod, close to the seam just above the waistband of the ephod. [28]The rings of the breastpiece are to be tied to the rings of the ephod with blue cord, connecting it to the waistband, so that the breastpiece will not swing out from the ephod.

[29]"Whenever Aaron enters the Holy Place, he will bear the names of the sons of Israel

[a] 16 That is, about 9 inches or about 23 centimeters   [b] 20 The precise identification of some of these precious stones is uncertain.

27:20, 21 | The priests kept the seven **lamps** of the menorah (25:31-39) burning with the olive **oil** provided by the people. For **the ark of the covenant law**, see note on 25:10-22. The lampstand was in front of the ark, although a **curtain** separated the two sections of the tabernacle.

28:1 | The preparation for formally establishing Israel's priesthood begins here. **Aaron** and **his sons** were appointed by Yahweh. Their principal function, according to the Lord, was to **serve** God through the administration of the temple and its sacrifices. From this point forward, all true **priests** in Israel were to be descended from Aaron's line (Heb. 5:4).

28:2–39 | The priestly **garments** were made by **skilled workers** and included some of the same materials as the curtains of the tabernacle (28:8, 15, 33, 39, 42), plus gold and precious stones (28:17–20). The high priest's clothing in particular signified dignity and honor (28:40) and served as a constant reminder of the Lord's holiness.

28:6–21 | The **ephod** was a two-part, sleeveless outer garment that covered the priest's upper body. The names of Israel's 12 tribes were engraved on the **stones** at the shoulders so that as Aaron entered the tabernacle, he would bear Israel's **names** before the Lord. Aaron's **breastpiece** bore 12 precious gems. Each stone was also inscribed with the name of one of the **sons of Israel**, showing that the priest represented all 12 tribes.

Historically Speaking

Urim and Thummim • 28:30

The Urim and the Thummim, meaning "the most dazzling light," were a means by which the high priest might find answers from the Lord (see also Lev. 8:8; Num. 27:21; Deut. 33:8; 1 Sam. 28:6; 30:7, 8 [implied]; Ezra 2:63; Neh. 7:65). When a divine answer was needed, the priest would turn toward the Most Holy Place and ask Yahweh for direction. When the Lord spoke, the priest would give the inquirer (usually a nation's ruler) the answer in an oracle. A brilliant flash of dazzling light (the actual meaning of the Hebrew words *urim-we-tummim*) from the stones of the breastplate would validate the answer!

over his heart on the breastpiece of decision as a continuing memorial before the LORD. ³⁰ Also put the Urim and the Thummim in the breastpiece, so they may be over Aaron's heart whenever he enters the presence of the LORD. Thus Aaron will always bear the means of making decisions for the Israelites over his heart before the LORD.

Other Priestly Garments

³¹ "Make the robe of the ephod entirely of blue cloth, ³² with an opening for the head in its center. There shall be a woven edge like a collar*ᵃ* around this opening, so that it will not tear. ³³ Make pomegranates of blue, purple and scarlet yarn around the hem of the robe, with gold bells between them. ³⁴ The gold bells and the pomegranates are to alternate around the hem of the robe. ³⁵ Aaron must wear it when he ministers. The sound of the bells will be heard when he enters the Holy Place before the LORD and when he comes out, so that he will not die.

³⁶ "Make a plate of pure gold and engrave on it as on a seal: HOLY TO THE LORD. ³⁷ Fasten a blue cord to it to attach it to the turban; it is to be on the front of the turban. ³⁸ It will be on Aaron's forehead, and he will bear the guilt involved in the sacred gifts the Israelites consecrate, whatever their gifts may be. It will be on Aaron's forehead continually so that they will be acceptable to the LORD.

³⁹ "Weave the tunic of fine linen and make the turban of fine linen. The sash is

to be the work of an embroiderer. ⁴⁰ Make tunics, sashes and caps for Aaron's sons to give them dignity and honor. ⁴¹ After you put these clothes on your brother Aaron and his sons, anoint and ordain them. Consecrate them so they may serve me as priests.

⁴² "Make linen undergarments as a covering for the body, reaching from the waist to the thigh. ⁴³ Aaron and his sons must wear them whenever they enter the tent of meeting or approach the altar to minister in the Holy Place, so that they will not incur guilt and die.

"This is to be a lasting ordinance for Aaron and his descendants.

Consecration of the Priests

29 "This is what you are to do to consecrate them, so they may serve me as priests: Take a young bull and two rams without defect. ² And from the finest wheat flour make round loaves without yeast, thick loaves without yeast and with olive oil mixed in, and thin loaves without yeast and brushed with olive oil. ³ Put them in a basket and present them along with the bull and the two rams. ⁴ Then bring Aaron and his sons to the entrance to the tent of meeting and wash them with water. ⁵ Take the garments and dress Aaron with the tunic, the robe of the ephod, the ephod itself*ᵃ* and the breastpiece. Fasten the ephod on him by its skillfully woven waistband. ⁶ Put the turban on his head and attach the sacred emblem to the turban. ⁷ Take the anointing oil and anoint him by pouring it on his head. ⁸ Bring his sons and dress them in tunics ⁹ and fasten caps on them. Then tie sashes on Aaron and his sons.*ᵇ* The priesthood is theirs by a lasting ordinance.

"Then you shall ordain Aaron and his sons.

¹⁰ "Bring the bull to the front of the tent of meeting, and Aaron and his sons shall lay their hands on its head. ¹¹ Slaughter it in the LORD's presence at the entrance to the tent of meeting. ¹² Take some of the bull's blood and put it on the horns of the altar with your finger, and pour out the rest of it at the base of the altar. ¹³ Then take all the fat on the

ᵃ 32 The meaning of the Hebrew for this word is uncertain.   ᵇ 9 Hebrew; Septuagint on them

---

28:31–39 | The **hem** of Aaron's **robe** was interspersed with **gold bells**. The sound of the bells indicated to those outside the Most Holy Place that the high priest was alive—he had not been consumed by the Lord's anger while fulfilling his duties.

28:40–43 | Special **linen undergarments** were also made for Aaron's sons. These protected the priests from unintentional immodesty as they led the people in worship.

29:1–37 | The consecration of the **priests** was so significant

in Israel's history that an entire chapter is devoted to this dedication ceremony, which included a series of sacrifices. First, a **bull** was sacrificed for a **sin offering**. Then **two rams** were sacrificed, one for a **burnt offering** and the other, the **ordination ram**, for a **wave offering** and a **fellowship** offering. By placing **their hands** on the animal's **head**, the priests symbolically acknowledged their own sin and need of cleansing (Lev. 17:11; Heb. 9:22).

internal organs, the long lobe of the liver, and both kidneys with the fat on them, and burn them on the altar. ¹⁴But burn the bull's flesh and its hide and its intestines outside the camp. It is a sin offering.ᵃ

¹⁵"Take one of the rams, and Aaron and his sons shall lay their hands on its head. ¹⁶Slaughter it and take the blood and splash it against the sides of the altar. ¹⁷Cut the ram into pieces and wash the internal organs and the legs, putting them with the head and the other pieces. ¹⁸Then burn the entire ram on the altar. It is a burnt offering to the LORD, a pleasing aroma, a food offering presented to the LORD.

¹⁹"Take the other ram, and Aaron and his sons shall lay their hands on its head. ²⁰Slaughter it, take some of its blood and put it on the lobes of the right ears of Aaron and his sons, on the thumbs of their right hands, and on the big toes of their right feet. Then splash blood against the sides of the altar. ²¹And take some blood from the altar and some of the anointing oil and sprinkle it on Aaron and his garments and on his sons and their garments. Then he and his sons and their garments will be consecrated.

²²"Take from this ram the fat, the fat tail, the fat on the internal organs, the long lobe of the liver, both kidneys with the fat on them, and the right thigh. (This is the ram for the ordination.) ²³From the basket of bread made without yeast, which is before the LORD, take one round loaf, one thick loaf with olive oil mixed in, and one thin loaf. ²⁴Put all these in the hands of Aaron and his sons and have them wave them before the LORD as a wave offering. ²⁵Then take them from their hands and burn them on the altar along with the burnt offering for a pleasing aroma to the LORD, a food offering presented to the LORD. ²⁶After you take the breast of the ram for Aaron's ordination, wave it before the LORD as a wave offering, and it will be your share.

²⁷"Consecrate those parts of the ordination ram that belong to Aaron and his sons: the breast that was waved and the thigh that was presented. ²⁸This is always to be the perpetual share from the Israelites for Aaron and his sons. It is the contribution the Israelites are to make to the LORD from their fellowship offerings.

²⁹"Aaron's sacred garments will belong to his descendants so that they can be anointed and ordained in them. ³⁰The son who succeeds him as priest and comes to the tent of meeting to minister in the Holy Place is to wear them seven days.

³¹"Take the ram for the ordination and cook the meat in a sacred place. ³²At the entrance to the tent of meeting, Aaron and his sons are to eat the meat of the ram and the bread that is in the basket. ³³They are to eat these offerings by which atonement was made for their ordination and consecration. But no one else may eat them, because they are sacred. ³⁴And if any of the meat of the ordination ram or any bread is left over till morning, burn it up. It must not be eaten, because it is sacred.

³⁵"Do for Aaron and his sons everything I have commanded you, taking seven days to ordain them. ³⁶Sacrifice a bull each day as a sin offering to make atonement. Purify the altar by making atonement for it, and anoint it to consecrate it. ³⁷For seven days make atonement for the altar and consecrate it. Then the altar will be most holy, and whatever touches it will be holy.

³⁸"This is what you are to offer on the altar regularly each day: two lambs a year old. ³⁹Offer one in the morning and the other at twilight. ⁴⁰With the first lamb offer a tenth of an ephahᵇ of the finest flour mixed with a quarter of a hinᶜ of oil from pressed olives, and a quarter of a hin of wine as a drink offering. ⁴¹Sacrifice the other lamb at twilight with the same grain offering and its drink offering as in the morning—a pleasing aroma, a food offering presented to the LORD.

⁴²"For the generations to come this burnt offering is to be made regularly at the entrance to the tent of meeting, before the LORD. There I will meet you and speak to you; ⁴³there also I will meet with the Israelites, and the place will be consecrated by my glory.

⁴⁴"So I will consecrate the tent of meeting and the altar and will consecrate Aaron and his sons to serve me as priests. ⁴⁵Then I will dwell among the Israelites and be their God. ⁴⁶They will know that I am the LORD their God, who brought them out of Egypt so that I might dwell among them. I am the LORD their God.

ᵃ 14 Or purification offering; also in verse 36   ᵇ 40 That is, probably about 3 1/2 pounds or about 1.6 kilograms   ᶜ 40 That is, probably about 1 quart or about 1 liter

---

29:22-28 | The **wave offering** was waved back and forth between the altar and the priest, signaling it was a gift to the Lord. Then those items were burned on the altar, except the **breast of the ram**, which was to be eaten by Aaron and his sons. In this way, the Hebrew people contributed to the work of the Lord. The **fellowship** offering was something held out before the Lord; it was not tossed.

29:42-46 | **Tent of meeting** means a "rendezvous tent." There, the Lord promised to meet with His people. God's special presence was limited to the tent of meeting (tabernacle) at that time, whereas today, His presence is in every believer through the Holy Spirit.

The Altar of Incense

30 "Make an altar of acacia wood for burning incense. [2]It is to be square, a cubit long and a cubit wide, and two cubits high[a] — its horns of one piece with it. [3]Overlay the top and all the sides and the horns with pure gold, and make a gold molding around it. [4]Make two gold rings for the altar below the molding — two on each of the opposite sides — to hold the poles used to carry it. [5]Make the poles of acacia wood and overlay them with gold. [6]Put the altar in front of the curtain that shields the ark of the covenant law — before the atonement cover that is over the tablets of the covenant law — where I will meet with you.

[7]"Aaron must burn fragrant incense on the altar every morning when he tends the lamps. [8]He must burn incense again when he lights the lamps at twilight so incense will burn regularly before the LORD for the generations to come. [9]Do not offer on this altar any other incense or any burnt offering or grain offering, and do not pour a drink offering on it. [10]Once a year Aaron shall make atonement on its horns. This annual atonement must be made with the blood of the atoning sin offering[b] for the generations to come. It is most holy to the LORD."

Atonement Money

[11]Then the LORD said to Moses, [12]"When you take a census of the Israelites to count them, each one must pay the LORD a ransom for his life at the time he is counted. Then no plague will come on them when you number them. [13]Each one who crosses over to those already counted is to give a half shekel,[c] according to the sanctuary shekel, which weighs twenty gerahs. This half shekel is an offering to the LORD. [14]All who cross over, those twenty years old or more, are to give an offering to the LORD. [15]The rich are not to give more than a half shekel and the poor are not to give less when you make the offering to the LORD to atone for your lives. [16]Receive the atonement money from the Israelites and use it for the service of the tent of meeting. It will be a memorial

for the Israelites before the LORD, making atonement for your lives."

Basin for Washing

[17]Then the LORD said to Moses, [18]"Make a bronze basin, with its bronze stand, for washing. Place it between the tent of meeting and the altar, and put water in it. [19]Aaron and his sons are to wash their hands and feet with water from it. [20]Whenever they enter the tent of meeting, they shall wash with water so that they will not die. Also, when they approach the altar to minister by presenting a food offering to the LORD, [21]they shall wash their hands and feet so that they will not die. This is to be a lasting ordinance for Aaron and his descendants for the generations to come."

Anointing Oil

[22]Then the LORD said to Moses, [23]"Take the following fine spices: 500 shekels[d] of liquid myrrh, half as much (that is, 250 shekels) of fragrant cinnamon, 250 shekels[e] of fragrant calamus, [24]500 shekels of cassia — all according to the sanctuary shekel — and a hin[f] of olive oil. [25]Make these into a sacred anointing oil, a fragrant blend, the work of a perfumer. It will be the sacred anointing oil. [26]Then use it to anoint the tent of meeting, the ark of the covenant law, [27]the table and all its articles, the lampstand and its accessories, the altar of incense, [28]the altar of burnt offering and all its utensils, and the basin with its stand. [29]You shall consecrate them so they will be most holy, and whatever touches them will be holy.

[30]"Anoint Aaron and his sons and consecrate them so they may serve me as priests. [31]Say to the Israelites, 'This is to be my sacred anointing oil for the generations to come. [32]Do not pour it on anyone else's body and do not make any other oil using the same formula. It is sacred, and you are to consider it sacred. [33]Whoever makes

---

[a] 2 That is, about 1 1/2 feet long and wide and 3 feet high or about 45 centimeters long and wide and 90 centimeters high   [b] 10 Or purification offering   [c] 13 That is, about 1/5 ounce or about 5.8 grams; also in verse 15   [d] 23 That is, about 12 1/2 pounds or about 5.8 kilograms; also in verse 24   [e] 23 That is, about 6 1/4 pounds or about 2.9 kilograms   [f] 24 That is, probably about 1 gallon or about 3.8 liters

---

30:1–10 | The small **altar . . . for burning incense** was similar to the ark of the covenant (25:10–22); it was to have four **horns**, one at each corner, along with the same type of molding, rings, and poles for transport. Its **fragrant**, pure incense was intended to perpetually provide a holy aroma to the Lord. Annual atonement was to be made for the incense altar, perhaps to show the association of things with people.
30:11–16 | **A census of the Israelites** would be taken (Num. 1:2), and a **ransom** payment would be required from **each** person over the age of 20. That the payment was the same, whether one was rich or poor, was

perhaps a symbol that every life has equal value before the Lord.
30:17–21 | See note on 27:1–18. The business of sacrifice was dirty; constant washing of the priests' **hands and feet** in the **bronze basin** was necessary for purity and cleanliness. Purity for the believer is necessary as well, and Christ is the only source of continual cleansing from sins.
30:22–38 | **The sacred anointing oil** and the **incense** were exclusively for the priests' use. The oil is thought to represent Jesus as the Christ—the anointed of the Lord (Ps. 45:8). Christians understand the incense to be a symbol of the sweet life and sacrifice of Jesus (Eph. 5:2).

perfume like it and puts it on anyone other than a priest must be cut off from their people.' "

Incense

³⁴ Then the LORD said to Moses, "Take fragrant spices—gum resin, onycha and galbanum—and pure frankincense, all in equal amounts, ³⁵ and make a fragrant blend of incense, the work of a perfumer. It is to be salted and pure and sacred. ³⁶ Grind some of it to powder and place it in front of the ark of the covenant law in the tent of meeting, where I will meet with you. It shall be most holy to you. ³⁷ Do not make any incense with this formula for yourselves; consider it holy to the LORD. ³⁸ Whoever makes incense like it to enjoy its fragrance must be cut off from their people."

Bezalel and Oholiab

31 Then the LORD said to Moses, ² "See, I have chosen Bezalel son of Uri, the son of Hur, of the tribe of Judah, ³ and I have filled him with the Spirit of God, with wisdom, with understanding, with knowledge and with all kinds of skills— ⁴ to make artistic designs for work in gold, silver and bronze, ⁵ to cut and set stones, to work in wood, and to engage in all kinds of crafts. ⁶ Moreover, I have appointed Oholiab son of Ahisamak, of the tribe of Dan, to help him. Also I have given ability to all the skilled workers to make everything I have commanded you: ⁷ the tent of meeting, the ark of the covenant law with the atonement cover on it, and all the other furnishings of the tent— ⁸ the table and its articles, the pure gold lampstand and all its accessories, the altar of incense, ⁹ the altar of burnt offering and all its utensils, the basin with its stand— ¹⁰ and also the woven garments, both the sacred garments for Aaron the priest and the garments for his sons when they serve as priests, ¹¹ and the anointing oil and fragrant incense for the Holy Place. They are to make them just as I commanded you."

The Sabbath

¹² Then the LORD said to Moses, ¹³ "Say to the Israelites, 'You must observe my Sabbaths. This will be a sign between me and

Picture This   Wisdom • 31:3

Wisdom's roots run deep into OT soil. The Hebrew verb, meaning "to be wise" or "to act in wisdom," actually describes a skill! As one may have a skill for sports or music, so a person may be skilled in wise behavior and thinking. This explains the wording used in association with those who applied their craft toward the tabernacle: those who made the high priest's garments (28:3) and who wove the curtains for the tabernacle (35:35).

The word for wisdom used in 31:3 is found numerous times in the Book of Proverbs. This wisdom is the capacity for a skill or intellect that must be developed within an individual (Prov. 9:9). It is also used to describe the ability God gave Solomon for the express purpose of building the house of the Lord (2 Chron. 2:12).

When we pray for wisdom (James 1:5), we are actually asking God to develop in us a skill for facing the issues of life. Thankfully, He promises that when we ask for wisdom, He will be faithful to answer.

you for the generations to come, so you may know that I am the LORD, who makes you holy.

¹⁴ " 'Observe the Sabbath, because it is holy to you. Anyone who desecrates it is to be put to death; those who do any work on that day must be cut off from their people. ¹⁵ For six days work is to be done, but the seventh day is a day of sabbath rest, holy to the LORD. Whoever does any work on the Sabbath day is to be put to death. ¹⁶ The Israelites are to observe the Sabbath, celebrating it for the generations to come as a lasting covenant. ¹⁷ It will be a sign between me and the Israelites forever, for in six days the LORD made the heavens and the earth, and on the seventh day he rested and was refreshed.' "

¹⁸ When the LORD finished speaking to Moses on Mount Sinai, he gave him the two tablets of the covenant law, the tablets of stone inscribed by the finger of God.

The Golden Calf

32 When the people saw that Moses was so long in coming down from the mountain, they gathered around Aaron

---

31:1-5 | Bezalel, a master craftsman, had a particular skill that was needed for worship: he was **filled . . . with the Spirit of God** (a phrase typically used in the OT for prophets and kings). For those who are willing, the Lord can and will use every gift He provides His servants as a means to worship Him.
31:12-17 | Instituted on Mount Sinai, the Sabbath was **a sign** of the distinct and special relationship between the Lord and Israel.

The basic idea of Sabbath is not worship but **rest** from **work** (see note on 20:8-11).
32:1 | While Moses was experiencing a spiritual peak, the people of God hit bottom. Fearful that Moses would not return, and desiring something tangible to follow, they asked: **Come, make us gods who will go before us.** Within weeks of experiencing the presence of God at Mount Sinai (19), they were involved in an orgy of idolatry (Acts 7:40).

Tough Questions

What is the meaning of "the LORD relented"? • 32:14

These words may lead us to think that Moses got the better of the Lord; or worse, that God can be manipulated. However, the key to understanding this statement is in understanding the two types of judgment oracles (or announcements) of God within the Bible. One is final and one is conditional.

When the Lord announced judgment on the earth in the form of the great Flood (Gen. 6:13), this was a final decision, an irrevocable judgment with no further room for the people to repent. But when the Lord announced through Jonah the destruction of Nineveh, it was an opportunity for reversal—something Jonah clearly dreaded and acknowledged. Citing the very words of Exodus 34:5–7, Jonah called God "a God who relents from sending calamity" (Jonah 4:2). Even when God announced judgment on Sodom, He allowed Abraham to engage in a form of "bargaining" (Gen. 18:16–33). In that case, Abraham came up short (or rather, the number of righteous persons in Sodom was short!). Here, the judgment oracle Moses heard was more for Moses' sake than anything else. It was a test of Moses' character in this stressful situation.

God draws human beings into the process of His work and His plans. God led Moses to pray for the Hebrew people, and God did what Moses asked. But we cannot forget: in all of this, God did what He had always intended to do.

and said, "Come, make us gods[a] who will go before us. As for this fellow Moses who brought us up out of Egypt, we don't know what has happened to him."

2 Aaron answered them, "Take off the gold earrings that your wives, your sons and your daughters are wearing, and bring them to me." 3 So all the people took off their earrings and brought them to Aaron. 4 He took what they handed him and made it into an idol cast in the shape of a calf, fashioning it with a tool. Then they said, "These are your gods,[b] Israel, who brought you up out of Egypt."

5 When Aaron saw this, he built an altar in front of the calf and announced, "Tomorrow there will be a festival to the LORD." 6 So the next day the people rose early and sacrificed burnt offerings and presented fellowship offerings. Afterward they sat down to eat and drink and got up to indulge in revelry.

7 Then the LORD said to Moses, "Go down, because your people, whom you brought up out of Egypt, have become corrupt. 8 They have been quick to turn away from what I commanded them and have made themselves an idol cast in the shape of a calf. They have bowed down to it and sacrificed to it and have said, 'These are your gods, Israel, who brought you up out of Egypt.'

9 "I have seen these people," the LORD said to Moses, "and they are a stiff-necked people. 10 Now leave me alone so that my anger may burn against them and that I may destroy them. Then I will make you into a great nation."

11 But Moses sought the favor of the LORD his God. "LORD," he said, "why should your anger burn against your people, whom you brought out of Egypt with great power and a mighty hand? 12 Why should the Egyptians say, 'It was with evil intent that he brought them out, to kill them in the mountains and to wipe them off the face of the earth'? Turn from your fierce anger; relent and do not bring disaster on your people. 13 Remember your servants Abraham, Isaac and Israel, to whom you swore by your own self: 'I will make your descendants as numerous as the stars in the sky and I will give your descendants all this land I promised them, and it will be their inheritance forever.'" 14 Then the LORD relented and did not bring on his people the disaster he had threatened.

15 Moses turned and went down the mountain with the two tablets of the covenant law in his hands. They were inscribed on both sides, front and back. 16 The tablets were the

---

[a] 1 Or a god; also in verses 23 and 31   [b] 4 Or This is your god; also in verse 8

32:2–4 | Aaron suggested the people give him their **gold earrings**; then he melted the gold **into an idol cast in the shape of a calf**. This action clearly broke the first two commandments (see 20:3–6). Although the Egyptians worshiped cows, probably more pertinent here is that bovine imagery was directly associated with the Canaanite worship of Baal. This "golden calf" is a dark foreshadowing of Israel's future idolatry (1 Cor. 10:7).
32:5, 6 | **Aaron** may have intended a partial obedience—he would give the people what they asked for, and then he would use it to worship God. But by calling it **a festival to the LORD**, Aaron broke the third commandment (see 20:7). The people's behavior was not like a picnic. The Hebrew verb rendered **indulge in revelry** comes

from the same root as the name "Isaac," which sometimes refers to laughter (see Gen. 21:1–7) but can also refer to words that have sexual implications (such as "caressing"; see Gen. 26:8). Here, it implies sexual acts done in the worship of pagan gods. Immorality often accompanies idolatry, even today (Rom. 1:22–24).
32:7–14 | **Corrupt** and **stiff-necked** mean "unresponsive" and "stubborn" (33:3, 5; 34:9; Deut. 9:6, 13; 10:16; 31:27). God wanted to destroy the people and create a new **nation** of Moses. Moses appealed to: (1) God's responsibility, asserting that these are **your people**; (2) God's reputation (the Egyptians would make false conclusions); and (3) God's reliability, citing Yahweh's solemn oath to Israel's forefathers.

work of God; the writing was the writing of God, engraved on the tablets.

[17] When Joshua heard the noise of the people shouting, he said to Moses, "There is the sound of war in the camp."

[18] Moses replied:

"It is not the sound of victory,
    it is not the sound of defeat;
    it is the sound of singing that I hear."

[19] When Moses approached the camp and saw the calf and the dancing, his anger burned and he threw the tablets out of his hands, breaking them to pieces at the foot of the mountain. [20] And he took the calf the people had made and burned it in the fire; then he ground it to powder, scattered it on the water and made the Israelites drink it.

[21] He said to Aaron, "What did these people do to you, that you led them into such great sin?"

[22] "Do not be angry, my lord," Aaron answered. "You know how prone these people are to evil. [23] They said to me, 'Make us gods who will go before us. As for this fellow Moses who brought us up out of Egypt, we don't know what has happened to him.' [24] So I told them, 'Whoever has any gold jewelry, take it off.' Then they gave me the gold, and I threw it into the fire, and out came this calf!"

[25] Moses saw that the people were running wild and that Aaron had let them get out of control and so become a laughingstock to their enemies. [26] So he stood at the entrance to the camp and said, "Whoever is for the LORD, come to me." And all the Levites rallied to him.

[27] Then he said to them, "This is what the LORD, the God of Israel, says: 'Each man strap a sword to his side. Go back and forth through the camp from one end to the other, each killing his brother and friend and neighbor.' " [28] The Levites did as Moses commanded, and that day about three thousand of the people died. [29] Then Moses said, "You have been set apart to the LORD today, for you were against your own sons and brothers, and he has blessed you this day."

[30] The next day Moses said to the people, "You have committed a great sin. But now I will go up to the LORD; perhaps I can make atonement for your sin."

[31] So Moses went back to the LORD and said, "Oh, what a great sin these people have committed! They have made themselves gods of gold. [32] But now, please forgive their sin—but if not, then blot me out of the book you have written."

[33] The LORD replied to Moses, "Whoever has sinned against me I will blot out of my book. [34] Now go, lead the people to the place I spoke of, and my angel will go before you. However, when the time comes for me to punish, I will punish them for their sin."

[35] And the LORD struck the people with a plague because of what they did with the calf Aaron had made.

33 Then the LORD said to Moses, "Leave this place, you and the people you brought up out of Egypt, and go up to the land I promised on oath to Abraham, Isaac and Jacob, saying, 'I will give it to your descendants.' [2] I will send an angel before you and drive out the Canaanites, Amorites, Hittites, Perizzites, Hivites and Jebusites. [3] Go up to the land flowing with milk and honey. But I will not go with you, because you are a stiff-necked people and I might destroy you on the way."

[4] When the people heard these distressing words, they began to mourn and no one put on any ornaments. [5] For the LORD had said to Moses, "Tell the Israelites, 'You are a stiff-necked people. If I were to go with you even for a moment, I might destroy you. Now take off your ornaments and I will decide

---

32:15, 16 | The two tablets of the covenant law refer to the Ten Commandments. We know now that both tablets had *all* Ten Commandments on them. When ancient nations made treaties, the stipulations were entered onto two original documents, with each party taking one home to its temple for observation "by the gods." For Israel, the two complete tablets would stay together as a sign of their belief in one God.

32:19-28 | This passage reveals how serious sin is to the Lord. Moses angrily **breaking** the stone tablets symbolized that Israel had broken the covenant. Although Aaron shifted blame (**You know how prone these people are to evil**) and made a feeble explanation (**I threw it into the fire, and out came this calf!**), Moses was right to confront him before confronting the people. Purging the sin from the Israelite camp required the slaying of 3,000 people by **all the Levites**.

32:25, 26 | Part of leadership's responsibility is to protectively restrain their people from doing what will bring them harm or judgment. Aaron's failure to do this made **a laughingstock** of the Lord and His chosen people in front of their enemies.

32:30-32 | Moses interceded for the people he loved so much, hoping he could atone for their sin (see Paul's similar words respecting the salvation of the Jews in Rom. 9:3). Of course, as a sinner himself, Moses could not do so, but his words convey the picture of the sacrifice of Christ, which *was* able to make atonement for humanity (Mark 10:45).

33:1-6 | For the rest of Israel's journey to the Promised Land, God promised His protection and guidance through one He called **an angel** (this was not Himself). Losing God's immediate presence caused great mourning. As a sign of their remorse, **the Israelites stripped off their ornaments** (jewelry), the equivalent of putting on sackcloth and ashes. Later, in response to Moses' prayer (33:12–16), God agreed to go with them (33:17).

what to do with you.'" [6]So the Israelites stripped off their ornaments at Mount Horeb.

The Tent of Meeting

[7]Now Moses used to take a tent and pitch it outside the camp some distance away, calling it the "tent of meeting." Anyone inquiring of the LORD would go to the tent of meeting outside the camp. [8]And whenever Moses went out to the tent, all the people rose and stood at the entrances to their tents, watching Moses until he entered the tent. [9]As Moses went into the tent, the pillar of cloud would come down and stay at the entrance, while the LORD spoke with Moses. [10]Whenever the people saw the pillar of cloud standing at the entrance to the tent, they all stood and worshiped, each at the entrance to their tent. [11]The LORD would speak to Moses face to face, as one speaks to a friend. Then Moses would return to the camp, but his young aide Joshua son of Nun did not leave the tent.

Moses and the Glory of the LORD

[12]Moses said to the LORD, "You have been telling me, 'Lead these people,' but you have not let me know whom you will send with me. You have said, 'I know you by name and you have found favor with me.' [13]If you are pleased with me, teach me your ways so I may know you and continue to find favor with you. Remember that this nation is your people."

[14]The LORD replied, "My Presence will go with you, and I will give you rest."

[15]Then Moses said to him, "If your Presence does not go with us, do not send us up from here. [16]How will anyone know that you are pleased with me and with your people unless you go with us? What else will distinguish me and your people from all the other people on the face of the earth?"

[17]And the LORD said to Moses, "I will do the very thing you have asked, because I am pleased with you and I know you by name."

[18]Then Moses said, "Now show me your glory."

[19]And the LORD said, "I will cause all my goodness to pass in front of you, and I will proclaim my name, the LORD, in your presence. I will have mercy on whom I will have mercy, and I will have compassion on whom I will have compassion. [20]But," he said, "you cannot see my face, for no one may see me and live."

[21]Then the LORD said, "There is a place near me where you may stand on a rock. [22]When my glory passes by, I will put you in a cleft in the rock and cover you with my hand until I have passed by. [23]Then I will remove my hand and you will see my back; but my face must not be seen."

The New Stone Tablets

34 The LORD said to Moses, "Chisel out two stone tablets like the first ones, and I will write on them the words that were on the first tablets, which you broke. [2]Be ready in the morning, and then come up on Mount Sinai. Present yourself to me there on top of the mountain. [3]No one is to come with you or be seen anywhere on the mountain; not even the flocks and herds may graze in front of the mountain."

[4]So Moses chiseled out two stone tablets like the first ones and went up Mount Sinai early in the morning, as the LORD had commanded him; and he carried the two stone tablets in his hands. [5]Then the LORD came down in the cloud and stood there with him and proclaimed his name, the LORD. [6]And he passed in front of Moses, proclaiming, "The LORD, the LORD, the compassionate and gracious God, slow to anger, abounding in love and faithfulness, [7]maintaining love to thousands, and forgiving wickedness, rebellion and sin. Yet he does not leave the guilty unpunished; he punishes the children

---

33:7–11 | Here we see that **the pillar of cloud** was in fact an appearance of Yahweh. Moses had not been a part of the illicit worship, so his tent **outside the camp** became the only place the Lord would meet with Moses, His only contact. Amazingly, the Lord spoke to him **face to face, as one speaks to a friend**. The Lord's tender care for Moses is underscored in 33:17, where He says, "I know you by name."

33:12–34:7 | Moses had seen God's astounding acts during the Exodus, but now he wanted to see more—God's **glory**. God granted this bold request, passing His **goodness** before Moses and proclaiming His own **name**—the expression of His character. The Lord speaks of His manner as having **mercy** and showing **compassion**, words Paul used in Romans 9:15–18.

33:20–23 | There were limits to what Moses would see, for no one can look upon the Lord and live. God is Spirit—with no physical

features whatsoever—so the use of anthropological imagery (**my face . . . my back**) is simply a means to help humans understand what cannot be understood otherwise. Moses' passing view of the Lord's **back** was still more than ever had been seen (see John 1:18; 14:7)—until Jesus, in whom the transcendent God was revealed in human flesh.

34:5–9 | In this stunning self-revelation, Yahweh doubled the word **LORD** to say, "This is who I Am." **Compassionate** and **gracious** go together—He is extensively gracious. **Slow to anger** is a comic term in Hebrew; it means "long of nose" in the sense that it takes a great deal to make the Lord angry. The most important phrase is **abounding in love and faithfulness**. These words (in Grk.) describe Jesus in John 1:14 as "full of grace and truth." Parallel descriptions of the Lord are found throughout Scripture (Neh. 9:17; Ps. 86:15; 100:5; 103:8; 117:2; Joel 2:13; Jonah 4:2).

and their children for the sin of the parents to the third and fourth generation."

⁸Moses bowed to the ground at once and worshiped. ⁹"Lord," he said, "if I have found favor in your eyes, then let the Lord go with us. Although this is a stiff-necked people, forgive our wickedness and our sin, and take us as your inheritance."

¹⁰Then the LORD said: "I am making a covenant with you. Before all your people I will do wonders never before done in any nation in all the world. The people you live among will see how awesome is the work that I, the LORD, will do for you. ¹¹Obey what I command you today. I will drive out before you the Amorites, Canaanites, Hittites, Perizzites, Hivites and Jebusites. ¹²Be careful not to make a treaty with those who live in the land where you are going, or they will be a snare among you. ¹³Break down their altars, smash their sacred stones and cut down their Asherah poles.ᵃ ¹⁴Do not worship any other god, for the LORD, whose name is Jealous, is a jealous God.

¹⁵"Be careful not to make a treaty with those who live in the land; for when they prostitute themselves to their gods and sacrifice to them, they will invite you and you will eat their sacrifices. ¹⁶And when you choose some of their daughters as wives for your sons and those daughters prostitute themselves to their gods, they will lead your sons to do the same.

¹⁷"Do not make any idols.

¹⁸"Celebrate the Festival of Unleavened Bread. For seven days eat bread made without yeast, as I commanded you. Do this at the appointed time in the month of Aviv, for in that month you came out of Egypt.

¹⁹"The first offspring of every womb belongs to me, including all the firstborn males of your livestock, whether from herd or flock. ²⁰Redeem the firstborn donkey with a lamb, but if you do not redeem it, break its neck. Redeem all your firstborn sons.

"No one is to appear before me empty-handed.

²¹"Six days you shall labor, but on the seventh day you shall rest; even during the plowing season and harvest you must rest.

²²"Celebrate the Festival of Weeks with the firstfruits of the wheat harvest, and the Festival of Ingathering at the turn of the year.ᵇ ²³Three times a year all your men are to appear before the Sovereign LORD, the God of Israel. ²⁴I will drive out nations before you and enlarge your territory, and no one will covet your land when you go up three times each year to appear before the LORD your God.

²⁵"Do not offer the blood of a sacrifice to me along with anything containing yeast, and do not let any of the sacrifice from the Passover Festival remain until morning.

²⁶"Bring the best of the firstfruits of your soil to the house of the LORD your God.

"Do not cook a young goat in its mother's milk."

²⁷Then the LORD said to Moses, "Write down these words, for in accordance with these words I have made a covenant with you and with Israel." ²⁸Moses was there with the LORD forty days and forty nights without eating bread or drinking water. And he wrote on the tablets the words of the covenant—the Ten Commandments.

The Radiant Face of Moses

²⁹When Moses came down from Mount Sinai with the two tablets of the covenant law in his hands, he was not aware that his face was radiant because he had spoken with the LORD. ³⁰When Aaron and all the Israelites saw Moses, his face was radiant, and they were afraid to come near him. ³¹But Moses called to them; so Aaron and all the leaders of the community came back to him, and he spoke to them. ³²Afterward all the Israelites came near him, and he gave them all the commands the LORD had given him on Mount Sinai.

³³When Moses finished speaking to them, he put a veil over his face. ³⁴But whenever he entered the LORD's presence to speak with him, he removed the veil until he came out. And when he came out and told the Israelites what he had been commanded, ³⁵they saw that his face was radiant. Then Moses would put the veil back over his face until he went in to speak with the LORD.

Sabbath Regulations

35 Moses assembled the whole Israelite community and said to them, "These are the things the LORD has commanded you to do: ²For six days, work is to be done, but

---

ᵃ 13 That is, wooden symbols of the goddess Asherah   ᵇ 22 That is, in the autumn

---

34:10–28 | In this renewed **covenant**, the Hebrew people were not to intermarry with the unbelieving peoples of the land or make alliances with them. To align with them would mean to eventually act like them, turning the children of Israel to idolatry (Hosea 4:13, 14).

34:29–35 | Moses' experience of the Holy had so transformed him that he wore a **veil** so no one could look upon him. In one sense, when we spend time communing with God, we too "shine" with His glory (2 Cor. 3:7, 18).

the seventh day shall be your holy day, a day of sabbath rest to the LORD. Whoever does any work on it is to be put to death. [3]Do not light a fire in any of your dwellings on the Sabbath day."

Materials for the Tabernacle

[4]Moses said to the whole Israelite community, "This is what the LORD has commanded: [5]From what you have, take an offering for the LORD. Everyone who is willing is to bring to the LORD an offering of gold, silver and bronze; [6]blue, purple and scarlet yarn and fine linen; goat hair; [7]ram skins dyed red and another type of durable leather[a]; acacia wood; [8]olive oil for the light; spices for the anointing oil and for the fragrant incense; [9]and onyx stones and other gems to be mounted on the ephod and breastpiece.

[10]"All who are skilled among you are to come and make everything the LORD has commanded: [11]the tabernacle with its tent and its covering, clasps, frames, crossbars, posts and bases; [12]the ark with its poles and the atonement cover and the curtain that shields it; [13]the table with its poles and all its articles and the bread of the Presence; [14]the lampstand that is for light with its accessories, lamps and oil for the light; [15]the altar of incense with its poles, the anointing oil and the fragrant incense; the curtain for the doorway at the entrance to the tabernacle; [16]the altar of burnt offering with its bronze grating, its poles and all its utensils; the bronze basin with its stand; [17]the curtains of the courtyard with its posts and bases, and the curtain for the entrance to the courtyard; [18]the tent pegs for the tabernacle and for the courtyard, and their ropes; [19]the woven garments worn for ministering in the sanctuary—both the sacred garments for Aaron the priest and the garments for his sons when they serve as priests."

[20]Then the whole Israelite community withdrew from Moses' presence, [21]and everyone who was willing and whose heart moved them came and brought an offering to the LORD for the work on the tent of meeting, for all its service, and for the sacred garments. [22]All who were willing, men and women alike, came and brought gold jewelry of all kinds: brooches, earrings, rings and ornaments. They all presented their gold as a wave offering to the LORD. [23]Everyone who had blue, purple or scarlet yarn or fine linen, or goat hair, ram skins dyed red or the other durable leather brought them. [24]Those presenting an offering of silver or bronze brought it as an offering to the LORD, and everyone who had acacia wood for any part of the work brought it. [25]Every skilled woman spun with her hands and brought what she had spun—blue, purple or scarlet yarn or fine linen. [26]And all the women who were willing and had the skill spun the goat hair. [27]The leaders brought onyx stones and other gems to be mounted on the ephod and breastpiece. [28]They also brought spices and olive oil for the light and for the anointing oil and for the fragrant incense. [29]All the Israelite men and women who were willing brought to the LORD freewill offerings for all the work the LORD through Moses had commanded them to do.

Bezalel and Oholiab

[30]Then Moses said to the Israelites, "See, the LORD has chosen Bezalel son of Uri, the son of Hur, of the tribe of Judah, [31]and he has filled him with the Spirit of God, with wisdom, with understanding, with knowledge and with all kinds of skills—[32]to make artistic designs for work in gold, silver and bronze, [33]to cut and set stones, to work in wood and to engage in all kinds of artistic crafts. [34]And he has given both him and Oholiab son of Ahisamak, of the tribe of Dan, the ability to teach others. [35]He has filled them with skill to do all kinds of work as engravers, designers, embroiderers in blue, purple and scarlet yarn and fine linen, and weavers—all of them skilled workers and designers. **36** [1]So Bezalel, Oholiab and every skilled person to whom the LORD has given skill and ability to know how to carry out all the work of constructing the sanctuary are to do the work just as the LORD has commanded."

---

[a] 7 Possibly the hides of large aquatic mammals; also in verse 23

35:1 | Starting here and continuing through the rest of the book, the people begin to prepare for the presence of the Lord, who will dwell with them in the tabernacle. Moses also begins to prepare the people for the completion of the tabernacle work.

35:4–9 | Exodus 25–27 gave the blueprint for the tabernacle. Here is the "budget." God had already prepared the people for this freewill **offering for the Lord** when they left Egypt (11:2, 3; 12:35, 36). Those who give from a **willing** heart will be stirred to keep giving.

35:10–19 | **All who are skilled** would **make everything the Lord . . . commanded** for the **tabernacle**, right down to its **bases** and **tent pegs**. No detail would be left to chance.

35:21–29 | **Willing** literally means "whose hearts were lifted up." The people gave for the work because they understood that God had freed them from slavery and made them rich (12:35, 36); therefore, what they had belonged to Him. The **leaders** also set a godly example of giving that the people followed.

[2]Then Moses summoned Bezalel and Oholiab and every skilled person to whom the LORD had given ability and who was willing to come and do the work. [3]They received from Moses all the offerings the Israelites had brought to carry out the work of constructing the sanctuary. And the people continued to bring freewill offerings morning after morning. [4]So all the skilled workers who were doing all the work on the sanctuary left what they were doing [5]and said to Moses, "The people are bringing more than enough for doing the work the LORD commanded to be done."

[6]Then Moses gave an order and they sent this word throughout the camp: "No man or woman is to make anything else as an offering for the sanctuary." And so the people were restrained from bringing more, [7]because what they already had was more than enough to do all the work.

The Tabernacle

[8]All those who were skilled among the workers made the tabernacle with ten curtains of finely twisted linen and blue, purple and scarlet yarn, with cherubim woven into them by expert hands. [9]All the curtains were the same size—twenty-eight cubits long and four cubits wide.[a] [10]They joined five of the curtains together and did the same with the other five. [11]Then they made loops of blue material along the edge of the end curtain in one set, and the same was done with the end curtain in the other set. [12]They also made fifty loops on one curtain and fifty loops on the end curtain of the other set, with the loops opposite each other. [13]Then they made fifty gold clasps and used them to fasten the two sets of curtains together so that the tabernacle was a unit.

[14]They made curtains of goat hair for the tent over the tabernacle—eleven altogether. [15]All eleven curtains were the same size—thirty cubits long and four cubits wide.[b] [16]They joined five of the curtains into one set and the other six into another set. [17]Then they made fifty loops along the edge of the end curtain in one set and also along the edge of the end curtain in the other set. [18]They made fifty bronze clasps to fasten the tent together as a unit. [19]Then they made for the tent a covering of ram skins dyed red, and over that a covering of the other durable leather.[c]

[20]They made upright frames of acacia wood for the tabernacle. [21]Each frame was ten cubits long and a cubit and a half wide,[d] [22]with two projections set parallel to each other. They made all the frames of the tabernacle in this way. [23]They made twenty frames for the south side of the tabernacle [24]and made forty silver bases to go under them—two bases for each frame, one under each projection. [25]For the other side, the north side of the tabernacle, they made twenty frames [26]and forty silver bases—two under each frame. [27]They made six frames for the far end, that is, the west end of the tabernacle, [28]and two frames were made for the corners of the tabernacle at the far end. [29]At these two corners the frames were double from the bottom all the way to the top and fitted into a single ring; both were made alike. [30]So there were eight frames and sixteen silver bases—two under each frame.

[31]They also made crossbars of acacia wood: five for the frames on one side of the tabernacle, [32]five for those on the other side, and five for the frames on the west, at the far end of the tabernacle. [33]They made the center crossbar so that it extended from end to end at the middle of the frames. [34]They overlaid the frames with gold and made gold rings to hold the crossbars. They also overlaid the crossbars with gold.

[35]They made the curtain of blue, purple and scarlet yarn and finely twisted linen, with cherubim woven into it by a skilled worker. [36]They made four posts of acacia wood for it and overlaid them with gold. They made gold hooks for them and cast their four silver bases. [37]For the entrance to the tent they made a curtain of blue, purple and scarlet yarn and finely twisted linen—the work of an embroiderer; [38]and they made five posts with hooks for them. They overlaid the tops of the posts and their bands with gold and made their five bases of bronze.

---

[a] 9 That is, about 42 feet long and 6 feet wide or about 13 meters long and 1.8 meters wide   [b] 15 That is, about 45 feet long and 6 feet wide or about 14 meters long and 1.8 meters wide   [c] 19 Possibly the hides of large aquatic mammals (see 35:7)   [d] 21 That is, about 15 feet long and 2 1/4 feet wide or about 4.5 meters long and 68 centimeters wide

---

35:30–36:7 | God deserves the best that can be found in all of His creation. Not only were the finest raw materials used in the furnishing and construction of the tabernacle but also the most skilled craftsmen. The lead **skilled person** was **Bezalel**, one so gifted that he was placed in charge of all the construction and craft. He was assisted by Oholiab. The people gave of their possessions just as enthusiastically, to the point that they had to be **restrained** from giving.

36:8–38 | Compared with 26:1–37, there is very little difference in these instructions except that this time, the tabernacle is the initial reference point rather than the ark.

The Ark

37 Bezalel made the ark of acacia wood—two and a half cubits long, a cubit and a half wide, and a cubit and a half high.[a] [2] He overlaid it with pure gold, both inside and out, and made a gold molding around it. [3] He cast four gold rings for it and fastened them to its four feet, with two rings on one side and two rings on the other. [4] Then he made poles of acacia wood and overlaid them with gold. [5] And he inserted the poles into the rings on the sides of the ark to carry it.

[6] He made the atonement cover of pure gold—two and a half cubits long and a cubit and a half wide. [7] Then he made two cherubim out of hammered gold at the ends of the cover. [8] He made one cherub on one end and the second cherub on the other; at the two ends he made them of one piece with the cover. [9] The cherubim had their wings spread upward, overshadowing the cover with them. The cherubim faced each other, looking toward the cover.

The Table

[10] They[b] made the table of acacia wood—two cubits long, a cubit wide and a cubit and a half high.[c] [11] Then they overlaid it with pure gold and made a gold molding around it. [12] They also made around it a rim a handbreadth[d] wide and put a gold molding on the rim. [13] They cast four gold rings for the table and fastened them to the four corners, where the four legs were. [14] The rings were put close to the rim to hold the poles used in carrying the table. [15] The poles for carrying the table were made of acacia wood and were overlaid with gold. [16] And they made from pure gold the articles for the table—its plates and dishes and bowls and its pitchers for the pouring out of drink offerings.

The Lampstand

[17] They made the lampstand of pure gold. They hammered out its base and shaft, and made its flowerlike cups, buds and blossoms of one piece with them. [18] Six branches extended from the sides of the lampstand—three on one side and three on the other. [19] Three cups shaped like almond flowers with buds and blossoms were on one branch, three on the next branch and the same for all six branches extending from the lampstand. [20] And on the lampstand were four cups shaped like almond flowers with buds and blossoms. [21] One bud was under the first pair of branches extending from the lampstand, a second bud under the second pair, and a third bud under the third pair—six branches in all. [22] The buds and the branches were all of one piece with the lampstand, hammered out of pure gold.

[23] They made its seven lamps, as well as its wick trimmers and trays, of pure gold. [24] They made the lampstand and all its accessories from one talent[e] of pure gold.

The Altar of Incense

[25] They made the altar of incense out of acacia wood. It was square, a cubit long and a cubit wide and two cubits high[f]—its horns of one piece with it. [26] They overlaid the top and all the sides and the horns with pure gold, and made a gold molding around it. [27] They made two gold rings below the molding—two on each of the opposite sides—to hold the poles used to carry it. [28] They made the poles of acacia wood and overlaid them with gold.

[29] They also made the sacred anointing oil and the pure, fragrant incense—the work of a perfumer.

The Altar of Burnt Offering

38 They[g] built the altar of burnt offering of acacia wood, three cubits[h] high; it was square, five cubits long and five cubits wide.[i] [2] They made a horn at each of the four corners, so that the horns and the altar were of one piece, and they overlaid the altar with bronze. [3] They made all its utensils of bronze—its pots, shovels, sprinkling bowls, meat forks and firepans. [4] They made a grating for the altar, a bronze network, to be under its ledge, halfway up the altar. [5] They cast bronze rings to hold the poles for the four corners of the bronze grating. [6] They made the poles of acacia wood and overlaid them with bronze. [7] They inserted the poles into the rings so they would be on the sides of the altar for carrying it. They made it hollow, out of boards.

---

[a] 1 That is, about 3 3/4 feet long and 2 1/4 feet wide and high or about 1.1 meters long and 68 centimeters wide and high; similarly in verse 6   [b] 10 Or *He*; also in verses 11-29   [c] 10 That is, about 3 feet long, 1 1/2 feet wide and 2 1/4 feet high or about 90 centimeters long, 45 centimeters wide and 68 centimeters high   [d] 12 That is, about 3 inches or about 7.5 centimeters   [e] 24 That is, about 75 pounds or about 34 kilograms   [f] 25 That is, about 1 1/2 feet long and wide and 3 feet high or about 45 centimeters long and wide and 90 centimeters high   [g] 1 Or *He*; also in verses 2-9   [h] 1 That is, about 4 1/2 feet or about 1.4 meters   [i] 1 That is, about 7 1/2 feet or about 2.3 meters long and wide

---

37:1–39:42 | **Bezalel** (see 31:2) is the subject of each of the verbs in the paragraphs that follow (e.g., **He made** and **They** [Bezalel and his helpers] **made** in 37:1–8, 10, 17, 25, 29). He and his assistant, Oholiab (31:6), employed and directed many skilled Hebrews. The summary statements in 39:32, 42 speak of the Lord's approval and Moses' blessing on all who labored.

The Basin for Washing

[8] They made the bronze basin and its bronze stand from the mirrors of the women who served at the entrance to the tent of meeting.

The Courtyard

[9] Next they made the courtyard. The south side was a hundred cubits[a] long and had curtains of finely twisted linen, [10] with twenty posts and twenty bronze bases, and with silver hooks and bands on the posts. [11] The north side was also a hundred cubits long and had twenty posts and twenty bronze bases, with silver hooks and bands on the posts. [12] The west end was fifty cubits[b] wide and had curtains, with ten posts and ten bases, with silver hooks and bands on the posts. [13] The east end, toward the sunrise, was also fifty cubits wide. [14] Curtains fifteen cubits[c] long were on one side of the entrance, with three posts and three bases, [15] and curtains fifteen cubits long were on the other side of the entrance to the courtyard, with three posts and three bases. [16] All the curtains around the courtyard were of finely twisted linen. [17] The bases for the posts were bronze. The hooks and bands on the posts were silver, and their tops were overlaid with silver; so all the posts of the courtyard had silver bands.

[18] The curtain for the entrance to the courtyard was made of blue, purple and scarlet yarn and finely twisted linen—the work of an embroiderer. It was twenty cubits[d] long and, like the curtains of the courtyard, five cubits[e] high, [19] with four posts and four bronze bases. Their hooks and bands were silver, and their tops were overlaid with silver. [20] All the tent pegs of the tabernacle and of the surrounding courtyard were bronze.

The Materials Used

[21] These are the amounts of the materials used for the tabernacle, the tabernacle of the covenant law, which were recorded at Moses' command by the Levites under the direction of Ithamar son of Aaron, the priest. [22] (Bezalel son of Uri, the son of Hur, of the tribe of Judah, made everything the LORD commanded Moses; [23] with him was Oholiab son of Ahisamak, of the tribe of Dan—an engraver and designer, and an embroiderer in blue, purple and scarlet yarn and fine linen.) [24] The total amount of the gold from the wave offering used for all the work on the sanctuary was 29 talents and 730 shekels,[f] according to the sanctuary shekel.

[25] The silver obtained from those of the community who were counted in the census was 100 talents[g] and 1,775 shekels,[h] according to the sanctuary shekel— [26] one beka per person, that is, half a shekel,[i] according to the sanctuary shekel, from everyone who had crossed over to those counted, twenty years old or more, a total of 603,550 men. [27] The 100 talents of silver were used to cast the bases for the sanctuary and for the curtain—100 bases from the 100 talents, one talent for each base. [28] They used the 1,775 shekels to make the hooks for the posts, to overlay the tops of the posts, and to make their bands.

[29] The bronze from the wave offering was 70 talents and 2,400 shekels.[j] [30] They used it to make the bases for the entrance to the tent of meeting, the bronze altar with its bronze grating and all its utensils, [31] the bases for the surrounding courtyard and those for its entrance and all the tent pegs for the tabernacle and those for the surrounding courtyard.

The Priestly Garments

39 From the blue, purple and scarlet yarn they made woven garments for ministering in the sanctuary. They also made sacred garments for Aaron, as the LORD commanded Moses.

The Ephod

[2] They[k] made the ephod of gold, and of blue, purple and scarlet yarn, and of finely twisted linen. [3] They hammered out thin sheets of gold and cut strands to be worked into the blue, purple and scarlet yarn and fine linen—the work of skilled hands. [4] They made shoulder pieces for the ephod, which were attached to two of its corners, so it could be fastened. [5] Its skillfully woven waistband was like it—of one piece with the ephod and made with gold, and with blue, purple and scarlet yarn, and with finely twisted linen, as the LORD commanded Moses.

---

[a] 9 That is, about 150 feet or about 45 meters   [b] 12 That is, about 75 feet or about 23 meters   [c] 14 That is, about 22 feet or about 6.8 meters   [d] 18 That is, about 30 feet or about 9 meters   [e] 18 That is, about 7 1/2 feet or about 2.3 meters   [f] 24 The weight of the gold was a little over a ton or about 1 metric ton.   [g] 25 That is, about 3 3/4 tons or about 3.4 metric tons; also in verse 27   [h] 25 That is, about 44 pounds or about 20 kilograms; also in verse 28   [i] 26 That is, about 1/5 ounce or about 5.7 grams   [j] 29 The weight of the bronze was about 2 1/2 tons or about 2.4 metric tons.   [k] 2 Or He; also in verses 7, 8 and 22

38:21–31 | Historians estimated that in following God's instructions to Moses, **Bezalel** and **Oholiab** used more than eight tons of gold, silver, and bronze when they built the tabernacle and crafted articles for it.

⁶They mounted the onyx stones in gold filigree settings and engraved them like a seal with the names of the sons of Israel. ⁷Then they fastened them on the shoulder pieces of the ephod as memorial stones for the sons of Israel, as the LORD commanded Moses.

The Breastpiece

⁸They fashioned the breastpiece—the work of a skilled craftsman. They made it like the ephod: of gold, and of blue, purple and scarlet yarn, and of finely twisted linen. ⁹It was square—a span*a* long and a span wide—and folded double. ¹⁰Then they mounted four rows of precious stones on it. The first row was carnelian, chrysolite and beryl; ¹¹the second row was turquoise, lapis lazuli and emerald; ¹²the third row was jacinth, agate and amethyst; ¹³the fourth row was topaz, onyx and jasper.*b* They were mounted in gold filigree settings. ¹⁴There were twelve stones, one for each of the names of the sons of Israel, each engraved like a seal with the name of one of the twelve tribes.

¹⁵For the breastpiece they made braided chains of pure gold, like a rope. ¹⁶They made two gold filigree settings and two gold rings, and fastened the rings to two of the corners of the breastpiece. ¹⁷They fastened the two gold chains to the rings at the corners of the breastpiece, ¹⁸and the other ends of the chains to the two settings, attaching them to the shoulder pieces of the ephod at the front. ¹⁹They made two gold rings and attached them to the other two corners of the breastpiece on the inside edge next to the ephod. ²⁰Then they made two more gold rings and attached them to the bottom of the shoulder pieces on the front of the ephod, close to the seam just above the waistband of the ephod. ²¹They tied the rings of the breastpiece to the rings of the ephod with blue cord, connecting it to the waistband so that the breastpiece would not swing out from the ephod—as the LORD commanded Moses.

Other Priestly Garments

²²They made the robe of the ephod entirely of blue cloth—the work of a weaver— ²³with an opening in the center of the robe like the opening of a collar,*c* and a band around this opening, so that it would not tear. ²⁴They made pomegranates of blue, purple and scarlet yarn and finely twisted linen around the hem of the robe. ²⁵And they made bells of pure gold and attached them around the hem between the pomegranates. ²⁶The bells and pomegranates alternated around the hem of the robe to be worn for ministering, as the LORD commanded Moses.

²⁷For Aaron and his sons, they made tunics of fine linen—the work of a weaver— ²⁸and the turban of fine linen, the linen caps and the undergarments of finely twisted linen. ²⁹The sash was made of finely twisted linen and blue, purple and scarlet yarn— the work of an embroiderer—as the LORD commanded Moses.

³⁰They made the plate, the sacred emblem, out of pure gold and engraved on it, like an inscription on a seal: HOLY TO THE LORD. ³¹Then they fastened a blue cord to it to attach it to the turban, as the LORD commanded Moses.

Moses Inspects the Tabernacle

³²So all the work on the tabernacle, the tent of meeting, was completed. The Israelites did everything just as the LORD commanded Moses. ³³Then they brought the tabernacle to Moses: the tent and all its furnishings, its clasps, frames, crossbars, posts and bases; ³⁴the covering of ram skins dyed red and the covering of another durable leather*d* and the shielding curtain; ³⁵the ark of the covenant law with its poles and the atonement cover; ³⁶the table with all its articles and the bread of the Presence; ³⁷the pure gold lampstand with its row of lamps and all its accessories, and the olive oil for the light; ³⁸the gold altar, the anointing oil, the fragrant incense, and the curtain for the entrance to the tent; ³⁹the bronze altar with its bronze grating, its poles and all its utensils; the basin with its stand; ⁴⁰the curtains of the courtyard with its posts and bases, and the curtain for the entrance to the courtyard; the ropes and tent pegs for the courtyard; all the furnishings for the tabernacle, the tent of meeting; ⁴¹and the woven garments worn for ministering in the sanctuary, both the sacred garments for Aaron the priest and the garments for his sons when serving as priests.

---

a 9 That is, about 9 inches or about 23 centimeters   *b* 13 The precise identification of some of these precious stones is uncertain.   *c* 23 The meaning of the Hebrew for this word is uncertain.   *d* 34 Possibly the hides of large aquatic mammals

---

39:1–31 | Seven times this passage states that **Bezalel** (38:22) and his helpers fashioned the priestly garments **as the LORD commanded Moses**. Besides the detail in these descriptions, phrases such as **the work of a weaver** and **skillfully sewed** reinforce the immense care that they took. The workers sewed **gold . . . yarn** into the fabric of the **ephod**, evidence of the garment's beauty and costliness. Nothing is too good for the Lord (Rom. 12:1, 2).

⁴²The Israelites had done all the work just as the Lord had commanded Moses. ⁴³Moses inspected the work and saw that they had done it just as the Lord had commanded. So Moses blessed them.

Setting Up the Tabernacle

40 Then the Lord said to Moses: ²"Set up the tabernacle, the tent of meeting, on the first day of the first month. ³Place the ark of the covenant law in it and shield the ark with the curtain. ⁴Bring in the table and set out what belongs on it. Then bring in the lampstand and set up its lamps. ⁵Place the gold altar of incense in front of the ark of the covenant law and put the curtain at the entrance to the tabernacle.

⁶"Place the altar of burnt offering in front of the entrance to the tabernacle, the tent of meeting; ⁷place the basin between the tent of meeting and the altar and put water in it. ⁸Set up the courtyard around it and put the curtain at the entrance to the courtyard.

⁹"Take the anointing oil and anoint the tabernacle and everything in it; consecrate it and all its furnishings, and it will be holy. ¹⁰Then anoint the altar of burnt offering and all its utensils; consecrate the altar, and it will be most holy. ¹¹Anoint the basin and its stand and consecrate them.

¹²"Bring Aaron and his sons to the entrance to the tent of meeting and wash them with water. ¹³Then dress Aaron in the sacred garments, anoint him and consecrate him so he may serve me as priest. ¹⁴Bring his sons and dress them in tunics. ¹⁵Anoint them just as you anointed their father, so they may serve me as priests. Their anointing will be to a priesthood that will continue throughout their generations." ¹⁶Moses did everything just as the Lord commanded him.

¹⁷So the tabernacle was set up on the first day of the first month in the second year. ¹⁸When Moses set up the tabernacle, he put the bases in place, erected the frames, inserted the crossbars and set up the posts. ¹⁹Then he spread the tent over the tabernacle and put the covering over the tent, as the Lord commanded him.

²⁰He took the tablets of the covenant law and placed them in the ark, attached the poles to the ark and put the atonement cover over it. ²¹Then he brought the ark into the tabernacle and hung the shielding curtain and shielded the ark of the covenant law, as the Lord commanded him.

²²Moses placed the table in the tent of meeting on the north side of the tabernacle outside the curtain ²³and set out the bread on it before the Lord, as the Lord commanded him.

²⁴He placed the lampstand in the tent of meeting opposite the table on the south side of the tabernacle ²⁵and set up the lamps before the Lord, as the Lord commanded him.

²⁶Moses placed the gold altar in the tent of meeting in front of the curtain ²⁷and burned fragrant incense on it, as the Lord commanded him.

²⁸Then he put up the curtain at the entrance to the tabernacle. ²⁹He set the altar of burnt offering near the entrance to the tabernacle, the tent of meeting, and offered on it burnt offerings and grain offerings, as the Lord commanded him.

³⁰He placed the basin between the tent of meeting and the altar and put water in it for washing, ³¹and Moses and Aaron and his sons used it to wash their hands and feet. ³²They washed whenever they entered the tent of meeting or approached the altar, as the Lord commanded Moses.

³³Then Moses set up the courtyard around the tabernacle and altar and put up the curtain at the entrance to the courtyard. And so Moses finished the work.

The Glory of the Lord

³⁴Then the cloud covered the tent of meeting, and the glory of the Lord filled the tabernacle. ³⁵Moses could not enter the tent of meeting because the cloud had settled on it, and the glory of the Lord filled the tabernacle.

³⁶In all the travels of the Israelites, whenever the cloud lifted from above the tabernacle, they would set out; ³⁷but if the cloud did not lift, they did not set out—until the day it lifted. ³⁸So the cloud of the Lord was over the tabernacle by day, and fire was in the cloud by night, in the sight of all the Israelites during all their travels.

40:1–33 | The tabernacle was raised up about a year after the Exodus from Egypt—10 months after they arrived at Sinai. Moses' faithfulness to the Lord's commands until the work was **finished** is recognized here. The writer of Hebrews also highlights Moses' faithfulness in the building of the tabernacle (Heb. 3:2; see Num. 12:7). It is never enough to start strong for God; His servants must also seek to finish well (2 Tim. 4:7, 8).

40:34, 35 | As it was at Mount Sinai (see 24:16–18; 34:5–9, 29–35), the **glory of the Lord** was evidence of God's presence with His people (1 Kgs. 8:10, 11). This abiding glory and presence is what some refer to as "the Shekinah Glory" (see John 1:14). God continued to guide the Hebrew people as a pillar of cloud by day and a pillar of fire by night throughout all their journeys (13:21, 22).

דַנְרַל רוֹמְזִמ חַצְנֻמְל

עִיקְרָה דִיָגֵמ וּדְי הַשֶׁעֲמֻ לֵא־דוֹבְכ סִירְפַסְמ סַיִמַשׁה

תַעֵד דַּהֵתִּי הַלָיֻלַל הַלָיְלוּ רֻמֵא עִיבַּי סֻיְל סֻנִי

סַלוֹק עָמְשַׁנ יַלְב סֵירְכַּד וַיֵ רַמֵא־ןֻיֵא

סַהַב לַהָא־סֵט שֻׁמַּשׁ סַהֻיִלֻמ לַבַּת הַצְקַבּוּ סַוָּק אַצָּי וַזְרָאַה־לְכַּב

תַרָא זַנְרַל רוֹבִנַכ שֻׁישֻׂי וַתַפְחֶמ אֲצָי נַתַזַכ אוֹהוּ

LEVITICUS

I am the Lord your God;

consecrate yourselves

and be holy, because I am holy.

LEVITICUS 11:44

LEVITICUS

BOOK INTRODUCTION

Sometimes in life, the excitement is in the journey. Not that rescuing a couple million Hebrew slaves from Egypt was boring, but Moses' real work began on the far side of the Red Sea, in the sunbaked wilderness of Sinai: he had to explain to the people *why* they were there.

Sun, sand, serpents, scorpions—a case could have been made for staying in the predictable, if not altogether comfortable, confines of Egypt. In the Sinai wilderness, life was neither predictable nor comfortable. And it was Moses' job to explain why that was better. His explanation began in the second half of the Book of Exodus and continued in Leviticus. In Exodus, Moses presented the instruction of Yahweh concerning who He is; the laws, judgments, and statutes by which He wanted them to live; and the Lord's direction concerning their central place of worship—the tabernacle.

In Leviticus, however, the heart of the matter is revealed: holiness. The Hebrew people needed to confront key questions: How can a holy God and an unholy people be in the same space together? How may they have a relationship? And what does *holy* mean anyway?

The three great events after Creation were (1) the Fall, (2) the Flood, and (3) the dispersion from Babel. Although God created human beings to represent His wonder and majesty, they had fallen profoundly in Eden. The Lord then raised up Israel as a distinct people group; the descendants of Abraham and Sarah were the means whereby He would draw other people to His holy worship. For this to work, the Hebrew people had to be holy—they were to be set apart *for the Lord* as a light to the Gentiles, a repository of the knowledge of God. Because of their spiritual and physical blessings and their moral purity, they would stand out among the nations of the world and draw the nations to the God who dwelt in their midst.

WHAT IT SAYS | *In the Desert School of Holiness*

The word *Leviticus* means "concerning the Levites." It fell to the tribe of Levi, whose members served as Israel's priests under Aaron (the high priest), to teach the Israelites how to be holy before the Lord. The Book of Leviticus concerns the responsibilities and duties the Levites had as intermediaries between the people and God. The necessary instructions on how to worship—ceremonies, rituals, sacrifices, washings, offerings—are all here. The challenge

To view Dr. Jeremiah's video introduction to Leviticus, go to www.JeremiahStudyBible.com/Leviticus/Intro

for Moses, Aaron, and the Levitical priests would be to convince the Israelites that Yahweh's laws were good for them.

As they called the people back to the beginning of human history, they recalled the perfection of God and the perfection of His creation. As the Israelites conformed their lives to the will of God, they would see the difference between their holy God and the gods of the Egyptians and their new pagan neighbors in Canaan. The goal was to let a focus on *ritual* holiness and perfection draw them ever closer to *moral* holiness and perfection. By making the perfection of God the focus of their lives, they would be more likely to reflect Him to the Gentile nations.

What the Israelites did not realize was that the law they agreed to pursue would actually serve as a guide and guard "until Christ came that [they] might be justified by faith" (Gal. 3:24). They would discover that keeping the law would not produce the perfection that God required. The laws of God were perfect, but the people themselves could never be by their own efforts.

What It Means | *Approaching a Holy God*

Leviticus is very much a how-to book for ceremonies and worship practices within the OT system. But this third book of the Pentateuch also illustrates that God was concerned that His people do what is right, and do it in the right way. Here are its five interlocking themes:

- **Holiness:** The word *holy* occurs 67 times in Leviticus, more than in any other book in the Bible. Leviticus reveals that a God who is set apart from all other "gods" must have a similar people (11:44, 45; 19:2; 20:7, 8; 1 Pet. 1:15, 16). The ceremonies detailed in this book are about serving Him as a holy and righteous God—as a God who sanctifies, or "makes . . . holy," His people (20:7, 8).
- **Worship:** Approaching a holy God is not a casual undertaking. Dealing with the sin that separates people from God requires sacrifice, which reflects death as the consequence of sin. It also requires payment for sin, through the offering of sacrifices without "defect" or "blemish." The sacrificial system was a lesson concerning the importance and cost of maintaining fellowship with the holy God (22:17–25; Matt. 5:48).
- **Law:** Leviticus is filled with regulations and ordinances, all of which reveal our inability as humans to be perfect on our own. The Levitical laws would set the stage for laws that would one day be written on the hearts of God's people rather than on stone, replacing external obligation with internal motivation (Jer. 31:33).
- **Presence:** God's willingness to dwell in the midst of a sinful people—camped in Israel in the Most Holy Place in the tabernacle—would be a sign of His forgiveness and grace toward those He redeemed to Himself. It also foreshadowed the day when God would come to "tabernacle" (dwell) among humanity in human flesh and later in human hearts (Matt. 5:8; John 1:14; Heb. 10:22).
- **Atonement:** Sins can be atoned for in the manner of God's choosing (16—17; see 17:11). In the NIV the word atonement is found 56 times in Leviticus, with the basic meaning "to cover," or "to make a covering." Old Testament atonement did not remove sins, but it covered sins until, ultimately, a final sacrifice would be made when the perfect Lamb of God offered Himself once and for all (Heb. 9:1–15, 24–28; 10:1–14).

What It Means for You | *Because He Is Near*

It was no easy feat for the infant nation of Israel to learn God's ways and become a set-apart people. In fact, they took many wrong turns on the way to the Promised Land. They had to learn the implications of living their lives with a holy God in their midst.

This is true for believers today as well. Even though every Christian has God's Spirit living within, we need to be reminded of His nearness and cultivate a sense of His presence. Paul wrote that believers should "pray continually" (1 Thess. 5:17). Scripture also urges us to "purify ourselves from everything that contaminates body and spirit, perfecting holiness out of reverence for God" (2 Cor. 7:1). Finally, we have the matchless promise that "if we walk in the light, as he is in the light, we have fellowship with one another, and the blood of Jesus, his Son, purifies us from all sin" (1 John 1:7). The sure knowledge of God's constant presence should not only flood our lives with comfort but also fill us with a healthy dread of offending Him and grieving His Spirit. It should also change the way we deal with one another. As Paul reminded us in Philippians 4:5, "Let your gentleness be evident to all. The Lord is near."

To access Dr. Jeremiah's digital library on Leviticus, go to
www.JeremiahStudyBible.com/Leviticus/library

LEVITICUS

The Burnt Offering

1 The LORD called to Moses and spoke to him from the tent of meeting. He said, 2 "Speak to the Israelites and say to them: 'When anyone among you brings an offering to the LORD, bring as your offering an animal from either the herd or the flock.

3 " 'If the offering is a burnt offering from the herd, you are to offer a male without defect. You must present it at the entrance to the tent of meeting so that it will be acceptable to the LORD. 4 You are to lay your hand on the head of the burnt offering, and it will be accepted on your behalf to make atonement for you. 5 You are to slaughter the young bull before the LORD, and then Aaron's sons the priests shall bring the blood and splash it against the sides of the altar at the entrance to the tent of meeting. 6 You are to skin the burnt offering and cut it into pieces. 7 The sons of Aaron the priest are to put fire on the altar and arrange wood on the fire. 8 Then Aaron's sons the priests shall arrange the pieces, including the head and the fat, on the wood that is burning on the altar. 9 You are to wash the internal organs and the legs with water, and the priest is to burn all of it on the altar. It is a burnt offering, a food offering, an aroma pleasing to the LORD.

10 " 'If the offering is a burnt offering from the flock, from either the sheep or the goats, you are to offer a male without defect. 11 You are to slaughter it at the north side of the altar before the LORD, and Aaron's sons the priests shall splash its blood against the

---

Historically Speaking — Designs of the Tent of Meeting and Temple • 1:1

The three-part design of the tent of meeting and, later, the temple of Solomon was also found in temple structures in other ancient cultures from ancient Cush (Southern Sudan) to Aram Naharaim (the region of modern Syria).

- The outer courtyard was a sacred space marked off by curtains and poles at its perimeter. The very process of repositioning the tent of meeting meant that "common ground" became "sacred ground" when the tent of meeting was erected. Ordinary people of faith could enter the outer courtyard to offer sacrifices, to pray, and to praise God for His goodness and for answers to prayer. There was no distinctive place for women or for foreigners (as was later the case in Herod's latter stage of the second temple at the time of Jesus); all people had access to the outer courtyard. The two great holy pieces in the outer courtyard were the altar of burnt offering and the bronze basin for washing.

- The Holy Place was the larger portion under the cover of the great tented structure in the courtyard. Only priests could enter here and minister, and they did their work on behalf of the people. The great holy pieces in this sacred place were the table for the bread of the Presence, the lampstand, and the altar of incense.

- The Most Holy Place was the smaller portion of the great tented structure, and it housed one sacred piece alone—the ark of the covenant, with its beautiful cover, the atonement cover. It was to this innermost room that only one person could enter, and he only one time a year. On the Day of Atonement, the high priest would bring blood from one of two goats and would sprinkle it on the atonement cover to symbolize a "covering" for the sins of the people. The other goat was driven into the wilderness. Both goats had the sins of the nation symbolically transferred to them.

The three levels of separation in the tent of meeting and its courts speak of the exquisite holiness of God—that He is not approachable in ordinary ways. Yet the fact that He may be approached at all is a wonder of His grace. The tent of meeting was a visible, tangible symbol of holiness and grace. The structure was beautiful and costly, orderly, and well-constructed. It was also transportable, as this was the movable shrine that always made God near—and central to Israel—in the wilderness years.

The most remarkable thing about the tent of meeting (and the later temple) was not the holy pieces that were found there but what was lacking: these were the only religious structures in the ancient Near East in which there was not an idol on display! God allowed no images of gods—not even of Himself (Ex. 20:4–6). This lack of an idol made the Israelite worship centers unique in the ancient world.

Christians are God's portable shrines today (1 Cor. 3:16–19; 2 Cor. 6:16). It is in and through His people that He makes Himself known today; it is from His people that He seeks His true worship.

1:1—7:38 | The concept of substitutionary death to atone for sin is not only a NT teaching; it is strongly foreshadowed by these offerings. The true significance of the OT sacrifices is found in the sacrificial death of Christ (John 1:29).
1:2 | Of the five offerings described in the first six chapters of Leviticus, only the sin offering (4:1–5:13) and the guilt offering (5:14–6:7) were required; the burnt (1:1-17), grain (2:1-16), and fellowship offerings (3:1-17) were freewill, or voluntary, offerings. The root of the words **brings** and **offering** means "draw near." Through these sacrifices, the people of Israel drew near to the Lord.

sides of the altar. [12]You are to cut it into pieces, and the priest shall arrange them, including the head and the fat, on the wood that is burning on the altar. [13]You are to wash the internal organs and the legs with water, and the priest is to bring all of them and burn them on the altar. It is a burnt offering, a food offering, an aroma pleasing to the LORD.

[14] "'If the offering to the LORD is a burnt offering of birds, you are to offer a dove or a young pigeon. [15]The priest shall bring it to the altar, wring off the head and burn it on the altar; its blood shall be drained out on the side of the altar. [16]He is to remove the crop and the feathers[a] and throw them down east of the altar where the ashes are. [17]He shall tear it open by the wings, not dividing it completely, and then the priest shall burn it on the wood that is burning on the altar. It is a burnt offering, a food offering, an aroma pleasing to the LORD.

The Grain Offering

2 "'When anyone brings a grain offering to the LORD, their offering is to be of the finest flour. They are to pour olive oil on it, put incense on it [2]and take it to Aaron's sons the priests. The priest shall take a handful of the flour and oil, together with all the incense, and burn this as a memorial[b] portion on the altar, a food offering, an aroma pleasing to the LORD. [3]The rest of the grain offering belongs to Aaron and his sons; it is a most holy part of the food offerings presented to the LORD.

[4] "'If you bring a grain offering baked in an oven, it is to consist of the finest flour: either thick loaves made without yeast and with olive oil mixed in or thin loaves made without yeast and brushed with olive oil. [5]If your grain offering is prepared on a griddle, it is to be made of the finest flour mixed with oil, and without yeast. [6]Crumble it and pour oil on it; it is a grain offering. [7]If your grain offering is cooked in a pan, it is to be made of the finest flour and some olive oil. [8]Bring the grain offering made of these things to the LORD; present it to the priest, who shall take it to the altar. [9]He shall take out the memorial portion from the grain offering and burn it on the altar as a food offering, an aroma pleasing to the LORD. [10]The rest of the grain offering belongs to Aaron and his sons; it is a most holy part of the food offerings presented to the LORD.

[11] "'Every grain offering you bring to the LORD must be made without yeast, for you are not to burn any yeast or honey in a food offering presented to the LORD. [12]You may bring them to the LORD as an offering of the firstfruits, but they are not to be offered on the altar as a pleasing aroma. [13]Season all your grain offerings with salt. Do not leave the salt of the covenant of your God out of your grain offerings; add salt to all your offerings.

[14] "'If you bring a grain offering of firstfruits to the LORD, offer crushed heads of new grain roasted in the fire. [15]Put oil and incense on it; it is a grain offering. [16]The priest shall burn the memorial portion of the crushed grain and the oil, together with all the incense, as a food offering presented to the LORD.

The Fellowship Offering

3 "'If your offering is a fellowship offering, and you offer an animal from the herd, whether male or female, you are to

---

[a] 16 Or crop with its contents; the meaning of the Hebrew for this word is uncertain.
[b] 2 Or representative; also in verses 9 and 16

1:3–9 | A **burnt offering** was to be a **male** animal, which was considered a more valuable offering than a female. The animal also had to be **without defect**, symbolizing the sinless humanity of Christ (2 Cor. 5:21; Heb. 4:15). The burnt offering—the most common offering—consumed the whole animal except for the skin, reflecting the worshiper's complete devotion to God.

1:4 | Laying a **hand on the head of the burnt offering** symbolically transferred the sin of the one making the sacrifice onto the animal. This sacrifice was substitutionary, meaning that it was **accepted on** the person's behalf. It did not save the person; it simply atoned for, or "covered," the worshiper's sin and restored his or her relationship with God. These sacrifices point to the ultimate resolution of the problem of sin: Christ's **atonement**.

1:10–13 | God's holiness demanded a pure sacrifice; the lamb or baby goat **without defect** was a prophetic symbol of the once-for-all sacrifice of the perfect Lamb of God (John 1:29; 1 Pet. 1:19).

1:14–17 | The animal could vary according to a person's economic status—the Lord graciously included provisions that allowed poor people to offer birds if they could not afford an animal from the herd (1:3–9) or the flock (1:10–13). Nevertheless, the law still closely regulated the sacrifice, including the type of bird (**a dove or a young pigeon**). Similar provisions appear throughout Leviticus (5:7–10;

12:6–8; 14:21–23, 31, 32).

2:1–16 | This is the only sacrifice in Leviticus 1:1–6:7 that was not animal and did not involve blood. Instead, it consisted of the **finest flour** (2:1–3), loaves baked with **olive oil** and **without yeast** (2:4–13), or **crushed heads of new grain** from the **firstfruits** of the harvest (2:14–16). The **grain offering** often accompanied the burnt offering (Num. 28:1–15). Further instructions are in Leviticus 6:14–23. All grain offerings were to be seasoned with **salt**, which represented preservation.

2:1 | **When anyone** expresses a marvelous inclusiveness. Women and men, foreigners and native-born Israelites could bring this offering to God, which showed one's dedication to God. The **grain offering** also acknowledged that all of life's gifts are ultimately from the Lord. This was the intent of Cain's offering (Gen. 4:3); unfortunately, his heart was not right before God.

2:4–13 | Perhaps because these offerings could ferment, they were not to include **yeast** or **honey**. The Bible sometimes uses yeast as a symbol for the pervasive spread of sin (1 Cor. 5:6, 7; Gal. 5:9; but see Luke 13:21 where yeast represents the kingdom of God). These offerings were to include both **olive oil** and **salt**, flavoring agents that would enhance the offering's taste (Matt. 5:13; Mark 9:49, 50; Col. 4:6).

present before the LORD an animal without defect. [2]You are to lay your hand on the head of your offering and slaughter it at the entrance to the tent of meeting. Then Aaron's sons the priests shall splash the blood against the sides of the altar. [3]From the fellowship offering you are to bring a food offering to the LORD: the internal organs and all the fat that is connected to them, [4]both kidneys with the fat on them near the loins, and the long lobe of the liver, which you will remove with the kidneys. [5]Then Aaron's sons are to burn it on the altar on top of the burnt offering that is lying on the burning wood; it is a food offering, an aroma pleasing to the LORD.

[6]" 'If you offer an animal from the flock as a fellowship offering to the LORD, you are to offer a male or female without defect. [7]If you offer a lamb, you are to present it before the LORD, [8]lay your hand on its head and slaughter it in front of the tent of meeting. Then Aaron's sons shall splash its blood against the sides of the altar. [9]From the fellowship offering you are to bring a food offering to the LORD: its fat, the entire fat tail cut off close to the backbone, the internal organs and all the fat that is connected to them, [10]both kidneys with the fat on them near the loins, and the long lobe of the liver, which you will remove with the kidneys. [11]The priest shall burn them on the altar as a food offering presented to the LORD.

[12]" 'If your offering is a goat, you are to present it before the LORD, [13]lay your hand on its head and slaughter it in front of the tent of meeting. Then Aaron's sons shall splash its blood against the sides of the altar. [14]From what you offer you are to present this food offering to the LORD: the internal organs and all the fat that is connected to them, [15]both kidneys with the fat on them near the loins, and the long lobe of the liver, which you will remove with the kidneys. [16]The priest shall burn them on the altar as

a food offering, a pleasing aroma. All the fat is the LORD's.

[17]" 'This is a lasting ordinance for the generations to come, wherever you live: You must not eat any fat or any blood.' "

The Sin Offering

4 The LORD said to Moses, [2]"Say to the Israelites: 'When anyone sins unintentionally and does what is forbidden in any of the LORD's commands—

[3]" 'If the anointed priest sins, bringing guilt on the people, he must bring to the LORD a young bull without defect as a sin offering[a] for the sin he has committed. [4]He is to present the bull at the entrance to the tent of meeting before the LORD. He is to lay his hand on its head and slaughter it there before the LORD. [5]Then the anointed priest shall take some of the bull's blood and carry it into the tent of meeting. [6]He is to dip his finger into the blood and sprinkle some of it seven times before the LORD, in front of the curtain of the sanctuary. [7]The priest shall then put some of the blood on the horns of the altar of fragrant incense that is before the LORD in the tent of meeting. The rest of the bull's blood he shall pour out at the base of the altar of burnt offering at the entrance to the tent of meeting. [8]He shall remove all the fat from the bull of the sin offering—all the fat that is connected to the internal organs, [9]both kidneys with the fat on them near the loins, and the long lobe of the liver, which he will remove with the kidneys— [10]just as the fat is removed from the ox[b] sacrificed as a fellowship offering. Then the priest shall burn them on the altar of burnt offering. [11]But the hide of the bull and all its flesh, as well as the head and legs, the internal organs and the intestines— [12]that is, all the rest of the bull—he must take outside the

---

[a] 3 Or purification offering; here and throughout this chapter   [b] 10 The Hebrew word can refer to either male or female.

3:1–7 | The **fellowship** (Heb., "wholeness, completeness") **offering**, an occasion of thanksgiving (7:11, 12), was the third freewill offering and was ultimately fulfilled in Christ, whose sacrifice enables believers to have peace with God (Col. 1:20). The animal could be **male or female**. Uniquely, the person presenting this offering could eat a portion of it—a depiction of fellowship with God (7:15).
3:9–16 | Because the **fat** was the prized portion of meat, worshipers were offering God their best. When burned, the fat and the **kidneys** produced a **pleasing aroma** to the Lord (3:9–16; 2 Cor. 2:16; Eph. 5:2; Phil. 4:18). By burning the **liver**, which neighboring cultures used when seeking omens (Ezek. 21:21), worshipers of God were demonstrating faith in Him alone and eliminating any hint of pagan practice.
3:17 | The command to **not eat any fat or any blood** reflects that the best parts belong to God (3:16). The prohibition

against consuming blood is explained in 17:11.
4:1–5:13 | Inadvertent sins are as much an affront to a holy God as intentional ones, so the fourth offering—the **sin offering**—covered unintentional sins. This was the first offering that was mandatory, because everyone is guilty. Offerings for the high priest, the whole Israelite community (in cases of collective sin), a leader, and a member of the Israelite community are described in 4:1–35.
4:3–12 | The **anointed priest** was the high priest (16:32; Ex. 29:29; 40:15). His sin endangered the nation, bringing **guilt on the people**, because he represented them before the Lord; thus, he had to atone for his own sin, not just theirs.
4:6, 7 | The **blood** of the sacrifices was poured **at the base of the altar**, a sign that the effect of the sacrifice was in place. The priest was to **sprinkle** some of the blood **seven times**, a number symbolizing the fullness of God's forgiveness.

camp to a place ceremonially clean, where the ashes are thrown, and burn it there in a wood fire on the ash heap.

13 " 'If the whole Israelite community sins unintentionally and does what is forbidden in any of the LORD's commands, even though the community is unaware of the matter, when they realize their guilt 14 and the sin they committed becomes known, the assembly must bring a young bull as a sin offering and present it before the tent of meeting. 15 The elders of the community are to lay their hands on the bull's head before the LORD, and the bull shall be slaughtered before the LORD. 16 Then the anointed priest is to take some of the bull's blood into the tent of meeting. 17 He shall dip his finger into the blood and sprinkle it before the LORD seven times in front of the curtain. 18 He is to put some of the blood on the horns of the altar that is before the LORD in the tent of meeting. The rest of the blood he shall pour out at the base of the altar of burnt offering at the entrance to the tent of meeting. 19 He shall remove all the fat from it and burn it on the altar, 20 and do with this bull just as he did with the bull for the sin offering. In this way the priest will make atonement for the community, and they will be forgiven. 21 Then he shall take the bull outside the camp and burn it as he burned the first bull. This is the sin offering for the community.

22 " 'When a leader sins unintentionally and does what is forbidden in any of the commands of the LORD his God, when he realizes his guilt 23 and the sin he has committed becomes known, he must bring as his offering a male goat without defect. 24 He is to lay his hand on the goat's head and slaughter it at the place where the burnt offering is slaughtered before the LORD. It is a sin offering. 25 Then the priest shall take some of the blood of the sin offering with his finger and put it on the horns of the altar of burnt offering and pour out the rest of the blood at the base of the altar. 26 He shall burn all the fat on the altar as he burned the

fat of the fellowship offering. In this way the priest will make atonement for the leader's sin, and he will be forgiven.

27 " 'If any member of the community sins unintentionally and does what is forbidden in any of the LORD's commands, when they realize their guilt 28 and the sin they have committed becomes known, they must bring as their offering for the sin they committed a female goat without defect. 29 They are to lay their hand on the head of the sin offering and slaughter it at the place of the burnt offering. 30 Then the priest is to take some of the blood with his finger and put it on the horns of the altar of burnt offering and pour out the rest of the blood at the base of the altar. 31 They shall remove all the fat, just as the fat is removed from the fellowship offering, and the priest shall burn it on the altar as an aroma pleasing to the LORD. In this way the priest will make atonement for them, and they will be forgiven.

32 " 'If someone brings a lamb as their sin offering, they are to bring a female without defect. 33 They are to lay their hand on its head and slaughter it for a sin offering at the place where the burnt offering is slaughtered. 34 Then the priest shall take some of the blood of the sin offering with his finger and put it on the horns of the altar of burnt offering and pour out the rest of the blood at the base of the altar. 35 They shall remove all the fat, just as the fat is removed from the lamb of the fellowship offering, and the priest shall burn it on the altar on top of the food offerings presented to the LORD. In this way the priest will make atonement for them for the sin they have committed, and they will be forgiven.

5 " 'If anyone sins because they do not speak up when they hear a public charge to testify regarding something they have seen or learned about, they will be held responsible.

2 " 'If anyone becomes aware that they are guilty—if they unwittingly touch anything ceremonially unclean (whether the carcass

---

4:11, 12 | Just as the **bull** was taken **outside the camp to a place ceremonially clean** and burned, a picture of sin's removal from the camp, so Jesus was taken outside the city gates of Jerusalem to be sacrificed on the cross (Heb. 13:11–13).
4:13–21 | The offering for the unintentional sin of the **whole Israelite community** was the same as that for the sin of the high priest: **a young bull**. Just as the people were to offer this sacrifice when they became aware of **their guilt** and their sin became **known**, Christians today should confess their sins to God as soon as they recognize them so that fellowship with God can be restored (Heb. 9:13, 14).

4:22–35 | The offerings for the **leader** differed from those for a **priest** and a **member of the community**, perhaps to remind the leader of the nation of the serious demands and responsibilities of his position.
5:1–4 | Four examples of unintentional sin requiring a sin offering were (1) failing to **speak up** when a person would **hear a public charge to testify**; (2) touching **anything ceremonially unclean** such as an animal carcass; (3) touching **human uncleanness**; (4) **thoughtlessly** taking **an oath**. None of these was a defiant act; they were still, however, trespasses against a holy God.

of an unclean animal, wild or domestic, or of any unclean creature that moves along the ground) and they are unaware that they have become unclean, but then they come to realize their guilt; ³or if they touch human uncleanness (anything that would make them unclean) even though they are unaware of it, but then they learn of it and realize their guilt; ⁴or if anyone thoughtlessly takes an oath to do anything, whether good or evil (in any matter one might carelessly swear about) even though they are unaware of it, but then they learn of it and realize their guilt— ⁵when anyone becomes aware that they are guilty in any of these matters, they must confess in what way they have sinned. ⁶As a penalty for the sin they have committed, they must bring to the LORD a female lamb or goat from the flock as a sin offering*a*; and the priest shall make atonement for them for their sin.

⁷ "'Anyone who cannot afford a lamb is to bring two doves or two young pigeons to the LORD as a penalty for their sin—one for a sin offering and the other for a burnt offering. ⁸They are to bring them to the priest, who shall first offer the one for the sin offering. He is to wring its head from its neck, not dividing it completely, ⁹and is to splash some of the blood of the sin offering against the side of the altar; the rest of the blood must be drained out at the base of the altar. It is a sin offering. ¹⁰The priest shall then offer the other as a burnt offering in the prescribed way and make atonement for them for the sin they have committed, and they will be forgiven.

¹¹ "'If, however, they cannot afford two doves or two young pigeons, they are to bring as an offering for their sin a tenth of an ephah*b* of the finest flour for a sin offering. They must not put olive oil or incense on it, because it is a sin offering. ¹²They are to bring it to the priest, who shall take a handful of it as a memorial*c* portion and burn it on the altar on top of the food offerings presented to the LORD. It is a sin offering. ¹³In this way the priest will make atonement for them for any of these sins they have committed, and they will be forgiven. The rest of the offering will belong to the priest, as in the case of the grain offering.'"

The Guilt Offering

¹⁴The LORD said to Moses: ¹⁵"When anyone is unfaithful to the LORD by sinning unintentionally in regard to any of the LORD's holy things, they are to bring to the LORD as a penalty a ram from the flock, one without defect and of the proper value in silver, according to the sanctuary shekel.*d* It is a guilt offering. ¹⁶They must make restitution for what they have failed to do in regard to the holy things, pay an additional penalty of a fifth of its value and give it all to the priest. The priest will make atonement for them with the ram as a guilt offering, and they will be forgiven.

¹⁷"If anyone sins and does what is forbidden in any of the LORD's commands, even though they do not know it, they are guilty and will be held responsible. ¹⁸They are to bring to the priest as a guilt offering a ram from the flock, one without defect and of the proper value. In this way the priest will make atonement for them for the wrong they have committed unintentionally, and they will be forgiven. ¹⁹It is a guilt offering; they have been guilty of*e* wrongdoing against the LORD."

6*f* The LORD said to Moses: ²"If anyone sins and is unfaithful to the LORD by deceiving a neighbor about something entrusted to them or left in their care or about something stolen, or if they cheat their neighbor, ³or if they find lost property and lie about it, or if they swear falsely about any such sin that people may commit— ⁴when they sin in any of these ways and realize their guilt, they must return what they have stolen or taken by extortion, or what was entrusted to them, or the lost property they found, ⁵or whatever it was they swore falsely about. They must make restitution in full, add a

---

a 6 Or purification offering; here and throughout this chapter   *b* 11 That is, probably about 3 1/2 pounds or about 1.6 kilograms   *c* 12 Or representative   *d* 15 That is, about 2/5 ounce or about 12 grams   *e* 19 Or offering; atonement has been made for their   *f* In Hebrew texts 6:1-7 is numbered 5:20-26, and 6:8-30 is numbered 6:1-23.

5:5, 6 | Offering a sacrifice was not enough. The **guilty** person first needed to **confess** his or her sin. Forgiveness always requires confession (Ps. 32:5; Prov. 28:13; 1 John 1:9).
5:7-13 | Like the **burnt offering**, the required **sin offering** provided options for those who could not **afford a lamb**.
5:14—6:7 | The **guilt offering** atoned for unintentional sins against **the LORD's holy things**, although in addition to sacrificing a **ram . . . without defect**, the person had to **make restitution** (pay what was owed, plus give the priest **a fifth of its value**; 22:14-16). The nature of the sin dictated the requirements of the restitution.

5:15 | In the sacrificial system in general, different animals were designated for different offerings according to their relative value. A bull was considered the most costly offering because the people of Israel raised them for meat.
6:1-7 | Sins against a **neighbor** included cheating, stealing, or damaging property; these sins were considered unfaithfulness **to the LORD** as well (Gen. 39:9; Ps. 51:4; Matt. 25:41-46; Luke 19:8). **Restitution** was commanded **on the day** of **their guilt offering** so that things were made right with God and with the offended party.

fifth of the value to it and give it all to the owner on the day they present their guilt offering. [6] And as a penalty they must bring to the priest, that is, to the LORD, their guilt offering, a ram from the flock, one without defect and of the proper value. [7] In this way the priest will make atonement for them before the LORD, and they will be forgiven for any of the things they did that made them guilty."

The Burnt Offering

[8] The LORD said to Moses: [9] "Give Aaron and his sons this command: 'These are the regulations for the burnt offering: The burnt offering is to remain on the altar hearth throughout the night, till morning, and the fire must be kept burning on the altar. [10] The priest shall then put on his linen clothes, with linen undergarments next to his body, and shall remove the ashes of the burnt offering that the fire has consumed on the altar and place them beside the altar. [11] Then he is to take off these clothes and put on others, and carry the ashes outside the camp to a place that is ceremonially clean. [12] The fire on the altar must be kept burning; it must not go out. Every morning the priest is to add firewood and arrange the burnt offering on the fire and burn the fat of the fellowship offerings on it. [13] The fire must be kept burning on the altar continuously; it must not go out.

The Grain Offering

[14] " 'These are the regulations for the grain offering: Aaron's sons are to bring it before the LORD, in front of the altar. [15] The priest is to take a handful of the finest flour and some olive oil, together with all the incense on the grain offering, and burn the memorial[a] portion on the altar as an aroma pleasing to the LORD. [16] Aaron and his sons shall eat the rest of it, but it is to be eaten without yeast in the sanctuary area; they are to eat it in the courtyard of the tent of meeting. [17] It must not be baked with yeast; I have given it as their share of the food offerings presented to me. Like the sin offering[b] and the guilt

The apostle Peter reminds us that Christians are the new priests of God (1 Pet. 2:5, 9). Like the priesthood of old, Christians should worship God formally at set times—through corporate worship services—and continually throughout the day, remaining in constant relationship with Him. It is easy to figure out which one we do best. Our calendar-controlled world gives us every reason to schedule worship right alongside piano lessons, golf dates, business lunches, family recreation nights, and a host of other weekly activities. But we need help in learning to worship God unceasingly.

offering, it is most holy. [18] Any male descendant of Aaron may eat it. For all generations to come it is his perpetual share of the food offerings presented to the LORD. Whatever touches them will become holy.[c] "

[19] The LORD also said to Moses, [20] "This is the offering Aaron and his sons are to bring to the LORD on the day he[d] is anointed: a tenth of an ephah[e] of the finest flour as a regular grain offering, half of it in the morning and half in the evening. [21] It must be prepared with oil on a griddle; bring it well-mixed and present the grain offering broken[f] in pieces as an aroma pleasing to the LORD. [22] The son who is to succeed him as anointed priest shall prepare it. It is the LORD's perpetual share and is to be burned completely. [23] Every grain offering of a priest shall be burned completely; it must not be eaten."

The Sin Offering

[24] The LORD said to Moses, [25] "Say to Aaron and his sons: 'These are the regulations for the sin offering: The sin offering is to be slaughtered before the LORD in the place the burnt offering is slaughtered; it is most holy. [26] The priest who offers it shall eat it; it is to be eaten in the sanctuary area, in the

---

[a] 15 Or representative   [b] 17 Or purification offering; also in verses 25 and 30   [c] 18 Or Whoever touches them must be holy; similarly in verse 27,   [d] 20 Or each   [e] 20 That is, probably about 3 1/2 pounds or about 1.6 kilograms   [f] 21 The meaning of the Hebrew for this word is uncertain.

6:8–13 | These additional stipulations concerning the **burnt offering** (1:1–17) describe the priest's clothing and conduct. The priests changed **clothes** for different tasks. The **ashes** from the offerings were considered holy, yet they were still possible sources of fire, so proper disposal was prudent.
6:12, 13 | The Lord's elaborate plans for worship in the tabernacle involved appointed times and places as well as perpetual acts of worship day and night before the Lord, which included **the fire on the altar** and the burning of incense (Ex. 30:8) as well as the maintenance of the lamps (Ex. 27:20, 21) and the bread of the Presence (24:5–9). The continual fire represented God's presence among His people.

6:14–18 | The priests were to display reverence in eating what was left over of the **grain offering**, doing so **in the sanctuary area (the courtyard of the tent of meeting)**. The bread was **to be eaten without yeast** (1 Cor. 9:13).
6:19–23 | The priests were worshipers too and were not exempt from sacrifice. Their own **grain offering** was to **be burned completely**, unlike the grain offering of the people.
6:24–30 | **Any male in a priest's family may eat it** suggests that in some instances, members of the priests' families would eat the sacrifices too; although in this case, the priest alone was commanded to eat his portion.

courtyard of the tent of meeting. [27]Whatever touches any of the flesh will become holy, and if any of the blood is spattered on a garment, you must wash it in the sanctuary area. [28]The clay pot the meat is cooked in must be broken; but if it is cooked in a bronze pot, the pot is to be scoured and rinsed with water. [29]Any male in a priest's family may eat it; it is most holy. [30]But any sin offering whose blood is brought into the tent of meeting to make atonement in the Holy Place must not be eaten; it must be burned up.

The Guilt Offering

7 " 'These are the regulations for the guilt offering, which is most holy: [2]The guilt offering is to be slaughtered in the place where the burnt offering is slaughtered, and its blood is to be splashed against the sides of the altar. [3]All its fat shall be offered: the fat tail and the fat that covers the internal organs, [4]both kidneys with the fat on them near the loins, and the long lobe of the liver, which is to be removed with the kidneys. [5]The priest shall burn them on the altar as a food offering presented to the LORD. It is a guilt offering. [6]Any male in a priest's family may eat it, but it must be eaten in the sanctuary area; it is most holy.

[7]" 'The same law applies to both the sin offering[a] and the guilt offering: They belong to the priest who makes atonement with them. [8]The priest who offers a burnt offering for anyone may keep its hide for himself. [9]Every grain offering baked in an oven or cooked in a pan or on a griddle belongs to the priest who offers it, [10]and every grain offering, whether mixed with olive oil or dry, belongs equally to all the sons of Aaron.

The Fellowship Offering

[11]" 'These are the regulations for the fellowship offering anyone may present to the LORD:

[12]" 'If they offer it as an expression of thankfulness, then along with this thank offering they are to offer thick loaves made without yeast and with olive oil mixed in, thin loaves made without yeast and brushed with oil, and thick loaves of the finest flour well-kneaded and with oil mixed in. [13]Along with their fellowship offering of thanksgiving they are to present an offering with thick loaves of bread made with yeast. [14]They are to bring one of each kind as an offering, a contribution to the LORD; it belongs to the priest who splashes the blood of the fellowship offering against the altar. [15]The meat of their fellowship offering of thanksgiving must be eaten on the day it is offered; they must leave none of it till morning.

[16]" 'If, however, their offering is the result of a vow or is a freewill offering, the sacrifice shall be eaten on the day they offer it, but anything left over may be eaten on the next day. [17]Any meat of the sacrifice left over till the third day must be burned up. [18]If any meat of the fellowship offering is eaten on the third day, the one who offered it will not be accepted. It will not be reckoned to their credit, for it has become impure; the person who eats any of it will be held responsible.

[19]" 'Meat that touches anything ceremonially unclean must not be eaten; it must be burned up. As for other meat, anyone ceremonially clean may eat it. [20]But if anyone who is unclean eats any meat of the fellowship offering belonging to the LORD, they must be cut off from their people. [21]Anyone who touches something unclean—whether human uncleanness or an unclean animal or any unclean creature that moves along the ground[b]—and then eats any of the meat of the fellowship offering belonging to the LORD must be cut off from their people.' "

Eating Fat and Blood Forbidden

[22]The LORD said to Moses, [23] "Say to the Israelites: 'Do not eat any of the fat of cattle, sheep or goats. [24]The fat of an animal

---

[a] 7 Or purification offering; also in verse 37   [b] 21 A few Hebrew manuscripts, Samaritan Pentateuch, Syriac and Targum (see 5:2); most Hebrew manuscripts any unclean, detestable thing

---

7:1–10 | More details are given for the **guilt offering**, including the requirements for the priests who ate these sacrifices and further instructions concerning the priestly portion of the burnt and the grain offerings.

7:7 | **The same law applies to both** meant that whatever the priest was allowed from the **sin offering**, he could have from the **guilt offering** (5:5, 6).

7:11–36 | **The regulations for the fellowship offering** include the types (7:12–14), the timing (7:15–18), issues concerning who and what was ceremonially clean and unclean (7:19–21), God's portion and the penalty for eating it (7:22–27), and the portion for the priests (7:28–36).

7:11–18 | The **fellowship offering** was made for a variety of reasons: **as an expression of thankfulness**; because of a **vow**; simply a **freewill offering**. (See note on 3:1–7.) Each type had its own rules. For example, the thanksgiving offering had to be eaten **the day** it was offered. In contrast, the vow and freewill offerings could have leftovers, but they had to be eaten **on the next day**, before spoiling, or burned **on the third day**.

7:19–21 | To **be cut off** was to be completely excluded from the community life of the Israelites and removed from God's covenant, either through banishment or execution (Gen. 17:14). Such harsh punishment was always the consequence when a person failed to treat what was holy with proper reverence (Heb. 10:26–31). Paul encouraged believers to demonstrate the same type of reverence and self-examination before partaking of the Lord's Supper (1 Cor. 11:27–29).

found dead or torn by wild animals may be used for any other purpose, but you must not eat it. ²⁵ Anyone who eats the fat of an animal from which a food offering may be*ᵃ* presented to the LORD must be cut off from their people. ²⁶ And wherever you live, you must not eat the blood of any bird or animal. ²⁷ Anyone who eats blood must be cut off from their people.' "

The Priests' Share

²⁸ The LORD said to Moses, ²⁹ "Say to the Israelites: 'Anyone who brings a fellowship offering to the LORD is to bring part of it as their sacrifice to the LORD. ³⁰ With their own hands they are to present the food offering to the LORD; they are to bring the fat, together with the breast, and wave the breast before the LORD as a wave offering. ³¹ The priest shall burn the fat on the altar, but the breast belongs to Aaron and his sons. ³² You are to give the right thigh of your fellowship offerings to the priest as a contribution. ³³ The son of Aaron who offers the blood and the fat of the fellowship offering shall have the right thigh as his share. ³⁴ From the fellowship offerings of the Israelites, I have taken the breast that is waved and the thigh that is presented and have given them to Aaron the priest and his sons as their perpetual share from the Israelites.' "

³⁵ This is the portion of the food offerings presented to the LORD that were allotted to Aaron and his sons on the day they were presented to serve the LORD as priests. ³⁶ On the day they were anointed, the LORD commanded that the Israelites give this to them as their perpetual share for the generations to come.

³⁷ These, then, are the regulations for the burnt offering, the grain offering, the sin offering, the guilt offering, the ordination offering and the fellowship offering, ³⁸ which the LORD gave Moses at Mount Sinai in the Desert of Sinai on the day he

commanded the Israelites to bring their offerings to the LORD.

The Ordination of Aaron and His Sons

8 The LORD said to Moses, ² "Bring Aaron and his sons, their garments, the anointing oil, the bull for the sin offering,*ᵇ* the two rams and the basket containing bread made without yeast, ³ and gather the entire assembly at the entrance to the tent of meeting." ⁴ Moses did as the LORD commanded him, and the assembly gathered at the entrance to the tent of meeting.

⁵ Moses said to the assembly, "This is what the LORD has commanded to be done." ⁶ Then Moses brought Aaron and his sons forward and washed them with water. ⁷ He put the tunic on Aaron, tied the sash around him, clothed him with the robe and put the ephod on him. He also fastened the ephod with a decorative waistband, which he tied around him. ⁸ He placed the breastpiece on him and put the Urim and Thummim in the breastpiece. ⁹ Then he placed the turban on Aaron's head and set the gold plate, the sacred emblem, on the front of it, as the LORD commanded Moses.

¹⁰ Then Moses took the anointing oil and anointed the tabernacle and everything in it, and so consecrated them. ¹¹ He sprinkled some of the oil on the altar seven times, anointing the altar and all its utensils and the basin with its stand, to consecrate them. ¹² He poured some of the anointing oil on Aaron's head and anointed him to consecrate him. ¹³ Then he brought Aaron's sons forward, put tunics on them, tied sashes around them and fastened caps on them, as the LORD commanded Moses.

¹⁴ He then presented the bull for the sin offering, and Aaron and his sons laid their hands on its head. ¹⁵ Moses slaughtered the bull and took some of the blood, and with his finger he put it on all the horns of the

---

ᵃ 25 Or offering is   ᵇ 2 Or purification offering; also in verse 14

7:22–27 | God reiterated that His people were not to consume **the blood of any bird or animal** (3:17; 17:11). Shed blood was the basis for atonement and was to be used only to that end.
7:28–36 | In a **wave offering,** the worshiper held the offering high and moved it in a horizontal motion, while the **contribution** to the priest was held high in a vertical motion. Both gestures showed that the offering was for the Lord. These offerings are also mentioned in 8:25–29; 9:21; 10:14, 15 and in the consecration of Aaron's sons in Exodus 29:22–28.
7:37, 38 | This summary of sacrifices from the preceding chapters is a reminder that God prescribed these offerings as an act of mercy—to enable His people to approach Him and please Him. All these **offerings** were fulfilled in the perfect sacrifice of Christ on the cross.
8:1–36 | The ordination ceremony for Aaron and his sons followed

the directions the Lord had given Moses in Exodus 29:1–37 and included a sin offering (8:14–17), a burnt offering (8:18–21), and the **ram for the ordination,** which featured a wave offering (8:22–29). The priestly **garments,** including the **ephod** and **breastpiece,** are described in Exodus 28:1–43.
8:8 | The **Urim and Thummim** (Ex. 28:15–30; Num. 27:21; Deut. 33:8; 1 Sam. 28:6; Ezra 2:63; Neh. 7:65) are thought to have been carried in a pocket in the high priest's ephod. It is uncertain exactly how they worked (see sidebar on Ex. 28:30 for one line of thinking), but some scholars believe these two special stones were flat on one side and rounded on the other, and when they were cast to the ground, God would reveal an answer: either yes (perhaps both landing flat side down), no (perhaps both landing rounded side down), or no answer at all (if they did not land on the same side).

altar to purify the altar. He poured out the rest of the blood at the base of the altar. So he consecrated it to make atonement for it. [16]Moses also took all the fat around the internal organs, the long lobe of the liver, and both kidneys and their fat, and burned it on the altar. [17]But the bull with its hide and its flesh and its intestines he burned up outside the camp, as the LORD commanded Moses.

[18]He then presented the ram for the burnt offering, and Aaron and his sons laid their hands on its head. [19]Then Moses slaughtered the ram and splashed the blood against the sides of the altar. [20]He cut the ram into pieces and burned the head, the pieces and the fat. [21]He washed the internal organs and the legs with water and burned the whole ram on the altar. It was a burnt offering, a pleasing aroma, a food offering presented to the LORD, as the LORD commanded Moses.

[22]He then presented the other ram, the ram for the ordination, and Aaron and his sons laid their hands on its head. [23]Moses slaughtered the ram and took some of its blood and put it on the lobe of Aaron's right ear, on the thumb of his right hand and on the big toe of his right foot. [24]Moses also brought Aaron's sons forward and put some of the blood on the lobes of their right ears, on the thumbs of their right hands and on the big toes of their right feet. Then he splashed blood against the sides of the altar. [25]After that, he took the fat, the fat tail, all the fat around the internal organs, the long lobe of the liver, both kidneys and their fat and the right thigh. [26]And from the basket of bread made without yeast, which was before the LORD, he took one thick loaf, one thick loaf with olive oil mixed in, and one thin loaf, and he put these on the fat portions and on the right thigh. [27]He put all these in the hands of Aaron and his sons, and they waved them before the LORD as a wave offering. [28]Then Moses took them from their hands and burned them on the altar on top of the burnt offering as an ordination offering, a pleasing aroma, a food offering presented to the LORD. [29]Moses also took the breast, which was his share of the ordination

ram, and waved it before the LORD as a wave offering, as the LORD commanded Moses. [30]Then Moses took some of the anointing oil and some of the blood from the altar and sprinkled them on Aaron and his garments and on his sons and their garments. So he consecrated Aaron and his garments and his sons and their garments.

[31]Moses then said to Aaron and his sons, "Cook the meat at the entrance to the tent of meeting and eat it there with the bread from the basket of ordination offerings, as I was commanded: 'Aaron and his sons are to eat it.' [32]Then burn up the rest of the meat and the bread. [33]Do not leave the entrance to the tent of meeting for seven days, until the days of your ordination are completed, for your ordination will last seven days. [34]What has been done today was commanded by the LORD to make atonement for you. [35]You must stay at the entrance to the tent of meeting day and night for seven days and do what the LORD requires, so you will not die; for that is what I have been commanded."

[36]So Aaron and his sons did everything the LORD commanded through Moses.

The Priests Begin Their Ministry

9 On the eighth day Moses summoned Aaron and his sons and the elders of Israel. [2]He said to Aaron, "Take a bull calf for your sin offering[a] and a ram for your burnt offering, both without defect, and present them before the LORD. [3]Then say to the Israelites: 'Take a male goat for a sin offering, a calf and a lamb—both a year old and without defect—for a burnt offering, [4]and an ox[b] and a ram for a fellowship offering to sacrifice before the LORD, together with a grain offering mixed with olive oil. For today the LORD will appear to you.'"

[5]They took the things Moses commanded to the front of the tent of meeting, and the entire assembly came near and stood before the LORD. [6]Then Moses said, "This is what the LORD has commanded you to do, so that the glory of the LORD may appear to you."

---

[a] 2 Or purification offering; here and throughout this chapter can refer to either male or female; also in verses 18 and 19.   [b] 4 The Hebrew word

---

8:23 | Moses took **blood** and consecrated **Aaron's right ear**, perhaps as a symbol of listening attentively to God. Moses also put blood **on the thumb of** Aaron's **right hand** as well as **on the big toe of his right foot**, presumably to represent the way a priest should live—pleasing to God in service and behavior.
8:33–36 | To emphasize the importance of following God's law, Aaron and his sons remained **at the entrance to the tent of meeting** for the seven days of their **ordination**. Their failure to obey the law would lead to death.

9:1–22 | **On the eighth day**, Aaron began his ministry as priest. He made a sin and burnt offering for himself (9:2, 8–14) and then the sin, burnt, fellowship, and grain offerings for the people (9:3, 4, 15–20), as well as the **wave offering**. The text highlights his obedience: all was done **as Moses commanded**. Aaron also fulfilled another priestly duty: **he lifted his hands toward the people and blessed them**. He probably used the blessing of Numbers 6:24–26, which is now called the Aaronic Blessing.

⁷Moses said to Aaron, "Come to the altar and sacrifice your sin offering and your burnt offering and make atonement for yourself and the people; sacrifice the offering that is for the people and make atonement for them, as the LORD has commanded."

⁸So Aaron came to the altar and slaughtered the calf as a sin offering for himself. ⁹His sons brought the blood to him, and he dipped his finger into the blood and put it on the horns of the altar; the rest of the blood he poured out at the base of the altar. ¹⁰On the altar he burned the fat, the kidneys and the long lobe of the liver from the sin offering, as the LORD commanded Moses; ¹¹the flesh and the hide he burned up outside the camp.

¹²Then he slaughtered the burnt offering. His sons handed him the blood, and he splashed it against the sides of the altar. ¹³They handed him the burnt offering piece by piece, including the head, and he burned them on the altar. ¹⁴He washed the internal organs and the legs and burned them on top of the burnt offering on the altar.

¹⁵Aaron then brought the offering that was for the people. He took the goat for the people's sin offering and slaughtered it and offered it for a sin offering as he did with the first one.

¹⁶He brought the burnt offering and offered it in the prescribed way. ¹⁷He also brought the grain offering, took a handful of it and burned it on the altar in addition to the morning's burnt offering.

¹⁸He slaughtered the ox and the ram as the fellowship offering for the people. His sons handed him the blood, and he splashed it against the sides of the altar. ¹⁹But the fat portions of the ox and the ram—the fat tail, the layer of fat, the kidneys and the long lobe of the liver— ²⁰these they laid on the breasts, and then Aaron burned the fat on the altar. ²¹Aaron waved the breasts and the right thigh before the LORD as a wave offering, as Moses commanded.

²²Then Aaron lifted his hands toward the people and blessed them. And having sacrificed the sin offering, the burnt offering and the fellowship offering, he stepped down. ²³Moses and Aaron then went into the tent of meeting. When they came out, they blessed the people; and the glory of the LORD appeared to all the people. ²⁴Fire came out from the presence of the LORD and consumed the burnt offering and the fat portions on the altar. And when all the people saw it, they shouted for joy and fell facedown.

The Death of Nadab and Abihu

10 Aaron's sons Nadab and Abihu took their censers, put fire in them and added incense; and they offered unauthorized fire before the LORD, contrary to his command. ²So fire came out from the presence of the LORD and consumed them, and they died before the LORD. ³Moses then said to Aaron, "This is what the LORD spoke of when he said:

"'Among those who approach me
    I will be proved holy;
in the sight of all the people
    I will be honored.'"

Aaron remained silent.

⁴Moses summoned Mishael and Elzaphan, sons of Aaron's uncle Uzziel, and said to them, "Come here; carry your cousins outside the camp, away from the front of the sanctuary." ⁵So they came and carried them, still in their tunics, outside the camp, as Moses ordered.

⁶Then Moses said to Aaron and his sons Eleazar and Ithamar, "Do not let your hair become unkempt[a] and do not tear your clothes, or you will die and the LORD will be angry with the whole community. But your relatives, all the Israelites, may mourn for

---

[a] 6 Or Do not uncover your heads

9:23, 24 | As God had promised (9:4, 6), **the glory of the LORD appeared to all the people** when Aaron made his first sacrifice. What this manifestation was like is unclear, but the crowd's response indicates that this was an extraordinary event that demonstrated the wonder and worthiness of God.

9:24 | When the OT refers to **fire . . . from the presence of the LORD**, lightning is an accurate image, as in the story of Elijah on Mount Carmel (1 Kgs. 18:38).

10:1–20 | On what was perhaps the first day of his high priestly ministry, Aaron experienced the deaths of his two eldest sons at the Lord's hands. Previously, God's fire had consumed sacrifices in holy approval of the people's obedience (9:24); here, however, His fire consumed the violators in immediate judgment. The Lord's holiness demands that He be obeyed in every detail.

10:1, 2 | Just as with Sodom and Gomorrah (Gen. 19:24),

fire came down from heaven and consumed **Nadab** and **Abihu**. The specifics of their fire are unknown, but these young men knowingly **offered unauthorized** (lit., "strange") **fire before the LORD**, violating God's commands.

10:3 | The experience of Nadab and Abihu is a staunch reminder that those who **approach** the Lord must regard him as **holy**, for as God says, **in the sight of all the people I will be honored.** By his silence, Aaron acknowledged that the Lord was justified in slaying his sons.

10:6, 7 | Leaving one's hair **unkempt** and tearing **clothes** were mourning practices at the time. As priests who were ministering before the Lord (21:10–12), Aaron and his surviving sons, **Eleazar and Ithamar**, were to remain at the **entrance to the tent of meeting** and perform their work. Others would **mourn** in their place.

those the LORD has destroyed by fire. [7]Do not leave the entrance to the tent of meeting or you will die, because the LORD's anointing oil is on you." So they did as Moses said.

[8]Then the LORD said to Aaron, [9]"You and your sons are not to drink wine or other fermented drink whenever you go into the tent of meeting, or you will die. This is a lasting ordinance for the generations to come, [10]so that you can distinguish between the holy and the common, between the unclean and the clean, [11]and so you can teach the Israelites all the decrees the LORD has given them through Moses."

[12]Moses said to Aaron and his remaining sons, Eleazar and Ithamar, "Take the grain offering left over from the food offerings prepared without yeast and presented to the LORD and eat it beside the altar, for it is most holy. [13]Eat it in the sanctuary area, because it is your share and your sons' share of the food offerings presented to the LORD; for so I have been commanded. [14]But you and your sons and your daughters may eat the breast that was waved and the thigh that was presented. Eat them in a ceremonially clean place; they have been given to you and your children as your share of the Israelites' fellowship offerings. [15]The thigh that was presented and the breast that was waved must be brought with the fat portions of the food offerings, to be waved before the LORD as a wave offering. This will be the perpetual share for you and your children, as the LORD has commanded."

[16]When Moses inquired about the goat of the sin offering[a] and found that it had been burned up, he was angry with Eleazar and Ithamar, Aaron's remaining sons, and asked, [17]"Why didn't you eat the sin offering in the sanctuary area? It is most holy; it was given to you to take away the guilt of the community by making atonement for them before the LORD. [18]Since its blood was not taken into the Holy Place, you should have eaten the goat in the sanctuary area, as I commanded."

[19]Aaron replied to Moses, "Today they sacrificed their sin offering and their burnt offering before the LORD, but such things as this have happened to me. Would the LORD have been pleased if I had eaten the sin offering today?" [20]When Moses heard this, he was satisfied.

Clean and Unclean Food

11 The LORD said to Moses and Aaron, [2]"Say to the Israelites: 'Of all the animals that live on land, these are the ones you may eat: [3]You may eat any animal that has a divided hoof and that chews the cud.

[4]"'There are some that only chew the cud or only have a divided hoof, but you must not eat them. The camel, though it chews the cud, does not have a divided hoof; it is ceremonially unclean for you. [5]The hyrax, though it chews the cud, does not have a divided hoof; it is unclean for you. [6]The rabbit, though it chews the cud, does not have a divided hoof; it is unclean for you. [7]And the pig, though it has a divided hoof, does not chew the cud; it is unclean for you. [8]You must not eat their meat or touch their carcasses; they are unclean for you.

[9]"'Of all the creatures living in the water of the seas and the streams you may eat any that have fins and scales. [10]But all creatures in the seas or streams that do not have fins and scales—whether among all the swarming things or among all the other living creatures in the water—you are to regard as unclean. [11]And since you are to regard them as unclean, you must not eat their meat; you must regard their carcasses as unclean. [12]Anything living in the water that does not have fins and scales is to be regarded as unclean by you.

[13]"'These are the birds you are to regard as unclean and not eat because they are unclean: the eagle,[b] the vulture, the black vulture, [14]the red kite, any kind of black kite, [15]any kind of raven, [16]the horned owl, the

---

[a] 16 Or *purification offering*; also in verses 17 and 19   [b] 13 The precise identification of some of the birds, insects and animals in this chapter is uncertain.

10:8–11 | The priests who served in the tent of meeting were not to **drink wine or other fermented drink** before conducting their sacred duties, because they were more likely to make serious errors that might lead to their death, as Nadab and Abihu had done (Prov. 20:1).
10:16–20 | **Moses** was initially **angry** with Eleazar and Ithamar when he discovered they had **burned up** the entire carcass of the people's **sin offering** (9:15) instead of eating it as prescribed (6:26)—until Aaron explained that the tragic events of the day had eradicated their hunger. God had mercy on them because they had done everything else properly.
10:19, 20 | Aaron's explanation for their failure to eat their portion of the offering was grief rather than defiance; thus Moses' anger was relieved. Good leaders learn to balance fault and penalty; some

mistakes merit grace rather than severe consequences.
11:1–8 | Of the four-legged animals, only those with a **divided hoof** that also chew the **cud** were permissible to eat. This included cattle, sheep, goats, and deer and excluded camels, rabbits, and pigs. The prohibition against eating **their meat** also meant not touching **their carcasses**. Even the carcasses of clean animals were considered unclean (11:39, 40; Deut. 14:3–8).
11:9–23 | These are rules regarding which creatures were permissible to eat. "Clean fish" were defined by two simple tests: **fins** and **scales**. This is similar to the two tests for mammals: split hoof and cud chewer. All types of crustaceans were excluded, as well as certain types of birds. The list of insects focuses more on those that were clean to eat (Deut. 14:9–20).

Tough Questions
Why did God forbid certain animals for food? • 11:1–23

The distinction among animals that could or could not be eaten (clean or unclean) was not an arbitrary test of religious obedience. Nor was the distinction made as motivation for or guidance in "healthy eating."

The dietary laws were a part of the laws of separation. Instructions concerning diet joined with the work/rest laws (the Sabbath; Ex. 20:8–11) and the clothing laws (no mixing of fabrics; Deut. 22:11) to help the people of Israel understand themselves as distinct from their neighbors. Without these laws, the Israelites might easily assimilate with pagan nations and be lost as a distinct community. The people of Israel had to maintain their special status as the people of God. Both chapters on unclean foods are either concluded (11:44, 45) or introduced (Deut. 14:1, 2) with an affirmation of Israel being chosen as consecrated (holy, or set apart) for the Lord.

There was nothing intrinsically significant in the "clean" animals as against the "unclean." But by maintaining distinctions about which animals should be used for food, the Israelites (then and now) were given a sense of differentiation from the other peoples of the world. Animals used in sacrifice came, of course, only from the clean animals.

Today, believers are distinguished not by abstaining from certain kinds of food but by "righteousness, peace and joy in the Holy Spirit" (Rom. 14:17).

screech owl, the gull, any kind of hawk, [17]the little owl, the cormorant, the great owl, [18]the white owl, the desert owl, the osprey, [19]the stork, any kind of heron, the hoopoe and the bat.

[20] "'All flying insects that walk on all fours are to be regarded as unclean by you. [21]There are, however, some flying insects that walk on all fours that you may eat: those that have jointed legs for hopping on the ground. [22]Of these you may eat any kind of locust, katydid, cricket or grasshopper. [23]But all other flying insects that have four legs you are to regard as unclean.

[24] "'You will make yourselves unclean by these; whoever touches their carcasses will be unclean till evening. [25]Whoever picks up one of their carcasses must wash their clothes, and they will be unclean till evening.

[26] "'Every animal that does not have a divided hoof or that does not chew the cud is unclean for you; whoever touches the carcass of any of them will be unclean. [27]Of all the animals that walk on all fours, those that walk on their paws are unclean for you; whoever touches their carcasses will be unclean till evening. [28]Anyone who picks up their carcasses must wash their clothes, and they will be unclean till evening. These animals are unclean for you.

[29] "'Of the animals that move along the ground, these are unclean for you: the weasel, the rat, any kind of great lizard, [30]the gecko, the monitor lizard, the wall lizard, the skink and the chameleon. [31]Of all those that move along the ground, these are unclean for you. Whoever touches them when they are dead will be unclean till evening. [32]When one of them dies and falls on something, that article, whatever its use, will be unclean, whether it is made of wood, cloth, hide or sackcloth. Put it in water; it will be unclean till evening, and then it will be clean. [33]If one of them falls into a clay pot, everything in it will be unclean, and you must break the pot. [34]Any food you are allowed to eat that has come into contact with water from any such pot is unclean, and any liquid that is drunk from such a pot is unclean. [35]Anything that one of their carcasses falls on becomes unclean; an oven or cooking pot must be broken up. They are unclean, and you are to regard them as unclean. [36]A spring, however, or a cistern for collecting water remains clean, but anyone who touches one of these carcasses is unclean. [37]If a carcass falls on any seeds that are to be planted, they remain clean. [38]But if water has been put on the seed and a carcass falls on it, it is unclean for you.

[39] "'If an animal that you are allowed to eat dies, anyone who touches its carcass will be unclean till evening. [40]Anyone who eats some of its carcass must wash their clothes, and they will be unclean till evening. Anyone who picks up the carcass must wash their clothes, and they will be unclean till evening.

11:10–43 | For things to be regarded as **unclean** was the strongest prohibition of all, describing an action or object that evokes revulsion and repugnance. This learned aversion to certain foods would keep the people of Israel separate from the nations who lived near them.

11:24–43 | A person could also become **unclean** by touching a **carcass**, or reptiles, or anything on which a reptile might fall. Cleansing was accomplished by washing in water, although some unclean items had to be broken. To be only **unclean till evening** (as opposed to a week, as with Miriam in Num. 12) suggests a lighter offense.

41 " 'Every creature that moves along the ground is to be regarded as unclean; it is not to be eaten. 42 You are not to eat any creature that moves along the ground, whether it moves on its belly or walks on all fours or on many feet; it is unclean. 43 Do not defile yourselves by any of these creatures. Do not make yourselves unclean by means of them or be made unclean by them. 44 I am the LORD your God; consecrate yourselves and be holy, because I am holy. Do not make yourselves unclean by any creature that moves along the ground. 45 I am the LORD, who brought you up out of Egypt to be your God; therefore be holy, because I am holy.

46 " 'These are the regulations concerning animals, birds, every living thing that moves about in the water and every creature that moves along the ground. 47 You must distinguish between the unclean and the clean, between living creatures that may be eaten and those that may not be eaten.' "

Purification After Childbirth

12 The LORD said to Moses, 2 "Say to the Israelites: 'A woman who becomes pregnant and gives birth to a son will be ceremonially unclean for seven days, just as she is unclean during her monthly period. 3 On the eighth day the boy is to be circumcised. 4 Then the woman must wait thirty-three days to be purified from her bleeding. She must not touch anything sacred or go to the sanctuary until the days of her purification are over. 5 If she gives birth to a daughter, for two weeks the woman will be unclean, as during her period. Then she must wait sixty-six days to be purified from her bleeding.

6 " 'When the days of her purification for a son or daughter are over, she is to bring to the priest at the entrance to the tent of meeting a year-old lamb for a burnt offering and a young pigeon or a dove for a sin offering.[a] 7 He shall offer them before the LORD to make atonement for her, and then she will be ceremonially clean from her flow of blood.

" 'These are the regulations for the woman who gives birth to a boy or a girl. 8 But if she cannot afford a lamb, she is to bring two doves or two young pigeons, one for a burnt offering and the other for a sin offering. In this way the priest will make atonement for her, and she will be clean.' "

Regulations About Defiling Skin Diseases

13 The LORD said to Moses and Aaron, 2 "When anyone has a swelling or a rash or a shiny spot on their skin that may be a defiling skin disease,[b] they must be brought to Aaron the priest or to one of his sons[c] who is a priest. 3 The priest is to examine the sore on the skin, and if the hair in the sore has turned white and the sore appears to be more than skin deep, it is a defiling skin disease. When the priest examines that person, he shall pronounce them ceremonially unclean. 4 If the shiny spot on the skin is white but does not appear to be more than skin deep and the hair in it has not turned white, the priest is to isolate the affected person for seven days. 5 On the seventh day the priest is to examine them, and if he sees that the sore is unchanged and has not spread in the skin, he is to isolate them for another seven days. 6 On the seventh day the priest is to examine them again, and if the sore has faded and has not spread in the skin, the priest shall pronounce them clean; it is only a rash. They must wash their clothes, and they will be clean. 7 But if the rash does spread in their skin after they have shown themselves to the priest to be pronounced clean, they must appear before the priest again. 8 The priest is to examine that person, and if the rash has spread in the skin, he shall pronounce them unclean; it is a defiling skin disease.

9 "When anyone has a defiling skin disease, they must be brought to the priest.

---

[a] 6 Or purification offering; also in verse 8   [b] 2 The Hebrew word for defiling skin disease, traditionally translated "leprosy," was used for various diseases affecting the skin; here and throughout verses 3-46.   [c] 2 Or descendants

---

11:44, 45 | By the words **therefore be holy, because I am holy**, it is apparent that the ceremonial laws were designed to teach Israel the significance of God's holiness, that He must be worshiped on His own terms, and that the people of Israel were different from other nations (Ex. 3:14, 15; 6:7; 1 Pet. 1:15, 16).
12:1-8 | The theme of this chapter is not personal holiness but **purification** for the mother after childbirth. Nothing here teaches or implies that human sexuality is "dirty," that pregnancy is defiling, or that babies are impure. On the contrary, Scripture presents children as blessings from God (Ps. 113:9; 127:3-5; 128:3; Prov. 17:6; Matt. 19:14).
12:2-5 | Being **ceremonially unclean** did not mean someone was sinful. Women became unclean because of the bleeding in

childbirth or menstruation (**unclean during her monthly period**; 15:19-30). These rites constantly reminded the Israelite people of the sacredness of blood (17:11, 14; Gen. 9:4; Deut. 12:23).
12:3 | Male converts to the Israelite faith were **circumcised** to indicate their acceptance into the community (Gen. 34:13-24; Ex. 12:48), as well as every Israelite baby **boy**. The name of the child would officially be announced on this occasion as well.
12:6-8 | Those who could not afford to offer a **lamb** in the ritual of **purification** brought a **young pigeon or a dove**. This was Mary's offering when Jesus was born (Luke 2:22-24), perhaps an indication that Jesus identified with the poor. A similar provision appears in the discussion of the sacrifices for a person cleansed of a defiling skin disease (14:21-23, 31, 32).

¹⁰The priest is to examine them, and if there is a white swelling in the skin that has turned the hair white and if there is raw flesh in the swelling, ¹¹it is a chronic skin disease and the priest shall pronounce them unclean. He is not to isolate them, because they are already unclean.

¹²"If the disease breaks out all over their skin and, so far as the priest can see, it covers all the skin of the affected person from head to foot, ¹³the priest is to examine them, and if the disease has covered their whole body, he shall pronounce them clean. Since it has all turned white, they are clean. ¹⁴But whenever raw flesh appears on them, they will be unclean. ¹⁵When the priest sees the raw flesh, he shall pronounce them unclean. The raw flesh is unclean; they have a defiling disease. ¹⁶If the raw flesh changes and turns white, they must go to the priest. ¹⁷The priest is to examine them, and if the sores have turned white, the priest shall pronounce the affected person clean; then they will be clean.

¹⁸"When someone has a boil on their skin and it heals, ¹⁹and in the place where the boil was, a white swelling or reddish-white spot appears, they must present themselves to the priest. ²⁰The priest is to examine it, and if it appears to be more than skin deep and the hair in it has turned white, the priest shall pronounce that person unclean. It is a defiling skin disease that has broken out where the boil was. ²¹But if, when the priest examines it, there is no white hair in it and it is not more than skin deep and has faded, then the priest is to isolate them for seven days. ²²If it is spreading in the skin, the priest shall pronounce them unclean; it is a defiling disease. ²³But if the spot is unchanged and has not spread, it is only a scar from the boil, and the priest shall pronounce them clean.

²⁴"When someone has a burn on their skin and a reddish-white or white spot appears in the raw flesh of the burn, ²⁵the priest is to examine the spot, and if the hair in it has turned white, and it appears to be more than skin deep, it is a defiling disease that has broken out in the burn. The priest shall pronounce them unclean; it is a defiling skin disease. ²⁶But if the priest examines it and there is no white hair in the spot

and if it is not more than skin deep and has faded, then the priest is to isolate them for seven days. ²⁷On the seventh day the priest is to examine that person, and if it is spreading in the skin, the priest shall pronounce them unclean; it is a defiling skin disease. ²⁸If, however, the spot is unchanged and has not spread in the skin but has faded, it is a swelling from the burn, and the priest shall pronounce them clean; it is only a scar from the burn.

²⁹"If a man or woman has a sore on their head or chin, ³⁰the priest is to examine the sore, and if it appears to be more than skin deep and the hair in it is yellow and thin, the priest shall pronounce them unclean; it is a defiling skin disease on the head or chin. ³¹But if, when the priest examines the sore, it does not seem to be more than skin deep and there is no black hair in it, then the priest is to isolate the affected person for seven days. ³²On the seventh day the priest is to examine the sore, and if it has not spread and there is no yellow hair in it and it does not appear to be more than skin deep, ³³then the man or woman must shave themselves, except for the affected area, and the priest is to keep them isolated another seven days. ³⁴On the seventh day the priest is to examine the sore, and if it has not spread in the skin and appears to be no more than skin deep, the priest shall pronounce them clean. They must wash their clothes, and they will be clean. ³⁵But if the sore does spread in the skin after they are pronounced clean, ³⁶the priest is to examine them, and if he finds that the sore has spread in the skin, he does not need to look for yellow hair; they are unclean. ³⁷If, however, the sore is unchanged so far as the priest can see, and if black hair has grown in it, the affected person is healed. They are clean, and the priest shall pronounce them clean.

³⁸"When a man or woman has white spots on the skin, ³⁹the priest is to examine them, and if the spots are dull white, it is a harmless rash that has broken out on the skin; they are clean.

⁴⁰"A man who has lost his hair and is bald is clean. ⁴¹If he has lost his hair from the front of his scalp and has a bald forehead, he is clean. ⁴²But if he has a reddish-white sore

---

13:1–46 | Only the priests could pronounce that a person with **a defiling skin disease** was cured (Mark 1:44; Luke 17:14). To be ill with leprosy (or any of the skin diseases encompassed by the Hebrew term) was no more a sign of personal sin than to be ill with cancer today, but because the disease could spread, various means

were used to quarantine the infected person in hopes of preventing an epidemic. Sin that goes unchecked among a people may similarly become an epidemic.

13:1–8 | The infected person was isolated for as long as two weeks to allow the symptoms time to improve.

on his bald head or forehead, it is a defiling disease breaking out on his head or forehead. [43] The priest is to examine him, and if the swollen sore on his head or forehead is reddish-white like a defiling skin disease, [44] the man is diseased and is unclean. The priest shall pronounce him unclean because of the sore on his head.

[45] "Anyone with such a defiling disease must wear torn clothes, let their hair be unkempt,[a] cover the lower part of their face and cry out, 'Unclean! Unclean!' [46] As long as they have the disease they remain unclean. They must live alone; they must live outside the camp.

Regulations About Defiling Molds

[47] "As for any fabric that is spoiled with a defiling mold—any woolen or linen clothing, [48] any woven or knitted material of linen or wool, any leather or anything made of leather—[49] if the affected area in the fabric, the leather, the woven or knitted material, or any leather article, is greenish or reddish, it is a defiling mold and must be shown to the priest. [50] The priest is to examine the affected area and isolate the article for seven days. [51] On the seventh day he is to examine it, and if the mold has spread in the fabric, the woven or knitted material, or the leather, whatever its use, it is a persistent defiling mold; the article is unclean. [52] He must burn the fabric, the woven or knitted material of wool or linen, or any leather article that has been spoiled; because the defiling mold is persistent, the article must be burned.

[53] "But if, when the priest examines it, the mold has not spread in the fabric, the woven or knitted material, or the leather article, [54] he shall order that the spoiled article be washed. Then he is to isolate it for another seven days. [55] After the article has been washed, the priest is to examine it again, and if the mold has not changed its appearance, even though it has not spread, it is unclean. Burn it, no matter which side of the fabric has been spoiled. [56] If, when the priest examines it, the mold has faded after the article has been washed, he is to

tear the spoiled part out of the fabric, the leather, or the woven or knitted material. [57] But if it reappears in the fabric, in the woven or knitted material, or in the leather article, it is a spreading mold; whatever has the mold must be burned. [58] Any fabric, woven or knitted material, or any leather article that has been washed and is rid of the mold, must be washed again. Then it will be clean."

[59] These are the regulations concerning defiling molds in woolen or linen clothing, woven or knitted material, or any leather article, for pronouncing them clean or unclean.

Cleansing From Defiling Skin Diseases

14 The LORD said to Moses, [2] "These are the regulations for any diseased person at the time of their ceremonial cleansing, when they are brought to the priest: [3] The priest is to go outside the camp and examine them. If they have been healed of their defiling skin disease,[b] [4] the priest shall order that two live clean birds and some cedar wood, scarlet yarn and hyssop be brought for the person to be cleansed. [5] Then the priest shall order that one of the birds be killed over fresh water in a clay pot. [6] He is then to take the live bird and dip it, together with the cedar wood, the scarlet yarn and the hyssop, into the blood of the bird that was killed over the fresh water. [7] Seven times he shall sprinkle the one to be cleansed of the defiling disease, and then pronounce them clean. After that, he is to release the live bird in the open fields.

[8] "The person to be cleansed must wash their clothes, shave off all their hair and bathe with water; then they will be ceremonially clean. After this they may come into the camp, but they must stay outside their tent for seven days. [9] On the seventh day they must shave off all their hair; they must shave their head, their beard, their eyebrows and the rest of their hair. They must

---

[a] 45 Or clothes, uncover their head   [b] 3 The Hebrew word for defiling skin disease, traditionally translated "leprosy," was used for various diseases affecting the skin; also in verses 7, 32, 54 and 57.

13:45, 46 | A person with a **defiling disease** had to live **outside the camp.** The law demanded that anyone with this disease must be removed from the general population and cry, **Unclean! Unclean!** so that others could avoid him or her. The sadness of those who suffered in this way was incalculable.

13:47-59 | In addition to serving as physicians, the priests also conducted the inspection for **defiling mold** on clothing and in houses (14:33-53).

14:1-32 | This section lists the cleansing rituals to be performed after a person with a defiling skin disease was declared clean

according to the procedures described in 13:1-46. This complex process involved numerous offerings (14:4-7, 10-32) as well as washing, shaving, and waiting a week to return to the camp (14:8, 9).

14:4 | These objects provided symbolic cleansing for a person who had been healed of a defiling skin disease. **Cedar wood** was a durable and decay-resistant wood. **Scarlet yarn** was probably used to tie the hyssop branch to the wood as a symbol of the sacrificial blood that brought victory over sin and death. **Hyssop** was an herb used for flavoring, fragrance, and medicinal purposes.

wash their clothes and bathe themselves with water, and they will be clean.

¹⁰ "On the eighth day they must bring two male lambs and one ewe lamb a year old, each without defect, along with three-tenths of an ephah* of the finest flour mixed with olive oil for a grain offering, and one log* of oil. ¹¹ The priest who pronounces them clean shall present both the one to be cleansed and their offerings before the LORD at the entrance to the tent of meeting.

¹² "Then the priest is to take one of the male lambs and offer it as a guilt offering, along with the log of oil; he shall wave them before the LORD as a wave offering. ¹³ He is to slaughter the lamb in the sanctuary area where the sin offering* and the burnt offering are slaughtered. Like the sin offering, the guilt offering belongs to the priest; it is most holy. ¹⁴ The priest is to take some of the blood of the guilt offering and put it on the lobe of the right ear of the one to be cleansed, on the thumb of their right hand and on the big toe of their right foot. ¹⁵ The priest shall then take some of the log of oil, pour it in the palm of his own left hand, ¹⁶ dip his right forefinger into the oil in his palm, and with his finger sprinkle some of it before the LORD seven times. ¹⁷ The priest is to put some of the oil remaining in his palm on the lobe of the right ear of the one to be cleansed, on the thumb of their right hand and on the big toe of their right foot, on top of the blood of the guilt offering. ¹⁸ The rest of the oil in his palm the priest shall put on the head of the one to be cleansed and make atonement for them before the LORD.

¹⁹ "Then the priest is to sacrifice the sin offering and make atonement for the one to be cleansed from their uncleanness. After that, the priest shall slaughter the burnt offering ²⁰ and offer it on the altar, together with the grain offering, and make atonement for them, and they will be clean.

²¹ "If, however, they are poor and cannot afford these, they must take one male lamb as a guilt offering to be waved to make atonement for them, together with a tenth of an ephah* of the finest flour mixed with olive oil for a grain offering, a log of oil, ²² and two doves or two young pigeons, such as they can afford, one for a sin offering and the other for a burnt offering.

²³ "On the eighth day they must bring them for their cleansing to the priest at the entrance to the tent of meeting, before the LORD. ²⁴ The priest is to take the lamb for the guilt offering, together with the log of oil, and wave them before the LORD as a wave offering. ²⁵ He shall slaughter the lamb for the guilt offering and take some of its blood and put it on the lobe of the right ear of the one to be cleansed, on the thumb of their right hand and on the big toe of their right foot. ²⁶ The priest is to pour some of the oil into the palm of his own left hand, ²⁷ and with his right forefinger sprinkle some of the oil from his palm seven times before the LORD. ²⁸ Some of the oil in his palm he is to put on the same places he put the blood of the guilt offering — on the lobe of the right ear of the one to be cleansed, on the thumb of their right hand and on the big toe of their right foot. ²⁹ The rest of the oil in his palm the priest shall put on the head of the one to be cleansed, to make atonement for them before the LORD. ³⁰ Then he shall sacrifice the doves or the young pigeons, such as the person can afford, ³¹ one as a sin offering and the other as a burnt offering, together with the grain offering. In this way the priest will make atonement before the LORD on behalf of the one to be cleansed."

³² These are the regulations for anyone who has a defiling skin disease and who cannot afford the regular offerings for their cleansing.

Cleansing From Defiling Molds

³³ The LORD said to Moses and Aaron, ³⁴ "When you enter the land of Canaan, which I am giving you as your possession, and I put a spreading mold in a house in

---

ᵃ 10 That is, probably about 11 pounds or about 5 kilograms   ᵇ 10 That is, about 1/3 quart or about 0.3 liter; also in verses 12, 15, 21 and 24   ᶜ 13 Or purification offering; also in verses 19, 22 and 31   ᵈ 21 That is, probably about 3 1/2 pounds or about 1.6 kilograms

---

14:10 | On the eighth day after his birth, every Israelite male was circumcised. Here, that day represents the rebirth of the person who had a defiling skin disease into the covenant community of faith. Because sickness and death are a result of humankind's sin, a sacrifice is the means for the cleansed person to enter into full fellowship in the community.

14:19, 20 | Three offerings completed the sacrificial procedure: (1) **the sin offering** of one ewe lamb (14:10); (2) **the burnt offering** of a male lamb (14:12); and (3) the burnt offering (the other male lamb of 14:10), accompanied by **the grain offering.**

14:21–32 | People who were **poor** had to bring a **male lamb** for the

guilt offering—the same as any other Israelite. The sin and burnt offerings could be made with less expensive animals, indicating that the poor person had the same value as a rich person. There was nothing special about the animals used for sacrifices, except that they had to be "clean." A person was not forgiven more when bringing a more valuable animal.

14:33–53 | This section is an extension of the law concerning clothing and personal articles defiled with mold (13:47–59). Since the passage refers to houses made of stones and not the tents in which the people lived at the time, these laws referred to the people's future residences in the **land of Canaan.**

that land, [35]the owner of the house must go and tell the priest, 'I have seen something that looks like a defiling mold in my house.' [36]The priest is to order the house to be emptied before he goes in to examine the mold, so that nothing in the house will be pronounced unclean. After this the priest is to go in and inspect the house. [37]He is to examine the mold on the walls, and if it has greenish or reddish depressions that appear to be deeper than the surface of the wall, [38]the priest shall go out the doorway of the house and close it up for seven days. [39]On the seventh day the priest shall return to inspect the house. If the mold has spread on the walls, [40]he is to order that the contaminated stones be torn out and thrown into an unclean place outside the town. [41]He must have all the inside walls of the house scraped and the material that is scraped off dumped into an unclean place outside the town. [42]Then they are to take other stones to replace these and take new clay and plaster the house.

[43]"If the defiling mold reappears in the house after the stones have been torn out and the house scraped and plastered, [44]the priest is to go and examine it and, if the mold has spread in the house, it is a persistent defiling mold; the house is unclean. [45]It must be torn down—its stones, timbers and all the plaster—and taken out of the town to an unclean place.

[46]"Anyone who goes into the house while it is closed up will be unclean till evening. [47]Anyone who sleeps or eats in the house must wash their clothes.

[48]"But if the priest comes to examine it and the mold has not spread after the house has been plastered, he shall pronounce the house clean, because the defiling mold is gone. [49]To purify the house he is to take two birds and some cedar wood, scarlet yarn and hyssop. [50]He shall kill one of the birds over fresh water in a clay pot. [51]Then he is to take the cedar wood, the hyssop, the scarlet yarn and the live bird, dip them into the blood of the dead bird and the fresh water, and sprinkle the house seven times. [52]He shall purify the house with the bird's blood, the fresh water, the live bird, the cedar wood, the hyssop and the scarlet yarn.

[53]Then he is to release the live bird in the open fields outside the town. In this way he will make atonement for the house, and it will be clean."

[54]These are the regulations for any defiling skin disease, for a sore, [55]for defiling molds in fabric or in a house, [56]and for a swelling, a rash or a shiny spot, [57]to determine when something is clean or unclean.

These are the regulations for defiling skin diseases and defiling molds.

Discharges Causing Uncleanness

15 The LORD said to Moses and Aaron, [2]"Speak to the Israelites and say to them: 'When any man has an unusual bodily discharge, such a discharge is unclean. [3]Whether it continues flowing from his body or is blocked, it will make him unclean. This is how his discharge will bring about uncleanness:

[4]"'Any bed the man with a discharge lies on will be unclean, and anything he sits on will be unclean. [5]Anyone who touches his bed must wash their clothes and bathe with water, and they will be unclean till evening. [6]Whoever sits on anything that the man with a discharge sat on must wash their clothes and bathe with water, and they will be unclean till evening.

[7]"'Whoever touches the man who has a discharge must wash their clothes and bathe with water, and they will be unclean till evening.

[8]"'If the man with the discharge spits on anyone who is clean, they must wash their clothes and bathe with water, and they will be unclean till evening.

[9]"'Everything the man sits on when riding will be unclean, [10]and whoever touches any of the things that were under him will be unclean till evening; whoever picks up those things must wash their clothes and bathe with water, and they will be unclean till evening.

[11]"'Anyone the man with a discharge touches without rinsing his hands with water must wash their clothes and bathe with water, and they will be unclean till evening.

[12]"'A clay pot that the man touches must be broken, and any wooden article is to be rinsed with water.

14:34 | A **spreading mold** could also affect a **house**. As with clothing defiled with mold (13:47–59), this probably refers to a form of mildew or fungus.
14:43–53 | If the **defiling mold** was eradicated, the priest would perform ceremonies similar to those for the cleansed person. If not, the dwelling was to be destroyed (**torn**

down), and anyone who lived and ate there was to **wash their clothes**.
15:2–15 | Males could become unclean through **an unusual bodily discharge**. The discharge likely describes something stemming from some sort of disease or illness. Whatever the afflicted man touched or spat on was also unclean.

13 " 'When a man is cleansed from his discharge, he is to count off seven days for his ceremonial cleansing; he must wash his clothes and bathe himself with fresh water, and he will be clean. 14 On the eighth day he must take two doves or two young pigeons and come before the LORD to the entrance to the tent of meeting and give them to the priest. 15 The priest is to sacrifice them, the one for a sin offering[a] and the other for a burnt offering. In this way he will make atonement before the LORD for the man because of his discharge.

16 " 'When a man has an emission of semen, he must bathe his whole body with water, and he will be unclean till evening. 17 Any clothing or leather that has semen on it must be washed with water, and it will be unclean till evening. 18 When a man has sexual relations with a woman and there is an emission of semen, both of them must bathe with water, and they will be unclean till evening.

19 " 'When a woman has her regular flow of blood, the impurity of her monthly period will last seven days, and anyone who touches her will be unclean till evening.

20 " 'Anything she lies on during her period will be unclean, and anything she sits on will be unclean. 21 Anyone who touches her bed will be unclean; they must wash their clothes and bathe with water, and they will be unclean till evening. 22 Anyone who touches anything she sits on will be unclean; they must wash their clothes and bathe with water, and they will be unclean till evening. 23 Whether it is the bed or anything she was sitting on, when anyone touches it, they will be unclean till evening.

24 " 'If a man has sexual relations with her and her monthly flow touches him, he will be unclean for seven days; any bed he lies on will be unclean.

25 " 'When a woman has a discharge of blood for many days at a time other than her monthly period or has a discharge that continues beyond her period, she will be unclean as long as she has the discharge, just as in the days of her period. 26 Any bed she lies on while her discharge continues will be unclean, as is her bed during her monthly period, and anything she sits on will be unclean, as during her period. 27 Anyone who touches them will be unclean; they must wash their clothes and bathe with water, and they will be unclean till evening.

28 " 'When she is cleansed from her discharge, she must count off seven days, and after that she will be ceremonially clean. 29 On the eighth day she must take two doves or two young pigeons and bring them to the priest at the entrance to the tent of meeting. 30 The priest is to sacrifice one for a sin offering and the other for a burnt offering. In this way he will make atonement for her before the LORD for the uncleanness of her discharge.

31 " 'You must keep the Israelites separate from things that make them unclean, so they will not die in their uncleanness for defiling my dwelling place,[b] which is among them.' "

32 These are the regulations for a man with a discharge, for anyone made unclean by an emission of semen, 33 for a woman in her monthly period, for a man or a woman with a discharge, and for a man who has sexual relations with a woman who is ceremonially unclean.

The Day of Atonement

16 The LORD spoke to Moses after the death of the two sons of Aaron who died when they approached the LORD. 2 The LORD said to Moses: "Tell your brother Aaron that he is not to come whenever he chooses into the Most Holy Place behind the curtain in front of the atonement cover on the ark, or else he will die. For I will appear in the cloud over the atonement cover.

3 "This is how Aaron is to enter the Most Holy Place: He must first bring a young bull for a sin offering[c] and a ram for a burnt offering. 4 He is to put on the sacred linen tunic, with linen undergarments next to his

---

a 15 Or purification offering; also in verse 30   b 31 Or my tabernacle
c 3 Or purification offering; here and throughout this chapter

---

15:16–18 | This passage refers to ceremonial uncleanness; it does not suggest that sexual intercourse within marriage is impure. Because intercourse involves bodily fluids, the husband and wife were to **bathe** afterward for purification. In this case, no sacrifices were required for cleansing, only washing in water.
15:19–30 | While a woman's irregular **discharge** mandated an **offering**, ordinary, monthly discharges such as menstruation were not associated with sin or wrongdoing, and therefore no offering was required. Cleansing was commanded, however, because in that era, bathing and washing clothes were infrequent, and a failure to clean up might lead to disease. Contemporary readers

should view these rituals as protective rather than punitive.
15:24 | A husband who had intercourse with his wife during her menstrual period was unclean for a week. The issue here is not prohibition due to sin but uncleanness.
16:1–34 | This chapter may be the most significant in Leviticus, because it points to the cross of Jesus the Christ. The Day of Atonement fell in September or October on the Hebrew calendar and was the annual event in which **atonement** was made for **all the sins of the Israelites**. While they fasted as a nation, the people were to consider their lives and confess sins, attitudes, and behavior patterns (**deny yourselves**).

Historically Speaking   The Day of Atonement • 16:1–34

The Day of Atonement (called Yom Kippur today) was the most holy day in the religious calendar of the Israelite people—and remains so in our day. There was a great deal that priests had to do on this day, as is indicated in chapter 16. But the most interesting actions concerned two goats. The Book of Leviticus begins with seven chapters describing five offerings that the people were to bring before God in His holy worship. In these offerings was the means for a person to ask forgiveness of known sins and to celebrate great love for God. But what was a person to do regarding sins that she or he might not even be aware of? On one day of the year—a day of solemnity, reflection, fasting, and prayer—all sins were atoned for by the Lord's gracious provision.

Two goats were brought to the priests, and the sins of the nation were transferred to each animal in a different way. One was driven into the wilderness as a symbol that the sins of the people had been driven away from their presence; the second goat was slain, and its blood was caught in a vessel and then sprinkled by the high priest on the atonement cover in the Most Holy Place.

All was possible because of the death of Christ; it was in His death that these sacrifices had their ultimate meaning (Heb. 9:12).

body; he is to tie the linen sash around him and put on the linen turban. These are sacred garments; so he must bathe himself with water before he puts them on. [5] From the Israelite community he is to take two male goats for a sin offering and a ram for a burnt offering.

[6] "Aaron is to offer the bull for his own sin offering to make atonement for himself and his household. [7] Then he is to take the two goats and present them before the LORD at the entrance to the tent of meeting. [8] He is to cast lots for the two goats—one lot for the LORD and the other for the scapegoat.[a] [9] Aaron shall bring the goat whose lot falls to the LORD and sacrifice it for a sin offering. [10] But the goat chosen by lot as the scapegoat shall be presented alive before the LORD to be used for making atonement by sending it into the wilderness as a scapegoat.

[11] "Aaron shall bring the bull for his own sin offering to make atonement for himself and his household, and he is to slaughter the bull for his own sin offering. [12] He is to take a censer full of burning coals from the altar before the LORD and two handfuls of finely ground fragrant incense and take them behind the curtain. [13] He is to put the incense on the fire before the LORD, and the smoke of the incense will conceal the atonement cover above the tablets of the covenant law, so that he will not die. [14] He is to take some of the bull's blood and with his finger sprinkle

it on the front of the atonement cover; then he shall sprinkle some of it with his finger seven times before the atonement cover.

[15] "He shall then slaughter the goat for the sin offering for the people and take its blood behind the curtain and do with it as he did with the bull's blood: He shall sprinkle it on the atonement cover and in front of it. [16] In this way he will make atonement for the Most Holy Place because of the uncleanness and rebellion of the Israelites, whatever their sins have been. He is to do the same for the tent of meeting, which is among them in the midst of their uncleanness. [17] No one is to be in the tent of meeting from the time Aaron goes in to make atonement in the Most Holy Place until he comes out, having made atonement for himself, his household and the whole community of Israel.

[18] "Then he shall come out to the altar that is before the LORD and make atonement for it. He shall take some of the bull's blood and some of the goat's blood and put it on all the horns of the altar. [19] He shall sprinkle some of the blood on it with his finger seven times to cleanse it and to consecrate it from the uncleanness of the Israelites.

[20] "When Aaron has finished making atonement for the Most Holy Place, the tent of meeting and the altar, he shall bring forward the live goat. [21] He is to lay both hands

---

[a] 8 The meaning of the Hebrew for this word is uncertain; also in verses 10 and 26.

16:5–10 | The Day of Atonement rituals featured two male goats: a **sin offering** and a **scapegoat**. The first was sacrificed to cleanse the Most Holy Place from the sins of the Israelites that had tainted it (16:15–19). The high priest would take blood from this goat and sprinkle it on and before the atonement cover (Heb. 9:13, 14). Then he would place his hands on the second goat, confess Israel's sins, and send it into the wilderness as a sign of the removal of sin. Both animals symbolized Christ (Heb. 7:27, 28; 9:7). The Hebrew verb *kapar* ("to cover") refers to the atonement cover and is the root of (Yom) Kippur (23:26–32). Jesus

"covered" (made atonement) and "took away" people's sins.
16:6 | As a sinful man, even Aaron the high priest of Israel had to bring a **sin offering to make atonement for himself and his household** (Heb. 5:1–3), but Jesus, the sinless high priest, did not (Heb. 9:11–28).
16:8 | In the OT, guidance was obtained by the casting of **lots**. This practice also appears in the NT (Acts 1:26), but Jesus told the disciples that when the Holy Spirit came, He would lead them in truth instead (John 14:16, 17).

on the head of the live goat and confess over it all the wickedness and rebellion of the Israelites—all their sins—and put them on the goat's head. He shall send the goat away into the wilderness in the care of someone appointed for the task. ²²The goat will carry on itself all their sins to a remote place; and the man shall release it in the wilderness.

²³ "Then Aaron is to go into the tent of meeting and take off the linen garments he put on before he entered the Most Holy Place, and he is to leave them there. ²⁴He shall bathe himself with water in the sanctuary area and put on his regular garments. Then he shall come out and sacrifice the burnt offering for himself and the burnt offering for the people, to make atonement for himself and for the people. ²⁵He shall also burn the fat of the sin offering on the altar.

²⁶ "The man who releases the goat as a scapegoat must wash his clothes and bathe himself with water; afterward he may come into the camp. ²⁷The bull and the goat for the sin offerings, whose blood was brought into the Most Holy Place to make atonement, must be taken outside the camp; their hides, flesh and intestines are to be burned up. ²⁸The man who burns them must wash his clothes and bathe himself with water; afterward he may come into the camp.

²⁹ "This is to be a lasting ordinance for you: On the tenth day of the seventh month you must deny yourselves*a* and not do any work—whether native-born or a foreigner residing among you— ³⁰because on this day atonement will be made for you, to cleanse you. Then, before the LORD, you will be clean from all your sins. ³¹It is a day of sabbath rest, and you must deny yourselves; it is a lasting ordinance. ³²The priest who is anointed and ordained to succeed his father as high priest is to make atonement. He is to put on the sacred linen garments ³³and make atonement for the Most Holy Place, for the tent of meeting and the altar, and for the priests and all the members of the community.

³⁴ "This is to be a lasting ordinance for you: Atonement is to be made once a year for all the sins of the Israelites."

And it was done, as the LORD commanded Moses.

Eating Blood Forbidden

17 The LORD said to Moses, ² "Speak to Aaron and his sons and to all the Israelites and say to them: 'This is what the LORD has commanded: ³Any Israelite who sacrifices an ox,*b* a lamb or a goat in the camp or outside of it ⁴instead of bringing it to the entrance to the tent of meeting to present it as an offering to the LORD in front of the tabernacle of the LORD—that person shall be considered guilty of bloodshed; they have shed blood and must be cut off from their people. ⁵This is so the Israelites will bring to the LORD the sacrifices they are now making in the open fields. They must bring them to the priest, that is, to the LORD, at the entrance to the tent of meeting and sacrifice them as fellowship offerings. ⁶The priest is to splash the blood against the altar of the LORD at the entrance to the tent of meeting and burn the fat as an aroma pleasing to the LORD. ⁷They must no longer offer any of their sacrifices to the goat idols*c* to whom they prostitute themselves. This is to be a lasting ordinance for them and for the generations to come.'

⁸ "Say to them: 'Any Israelite or any foreigner residing among them who offers a burnt offering or sacrifice ⁹and does not bring it to the entrance to the tent of meeting to sacrifice it to the LORD must be cut off from the people of Israel.

¹⁰ " 'I will set my face against any Israelite or any foreigner residing among them who eats blood, and I will cut them off from the people. ¹¹For the life of a creature is in the blood, and I have given it to you to make atonement for yourselves on the altar; it is the blood that makes atonement for one's life.*d* ¹²Therefore I say to the Israelites, "None of you may eat blood, nor may any foreigner residing among you eat blood."

¹³ " 'Any Israelite or any foreigner residing among you who hunts any animal or bird

---

a 29 Or *must fast; also in verse 31*   *b* 3 The Hebrew word can refer to either male or female.   *c* 7 Or *the demons*   *d* 11 Or *atonement by the life in the blood*

16:32-34 | The work of the priest on the Day of Atonement to cleanse Israel's people from sin pointed toward the far greater work of Jesus on the cross and His once-for-all sacrifice (Heb. 10:19–22).
17:1-9 | The sacrifice of animals and produce from the land was not unique to the people of Israel, but the Lord whom they sacrificed to is unique. These laws were intended to ensure that the Israelites would not **offer any of their sacrifices to the goat idols**. Failure to bring all sacrifices to the **entrance to the tent of meeting** merited death or banishment, apparently because

stopping short in this regard might lead to heretical acts.
17:11-16 | The shedding of **blood** is necessary for forgiveness of sin. The NT affirms this truth (Heb. 9:22).
17:11 | Oxygen, the body's most critical nutrient, is carried through the **blood**. The human body can live on when all other parts of the body fail, but when the heart stops, death is inevitable. That is why atonement was made through blood. The OT sacrifices that had to be offered each day pointed toward the ultimate, once-for-all blood sacrifice of Christ.

that may be eaten must drain out the blood and cover it with earth, [14]because the life of every creature is its blood. That is why I have said to the Israelites, "You must not eat the blood of any creature, because the life of every creature is its blood; anyone who eats it must be cut off."

[15]" 'Anyone, whether native-born or foreigner, who eats anything found dead or torn by wild animals must wash their clothes and bathe with water, and they will be ceremonially unclean till evening; then they will be clean. [16]But if they do not wash their clothes and bathe themselves, they will be held responsible.' "

Unlawful Sexual Relations

18 The LORD said to Moses, [2]"Speak to the Israelites and say to them: 'I am the LORD your God. [3]You must not do as they do in Egypt, where you used to live, and you must not do as they do in the land of Canaan, where I am bringing you. Do not follow their practices. [4]You must obey my laws and be careful to follow my decrees. I am the LORD your God. [5]Keep my decrees and laws, for the person who obeys them will live by them. I am the LORD.

[6]" 'No one is to approach any close relative to have sexual relations. I am the LORD.

[7]" 'Do not dishonor your father by having sexual relations with your mother. She is your mother; do not have relations with her.

[8]" 'Do not have sexual relations with your father's wife; that would dishonor your father.

[9]" 'Do not have sexual relations with your sister, either your father's daughter or your mother's daughter, whether she was born in the same home or elsewhere.

[10]" 'Do not have sexual relations with your son's daughter or your daughter's daughter; that would dishonor you.

[11]" 'Do not have sexual relations with the daughter of your father's wife, born to your father; she is your sister.

[12]" 'Do not have sexual relations with your father's sister; she is your father's close relative.

[13]" 'Do not have sexual relations with your mother's sister, because she is your mother's close relative.

[14]" 'Do not dishonor your father's brother by approaching his wife to have sexual relations; she is your aunt.

[15]" 'Do not have sexual relations with your daughter-in-law. She is your son's wife; do not have relations with her.

[16]" 'Do not have sexual relations with your brother's wife; that would dishonor your brother.

[17]" 'Do not have sexual relations with both a woman and her daughter. Do not have sexual relations with either her son's daughter or her daughter's daughter; they are her close relatives. That is wickedness.

[18]" 'Do not take your wife's sister as a rival wife and have sexual relations with her while your wife is living.

[19]" 'Do not approach a woman to have sexual relations during the uncleanness of her monthly period.

[20]" 'Do not have sexual relations with your neighbor's wife and defile yourself with her.

[21]" 'Do not give any of your children to be sacrificed to Molek, for you must not profane the name of your God. I am the LORD.

[22]" 'Do not have sexual relations with a man as one does with a woman; that is detestable.

[23]" 'Do not have sexual relations with an animal and defile yourself with it. A woman must not present herself to an animal to have sexual relations with it; that is a perversion.

[24]" 'Do not defile yourselves in any of these ways, because this is how the nations that I am going to drive out before you became defiled. [25]Even the land was defiled; so I punished it for its sin, and the land vomited out its inhabitants. [26]But you must keep my decrees and my laws. The native-born and the foreigners residing among you must not do any of these detestable things, [27]for all these things were done by the people who lived in the land before you, and the land became defiled. [28]And if you defile the land, it will vomit you out as it vomited out the nations that were before you.

[29]" 'Everyone who does any of these detestable things—such persons must be cut off from their people. [30]Keep my requirements and do not follow any of the detestable customs that were practiced before

---

18:4, 5 | The principal term in the Pentateuch for the Law is *Torah*—the word used to describe God's gracious covenant with Israel at Mount Sinai (Ex. 20). The people were not simply to **obey** and **follow** God's **decrees**, but to **keep** them and **live by them**, enjoying life as God's great gift.
18:6-23 | The Bible gives clear standards regarding sexual conduct, as God prohibits incest (18:6-18), adultery (18:20),

homosexuality (18:22), and bestiality (18:23). The penalties for breaking these commands are in 20:10-21.
18:21 | God expressly prohibited the terrible practice of sacrificing a child to a deity (Deut. 18:9-12). Some neighboring peoples sacrificed their children to the god **Molek**. The penalty for this heinous sin was death (20:2-5).

you came and do not defile yourselves with them. I am the LORD your God.'"

Various Laws

19 The LORD said to Moses, [2] "Speak to the entire assembly of Israel and say to them: 'Be holy because I, the LORD your God, am holy.

[3] " 'Each of you must respect your mother and father, and you must observe my Sabbaths. I am the LORD your God.

[4] " 'Do not turn to idols or make metal gods for yourselves. I am the LORD your God.

[5] " 'When you sacrifice a fellowship offering to the LORD, sacrifice it in such a way that it will be accepted on your behalf. [6]It shall be eaten on the day you sacrifice it or on the next day; anything left over until the third day must be burned up. [7]If any of it is eaten on the third day, it is impure and will not be accepted. [8]Whoever eats it will be held responsible because they have desecrated what is holy to the LORD; they must be cut off from their people.

[9] " 'When you reap the harvest of your land, do not reap to the very edges of your field or gather the gleanings of your harvest. [10]Do not go over your vineyard a second time or pick up the grapes that have fallen. Leave them for the poor and the foreigner. I am the LORD your God.

[11] " 'Do not steal.

" 'Do not lie.

" 'Do not deceive one another.

[12] " 'Do not swear falsely by my name and so profane the name of your God. I am the LORD.

[13] " 'Do not defraud or rob your neighbor.

" 'Do not hold back the wages of a hired worker overnight.

[14] " 'Do not curse the deaf or put a stumbling block in front of the blind, but fear your God. I am the LORD.

[15] " 'Do not pervert justice; do not show partiality to the poor or favoritism to the great, but judge your neighbor fairly.

[16] " 'Do not go about spreading slander among your people.

" 'Do not do anything that endangers your neighbor's life. I am the LORD.

[17] " 'Do not hate a fellow Israelite in your heart. Rebuke your neighbor frankly so you will not share in their guilt.

[18] " 'Do not seek revenge or bear a grudge against anyone among your people, but love your neighbor as yourself. I am the LORD.

[19] " 'Keep my decrees.

" 'Do not mate different kinds of animals.

" 'Do not plant your field with two kinds of seed.

" 'Do not wear clothing woven of two kinds of material.

[20] " 'If a man sleeps with a female slave who is promised to another man but who has not been ransomed or given her freedom, there must be due punishment.[a] Yet they are not to be put to death, because she had not been freed. [21]The man, however, must bring a ram to the entrance to the tent of meeting for a guilt offering to the LORD. [22]With the ram of the guilt offering the priest is to make atonement for him before the LORD for the sin he has committed, and his sin will be forgiven.

[23] " 'When you enter the land and plant any kind of fruit tree, regard its fruit as forbidden.[b] For three years you are to consider it forbidden[b]; it must not be eaten. [24]In the fourth year all its fruit will be holy, an offering of praise to the LORD. [25]But in the fifth year you may eat its fruit. In this way your harvest will be increased. I am the LORD your God.

[26] " 'Do not eat any meat with the blood still in it.

" 'Do not practice divination or seek omens.

[27] " 'Do not cut the hair at the sides of your head or clip off the edges of your beard.

[28] " 'Do not cut your bodies for the dead or put tattoo marks on yourselves. I am the LORD.

[a] 20 Or be an inquiry   [b] 23 Hebrew uncircumcised

19:2 | From beginning to end, Scripture continually reminds readers that God is holy (Ex. 15:11; 1 Sam. 2:2; Ps. 22:3; 99:3, 5, 9). The holiness of God is the basis for the practical holiness promoted in the laws and instructions within Scripture.

19:3 | Holiness begins in the home. Children who **respect** their **mother and father** are far more inclined to respect God than those who disrespect their parents.

19:9, 10 | The law had a special provision for **the poor and the foreigner**, permitting them to **gather** the leftover crops from the fields and the fallen grapes in the vineyards (23:22; Deut. 24:19–22; Ruth 2:2–23). When possible, God's people should enable the poor to provide for their own needs with dignity.

19:11–18 | The command to **love your neighbor as yourself** (Matt. 5:43; 19:19; 22:39; Mark 12:31, 33; Luke 10:27; Rom. 13:9; Gal. 5:14;

James 2:8) is expanded to "love [the foreigner] as yourself" (19:34). These laws promote honesty, fair treatment, and community harmony as well as justice in a court of law for both the **poor** and the **great**.

19:11 | The Bible repeatedly condemns lying (Prov. 12:22; Eph. 4:25) as well as deceit.

19:13 | God calls His people to fairness, instructing employers to pay a worker's **wages** right away (Deut. 24:14, 15). The Israelites did not always obey this law (Jer. 22:13).

19:15 | The prohibitions against perverting **justice** (19:35) and showing **partiality** toward the **poor** or the **great** are not only wise (Prov. 24:23; 28:21) but they derive from the character of the Lord Himself (Deut. 1:17; 10:17; 16:19; 32:4).

19:18 | The command to **love your neighbor as yourself** was central to OT law and one of the two primary commandments (Matt. 22:39).

ESSENTIALS
of the Christian Faith

Loving Others
Leviticus 19:18

When a Pharisee, an expert in the law, asked Jesus which was the greatest commandment, He replied with twice the answer, noting not only the greatest commandment ("love the Lord your God") but the second greatest as well: "And the second is like it: 'Love your neighbor as yourself'" (Matt. 22:37–39).

This was the perfect answer to one who was trying to trap Him in a legal technicality—and to a group of legalists who prided themselves on ranking God's commands and their traditions. Jesus bypassed their detailed ledgers and told them they really only needed to be concerned with two things: loving God and loving their neighbor. By fulfilling these two commands, they would be fulfilling all the rest. Put another way, efforts to keep the lesser laws without keeping these two greatest laws were misspent at best and hypocritical at worst.

In addition to summarizing the content of the Ten Commandments, Jesus was doing something else with His answer: He was reminding the Sadducees and Pharisees of the danger of mixing man's traditions with God's laws.

The command for God's people to love their neighbors was first set forth in Leviticus 19:18: "Love your neighbor as yourself." Lest God's chosen people should think this command extended only to each other, however, verse 34 adds: "The foreigner residing among you must be treated as your native-born. Love them as yourself." So, the Israelites were commanded by God to love native-born and non-Israelite people alike. Rather than viewing the world as "us" and "them"—Israelite and foreigner—God was requiring them to love even those who were different. The distinction between Israelite and non-Israelite would continue, but the treatment of non-Israelites in Israel's midst was to be loving, not hateful. All of those "foreigners" among them were their neighbors according to the Lord's perspective.

By the time Jesus began His ministry, however, a strange change had occurred in the religious tradition. Leviticus 19:18 was being misquoted as "Love your neighbor and hate your enemy." That is the way Jesus quoted the Pharisees in the Sermon on the Mount (Matt. 5:43). This change was probably born out of the Jewish leaders' long memories of oppression. They suffered at the hands of the Egyptians for 400 years, then were attacked by numerous border nations for several hundred more years once they settled in Canaan, then were hauled into captivity by Assyria and Babylon, then were oppressed by the Greeks, and finally, in Jesus' day, by the Romans. So they were clear about "us" and "them." They had decided it was God's will for Jews to love Jews but to hate everybody else. They had rewritten Leviticus 19:18 and chosen to avoid verse 34 altogether.

But Jesus corrected them: "But I tell you, love your enemies and pray for those who persecute you, that you may be children of your Father in heaven. . . . If you love those who love you, what reward will you get?" (Matt. 5:44–46). Jesus made it clear: we are to love like God loves—without distinction.

On another occasion, an expert in the law asked Jesus His opinion of the "us" versus "them" question. Jesus' answer resulted in the famous parable of the Good Samaritan. When Jesus asked who the real neighbor in the story was, the expert answered correctly: the one who had mercy. Jesus said, "Go and do likewise" (Luke 10:25–37).

A neighbor is anyone who has a need that we are in a position to meet—cultural, racial, economic, and religious dividing lines notwithstanding. Our keeping of the second commandment demonstrates our commitment to the first commandment: to love God.

For Further Reading: Ps. 67; 98; Matt. 5:48; 22:40; Heb. 13:1–25; 1 Pet. 4:8; 1 John 4:7, 8

Never Out of Style • 19:30

Some words go out of style. If we could go back in time and eavesdrop on our great-grandparents, we might hear *hark, hither, alas, fain, betwixt, mayhap, nigh,* and *yon.* Those words have been replaced by others. But another set of nearly forgotten terms is not so expendable: *holy, reverence, God-fearing, devout,* and *pious.* How did we manage to lose those words?

The loss of reverence is particularly disturbing. We are to "worship God acceptably with reverence and awe" (Heb. 12:28). The Lord told the Israelites, "Observe my Sabbaths and have reverence for my sanctuary. I am the LORD" (19:30). The psalmist said, "God is greatly feared; he is more awesome than all who surround him" (Ps. 89:7). Proverbs 28:14 says, "Blessed is the one who always trembles before God." To the people of Malachi's day, the Lord demanded: "If I am a master, where is the respect due me?" (Mal. 1:6).

The term *reverence* in Scripture comes from a verb that means "to fear." This verb is used at times to describe "fright" or "terror" (Gen. 3:10; Ex. 14:10), but it is also used to describe the awe, wonder, and respect one rightly experiences when encountering the living God (19:14, 32). A remarkable use of the verb is in the words of God to Abraham at the binding of Isaac: "Now I know that you fear God" (Gen. 22:12). Abraham was not afraid of God in a disarming way; Abraham held God in highest honor and reverence.

---

29 " 'Do not degrade your daughter by making her a prostitute, or the land will turn to prostitution and be filled with wickedness.

30 " 'Observe my Sabbaths and have reverence for my sanctuary. I am the LORD.

31 " 'Do not turn to mediums or seek out spiritists, for you will be defiled by them. I am the LORD your God.

32 " 'Stand up in the presence of the aged, show respect for the elderly and revere your God. I am the LORD.

33 " 'When a foreigner resides among you in your land, do not mistreat them. 34 The foreigner residing among you must be treated as your native-born. Love them as yourself, for you were foreigners in Egypt. I am the LORD your God.

35 " 'Do not use dishonest standards when measuring length, weight or quantity. 36 Use honest scales and honest weights, an honest ephah[a] and an honest hin.[b] I am the LORD your God, who brought you out of Egypt.

37 " 'Keep all my decrees and all my laws and follow them. I am the LORD.' "

Punishments for Sin

20 The LORD said to Moses, 2 "Say to the Israelites: 'Any Israelite or any foreigner residing in Israel who sacrifices any of his children to Molek is to be put to death.

The members of the community are to stone him. 3 I myself will set my face against him and will cut him off from his people; for by sacrificing his children to Molek, he has defiled my sanctuary and profaned my holy name. 4 If the members of the community close their eyes when that man sacrifices one of his children to Molek and if they fail to put him to death, 5 I myself will set my face against him and his family and will cut them off from their people together with all who follow him in prostituting themselves to Molek.

6 " 'I will set my face against anyone who turns to mediums and spiritists to prostitute themselves by following them, and I will cut them off from their people.

7 " 'Consecrate yourselves and be holy, because I am the LORD your God. 8 Keep my decrees and follow them. I am the LORD, who makes you holy.

9 " 'Anyone who curses their father or mother is to be put to death. Because they have cursed their father or mother, their blood will be on their own head.

10 " 'If a man commits adultery with another man's wife — with the wife of his

---

a 36 An ephah was a dry measure having the capacity of about 3/5 of a bushel or about 22 liters.   b 36 A hin was a liquid measure having the capacity of about 1 gallon or about 3.8 liters.

19:26–31 | Here, pagan religious customs are forbidden, including mourning rites (19:27, 28), cultic prostitution (19:29), and necromancy (19:26, 31; Deut. 18:11, 12). Tattoos have been found in most cultures worldwide and date as far back as 3200 BC. Their use among Mediterranean and Egyptian people is probably what led to their prohibition, along with cutting **bodies for the dead.** These cuttings were something like present-day piercings but with occult associations.

19:36 | The term *rendered honest* in Hebrew is the principal term for "righteousness." The laws concerning **honest scales** and **weights** are important both for fairness in commerce and for understanding the important biblical concept of justice. Scales and

weights that were "righteous" conformed to a standard that satisfied the Lord's demands.

20:1–27 | The laws in earlier chapters (specifically 18—19) addressed would-be offenders and specific actions, but the ones in this chapter address the entire community and give specific punishments for certain crimes, most of which receive **death** (Ex. 21:12–17). These harsh penalties were essential to prevent sin from infecting God's people.

20:6 | The Lord strictly forbade occult practices (19:31) and consistently condemned **mediums** (20:27), commanding the death penalty for those who consult them. Trafficking with Satan in any form is dangerous.

neighbor—both the adulterer and the adulteress are to be put to death.

11 " 'If a man has sexual relations with his father's wife, he has dishonored his father. Both the man and the woman are to be put to death; their blood will be on their own heads.

12 " 'If a man has sexual relations with his daughter-in-law, both of them are to be put to death. What they have done is a perversion; their blood will be on their own heads.

13 " 'If a man has sexual relations with a man as one does with a woman, both of them have done what is detestable. They are to be put to death; their blood will be on their own heads.

14 " 'If a man marries both a woman and her mother, it is wicked. Both he and they must be burned in the fire, so that no wickedness will be among you.

15 " 'If a man has sexual relations with an animal, he is to be put to death, and you must kill the animal.

16 " 'If a woman approaches an animal to have sexual relations with it, kill both the woman and the animal. They are to be put to death; their blood will be on their own heads.

17 " 'If a man marries his sister, the daughter of either his father or his mother, and they have sexual relations, it is a disgrace. They are to be publicly removed from their people. He has dishonored his sister and will be held responsible.

18 " 'If a man has sexual relations with a woman during her monthly period, he has exposed the source of her flow, and she has also uncovered it. Both of them are to be cut off from their people.

19 " 'Do not have sexual relations with the sister of either your mother or your father, for that would dishonor a close relative; both of you would be held responsible.

20 " 'If a man has sexual relations with his aunt, he has dishonored his uncle. They will be held responsible; they will die childless.

21 " 'If a man marries his brother's wife, it is an act of impurity; he has dishonored his brother. They will be childless.

22 " 'Keep all my decrees and laws and follow them, so that the land where I am bringing you to live may not vomit you out. 23 You must not live according to the customs of the nations I am going to drive out before you. Because they did all these things, I abhorred them. 24 But I said to you, "You will possess their land; I will give it to you as an inheritance, a land flowing with milk and honey." I am the LORD your God, who has set you apart from the nations.

25 " 'You must therefore make a distinction between clean and unclean animals and between unclean and clean birds. Do not defile yourselves by any animal or bird or anything that moves along the ground—those that I have set apart as unclean for you. 26 You are to be holy to me because I, the LORD, am holy, and I have set you apart from the nations to be my own.

27 " 'A man or woman who is a medium or spiritist among you must be put to death. You are to stone them; their blood will be on their own heads.' "

Rules for Priests

21 The LORD said to Moses, "Speak to the priests, the sons of Aaron, and say to them: 'A priest must not make himself ceremonially unclean for any of his people who die, 2 except for a close relative, such as his mother or father, his son or daughter, his brother, 3 or an unmarried sister who is dependent on him since she has no husband—for her he may make himself unclean. 4 He must not make himself unclean for people related to him by marriage,[a] and so defile himself.

5 " 'Priests must not shave their heads or shave off the edges of their beards or cut their bodies. 6 They must be holy to their God and must not profane the name of their

---

a 4 Or unclean as a leader among his people

20:7, 8 | The LORD, who makes you holy is a translation of a divine title that means "Yahweh Who Makes You Holy." While the people had to **consecrate** themselves and keep God's **decrees**, God was the One who ultimately sanctified them. The process of any believer being conformed into His image is a cooperative process: His people participate in the work, but only God accomplishes it.
20:9, 10 | The Ten Commandments required children to honor their parents and prohibited **adultery** (Ex. 20:12, 14). The penalty for violating either commandment was death (20:10; Ex. 21:17). God's laws show how seriously He takes marriage and family.
20:17 | Incest was condemned, and offenders were to be **publicly removed from their people.** The fact that David did not properly

punish his son Amnon for raping David's daughter Tamar caused severe consequences later (2 Sam. 13–15).
20:22–26 | Verses 22–24 are similar to 18:24–30. The command to **make a distinction between** the **clean** and the **unclean** indicates that God had **set** Israel **apart from the nations**; a holy God must have a holy people.
21:1–23 | Special ordinances regulated the lives of priests to preserve their holiness. For example, a priest was neither permitted to touch **any of his people who die** except for that of a **close relative**, nor to marry a former prostitute, a **widow**, or a **divorced woman.** The **high priest** had to meet even higher standards. Levites with any physical **defect** could not serve as priests.

God. Because they present the food offerings to the LORD, the food of their God, they are to be holy.

⁷ " 'They must not marry women defiled by prostitution or divorced from their husbands, because priests are holy to their God. ⁸Regard them as holy, because they offer up the food of your God. Consider them holy, because I the LORD am holy—I who make you holy.

⁹ " 'If a priest's daughter defiles herself by becoming a prostitute, she disgraces her father; she must be burned in the fire.

¹⁰ " 'The high priest, the one among his brothers who has had the anointing oil poured on his head and who has been ordained to wear the priestly garments, must not let his hair become unkempt[a] or tear his clothes. ¹¹He must not enter a place where there is a dead body. He must not make himself unclean, even for his father or mother, ¹²nor leave the sanctuary of his God or desecrate it, because he has been dedicated by the anointing oil of his God. I am the LORD.

¹³ " 'The woman he marries must be a virgin. ¹⁴He must not marry a widow, a divorced woman, or a woman defiled by prostitution, but only a virgin from his own people, ¹⁵so that he will not defile his offspring among his people. I am the LORD, who makes him holy.' "

¹⁶The LORD said to Moses, ¹⁷ "Say to Aaron: 'For the generations to come none of your descendants who has a defect may come near to offer the food of his God. ¹⁸No man who has any defect may come near: no man who is blind or lame, disfigured or deformed; ¹⁹no man with a crippled foot or hand, ²⁰or who is a hunchback or a dwarf, or who has any eye defect, or who has festering or running sores or damaged testicles. ²¹No descendant of Aaron the priest who has any defect is to come near to present the food offerings to the LORD. He has a defect; he must not come near to offer the food of his God. ²²He may eat the most holy food of his God, as well as the holy food; ²³yet because of his defect, he must not go near the curtain or approach the altar, and so desecrate my sanctuary. I am the LORD, who makes them holy.' "

²⁴So Moses told this to Aaron and his sons and to all the Israelites.

22 The LORD said to Moses, ² "Tell Aaron and his sons to treat with respect the sacred offerings the Israelites consecrate to me, so they will not profane my holy name. I am the LORD.

³ "Say to them: 'For the generations to come, if any of your descendants is ceremonially unclean and yet comes near the sacred offerings that the Israelites consecrate to the LORD, that person must be cut off from my presence. I am the LORD.

⁴ " 'If a descendant of Aaron has a defiling skin disease[b] or a bodily discharge, he may not eat the sacred offerings until he is cleansed. He will also be unclean if he touches something defiled by a corpse or by anyone who has an emission of semen, ⁵or if he touches any crawling thing that makes him unclean, or any person who makes him unclean, whatever the uncleanness may be. ⁶The one who touches any such thing will be unclean till evening. He must not eat any of the sacred offerings unless he has bathed himself with water. ⁷When the sun goes down, he will be clean, and after that he may eat the sacred offerings, for they are his food. ⁸He must not eat anything found dead or torn by wild animals, and so become unclean through it. I am the LORD.

⁹ " 'The priests are to perform my service in such a way that they do not become guilty and die for treating it with contempt. I am the LORD, who makes them holy.

¹⁰ " 'No one outside a priest's family may eat the sacred offering, nor may the guest of a priest or his hired worker eat it. ¹¹But if a priest buys a slave with money, or if slaves are born in his household, they may eat his food. ¹²If a priest's daughter marries anyone other than a priest, she may not eat any of the sacred contributions. ¹³But if a priest's daughter becomes a widow or is divorced, yet has no children, and she returns to live in her father's household as in her youth, she may eat her father's food. No unauthorized person, however, may eat it.

---

[a] *10* Or *not uncover his head*   [b] *4* The Hebrew word for defiling skin disease, traditionally translated "leprosy," was used for various diseases affecting the skin.

21:5, 6 | God's people are not supposed to "grieve like the rest of mankind, who have no hope" (1 Thess. 4:13); even the believer's grief should glorify God. Thus the priests must not mourn the way pagans did—shaving **heads or . . . beards,** or cutting **their bodies** (19:27, 28; Deut. 14:1). Any association with pagan practices would **profane the name of their God** and make them unfit to present the **food offerings** at the altar.
22:1–16 | These ordinances regarding the presentation and personnel involved in the offerings reveal how seriously the Lord viewed the sacrifices. Priests were not permitted to minister until they were cleansed. They also had to ensure that only priests and their families ate the offerings—**no one outside a priest's family** was permitted to do so. Unintentional consumption of the priestly food could be forgiven with a **guilt** offering (5:14–19), but an intentional lack of regard for the **sacred offerings that the Israelites consecrate** to God would cause one to **be cut off from** God's **presence** or even die.

¹⁴ " 'Anyone who eats a sacred offering by mistake must make restitution to the priest for the offering and add a fifth of the value to it. ¹⁵ The priests must not desecrate the sacred offerings the Israelites present to the LORD ¹⁶ by allowing them to eat the sacred offerings and so bring upon them guilt requiring payment. I am the LORD, who makes them holy.' "

Unacceptable Sacrifices

¹⁷ The LORD said to Moses, ¹⁸ "Speak to Aaron and his sons and to all the Israelites and say to them: 'If any of you—whether an Israelite or a foreigner residing in Israel—presents a gift for a burnt offering to the LORD, either to fulfill a vow or as a freewill offering, ¹⁹ you must present a male without defect from the cattle, sheep or goats in order that it may be accepted on your behalf. ²⁰ Do not bring anything with a defect, because it will not be accepted on your behalf. ²¹ When anyone brings from the herd or flock a fellowship offering to the LORD to fulfill a special vow or as a freewill offering, it must be without defect or blemish to be acceptable. ²² Do not offer to the LORD the blind, the injured or the maimed, or anything with warts or festering or running sores. Do not place any of these on the altar as a food offering presented to the LORD. ²³ You may, however, present as a freewill offering an ox^a or a sheep that is deformed or stunted, but it will not be accepted in fulfillment of a vow. ²⁴ You must not offer to the LORD an animal whose testicles are bruised, crushed, torn or cut. You must not do this in your own land, ²⁵ and you must not accept such animals from the hand of a foreigner and offer them as the food of your God. They will not be accepted on your behalf, because they are deformed and have defects.' "

²⁶ The LORD said to Moses, ²⁷ "When a calf, a lamb or a goat is born, it is to remain with its mother for seven days. From the eighth day on, it will be acceptable as a food offering presented to the LORD. ²⁸ Do not slaughter a cow or a sheep and its young on the same day.

²⁹ "When you sacrifice a thank offering to the LORD, sacrifice it in such a way that it will be accepted on your behalf. ³⁰ It must be eaten that same day; leave none of it till morning. I am the LORD.

³¹ "Keep my commands and follow them. I am the LORD. ³² Do not profane my holy name, for I must be acknowledged as holy by the Israelites. I am the LORD, who made you holy ³³ and who brought you out of Egypt to be your God. I am the LORD."

The Appointed Festivals

23 The LORD said to Moses, ² "Speak to the Israelites and say to them: 'These are my appointed festivals, the appointed festivals of the LORD, which you are to proclaim as sacred assemblies.

The Sabbath

³ " 'There are six days when you may work, but the seventh day is a day of sabbath rest, a day of sacred assembly. You are not to do any work; wherever you live, it is a sabbath to the LORD.

The Passover and the Festival of Unleavened Bread

⁴ " 'These are the LORD's appointed festivals, the sacred assemblies you are to proclaim at their appointed times: ⁵ The LORD's Passover begins at twilight on the fourteenth day of the first month. ⁶ On the fifteenth day of that month the LORD's Festival of Unleavened Bread begins; for seven days you must eat bread made without yeast. ⁷ On the first day hold a sacred assembly and do no regular work. ⁸ For seven days present a food offering to the LORD. And on the seventh day hold a sacred assembly and do no regular work.' "

---

^{a} 23 The Hebrew word can refer to either male or female.

22:17–32 | This section discusses unacceptable sacrifices, beginning with a general statement about **freewill** offerings (22:18, 21). The prohibition against defective sacrificial animals (22:22–25) is similar to those excluding priests who are disfigured or have deformities (21:18–20).

22:19–21 | Sacrificial animals had to be **without defect** as befitting a holy God. Christ was the ultimate sacrificial Lamb, perfect in every respect (Mal. 1:7–14; Heb. 9:17; 1 Pet. 1:19)—and the only One permanently acceptable to God.

23:1–44 | This chapter lists, in order by date, the appointed festivals of Israel: Sabbath, Passover and Festival of Unleavened Bread, Offering of Firstfruits, Festival of Weeks, Festival of Trumpets, Day of Atonement, and Festival of Tabernacles. Numbers 28 and 29 describe the offerings presented on these days. The

Festival of Purim was established after the events described in Esther 9:17–32, long after Moses. The Hanukkah celebration was established even later and is described in the noncanonical books of 1 and 2 Maccabees.

23:3 | The first sacred assembly mentioned is the Sabbath, a weekly day of rest first observed by God at creation (Gen. 2:2, 3). Later, God prescribed the Sabbath through Moses (Ex. 20:8–11; 23:10–12; 31:12–17; Deut. 5:12–15). The **sabbath rest** was to be observed anywhere the faithful Israelite happened to be on that day (**wherever you live**).

23:5–8 | The **Passover** commences the **Festival of Unleavened Bread**, celebrating the Lord's deliverance of Israel out of Egypt (Ex. 12:14–20; 43–49; 13:3–10; Num. 28:16–25). This festival occurs in March or April, and is followed by the Offering of Firstfruits.

JEWISH APPOINTED FESTIVALS AND CELEBRATIONS • 23:1–44			
Feast/Event	**Passage**	**Meaning**	**Christ**
Sabbath	23:3; see Ex. 20:8–11	Rest	Christ Is Our Rest (Heb. 4:9, 10)
Passover	23:4–8	Deliverance	Christ Is Our Pass-over (1 Cor. 5:7)
Festival of Unleavened Bread	23:4–8	Sustenance	Christ Is the Bread of Life (John 6:35)
Offering the Firstfruits	23:9–14	First harvest	Christ's Resurrec-tion (1 Cor. 15:23)
Festival of Weeks	23:15–16	Full harvest	Christ's Church Begins (Acts 2)
Festival of Trumpets	23:23–25	Joy in God's goodness	Christ's Return (1 Thess. 4:15–18)
Day of Atonement	16; 23:26–32	Atonement for sin	Christ's Atoning Death (Rom. 3:24–26)
Festival of Taber-nacles/Harvest	23:33–36	Provision in the wilderness	Christ Is Our Provi-sion (John 6:32, 33)

Offering the Firstfruits

⁹The LORD said to Moses, ¹⁰ "Speak to the Israelites and say to them: 'When you enter the land I am going to give you and you reap its harvest, bring to the priest a sheaf of the first grain you harvest. ¹¹He is to wave the sheaf before the LORD so it will be accepted on your behalf; the priest is to wave it on the day after the Sabbath. ¹²On the day you wave the sheaf, you must sacrifice as a burnt offering to the LORD a lamb a year old without defect, ¹³together with its grain offering of two-tenths of an ephah*ᵃ* of the finest flour mixed with olive oil—a food offering presented to the LORD, a pleasing aroma—and its drink offering of a quarter of a hin*ᵇ* of wine. ¹⁴You must not eat any bread, or roasted or new grain, until the very day you bring this offering to your God. This is to be a lasting ordinance for the generations to come, wherever you live.

The Festival of Weeks

¹⁵ "'From the day after the Sabbath, the day you brought the sheaf of the wave offering, count off seven full weeks. ¹⁶Count off fifty days up to the day after the seventh Sabbath, and then present an offering of new grain to the LORD. ¹⁷From wherever you live, bring two loaves made of two-tenths of an ephah of the finest flour, baked with

yeast, as a wave offering of firstfruits to the LORD. ¹⁸Present with this bread seven male lambs, each a year old and without defect, one young bull and two rams. They will be a burnt offering to the LORD, together with their grain offerings and drink offerings—a food offering, an aroma pleasing to the LORD. ¹⁹Then sacrifice one male goat for a sin offering*ᶜ* and two lambs, each a year old, for a fellowship offering. ²⁰The priest is to wave the two lambs before the LORD as a wave offering, together with the bread of the firstfruits. They are a sacred offering to the LORD for the priest. ²¹On that same day you are to proclaim a sacred assembly and do no regular work. This is to be a lasting ordinance for the generations to come, wherever you live.

²² "'When you reap the harvest of your land, do not reap to the very edges of your field or gather the gleanings of your harvest. Leave them for the poor and for the foreigner residing among you. I am the LORD your God.'"

The Festival of Trumpets

²³The LORD said to Moses, ²⁴ "Say to the Israelites: 'On the first day of the seventh month you are to have a day of sabbath rest, a sacred assembly commemorated with

---

ᵃ 13 That is, probably about 7 pounds or about 3.2 kilograms; also in verse 17
ᵇ 13 That is, about 1 quart or about 1 liter   *ᶜ 19* Or *purification offering*

23:9–14 | The Offering of Firstfruits celebrated the first grain harvest of each year—the barley harvest—by commemorating God's faithfulness to His people. The priest waved **before the LORD** the **sheaf of the first grain** as the people pledged that what belonged to God would be given back to Him. The Offering of the Firstfruits coincided with Christ's resurrection (1 Cor. 15:23).

23:15–22 | The Festival of Weeks, celebrating the wheat harvest (Ex. 34:22; Num. 28:26–31; Deut. 16:9, 10), was one of the three great festivals the Israelite people later celebrated in Jerusalem. Because it occurred **fifty days** from the Passover Sabbath, it was also called "Pentecost," meaning "fiftieth." During the Pentecost following the resurrection of Christ, the church was born (Acts 2).

trumpet blasts. [25]Do no regular work, but present a food offering to the LORD.' "

The Day of Atonement

[26]The LORD said to Moses, [27]"The tenth day of this seventh month is the Day of Atonement. Hold a sacred assembly and deny yourselves,[a] and present a food offering to the LORD. [28]Do not do any work on that day, because it is the Day of Atonement, when atonement is made for you before the LORD your God. [29]Those who do not deny themselves on that day must be cut off from their people. [30]I will destroy from among their people anyone who does any work on that day. [31]You shall do no work at all. This is to be a lasting ordinance for the generations to come, wherever you live. [32]It is a day of sabbath rest for you, and you must deny yourselves. From the evening of the ninth day of the month until the following evening you are to observe your sabbath."

The Festival of Tabernacles

[33]The LORD said to Moses, [34]"Say to the Israelites: 'On the fifteenth day of the seventh month the LORD's Festival of Tabernacles begins, and it lasts for seven days. [35]The first day is a sacred assembly; do no regular work. [36]For seven days present food offerings to the LORD, and on the eighth day hold a sacred assembly and present a food offering to the LORD. It is the closing special assembly; do no regular work.

[37](" 'These are the LORD's appointed festivals, which you are to proclaim as sacred assemblies for bringing food offerings to the LORD—the burnt offerings and grain offerings, sacrifices and drink offerings required for each day. [38]These offerings are in addition to those for the LORD's Sabbaths and[b] in addition to your gifts and whatever you have vowed and all the freewill offerings you give to the LORD.)

[39]" 'So beginning with the fifteenth day of the seventh month, after you have gathered the crops of the land, celebrate the festival to the LORD for seven days; the first day is a day of sabbath rest, and the eighth day also is a day of sabbath rest. [40]On the first day you are to take branches from luxuriant trees—from palms, willows and other leafy trees—and rejoice before the LORD your God for seven days. [41]Celebrate this as a festival to the LORD for seven days each year. This is to be a lasting ordinance for the generations to come; celebrate it in the seventh month. [42]Live in temporary shelters for seven days: All native-born Israelites are to live in such shelters [43]so your descendants will know that I had the Israelites live in temporary shelters when I brought them out of Egypt. I am the LORD your God.' "

[44]So Moses announced to the Israelites the appointed festivals of the LORD.

Olive Oil and Bread Set Before the LORD

24 The LORD said to Moses, [2]"Command the Israelites to bring you clear oil of pressed olives for the light so that the lamps may be kept burning continually. [3]Outside the curtain that shields the ark of the covenant law in the tent of meeting, Aaron is to tend the lamps before the LORD from evening till morning, continually. This is to be a lasting ordinance for the generations to come. [4]The lamps on the pure gold lampstand before the LORD must be tended continually.

[5]"Take the finest flour and bake twelve loaves of bread, using two-tenths of an ephah[c] for each loaf. [6]Arrange them in two stacks, six in each stack, on the table of pure gold before the LORD. [7]By each stack put some pure incense as a memorial[d] portion to represent the bread and to be a food offering presented to the LORD. [8]This bread is to be set out before the LORD regularly, Sabbath after Sabbath, on behalf of the Israelites, as a lasting covenant. [9]It belongs

---

[a] 27 Or and fast; similarly in verses 29 and 32   [b] 38 Or These festivals are in addition to the LORD's Sabbaths, and these offerings are   [c] 5 That is, probably about 7 pounds or about 3.2 kilograms   [d] 7 Or representative

---

23:23–25 | **The seventh month** on the Hebrew calendar is September or October on standard calendars. The Festival of Trumpets mentioned here (known in modern times as Rosh Hashanah, the Jewish New Year) is the first of three festivals during this season (Num. 29:1–6) and signals a month-long **sabbath rest**. The others are the Day of Atonement and the Festival of Tabernacles.
23:26–32 | For more on the **Day of Atonement**, see 16:1–34 and Numbers 29:7–11.
23:33–43 | The **Festival of Tabernacles** (also called the Festival of Ingathering; Ex. 23:16) was held exactly seven weeks after the beginning of the fall harvest; it was also known as the Feast of Booths because the Israelites were to live in temporary shelters **for seven days** (Num. 29:12–40; Deut. 16:13–17). These structures, made of tree branches—palms, willows, and other leafy trees—would remind God's

children of His providential care during their time in the wilderness.
24:1–4 | The **gold lampstand** provided light in the tent of meeting, which had no openings for natural light. Hammered out of pure gold and made in one piece, this piece had a central shaft and six branches (Ex. 25:31–39; 30:7, 8; 37:17–24; 40:24, 25). The seven **lamps** were fueled by **clear oil of pressed olives** (Ex. 27:20, 21) and were to burn **continually**.
24:5–9 | The **bread . . . set out** on the table (bread of the Presence; Ex. 25:30) was a perpetual sign of worship, along with the fire on the altar (6:12) and the incense the priests burned morning and night in the Most Holy Place (Ex. 30:8). This bread, signifying Jesus as the Bread of Life (John 6:35), was replaced on each Sabbath. **Pure incense**—one of the gifts given to young Jesus by the wise men from the East (Isa. 60:6; Matt. 2:11)—was poured over the loaves as a **memorial**.

to Aaron and his sons, who are to eat it in the sanctuary area, because it is a most holy part of their perpetual share of the food offerings presented to the LORD."

A Blasphemer Put to Death

[10] Now the son of an Israelite mother and an Egyptian father went out among the Israelites, and a fight broke out in the camp between him and an Israelite. [11] The son of the Israelite woman blasphemed the Name with a curse; so they brought him to Moses. (His mother's name was Shelomith, the daughter of Dibri the Danite.) [12] They put him in custody until the will of the LORD should be made clear to them.

[13] Then the LORD said to Moses: [14] "Take the blasphemer outside the camp. All those who heard him are to lay their hands on his head, and the entire assembly is to stone him. [15] Say to the Israelites: 'Anyone who curses their God will be held responsible; [16] anyone who blasphemes the name of the LORD is to be put to death. The entire assembly must stone them. Whether foreigner or native-born, when they blaspheme the Name they are to be put to death.

[17] "'Anyone who takes the life of a human being is to be put to death. [18] Anyone who takes the life of someone's animal must make restitution—life for life. [19] Anyone who injures their neighbor is to be injured in the same manner: [20] fracture for fracture, eye for eye, tooth for tooth. The one who has inflicted the injury must suffer the same injury. [21] Whoever kills an animal must make restitution, but whoever kills a human being is to be put to death. [22] You are to have the same law for the foreigner and the native-born. I am the LORD your God.'"

[23] Then Moses spoke to the Israelites, and they took the blasphemer outside the camp and stoned him. The Israelites did as the LORD commanded Moses.

The Sabbath Year

25 The LORD said to Moses at Mount Sinai, [2] "Speak to the Israelites and say to them: 'When you enter the land I am going to give you, the land itself must observe a sabbath to the LORD. [3] For six years

sow your fields, and for six years prune your vineyards and gather their crops. [4] But in the seventh year the land is to have a year of sabbath rest, a sabbath to the LORD. Do not sow your fields or prune your vineyards. [5] Do not reap what grows of itself or harvest the grapes of your untended vines. The land is to have a year of rest. [6] Whatever the land yields during the sabbath year will be food for you—for yourself, your male and female servants, and the hired worker and temporary resident who live among you, [7] as well as for your livestock and the wild animals in your land. Whatever the land produces may be eaten.

The Year of Jubilee

[8] "'Count off seven sabbath years—seven times seven years—so that the seven sabbath years amount to a period of forty-nine years. [9] Then have the trumpet sounded everywhere on the tenth day of the seventh month; on the Day of Atonement sound the trumpet throughout your land. [10] Consecrate the fiftieth year and proclaim liberty throughout the land to all its inhabitants. It shall be a jubilee for you; each of you is to return to your family property and to your own clan. [11] The fiftieth year shall be a jubilee for you; do not sow and do not reap what grows of itself or harvest the untended vines. [12] For it is a jubilee and is to be holy for you; eat only what is taken directly from the fields.

[13] "'In this Year of Jubilee everyone is to return to their own property.

[14] "'If you sell land to any of your own people or buy land from them, do not take advantage of each other. [15] You are to buy from your own people on the basis of the number of years since the Jubilee. And they are to sell to you on the basis of the number of years left for harvesting crops. [16] When the years are many, you are to increase the price, and when the years are few, you are to decrease the price, because what is really being sold to you is the number of crops. [17] Do not take advantage of each other, but fear your God. I am the LORD your God.

[18] "'Follow my decrees and be careful to obey my laws, and you will live safely in the land. [19] Then the land will yield its fruit, and

24:10–23 | The law regarding the penalty for a **blasphemer** (one who curses God) is unique because it was demonstrated with a story. The penalty of **death** fit the crime because blasphemy insults a holy and perfect God (Ex. 22:28).
25:1–7 | In addition to a Sabbath day, every **seventh year** the people of Israel observed a **sabbath year**. This was a **year of rest** for their **land** to remind them that their land

was a gift from the Lord that ultimately belonged to Him. The instructions for the sabbath year served to restore the social order, allowing those who had become poor to escape their poverty.
25:8–17 | The fiftieth year was the **Year of Jubilee**. As in the sabbath year, the land would lie fallow. It was also a year of **liberty**, when all property was returned to its original owners.

The Year of Jubilee • 25:8–17

One of the remarkable declarations in Leviticus is that of the Year of Jubilee, which was celebrated every fiftieth year (seven sets of seven years, plus one more year). In that year was today's equivalent of a grand reboot in which some of the difficulties of human circumstance could be made right again.

One of the values the Lord established among His people in the ideals of the Law was a clear line of inheritance so that a family could continue to have its proper place in the greater scheme of things. But what happened if a person was forced to sell land or was not able to maintain it properly? What would be a remedy for those who were impoverished through storm, war, or misadventure? How could things be "fixed" so that families were safe in their ancestral holdings?

God's plan for all this is found in the Year of Jubilee. Here, the Lord commanded that people be permitted to return to their ancestral property and to their families (25:10, 13). In this way, there was no long-lasting harm from adversities that might cause a person to dispose of land because of immediate needs.

you will eat your fill and live there in safety. ²⁰You may ask, "What will we eat in the seventh year if we do not plant or harvest our crops?" ²¹I will send you such a blessing in the sixth year that the land will yield enough for three years. ²²While you plant during the eighth year, you will eat from the old crop and will continue to eat from it until the harvest of the ninth year comes in.

²³ "'The land must not be sold permanently, because the land is mine and you reside in my land as foreigners and strangers. ²⁴Throughout the land that you hold as a possession, you must provide for the redemption of the land.

²⁵ "'If one of your fellow Israelites becomes poor and sells some of their property, their nearest relative is to come and redeem what they have sold. ²⁶If, however, there is no one to redeem it for them but later on they prosper and acquire sufficient means to redeem it themselves, ²⁷they are to determine the value for the years since they sold it and refund the balance to the one to whom they sold it; they can then go back to their own property. ²⁸But if they do not acquire the means to repay, what was sold will remain in the possession of the buyer until the Year of Jubilee. It will be returned in the Jubilee, and they can then go back to their property.

²⁹ "'Anyone who sells a house in a walled city retains the right of redemption a full year after its sale. During that time the seller may redeem it. ³⁰If it is not redeemed before a full year has passed, the house in the walled city shall belong permanently to the buyer and the buyer's descendants. It is not to be returned in the Jubilee. ³¹But houses in villages without walls around them are to be considered as belonging to the open country. They can be redeemed, and they are to be returned in the Jubilee.

³² "'The Levites always have the right to redeem their houses in the Levitical towns, which they possess. ³³So the property of the Levites is redeemable—that is, a house sold in any town they hold—and is to be returned in the Jubilee, because the houses in the towns of the Levites are their property among the Israelites. ³⁴But the pastureland belonging to their towns must not be sold; it is their permanent possession.

³⁵ "'If any of your fellow Israelites become poor and are unable to support themselves among you, help them as you would a foreigner and stranger, so they can continue to live among you. ³⁶Do not take interest or any profit from them, but fear your God, so that they may continue to live among you. ³⁷You must not lend them money at interest or sell them food at a profit. ³⁸I am the LORD your God, who brought you out of Egypt to give you the land of Canaan and to be your God.

³⁹ "'If any of your fellow Israelites become poor and sell themselves to you, do not make them work as slaves. ⁴⁰They are to be treated as hired workers or temporary residents

---

25:18–22 | Naturally, the Israelites would be apprehensive after two successive years of neither planting nor harvesting crops. God promised blessings in **the land** for obedience: freedom from want and war (26:3–13; Deut. 28:1–14), including crops **in the sixth year** yielding **enough for three years**, an astonishing promise!
25:23–34 | Because the land belonged to God, the Israelites could not **permanently** sell their inherited portion. If a person had to sell his land, it was returned to him in the Year of Jubilee.
25:35–38 | An Israelite was prohibited from exacting **interest** from a fellow Israelite but could charge interest to a **foreigner** from another country (a **stranger**) who borrowed money (Deut. 23:20).

The rich were not to oppress the **poor** but were to show compassion instead, based on God's compassion to Israel. Unfortunately, this law was not always followed (Neh. 5:1–13).
25:39–46 | The enslavement of **fellow Israelites** was to be rare; if servitude was unavoidable, it was to be handled with grace and kindness, treating the individuals as **hired workers** rather than as **slaves**. Israelites were permitted to buy slaves from surrounding nations or from the **temporary residents** living among them. These Gentile servants were exempt from the restrictions detailed here; they could be enslaved for life and inherited as **property**.

among you; they are to work for you until the Year of Jubilee. [41]Then they and their children are to be released, and they will go back to their own clans and to the property of their ancestors. [42]Because the Israelites are my servants, whom I brought out of Egypt, they must not be sold as slaves. [43]Do not rule over them ruthlessly, but fear your God.

[44]" 'Your male and female slaves are to come from the nations around you; from them you may buy slaves. [45]You may also buy some of the temporary residents living among you and members of their clans born in your country, and they will become your property. [46]You can bequeath them to your children as inherited property and can make them slaves for life, but you must not rule over your fellow Israelites ruthlessly.

[47]" 'If a foreigner residing among you becomes rich and any of your fellow Israelites become poor and sell themselves to the foreigner or to a member of the foreigner's clan, [48]they retain the right of redemption after they have sold themselves. One of their relatives may redeem them: [49]An uncle or a cousin or any blood relative in their clan may redeem them. Or if they prosper, they may redeem themselves. [50]They and their buyer are to count the time from the year they sold themselves up to the Year of Jubilee. The price for their release is to be based on the rate paid to a hired worker for that number of years. [51]If many years remain, they must pay for their redemption a larger share of the price paid for them. [52]If only a few years remain until the Year of Jubilee, they are to compute that and pay for their redemption accordingly. [53]They are to be treated as workers hired from year to year; you must see to it that those to whom they owe service do not rule over them ruthlessly.

[54]" 'Even if someone is not redeemed in any of these ways, they and their children are to be released in the Year of Jubilee, [55]for the Israelites belong to me as servants. They are my servants, whom I brought out of Egypt. I am the LORD your God.

Reward for Obedience

26 " 'Do not make idols or set up an image or a sacred stone for yourselves, and do not place a carved stone in your land to bow down before it. I am the LORD your God.

[2]" 'Observe my Sabbaths and have reverence for my sanctuary. I am the LORD.

[3]" 'If you follow my decrees and are careful to obey my commands, [4]I will send you rain in its season, and the ground will yield its crops and the trees their fruit. [5]Your threshing will continue until grape harvest and the grape harvest will continue until planting, and you will eat all the food you want and live in safety in your land.

[6]" 'I will grant peace in the land, and you will lie down and no one will make you afraid. I will remove wild beasts from the land, and the sword will not pass through your country. [7]You will pursue your enemies, and they will fall by the sword before you. [8]Five of you will chase a hundred, and a hundred of you will chase ten thousand, and your enemies will fall by the sword before you.

[9]" 'I will look on you with favor and make you fruitful and increase your numbers, and I will keep my covenant with you. [10]You will still be eating last year's harvest when you will have to move it out to make room for the new. [11]I will put my dwelling place[a] among you, and I will not abhor you. [12]I will walk among you and be your God, and you will be my people. [13]I am the LORD your God, who brought you out of Egypt so that you would no longer be slaves to the Egyptians; I broke the bars of your yoke and enabled you to walk with heads held high.

Punishment for Disobedience

[14]" 'But if you will not listen to me and carry out all these commands, [15]and if you reject my decrees and abhor my laws and fail

---

a 11 Or my tabernacle

25:43 | Those who are in authority over others are not to treat their subordinates harshly (**ruthlessly**) but according to the **fear** of God. This remains an important verse for those in positions of leadership of any kind.

25:47-55 | A person could be redeemed from bondage (25:48), from poverty (25:25), or from widowhood (Deut. 25:5, 6). The redeemer was a **blood relative** who agreed to marry the widowed woman or to buy back the enslaved person or the mortgaged property, providing help and security in adversity.

26:1-46 | Poems like this are found in each of the books of the Pentateuch: the Blessings of Jacob (Gen. 49), the Song of Moses and Miriam (Ex. 15), the Messages of Balaam (Num. 23, 24), the Song of Moses (Deut. 32), and the Blessing of Moses (Deut. 33).

26:1 | **Idols**, **image**, **sacred stone**, and **carved stone** were forms of pagan idol worship at that time. Although idols today often look different than these, the Lord forbids His people in any age to worship any god other than Himself.

26:4 | Among God's blessings if the Israelites walked in His ways would be **rain**. Agrarian Israel would be dependent on rainfall from heaven rather than a great river, as Egypt was on the Nile.

26:6-10 | After promising abundant food in 26:4, 5, God promised a time of **peace** and protection, both from natural predators and human enemies.

26:11-13 | God's covenant promise to His people included His presence among them (Ex. 6:2-9), visually represented by God's **dwelling place**, or tabernacle (Rev. 21:3).

to carry out all my commands and so violate my covenant, [16]then I will do this to you: I will bring on you sudden terror, wasting diseases and fever that will destroy your sight and sap your strength. You will plant seed in vain, because your enemies will eat it. [17]I will set my face against you so that you will be defeated by your enemies; those who hate you will rule over you, and you will flee even when no one is pursuing you.

[18] " 'If after all this you will not listen to me, I will punish you for your sins seven times over. [19]I will break down your stubborn pride and make the sky above you like iron and the ground beneath you like bronze. [20]Your strength will be spent in vain, because your soil will not yield its crops, nor will the trees of your land yield their fruit.

[21] " 'If you remain hostile toward me and refuse to listen to me, I will multiply your afflictions seven times over, as your sins deserve. [22]I will send wild animals against you, and they will rob you of your children, destroy your cattle and make you so few in number that your roads will be deserted.

[23] " 'If in spite of these things you do not accept my correction but continue to be hostile toward me, [24]I myself will be hostile toward you and will afflict you for your sins seven times over. [25]And I will bring the sword on you to avenge the breaking of the covenant. When you withdraw into your cities, I will send a plague among you, and you will be given into enemy hands. [26]When I cut off your supply of bread, ten women will be able to bake your bread in one oven, and they will dole out the bread by weight. You will eat, but you will not be satisfied.

[27] " 'If in spite of this you still do not listen to me but continue to be hostile toward me, [28]then in my anger I will be hostile toward you, and I myself will punish you for your sins seven times over. [29]You will eat the flesh of your sons and the flesh of your daughters. [30]I will destroy your high places, cut down your incense altars and pile your dead bodies[a] on the lifeless forms of your idols, and I will abhor you. [31]I will turn your cities into ruins and lay waste your sanctuaries, and I will take no delight in the pleasing aroma of your offerings. [32]I myself will lay waste the land, so that your enemies who live there will be appalled. [33]I will scatter you among the nations and will draw out my sword and pursue you. Your land will be laid waste, and your cities will lie in ruins. [34]Then the land will enjoy its sabbath years all the time that it lies desolate and you are in the country of your enemies; then the land will rest and enjoy its sabbaths. [35]All the time that it lies desolate, the land will have the rest it did not have during the sabbaths you lived in it.

[36] " 'As for those of you who are left, I will make their hearts so fearful in the lands of their enemies that the sound of a wind-blown leaf will put them to flight. They will run as though fleeing from the sword, and they will fall, even though no one is pursuing them. [37]They will stumble over one another as though fleeing from the sword, even though no one is pursuing them. So you will not be able to stand before your enemies. [38]You will perish among the nations; the land of your enemies will devour you. [39]Those of you who are left will waste away in the lands of their enemies because of their sins; also because of their ancestors' sins they will waste away.

[40] " 'But if they will confess their sins and the sins of their ancestors—their unfaithfulness and their hostility toward me, [41]which made me hostile toward them so that I sent them into the land of their enemies—then when their uncircumcised hearts are humbled and they pay for their sin, [42]I will remember my covenant with Jacob and my covenant with Isaac and my covenant with Abraham, and I will remember the land. [43]For the land will be deserted by them and will enjoy its sabbaths while it lies desolate without them. They will pay for their sins because they rejected my laws and abhorred my decrees. [44]Yet in spite of this, when they are in the land of their enemies, I will not reject them or abhor them so as to destroy them completely, breaking my covenant with them. I am the LORD their God. [45]But for their sake I will remember the covenant with their ancestors whom I brought out of Egypt in the sight of the nations to be their God. I am the LORD.' "

---

[a] 30 Or your funeral offerings

26:14–39 | Here the Lord lists the punishments for the Israelites' disobedience: terror, disease, famine, and subjection to their enemies. **I will scatter you among the nations** foreshadows the exile at the hands of the Assyrians and then the Babylonians—a circumstance that would bring **sabbath years** to the land (26:34, 35).

26:40–45 | Even in these punishments, the Lord, who is rich in mercy, promised to restore the nation if its people would **confess their sins**. God always responds to true repentance with forgiveness. He would also save a remnant (**I will not reject them . . . so as to destroy them completely**) of His chosen people.

⁴⁶These are the decrees, the laws and the regulations that the LORD established at Mount Sinai between himself and the Israelites through Moses.

Redeeming What Is the LORD's

27 The LORD said to Moses, ²"Speak to the Israelites and say to them: 'If anyone makes a special vow to dedicate a person to the LORD by giving the equivalent value, ³set the value of a male between the ages of twenty and sixty at fifty shekels*ᵃ* of silver, according to the sanctuary shekel*ᵇ*; ⁴for a female, set her value at thirty shekels*ᶜ*; ⁵for a person between the ages of five and twenty, set the value of a male at twenty shekels*ᵈ* and of a female at ten shekels*ᵉ*; ⁶for a person between one month and five years, set the value of a male at five shekels*ᶠ* of silver and that of a female at three shekels*ᵍ* of silver; ⁷for a person sixty years old or more, set the value of a male at fifteen shekels*ʰ* and of a female at ten shekels. ⁸If anyone making the vow is too poor to pay the specified amount, the person being dedicated is to be presented to the priest, who will set the value according to what the one making the vow can afford.

⁹" 'If what they vowed is an animal that is acceptable as an offering to the LORD, such an animal given to the LORD becomes holy. ¹⁰They must not exchange it or substitute a good one for a bad one, or a bad one for a good one; if they should substitute one animal for another, both it and the substitute become holy. ¹¹If what they vowed is a ceremonially unclean animal—one that is not acceptable as an offering to the LORD—the animal must be presented to the priest, ¹²who will judge its quality as good or bad. Whatever value the priest then sets, that is what it will be. ¹³If the owner wishes to redeem the animal, a fifth must be added to its value.

¹⁴" 'If anyone dedicates their house as something holy to the LORD, the priest will judge its quality as good or bad. Whatever value the priest then sets, so it will remain. ¹⁵If the one who dedicates their house wishes to redeem it, they must add a fifth to its value, and the house will again become theirs.

¹⁶" 'If anyone dedicates to the LORD part of their family land, its value is to be set according to the amount of seed required for it—fifty shekels of silver to a homer*ⁱ* of barley seed. ¹⁷If they dedicate a field during the Year of Jubilee, the value that has been set remains. ¹⁸But if they dedicate a field after the Jubilee, the priest will determine the value according to the number of years that remain until the next Year of Jubilee, and its set value will be reduced. ¹⁹If the one who dedicates the field wishes to redeem it, they must add a fifth to its value, and the field will again become theirs. ²⁰If, however, they do not redeem the field, or if they have sold it to someone else, it can never be redeemed. ²¹When the field is released in the Jubilee, it will become holy, like a field devoted to the LORD; it will become priestly property.

²²" 'If anyone dedicates to the LORD a field they have bought, which is not part of their family land, ²³the priest will determine its value up to the Year of Jubilee, and the owner must pay its value on that day as something holy to the LORD. ²⁴In the Year of Jubilee the field will revert to the person from whom it was bought, the one whose land it was. ²⁵Every value is to be set according to the sanctuary shekel, twenty gerahs to the shekel.

²⁶" 'No one, however, may dedicate the firstborn of an animal, since the firstborn already belongs to the LORD; whether an ox*ʲ* or a sheep, it is the LORD's. ²⁷If it is one of the unclean animals, it may be bought back at its set value, adding a fifth of the value to it. If it is not redeemed, it is to be sold at its set value.

²⁸" 'But nothing that a person owns and devotes*ᵏ* to the LORD—whether a human being or an animal or family land—may be sold or redeemed; everything so devoted is most holy to the LORD.

²⁹" 'No person devoted to destruction*ᵃ* may be ransomed; they are to be put to death.

ᵃ 3 That is, about 1 1/4 pounds or about 575 grams; also in verse 16   *ᵇ* 3 That is, about 2/5 ounce or about 12 grams; also in verse 25   *ᶜ* 4 That is, about 12 ounces or about 345 grams   *ᵈ* 5 That is, about 8 ounces or about 230 grams   *ᵉ* 5 That is, about 4 ounces or about 115 grams; also in verse 7   *ᶠ* 6 That is, about 2 ounces or about 58 grams   *ᵍ* 6 That is, about 1 1/4 ounces or about 35 grams   *ʰ* 7 That is, about 6 ounces or about 175 grams   *ⁱ* 16 That is, probably about 300 pounds or about 135 kilograms   *ʲ* 26 The Hebrew word can refer to either male or female.   *ᵏ* 28 The Hebrew term refers to the irrevocable giving over of things or persons to the LORD.   *ᵃ* 29 The Hebrew term refers to the irrevocable giving over of things or persons to the LORD, often by totally destroying them.

27:1-34 | The concluding chapter includes rules for redeeming people (27:2-8), animals (27:9-13), houses (27:14, 15), and **family land** (27:16-25) that had been dedicated to God. If someone vowed any possession or property to the Lord's use, an extra **fifth** of its value had to be paid to **redeem** it, or get it back (27:9-25). A **firstborn** animal could not be dedicated to God because it already belonged to him (Ex. 13:2).

27:28, 29 | What a man owned but **devoted** to the Lord (set aside for exclusive use), including those things **devoted to destruction**, was given over to Him and could not be redeemed. To be dedicated to the Lord meant to be consecrated for holy use at sacred places.

30 " 'A tithe of everything from the land, whether grain from the soil or fruit from the trees, belongs to the LORD; it is holy to the LORD. 31 Whoever would redeem any of their tithe must add a fifth of the value to it. 32 Every tithe of the herd and flock— every tenth animal that passes under the shepherd's rod—will be holy to the LORD.

33 No one may pick out the good from the bad or make any substitution. If anyone does make a substitution, both the animal and its substitute become holy and cannot be redeemed.' "

34 These are the commands the LORD gave Moses at Mount Sinai for the Israelites.

27:30–32 | To fail to give faithfully and generously is to rob God of what is rightfully His and limit one's blessings. Because Israel was a theocracy, religious and civic aspects were combined, so this **tithe** (Deut. 14:22, 23; Mal. 3:10; Luke 11:42)—used in sacrifices—also helped support the government infrastructure.

NUMBERS

NUMBERS

"TELL AARON AND HIS SONS,

'This is how you are to bless the Israelites.

Say to them: "The LORD bless you and keep you;

the LORD make his face shine on you and be gracious to you;

the LORD turn his face toward you and give you peace."'"

NUMBERS 6:23–26

הנדיל הומזם חזצנמל

עיקרה דיזמ ויכי קשעמו לא־דובכ סידרפסכם סימשה

תעד־דוחי הלולל הלילו חמא עיבי סול סני

סלוק עמשן ילב סירכבד וזאו המא־וזא

סדכ להא קש שמעל סדולו לבת הצקכי בק אצי ודראה־לכב

דכ אזח

NUMBERS

Somewhere on the way to the Promised Land, something went terribly wrong. Why would it take the infant nation of Israel *38 years* to travel a distance that should have taken only a few weeks at most? The distance was just under 300 miles. At a modest pace of 10 miles per day, the whole journey should have taken only 30 days. And yet that one month's travel turned into nearly four decades of travail. For the adults age 20 and over who left Egypt, it consumed the rest of their lives. They never made it to the Promised Land at all.

For many long periods the Israelites were in encampments, not wandering. Still, the reason for this seemingly interminable period forms the heart of this book: the Exodus generation of adults had a spiritual crisis halfway from Sinai to Canaan. It was not a question of geography or topography; it was a question of faith. The trip from prison land to Promised Land was spiritual at its core. It was a test to see whether the Hebrews would trust Yahweh to meet their needs and deliver them safely to their new home in Canaan.

The Exodus generation failed the test and died on the threshold of blessing and promise. Their children, those under the age of 20 and those born in the wilderness years, would lead the nation into Canaan.

The story of Numbers is so important from a spiritual perspective that two NT writers warn their readers about failing similar tests. The apostle Paul advised the church in Corinth about yielding to temptations to grumbling, immorality, and idol worship like the Hebrews did (1 Cor. 10:1–11). The author of Hebrews warned his readers about a failure to move in and claim the spiritual rest God had promised (Heb. 3:7—4:11). He draws from the story in the Book of Numbers to remind his readers that promises must be grasped and acted on before they can be realized.

Numbers is far more than Moses' travelogue or a record of Israel's population growth. It must be read with spiritual eyes wide open.

WHAT IT SAYS | *A Nation Transformed*

For more than a year, the Hebrew slaves underwent a transformation. They shuffled into the shadow of Mount Sinai as an unorganized family—the descendants of Jacob—but they left in a wholly different manner. While at Sinai, Moses grouped them by tribes, according to the 12 sons of Jacob. The tribes camped around the periphery of a

To view Dr. Jeremiah's video introduction to Numbers, go to www.JeremiahStudyBible.com/Numbers/Intro

square, three tribes to a side, with the tabernacle erected in the middle of the square. And each grouping of tribes had a lead tribe responsible for their group.

Once organized, it was possible for the new nation to meet their King, the God of their fathers Abraham, Isaac, and Jacob. They entered into a covenantal agreement with Him to receive and to obey His laws, summarized in the Ten Commandments Moses brought down from the mountain. And they learned what it meant to be separate from the world, illustrated by their separation from the pagan ways of Egypt.

The difference between the Hebrews' arrival at Sinai and their departure could not have been more stark! They arrived as refugees and left as a military nation. They were as organized in their march to Canaan as in their camp at Sinai. In a little over a year, the children of Israel had become a nation under the rule of God.

WHAT IT MEANS | *A Crisis of Faith*

Numbers can be grouped into two movements based on the two censuses: chapters 1—25 and chapters 26—36. The book is undergirded by four central themes:

- **Covenant:** The Law of God—the covenant by which Israel was to be ruled— plays a critical role in Israel's history. The covenant was given by God at Mount Sinai, beginning with the Ten Commandments (Ex. 20:1–17). Throughout the rest of Exodus, all of Leviticus, and Numbers 1:1—10:10, commandments, statutes, and judgments were added. These laws were focused particularly on worship, emphasizing instructions concerning the tabernacle and sacrifice. More laws were added at Kadesh (15; 18—19), and again in the plains of Moab (27—30; 35—36).
- **Land:** The land that the Lord promised to Abraham and his descendants forever (Gen. 12:7; 13:15; 15:7–21) was the land of Canaan, and the people were to possess what had been promised to them. But the land where they would finally dwell would involve many battles. The two descriptions of census and organization in Numbers (1—3; 26) were for preparing an army. Israel's battle to inherit their land is a type of the Christian's preparation for victory in spiritual warfare (1 Cor. 10:1– 13; 2 Cor. 10:1–6; Eph. 6:10–17; Heb. 3:7—4:11).
- **Faith:** Israel's crisis of faith came at Kadesh. That is when the people rebelled against Moses and the Lord upon hearing the evil report of the 10 faithless spies—a report of insurmountable problems in the land (13—14). Israel learned the lesson that faith is manifested by obedience to God's commands. As a result of their disobedience, the adult Israelites (except for the faithful spies Joshua and Caleb) were barred from entering the Promised Land (14:22, 23).
- **Promises:** The promises of God are not invalidated by the failures of humanity. People's actions can delay the realization of God's promised blessing but not cancel them. Just as God waited 38 years for a new generation of Israelites to inherit the land, so Israel has been waiting nearly 2,000 years to re-inhabit the land under God's blessing. The apostle Paul takes up the issue of Israel and God's promises in Romans 9—11.

WHAT IT MEANS TO YOU | *Tipping Points*

What happened one night at a crossroads called Kadesh changed the destiny of millions and erased the hopes of a whole generation. There is no way to overstate what a devastating effect the negative, faithless report of 10 men had on the nation. Israel was at a tipping point that night: the words of the returned spies would either tip the people toward the Promised Land—or toward death and futility.

People all around us in the course of our day may be—for one reason or another— at an intersection in their lives. Our attitude, our outlook, our faith, our words, our courage at their crossroads could actually lift their lives, sending them in a positive direction. Conversely, our negative, discouraging, cynical talk might easily nudge the confused or disheartened down a longer road into doubt or despair. Is it any wonder that the Lord spoke so soberly about the power of our words and our responsibility in speaking them? Jesus said, "But I tell you that everyone will have to give account on the day of judgment for every empty word they have spoken" (Matt. 12:36).

To access Dr. Jeremiah's digital library on Numbers, go to
www.JeremiahStudyBible.com/Numbers/library

SONS OF JACOB AND THE 12 TRIBES						
Birth Order	Son	Grandson	Mother	Meaning	Location of Tribe	Tabernacle Side
1	Reuben		Leah	"See, a son"	Northeastern side of Dead Sea	South
2	Simeon		Leah	"One who hears"	South of Judah	South
3	Levi		Leah	"Attached"	No territory	
4	Judah		Leah	"Praise"	Central, includes Jerusalem	East
5	Dan		Bilha	"He has vindicated"	Northernmost	North
6	Naphtali		Bilhah	"My struggle"	East of Asher	North
7	Gad		Zilpah	"Troop" or "Good fortune"	North of Reuben	South
8	Asher		Zilpah	"Happy"	Northern coast	North
9	Issachar		Leah	"Reward"	North of Manasseh	East
10	Zebulun		Leah	"Honor"	Southeast of Asher	East
11	Joseph		Rachel	"May he add"	Territory to Sons	
		Manasseh	Asenath	"Forget"	Both sides of the Jordan	West
		Ephraim	Asenath	"Twice fruitful"	Small area north of Benjamin	West
12	Benjamin		Rachel	"Son of my right hand"	North of Judah	West

NUMBERS

The Census

1 The LORD spoke to Moses in the tent of meeting in the Desert of Sinai on the first day of the second month of the second year after the Israelites came out of Egypt. He said: ² "Take a census of the whole Israelite community by their clans and families, listing every man by name, one by one. ³ You and Aaron are to count according to their divisions all the men in Israel who are twenty years old or more and able to serve in the army. ⁴ One man from each tribe, each of them the head of his family, is to help you. ⁵ These are the names of the men who are to assist you:

from Reuben, Elizur son of Shedeur;
⁶ from Simeon, Shelumiel son of Zurishaddai;
⁷ from Judah, Nahshon son of Amminadab;
⁸ from Issachar, Nethanel son of Zuar;
⁹ from Zebulun, Eliab son of Helon;
¹⁰ from the sons of Joseph:
from Ephraim, Elishama son of Ammihud;
from Manasseh, Gamaliel son of Pedahzur;
¹¹ from Benjamin, Abidan son of Gideoni;
¹² from Dan, Ahiezer son of Ammishaddai;
¹³ from Asher, Pagiel son of Okran;
¹⁴ from Gad, Eliasaph son of Deuel;
¹⁵ from Naphtali, Ahira son of Enan."

¹⁶ These were the men appointed from the community, the leaders of their ancestral tribes. They were the heads of the clans of Israel.

¹⁷ Moses and Aaron took these men whose names had been specified, ¹⁸ and they called the whole community together on the first day of the second month. The people registered their ancestry by their clans and families, and the men twenty years old or more were listed by name, one by one, ¹⁹ as the LORD commanded Moses. And so he counted them in the Desert of Sinai:

²⁰ From the descendants of Reuben the firstborn son of Israel:

All the men twenty years old or more who were able to serve in the army were listed by name, one by one, according to the records of their clans and families. ²¹ The number from the tribe of Reuben was 46,500.

²² From the descendants of Simeon:

All the men twenty years old or more who were able to serve in the army were counted and listed by name, one by one, according to the records of their clans and families. ²³ The number from the tribe of Simeon was 59,300.

²⁴ From the descendants of Gad:

All the men twenty years old or more who were able to serve in the army were listed by name, according to the records of their clans and families. ²⁵ The number from the tribe of Gad was 45,650.

²⁶ From the descendants of Judah:

All the men twenty years old or more who were able to serve in the army were listed by name, according to the records of their clans and families. ²⁷ The number from the tribe of Judah was 74,600.

²⁸ From the descendants of Issachar:

All the men twenty years old or more who were able to serve in the army were listed by name, according to the records of their clans and families. ²⁹ The number from the tribe of Issachar was 54,400.

³⁰ From the descendants of Zebulun:

All the men twenty years old or more who were able to serve in the army were listed by name, according to the records of their clans and families.

1:1 | Over 150 times in this book, Moses wrote that the Lord gave him specific instructions. Numbers begins this way (**The LORD spoke to Moses**) and concludes with the statement, "These are the commands and regulations the LORD gave through Moses to the Israelites" (36:13).
1:2–16 | After making the covenant and giving the Law at Sinai, the Lord told Moses to **take a census of the whole Israelite community**. Its purpose was not taxation or political control but preparation for military service—the next phase in Israel's development. This census began one month after the tabernacle was erected at Mount Sinai (Ex.

40:17), in the second year of Israel's history as a nation (1:1; 9:1).
1:17–46 | Except for Joshua and Caleb, all these men (603,550) **who were able to serve in the army** (Ex. 12:37) would die during Israel's years in the wilderness.
1:19 | Like Abram (Abraham) in Genesis 12:4, **Moses obeyed as the LORD commanded**. The Book of Numbers, however, describes a litany of events in which the people did not heed the Lord (e.g., 13–14), and even a sad occasion when Moses did not (20:1–13). Obedience has to be ongoing; occasional obedience is not enough for the children of God.

[31] The number from the tribe of Zebulun was 57,400.

[32] From the sons of Joseph:

From the descendants of Ephraim:

All the men twenty years old or more who were able to serve in the army were listed by name, according to the records of their clans and families. [33] The number from the tribe of Ephraim was 40,500.

[34] From the descendants of Manasseh:

All the men twenty years old or more who were able to serve in the army were listed by name, according to the records of their clans and families. [35] The number from the tribe of Manasseh was 32,200.

[36] From the descendants of Benjamin:

All the men twenty years old or more who were able to serve in the army were listed by name, according to the records of their clans and families. [37] The number from the tribe of Benjamin was 35,400.

[38] From the descendants of Dan:

All the men twenty years old or more who were able to serve in the army were listed by name, according to the records of their clans and families. [39] The number from the tribe of Dan was 62,700.

[40] From the descendants of Asher:

All the men twenty years old or more who were able to serve in the army were listed by name, according to the records of their clans and families. [41] The number from the tribe of Asher was 41,500.

[42] From the descendants of Naphtali:

All the men twenty years old or more who were able to serve in the army were listed by name, according to the records of their clans and families. [43] The number from the tribe of Naphtali was 53,400.

[44] These were the men counted by Moses and Aaron and the twelve leaders of Israel, each one representing his family. [45] All the Israelites twenty years old or more who were able to serve in Israel's army were counted according to their families. [46] The total number was 603,550.

[47] The ancestral tribe of the Levites, however, was not counted along with the others. [48] The LORD had said to Moses: [49] "You must not count the tribe of Levi or include them in the census of the other Israelites. [50] Instead, appoint the Levites to be in charge of the tabernacle of the covenant law—over all its furnishings and everything belonging to it. They are to carry the tabernacle and all its furnishings; they are to take care of it and encamp around it. [51] Whenever the tabernacle is to move, the Levites are to take it down, and whenever the tabernacle is to be set up, the Levites shall do it. Anyone else who approaches it is to be put to death. [52] The Israelites are to set up their tents by divisions, each of them in their own camp under their standard. [53] The Levites, however, are to set up their tents around the tabernacle of the covenant law so that my wrath will not fall on the Israelite community. The Levites are to be responsible for the care of the tabernacle of the covenant law."

[54] The Israelites did all this just as the LORD commanded Moses.

The Arrangement of the Tribal Camps

2 The LORD said to Moses and Aaron: [2] "The Israelites are to camp around the tent of meeting some distance from it, each of them under their standard and holding the banners of their family."

[3] On the east, toward the sunrise, the divisions of the camp of Judah are to encamp under their standard. The leader of the people of Judah is Nahshon son of Amminadab. [4] His division numbers 74,600.

[5] The tribe of Issachar will camp next to them. The leader of the people of Issachar is Nethanel son of Zuar. [6] His division numbers 54,400.

1:47–53 | The **tribe of Levi** was not included because they were exempt from military service. They alone had the special task of transporting and encamping around the **tabernacle**, protecting it from desecration by the Israelites and also protecting the Israelites from God's wrath should any non-Levite (**anyone else**) touch the tabernacle (3:10, 38; 18:7; 16:3–33).
1:50 | **Tabernacle** ("tent") emphasizes the temporary nature of this house of God, and **the covenant law** signifies God's covenantal relationship with Israel. See note on Exodus 25:10–22.

2:1–34 | *See "Sons of Jacob and the 12 Tribes" chart on page 171.*
2:3–9 | The lead tribe on the **east** of the tent of meeting was **Judah**, followed by the tribes of **Issachar** and **Zebulun**. This group represented Leah's fourth, fifth, and sixth sons (Gen. 29:35; 30:17–20). Although he was the fourth-born of Jacob's sons, Judah is listed first and was honored above his older brothers because of their reprehensible actions (Gen. 34; 35:22). The tribe of Judah had the largest division (army) of the 12.

⁷The tribe of Zebulun will be next. The leader of the people of Zebulun is Eliab son of Helon. ⁸His division numbers 57,400.

⁹All the men assigned to the camp of Judah, according to their divisions, number 186,400. They will set out first.

¹⁰On the south will be the divisions of the camp of Reuben under their standard. The leader of the people of Reuben is Elizur son of Shedeur. ¹¹His division numbers 46,500.

¹²The tribe of Simeon will camp next to them. The leader of the people of Simeon is Shelumiel son of Zurishaddai. ¹³His division numbers 59,300.

¹⁴The tribe of Gad will be next. The leader of the people of Gad is Eliasaph son of Deuel.ᵃ ¹⁵His division numbers 45,650.

¹⁶All the men assigned to the camp of Reuben, according to their divisions, number 151,450. They will set out second.

¹⁷Then the tent of meeting and the camp of the Levites will set out in the middle of the camps. They will set out in the same order as they encamp, each in their own place under their standard.

¹⁸On the west will be the divisions of the camp of Ephraim under their standard. The leader of the people of Ephraim is Elishama son of Ammihud. ¹⁹His division numbers 40,500.

²⁰The tribe of Manasseh will be next to them. The leader of the people of Manasseh is Gamaliel son of Pedahzur. ²¹His division numbers 32,200.

²²The tribe of Benjamin will be next. The leader of the people of Benjamin is Abidan son of Gideoni. ²³His division numbers 35,400.

²⁴All the men assigned to the camp of Ephraim, according to their divisions, number 108,100. They will set out third.

²⁵On the north will be the divisions of the camp of Dan under their standard. The leader of the people of Dan is Ahiezer son of Ammishaddai. ²⁶His division numbers 62,700.

²⁷The tribe of Asher will camp next to them. The leader of the people of Asher is Pagiel son of Okran. ²⁸His division numbers 41,500.

²⁹The tribe of Naphtali will be next. The leader of the people of Naphtali is Ahira son of Enan. ³⁰His division numbers 53,400.

³¹All the men assigned to the camp of Dan number 157,600. They will set out last, under their standards.

³²These are the Israelites, counted according to their families. All the men in the camps, by their divisions, number 603,550. ³³The Levites, however, were not counted along with the other Israelites, as the LORD commanded Moses.

³⁴So the Israelites did everything the LORD commanded Moses; that is the way they encamped under their standards, and that is the way they set out, each of them with their clan and family.

The Levites

3 This is the account of the family of Aaron and Moses at the time the LORD spoke to Moses at Mount Sinai.

²The names of the sons of Aaron were Nadab the firstborn and Abihu, Eleazar and Ithamar. ³Those were the names of Aaron's sons, the anointed priests, who were ordained to serve as priests. ⁴Nadab and Abihu, however, died before the LORD when they made an offering with unauthorized

---

ᵃ 14 Many manuscripts of the Masoretic Text, Samaritan Pentateuch and Vulgate (see also 1:14); most manuscripts of the Masoretic Text *Reuel*

2:10–16 | The lead tribe on the **south** of the tent of meeting was **Reuben**, followed by the tribes of **Simeon** and **Gad**. Reuben was Leah's firstborn (Gen. 29:32); Simeon, her second (Gen. 29:33); and Gad was Leah's son through her maid Zilpah (Gen. 30:11).
2:17 | Once the first two triads of tribes were in motion, the Levites disassembled and packed elements of the **tent of meeting**, a gracious expression for the tent that was the "meeting place" between Yahweh and His people. The Israelites set out with the **camp of the Levites . . . in the middle** so that God's presence was ever central for Israel's division (army) and its people.
2:18–24 | The lead tribe on the **west** was **Ephraim**, one of the "Rachel Tribes." Ephraim and Manasseh were grandsons of her firstborn, Joseph (Gen. 30:22–24; 48); Benjamin was her second son (Gen. 35:16–20).

2:25–31 | The lead tribe on the **north** of the tent of meeting was **Dan**, followed by **Asher** and **Naphtali**. Dan and Naphtali were sons of Rachel through her servant Bilhah (Gen. 30:6–8); Asher was the son of Leah through her servant Zilpah (Gen. 30:13).
2:32, 33 | According to Moses' account, the sum of the fighting men in Israel was 603,550. Counting women, children, and males who were excluded from fighting, the total population could have been as high as two and a half million people—or significantly less, depending on how one interprets the text.
3:2–4 | The disobedience of Aaron's oldest sons, **Nadab** and **Abihu**, is recalled here (Lev. 10:1, 2). Their younger brothers **Eleazar** and **Ithamar** took their place and ministered alongside of their father. All future priests would be descendants of these two men.

The People Called the Levites • 3:1–51

The Levites were one of the tribes of Israel, the descendants of Jacob's son Levi. They were different from all the other tribes in several ways:

1. They were assigned the task of leading God's people in worship and caring for and guarding the tabernacle (3:38). Only Levites could serve as priests, and Levites could not have occupations other than serving in the tabernacle.
2. They did not serve in the army, so when they were counted in the census, their numbers were not added to those of the fighting men (1:47; 3:14–39).
3. They did not inherit a parcel of land but instead were instructed to live in towns among the other tribes (35:1–8). This gave every Israelite easy access to a priest. Because they did not own land, they lived off of the offerings and sacrifices people brought to the tabernacle and (later) the temple.
4. They represented the firstborn of each family. Rather than the firstborn son of each family being dedicated to God's service, the entire tribe of Levi was dedicated (3:40–51). This substitution was a prototype of Christ's substitutionary death for the sake of all sinners.

fire before him in the Desert of Sinai. They had no sons, so Eleazar and Ithamar served as priests during the lifetime of their father Aaron.

⁵The LORD said to Moses, ⁶"Bring the tribe of Levi and present them to Aaron the priest to assist him. ⁷They are to perform duties for him and for the whole community at the tent of meeting by doing the work of the tabernacle. ⁸They are to take care of all the furnishings of the tent of meeting, fulfilling the obligations of the Israelites by doing the work of the tabernacle. ⁹Give the Levites to Aaron and his sons; they are the Israelites who are to be given wholly to him.ᵃ ¹⁰Appoint Aaron and his sons to serve as priests; anyone else who approaches the sanctuary is to be put to death."

¹¹The LORD also said to Moses, ¹²"I have taken the Levites from among the Israelites in place of the first male offspring of every Israelite woman. The Levites are mine, ¹³for all the firstborn are mine. When I struck down all the firstborn in Egypt, I set apart for myself every firstborn in Israel, whether human or animal. They are to be mine. I am the LORD."

¹⁴The LORD said to Moses in the Desert of Sinai, ¹⁵"Count the Levites by their families and clans. Count every male a month old or more." ¹⁶So Moses counted them, as he was commanded by the word of the LORD.

¹⁷These were the names of the sons of Levi:

Gershon, Kohath and Merari.

¹⁸These were the names of the Gershonite clans:

Libni and Shimei.

¹⁹The Kohathite clans:

Amram, Izhar, Hebron and Uzziel.

²⁰The Merarite clans:

Mahli and Mushi.

These were the Levite clans, according to their families.

²¹To Gershon belonged the clans of the Libnites and Shimeites; these were the Gershonite clans. ²²The number of all the males a month old or more who were counted was 7,500. ²³The Gershonite clans were to camp on the west, behind the tabernacle. ²⁴The leader of the families of the Gershonites was Eliasaph son of Lael. ²⁵At the tent of meeting the Gershonites were responsible for the care of the tabernacle and tent, its coverings, the curtain at the entrance to the tent of meeting, ²⁶the curtains of the courtyard, the curtain at the entrance to the courtyard surrounding the tabernacle and altar, and the ropes—and everything related to their use.

²⁷To Kohath belonged the clans of the Amramites, Izharites, Hebronites and Uzzielites; these were the Kohathite clans. ²⁸The number of all the males a month old or more was 8,600.ᵇ The Kohathites were

---

ᵃ 9 Most manuscripts of the Masoretic Text; some manuscripts of the Masoretic Text, Samaritan Pentateuch and Septuagint (see also 8:16) *to me*   ᵇ 28 Hebrew; some Septuagint manuscripts *8,300*

3:5–13 | The descendants of Levi were set apart to serve God because He declared, **The Levites are mine** (Deut. 10:8). This whole tribe was selected rather than the **firstborn** of every family (3:40–51; 8:14).
3:14–39 | The Levites were also numbered, divided into three clans according to their relationship to Levi's three sons: **Gershon**, **Kohath**, and **Merari** (Ex. 6:16–22). The major duties of the clans

are spelled out, as are their respective positions of encampment around the tabernacle. The Gershonites were **to camp on the west**, the Kohathites on the **south side**, and the Merarites on the **north side**. To the **east** of the tabernacle were the encampments of **Moses and Aaron and his sons**. The **total number** of males who were **a month old or more** was 22,000 (3:39).

responsible for the care of the sanctuary. [29]The Kohathite clans were to camp on the south side of the tabernacle. [30]The leader of the families of the Kohathite clans was Elizaphan son of Uzziel. [31]They were responsible for the care of the ark, the table, the lampstand, the altars, the articles of the sanctuary used in ministering, the curtain, and everything related to their use. [32]The chief leader of the Levites was Eleazar son of Aaron, the priest. He was appointed over those who were responsible for the care of the sanctuary.

[33]To Merari belonged the clans of the Mahlites and the Mushites; these were the Merarite clans. [34]The number of all the males a month old or more who were counted was 6,200. [35]The leader of the families of the Merarite clans was Zuriel son of Abihail; they were to camp on the north side of the tabernacle. [36]The Merarites were appointed to take care of the frames of the tabernacle, its crossbars, posts, bases, all its equipment, and everything related to their use, [37]as well as the posts of the surrounding courtyard with their bases, tent pegs and ropes.

[38]Moses and Aaron and his sons were to camp to the east of the tabernacle, toward the sunrise, in front of the tent of meeting. They were responsible for the care of the sanctuary on behalf of the Israelites. Anyone else who approached the sanctuary was to be put to death.

[39]The total number of Levites counted at the LORD's command by Moses and Aaron according to their clans, including every male a month old or more, was 22,000.

[40]The LORD said to Moses, "Count all the firstborn Israelite males who are a month old or more and make a list of their names. [41]Take the Levites for me in place of all the firstborn of the Israelites, and the livestock of the Levites in place of all the firstborn of the livestock of the Israelites. I am the LORD."

[42]So Moses counted all the firstborn of the Israelites, as the LORD commanded him. [43]The total number of firstborn males a month old or more, listed by name, was 22,273.

[44]The LORD also said to Moses, [45]"Take the Levites in place of all the firstborn of Israel, and the livestock of the Levites in place of their livestock. The Levites are to be mine. I am the LORD. [46]To redeem the 273 firstborn Israelites who exceed the number of the Levites, [47]collect five shekels[a] for each one, according to the sanctuary shekel, which weighs twenty gerahs. [48]Give the money for the redemption of the additional Israelites to Aaron and his sons."

[49]So Moses collected the redemption money from those who exceeded the number redeemed by the Levites. [50]From the firstborn of the Israelites he collected silver weighing 1,365 shekels,[b] according to the sanctuary shekel. [51]Moses gave the redemption money to Aaron and his sons, as he was commanded by the word of the LORD.

The Kohathites

4 The LORD said to Moses and Aaron: [2]"Take a census of the Kohathite branch of the Levites by their clans and families. [3]Count all the men from thirty to fifty years of age who come to serve in the work at the tent of meeting.

[4]"This is the work of the Kohathites at the tent of meeting: the care of the most holy things. [5]When the camp is to move, Aaron and his sons are to go in and take down the shielding curtain and put it over the ark of the covenant law. [6]Then they are to cover the curtain with a durable leather,[c] spread a cloth of solid blue over that and put the poles in place.

[7]"Over the table of the Presence they are to spread a blue cloth and put on it the plates, dishes and bowls, and the jars for drink offerings; the bread that is continually there is to remain on it. [8]They are to spread a scarlet cloth over them, cover that with the durable leather and put the poles in place.

[9]"They are to take a blue cloth and cover the lampstand that is for light, together with its lamps, its wick trimmers and trays, and all its jars for the olive oil used to supply it.

---

[a] 47 That is, about 2 ounces or about 58 grams   [b] 50 That is, about 35 pounds or about 16 kilograms   [c] 6 Possibly the hides of large aquatic mammals; also in verses 8, 10, 11, 12, 14 and 25

4:1–3 | Hebrew priests began leading worship in the tabernacle at age 30 and ministered until age 50. These requirements meant that of the 22,000 Levites, only about 8,600 were eligible for service, although the Levites did serve in various capacities at younger ages (8:24).

4:4–15 | God specifically instructed the sons of Kohath (3:27–31) on how to move the **ark of the covenant law** and care for its

sacred implements. They should first cover the ark with **durable leather** (to protect it from rain) and a **solid blue** covering (perhaps representing heaven), and then **put the poles in place** so the ark would rest on them as the priests carried it on their shoulders (7:9; Ex. 25:13). The command **They must not touch the holy things or they will die** was later violated with disastrous results (2 Sam. 6:6–8).

¹⁰ Then they are to wrap it and all its accessories in a covering of the durable leather and put it on a carrying frame.

¹¹ "Over the gold altar they are to spread a blue cloth and cover that with the durable leather and put the poles in place.

¹² "They are to take all the articles used for ministering in the sanctuary, wrap them in a blue cloth, cover that with the durable leather and put them on a carrying frame.

¹³ "They are to remove the ashes from the bronze altar and spread a purple cloth over it. ¹⁴ Then they are to place on it all the utensils used for ministering at the altar, including the firepans, meat forks, shovels and sprinkling bowls. Over it they are to spread a covering of the durable leather and put the poles in place.

¹⁵ "After Aaron and his sons have finished covering the holy furnishings and all the holy articles, and when the camp is ready to move, only then are the Kohathites to come and do the carrying. But they must not touch the holy things or they will die. The Kohathites are to carry those things that are in the tent of meeting.

¹⁶ "Eleazar son of Aaron, the priest, is to have charge of the oil for the light, the fragrant incense, the regular grain offering and the anointing oil. He is to be in charge of the entire tabernacle and everything in it, including its holy furnishings and articles."

¹⁷ The Lord said to Moses and Aaron, ¹⁸ "See that the Kohathite tribal clans are not destroyed from among the Levites. ¹⁹ So that they may live and not die when they come near the most holy things, do this for them: Aaron and his sons are to go into the sanctuary and assign to each man his work and what he is to carry. ²⁰ But the Kohathites must not go in to look at the holy things, even for a moment, or they will die."

The Gershonites

²¹ The Lord said to Moses, ²² "Take a census also of the Gershonites by their families and clans. ²³ Count all the men from thirty to fifty years of age who come to serve in the work at the tent of meeting. ²⁴ "This is the service of the Gershonite clans in their carrying and their other work: ²⁵ They are to carry the curtains of the tabernacle, that is, the tent of meeting, its covering and its outer covering of durable leather, the curtains for the entrance to the tent of meeting, ²⁶ the curtains of the courtyard surrounding the tabernacle and altar, the curtain for the entrance to the courtyard, the ropes and all the equipment used in the service of the tent. The Gershonites are to do all that needs to be done with these things. ²⁷ All their service, whether carrying or doing other work, is to be done under the direction of Aaron and his sons. You shall assign to them as their responsibility all they are to carry. ²⁸ This is the service of the Gershonite clans at the tent of meeting. Their duties are to be under the direction of Ithamar son of Aaron, the priest.

The Merarites

²⁹ "Count the Merarites by their clans and families. ³⁰ Count all the men from thirty to fifty years of age who come to serve in the work at the tent of meeting. ³¹ As part of all their service at the tent, they are to carry the frames of the tabernacle, its crossbars, posts and bases, ³² as well as the posts of the surrounding courtyard with their bases, tent pegs, ropes, all their equipment and everything related to their use. Assign to each man the specific things he is to carry. ³³ This is the service of the Merarite clans as they work at the tent of meeting under the direction of Ithamar son of Aaron, the priest."

The Numbering of the Levite Clans

³⁴ Moses, Aaron and the leaders of the community counted the Kohathites by their clans and families. ³⁵ All the men from thirty to fifty years of age who came to serve in the work at the tent of meeting, ³⁶ counted by clans, were 2,750. ³⁷ This was the total of all those in the Kohathite clans who served at the tent of meeting. Moses and Aaron counted them according to the Lord's command through Moses.

³⁸ The Gershonites were counted by their clans and families. ³⁹ All the men from thirty to fifty years of age who came to serve in the work at the tent of meeting, ⁴⁰ counted by their clans and families, were 2,630. ⁴¹ This was the total of those in the Gershonite clans who served at the tent of meeting. Moses and Aaron counted them according to the Lord's command.

⁴² The Merarites were counted by their clans and families. ⁴³ All the men from thirty

---

4:16-20 | Special instructions were given regarding Eleazar's duties and also the preservation of the **Kohathites**.
4:21-33 | The **Gershonites** and their **families and clans** (3:21-26) were responsible to carry the tabernacle's **curtains** and coverings. The **Merarites** (3:33-37) and their **families and clans** carried the frames of the tabernacle (its **crossbars, posts and bases** and their related attachments).

Historically Speaking
The Law of Jealousy • 5:11–31

Adultery was forbidden in Israel in the Ten Commandments (Ex. 20:14; Deut. 5:18) and was punishable by death (Lev. 20:10). This passage in Numbers concerns the law of jealousy, a ritual that either proved or exonerated a man's wife of immorality. It seems unfair to us today, but the fact that there was a remedy for a wife suspected of immorality was actually a gain for women in biblical times.

This unusual ritual was similar to pagan trials, except that the law expressly forbade magic (Deut. 18:9–13). Therefore, it should be understood in terms of the symbolic value of its elements, not the properties in the liquid mixture.

"Bitter" does not refer to the taste of the water but the effects in the woman's body. If the woman was guilty, God would send her bitter suffering, likely a miscarriage; if she was innocent, children.

to fifty years of age who came to serve in the work at the tent of meeting, ⁴⁴counted by their clans, were 3,200. ⁴⁵This was the total of those in the Merarite clans. Moses and Aaron counted them according to the LORD's command through Moses.

⁴⁶So Moses, Aaron and the leaders of Israel counted all the Levites by their clans and families. ⁴⁷All the men from thirty to fifty years of age who came to do the work of serving and carrying the tent of meeting ⁴⁸numbered 8,580. ⁴⁹At the LORD's command through Moses, each was assigned his work and told what to carry.

Thus they were counted, as the LORD commanded Moses.

The Purity of the Camp

5 The LORD said to Moses, ²"Command the Israelites to send away from the camp anyone who has a defiling skin disease*ᵃ* or a discharge of any kind, or who is ceremonially unclean because of a dead body. ³Send away male and female alike; send them outside the camp so they will not defile their camp, where I dwell among them." ⁴The Israelites did so; they sent them outside the camp. They did just as the LORD had instructed Moses.

Restitution for Wrongs

⁵The LORD said to Moses, ⁶"Say to the Israelites: 'Any man or woman who wrongs another in any way*ᵇ* and so is unfaithful to the LORD is guilty ⁷and must confess the sin they have committed. They must make full restitution for the wrong they have done, add a fifth of the value to it and give it all to the person they have wronged. ⁸But if that person has no close relative to whom restitution can be made for the wrong, the restitution belongs to the LORD and must be given to the priest, along with the ram with which atonement is made for the wrongdoer. ⁹All the sacred contributions the Israelites bring to a priest will belong to him. ¹⁰Sacred things belong to their owners, but what they give to the priest will belong to the priest.' "

The Test for an Unfaithful Wife

¹¹Then the LORD said to Moses, ¹²"Speak to the Israelites and say to them: 'If a man's wife goes astray and is unfaithful to him ¹³so that another man has sexual relations with her, and this is hidden from her husband and her impurity is undetected (since there is no witness against her and she has not been caught in the act), ¹⁴and if feelings of jealousy come over her husband and he suspects his wife and she is impure—or if he is jealous and suspects her even though she is not impure— ¹⁵then he is to take his wife to the priest. He must also take an offering of a tenth of an ephah*ᶜ* of barley flour on her behalf. He must not pour olive oil on it or put incense on it, because it is a grain offering for jealousy, a reminder-offering to draw attention to wrongdoing.

¹⁶"'The priest shall bring her and have her stand before the LORD. ¹⁷Then he shall take some holy water in a clay jar and put some dust from the tabernacle floor into the water. ¹⁸After the priest has had the woman stand before the LORD, he shall loosen her hair and place in her hands the reminder-offering, the grain offering for jealousy, while he himself holds the bitter water that brings a curse. ¹⁹Then the priest shall put the woman under oath and say to her,

ᵃ 2 The Hebrew word for defiling skin disease, traditionally translated "leprosy," was used for various diseases affecting the skin.   ᵇ 6 Or woman who commits any wrong common to mankind   ᶜ 15 That is, probably about 3 1/2 pounds or about 1.6 kilograms

---

5:1–4 | Beginning in chapter 5, the inward life of the people is emphasized. To live near the dwelling place of Holy God, the people had to be holy. Therefore, all who were declared unclean according to the instructions in Leviticus were **sent . . . outside the camp** (Lev. 13:3, 8, 46).
5:5–10 | True repentance required one to not only **confess the sin**

but make atonement (Ps. 32:5). Similar to the guilt offering (Lev. 5:14—6:7), a person had to make **full restitution**, adding a **fifth of the value** to someone he or she had wronged. If the wronged one was deceased and had no relative to receive the restitution, it would go to the priest as God's representative. A sin against a fellow Israelite meant the man or woman was **unfaithful to the LORD**.

"If no other man has had sexual relations with you and you have not gone astray and become impure while married to your husband, may this bitter water that brings a curse not harm you. ²⁰But if you have gone astray while married to your husband and you have made yourself impure by having sexual relations with a man other than your husband" — ²¹here the priest is to put the woman under this curse — "may the LORD cause you to become a curse^a among your people when he makes your womb miscarry and your abdomen swell. ²²May this water that brings a curse enter your body so that your abdomen swells or your womb miscarries."

" 'Then the woman is to say, "Amen. So be it."

²³ " 'The priest is to write these curses on a scroll and then wash them off into the bitter water. ²⁴He shall make the woman drink the bitter water that brings a curse, and this water that brings a curse and causes bitter suffering will enter her. ²⁵The priest is to take from her hands the grain offering for jealousy, wave it before the LORD and bring it to the altar. ²⁶The priest is then to take a handful of the grain offering as a memorial^b offering and burn it on the altar; after that, he is to have the woman drink the water. ²⁷If she has made herself impure and been unfaithful to her husband, this will be the result: When she is made to drink the water that brings a curse and causes bitter suffering, it will enter her, her abdomen will swell and her womb will miscarry, and she will become a curse. ²⁸If, however, the woman has not made herself impure, but is clean, she will be cleared of guilt and will be able to have children.

²⁹ " 'This, then, is the law of jealousy when a woman goes astray and makes herself impure while married to her husband, ³⁰or when feelings of jealousy come over a man because he suspects his wife. The priest is to have her stand before the LORD and is to apply this entire law to her. ³¹The husband will be innocent of any wrongdoing, but the woman will bear the consequences of her sin.' "

The Nazirite

6 The LORD said to Moses, ²"Speak to the Israelites and say to them: 'If a man or woman wants to make a special vow, a vow

The Vow of the Nazirite • 6:1–12

Unless a person was born into it by divine appointment (such as Samson and John the Baptist), the Nazirite vow was a voluntary commitment a man or a woman made to the Lord in the desire to be particularly dedicated or separated to Him. The period of the vow was usually brief, perhaps a month. There were three particulars in the vow of the Nazirite:

1. No consumption of wine or anything related to the vine.
2. No cutting of the hair.
3. No contact whatsoever with a dead body, even if a family member's remains had to be prepared for burial.

The apostle Paul seems to have taken such a vow in Acts 21:24–26.

of dedication to the LORD as a Nazirite, ³they must abstain from wine and other fermented drink and must not drink vinegar made from wine or other fermented drink. They must not drink grape juice or eat grapes or raisins. ⁴As long as they remain under their Nazirite vow, they must not eat anything that comes from the grapevine, not even the seeds or skins.

⁵ " 'During the entire period of their Nazirite vow, no razor may be used on their head. They must be holy until the period of their dedication to the LORD is over; they must let their hair grow long.

⁶ " 'Throughout the period of their dedication to the LORD, the Nazirite must not go near a dead body. ⁷Even if their own father or mother or brother or sister dies, they must not make themselves ceremonially unclean on account of them, because the symbol of their dedication to God is on their head. ⁸Throughout the period of their dedication, they are consecrated to the LORD.

⁹ " 'If someone dies suddenly in the Nazirite's presence, thus defiling the hair that symbolizes their dedication, they must shave their head on the seventh day — the day of their cleansing. ¹⁰Then on the eighth day they must bring two doves or two young pigeons to the priest at the entrance to the tent of meeting. ¹¹The priest is to offer one as a sin offering^c and the other as a burnt

---

^a 21 That is, may he cause your name to be used in cursing (see Jer. 29:22); or, may others see that you are cursed; similarly in verse 27.   ^b 26 Or representative
^c 11 Or purification offering; also in verses 14 and 16

5:22 | The woman's response is the first use of **Amen** in the Bible. Its basic meaning is "So let it be!" This strong term of affirmation, when used in response to the person and words of God, is a way of saying yes to the Lord. In the Psalms, it is a term for praise (Ps. 72:19).

6:1–12 | The **Nazirite vow** was somewhat similar to fasting today, as it involved pulling away from ordinary pleasures and being more fully devoted to God and His work (Amos 2:11, 12).

offering to make atonement for the Nazirite because they sinned by being in the presence of the dead body. That same day they are to consecrate their head again. [12]They must rededicate themselves to the LORD for the same period of dedication and must bring a year-old male lamb as a guilt offering. The previous days do not count, because they became defiled during their period of dedication.

[13]" 'Now this is the law of the Nazirite when the period of their dedication is over. They are to be brought to the entrance to the tent of meeting. [14]There they are to present their offerings to the LORD: a year-old male lamb without defect for a burnt offering, a year-old ewe lamb without defect for a sin offering, a ram without defect for a fellowship offering, [15]together with their grain offerings and drink offerings, and a basket of bread made with the finest flour and without yeast—thick loaves with olive oil mixed in, and thin loaves brushed with olive oil.

[16]" 'The priest is to present all these before the LORD and make the sin offering and the burnt offering. [17]He is to present the basket of unleavened bread and is to sacrifice the ram as a fellowship offering to the LORD, together with its grain offering and drink offering.

[18]" 'Then at the entrance to the tent of meeting, the Nazirite must shave off the hair that symbolizes their dedication. They are to take the hair and put it in the fire that is under the sacrifice of the fellowship offering.

[19]" 'After the Nazirite has shaved off the hair that symbolizes their dedication, the priest is to place in their hands a boiled shoulder of the ram, and one thick loaf and one thin loaf from the basket, both made without yeast. [20]The priest shall then wave these before the LORD as a wave offering; they are holy and belong to the priest, together with the breast that was waved and the thigh that was presented. After that, the Nazirite may drink wine.

[21]" 'This is the law of the Nazirite who vows offerings to the LORD in accordance with their dedication, in addition to whatever else they can afford. They must fulfill the vows they have made, according to the law of the Nazirite.' "

The Priestly Blessing

[22]The LORD said to Moses, [23]"Tell Aaron and his sons, 'This is how you are to bless the Israelites. Say to them:

[24]" ' "The LORD bless you
  and keep you;
[25]the LORD make his face shine on you
  and be gracious to you;
[26]the LORD turn his face toward you
  and give you peace." '

[27]"So they will put my name on the Israelites, and I will bless them."

Offerings at the Dedication of the Tabernacle

7 When Moses finished setting up the tabernacle, he anointed and consecrated it and all its furnishings. He also anointed and consecrated the altar and all its utensils. [2]Then the leaders of Israel, the heads of families who were the tribal leaders in charge of those who were counted, made offerings. [3]They brought as their gifts before the LORD six covered carts and twelve oxen—an ox from each leader and a cart from every two. These they presented before the tabernacle.

[4]The LORD said to Moses, [5]"Accept these from them, that they may be used in the work at the tent of meeting. Give them to the Levites as each man's work requires."

[6]So Moses took the carts and oxen and gave them to the Levites. [7]He gave two carts and four oxen to the Gershonites, as their work required, [8]and he gave four carts and eight oxen to the Merarites, as their work required. They were all under the direction of Ithamar son of Aaron, the priest. [9]But Moses did not give any to the Kohathites, because they were to carry on their shoulders the holy things, for which they were responsible.

6:13–17 | When the time of dedication was over, the Nazirite was to present **a burnt offering**, symbolizing complete surrender to Yahweh (Lev. 1:10–13), **a sin offering** to atone for any sins committed unwittingly during the time of the vow (Lev. 4), and **a fellowship offering**, demonstrating that the person and the Lord were in harmony (Lev. 3:6–11; 7:11–14).
6:22–27 | God's gracious provision to Aaron and his sons for the blessing of the people of God is called "the Aaronic benediction." **Make his face shine on you** asks for God to delight in His people and show them favor. This favor results in **peace**. More than the

absence of war, this refers to someone's overall well-being—where everything is as it ought to be (Deut. 28:3–6).
7:1–9:15 | The events recorded here precede the ones of chapters 1–6.
7:1–9 | This chapter points back a month to when **the tabernacle** was completed and dedicated, the first day of the second year of the Exodus (Ex. 40:2). Moses distributed **oxen** and **carts** to the Levitical clans of the Gershonites and Merarites, but none to the Kohathites (3:16–39; 4:1–33) because they were to carry the holy things **on their shoulders** (4:15).

[10]When the altar was anointed, the leaders brought their offerings for its dedication and presented them before the altar. [11]For the LORD had said to Moses, "Each day one leader is to bring his offering for the dedication of the altar."

[12]The one who brought his offering on the first day was Nahshon son of Amminadab of the tribe of Judah.

[13]His offering was one silver plate weighing a hundred and thirty shekels[a] and one silver sprinkling bowl weighing seventy shekels,[b] both according to the sanctuary shekel, each filled with the finest flour mixed with olive oil as a grain offering; [14]one gold dish weighing ten shekels,[c] filled with incense; [15]one young bull, one ram and one male lamb a year old for a burnt offering; [16]one male goat for a sin offering[d]; [17]and two oxen, five rams, five male goats and five male lambs a year old to be sacrificed as a fellowship offering. This was the offering of Nahshon son of Amminadab.

[18]On the second day Nethanel son of Zuar, the leader of Issachar, brought his offering. [19]The offering he brought was one silver plate weighing a hundred and thirty shekels and one silver sprinkling bowl weighing seventy shekels, both according to the sanctuary shekel, each filled with the finest flour mixed with olive oil as a grain offering; [20]one gold dish weighing ten shekels, filled with incense; [21]one young bull, one ram and one male lamb a year old for a burnt offering; [22]one male goat for a sin offering; [23]and two oxen, five rams, five male goats and five male lambs a year old to be sacrificed as a fellowship offering. This was the offering of Nethanel son of Zuar.

[24]On the third day, Eliab son of Helon, the leader of the people of Zebulun, brought his offering. [25]His offering was one silver plate weighing a hundred and thirty shekels and one silver sprinkling bowl weighing seventy shekels, both according to the sanctuary shekel, each filled with the finest flour mixed with olive oil as a grain offering; [26]one gold dish weighing ten shekels, filled with incense; [27]one young bull, one ram and one male lamb a year old for a burnt offering; [28]one male goat for a sin offering; [29]and two oxen, five rams, five male goats and five male lambs a year old to be sacrificed as a fellowship offering. This was the offering of Eliab son of Helon.

[30]On the fourth day Elizur son of Shedeur, the leader of the people of Reuben, brought his offering. [31]His offering was one silver plate weighing a hundred and thirty shekels and one silver sprinkling bowl weighing seventy shekels, both according to the sanctuary shekel, each filled with the finest flour mixed with olive oil as a grain offering; [32]one gold dish weighing ten shekels, filled with incense; [33]one young bull, one ram and one male lamb a year old for a burnt offering; [34]one male goat for a sin offering; [35]and two oxen, five rams, five male goats and five male lambs a year old to be sacrificed as a fellowship offering. This was the offering of Elizur son of Shedeur.

[36]On the fifth day Shelumiel son of Zurishaddai, the leader of the people of Simeon, brought his offering. [37]His offering was one silver plate weighing a hundred and thirty shekels and one silver sprinkling bowl weighing seventy shekels, both according to the sanctuary shekel, each filled with the finest flour mixed with olive oil as a grain offering; [38]one gold dish weighing ten shekels, filled with incense; [39]one young bull, one ram and one male lamb a year old for a burnt offering; [40]one male goat for a sin offering; [41]and two oxen, five rams, five male goats and five male lambs a year old to be sacrificed as a fellowship offering. This was the offering of Shelumiel son of Zurishaddai.

---

a 13 That is, about 3 1/4 pounds or about 1.5 kilograms; also elsewhere in this chapter   *b 13* That is, about 1 3/4 pounds or about 800 grams; also elsewhere in this chapter   *c 14* That is, about 4 ounces or about 115 grams; also elsewhere in this chapter   *d 16* Or *purification offering*; also elsewhere in this chapter

---

7:10-88 | The gifts of the **dedication** offering from each tribe were presented in sequence on the first 12 days of the month. Each leader brought identical gifts to Yahweh, including a **silver plate** and a **silver sprinkling bowl**, both filled with flour and olive oil as a **grain offering**; a **gold dish** filled with **incense**; three animals as a **burnt offering**; a young goat as a **sin offering**; and an impressive number of animals as a **fellowship offering**. The fact that each of the identical offerings is listed separately suggests: (1) a congregational pattern of worship; (2) the significance of the offerings from each tribe; (3) the delight of each tribe as its offerings were honored.

⁴²On the sixth day Eliasaph son of Deuel, the leader of the people of Gad, brought his offering. ⁴³His offering was one silver plate weighing a hundred and thirty shekels and one silver sprinkling bowl weighing seventy shekels, both according to the sanctuary shekel, each filled with the finest flour mixed with olive oil as a grain offering; ⁴⁴one gold dish weighing ten shekels, filled with incense; ⁴⁵one young bull, one ram and one male lamb a year old for a burnt offering; ⁴⁶one male goat for a sin offering; ⁴⁷and two oxen, five rams, five male goats and five male lambs a year old to be sacrificed as a fellowship offering. This was the offering of Eliasaph son of Deuel.

⁴⁸On the seventh day Elishama son of Ammihud, the leader of the people of Ephraim, brought his offering. ⁴⁹His offering was one silver plate weighing a hundred and thirty shekels and one silver sprinkling bowl weighing seventy shekels, both according to the sanctuary shekel, each filled with the finest flour mixed with olive oil as a grain offering; ⁵⁰one gold dish weighing ten shekels, filled with incense; ⁵¹one young bull, one ram and one male lamb a year old for a burnt offering; ⁵²one male goat for a sin offering; ⁵³and two oxen, five rams, five male goats and five male lambs a year old to be sacrificed as a fellowship offering. This was the offering of Elishama son of Ammihud.

⁵⁴On the eighth day Gamaliel son of Pedahzur, the leader of the people of Manasseh, brought his offering. ⁵⁵His offering was one silver plate weighing a hundred and thirty shekels and one silver sprinkling bowl weighing seventy shekels, both according to the sanctuary shekel, each filled with the finest flour mixed with olive oil as a grain offering; ⁵⁶one gold dish weighing ten shekels, filled with incense; ⁵⁷one young bull, one ram and one male lamb a year old for a burnt offering; ⁵⁸one male goat for a sin offering; ⁵⁹and two oxen, five rams, five male goats and five male lambs a year old to be sacrificed as a fellowship offering. This was the offering of Gamaliel son of Pedahzur.

⁶⁰On the ninth day Abidan son of Gideoni, the leader of the people of Benjamin, brought his offering. ⁶¹His offering was one silver plate weighing a hundred and thirty shekels and one silver sprinkling bowl weighing seventy shekels, both according to the sanctuary shekel, each filled with the finest flour mixed with olive oil as a grain offering; ⁶²one gold dish weighing ten shekels, filled with incense; ⁶³one young bull, one ram and one male lamb a year old for a burnt offering; ⁶⁴one male goat for a sin offering; ⁶⁵and two oxen, five rams, five male goats and five male lambs a year old to be sacrificed as a fellowship offering. This was the offering of Abidan son of Gideoni.

⁶⁶On the tenth day Ahiezer son of Ammishaddai, the leader of the people of Dan, brought his offering. ⁶⁷His offering was one silver plate weighing a hundred and thirty shekels and one silver sprinkling bowl weighing seventy shekels, both according to the sanctuary shekel, each filled with the finest flour mixed with olive oil as a grain offering; ⁶⁸one gold dish weighing ten shekels, filled with incense; ⁶⁹one young bull, one ram and one male lamb a year old for a burnt offering; ⁷⁰one male goat for a sin offering; ⁷¹and two oxen, five rams, five male goats and five male lambs a year old to be sacrificed as a fellowship offering. This was the offering of Ahiezer son of Ammishaddai.

⁷²On the eleventh day Pagiel son of Okran, the leader of the people of Asher, brought his offering. ⁷³His offering was one silver plate weighing a hundred and thirty shekels and one silver sprinkling bowl weighing seventy shekels, both according to the sanctuary shekel, each filled with the finest flour mixed with olive oil as a grain offering; ⁷⁴one gold dish weighing ten shekels, filled with incense; ⁷⁵one young bull, one ram and one male lamb a year old for a burnt offering; ⁷⁶one male goat for a sin offering; ⁷⁷and two oxen, five rams, five male goats and five male lambs a year old to be sacrificed as a fellowship offering. This was the offering of Pagiel son of Okran.

⁷⁸On the twelfth day Ahira son of Enan, the leader of the people of Naphtali, brought his offering.

⁷⁹His offering was one silver plate weighing a hundred and thirty shekels and one silver sprinkling bowl weighing seventy shekels, both according to the sanctuary shekel, each filled with the finest flour mixed with olive oil as a grain offering; ⁸⁰one gold dish weighing ten shekels, filled with incense; ⁸¹one young bull, one ram and one male lamb a year old for a burnt offering; ⁸²one male goat for a sin offering; ⁸³and two oxen, five rams, five male goats and five male lambs a year old to be sacrificed as a fellowship offering. This was the offering of Ahira son of Enan.

⁸⁴These were the offerings of the Israelite leaders for the dedication of the altar when it was anointed: twelve silver plates, twelve silver sprinkling bowls and twelve gold dishes. ⁸⁵Each silver plate weighed a hundred and thirty shekels, and each sprinkling bowl seventy shekels. Altogether, the silver dishes weighed two thousand four hundred shekels,ᵃ according to the sanctuary shekel. ⁸⁶The twelve gold dishes filled with incense weighed ten shekels each, according to the sanctuary shekel. Altogether, the gold dishes weighed a hundred and twenty shekels.ᵇ ⁸⁷The total number of animals for the burnt offering came to twelve young bulls, twelve rams and twelve male lambs a year old, together with their grain offering. Twelve male goats were used for the sin offering. ⁸⁸The total number of animals for the sacrifice of the fellowship offering came to twenty-four oxen, sixty rams, sixty male goats and sixty male lambs a year old. These were the offerings for the dedication of the altar after it was anointed.

⁸⁹When Moses entered the tent of meeting to speak with the LORD, he heard the voice speaking to him from between the two cherubim above the atonement cover on the ark of the covenant law. In this way the LORD spoke to him.

Setting Up the Lamps

8 The LORD said to Moses, ²"Speak to Aaron and say to him, 'When you set up the lamps, see that all seven light up the area in front of the lampstand.'"

³Aaron did so; he set up the lamps so that they faced forward on the lampstand, just as the LORD commanded Moses. ⁴This is how the lampstand was made: It was made of hammered gold—from its base to its blossoms. The lampstand was made exactly like the pattern the LORD had shown Moses.

The Setting Apart of the Levites

⁵The LORD said to Moses: ⁶"Take the Levites from among all the Israelites and make them ceremonially clean. ⁷To purify them, do this: Sprinkle the water of cleansing on them; then have them shave their whole bodies and wash their clothes. And so they will purify themselves. ⁸Have them take a young bull with its grain offering of the finest flour mixed with olive oil; then you are to take a second young bull for a sin offering.ᶜ ⁹Bring the Levites to the front of the tent of meeting and assemble the whole Israelite community. ¹⁰You are to bring the Levites before the LORD, and the Israelites are to lay their hands on them. ¹¹Aaron is to present the Levites before the LORD as a wave offering from the Israelites, so that they may be ready to do the work of the LORD.

¹²"Then the Levites are to lay their hands on the heads of the bulls, using one for a sin offering to the LORD and the other for a burnt offering, to make atonement for the Levites. ¹³Have the Levites stand in front of Aaron and his sons and then present them as a wave offering to the LORD. ¹⁴In this way you are to set the Levites apart from the other Israelites, and the Levites will be mine.

¹⁵"After you have purified the Levites and presented them as a wave offering, they are to come to do their work at the tent of meeting. ¹⁶They are the Israelites who are to be given wholly to me. I have taken them as my own in place of the firstborn, the first male offspring from every Israelite woman. ¹⁷Every firstborn male in Israel, whether human or animal, is mine. When I struck down all the firstborn in Egypt, I set

---

ᵃ 85 That is, about 60 pounds or about 28 kilograms   ᵇ 86 That is, about 3 pounds or about 1.4 kilograms   ᶜ 8 Or purification offering; also in verse 12

7:84–88 | This summary of all the offerings given during the 12 days marks the significance and solemnity of this signature week in the life of Israel.

8:1–4 | Moses had given the artisans of Israel detailed instructions on how to build the **lampstand** (Heb., menorah; Ex. 25:31–40), and they had fully complied (Ex. 37:17–24). This section contains instructions concerning the placement of the **seven lamps** of the lampstand (Ex. 25:37; Lev. 24:2–4). To situate each oil lamp so that

its light **faced forward** on the lampstand would maximize visibility in the otherwise dark room, allowing the priests to see both the incense altar and the bread of the Presence.

8:5–22 | Here the **Levites** were set apart **as gifts to Aaron and his sons**. They would assist the priests in **the work at the tent of meeting**. The dedication process included having water sprinkled on them, shaving their entire bodies, and washing their clothes—all symbols of cleansing. They were presented as a **wave offering**.

fyi — Following God Even When Stuck • 9:17, 18

We no longer have the Lord's visible cloud above us, but we have His invisible Spirit within us and His infallible Word in our hands. We have His providential ordering of our circumstances and His promise to direct us in all our ways. If we seem stuck for the moment, even if it appears to be for a prolonged period, we are better off to remain stuck in God's will than to wander off on our own. Sometimes we can make a lot of progress while standing still, even though it does not appear so at the time. If as best you can determine, you are in God's will, try not to worry about the pace of things. Just take one day at a time.

them apart for myself. [18] And I have taken the Levites in place of all the firstborn sons in Israel. [19] From among all the Israelites, I have given the Levites as gifts to Aaron and his sons to do the work at the tent of meeting on behalf of the Israelites and to make atonement for them so that no plague will strike the Israelites when they go near the sanctuary."

[20] Moses, Aaron and the whole Israelite community did with the Levites just as the LORD commanded Moses. [21] The Levites purified themselves and washed their clothes. Then Aaron presented them as a wave offering before the LORD and made atonement for them to purify them. [22] After that, the Levites came to do their work at the tent of meeting under the supervision of Aaron and his sons. They did with the Levites just as the LORD commanded Moses.

[23] The LORD said to Moses, [24] "This applies to the Levites: Men twenty-five years old or more shall come to take part in the work at the tent of meeting, [25] but at the age of fifty, they must retire from their regular service and work no longer. [26] They may assist their brothers in performing their duties at the tent of meeting, but they themselves must not do the work. This, then, is how you are to assign the responsibilities of the Levites."

The Passover

9 The LORD spoke to Moses in the Desert of Sinai in the first month of the second year after they came out of Egypt. He said, [2] "Have the Israelites celebrate the Passover at the appointed time. [3] Celebrate it at the appointed time, at twilight on the fourteenth day of this month, in accordance with all its rules and regulations."

[4] So Moses told the Israelites to celebrate the Passover, [5] and they did so in the Desert of Sinai at twilight on the fourteenth day of the first month. The Israelites did everything just as the LORD commanded Moses.

[6] But some of them could not celebrate the Passover on that day because they were ceremonially unclean on account of a dead body. So they came to Moses and Aaron that same day [7] and said to Moses, "We have become unclean because of a dead body, but why should we be kept from presenting the LORD's offering with the other Israelites at the appointed time?"

[8] Moses answered them, "Wait until I find out what the LORD commands concerning you."

[9] Then the LORD said to Moses, [10] "Tell the Israelites: 'When any of you or your descendants are unclean because of a dead body or are away on a journey, they are still to celebrate the LORD's Passover, [11] but they are to do it on the fourteenth day of the second month at twilight. They are to eat the lamb, together with unleavened bread and bitter herbs. [12] They must not leave any of it till morning or break any of its bones. When they celebrate the Passover, they must follow all the regulations. [13] But if anyone who is ceremonially clean and not on a journey fails to celebrate the Passover, they must be cut off from their people for not presenting the LORD's offering at the appointed time. They will bear the consequences of their sin.

[14] "'A foreigner residing among you is also to celebrate the LORD's Passover in accordance with its rules and regulations. You must have the same regulations for both the foreigner and the native-born.'"

8:23–26 | The Levites began serving in the tabernacle at age 25, but not until age 30 were they allowed to carry the tabernacle (4:3). The five years of service probably prepared them for the task, similar to a mentoring period. The age was lowered to 20 during the time of David (1 Chron. 23:27).

9:1–5 | This second **Passover** would still follow the ordinances established by the Lord when the Israelites were in Egypt (Ex. 12:1–16; Deut. 16:1, 2).

9:6–13 | The ceremonial uncleanness of these men presented a problem for them on the day of Passover. Here is an example of Yahweh making a new provision for the good of people in particular

situations (something seen again in chapters 27 and 36 regarding the daughters of Zelophehad). This was especially important here, because a person who ignored his opportunity to keep the Passover would be **cut off** from the community (Ex. 12:15). However, the Lord's gracious exceptions were never to be taken as reasons to disregard His commands.

9:14 | Foreigners living with the Israelites were allowed to celebrate the Passover but had to follow the prescribed rites (including circumcision; Ex. 12:48). **The same regulations** means that foreigners were not to improvise, nor were they to incorporate Israel's rites with their own. They were to do all the things required of the Hebrew people.

The Cloud Above the Tabernacle

[15] On the day the tabernacle, the tent of the covenant law, was set up, the cloud covered it. From evening till morning the cloud above the tabernacle looked like fire. [16] That is how it continued to be; the cloud covered it, and at night it looked like fire. [17] Whenever the cloud lifted from above the tent, the Israelites set out; wherever the cloud settled, the Israelites encamped. [18] At the LORD's command the Israelites set out, and at his command they encamped. As long as the cloud stayed over the tabernacle, they remained in camp. [19] When the cloud remained over the tabernacle a long time, the Israelites obeyed the LORD's order and did not set out. [20] Sometimes the cloud was over the tabernacle only a few days; at the LORD's command they would encamp, and then at his command they would set out. [21] Sometimes the cloud stayed only from evening till morning, and when it lifted in the morning, they set out. Whether by day or by night, whenever the cloud lifted, they set out. [22] Whether the cloud stayed over the tabernacle for two days or a month or a year, the Israelites would remain in camp and not set out; but when it lifted, they would set out. [23] At the LORD's command they encamped, and at the LORD's command they set out. They obeyed the LORD's order, in accordance with his command through Moses.

The Silver Trumpets

10 The LORD said to Moses: [2] "Make two trumpets of hammered silver, and use them for calling the community together and for having the camps set out. [3] When both are sounded, the whole community is to assemble before you at the entrance to the tent of meeting. [4] If only one is sounded, the leaders—the heads of the clans of Israel—are to assemble before you. [5] When a trumpet blast is sounded, the tribes camping on the east are to set out. [6] At the sounding of a second blast, the camps on the south are to set out. The blast will be the signal for setting out. [7] To gather the assembly, blow the trumpets, but not with the signal for setting out.

Picture This **Trumpets in the Bible • 10:1**

Trumpets in the Bible were of two types. They could be animal horns of various lengths, called the *shofar* in Hebrew. Trumpets could also be made of silver, and these could be of various lengths. Both the biblical *shofar* and the silver trumpet were like a bugle in that they were each capable of only a few intervals.

Moses was instructed after the Exodus to have artisans make silver trumpets for use in the tabernacle. When the Levites wanted to gather the people for worship, they would sound the trumpet (10:1-10; 1 Chron. 16:6, 42). The trumpet was also used to call people to battle (10:9; Judg. 3:27; 1 Sam. 13:3; Neh. 4:20). Later, trumpets were used in the music of worship (1 Chron. 13:8; 2 Chron. 5:13; Ps. 150:3).

---

[8] "The sons of Aaron, the priests, are to blow the trumpets. This is to be a lasting ordinance for you and the generations to come. [9] When you go into battle in your own land against an enemy who is oppressing you, sound a blast on the trumpets. Then you will be remembered by the LORD your God and rescued from your enemies. [10] Also at your times of rejoicing—your appointed festivals and New Moon feasts—you are to sound the trumpets over your burnt offerings and fellowship offerings, and they will be a memorial for you before your God. I am the LORD your God."

The Israelites Leave Sinai

[11] On the twentieth day of the second month of the second year, the cloud lifted from above the tabernacle of the covenant law. [12] Then the Israelites set out from the Desert of Sinai and traveled from place to place until the cloud came to rest in the Desert of Paran. [13] They set out, this first time, at the LORD's command through Moses.

[14] The divisions of the camp of Judah went first, under their standard. Nahshon son of Amminadab was in command. [15] Nethanel son of Zuar was over the division of the tribe of Issachar, [16] and Eliab son of Helon was over the division of the tribe of Zebulun.

9:15-23 | God's presence among the children of Israel was symbolically manifested in the mysterious **cloud**, which at night **looked like fire**. By means of the hovering cloud by day and the covering fire by night, Yahweh directed the encampments and travel of His people in the wilderness journey. These were powerful symbols communicating protection and comfort to the people.
10:1-10 | The Lord told Moses to make **two trumpets of hammered silver** for the priests to use to signal the entire camp. Blowing **both** trumpets at the same time was the signal for the whole community;

blowing **one** signaled the leaders (2 Chron. 13:12; Jer. 4:5; Joel 2:15).
10:11-28 | The people finally began to **set out** for the Promised Land, 13 months after the Exodus and 11 months after they first came to Mount **Sinai**. The additional time was necessary to transform a huge band of refugees into a functioning people group that would work together in the arduous task of their collective journey. Moses must have done an enormous amount of organizing and training—and he followed the good advice of Jethro, using many aides (Ex. 18:17-26).

¹⁷ Then the tabernacle was taken down, and the Gershonites and Merarites, who carried it, set out.

¹⁸ The divisions of the camp of Reuben went next, under their standard. Elizur son of Shedeur was in command. ¹⁹ Shelumiel son of Zurishaddai was over the division of the tribe of Simeon, ²⁰ and Eliasaph son of Deuel was over the division of the tribe of Gad. ²¹ Then the Kohathites set out, carrying the holy things. The tabernacle was to be set up before they arrived.

²² The divisions of the camp of Ephraim went next, under their standard. Elishama son of Ammihud was in command. ²³ Gamaliel son of Pedahzur was over the division of the tribe of Manasseh, ²⁴ and Abidan son of Gideoni was over the division of the tribe of Benjamin.

²⁵ Finally, as the rear guard for all the units, the divisions of the camp of Dan set out under their standard. Ahiezer son of Ammishaddai was in command. ²⁶ Pagiel son of Okran was over the division of the tribe of Asher, ²⁷ and Ahira son of Enan was over the division of the tribe of Naphtali. ²⁸ This was the order of march for the Israelite divisions as they set out.

²⁹ Now Moses said to Hobab son of Reuel the Midianite, Moses' father-in-law, "We are setting out for the place about which the LORD said, 'I will give it to you.' Come with us and we will treat you well, for the LORD has promised good things to Israel."

³⁰ He answered, "No, I will not go; I am going back to my own land and my own people."

³¹ But Moses said, "Please do not leave us. You know where we should camp in the wilderness, and you can be our eyes. ³² If you come with us, we will share with you whatever good things the LORD gives us."

³³ So they set out from the mountain of the LORD and traveled for three days. The ark of the covenant of the LORD went before them during those three days to find them a place to rest. ³⁴ The cloud of the LORD was over them by day when they set out from the camp.

³⁵ Whenever the ark set out, Moses said,

"Rise up, LORD!
    May your enemies be scattered;
    may your foes flee before you."

³⁶ Whenever it came to rest, he said,

"Return, LORD,
    to the countless thousands of Israel."

Fire From the LORD

11 Now the people complained about their hardships in the hearing of the LORD, and when he heard them his anger was aroused. Then fire from the LORD burned among them and consumed some of the outskirts of the camp. ² When the people cried out to Moses, he prayed to the LORD and the fire died down. ³ So that place was called Taberah,^a because fire from the LORD had burned among them.

Quail From the LORD

⁴ The rabble with them began to crave other food, and again the Israelites started wailing and said, "If only we had meat to eat! ⁵ We remember the fish we ate in Egypt at no cost — also the cucumbers, melons, leeks, onions and garlic. ⁶ But now we have lost our appetite; we never see anything but this manna!"

⁷ The manna was like coriander seed and looked like resin. ⁸ The people went around gathering it, and then ground it in a hand mill or crushed it in a mortar. They cooked it in a pot or made it into loaves. And it tasted

---

^a 3 Taberah means burning.

10:29-32 | Moses urged his brother-in-law **Hobab** to go with the Israelites, knowing that his knowledge of "**wilderness** survival" could help the people on their journey. This younger brother of Zipporah would be the family leader after his father, **Reuel** (also known as Jethro; Ex. 2:16–22). For him to leave his responsibilities would have been as difficult as it was for Abram (Gen. 12:1). Moreover, for Hobab to join Israel would mean his conversion to the true worship of Yahweh—an example of evangelization in the days of the Law. Hobab must have agreed, because Judges 1:16 reports these Midianites dwelling among the Hebrew people in the land of Israel.
10:33-36 | Now that the journey to Canaan had commenced, Moses the songwriter crafted poetic texts that celebrated both the leading of the Lord for their departure and the direction of the Lord upon their settlement: **Rise up, LORD!** . . . **Return, LORD**. In both words and symbols—including **the ark** and **the cloud**—Yahweh assured the people that they were under His protective care and guidance.

11:1-3 | It is difficult to imagine words more startling than **Now the people complained**, given the extent of the Lord's protection, guidance, and care as celebrated in their departure from Mount Sinai (10:33–36). Until now, the people had been obedient to all the Lord's commands, but in a turning-point moment, they resumed their former ingratitude and lack of faith (Ex. 15:22—17:7). God's grace is revealed in that His **fire** only **consumed some of the outskirts of the camp** rather than all the people (Ps. 78:21).
11:4-6 | **The rabble with them** (Ex. 12:38) were people of various ethnicities, perhaps including some Egyptians. Some were, or would become, people of faith because of their contacts with believing Hebrews. (One woman from Cush became the second wife of Moses; 12:1). Their craving for **other food** (the abundance and varieties of foods in Egypt) caused the Israelites to forget God's goodness and faithfulness to them, including His wonderful provision of manna (Ps. 78:18).

Tough Questions — **Did God really provide manna for up to two million people?** • 11:6

The thing about miracles is that they are *miracles*. This means that attempts at natural explanations are not helpful. Some have suggested that manna was actually the by-product of a secretion of certain insects feeding on tamarisk trees, or a secretion from the trees themselves. The implausibility of this explanation is enormous: such trees and insects would have to be present in all places that the people of Israel encamped; they would have to constantly produce during the 40 years Israel was in the wilderness; the secretions would need to be so abundant that they could provide food for the myriad of people; the secretions would need to be doubled on Friday, nonexistent on Saturday, and capable of being preserved for a second day only on Saturday. It would take more faith to believe this story than to believe in the account in Scripture.

Manna means "What is it?" It was unknown before Israel was in the wilderness, and it never recurred after they left and entered Canaan.

like something made with olive oil. [9]When the dew settled on the camp at night, the manna also came down.

[10]Moses heard the people of every family wailing at the entrance to their tents. The LORD became exceedingly angry, and Moses was troubled. [11]He asked the LORD, "Why have you brought this trouble on your servant? What have I done to displease you that you put the burden of all these people on me? [12]Did I conceive all these people? Did I give them birth? Why do you tell me to carry them in my arms, as a nurse carries an infant, to the land you promised on oath to their ancestors? [13]Where can I get meat for all these people? They keep wailing to me, 'Give us meat to eat!' [14]I cannot carry all these people by myself; the burden is too heavy for me. [15]If this is how you are going to treat me, please go ahead and kill me—if I have found favor in your eyes—and do not let me face my own ruin."

[16]The LORD said to Moses: "Bring me seventy of Israel's elders who are known to you as leaders and officials among the people. Have them come to the tent of meeting, that they may stand there with you. [17]I will come down and speak with you there, and I will take some of the power of the Spirit that is on you and put it on them. They will share the burden of the people with you so that you will not have to carry it alone.

[18]"Tell the people: 'Consecrate yourselves in preparation for tomorrow, when you will

eat meat. The LORD heard you when you wailed, "If only we had meat to eat! We were better off in Egypt!" Now the LORD will give you meat, and you will eat it. [19]You will not eat it for just one day, or two days, or five, ten or twenty days, [20]but for a whole month—until it comes out of your nostrils and you loathe it—because you have rejected the LORD, who is among you, and have wailed before him, saying, "Why did we ever leave Egypt?" ' "

[21]But Moses said, "Here I am among six hundred thousand men on foot, and you say, 'I will give them meat to eat for a whole month!' [22]Would they have enough if flocks and herds were slaughtered for them? Would they have enough if all the fish in the sea were caught for them?"

[23]The LORD answered Moses, "Is the LORD's arm too short? Now you will see whether or not what I say will come true for you."

[24]So Moses went out and told the people what the LORD had said. He brought together seventy of their elders and had them stand around the tent. [25]Then the LORD came down in the cloud and spoke with him, and he took some of the power of the Spirit that was on him and put it on the seventy elders. When the Spirit rested on them, they prophesied—but did not do so again.

[26]However, two men, whose names were Eldad and Medad, had remained in the camp. They were listed among the elders, but did not go out to the tent. Yet the Spirit also rested

---

11:10–20 | Moses reacted to the **wailing** with displeasure at the people and pity for himself. God responded to the people's complaint and Moses' cry for help in two ways: He told Moses to appoint 70 men who would also **share the burden of the people**, and God gave the people what they wanted—only He gave them so much **meat** that they began to **loathe** it (Ps. 78:29; 106:15).

11:21–23 | Every answer to prayer should be cherished, remembered, and "banked" in one's memory so that it may be drawn on in future times of trial. **Is the LORD's arm too short?** is a figure of speech, with God's arm referring to His power. Because God had

miraculously provided manna for the people, Moses should never have doubted that He could supply meat for more than 600,000 men for **a whole month**.

11:24, 25 | The Lord signaled both His pleasure and His purpose when He **came down in the cloud** and divinely empowered the 70 elders by His **Spirit**. This is an extraordinary example of Spirit endowment in the OT.

11:26–29 | **Joshua** deferred to Moses' leadership, making Moses wish that everyone in the nation was spirit-empowered like his leaders were. What a privilege that since Jesus' return to heaven, all God's people have the Holy Spirit!

on them, and they prophesied in the camp. [27]A young man ran and told Moses, "Eldad and Medad are prophesying in the camp."

[28]Joshua son of Nun, who had been Moses' aide since youth, spoke up and said, "Moses, my lord, stop them!"

[29]But Moses replied, "Are you jealous for my sake? I wish that all the LORD's people were prophets and that the LORD would put his Spirit on them!" [30]Then Moses and the elders of Israel returned to the camp.

[31]Now a wind went out from the LORD and drove quail in from the sea. It scattered them up to two cubits*a* deep all around the camp, as far as a day's walk in any direction. [32]All that day and night and all the next day the people went out and gathered quail. No one gathered less than ten homers.*b* Then they spread them out all around the camp. [33]But while the meat was still between their teeth and before it could be consumed, the anger of the LORD burned against the people, and he struck them with a severe plague. [34]Therefore the place was named Kibroth Hattaavah,*c* because there they buried the people who had craved other food.

[35]From Kibroth Hattaavah the people traveled to Hazeroth and stayed there.

Miriam and Aaron Oppose Moses

12 Miriam and Aaron began to talk against Moses because of his Cushite wife, for he had married a Cushite. [2]"Has the LORD spoken only through Moses?" they asked. "Hasn't he also spoken through us?" And the LORD heard this.

[3](Now Moses was a very humble man, more humble than anyone else on the face of the earth.)

[4]At once the LORD said to Moses, Aaron and Miriam, "Come out to the tent of meeting, all three of you." So the three of them went out. [5]Then the LORD came down in a pillar of cloud; he stood at the entrance to the tent and summoned Aaron and Miriam. When the two of them stepped forward, [6]he said, "Listen to my words:

"When there is a prophet among you,
    I, the LORD, reveal myself to them in
        visions,
    I speak to them in dreams.
[7]But this is not true of my servant
        Moses;
    he is faithful in all my house.
[8]With him I speak face to face,
    clearly and not in riddles;
    he sees the form of the LORD.
Why then were you not afraid
    to speak against my servant Moses?"

[9]The anger of the LORD burned against them, and he left them.

[10]When the cloud lifted from above the tent, Miriam's skin was leprous*d*—it became as white as snow. Aaron turned toward her and saw that she had a defiling skin disease, [11]and he said to Moses, "Please, my lord, I ask you not to hold against us the sin we have so foolishly committed. [12]Do not let her be like a stillborn infant coming from its mother's womb with its flesh half eaten away."

[13]So Moses cried out to the LORD, "Please, God, heal her!"

[14]The LORD replied to Moses, "If her father had spit in her face, would she not have been in disgrace for seven days? Confine

---

a 31 That is, about 3 feet or about 90 centimeters   *b 32* That is, possibly about 1 3/4 tons or about 1.6 metric tons   *c 34* Kibroth Hattaavah means graves of craving.   *d 10* The Hebrew for leprous was used for various diseases affecting the skin.

11:31–35 | As promised, the Lord provided meat in the form of **quail**—in nearly plague-like amounts (Ps. 78:26–28; 105:40). The narrative is so vivid: **the meat was still between their teeth** when the Lord brought a **plague** of another sort (Ps. 78:29–31). Place names like **Kibroth Hattaavah** were markers of disobedience and ingratitude; the name means "Graves of Craving."

12:1–16 | Moses also faced complaints from his older siblings. **Miriam** and **Aaron** attacked his leadership because he had married a **Cushite** woman. The real nature of their complaint, however, stemmed from jealousy over Moses' special leadership role. Miriam, whose name comes first, was likely the principal in this protest.

12:1 | The Hebrew word translated **Cushite** or "Ethiopian" is *Cush*; it is now known that Cush was the actual name of a nation and a people south of Egypt (modern Sudan). As the new wife of Moses, she would have had to be a woman of true faith in Yahweh. It is possible that his first wife, Zipporah, had died; it is even more likely that the marriage had ended (Ex. 2:21; 18:1–5).

12:3 | The parenthetical words **Moses was a very humble man, more humble than anyone else** may suggest that his strength came through his humility (2 Cor. 12:9), but one who was so humble

would not likely state the case. The word *humble* is much better rendered as "terribly *broken."* The attacks on Moses from the people were one thing; attacks from his siblings were heartbreaking.

12:6–8 | This poem is astonishing in its content. Yahweh had revealed Himself to numerous people in a variety of ways, but to Moses He spoke **clearly and not in riddles** (metaphors and symbols); only of Moses could it be said, **he sees the form of the LORD.** None of the prophets in Hebrew Scripture had the privileges of divine encounter to match that of Moses.

12:9–12 | In anger, the **LORD** struck **Miriam** with leprosy (Deut. 24:9). Miriam's **flesh** was so **eaten away** that she looked to Aaron like a **stillborn infant** that had been born early. For the high priest, **Aaron,** to need priestly intercession from Moses must have seemed ironic, but it was an admittance of his sin.

12:13–16 | Although God removed Miriam's leprosy, she had to remain **outside the camp for seven days** (Lev. 13:1–6; 14:1–8; 15:8) because she was defiled. This meant shame for her and delay for the people because they had to wait for her restoration before they could move on. A rebellious sinner is always capable of holding back the progress of God's people.

For Reflection — Know Your Enemy • 13:18

Sun Tzu, an ancient Chinese military strategist (died c. 496 BC) is often credited with the saying, "Know your enemy." But this common-sense idea is even older than Sun Tzu. Moses sent the 12 spies from Kadesh into Canaan to "see . . . whether the people who live there are strong or weak, few or many." Joshua did the same from the east bank of the Jordan River before entering Canaan, sending spies to assess the strength of Jericho (Josh. 2:1). Even Jesus Christ recommended such knowledge: "Suppose a king is about to go to war against another king. Won't he first sit down and consider whether he is able with ten thousand men to oppose the one coming against him with twenty thousand?" (Luke 14:31).

If the idea of knowing one's enemy makes military sense and common sense, it makes even more sense in the spiritual arena because our spiritual enemy is stronger and the stakes are higher. The biblical writers spare no effort in giving us intelligence on the nature of our true enemy, Satan himself. Indeed, they covered both the requirements for victory: know yourself *and* know your enemy. Our task is to embrace what the Bible tells us and be prepared for the battles we will certainly face.

her outside the camp for seven days; after that she can be brought back." [15] So Miriam was confined outside the camp for seven days, and the people did not move on till she was brought back.

[16] After that, the people left Hazeroth and encamped in the Desert of Paran.

Exploring Canaan

13 The LORD said to Moses, [2] "Send some men to explore the land of Canaan, which I am giving to the Israelites. From each ancestral tribe send one of its leaders."

[3] So at the LORD's command Moses sent them out from the Desert of Paran. All of them were leaders of the Israelites. [4] These are their names:

from the tribe of Reuben, Shammua son of Zakkur;
[5] from the tribe of Simeon, Shaphat son of Hori;
[6] from the tribe of Judah, Caleb son of Jephunneh;
[7] from the tribe of Issachar, Igal son of Joseph;
[8] from the tribe of Ephraim, Hoshea son of Nun;
[9] from the tribe of Benjamin, Palti son of Raphu;
[10] from the tribe of Zebulun, Gaddiel son of Sodi;
[11] from the tribe of Manasseh (a tribe of Joseph), Gaddi son of Susi;
[12] from the tribe of Dan, Ammiel son of Gemalli;
[13] from the tribe of Asher, Sethur son of Michael;
[14] from the tribe of Naphtali, Nahbi son of Vophsi;
[15] from the tribe of Gad, Geuel son of Maki.

[16] These are the names of the men Moses sent to explore the land. (Moses gave Hoshea son of Nun the name Joshua.)

[17] When Moses sent them to explore Canaan, he said, "Go up through the Negev and on into the hill country. [18] See what the land is like and whether the people who live there are strong or weak, few or many. [19] What kind of land do they live in? Is it good or bad? What kind of towns do they live in? Are they unwalled or fortified? [20] How is the soil? Is it fertile or poor? Are there trees in it or not? Do your best to bring back some of the fruit of the land." (It was the season for the first ripe grapes.)

[21] So they went up and explored the land from the Desert of Zin as far as Rehob, toward Lebo Hamath. [22] They went up through the Negev and came to Hebron, where Ahiman, Sheshai and Talmai, the descendants of Anak, lived. (Hebron had been built seven years before Zoan in Egypt.) [23] When they reached the Valley of Eshkol,[a] they cut off a branch bearing a single cluster of grapes.

---

[a] 23 *Eshkol* means *cluster*; also in verse 24.

13:1-20 | Here we have the instruction of the Lord to send out the leaders to **explore** the land (Deut. 1:22, 23).

13:3–16 | The 12 men honored to represent each tribe are named here, but because of the way their story ends, 10 of the names are remembered today with sorrow and shame (Deut. 9:23). **Caleb**, the leader of the tribe of Judah, and **Joshua** brought back the (truthful) minority report—that God would help them conquer the land as He had promised (14:6). Consequently, they were the only ones who were allowed to enter the Promised Land.

13:16 | Moses gave **Hoshea son of Nun** (13:8) a new name, **Joshua**—a mark of esteem and perhaps of adoption as his protégé.

13:21–29 | After traveling the extent of the land for **forty days**, the spies should have emphasized the benefits of the land: a good land, flowing **with milk and honey** (Ex. 3:8, 17). When they returned to the people, however, the majority report focused primarily on obstacles—powerful cities and powerful defenders, exaggerating the latter.

Historically Speaking — The Anakim and Nephilim • 13:31-33

The Anakim were a people group of large size who lived in the region of Hebron and in some areas of Philistia. The word *'anaq* actually refers to one with a "long neck." Goliath may have come from the Anakim. He likely suffered from pituitary gland-induced gigantism, a malady marked by poor vision and a soft, bulbous forehead. When the young David came to the battlefield without armor and shield, it is possible the giant could hardly believe his (poor) eyes. Thus he removed the visor of his helmet to get a better look—and the stone of David's sling (a real military weapon at the time) killed him.

The *Nephilim* are something else altogether. These are the "fallen ones" (the literal meaning of the word rendered "giants" in Gen. 6:1-4). These were the offspring of the unsuitable alliance between fallen angels and the women of earth. So the *Nephilim* ("giants" or "fallen ones") would have all drowned in the great Flood (Gen. 6:5–8:22) along with the women. The angelic beings who provoked the deluge could not be drowned but were imprisoned by the Lord in a special place (a "pit"), where they await final judgment. This appears to be the importance of the passages in Jude, and 2 Peter (to be read in that order) in regard to Genesis 6 (Jude 6; 2 Pet. 2:4).

Ultimately, any reference to *Nephilim* living past the Flood (as in the false words of the spies in Numbers) is untrue.

Two of them carried it on a pole between them, along with some pomegranates and figs. ²⁴ That place was called the Valley of Eshkol because of the cluster of grapes the Israelites cut off there. ²⁵ At the end of forty days they returned from exploring the land.

Report on the Exploration

²⁶ They came back to Moses and Aaron and the whole Israelite community at Kadesh in the Desert of Paran. There they reported to them and to the whole assembly and showed them the fruit of the land. ²⁷ They gave Moses this account: "We went into the land to which you sent us, and it does flow with milk and honey! Here is its fruit. ²⁸ But the people who live there are powerful, and the cities are fortified and very large. We even saw descendants of Anak there. ²⁹ The Amalekites live in the Negev; the Hittites, Jebusites and Amorites live in the hill country; and the Canaanites live near the sea and along the Jordan."

³⁰ Then Caleb silenced the people before Moses and said, "We should go up and take possession of the land, for we can certainly do it."

³¹ But the men who had gone up with him said, "We can't attack those people; they are stronger than we are." ³² And they spread among the Israelites a bad report about the land they had explored. They said, "The land we explored devours those living in it. All the people we saw there are of great size. ³³ We saw the Nephilim there (the descendants of Anak come from the Nephilim). We seemed like grasshoppers in our own eyes, and we looked the same to them."

The People Rebel

14 That night all the members of the community raised their voices and wept aloud. ² All the Israelites grumbled against Moses and Aaron, and the whole assembly said to them, "If only we had died in Egypt! Or in this wilderness! ³ Why is the LORD bringing us to this land only to let us fall by the sword? Our wives and children will be taken as plunder. Wouldn't it be better for us to go back to Egypt?" ⁴ And they said to each other, "We should choose a leader and go back to Egypt."

⁵ Then Moses and Aaron fell facedown in front of the whole Israelite assembly gathered there. ⁶ Joshua son of Nun and Caleb son of Jephunneh, who were among those who had explored the land, tore their clothes ⁷ and said to the entire Israelite assembly, "The land we passed through and explored is exceedingly good. ⁸ If the LORD is pleased

---

13:28 | The word **Anak** was synonymous with monstrous, marauding giants. While the spies saw a giant or two, the only formidable one was the giant inside their heads—*Fear*. The spies brought back a distorted picture and infected the whole nation with it. This fear was unfounded because God would help them drive the giants out of the land (14:7-9; Josh. 11:21, 22).

13:30 | Caleb saw Canaan not as an obstacle but as an opportunity (**We should go up . . . for we can certainly do it**). Caleb was a brave and faith-filled man among cowards. He serves as an example for believers in all times and places.

13:31-33 | Fear not only distorts the truth and deters faith, it devours people's judgment. This passage reveals the fear of the spies, which provoked them to lie about the land. Their **bad report** (14:36, 37) claimed that the land **devours those living in it** and that they saw **Nephilim** (giants), but they saw no such thing; Nephilim ceased to exist during the Flood.

14:1-4 | In the people's desire to **choose a leader and go back to Egypt**, they were rejecting both Moses as their leader and the promises of the Lord (Ex. 16:2; 17:3).

14:5 | **Moses and Aaron fell facedown**, a response that must have been in exceeding remorse or fervent prayer.

with us, he will lead us into that land, a land flowing with milk and honey, and will give it to us. ⁹Only do not rebel against the LORD. And do not be afraid of the people of the land, because we will devour them. Their protection is gone, but the LORD is with us. Do not be afraid of them."

¹⁰But the whole assembly talked about stoning them. Then the glory of the LORD appeared at the tent of meeting to all the Israelites. ¹¹The LORD said to Moses, "How long will these people treat me with contempt? How long will they refuse to believe in me, in spite of all the signs I have performed among them? ¹²I will strike them down with a plague and destroy them, but I will make you into a nation greater and stronger than they."

¹³Moses said to the LORD, "Then the Egyptians will hear about it! By your power you brought these people up from among them. ¹⁴And they will tell the inhabitants of this land about it. They have already heard that you, LORD, are with these people and that you, LORD, have been seen face to face, that your cloud stays over them, and that you go before them in a pillar of cloud by day and a pillar of fire by night. ¹⁵If you put all these people to death, leaving none alive, the nations who have heard this report about you will say, ¹⁶'The LORD was not able to bring these people into the land he promised them on oath, so he slaughtered them in the wilderness.'

¹⁷"Now may the LORD's strength be displayed, just as you have declared: ¹⁸'The LORD is slow to anger, abounding in love and forgiving sin and rebellion. Yet he does not leave the guilty unpunished; he punishes the children for the sin of the parents to the third and fourth generation.' ¹⁹In accordance with your great love, forgive the sin of these people, just as you have pardoned them from the time they left Egypt until now."

fyi True to His Vow • 14:26–38

God's words "As surely as I live" introduce a strong vow of the Lord's; they are irrevocable words. The severity and strength of the oath are emphasized by the words of verse 35: "I, the LORD, have spoken." The two statements form an *inclusio*—a frame for the passage.

Except for Joshua and Caleb, no one over 20 years of age—including Moses, Aaron, and Miriam—was allowed to enter the Promised Land. During the next 40 years after this incident, Joshua and Caleb essentially got up many mornings and went to yet another funeral of someone in their generation who had died. Their fellow spies died immediately when God sent a plague on them, indicating the severity of their sinful behavior. Others lost their opportunity to enter the land, but the instigators lost their lives at once.

²⁰The LORD replied, "I have forgiven them, as you asked. ²¹Nevertheless, as surely as I live and as surely as the glory of the LORD fills the whole earth, ²²not one of those who saw my glory and the signs I performed in Egypt and in the wilderness but who disobeyed me and tested me ten times— ²³not one of them will ever see the land I promised on oath to their ancestors. No one who has treated me with contempt will ever see it. ²⁴But because my servant Caleb has a different spirit and follows me wholeheartedly, I will bring him into the land he went to, and his descendants will inherit it. ²⁵Since the Amalekites and the Canaanites are living in the valleys, turn back tomorrow and set out toward the desert along the route to the Red Sea.ᵃ"

²⁶The LORD said to Moses and Aaron: ²⁷"How long will this wicked community grumble against me? I have heard the complaints of these grumbling Israelites. ²⁸So

ᵃ 25 Or the Sea of Reeds

14:6-10 | Joshua and **Caleb** declared **the land** as **exceedingly good**. They were also adamant that the Lord was truly able (Deut. 1:25). Nevertheless, the people **talked about stoning them**. Only the Lord's appearance prevented them from following through.

14:9 | The spies with the evil report had used a great deal of exaggeration to make their point (see notes on 13:28, 31–33). Here, rhetorical flourish is returned by Joshua and Caleb. It is as if they are saying of the enemy: They have no chance; **we will devour them**.

14:11, 12 | Numerous times in Scripture, a hurting believer will ask the Lord, **How long** will You wait before helping? Here, the words are expressed by God regarding the continued rejection of His people! The Lord would begin anew with Moses.

14:13-19 | As was the case in Exodus 32:11-14, following the apostasy of the worship of the golden calf, Moses again pleaded with God to forgive the people, even though they would have to suffer His punishment in some way. In this instance, Moses quoted the

Lord's own words that describe Him as **slow to anger, abounding in love and forgiving sin and rebellion** (Ex. 32:10; 34:6, 7; Neh. 9:17; Ps. 103:8). Moses' concern was for the glory and reputation of God among the nations—if He destroyed His chosen people, the pagan nations would doubt God's power and mercy.

14:20-25 | This generation would not enter Canaan because they believed their doubts and doubted their beliefs (1 Cor. 10:5). The hardening of their hearts was not restricted to this one occasion either; it apparently happened on **ten** different occasions. In contrast to the fear of the people was the fearless confidence of Caleb; God declared, **My servant Caleb . . . follows me wholeheartedly** (Deut. 1:36).

14:24 | The reason for Caleb's success is no secret. Thirty verses hold his entire life story in the Scriptures. Six times in those 30 verses we see a recurring theme: he had a **different spirit** (14:24; 32:12; Deut. 1:35, 36; Josh. 14:8, 9; 14:14). Caleb had a passion for God and followed Him with all his heart.

tell them, 'As surely as I live, declares the LORD, I will do to you the very thing I heard you say: ²⁹In this wilderness your bodies will fall—every one of you twenty years old or more who was counted in the census and who has grumbled against me. ³⁰Not one of you will enter the land I swore with uplifted hand to make your home, except Caleb son of Jephunneh and Joshua son of Nun. ³¹As for your children that you said would be taken as plunder, I will bring them in to enjoy the land you have rejected. ³²But as for you, your bodies will fall in this wilderness. ³³Your children will be shepherds here for forty years, suffering for your unfaithfulness, until the last of your bodies lies in the wilderness. ³⁴For forty years—one year for each of the forty days you explored the land—you will suffer for your sins and know what it is like to have me against you.' ³⁵I, the LORD, have spoken, and I will surely do these things to this whole wicked community, which has banded together against me. They will meet their end in this wilderness; here they will die."

³⁶So the men Moses had sent to explore the land, who returned and made the whole community grumble against him by spreading a bad report about it— ³⁷these men who were responsible for spreading the bad report about the land were struck down and died of a plague before the LORD. ³⁸Of the men who went to explore the land, only Joshua son of Nun and Caleb son of Jephunneh survived.

³⁹When Moses reported this to all the Israelites, they mourned bitterly. ⁴⁰Early the next morning they set out for the highest point in the hill country, saying, "Now we are ready to go up to the land the LORD promised. Surely we have sinned!"

⁴¹But Moses said, "Why are you disobeying the LORD's command? This will not succeed! ⁴²Do not go up, because the LORD is not with you. You will be defeated by your enemies, ⁴³for the Amalekites and the Canaanites will face you there. Because you have turned away from the LORD, he will not be with you and you will fall by the sword."

⁴⁴Nevertheless, in their presumption they went up toward the highest point in the hill country, though neither Moses nor the ark of the LORD's covenant moved from the camp. ⁴⁵Then the Amalekites and the Canaanites who lived in that hill country came down and attacked them and beat them down all the way to Hormah.

Supplementary Offerings

15 The LORD said to Moses, ²"Speak to the Israelites and say to them: 'After you enter the land I am giving you as a home ³and you present to the LORD food offerings from the herd or the flock, as an aroma pleasing to the LORD—whether burnt offerings or sacrifices, for special vows or freewill offerings or festival offerings— ⁴then the person who brings an offering shall present to the LORD a grain offering of a tenth of an ephah^a of the finest flour mixed with a quarter of a hin^b of olive oil. ⁵With each lamb for the burnt offering or the sacrifice, prepare a quarter of a hin of wine as a drink offering.

⁶"'With a ram prepare a grain offering of two-tenths of an ephah^c of the finest flour mixed with a third of a hin^d of olive oil, ⁷and a third of a hin of wine as a drink offering. Offer it as an aroma pleasing to the LORD.

⁸"'When you prepare a young bull as a burnt offering or sacrifice, for a special vow or a fellowship offering to the LORD, ⁹bring with the bull a grain offering of three-tenths of an ephah^e of the finest flour mixed with half a hin^f of olive oil, ¹⁰and also bring half a hin of wine as a drink offering. This will be a food offering, an aroma pleasing to the LORD. ¹¹Each bull or ram, each lamb or young goat, is to be prepared in this manner. ¹²Do this for each one, for as many as you prepare.

¹³"'Everyone who is native-born must do these things in this way when they present a food offering as an aroma pleasing to the LORD. ¹⁴For the generations to come, whenever a foreigner or anyone else living among you presents a food offering as an aroma pleasing to the LORD, they must do exactly as you do. ¹⁵The community is to

^a 4 That is, probably about 3 1/2 pounds or about 1.6 kilograms   ^b 4 That is, about 1 quart or about 1 liter; also in verse 5   ^c 6 That is, probably about 7 pounds or about 3.2 kilograms   ^d 6 That is, about 1 1/3 quarts or about 1.3 liters; also in verse 7   ^e 9 That is, probably about 11 pounds or about 5 kilograms   ^f 9 That is, about 2 quarts or about 1.9 liters; also in verse 10

14:39–45 | Actions come too late when the Lord is no longer in them. A chastened and shamed people were defeated when they took things into their own hands, attacking a group of **Amalekites** apart from the Lord's instruction.

15:1–16 | For the Lord to say **After you enter the land** demonstrates His ongoing grace to His erring people. Israel's future was there. And even though the adult generation had been sentenced to die before reaching the Promised Land (Heb. 3:17, 18), the next generation would need to understand the covenant's requirements, including its system of **offerings** (Ex. 23:14–19; Deut. 12:1–13).

15:14–16 | The **foreigner** (resident alien) who lived among the people of Israel was permitted to bring **aroma** offerings in the same manner as the native-born (9:14). This was OT evangelism at work.

have the same rules for you and for the foreigner residing among you; this is a lasting ordinance for the generations to come. You and the foreigner shall be the same before the LORD: [16]The same laws and regulations will apply both to you and to the foreigner residing among you.' "

[17]The LORD said to Moses, [18]"Speak to the Israelites and say to them: 'When you enter the land to which I am taking you [19]and you eat the food of the land, present a portion as an offering to the LORD. [20]Present a loaf from the first of your ground meal and present it as an offering from the threshing floor. [21]Throughout the generations to come you are to give this offering to the LORD from the first of your ground meal.

Offerings for Unintentional Sins

[22]" 'Now if you as a community unintentionally fail to keep any of these commands the LORD gave Moses— [23]any of the LORD's commands to you through him, from the day the LORD gave them and continuing through the generations to come— [24]and if this is done unintentionally without the community being aware of it, then the whole community is to offer a young bull for a burnt offering as an aroma pleasing to the LORD, along with its prescribed grain offering and drink offering, and a male goat for a sin offering.[a] [25]The priest is to make atonement for the whole Israelite community, and they will be forgiven, for it was not intentional and they have presented to the LORD for their wrong a food offering and a sin offering. [26]The whole Israelite community and the foreigners residing among them will be forgiven, because all the people were involved in the unintentional wrong.

[27]" 'But if just one person sins unintentionally, that person must bring a year-old female goat for a sin offering. [28]The priest is to make atonement before the LORD for the one who erred by sinning unintentionally, and when atonement has been made, that person will be forgiven. [29]One and the same law applies to everyone who sins

unintentionally, whether a native-born Israelite or a foreigner residing among you.

[30]" 'But anyone who sins defiantly, whether native-born or foreigner, blasphemes the LORD and must be cut off from the people of Israel. [31]Because they have despised the LORD's word and broken his commands, they must surely be cut off; their guilt remains on them.' "

The Sabbath-Breaker Put to Death

[32]While the Israelites were in the wilderness, a man was found gathering wood on the Sabbath day. [33]Those who found him gathering wood brought him to Moses and Aaron and the whole assembly, [34]and they kept him in custody, because it was not clear what should be done to him. [35]Then the LORD said to Moses, "The man must die. The whole assembly must stone him outside the camp." [36]So the assembly took him outside the camp and stoned him to death, as the LORD commanded Moses.

Tassels on Garments

[37]The LORD said to Moses, [38]"Speak to the Israelites and say to them: 'Throughout the generations to come you are to make tassels on the corners of your garments, with a blue cord on each tassel. [39]You will have these tassels to look at and so you will remember all the commands of the LORD, that you may obey them and not prostitute yourselves by chasing after the lusts of your own hearts and eyes. [40]Then you will remember to obey all my commands and will be consecrated to your God. [41]I am the LORD your God, who brought you out of Egypt to be your God. I am the LORD your God.' "

Korah, Dathan and Abiram

16 Korah son of Izhar, the son of Kohath, the son of Levi, and certain Reubenites—Dathan and Abiram, sons of Eliab, and On son of Peleth—became insolent[b] [2]and rose up against Moses. With them were 250

---

[a] 24 Or purification offering; also in verses 25 and 27   [b] 1 Or Peleth—took men

---

15:22-29 | Those who sinned **unintentionally** had provision for forgiveness. These several offerings (**burnt**, **grain**, **drink**, **sin**) were to be made in **atonement** for omitting or unintentionally sinning against any of the Lord's commands.

15:30, 31 | Sinning **defiantly**—literally, sinning "with a high hand"— is a sign of rebellion against the Lord, so no provisions were given for a person who defied Yahweh's grace in this way. Instead, they were to **surely be cut off** (Deut. 17:12; Ps. 19:13; Heb. 10:26).

15:32-36 | An illustration of presumptuous sin concerns a man who violated the **Sabbath**. His condemnation was a **death** sentence, because God's requirements about observing this day of rest were well known in Israel. A violation was deemed deliberate.

15:37-41 | The special identity of the people of Israel was to be fully woven into their everyday life, including what they wore. The **tassels on the corners of** their **garments** were not for fashion but to cause them to **remember all the commands of the LORD** and help them be **consecrated** (holy). This commandment is the basis for the prayer shawl worn by Jewish men to this day. See Deuteronomy 6:4-9 for other daily reminders of their status as the people of the Lord.

16:1-3 | A Levite named **Korah** and two Reubenites named **Dathan and Abiram** were jealous of Moses' and Aaron's positions among the people. A faction rose up, claiming these divinely designated leaders had exalted themselves, and unrest spread throughout the camp.

Israelite men, well-known community leaders who had been appointed members of the council. ³They came as a group to oppose Moses and Aaron and said to them, "You have gone too far! The whole community is holy, every one of them, and the LORD is with them. Why then do you set yourselves above the LORD's assembly?"

⁴When Moses heard this, he fell facedown. ⁵Then he said to Korah and all his followers: "In the morning the LORD will show who belongs to him and who is holy, and he will have that person come near him. The man he chooses he will cause to come near him. ⁶You, Korah, and all your followers are to do this: Take censers ⁷and tomorrow put burning coals and incense in them before the LORD. The man the LORD chooses will be the one who is holy. You Levites have gone too far!"

⁸Moses also said to Korah, "Now listen, you Levites! ⁹Isn't it enough for you that the God of Israel has separated you from the rest of the Israelite community and brought you near himself to do the work at the LORD's tabernacle and to stand before the community and minister to them? ¹⁰He has brought you and all your fellow Levites near himself, but now you are trying to get the priesthood too. ¹¹It is against the LORD that you and all your followers have banded together. Who is Aaron that you should grumble against him?"

¹²Then Moses summoned Dathan and Abiram, the sons of Eliab. But they said, "We will not come! ¹³Isn't it enough that you have brought us up out of a land flowing with milk and honey to kill us in the wilderness? And now you also want to lord it over us! ¹⁴Moreover, you haven't brought us into a land flowing with milk and honey or given us an inheritance of fields and vineyards. Do you want to treat these men like slaves*? No, we will not come!"

¹⁵Then Moses became very angry and said to the LORD, "Do not accept their offering. I have not taken so much as a donkey from them, nor have I wronged any of them."

¹⁶Moses said to Korah, "You and all your followers are to appear before the LORD tomorrow—you and they and Aaron. ¹⁷Each man is to take his censer and put incense in it—250 censers in all—and present it before the LORD. You and Aaron are to present your censers also." ¹⁸So each of them took his censer, put burning coals and incense in it, and stood with Moses and Aaron at the entrance to the tent of meeting. ¹⁹When Korah had gathered all his followers in opposition to them at the entrance to the tent of meeting, the glory of the LORD appeared to the entire assembly. ²⁰The LORD said to Moses and Aaron, ²¹"Separate yourselves from this assembly so I can put an end to them at once."

²²But Moses and Aaron fell facedown and cried out, "O God, the God who gives breath to all living things, will you be angry with the entire assembly when only one man sins?"

²³Then the LORD said to Moses, ²⁴"Say to the assembly, 'Move away from the tents of Korah, Dathan and Abiram.'"

²⁵Moses got up and went to Dathan and Abiram, and the elders of Israel followed him. ²⁶He warned the assembly, "Move back from the tents of these wicked men! Do not touch anything belonging to them, or you will be swept away because of all their sins." ²⁷So they moved away from the tents of Korah, Dathan and Abiram. Dathan and Abiram had come out and were standing with their wives, children and little ones at the entrances to their tents.

²⁸Then Moses said, "This is how you will know that the LORD has sent me to do all these things and that it was not my idea: ²⁹If these men die a natural death and suffer the fate of all mankind, then the LORD has not sent me. ³⁰But if the LORD brings about something totally new, and the earth opens its mouth and swallows them, with

---

a 14 Or to deceive these men; Hebrew Will you gouge out the eyes of these men

---

16:4–7 | Moses **fell facedown** (14:5), not in reverence to the Lord, but in exasperation at the people's sin. His challenge to **Korah** bears some resemblance to Elijah's challenge to the prophet-priests of Baal (1 Kgs. 18:20–40), only Moses' confrontation would **show who belongs to him** (the Lord).

16:8–11 | **Korah** and his fellow Levites had decided they were not content with the role God gave them and wanted to exalt themselves to higher positions. Yet as Moses said, their ministry at the **tabernacle** was already highly favored for having been selected from among all Israel, so their assault was on the Lord Himself—the One who had sovereignly appointed only Aaron's family as priests. **Levites** in this context refers to Levi's descendants. It is **enough** to be assigned to *any* work when a person is assigned by the Lord.

16:15 | Moses' words **I have not taken so much as a donkey from them, nor have I wronged any of them** show his brokenness at being accused of expecting preferential treatment. This is the reaction of someone whose leadership truly was not based on personal demands or privilege.

16:28–34 | In verse 30 is a splendid use of the Hebrew verb meaning "to create something new or remarkable" (Gen. 1:1, 21, 26). **Something totally new** was a new judgment: the divine sinkhole that opened suddenly and swallowed Abiram, **Korah**, and Dathan **and their households**, along with **their possessions**. This should have left no doubt as to who was God's appointed leader in Israel. Scripture is careful to note that Korah's sons did not join the rebellion (26:11).

everything that belongs to them, and they go down alive into the realm of the dead, then you will know that these men have treated the LORD with contempt."

³¹As soon as he finished saying all this, the ground under them split apart ³²and the earth opened its mouth and swallowed them and their households, and all those associated with Korah, together with their possessions. ³³They went down alive into the realm of the dead, with everything they owned; the earth closed over them, and they perished and were gone from the community. ³⁴At their cries, all the Israelites around them fled, shouting, "The earth is going to swallow us too!"

³⁵And fire came out from the LORD and consumed the 250 men who were offering the incense.

³⁶The LORD said to Moses, ³⁷ "Tell Eleazar son of Aaron, the priest, to remove the censers from the charred remains and scatter the coals some distance away, for the censers are holy— ³⁸the censers of the men who sinned at the cost of their lives. Hammer the censers into sheets to overlay the altar, for they were presented before the LORD and have become holy. Let them be a sign to the Israelites."

³⁹So Eleazar the priest collected the bronze censers brought by those who had been burned to death, and he had them hammered out to overlay the altar, ⁴⁰as the LORD directed him through Moses. This was to remind the Israelites that no one except a descendant of Aaron should come to burn incense before the LORD, or he would become like Korah and his followers.

⁴¹The next day the whole Israelite community grumbled against Moses and Aaron. "You have killed the LORD's people," they said.

⁴²But when the assembly gathered in opposition to Moses and Aaron and turned toward the tent of meeting, suddenly the cloud covered it and the glory of the LORD appeared. ⁴³Then Moses and Aaron went to the front of the tent of meeting, ⁴⁴and

the LORD said to Moses, ⁴⁵ "Get away from this assembly so I can put an end to them at once." And they fell facedown.

⁴⁶Then Moses said to Aaron, "Take your censer and put incense in it, along with burning coals from the altar, and hurry to the assembly to make atonement for them. Wrath has come out from the LORD; the plague has started." ⁴⁷So Aaron did as Moses said, and ran into the midst of the assembly. The plague had already started among the people, but Aaron offered the incense and made atonement for them. ⁴⁸He stood between the living and the dead, and the plague stopped. ⁴⁹But 14,700 people died from the plague, in addition to those who had died because of Korah. ⁵⁰Then Aaron returned to Moses at the entrance to the tent of meeting, for the plague had stopped.ᵃ

The Budding of Aaron's Staff

17ᵇ The LORD said to Moses, ²"Speak to the Israelites and get twelve staffs from them, one from the leader of each of their ancestral tribes. Write the name of each man on his staff. ³On the staff of Levi write Aaron's name, for there must be one staff for the head of each ancestral tribe. ⁴Place them in the tent of meeting in front of the ark of the covenant law, where I meet with you. ⁵The staff belonging to the man I choose will sprout, and I will rid myself of this constant grumbling against you by the Israelites."

⁶So Moses spoke to the Israelites, and their leaders gave him twelve staffs, one for the leader of each of their ancestral tribes, and Aaron's staff was among them. ⁷Moses placed the staffs before the LORD in the tent of the covenant law.

⁸The next day Moses entered the tent and saw that Aaron's staff, which represented the tribe of Levi, had not only sprouted but had budded, blossomed and produced almonds. ⁹Then Moses brought out all the staffs from the LORD's presence to all the

---

ᵃ 50 In Hebrew texts 16:36-50 is numbered 17:1-15.   ᵇ In Hebrew texts 17:1-13 is numbered 17:16-28.

16:35-40 | All 250 Levites challenging Aaron's leadership (16:8–11) were **consumed** by fire while **offering the incense** (8:16–19). This affirmed that the priesthood belonged only to Aaron and his line. Eleazar made a covering from the **censers to overlay the altar** as a visual reminder to the Israelites: beware the consequences of questioning the sovereign decisions of God by opposing His anointed leaders (Jude 11).
16:41-50 | It is nearly unbelievable that after the divine judgments—which were so clearly the work of Yahweh—the people held **Moses and Aaron** responsible for the calamities.
17:1-7 | The attack on Moses and Aaron by Korah and his accomplices left some people uncertain about whether Aaron and his

sons were the true priests of the Lord. **Twelve** wooden **staffs**, one for each tribe, were presented. The staffs were to have the name of each leader of Israel's tribes on them, and the Lord demanded that the one for the tribe of **Levi** bear **Aaron's name**. In the aftermath of the Levite uprising in chapter 16, this was an important reaffirmation of whose descendants would serve as priests from that tribe.
17:8, 9 | The staff that blossomed would further signal which tribe the Lord had designated to be Israel's priests (17:5). That Aaron's staff alone miraculously **produced almonds** on the same day it **sprouted** and **blossomed** unequivocally affirmed God's choice. As the first fruit tree that blooms in Canaan, the almond tree is known as the harbinger of spring. Its Hebrew name means "The Watchman" (Jer. 1:11, 12).

Israelites. They looked at them, and each of the leaders took his own staff.

[10] The LORD said to Moses, "Put back Aaron's staff in front of the ark of the covenant law, to be kept as a sign to the rebellious. This will put an end to their grumbling against me, so that they will not die." [11] Moses did just as the LORD commanded him.

[12] The Israelites said to Moses, "We will die! We are lost, we are all lost! [13] Anyone who even comes near the tabernacle of the LORD will die. Are we all going to die?"

Duties of Priests and Levites

18 The LORD said to Aaron, "You, your sons and your family are to bear the responsibility for offenses connected with the sanctuary, and you and your sons alone are to bear the responsibility for offenses connected with the priesthood. [2] Bring your fellow Levites from your ancestral tribe to join you and assist you when you and your sons minister before the tent of the covenant law. [3] They are to be responsible to you and are to perform all the duties of the tent, but they must not go near the furnishings of the sanctuary or the altar. Otherwise both they and you will die. [4] They are to join you and be responsible for the care of the tent of meeting—all the work at the tent—and no one else may come near where you are.

[5] "You are to be responsible for the care of the sanctuary and the altar, so that my wrath will not fall on the Israelites again. [6] I myself have selected your fellow Levites from among the Israelites as a gift to you, dedicated to the LORD to do the work at the tent of meeting. [7] But only you and your sons may serve as priests in connection with everything at the altar and inside the curtain. I am giving you the service of the priesthood as a gift. Anyone else who comes near the sanctuary is to be put to death."

Offerings for Priests and Levites

[8] Then the LORD said to Aaron, "I myself have put you in charge of the offerings presented to me; all the holy offerings the Israelites give me I give to you and your sons as your portion, your perpetual share. [9] You are to have the part of the most holy offerings that is kept from the fire. From all the gifts they bring me as most holy offerings, whether grain or sin[a] or guilt offerings, that part belongs to you and your sons. [10] Eat it as something most holy; every male shall eat it. You must regard it as holy.

[11] "This also is yours: whatever is set aside from the gifts of all the wave offerings of the Israelites. I give this to you and your sons and daughters as your perpetual share. Everyone in your household who is ceremonially clean may eat it.

[12] "I give you all the finest olive oil and all the finest new wine and grain they give the LORD as the firstfruits of their harvest. [13] All the land's firstfruits that they bring to the LORD will be yours. Everyone in your household who is ceremonially clean may eat it.

[14] "Everything in Israel that is devoted[b] to the LORD is yours. [15] The first offspring of every womb, both human and animal, that is offered to the LORD is yours. But you must redeem every firstborn son and every firstborn male of unclean animals. [16] When they are a month old, you must redeem them at the redemption price set at five shekels[c] of silver, according to the sanctuary shekel, which weighs twenty gerahs.

[17] "But you must not redeem the firstborn of a cow, a sheep or a goat; they are holy. Splash their blood against the altar and burn their fat as a food offering, an aroma pleasing to the LORD. [18] Their meat is to be yours, just as the breast of the wave offering and the right thigh are yours. [19] Whatever is set aside from the holy offerings the Israelites present to the LORD I give to you and your sons and daughters as your perpetual share. It is an everlasting covenant of salt before the LORD for both you and your offspring."

[20] The LORD said to Aaron, "You will have no inheritance in their land, nor will you have any share among them; I am your share and your inheritance among the Israelites.

[21] "I give to the Levites all the tithes in Israel as their inheritance in return for the work they do while serving at the tent of meeting. [22] From now on the Israelites must

---

[a] 9 Or *purification*   [b] 14 The Hebrew term refers to the irrevocable giving over of things or persons to the LORD.   [c] 16 That is, about 2 ounces or about 58 grams

---

17:10 | Other items in the **ark of the covenant law** were a jar of manna (Ex. 16:33, 34) and the two tablets with the Ten Commandments ("the covenant law"; Ex. 25:16; see note on Ex. 32:15, 16). The stunning thing about these three objects is that no one but Yahweh would ever see them once they were placed in the ark. These were "reminders" of His great mercy—not to the people but to the Lord!

18:1–20 | This passage describes the priestly duties and provisions that God communicated to **Aaron** (Ex. 40:13). One priority was that the priests make sure no one defiled the **sanctuary**. The priests would be punished (**bear the responsibility**) if it was desecrated. God gave the **Levites** to assist the priestly work and promised that the priests would receive a **portion** of the **offerings** since they did not inherit any land.

not go near the tent of meeting, or they will bear the consequences of their sin and will die. ²³It is the Levites who are to do the work at the tent of meeting and bear the responsibility for any offenses they commit against it. This is a lasting ordinance for the generations to come. They will receive no inheritance among the Israelites. ²⁴Instead, I give to the Levites as their inheritance the tithes that the Israelites present as an offering to the LORD. That is why I said concerning them: 'They will have no inheritance among the Israelites.'"

²⁵The LORD said to Moses, ²⁶ "Speak to the Levites and say to them: 'When you receive from the Israelites the tithe I give you as your inheritance, you must present a tenth of that tithe as the LORD's offering. ²⁷Your offering will be reckoned to you as grain from the threshing floor or juice from the winepress. ²⁸In this way you also will present an offering to the LORD from all the tithes you receive from the Israelites. From these tithes you must give the LORD's portion to Aaron the priest. ²⁹You must present as the LORD's portion the best and holiest part of everything given to you.'

³⁰ "Say to the Levites: 'When you present the best part, it will be reckoned to you as the product of the threshing floor or the winepress. ³¹You and your households may eat the rest of it anywhere, for it is your wages for your work at the tent of meeting. ³²By presenting the best part of it you will not be guilty in this matter; then you will not defile the holy offerings of the Israelites, and you will not die.'"

The Water of Cleansing

19 The LORD said to Moses and Aaron: ² "This is a requirement of the law that the LORD has commanded: Tell the Israelites to bring you a red heifer without defect or blemish and that has never been under a yoke. ³Give it to Eleazar the priest; it is to be taken outside the camp and slaughtered in his presence. ⁴Then Eleazar the priest is to take some of its blood on his finger and sprinkle it seven times toward the front of the tent of meeting. ⁵While he watches, the heifer is to be burned—its hide, flesh, blood and intestines. ⁶The priest is to take some cedar wood, hyssop and scarlet wool and throw them onto the burning heifer. ⁷After that, the priest must wash his clothes and bathe himself with water. He may then come into the camp, but he will be ceremonially unclean till evening. ⁸The man who burns it must also wash his clothes and bathe with water, and he too will be unclean till evening.

⁹ "A man who is clean shall gather up the ashes of the heifer and put them in a ceremonially clean place outside the camp. They are to be kept by the Israelite community for use in the water of cleansing; it is for purification from sin. ¹⁰The man who gathers up the ashes of the heifer must also wash his clothes, and he too will be unclean till evening. This will be a lasting ordinance both for the Israelites and for the foreigners residing among them.

¹¹ "Whoever touches a human corpse will be unclean for seven days. ¹²They must purify themselves with the water on the third day and on the seventh day; then they will be clean. But if they do not purify themselves on the third and seventh days, they will not be clean. ¹³If they fail to purify themselves after touching a human corpse, they defile the LORD's tabernacle. They must be cut off from Israel. Because the water of cleansing has not been sprinkled on them, they are unclean; their uncleanness remains on them.

¹⁴ "This is the law that applies when a person dies in a tent: Anyone who enters the tent and anyone who is in it will be unclean for seven days, ¹⁵and every open container without a lid fastened on it will be unclean.

¹⁶ "Anyone out in the open who touches someone who has been killed with a sword or someone who has died a natural death, or anyone who touches a human bone or a grave, will be unclean for seven days.

18:21–24 | This obligatory annual tithe, also known as "the Levites' tithe," was given from the fruit of the land, the flocks, and the herds. It recognized that everything belonged to God. **Tithes** were also a way to meet the needs of the **Levites**. Like the priests, they had no land; they were to devote their time to serving in the tabernacle rather than tending to livestock or property.

18:25–32 | Every member of God's chosen people was to worship Him by returning to Him a portion of His blessings. Even the Levites were to present God with a **tenth of that tithe** they received—and to make sure it was the **best** of what they received. Disobedience would result in death.

19:2–10 | A **red heifer** was a most unusual animal for sacrifice.

Typically, the animal's color is not mentioned. This sacrifice was to be made outside the camp (Heb. 13:11); the ashes were gathered for certain rituals of **purification** (Heb. 9:13).

19:11–16 | This passage may provide a clue as to why the priest in the parable of the Good Samaritan "passed by on the other side" (Luke 10:31). If the man was dead, the priest—putting temple ritual ahead of compassion—would have been temporarily prohibited from performing his duties after touching the body. Anyone who entered **a tent** in which someone had died, or who came in contact with a **corpse**, a human **bone**, or a **grave** was also considered **unclean**. The effect of death was so pervasive that it corrupted open containers in its proximity.

[17] "For the unclean person, put some ashes from the burned purification offering into a jar and pour fresh water over them. [18] Then a man who is ceremonially clean is to take some hyssop, dip it in the water and sprinkle the tent and all the furnishings and the people who were there. He must also sprinkle anyone who has touched a human bone or a grave or anyone who has been killed or anyone who has died a natural death. [19] The man who is clean is to sprinkle those who are unclean on the third and seventh days, and on the seventh day he is to purify them. Those who are being cleansed must wash their clothes and bathe with water, and that evening they will be clean. [20] But if those who are unclean do not purify themselves, they must be cut off from the community, because they have defiled the sanctuary of the LORD. The water of cleansing has not been sprinkled on them, and they are unclean. [21] This is a lasting ordinance for them.

"The man who sprinkles the water of cleansing must also wash his clothes, and anyone who touches the water of cleansing will be unclean till evening. [22] Anything that an unclean person touches becomes unclean, and anyone who touches it becomes unclean till evening."

Water From the Rock

20 In the first month the whole Israelite community arrived at the Desert of Zin, and they stayed at Kadesh. There Miriam died and was buried.

[2] Now there was no water for the community, and the people gathered in opposition to Moses and Aaron. [3] They quarreled with Moses and said, "If only we had died when our brothers fell dead before the LORD! [4] Why did you bring the LORD's community into this wilderness, that we and our livestock should die here? [5] Why did you bring us up out of Egypt to this terrible place? It has no grain or figs, grapevines or pomegranates. And there is no water to drink!"

[6] Moses and Aaron went from the assembly to the entrance to the tent of meeting and fell facedown, and the glory of the LORD appeared to them. [7] The LORD said to Moses, [8] "Take the staff, and you and your brother Aaron gather the assembly together. Speak to that rock before their eyes and it will pour out its water. You will bring water out of the rock for the community so they and their livestock can drink."

[9] So Moses took the staff from the LORD's presence, just as he commanded him. [10] He and Aaron gathered the assembly together in front of the rock and Moses said to them, "Listen, you rebels, must we bring you water out of this rock?" [11] Then Moses raised his arm and struck the rock twice with his staff. Water gushed out, and the community and their livestock drank.

[12] But the LORD said to Moses and Aaron, "Because you did not trust in me enough to honor me as holy in the sight of the Israelites, you will not bring this community into the land I give them."

[13] These were the waters of Meribah,[a] where the Israelites quarreled with the LORD and where he was proved holy among them.

Edom Denies Israel Passage

[14] Moses sent messengers from Kadesh to the king of Edom, saying:

"This is what your brother Israel says: You know about all the hardships that have come on us. [15] Our ancestors went down into Egypt, and we lived there many years. The Egyptians mistreated us and our ancestors, [16] but when we cried out to the LORD, he heard our cry and sent an angel and brought us out of Egypt.

"Now we are here at Kadesh, a town on the edge of your territory. [17] Please let us pass through your country. We will

---

[a] 13 Meribah means quarreling.

20:1–29 | The reports of Miriam's and Aaron's deaths serve as an inclusion—bookends—for this chapter. It also describes the transition of the high priesthood to **Eleazar**. In between these events, Moses disqualified himself from the Promised Land.

20:2–5 | This account recalls other incidents from Israel's time in the wilderness. They had previously lacked water and **quarreled** against God and their leaders (Ex. 17:1–7); now they repeated their complaint of 14:1–3.

20:6–12 | Moses disobeyed God by striking the rock **twice** instead of speaking to it. Perhaps he thought that he and Aaron (**must we . . . ?**) were expected to **bring water . . . out of the rock** rather than God. Because Moses **did not trust** God, his actions did not represent God as holy (**honor me**) before the people, and he was denied entry into the Promised Land.

20:13 | The name **Meribah** is a play on words, meaning "contention," "quarreling," or "striving" in Hebrew. This place name also appears in the earlier incident, right after the Exodus, in which God brought water from the rock for the people (Ex.17:7). That first location was called Massah, which means "testing" (Ps. 95:8).

20:14–21 | **Edom** is mentioned nearly 125 times in Scripture—every one of those references in the OT, and many of them pertaining to prophetic judgment, in part because of the king's response here (Ezek. 25:12, 13; Obad. 10–12). Edom is where the descendants of Jacob's brother Esau dwelt. Even though Moses promised that the Israelites would essentially pass through their territory quietly—leaving every **field** and all well **water** undisturbed—the **king** of their brother nation not only **refused to let them go through their territory** but threatened war (Deut. 2:1–8).

not go through any field or vineyard, or drink water from any well. We will travel along the King's Highway and not turn to the right or to the left until we have passed through your territory."

[18] But Edom answered:

"You may not pass through here; if you try, we will march out and attack you with the sword."

[19] The Israelites replied:

"We will go along the main road, and if we or our livestock drink any of your water, we will pay for it. We only want to pass through on foot—nothing else."

[20] Again they answered:

"You may not pass through."

Then Edom came out against them with a large and powerful army. [21] Since Edom refused to let them go through their territory, Israel turned away from them.

The Death of Aaron

[22] The whole Israelite community set out from Kadesh and came to Mount Hor. [23] At Mount Hor, near the border of Edom, the LORD said to Moses and Aaron, [24] "Aaron will be gathered to his people. He will not enter the land I give the Israelites, because both of you rebelled against my command at the waters of Meribah. [25] Get Aaron and his son Eleazar and take them up Mount Hor. [26] Remove Aaron's garments and put them on his son Eleazar, for Aaron will be gathered to his people; he will die there."

[27] Moses did as the LORD commanded: They went up Mount Hor in the sight of the whole community. [28] Moses removed Aaron's garments and put them on his son Eleazar. And Aaron died there on top of the mountain. Then Moses and Eleazar came down from the mountain, [29] and when the whole community learned that Aaron had died, all the Israelites mourned for him thirty days.

Arad Destroyed

21 When the Canaanite king of Arad, who lived in the Negev, heard that Israel was coming along the road to Atharim, he attacked the Israelites and captured some of them. [2] Then Israel made this vow to the LORD: "If you will deliver these people into our hands, we will totally destroy[a] their cities." [3] The LORD listened to Israel's plea and gave the Canaanites over to them. They completely destroyed them and their towns; so the place was named Hormah.[b]

The Bronze Snake

[4] They traveled from Mount Hor along the route to the Red Sea,[c] to go around Edom. But the people grew impatient on the way; [5] they spoke against God and against Moses, and said, "Why have you brought us up out of Egypt to die in the wilderness? There is no bread! There is no water! And we detest this miserable food!"

[6] Then the LORD sent venomous snakes among them; they bit the people and many Israelites died. [7] The people came to Moses and said, "We sinned when we spoke against the LORD and against you. Pray that the LORD will take the snakes away from us." So Moses prayed for the people.

[8] The LORD said to Moses, "Make a snake and put it up on a pole; anyone who is bitten can look at it and live." [9] So Moses made a bronze snake and put it up on a pole. Then when anyone was bitten by a snake and looked at the bronze snake, they lived.

---

[a] 2 The Hebrew term refers to the irrevocable giving over of things or persons to the LORD, often by totally destroying them; also in verse 3.   [b] 3 Hormah means destruction.   [c] 4 Or the Sea of Reeds

---

20:22–29 | The exact location of **Mount Hor** remains unknown. The text indicates that it is **near the border of Edom**. It was probably located northeast of Kadesh. This is where Aaron would die and **Eleazar** would succeed him as high priest, signified by the transfer of Aaron's **garments** onto his son (33:38; Ex. 29:29, 30; Deut. 32:50).
21:1–3 | While the Israelites had previously been defeated at **Hormah** (14:45), this time they were victorious, defeating **the king of Arad** after he attacked them. *Hormah* means "destruction," a fitting name because Israel **completely destroyed** the Canaanites who lived there. This victory is the first of many recorded in Numbers and serves as a foretaste of this new generation's readiness for battle.
21:4–9 | Jesus used the lens of OT experience to explain His death and the story of salvation to Nicodemus (John 3:14, 15). With the judgment of the **venomous snakes**, God provided a most unexpected remedy for sin (1 Cor. 10:9).

21:4–6 | Nothing is wrong with being discouraged, but being **impatient** can lead to something worse. The Israelites first murmured **against God and against Moses**, then they began to complain about everything, especially the **bread** (manna) from God, and this became outright rebellion. **Many . . . died** because of this faithless attitude.
21:7 | Moses became the people's mediator with God.
21:9 | The snake was a symbol of all that repelled the people of Israel. As such, the **bronze snake** atop a pole was a dramatic, horrific symbol. Yet only those who would look at it would live. The snake on the pole has the effect of Christ on the cross—visually horrible, but the only means of salvation (John 3:14, 15). Moses kept the bronze figure as a reminder of the people's sin and God's provision. Eventually, however, Hezekiah destroyed the serpent because the people had turned it into an idol (2 Kgs. 18:1–4).

Teaching Points   Finding Jesus in the Snake • 21:8, 9

It is astonishing to observe the comparisons between the bronze snake and Jesus—here in the Book of Numbers and in Christ's crucifixion:

- *Death comes as a punishment for sin.* In this passage, death was threatened as a punishment for speaking against God. At the cross, we know that if we do not have Christ, we are under the sentence of death for our sins.
- *God provides a remedy.* In the OT, it was a snake on a pole. In the NT, it was His Son on a post and crossbeam.
- *Those who looked at that which was lifted up were healed.*
- *The saving power was the result of faith, not works.*
- *The destiny of the individual was determined by their response.*
- *The remedy was made available to every person, without favoring any group over another.* For the venomous snakes in the Book of Numbers, God said through Moses to the entire camp, "Anyone who is bitten can look at it and live" (21:8). God has also said the same thing to all of us, that "whoever believes in him" will be saved (John 3:14–16).

The Journey to Moab

[10] The Israelites moved on and camped at Oboth. [11] Then they set out from Oboth and camped in Iye Abarim, in the wilderness that faces Moab toward the sunrise. [12] From there they moved on and camped in the Zered Valley. [13] They set out from there and camped alongside the Arnon, which is in the wilderness extending into Amorite territory. The Arnon is the border of Moab, between Moab and the Amorites. [14] That is why the Book of the Wars of the LORD says:

"... Zahab[a] in Suphah and the
     ravines,
the Arnon [15] and[b] the slopes of the
     ravines
that lead to the settlement of Ar
and lie along the border of Moab."

[16] From there they continued on to Beer, the well where the LORD said to Moses, "Gather the people together and I will give them water."
[17] Then Israel sang this song:

"Spring up, O well!
     Sing about it,
[18] about the well that the princes dug,
     that the nobles of the people sank—
     the nobles with scepters and staffs."

Then they went from the wilderness to Mattanah, [19] from Mattanah to Nahaliel, from Nahaliel to Bamoth, [20] and from Bamoth to the valley in Moab where the top of Pisgah overlooks the wasteland.

Defeat of Sihon and Og

[21] Israel sent messengers to say to Sihon king of the Amorites:

[22] "Let us pass through your country. We will not turn aside into any field or vineyard, or drink water from any well. We will travel along the King's Highway until we have passed through your territory."

[23] But Sihon would not let Israel pass through his territory. He mustered his entire army and marched out into the wilderness against Israel. When he reached Jahaz, he fought with Israel. [24] Israel, however, put him to the sword and took over his land from the Arnon to the Jabbok, but only as far as the Ammonites, because their border was fortified. [25] Israel captured all the cities of the Amorites and occupied them, including Heshbon and all its surrounding settlements. [26] Heshbon was the city of Sihon king of the Amorites, who had fought against the former king of Moab and had taken from him all his land as far as the Arnon.
[27] That is why the poets say:

"Come to Heshbon and let it be rebuilt;
     let Sihon's city be restored.

---

[a] 14 Septuagint; Hebrew Waheb   [b] 14,15 Or "I have been given from Suphah and the ravines / of the Arnon [15]to

---

21:16, 17 | This time, when the traveling Israelites needed water, they **continued on to Beer** (lit., "well") rather than complaining. They remembered God's promise to give them water and subsequently **sang** a **song** of praise (Ex. 15:1).
21:21–32 | Just as the Edomites had done, the **Amorites** refused

Israel's request for safe passage. The Amorite king, **Sihon**, then attacked Israel. Because the Amorites were not a brother nation as Edom was, the Israelites fought back and won. This was a just punishment for having taken land from the **king of Moab** (Deut. 2:26–37).

28 "Fire went out from Heshbon,
    a blaze from the city of Sihon.
It consumed Ar of Moab,
    the citizens of Arnon's heights.
29 Woe to you, Moab!
    You are destroyed, people of
        Chemosh!
He has given up his sons as fugitives
    and his daughters as captives
    to Sihon king of the Amorites.

30 "But we have overthrown them;
    Heshbon's dominion has been
        destroyed all the way to
            Dibon.
We have demolished them as far as
        Nophah,
    which extends to Medeba."

31 So Israel settled in the land of the Amorites.

32 After Moses had sent spies to Jazer, the Israelites captured its surrounding settlements and drove out the Amorites who were there. 33 Then they turned and went up along the road toward Bashan, and Og king of Bashan and his whole army marched out to meet them in battle at Edrei. 34 The LORD said to Moses, "Do not be afraid of him, for I have delivered him into your hands, along with his whole army and his land. Do to him what you did to Sihon king of the Amorites, who reigned in Heshbon." 35 So they struck him down, together with his sons and his whole army, leaving them no survivors. And they took possession of his land.

Balak Summons Balaam

22 Then the Israelites traveled to the plains of Moab and camped along the Jordan across from Jericho.

2 Now Balak son of Zippor saw all that Israel had done to the Amorites, 3 and Moab was terrified because there were so many people. Indeed, Moab was filled with dread because of the Israelites.

Historically Speaking | **Balaam • 22:5**

Balaam is mentioned in several Scripture texts as an example of a prophet for hire, a pagan diviner whose primary aim was personal gain (Deut. 23:4, 5; Josh. 13:22; 24:9, 10; Neh. 13:2; Micah 6:5; 2 Pet. 2:15; Jude 11; Rev. 2:14). In 1967, during an excavation of a temple in Deir Alla, Jordan, an inscription dating from c. 840–760 BC was found that preserves an oracle of Balaam, son of Beor. This is remarkable for two reasons: (1) It is the first mention found of Balaam from an ancient source outside of Scripture. (2) It demonstrates the importance of Balaam, for his messages were still being preserved centuries after his death.

No imagination is needed to see why Balak would have hired such a man to curse his enemies. But of course God will not be mocked, and the pagan diviner Balaam was subject to His sovereign control.

---

4 The Moabites said to the elders of Midian, "This horde is going to lick up everything around us, as an ox licks up the grass of the field."

So Balak son of Zippor, who was king of Moab at that time, 5 sent messengers to summon Balaam son of Beor, who was at Pethor, near the Euphrates River, in his native land. Balak said:

"A people has come out of Egypt; they cover the face of the land and have settled next to me. 6 Now come and put a curse on these people, because they are too powerful for me. Perhaps then I will be able to defeat them and drive them out of the land. For I know that whoever you bless is blessed, and whoever you curse is cursed."

7 The elders of Moab and Midian left, taking with them the fee for divination. When they came to Balaam, they told him what Balak had said. 8 "Spend the night here," Balaam said to them, "and I will report back to you with the

---

21:33–35 | In defeating **Og king of Bashan** and taking **possession of his land**, the Israelites continued to expand their territory. They now had control of the Transjordan from the Arnon River (the northern border of Moab) to Bashan and Gilead—from south to north. On today's maps, most of this territory lies in the modern country of Jordan, the region immediately east of the Jordan River. These victories gave the Israelites a fearsome reputation across the land (22:2, 3).

22:2–18 | Balak tried to purchase Balaam's prophetic ability, wanting him to pronounce a curse upon Israel. God's favor cannot be purchased; neither can His wrath be avoided with money. Others would learn these truths the hard way: Ananias and Sapphira (Acts 5:1–11) and Simon the sorcerer (Acts 8:9–24).

22:5, 6 | **Balaam son of Beor** was a pagan prophet who focused on animal divination, particularly the use of sheep liver, to seek the will of the gods (Rev. 2:14). All such divination practices were forbidden among the people of Israel (Lev. 19:26). Balaam was known internationally at the time, and his prophecies were celebrated by guilds of followers hundreds of years after his death.

22:7–20 | In the face of follow-up invitations and bribes from the king of Moab, **Balaam** sought **what else the LORD** might **tell** him, even though God had given him a definitive answer the first time (22:12). Fifteen centuries later, the apostle Peter precisely defined Balaam's character this way: he "loved the wages of wickedness" (2 Pet. 2:15; Jude 11).

answer the LORD gives me." So the Moabite officials stayed with him.

⁹God came to Balaam and asked, "Who are these men with you?"

¹⁰Balaam said to God, "Balak son of Zippor, king of Moab, sent me this message: ¹¹'A people that has come out of Egypt covers the face of the land. Now come and put a curse on them for me. Perhaps then I will be able to fight them and drive them away.' "

¹²But God said to Balaam, "Do not go with them. You must not put a curse on those people, because they are blessed."

¹³The next morning Balaam got up and said to Balak's officials, "Go back to your own country, for the LORD has refused to let me go with you."

¹⁴So the Moabite officials returned to Balak and said, "Balaam refused to come with us."

¹⁵Then Balak sent other officials, more numerous and more distinguished than the first. ¹⁶They came to Balaam and said:

"This is what Balak son of Zippor says: Do not let anything keep you from coming to me, ¹⁷because I will reward you handsomely and do whatever you say. Come and put a curse on these people for me."

¹⁸But Balaam answered them, "Even if Balak gave me all the silver and gold in his palace, I could not do anything great or small to go beyond the command of the LORD my God. ¹⁹Now spend the night here so that I can find out what else the LORD will tell me."

²⁰That night God came to Balaam and said, "Since these men have come to summon you, go with them, but do only what I tell you."

Balaam's Donkey

²¹Balaam got up in the morning, saddled his donkey and went with the Moabite officials. ²²But God was very angry when he went, and the angel of the LORD stood in the road to oppose him. Balaam was riding on his donkey, and his two servants were with him. ²³When the donkey saw the angel of the LORD standing in the road with a drawn sword in his hand, it turned off the road into a field. Balaam beat it to get it back on the road.

²⁴Then the angel of the LORD stood in a narrow path through the vineyards, with walls on both sides. ²⁵When the donkey saw the angel of the LORD, it pressed close to the wall, crushing Balaam's foot against it. So he beat the donkey again.

²⁶Then the angel of the LORD moved on ahead and stood in a narrow place where there was no room to turn, either to the right or to the left. ²⁷When the donkey saw the angel of the LORD, it lay down under Balaam, and he was angry and beat it with his staff. ²⁸Then the LORD opened the donkey's mouth, and it said to Balaam, "What have I done to you to make you beat me these three times?"

²⁹Balaam answered the donkey, "You have made a fool of me! If only I had a sword in my hand, I would kill you right now."

³⁰The donkey said to Balaam, "Am I not your own donkey, which you have always ridden, to this day? Have I been in the habit of doing this to you?"

"No," he said.

³¹Then the LORD opened Balaam's eyes, and he saw the angel of the LORD standing in the road with his sword drawn. So he bowed low and fell facedown.

³²The angel of the LORD asked him, "Why have you beaten your donkey these three times? I have come here to oppose you because your path is a reckless one before me.ᵃ ³³The donkey saw me and turned away from me these three times. If it had not turned away, I would certainly have killed you by now, but I would have spared it."

³⁴Balaam said to the angel of the LORD, "I have sinned. I did not realize you were standing in the road to oppose me. Now if you are displeased, I will go back."

ᵃ 32 The meaning of the Hebrew for this clause is uncertain.

22:22-27 | God was so angry with Balaam that He stationed Himself as the **angel of the LORD** in a narrow spot across the middle of the Moab road. This angel who **stood in the road to oppose** Balaam with **a drawn sword** is the same One who appeared to Moses in the burning bush (Ex. 3:2) and to Hagar in the wilderness (Gen. 16:7; 22:11, 15): a manifestation of God Himself—a preincarnate appearance of Jesus (Josh. 5:13–15).

22:28-35 | Once God opened the donkey's mouth and let it speak, Balaam's eyes were also opened to see God Himself—**the angel of the LORD.** Although the matter is of the utmost seriousness, there is humor in all of this. Balaam was the most noted "seer" (diviner) of his day; the donkey is the most proverbially "stupid" of beasts. Yet the dumb donkey saw the Lord, whom Balaam could not see on his own (2 Pet. 2:14–16).

22:31 | Like Abraham (Gen. 17:3), Joshua (Josh. 5:14) and others, Balaam **bowed low and fell facedown** when he saw **the angel of the LORD.** The sadness in this is that Balaam never shared the faith of Abraham or Joshua. One day, every creature will bow before Jesus (Phil. 2:10), but not all will do so because of personal faith.

³⁵The angel of the LORD said to Balaam, "Go with the men, but speak only what I tell you." So Balaam went with Balak's officials.

³⁶When Balak heard that Balaam was coming, he went out to meet him at the Moabite town on the Arnon border, at the edge of his territory. ³⁷Balak said to Balaam, "Did I not send you an urgent summons? Why didn't you come to me? Am I really not able to reward you?"

³⁸"Well, I have come to you now," Balaam replied. "But I can't say whatever I please. I must speak only what God puts in my mouth."

³⁹Then Balaam went with Balak to Kiriath Huzoth. ⁴⁰Balak sacrificed cattle and sheep, and gave some to Balaam and the officials who were with him. ⁴¹The next morning Balak took Balaam up to Bamoth Baal, and from there he could see the outskirts of the Israelite camp.

Balaam's First Message

23 Balaam said, "Build me seven altars here, and prepare seven bulls and seven rams for me." ²Balak did as Balaam said, and the two of them offered a bull and a ram on each altar.

³Then Balaam said to Balak, "Stay here beside your offering while I go aside. Perhaps the LORD will come to meet with me. Whatever he reveals to me I will tell you." Then he went off to a barren height.

⁴God met with him, and Balaam said, "I have prepared seven altars, and on each altar I have offered a bull and a ram."

⁵The LORD put a word in Balaam's mouth and said, "Go back to Balak and give him this word."

⁶So he went back to him and found him standing beside his offering, with all the Moabite officials. ⁷Then Balaam spoke his message:

"Balak brought me from Aram,
    the king of Moab from the eastern
        mountains.
'Come,' he said, 'curse Jacob for me;
    come, denounce Israel.'

⁸How can I curse
    those whom God has not cursed?
How can I denounce
    those whom the LORD has not
        denounced?
⁹From the rocky peaks I see them,
    from the heights I view them.
I see a people who live apart
    and do not consider themselves one
        of the nations.
¹⁰Who can count the dust of Jacob
    or number even a fourth of Israel?
Let me die the death of the righteous,
    and may my final end be like theirs!"

¹¹Balak said to Balaam, "What have you done to me? I brought you to curse my enemies, but you have done nothing but bless them!"

¹²He answered, "Must I not speak what the LORD puts in my mouth?"

Balaam's Second Message

¹³Then Balak said to him, "Come with me to another place where you can see them; you will not see them all but only the outskirts of their camp. And from there, curse them for me." ¹⁴So he took him to the field of Zophim on the top of Pisgah, and there he built seven altars and offered a bull and a ram on each altar.

¹⁵Balaam said to Balak, "Stay here beside your offering while I meet with him over there."

¹⁶The LORD met with Balaam and put a word in his mouth and said, "Go back to Balak and give him this word."

¹⁷So he went to him and found him standing beside his offering, with the Moabite officials. Balak asked him, "What did the LORD say?"

¹⁸Then he spoke his message:

"Arise, Balak, and listen;
    hear me, son of Zippor.
¹⁹God is not human, that he should lie,
    not a human being, that he should
        change his mind.
Does he speak and then not act?
    Does he promise and not fulfill?

22:41—23:12 | Instead of calling down a curse upon Israel as King **Balak** requested, Balaam's first **message**, or prophecy, from God (23:7–10) did **nothing but bless them**. As such, Israel could not be cursed by God. When the blessings of God are solidly in place, no power can change them (23:20).
23:5–12 | That Israel did **not consider themselves one of the nations** means they were a distinct people, and again, neither **Balaam** nor his prophecies had any power over them. In each of these messages, Yahweh spoke through the pagan prophet—an

amazing demonstration of the Lord's will and power (23:5, 12).
23:13–26 | The change in venue did not change the outcome: Balaam's second message (23:18–24) again emphasized that Israel was **blessed**, noting that God had brought Israel out of Egypt and that Balaam's usual **divination** or **evil omens** could not thwart their prosperity. The Lord's blessings on the Hebrew people from Abraham onward are irrevocable (23:8, 20; Gen. 12:2, 3; 15:12–21; 22:15–18). His promises to His people today are also unchangeable (Heb. 6:13–20).

²⁰I have received a command to bless;
   he has blessed, and I cannot
      change it.

²¹ "No misfortune is seen in Jacob,
   no misery observed[a] in Israel.
The LORD their God is with them;
   the shout of the King is among them.
²²God brought them out of Egypt;
   they have the strength of a wild ox.
²³There is no divination against[b] Jacob,
   no evil omens against[b] Israel.
It will now be said of Jacob
   and of Israel, 'See what God has
      done!'
²⁴The people rise like a lioness;
   they rouse themselves like a lion
that does not rest till it devours its prey
   and drinks the blood of its victims."

²⁵Then Balak said to Balaam, "Neither curse them at all nor bless them at all!" ²⁶Balaam answered, "Did I not tell you I must do whatever the LORD says?"

Balaam's Third Message

²⁷Then Balak said to Balaam, "Come, let me take you to another place. Perhaps it will please God to let you curse them for me from there." ²⁸And Balak took Balaam to the top of Peor, overlooking the wasteland.

²⁹Balaam said, "Build me seven altars here, and prepare seven bulls and seven rams for me." ³⁰Balak did as Balaam had said, and offered a bull and a ram on each altar.

24 Now when Balaam saw that it pleased the LORD to bless Israel, he did not resort to divination as at other times, but turned his face toward the wilderness. ²When Balaam looked out and saw Israel encamped tribe by tribe, the Spirit of God came on him ³and he spoke his message:

"The prophecy of Balaam son of Beor,
   the prophecy of one whose eye sees
      clearly,
⁴the prophecy of one who hears the
      words of God,
who sees a vision from the
      Almighty,[c]
who falls prostrate, and whose eyes
      are opened:

⁵ "How beautiful are your tents, Jacob,
   your dwelling places, Israel!

⁶ "Like valleys they spread out,
   like gardens beside a river,
like aloes planted by the LORD,
   like cedars beside the waters.
⁷Water will flow from their buckets;
   their seed will have abundant water.

"Their king will be greater than Agag;
   their kingdom will be exalted.

⁸ "God brought them out of Egypt;
   they have the strength of a wild ox.
They devour hostile nations
   and break their bones in pieces;
   with their arrows they pierce them.
⁹Like a lion they crouch and lie down,
   like a lioness—who dares to rouse
      them?

"May those who bless you be blessed
   and those who curse you be cursed!"

¹⁰Then Balak's anger burned against Balaam. He struck his hands together and said to him, "I summoned you to curse my enemies, but you have blessed them these three times. ¹¹Now leave at once and go home! I said I would reward you handsomely, but the LORD has kept you from being rewarded."

¹²Balaam answered Balak, "Did I not tell the messengers you sent me, ¹³'Even if Balak gave me all the silver and gold in his palace, I could not do anything of my own accord, good or bad, to go beyond the command of the LORD—and I must say only what the LORD says'? ¹⁴Now I am going back to my people, but come, let me warn you of what this people will do to your people in days to come."

Balaam's Fourth Message

¹⁵Then he spoke his message:

"The prophecy of Balaam son of Beor,
   the prophecy of one whose eye sees
      clearly,

---

[a] 21 Or He has not looked on Jacob's offenses / or on the wrongs found   [b] 23 Or in
[c] 4 Hebrew Shaddai; also in verse 16

23:21 | This is the first time in the OT that Yahweh is described as **King**. **23:27—24:2** | It did not matter where Balaam was when God was about to speak through him. From **the top of Peor**, Balaam began with pagan acts of worship, but then he abandoned them and **the Spirit of God came on him**. This was a most remarkable thing, considering that Balaam was not a man of true faith. The word of God is truth no matter how, or through whom, it is delivered!

24:15-24 | Balaam's fourth **message** spoke in more detail about the king (**scepter**) who was introduced in the third message (24:3-9): He was **not now** and **not near** but would come someday as a **ruler** over Moab and Edom (**the people of Sheth**). The other nations and peoples mentioned in Balaam's final three messages would face defeat: the Amalekites (**Amalek**), Kenites (Midianites), Assyrians (**Ashur**), and people of **Cyprus**.

[16]the prophecy of one who hears the
    words of God,
who has knowledge from the Most
    High,
who sees a vision from the Almighty,
    who falls prostrate, and whose eyes
    are opened:

[17] "I see him, but not now;
    I behold him, but not near.
A star will come out of Jacob;
    a scepter will rise out of Israel.
He will crush the foreheads of Moab,
    the skulls[a] of[b] all the people of Sheth.[c]
[18]Edom will be conquered;
    Seir, his enemy, will be conquered,
    but Israel will grow strong.
[19]A ruler will come out of Jacob
    and destroy the survivors of the city."

Balaam's Fifth Message
[20]Then Balaam saw Amalek and spoke
his message:

    "Amalek was first among the nations,
        but their end will be utter
           destruction."

Balaam's Sixth Message
[21]Then he saw the Kenites and spoke his
message:

    "Your dwelling place is secure,
        your nest is set in a rock;
[22]yet you Kenites will be destroyed
        when Ashur takes you captive."

Balaam's Seventh Message
[23]Then he spoke his message:

    "Alas! Who can live when God does
        this?[d]
[24]   Ships will come from the shores of
        Cyprus;
    they will subdue Ashur and Eber,
    but they too will come to ruin."

[25]Then Balaam got up and returned home,
and Balak went his own way.

Moab Seduces Israel
25 While Israel was staying in Shittim, the men began to indulge in sexual immorality with Moabite women, [2]who invited them to the sacrifices to their gods. The people ate the sacrificial meal and bowed down before these gods. [3]So Israel yoked themselves to the Baal of Peor. And the LORD's anger burned against them.

[4]The LORD said to Moses, "Take all the leaders of these people, kill them and expose them in broad daylight before the LORD, so that the LORD's fierce anger may turn away from Israel."

[5]So Moses said to Israel's judges, "Each of you must put to death those of your people who have yoked themselves to the Baal of Peor."

[6]Then an Israelite man brought into the camp a Midianite woman right before the eyes of Moses and the whole assembly of Israel while they were weeping at the entrance to the tent of meeting. [7]When Phinehas son of Eleazar, the son of Aaron, the priest, saw this, he left the assembly, took a spear in his hand [8]and followed the Israelite into the tent. He drove the spear into both of them, right through the Israelite man and into the woman's stomach. Then the plague against the Israelites was stopped; [9]but those who died in the plague numbered 24,000.

[10]The LORD said to Moses, [11]"Phinehas son of Eleazar, the son of Aaron, the priest, has turned my anger away from the Israelites. Since he was as zealous for my honor among them as I am, I did not put an end to them in my zeal. [12]Therefore tell him I am making my covenant of peace with him. [13]He and his descendants will have a covenant of a lasting priesthood, because he was zealous for the honor of his God and made atonement for the Israelites."

[14]The name of the Israelite who was killed with the Midianite woman was Zimri son of Salu, the leader of a Simeonite family. [15]And

---

[a] 17 Samaritan Pentateuch (see also Jer. 48:45); the meaning of the word in the Masoretic Text is uncertain.   [b] 17 Or possibly Moab, / batter   [c] 17 Or all the noisy boasters   [d] 23 Masoretic Text; with a different word division of the Hebrew The people from the islands will gather from the north.

24:17 | The Magi mentioned in Matthew 2 were likely Medes from the Mesopotamian region where Jews had lived in exile for 70 years. As scholars, they were no doubt familiar with and watching for fulfillment of this prophecy: **A star** (the Messiah) **will come out of Jacob; a scepter** (king) **will rise out of Israel**.
24:24 | **Eber** is another name for Israel (Gen. 10:21).
25:1-9 | The wicked **Moabite women** seduced Israelite men into immorality and idolatry, costing 24,000 people their lives. Moabites were so evil in the eyes of God that they were among the few people He said could never be admitted into the whole assembly of Israel.

The instigator of this sad situation was Balaam (31:16; Rev. 2:14).
25:3 | **Yoked** means "joined." This was not just participation in idolatry but unrestrained betrayal of the Lord that would have impact for generations to come (Ps. 106:28, 29).
25:7–13 | **Phinehas**, the grandson of Aaron, was **zealous for** God's **honor** and thrust a spear through the bodies of a couple engaged in immorality. This stopped the **plague**, but not before thousands of people died, punished for their immorality and idolatry (Ps. 106:30). Because of his action, Phinehas was promised a **lasting priesthood**.

Picture This
What was at stake at Baal of Peor? • 25—31

The "LORD's fierce anger" (25:4) demonstrates that this story does not describe a small offense. The plans of Balak and Balaam to destroy the people of Israel by means of the power of a curse (22—24) led to a new strategy. What Baalam could not incite by word, he was able to do in a more subtle manner (31:16), by persuading Moabite and Midianite women to seduce many Hebrew men not only to sexual acts but to the worship of the god Baal in ritual prostitution. In the mass frenzy, a Hebrew man and a Moabite woman were actually having sexual relations at the fabric door of the sacred place of the tabernacle. A righteous priest, Phinehas—incensed at the outrage—grabbed a javelin and thrust the weapon through both bodies. God honored Phinehas' zeal for Him with a covenantal promise that his family would be the principal line of God's priests.

Sexually charged acts in the worship of pagan gods were not momentary aberrations; in the subsequent history of Israel, these actions would recur—and would finally be their downfall.

the name of the Midianite woman who was put to death was Kozbi daughter of Zur, a tribal chief of a Midianite family.

¹⁶The LORD said to Moses, ¹⁷ "Treat the Midianites as enemies and kill them. ¹⁸They treated you as enemies when they deceived you in the Peor incident involving their sister Kozbi, the daughter of a Midianite leader, the woman who was killed when the plague came as a result of that incident."

The Second Census

26 After the plague the LORD said to Moses and Eleazar son of Aaron, the priest, ² "Take a census of the whole Israelite community by families—all those twenty years old or more who are able to serve in the army of Israel." ³So on the plains of Moab by the Jordan across from Jericho, Moses and Eleazar the priest spoke with them and said, ⁴ "Take a census of the men twenty years old or more, as the LORD commanded Moses."

These were the Israelites who came out of Egypt:

⁵The descendants of Reuben, the firstborn son of Israel, were:

through Hanok, the Hanokite clan;
through Pallu, the Palluite clan;
⁶through Hezron, the Hezronite clan;
through Karmi, the Karmite clan.

⁷These were the clans of Reuben; those numbered were 43,730.

⁸The son of Pallu was Eliab, ⁹and the sons of Eliab were Nemuel, Dathan and Abiram. The same Dathan and Abiram were the community officials who rebelled against Moses and Aaron and were among Korah's followers when they rebelled against the LORD. ¹⁰The earth opened its mouth and swallowed them along with Korah, whose followers died when the fire devoured the 250 men. And they served as a warning sign. ¹¹The line of Korah, however, did not die out.

¹²The descendants of Simeon by their clans were:

through Nemuel, the Nemuelite clan;
through Jamin, the Jaminite clan;
through Jakin, the Jakinite clan;
¹³through Zerah, the Zerahite clan;
through Shaul, the Shaulite clan.

¹⁴These were the clans of Simeon; those numbered were 22,200.

¹⁵The descendants of Gad by their clans were:

through Zephon, the Zephonite clan;
through Haggi, the Haggite clan;
through Shuni, the Shunite clan;
¹⁶through Ozni, the Oznite clan;
through Eri, the Erite clan;
¹⁷through Arodi,^a the Arodite clan;
through Areli, the Arelite clan.

¹⁸These were the clans of Gad; those numbered were 40,500.

¹⁹Er and Onan were sons of Judah, but they died in Canaan.
²⁰The descendants of Judah by their clans were:

through Shelah, the Shelanite clan;
through Perez, the Perezite clan;
through Zerah, the Zerahite clan.

---

^a 17 Samaritan Pentateuch and Syriac (see also Gen. 46:16); Masoretic Text *Arod*

25:14–18 | Balaam was involved in this further attempt to deceive Israel, as reported in Revelation 2:14: "Balaam . . . taught Balak to entice the Israelites to sin so that they ate food sacrificed to idols and committed sexual immorality." What Balaam and Balak could not do to Israel by divination, they tried to accomplish by deception. Because of this, the **Midianites** would be punished (31:1–24).

26:1, 2 | The Lord commanded that a new **census** be taken, because the first census (1:1–46) numbered the rebellious generation that had died in the wilderness. In counting the men of Israel who were **able to serve in the army**, this census prepared the nation for their conquest of Canaan.

21 The descendants of Perez were:
   through Hezron, the Hezronite clan;
   through Hamul, the Hamulite clan.
22 These were the clans of Judah; those numbered were 76,500.

23 The descendants of Issachar by their clans were:
   through Tola, the Tolaite clan;
   through Puah, the Puite[a] clan;
24 through Jashub, the Jashubite clan;
   through Shimron, the Shimronite clan.
25 These were the clans of Issachar; those numbered were 64,300.

26 The descendants of Zebulun by their clans were:
   through Sered, the Seredite clan;
   through Elon, the Elonite clan;
   through Jahleel, the Jahleelite clan.
27 These were the clans of Zebulun; those numbered were 60,500.

28 The descendants of Joseph by their clans through Manasseh and Ephraim were:

29 The descendants of Manasseh:
   through Makir, the Makirite clan (Makir was the father of Gilead);
   through Gilead, the Gileadite clan.
30 These were the descendants of Gilead:
   through Iezer, the Iezerite clan;
   through Helek, the Helekite clan;
   31 through Asriel, the Asrielite clan;
   through Shechem, the Shechemite clan;
   32 through Shemida, the Shemidaite clan;
   through Hepher, the Hepherite clan.
33 (Zelophehad son of Hepher had no sons; he had only daughters, whose names were Mahlah, Noah, Hoglah, Milkah and Tirzah.)
34 These were the clans of Manasseh; those numbered were 52,700.

35 These were the descendants of Ephraim by their clans:
   through Shuthelah, the Shuthelahite clan;
   through Beker, the Bekerite clan;
   through Tahan, the Tahanite clan.
36 These were the descendants of Shuthelah:
   through Eran, the Eranite clan.

37 These were the clans of Ephraim; those numbered were 32,500.

These were the descendants of Joseph by their clans.

38 The descendants of Benjamin by their clans were:
   through Bela, the Belaite clan;
   through Ashbel, the Ashbelite clan;
   through Ahiram, the Ahiramite clan;
   39 through Shupham,[b] the Shuphamite clan;
   through Hupham, the Huphamite clan.
40 The descendants of Bela through Ard and Naaman were:
   through Ard,[c] the Ardite clan;
   through Naaman, the Naamite clan.
41 These were the clans of Benjamin; those numbered were 45,600.

42 These were the descendants of Dan by their clans:
   through Shuham, the Shuhamite clan.
These were the clans of Dan: 43 All of them were Shuhamite clans; and those numbered were 64,400.

44 The descendants of Asher by their clans were:
   through Imnah, the Imnite clan;
   through Ishvi, the Ishvite clan;
   through Beriah, the Beriite clan;
45 and through the descendants of Beriah:
   through Heber, the Heberite clan;
   through Malkiel, the Malkielite clan.
46 (Asher had a daughter named Serah.)
47 These were the clans of Asher; those numbered were 53,400.

48 The descendants of Naphtali by their clans were:
   through Jahzeel, the Jahzeelite clan;
   through Guni, the Gunite clan;
   49 through Jezer, the Jezerite clan;
   through Shillem, the Shillemite clan.
50 These were the clans of Naphtali; those numbered were 45,400.

51 The total number of the men of Israel was 601,730.

---

[a] 23 Samaritan Pentateuch, Septuagint, Vulgate and Syriac (see also 1 Chron. 7:1); Masoretic Text *through Puvah, the Punite*   [b] 39 A few manuscripts of the Masoretic Text, Samaritan Pentateuch, Vulgate and Syriac (see also Septuagint); most manuscripts of the Masoretic Text *Shephupham*   [c] 40 Samaritan Pentateuch and Vulgate (see also Septuagint); Masoretic Text does not have *through Ard.*

26:5–14 | Both the tribes of **Reuben** and **Simeon** had declined in numbers between the first and second censuses (1:20–23). **Dathan and Abiram** in Korah's rebellions may have accounted for Reuben's loss. Simeon's loss was greater, having been singled out for its sinful actions at the site of Baal of Peor (25:14).
26:33 | The remark about **Zelophehad** only having daughters would factor into the laws of inheritance developed in 27:1–11 and 36:1–12.

⁵²The Lord said to Moses, ⁵³ "The land is to be allotted to them as an inheritance based on the number of names. ⁵⁴To a larger group give a larger inheritance, and to a smaller group a smaller one; each is to receive its inheritance according to the number of those listed. ⁵⁵Be sure that the land is distributed by lot. What each group inherits will be according to the names for its ancestral tribe. ⁵⁶Each inheritance is to be distributed by lot among the larger and smaller groups."

⁵⁷These were the Levites who were counted by their clans:

through Gershon, the Gershonite clan;
through Kohath, the Kohathite clan;
through Merari, the Merarite clan.
⁵⁸These also were Levite clans:
the Libnite clan,
the Hebronite clan,
the Mahlite clan,
the Mushite clan,
the Korahite clan.

(Kohath was the forefather of Amram; ⁵⁹the name of Amram's wife was Jochebed, a descendant of Levi, who was born to the Levites[a] in Egypt. To Amram she bore Aaron, Moses and their sister Miriam. ⁶⁰Aaron was the father of Nadab and Abihu, Eleazar and Ithamar. ⁶¹But Nadab and Abihu died when they made an offering before the Lord with unauthorized fire.)

⁶²All the male Levites a month old or more numbered 23,000. They were not counted along with the other Israelites because they received no inheritance among them.

⁶³These are the ones counted by Moses and Eleazar the priest when they counted the Israelites on the plains of Moab by the Jordan across from Jericho. ⁶⁴Not one of them was among those counted by Moses and Aaron the priest when they counted the Israelites in the Desert of Sinai. ⁶⁵For the Lord had told those Israelites they would surely die in the wilderness, and not one of them was left except Caleb son of Jephunneh and Joshua son of Nun.

Zelophehad's Daughters

27 The daughters of Zelophehad son of Hepher, the son of Gilead, the son of Makir, the son of Manasseh, belonged to the clans of Manasseh son of Joseph. The names of the daughters were Mahlah, Noah, Hoglah, Milkah and Tirzah. They came forward ²and stood before Moses, Eleazar the priest, the leaders and the whole assembly at the entrance to the tent of meeting and said, ³"Our father died in the wilderness. He was not among Korah's followers, who banded together against the Lord, but he died for his own sin and left no sons. ⁴Why should our father's name disappear from his clan because he had no son? Give us property among our father's relatives."

⁵So Moses brought their case before the Lord, ⁶and the Lord said to him, ⁷"What Zelophehad's daughters are saying is right. You must certainly give them property as an inheritance among their father's relatives and give their father's inheritance to them.

⁸"Say to the Israelites, 'If a man dies and leaves no son, give his inheritance to his daughter. ⁹If he has no daughter, give his inheritance to his brothers. ¹⁰If he has no brothers, give his inheritance to his father's brothers. ¹¹If his father had no brothers, give his inheritance to the nearest relative in his clan, that he may possess it. This is to have the force of law for the Israelites, as the Lord commanded Moses.' "

Joshua to Succeed Moses

¹²Then the Lord said to Moses, "Go up this mountain in the Abarim Range and see

---

[a] 59 Or Jochebed, a daughter of Levi, who was born to Levi

26:51 | The total net loss between the first and second census (603,550 versus 601,730) was a little less than 2,000 (1:46). Such a small decline is somewhat surprising in light of the numerous failures of the people in the wilderness. Despite their sin, God kept His promise to preserve the nation.
26:52–56 | In addition to preparing the people to serve in the army, the census also served to help determine how **the land** would be **allotted** once Israel entered Canaan. Each tribe would receive an amount of land in proportion to their **number** (population). While size would determine the amount of land, the locations would be determined **by lot**.
26:57–62 | As in the first census (3:14–39), this census of the **Levites** was done separately because they were to serve the tabernacle, not serve in the army or receive an inheritance. The number of Israelites eligible to serve in the army had decreased, but the (rounded) number of Levites had increased, from 22,000 (3:39) to 23,000.

26:63–65 | This summary section is enormously important. None of the first generation enumerated in the census of chapters 1–3 was included in this census, except for **Caleb** and **Joshua**. The rest had died.
27:1–11 | Since he had **no sons**, no inheritance would go to the household of **Zelophehad**, and his name in the family line would end (**disappear**). The Lord declared to Moses that the petition of Zelophehad's five daughters was **right**: they should receive their father's inheritance (**property**). This prompted special provisions for such situations. This revelation from Yahweh to Moses would have come through Eleazar the priest, by way of the Urim and Thummim (see note on 27:21).
27:12–20 | Upon Moses' request that Israel not be left **like sheep without a shepherd**, God appointed **Joshua** to be the nation's next leader and gave him some of Moses' **authority**.

the land I have given the Israelites. [13] After you have seen it, you too will be gathered to your people, as your brother Aaron was, [14] for when the community rebelled at the waters in the Desert of Zin, both of you disobeyed my command to honor me as holy before their eyes." (These were the waters of Meribah Kadesh, in the Desert of Zin.)

[15] Moses said to the LORD, [16] "May the LORD, the God who gives breath to all living things, appoint someone over this community [17] to go out and come in before them, one who will lead them out and bring them in, so the LORD's people will not be like sheep without a shepherd."

[18] So the LORD said to Moses, "Take Joshua son of Nun, a man in whom is the spirit of leadership,[a] and lay your hand on him. [19] Have him stand before Eleazar the priest and the entire assembly and commission him in their presence. [20] Give him some of your authority so the whole Israelite community will obey him. [21] He is to stand before Eleazar the priest, who will obtain decisions for him by inquiring of the Urim before the LORD. At his command he and the entire community of the Israelites will go out, and at his command they will come in."

[22] Moses did as the LORD commanded him. He took Joshua and had him stand before Eleazar the priest and the whole assembly. [23] Then he laid his hands on him and commissioned him, as the LORD instructed through Moses.

Daily Offerings

28 The LORD said to Moses, [2] "Give this command to the Israelites and say to them: 'Make sure that you present to me at the appointed time my food offerings, as an aroma pleasing to me.' [3] Say to them: 'This is the food offering you are to present to the LORD: two lambs a year old without defect, as a regular burnt offering each day. [4] Offer one lamb in the morning and the other at twilight, [5] together with a grain offering of a tenth of an ephah[b] of the finest flour mixed with a quarter of a hin[c] of oil from pressed olives. [6] This is the regular burnt offering instituted at Mount Sinai as a pleasing aroma, a food offering presented to the LORD. [7] The accompanying drink offering is to be a quarter of a hin of fermented drink with each lamb. Pour out the drink offering to the LORD at the sanctuary. [8] Offer the second

lamb at twilight, along with the same kind of grain offering and drink offering that you offer in the morning. This is a food offering, an aroma pleasing to the LORD.

Sabbath Offerings

[9] " 'On the Sabbath day, make an offering of two lambs a year old without defect, together with its drink offering and a grain offering of two-tenths of an ephah[d] of the finest flour mixed with olive oil. [10] This is the burnt offering for every Sabbath, in addition to the regular burnt offering and its drink offering.

Monthly Offerings

[11] " 'On the first of every month, present to the LORD a burnt offering of two young bulls, one ram and seven male lambs a year old, all without defect. [12] With each bull there is to be a grain offering of three-tenths of an ephah[e] of the finest flour mixed with oil; with the ram, a grain offering of two-tenths of an ephah of the finest flour mixed with oil; [13] and with each lamb, a grain offering of a tenth of an ephah of the finest flour mixed with oil. This is for a burnt offering, a pleasing aroma, a food offering presented to the LORD. [14] With each bull there is to be a drink offering of half a hin[f] of wine; with the ram, a third of a hin[g]; and with each lamb, a quarter of a hin. This is the monthly burnt offering to be made at each new moon during the year. [15] Besides the regular burnt offering with its drink offering, one male goat is to be presented to the LORD as a sin offering.[h]

The Passover

[16] " 'On the fourteenth day of the first month the LORD's Passover is to be held. [17] On the fifteenth day of this month there is to be a festival; for seven days eat bread made without yeast. [18] On the first day hold a sacred assembly and do no regular work. [19] Present to the LORD a food offering consisting of a burnt offering of two young bulls, one ram and seven male lambs a year old, all without defect. [20] With each bull offer a grain offering of three-tenths of an ephah of the finest flour mixed with oil; with the

---

[a] 18 Or the Spirit   [b] 5 That is, probably about 3 1/2 pounds or about 1.6 kilograms; also in verses 13, 21 and 29   [c] 5 That is, about 1 quart or about 1 liter; also in verses 7 and 14   [d] 9 That is, probably about 7 pounds or about 3.2 kilograms; also in verses 12, 20 and 28   [e] 12 That is, probably about 11 pounds or about 5 kilograms; also in verses 20 and 28   [f] 14 That is, about 2 quarts or about 1.9 liters   [g] 14 That is, about 1 1/3 quarts or about 1.3 liters   [h] 15 Or purification offering; also in verse 22

27:21 | God spoke to Moses "face to face" (12:8), but often Moses received divine revelation through Aaron the high priest that would then be confirmed by the **Urim** and the **Thummim** (see sidebar on Ex. 28:30). In a similar manner, **Eleazar the priest** would be a mediator for Joshua (Lev. 8:8).

From the opening pages of Genesis to the final chapters of Revelation, there is a red thread of redemption running through the Bible—blood, the image of sacrifice (Heb. 9:22), and red, the color of blood. Generation after generation, God used the sacrifice of innocent animals to foreshadow the ultimate sacrifice for sin that would come, the death of Jesus Christ, God's own Son.

When Adam and Eve first rebelled against God's command, it was necessary for one of two things to happen: either sinners needed to forfeit their lives to pay for their sins, or a sacrifice would have to be made in their place. For Adam and Eve, innocent animals were slain by the Lord to provide clothing to cover their shame—a powerful symbol of the Lord's grace (Gen. 3:21). Throughout the OT, this pattern of sacrifice continued in daily offerings, Sabbath offerings, monthly offerings, and offerings at festivals (28—29). And through the centuries, countless innocent animals were sacrificed to forestall the judgment of God upon the guilty.

Various sacrifices were offered for various reasons throughout the religious year, but their culmination was in (our) September/October: *Yom Kippur*, the Day of Atonement (29:7–11; Lev. 16; 23:26–32). On that day—one day out of every year—two goats were identified as the bearers of the sins of the people. One (called "the scapegoat") was driven into the wilderness—a brilliant symbol of the sins of the people being carried away because of the grace of the Lord. The second goat was slain. Then the high priest went into the Most Holy Place to portray a parallel act of God's grace in dealing with the sins of the nation. The high priest would sprinkle blood from the second goat over the atonement cover on the ark of the covenant, which contained the stone tablets of the covenant laws the people had broken. Thus, the sins of the people were "covered" for another year.

These OT sacrifices foreshadowed the death and resurrection of Jesus. They could never take away sins; they could only cover them (Heb. 10:4)—hiding them, as it were, from God's sight. The need for a permanent, perfect, once-for-all sacrifice still existed. This sacrifice would transfer the perfection of the One being sacrificed (Jesus) to imperfect sinners (us), and the sinners' imperfections would fall upon the perfect sacrifice. Only by such an exchange could God's wrath against sin be satisfied and turned away: "The blood of goats and bulls and the ashes of a heifer sprinkled on those who are ceremonially unclean sanctify them so that they are outwardly clean. How much more, then, will the blood of Christ, who through the eternal Spirit offered himself unblemished to God, cleanse our consciences from acts that lead to death, so that we may serve the living God!" (Heb. 9:13, 14).

This is the gospel! It is why Jesus Christ died: "to present you holy in [God's] sight, without blemish and free from accusation" (Col. 1:22). The reasons we may be "without blemish" are that God "forgave us all our sins" and "canceled the charge of our legal indebtedness . . . [by] nailing it to the cross" (Col. 2:13, 14).

But if the story ends here, we have a significant problem. The death of Christ that took away our sins also took away our life . . . if He remained in the grave. And what good is freedom from sin if we have no life by which to express that freedom?

Christ came into the world to "destroy the devil's work" (1 John 3:8). His death conquered death. And on that glorious morning when the stone covering the tomb was rolled away, Christ destroyed the ultimate work of the devil by not only conquering sin (freeing every believer from Satan's accusations) but by conquering death—restoring to us the gift of life, *free from the guilt of sin and free to pursue righteousness*. Christ was crucified "for our sins and was raised to life for our justification" (Rom. 4:25) so we could live a justified life (as in, just-as-if-I'd never sinned).

Christ was raised from the dead as the "firstfruits of those who have fallen asleep" (1 Cor. 15:20). All who die in Christ will follow Christ in resurrection to new life, both spiritually (Rom. 6:4) and physically at the end of the age (1 Cor. 15:50–57; 1 Thess. 4:16).

For Further Reading: Lev. 1:1–9; 9:1–9; Ps. 16:10; Matt. 27–28; Rom. 6:8–11; 1 Cor. 15:12–14; 1 Pet. 1:17–20

ram, two-tenths; [21] and with each of the seven lambs, one-tenth. [22] Include one male goat as a sin offering to make atonement for you. [23] Offer these in addition to the regular morning burnt offering. [24] In this way present the food offering every day for seven days as an aroma pleasing to the LORD; it is to be offered in addition to the regular burnt offering and its drink offering. [25] On the seventh day hold a sacred assembly and do no regular work.

The Festival of Weeks

[26] " 'On the day of firstfruits, when you present to the LORD an offering of new grain during the Festival of Weeks, hold a sacred assembly and do no regular work. [27] Present a burnt offering of two young bulls, one ram and seven male lambs a year old as an aroma pleasing to the LORD. [28] With each bull there is to be a grain offering of three-tenths of an ephah of the finest flour mixed with oil; with the ram, two-tenths; [29] and with each of the seven lambs, one-tenth. [30] Include one male goat to make atonement for you. [31] Offer these together with their drink offerings, in addition to the regular burnt offering and its grain offering. Be sure the animals are without defect.

The Festival of Trumpets

29 " 'On the first day of the seventh month hold a sacred assembly and do no regular work. It is a day for you to sound the trumpets. [2] As an aroma pleasing to the LORD, offer a burnt offering of one young bull, one ram and seven male lambs a year old, all without defect. [3] With the bull offer a grain offering of three-tenths of an ephah[a] of the finest flour mixed with olive oil; with the ram, two-tenths[b]; [4] and with each of the seven lambs, one-tenth.[c] [5] Include one male goat as a sin offering[d] to make atonement for you. [6] These are in addition to the monthly and daily burnt offerings with their grain offerings and drink offerings as specified. They are food offerings presented to the LORD, a pleasing aroma.

The Day of Atonement

[7] " 'On the tenth day of this seventh month hold a sacred assembly. You must deny yourselves[e] and do no work. [8] Present as an

aroma pleasing to the LORD a burnt offering of one young bull, one ram and seven male lambs a year old, all without defect. [9] With the bull offer a grain offering of three-tenths of an ephah of the finest flour mixed with oil; with the ram, two-tenths; [10] and with each of the seven lambs, one-tenth. [11] Include one male goat as a sin offering, in addition to the sin offering for atonement and the regular burnt offering with its grain offering, and their drink offerings.

The Festival of Tabernacles

[12] " 'On the fifteenth day of the seventh month, hold a sacred assembly and do no regular work. Celebrate a festival to the LORD for seven days. [13] Present as an aroma pleasing to the LORD a food offering consisting of a burnt offering of thirteen young bulls, two rams and fourteen male lambs a year old, all without defect. [14] With each of the thirteen bulls offer a grain offering of three-tenths of an ephah of the finest flour mixed with oil; with each of the two rams, two-tenths; [15] and with each of the fourteen lambs, one-tenth. [16] Include one male goat as a sin offering, in addition to the regular burnt offering with its grain offering and drink offering.

[17] " 'On the second day offer twelve young bulls, two rams and fourteen male lambs a year old, all without defect. [18] With the bulls, rams and lambs, offer their grain offerings and drink offerings according to the number specified. [19] Include one male goat as a sin offering, in addition to the regular burnt offering with its grain offering, and their drink offerings.

[20] " 'On the third day offer eleven bulls, two rams and fourteen male lambs a year old, all without defect. [21] With the bulls, rams and lambs, offer their grain offerings and drink offerings according to the number specified. [22] Include one male goat as a sin offering, in addition to the regular burnt offering with its grain offering and drink offering.

[23] " 'On the fourth day offer ten bulls, two rams and fourteen male lambs a year old, all without defect. [24] With the bulls, rams and

---

[a] 3 That is, probably about 11 pounds or about 5 kilograms; also in verses 9 and 14
[b] 3 That is, probably about 7 pounds or about 3.2 kilograms; also in verses 9 and 14
[c] 4 That is, probably about 3 1/2 pounds or about 1.6 kilograms; also in verses 10 and 15   [d] 5 Or purification offering; also elsewhere in this chapter   [e] 7 Or must fast

---

28:1—29:40 | This section gives instructions on the daily **offerings** Israel was to make (28:1-8) as well as regular ones (food offerings) on certain days: each **Sabbath**, on the **first of every month**, and at the different festivals (28:16—29:38). Leviticus 23:4-43 gives more information on these festivals. Detailing these offerings and occasions just before the nation took possession of the Promised Land highlights their importance. According to 10:10, trumpets were blown to accompany the offerings on the first of the month (New Moon feasts). **See the article "The Need for Atonement" on page 210.**

lambs, offer their grain offerings and drink offerings according to the number specified. [25]Include one male goat as a sin offering, in addition to the regular burnt offering with its grain offering and drink offering.

[26]" 'On the fifth day offer nine bulls, two rams and fourteen male lambs a year old, all without defect. [27]With the bulls, rams and lambs, offer their grain offerings and drink offerings according to the number specified. [28]Include one male goat as a sin offering, in addition to the regular burnt offering with its grain offering and drink offering.

[29]" 'On the sixth day offer eight bulls, two rams and fourteen male lambs a year old, all without defect. [30]With the bulls, rams and lambs, offer their grain offerings and drink offerings according to the number specified. [31]Include one male goat as a sin offering, in addition to the regular burnt offering with its grain offering and drink offering.

[32]" 'On the seventh day offer seven bulls, two rams and fourteen male lambs a year old, all without defect. [33]With the bulls, rams and lambs, offer their grain offerings and drink offerings according to the number specified. [34]Include one male goat as a sin offering, in addition to the regular burnt offering with its grain offering and drink offering.

[35]" 'On the eighth day hold a closing special assembly and do no regular work. [36]Present as an aroma pleasing to the LORD a food offering consisting of a burnt offering of one bull, one ram and seven male lambs a year old, all without defect. [37]With the bull, the ram and the lambs, offer their grain offerings and drink offerings according to the number specified. [38]Include one male goat as a sin offering, in addition to the regular burnt offering with its grain offering and drink offering.

[39]" 'In addition to what you vow and your freewill offerings, offer these to the LORD at your appointed festivals: your burnt offerings, grain offerings, drink offerings and fellowship offerings.' "

[40]Moses told the Israelites all that the LORD commanded him.[a]

Vows

30[b] Moses said to the heads of the tribes of Israel: "This is what the LORD commands: [2]When a man makes a vow to the LORD or takes an oath to obligate himself by a pledge, he must not break his word but must do everything he said.

[3]"When a young woman still living in her father's household makes a vow to the LORD or obligates herself by a pledge [4]and her father hears about her vow or pledge but says nothing to her, then all her vows and every pledge by which she obligated herself will stand. [5]But if her father forbids her when he hears about it, none of her vows or the pledges by which she obligated herself will stand; the LORD will release her because her father has forbidden her.

[6]"If she marries after she makes a vow or after her lips utter a rash promise by which she obligates herself [7]and her husband hears about it but says nothing to her, then her vows or the pledges by which she obligated herself will stand. [8]But if her husband forbids her when he hears about it, he nullifies the vow that obligates her or the rash promise by which she obligates herself, and the LORD will release her.

[9]"Any vow or obligation taken by a widow or divorced woman will be binding on her.

[10]"If a woman living with her husband makes a vow or obligates herself by a pledge under oath [11]and her husband hears about it but says nothing to her and does not forbid her, then all her vows or the pledges by which she obligated herself will stand. [12]But if her husband nullifies them when he hears about them, then none of the vows or pledges that came from her lips will stand. Her husband has nullified them, and the LORD will release her. [13]Her husband may confirm or nullify any vow she makes or any sworn pledge to deny herself.[c] [14]But if her husband says nothing to her about it from day to day, then he confirms all her vows or the pledges binding on her. He confirms them by saying nothing to her when he hears about them. [15]If, however, he nullifies them some time after he hears about them, then he must bear the consequences of her wrongdoing."

[16]These are the regulations the LORD gave Moses concerning relationships between a man and his wife, and between a father and his young daughter still living at home.

---

[a] 40 In Hebrew texts this verse (29:40) is numbered 30:1.   [b] In Hebrew texts 30:1-16 is numbered 30:2-17.   [c] 13 Or to fast

---

30:1, 2 | Vows were not required, but once made, they must be kept; thus to enter into one required serious thought. What is vowed before God is binding. Vows to Him are not trifling things (Deut. 23:21–23; Eccl. 5:1–7).

30:3–16 | A vow made by an unmarried **woman still living in her father's household** could be **forbidden** by her father, just as a **husband** could nullify the vow of his wife. In contrast, the vow of a **widow or divorced woman** was binding because she had no one to void it. These measures helped to protect women in their culture during OT times.

Vengeance on the Midianites

31 The LORD said to Moses, [2]"Take vengeance on the Midianites for the Israelites. After that, you will be gathered to your people."

[3]So Moses said to the people, "Arm some of your men to go to war against the Midianites so that they may carry out the LORD's vengeance on them. [4]Send into battle a thousand men from each of the tribes of Israel." [5]So twelve thousand men armed for battle, a thousand from each tribe, were supplied from the clans of Israel. [6]Moses sent them into battle, a thousand from each tribe, along with Phinehas son of Eleazar, the priest, who took with him articles from the sanctuary and the trumpets for signaling.

[7]They fought against Midian, as the LORD commanded Moses, and killed every man. [8]Among their victims were Evi, Rekem, Zur, Hur and Reba—the five kings of Midian. They also killed Balaam son of Beor with the sword. [9]The Israelites captured the Midianite women and children and took all the Midianite herds, flocks and goods as plunder. [10]They burned all the towns where the Midianites had settled, as well as all their camps. [11]They took all the plunder and spoils, including the people and animals, [12]and brought the captives, spoils and plunder to Moses and Eleazar the priest and the Israelite assembly at their camp on the plains of Moab, by the Jordan across from Jericho.

[13]Moses, Eleazar the priest and all the leaders of the community went to meet them outside the camp. [14]Moses was angry with the officers of the army—the commanders of thousands and commanders of hundreds—who returned from the battle.

[15]"Have you allowed all the women to live?" he asked them. [16]"They were the ones who followed Balaam's advice and enticed the Israelites to be unfaithful to the LORD in the Peor incident, so that a plague struck the LORD's people. [17]Now kill all the boys. And kill every woman who has slept with a man, [18]but save for yourselves every girl who has never slept with a man.

[19]"Anyone who has killed someone or touched someone who was killed must stay outside the camp seven days. On the third and seventh days you must purify yourselves and your captives. [20]Purify every garment as well as everything made of leather, goat hair or wood."

[21]Then Eleazar the priest said to the soldiers who had gone into battle, "This is what is required by the law that the LORD gave Moses: [22]Gold, silver, bronze, iron, tin, lead [23]and anything else that can withstand fire must be put through the fire, and then it will be clean. But it must also be purified with the water of cleansing. And whatever cannot withstand fire must be put through that water. [24]On the seventh day wash your clothes and you will be clean. Then you may come into the camp."

Dividing the Spoils

[25]The LORD said to Moses, [26]"You and Eleazar the priest and the family heads of the community are to count all the people and animals that were captured. [27]Divide the spoils equally between the soldiers who took part in the battle and the rest of the community. [28]From the soldiers who fought in the battle, set apart as tribute for the LORD one out of every five hundred, whether people, cattle, donkeys or sheep. [29]Take this tribute from their half share and give it to Eleazar the priest as the LORD's part. [30]From the Israelites' half, select one out of every fifty, whether people, cattle, donkeys, sheep or other animals. Give them to the Levites, who are responsible for the care of the LORD's tabernacle." [31]So Moses and Eleazar the priest did as the LORD commanded Moses.

[32]The plunder remaining from the spoils that the soldiers took was 675,000 sheep, [33]72,000 cattle, [34]61,000 donkeys [35]and 32,000 women who had never slept with a man.

[36]The half share of those who fought in the battle was:

337,500 sheep, [37]of which the tribute for the LORD was 675;

31:4–54 | Each of the nonpriestly tribes of Israel played an equal role in the fighting force, as **a thousand men from each of the tribes** were recruited when the Israelites went to war against the Midianites. After the battle, the **spoils** of the Midianites were **divided equally** between those who took part in the war and those who remained behind, for each played an important role in gaining the victory (31:15–54).
31:8 | Balaam's involvement with the Midianites in an attempt to deceive Israel (25:14–18; Rev. 2:14) cost him his life. God commanded His people to likewise take vengeance on the people of **Midian**. The victims' list here includes **five** of their **kings**. It turned

out that seeing the sword of the Lord was not enough to bring **Balaam** to repentance and faith in Yahweh. A human **sword** sent him to his eternal reckoning.
31:15–20 | Moses gave this command because the Midianites had caused the people of God to **be unfaithful to the LORD**. For the Israelites to kill everyone except the young virgins would prevent further Midianite influence and eliminate their threat to the Israelites' inheritance. The ones who carried out this punishment became unclean and had to be purified with the **water** mixed with the ashes of the red heifer (19:2–10).

[38] 36,000 cattle, of which the tribute for the LORD was 72;

[39] 30,500 donkeys, of which the tribute for the LORD was 61;

[40] 16,000 people, of whom the tribute for the LORD was 32.

[41] Moses gave the tribute to Eleazar the priest as the LORD's part, as the LORD commanded Moses.

[42] The half belonging to the Israelites, which Moses set apart from that of the fighting men— [43] the community's half— was 337,500 sheep, [44] 36,000 cattle, [45] 30,500 donkeys [46] and 16,000 people. [47] From the Israelites' half, Moses selected one out of every fifty people and animals, as the LORD commanded him, and gave them to the Levites, who were responsible for the care of the LORD's tabernacle.

[48] Then the officers who were over the units of the army—the commanders of thousands and commanders of hundreds— went to Moses [49] and said to him, "Your servants have counted the soldiers under our command, and not one is missing. [50] So we have brought as an offering to the LORD the gold articles each of us acquired—armlets, bracelets, signet rings, earrings and necklaces—to make atonement for ourselves before the LORD."

[51] Moses and Eleazar the priest accepted from them the gold—all the crafted articles. [52] All the gold from the commanders of thousands and commanders of hundreds that Moses and Eleazar presented as a gift to the LORD weighed 16,750 shekels.[a] [53] Each soldier had taken plunder for himself. [54] Moses and Eleazar the priest accepted the gold from the commanders of thousands and commanders of hundreds and brought it into the tent of meeting as a memorial for the Israelites before the LORD.

The Transjordan Tribes

32 The Reubenites and Gadites, who had very large herds and flocks, saw that the lands of Jazer and Gilead were suitable for livestock. [2] So they came to Moses and Eleazar the priest and to the leaders of the community, and said, [3] "Ataroth, Dibon, Jazer, Nimrah, Heshbon, Elealeh, Sebam, Nebo and Beon— [4] the land the LORD subdued before the people of Israel—are suitable for livestock, and your servants have livestock. [5] If we have found favor in your eyes," they said, "let this land be given to your servants as our possession. Do not make us cross the Jordan."

[6] Moses said to the Gadites and Reubenites, "Should your fellow Israelites go to war while you sit here? [7] Why do you discourage the Israelites from crossing over into the land the LORD has given them? [8] This is what your fathers did when I sent them from Kadesh Barnea to look over the land. [9] After they went up to the Valley of Eshkol and viewed the land, they discouraged the Israelites from entering the land the LORD had given them. [10] The LORD's anger was aroused that day and he swore this oath: [11] 'Because they have not followed me wholeheartedly, not one of those who were twenty years old or more when they came up out of Egypt will see the land I promised on oath to Abraham, Isaac and Jacob— [12] not one except Caleb son of Jephunneh the Kenizzite and Joshua son of Nun, for they followed the LORD wholeheartedly.' [13] The LORD's anger burned against Israel and he made them wander in the wilderness forty years, until the whole generation of those who had done evil in his sight was gone.

[14] "And here you are, a brood of sinners, standing in the place of your fathers and making the LORD even more angry with Israel. [15] If you turn away from following him, he will again leave all this people in the wilderness, and you will be the cause of their destruction."

[16] Then they came up to him and said, "We would like to build pens here for our livestock and cities for our women and children. [17] But we will arm ourselves for battle[b] and go ahead of the Israelites until we have brought them to their place. Meanwhile our women and children will live in fortified cities, for protection from the inhabitants of the

[a] 52 That is, about 420 pounds or about 190 kilograms   [b] 17 Septuagint; Hebrew will be quick to arm ourselves

---

32:1-7 | Because the herdsmen tribes of Reuben and Gad needed plenty of grazing land, they decided not to go over the Jordan into Canaan but to settle on the east side of the river. Moses was concerned that they wanted to enjoy their inheritance without fighting the battle, which would **discourage** the other tribes from taking the land, just as the spies had done at Kadesh Barnea (13:26–14:1). Discouragement is contagious.

32:1-5 | **The Reubenites**, unable to wait for the best, were the first tribe to demand its inheritance. In the terrible rebellion of Korah (16), Reuben was at the forefront.

32:8-10 | The land of discouragement is deadly territory, and this story demonstrates that to unwittingly dishearten others by a negative or critical spirit dampens their spiritual enthusiasm and displeases the Lord (Prov. 15:13, 15).

32:12 | **Joshua** and **Caleb** were different from the rest of the spies—faithful in their following of the Lord, fearless in the face of crisis, and filled with the Spirit of God.

land. ¹⁸We will not return to our homes until each of the Israelites has received their inheritance. ¹⁹We will not receive any inheritance with them on the other side of the Jordan, because our inheritance has come to us on the east side of the Jordan."

²⁰Then Moses said to them, "If you will do this—if you will arm yourselves before the LORD for battle ²¹and if all of you who are armed cross over the Jordan before the LORD until he has driven his enemies out before him— ²²then when the land is subdued before the LORD, you may return and be free from your obligation to the LORD and to Israel. And this land will be your possession before the LORD.

²³"But if you fail to do this, you will be sinning against the LORD; and you may be sure that your sin will find you out. ²⁴Build cities for your women and children, and pens for your flocks, but do what you have promised."

²⁵The Gadites and Reubenites said to Moses, "We your servants will do as our lord commands. ²⁶Our children and wives, our flocks and herds will remain here in the cities of Gilead. ²⁷But your servants, every man who is armed for battle, will cross over to fight before the LORD, just as our lord says."

²⁸Then Moses gave orders about them to Eleazar the priest and Joshua son of Nun and to the family heads of the Israelite tribes. ²⁹He said to them, "If the Gadites and Reubenites, every man armed for battle, cross over the Jordan with you before the LORD, then when the land is subdued before you, you must give them the land of Gilead as their possession. ³⁰But if they do not cross over with you armed, they must accept their possession with you in Canaan."

³¹The Gadites and Reubenites answered, "Your servants will do what the LORD has said. ³²We will cross over before the LORD into Canaan armed, but the property we inherit will be on this side of the Jordan."

³³Then Moses gave to the Gadites, the Reubenites and the half-tribe of Manasseh son of Joseph the kingdom of Sihon king of the Amorites and the kingdom of Og king of Bashan—the whole land with its cities and the territory around them.

³⁴The Gadites built up Dibon, Ataroth, Aroer, ³⁵Atroth Shophan, Jazer, Jogbehah, ³⁶Beth Nimrah and Beth Haran as fortified cities, and built pens for their flocks. ³⁷And the Reubenites rebuilt Heshbon, Elealeh and Kiriathaim, ³⁸as well as Nebo and Baal Meon (these names were changed) and Sibmah. They gave names to the cities they rebuilt.

³⁹The descendants of Makir son of Manasseh went to Gilead, captured it and drove out the Amorites who were there. ⁴⁰So Moses gave Gilead to the Makirites, the descendants of Manasseh, and they settled there. ⁴¹Jair, a descendant of Manasseh, captured their settlements and called them Havvoth Jair.ᵃ ⁴²And Nobah captured Kenath and its surrounding settlements and called it Nobah after himself.

Stages in Israel's Journey

33 Here are the stages in the journey of the Israelites when they came out of Egypt by divisions under the leadership of Moses and Aaron. ²At the LORD's command Moses recorded the stages in their journey. This is their journey by stages:

³The Israelites set out from Rameses on the fifteenth day of the first month, the day after the Passover. They marched out defiantly in full view of all the Egyptians, ⁴who were burying all their firstborn, whom the LORD had struck down among them; for the LORD had brought judgment on their gods.

⁵The Israelites left Rameses and camped at Sukkoth. ⁶They left Sukkoth and camped at Etham, on the edge of the desert. ⁷They left Etham, turned back to Pi Hahiroth, to the east of Baal Zephon, and camped near Migdol. ⁸They left Pi Hahirothᵇ and passed through the sea into the desert, and when they had traveled for three days in the Desert of Etham, they camped at Marah.

ᵃ 41 Or them the settlements of Jair   ᵇ 8 Many manuscripts of the Masoretic Text, Samaritan Pentateuch and Vulgate; most manuscripts of the Masoretic Text left from before Hahiroth

---

32:20-24 | These verses lay out the conditions by which the tribes of Reuben and Gad could have the land they wanted: they would have to send their armed men with the rest of Israel when Israel crossed into Canaan, and they would have to lead the troops. They could only return after the land was **subdued** and Israel's enemies driven out.
32:33 | The **half-tribe of Manasseh** also chose land on the east side of the Jordan. The same stipulations that Moses gave to the **Reubenites** and the **Gadites** would apply to this group (see note on

32:20-24). The other half of the tribe of Manasseh would receive land on the west side of the Jordan (Josh. 13:7).
33:1-49 | In listing the 40 different places the Israelites camped as they traveled from Egypt to the Promised Land, this section reveals God's faithfulness to Israel. Most of the locations are unknown today; they are not archaeological sites because they were temporary camps rather than cities. The number of sites corresponds to the number of years of their wandering.

⁹They left Marah and went to Elim, where there were twelve springs and seventy palm trees, and they camped there.

¹⁰They left Elim and camped by the Red Sea.ª

¹¹They left the Red Sea and camped in the Desert of Sin.

¹²They left the Desert of Sin and camped at Dophkah.

¹³They left Dophkah and camped at Alush.

¹⁴They left Alush and camped at Rephidim, where there was no water for the people to drink.

¹⁵They left Rephidim and camped in the Desert of Sinai.

¹⁶They left the Desert of Sinai and camped at Kibroth Hattaavah.

¹⁷They left Kibroth Hattaavah and camped at Hazeroth.

¹⁸They left Hazeroth and camped at Rithmah.

¹⁹They left Rithmah and camped at Rimmon Perez.

²⁰They left Rimmon Perez and camped at Libnah.

²¹They left Libnah and camped at Rissah.

²²They left Rissah and camped at Kehelathah.

²³They left Kehelathah and camped at Mount Shepher.

²⁴They left Mount Shepher and camped at Haradah.

²⁵They left Haradah and camped at Makheloth.

²⁶They left Makheloth and camped at Tahath.

²⁷They left Tahath and camped at Terah.

²⁸They left Terah and camped at Mithkah.

²⁹They left Mithkah and camped at Hashmonah.

³⁰They left Hashmonah and camped at Moseroth.

³¹They left Moseroth and camped at Bene Jaakan.

³²They left Bene Jaakan and camped at Hor Haggidgad.

³³They left Hor Haggidgad and camped at Jotbathah.

³⁴They left Jotbathah and camped at Abronah.

³⁵They left Abronah and camped at Ezion Geber.

³⁶They left Ezion Geber and camped at Kadesh, in the Desert of Zin.

³⁷They left Kadesh and camped at Mount Hor, on the border of Edom. ³⁸At the LORD's command Aaron the priest went up Mount Hor, where he died on the first day of the fifth month of the fortieth year after the Israelites came out of Egypt. ³⁹Aaron was a hundred and twenty-three years old when he died on Mount Hor.

⁴⁰The Canaanite king of Arad, who lived in the Negev of Canaan, heard that the Israelites were coming.

⁴¹They left Mount Hor and camped at Zalmonah.

⁴²They left Zalmonah and camped at Punon.

⁴³They left Punon and camped at Oboth.

⁴⁴They left Oboth and camped at Iye Abarim, on the border of Moab.

⁴⁵They left Iye Abarim and camped at Dibon Gad.

⁴⁶They left Dibon Gad and camped at Almon Diblathaim.

⁴⁷They left Almon Diblathaim and camped in the mountains of Abarim, near Nebo.

⁴⁸They left the mountains of Abarim and camped on the plains of Moab by the Jordan across from Jericho. ⁴⁹There on the plains of Moab they camped along the Jordan from Beth Jeshimoth to Abel Shittim.

⁵⁰On the plains of Moab by the Jordan across from Jericho the LORD said to Moses, ⁵¹"Speak to the Israelites and say to them: 'When you cross the Jordan into Canaan, ⁵²drive out all the inhabitants of the land before you. Destroy all their carved images and their cast idols, and demolish all their high places. ⁵³Take possession of the land and settle in it, for I have given you the land to possess. ⁵⁴Distribute the land by lot, according to your clans. To a larger group give a larger inheritance, and to a smaller group a smaller one. Whatever falls to them by lot will be theirs. Distribute it according to your ancestral tribes.

ª 10 Or the Sea of Reeds; also in verse 11

33:50–56 | The Israelites were commanded not only to **drive out all the inhabitants of the land** but to **destroy** their **carved images, cast idols,** and **high places**—the things associated with idol worship that could tempt God's people to idolatry. Because of this, there were serious warnings to Israel to be faithful in these charges. Not to obey God might cause Him to treat them as He had planned to do their enemies.

55 " 'But if you do not drive out the inhabitants of the land, those you allow to remain will become barbs in your eyes and thorns in your sides. They will give you trouble in the land where you will live. 56 And then I will do to you what I plan to do to them.' "

Boundaries of Canaan

34 The LORD said to Moses, 2 "Command the Israelites and say to them: 'When you enter Canaan, the land that will be allotted to you as an inheritance is to have these boundaries:

3 " 'Your southern side will include some of the Desert of Zin along the border of Edom. Your southern boundary will start in the east from the southern end of the Dead Sea, 4 cross south of Scorpion Pass, continue on to Zin and go south of Kadesh Barnea. Then it will go to Hazar Addar and over to Azmon, 5 where it will turn, join the Wadi of Egypt and end at the Mediterranean Sea.

6 " 'Your western boundary will be the coast of the Mediterranean Sea. This will be your boundary on the west.

7 " 'For your northern boundary, run a line from the Mediterranean Sea to Mount Hor 8 and from Mount Hor to Lebo Hamath. Then the boundary will go to Zedad, 9 continue to Ziphron and end at Hazar Enan. This will be your boundary on the north.

10 " 'For your eastern boundary, run a line from Hazar Enan to Shepham. 11 The boundary will go down from Shepham to Riblah on the east side of Ain and continue along the slopes east of the Sea of Galilee.ᵃ 12 Then the boundary will go down along the Jordan and end at the Dead Sea.

" 'This will be your land, with its boundaries on every side.' "

13 Moses commanded the Israelites: "Assign this land by lot as an inheritance. The LORD has ordered that it be given to the nine and a half tribes, 14 because the families of the tribe of Reuben, the tribe of Gad and the half-tribe of Manasseh have received their inheritance. 15 These two and a half tribes have received their inheritance east of the Jordan across from Jericho, toward the sunrise."

16 The LORD said to Moses, 17 "These are the names of the men who are to assign the land for you as an inheritance: Eleazar the priest and Joshua son of Nun. 18 And appoint one leader from each tribe to help assign the land. 19 These are their names:

Caleb son of Jephunneh,
  from the tribe of Judah;
20 Shemuel son of Ammihud,
  from the tribe of Simeon;
21 Elidad son of Kislon,
  from the tribe of Benjamin;
22 Bukki son of Jogli,
  the leader from the tribe of Dan;
23 Hanniel son of Ephod,
  the leader from the tribe of Manasseh
  son of Joseph;
24 Kemuel son of Shiphtan,
  the leader from the tribe of Ephraim
  son of Joseph;
25 Elizaphan son of Parnak,
  the leader from the tribe of Zebulun;
26 Paltiel son of Azzan,
  the leader from the tribe of Issachar;
27 Ahihud son of Shelomi,
  the leader from the tribe of Asher;
28 Pedahel son of Ammihud,
  the leader from the tribe of Naphtali."

29 These are the men the LORD commanded to assign the inheritance to the Israelites in the land of Canaan.

Towns for the Levites

35 On the plains of Moab by the Jordan across from Jericho, the LORD said to Moses, 2 "Command the Israelites to give the Levites towns to live in from the inheritance the Israelites will possess. And give them pasturelands around the towns. 3 Then they will have towns to live in and pasturelands for the cattle they own and all their other animals.

4 "The pasturelands around the towns that you give the Levites will extend a thousand cubitsᵇ from the town wall. 5 Outside the town, measure two thousand cubitsᶜ on the east side, two thousand on the south side, two thousand on the west and two thousand on the north, with the town in the center. They will have this area as pastureland for the towns.

ᵃ 11 Hebrew *Kinnereth*   ᵇ 4 That is, about 1,500 feet or about 450 meters
ᶜ 5 That is, about 3,000 feet or about 900 meters

34:1–15 | Yahweh gave the boundaries appointed for the people of Israel. The sheer quantity of land was evidence of God's grace.
34:16–29 | Under Israel's new leadership, the heads of the 10 other tribes would assist **Joshua** and **Eleazar** in dividing the land. None of these leaders was the son of a leader from the previous generation (1:5–15). These men would prove to be more faithful than their predecessors.
35:1–8 | In place of land, the tribe of Levi was given 48 **towns** spread throughout Israel with **pasturelands** where they could raise their **cattle** and **animals**. These towns are listed in Joshua 21:1–42.

Cities of Refuge

[6] "Six of the towns you give the Levites will be cities of refuge, to which a person who has killed someone may flee. In addition, give them forty-two other towns. [7] In all you must give the Levites forty-eight towns, together with their pasturelands. [8] The towns you give the Levites from the land the Israelites possess are to be given in proportion to the inheritance of each tribe: Take many towns from a tribe that has many, but few from one that has few."

[9] Then the LORD said to Moses: [10] "Speak to the Israelites and say to them: 'When you cross the Jordan into Canaan, [11] select some towns to be your cities of refuge, to which a person who has killed someone accidentally may flee. [12] They will be places of refuge from the avenger, so that anyone accused of murder may not die before they stand trial before the assembly. [13] These six towns you give will be your cities of refuge. [14] Give three on this side of the Jordan and three in Canaan as cities of refuge. [15] These six towns will be a place of refuge for Israelites and for foreigners residing among them, so that anyone who has killed another accidentally can flee there.

[16] "'If anyone strikes someone a fatal blow with an iron object, that person is a murderer; the murderer is to be put to death. [17] Or if anyone is holding a stone and strikes someone a fatal blow with it, that person is a murderer; the murderer is to be put to death. [18] Or if anyone is holding a wooden object and strikes someone a fatal blow with it, that person is a murderer; the murderer is to be put to death. [19] The avenger of blood shall put the murderer to death; when the avenger comes upon the murderer, the avenger shall put the murderer to death. [20] If anyone with malice aforethought shoves another or throws something at them intentionally so that they die [21] or if out of enmity one person hits another with their fist so that the other dies, that person is to be put to death; that person is a murderer. The avenger of blood shall put the murderer to death when they meet.

[22] "'But if without enmity someone suddenly pushes another or throws something at them unintentionally [23] or, without seeing them, drops on them a stone heavy enough to kill them, and they die, then since that other person was not an enemy and no harm was intended, [24] the assembly must judge between the accused and the avenger of blood according to these regulations. [25] The assembly must protect the one accused of murder from the avenger of blood and send the accused back to the city of refuge to which they fled. The accused must stay there until the death of the high priest, who was anointed with the holy oil.

[26] "'But if the accused ever goes outside the limits of the city of refuge to which they fled [27] and the avenger of blood finds them outside the city, the avenger of blood may kill the accused without being guilty of murder. [28] The accused must stay in the city of refuge until the death of the high priest; only after the death of the high priest may they return to their own property.

[29] "'This is to have the force of law for you throughout the generations to come, wherever you live.

[30] "'Anyone who kills a person is to be put to death as a murderer only on the testimony of witnesses. But no one is to be put to death on the testimony of only one witness.

[31] "'Do not accept a ransom for the life of a murderer, who deserves to die. They are to be put to death.

[32] "'Do not accept a ransom for anyone who has fled to a city of refuge and so allow them to go back and live on their own land before the death of the high priest.

[33] "'Do not pollute the land where you are. Bloodshed pollutes the land, and atonement cannot be made for the land on which blood has been shed, except by the blood of the one who shed it. [34] Do not defile the land where you live and where I dwell, for I, the LORD, dwell among the Israelites.'"

Inheritance of Zelophehad's Daughters

36 The family heads of the clan of Gilead son of Makir, the son of Manasseh, who were from the clans of the descendants of Joseph, came and spoke before Moses and the leaders, the heads of the Israelite families. [2] They said, "When the

---

35:6–15 | Six of the Levites' towns were designated **cities of refuge**, three east of the Jordan and three west of it (Deut. 19:1–13; see note on Josh. 20:1-9).

35:16–28 | God provided the cities of refuge to protect those who had **unintentionally** killed someone. The congregation would judge whether the person's motive was out of **malice** or **without enmity**. Someone who accidentally took the life of another had to stay in the city of refuge **until the death of the high priest**. He or she could be killed for leaving the city before then (Ex. 21:23, 24; Deut.19:1–13).

35:29–34 | The **law** took justice just as seriously as murder: a person could not be put to death by the **testimony of only one witness**; two were needed. Those who committed murder, however, were to be executed, and those who committed manslaughter had to stay in a city of refuge. These provisions were in place because the unjust taking of life **pollutes the land**.

LORD commanded my lord to give the land as an inheritance to the Israelites by lot, he ordered you to give the inheritance of our brother Zelophehad to his daughters. ³Now suppose they marry men from other Israelite tribes; then their inheritance will be taken from our ancestral inheritance and added to that of the tribe they marry into. And so part of the inheritance allotted to us will be taken away. ⁴When the Year of Jubilee for the Israelites comes, their inheritance will be added to that of the tribe into which they marry, and their property will be taken from the tribal inheritance of our ancestors."

⁵Then at the LORD's command Moses gave this order to the Israelites: "What the tribe of the descendants of Joseph is saying is right. ⁶This is what the LORD commands for Zelophehad's daughters: They may marry anyone they please as long as they marry within their father's tribal clan. ⁷No inheritance in Israel is to pass from one tribe to another, for every Israelite shall keep the tribal inheritance of their ancestors. ⁸Every daughter who inherits land in any Israelite tribe must marry someone in her father's tribal clan, so that every Israelite will possess the inheritance of their ancestors. ⁹No inheritance may pass from one tribe to another, for each Israelite tribe is to keep the land it inherits."

¹⁰So Zelophehad's daughters did as the LORD commanded Moses. ¹¹Zelophehad's daughters—Mahlah, Tirzah, Hoglah, Milkah and Noah—married their cousins on their father's side. ¹²They married within the clans of the descendants of Manasseh son of Joseph, and their inheritance remained in their father's tribe and clan.

¹³These are the commands and regulations the LORD gave through Moses to the Israelites on the plains of Moab by the Jordan across from Jericho.

36:1–13 | One unanswered question regarding the daughters of **Zelophehad** (27:1–11) was what would happen to their family's land if they married into a different tribe. Moses declared the decision of Yahweh: these women, and anyone else in the same situation, should only marry within their own tribe. Here is another example of new laws being made for people's good in particular circumstances (9:1–13).

36:7 | Because it was God's gift to each tribe, property could not be sold (**pass**) between tribes. This law stands in the background of the story of Ahab and Naboth. Naboth understood this principle, but Ahab sought to violate it (1 Kgs. 21:3).

36:10–12 | The Book of Numbers begins by discussing the obedience of the people (1–10), but much of the book speaks of Israel's disobedience, which led to the death of an entire generation in the wilderness. The book ends on a positive note, as **Zelophehad's daughters** obeyed the words of Moses and **married within the clans of the descendants of Manasseh son of Joseph**.

הָגְדֵל רוֹמֵזֵם הַצֶּנֶמֵל

עִקְרָה דִיגֵם וִלְדִי הַשַׁעֲמוּ לָא־דוּבֵכ סֵירֵכְפֵסֵם סֵנֹמְשָׁה

תַּעַד־הֵחֵן הֲלֵלֵל הֲלֵילוּ רֵמָא עֵיבֵי סוֹיֵל סֵנִי

סֵלוֹק עַמֵשַׁן ךִלֵב סֵירֵכֵד זֵאוֹ רֵמָא־זֵיא

סֵהֵב לֵהָא־סָשׁ שֵׁמֵל סֵהֵיֵלֵם לֵבַת הַצֵקֵבוּ סֵק אֵצֵי וֵרְאָה־לָכֵב

חֵרָא יֵהֲדֵל רוֹבֵבֵכ שֵׁיֵשׁ וֵהֵפֵחֵם אֵצֵי נֵתֵדֵכ אוֹדֵן

DEUTERONOMY

HEAR, O ISRAEL:

The LORD our God, the LORD is one.

Love the LORD your God with all your heart

and with all your soul and with all your strength.

These commandments that I give you today

are to be on your hearts. Impress them on your children.

Talk about them when you sit at home and when you walk along

the road, when you lie down and when you get up.

Tie them as symbols on your hands

and bind them on your foreheads.

Write them on the doorframes of your houses and on your gates.

DEUTERONOMY 6:4–9

DEUTERONOMY

BOOK INTRODUCTION

You might expect a man who had lived 120 years to look back on his life and see it as multiple chapters of a long book. Moses' years, however, divided neatly into three major parts: 40 years in the royal halls of Egypt, 40 years as shepherd of his father-in-law's flocks in Midian, and a final 40 years as the shepherd of God's flock as they moved from Sinai to the plains of Moab, ready to enter the Promised Land. Yet Moses' fondest desire through the weary decades of the wilderness experience would not be fulfilled: he would not be allowed to enter the Promised Land along with the new generation of Israelites. When Yahweh gave him clear instruction at Kadesh for getting water for the people, Moses violated the command (Num. 20:1–13), misrepresenting the Lord before all the people in a fit of anger. Through the heartbreaking discipline that followed, Moses learned that the shepherd was no less accountable than the sheep.

Although Moses was bruised by that incident, Yahweh Himself bound up His servant's wounds. The final scene of Moses and the Lord together in Moab, just before Moses' death, is poignant and bittersweet (34:1–8). Moses climbed Mount Nebo and the Lord was there, showing him all the land across the Jordan—from the north to the west and the south. The Lord told him, "This is the land I promised on oath to Abraham, Isaac and Jacob . . . I have let you see it with your eyes, but you will not cross over into it" (34:4).

There was no animosity, no bitterness, between them. With great honor for His friend, the Lord buried Moses Himself upon his death (34:6), the prophet's mission complete.

Before Moses died, he schooled Israel through the writing of the Book of Deuteronomy. Once the Exodus generation (excluding faithful spies Joshua and Caleb) died in the wilderness, there was a new generation to teach. This new generation was mature (60 years of age and younger) and sober—they had witnessed how serious God was that they trust Him (Num. 13—14). And they had learned to trust Yahweh through the victories over the nations who attacked them as they approached Moab. But some within the "new Israel" may not have yet committed to the covenant themselves. So Moses' task in his final days was to explain the covenant again (*Deuteronomy* means "a repetition or retelling of the law") and to lead the new nation to devote themselves to it.

To view Dr. Jeremiah's video introduction to Deuteronomy, go to ww.JeremiahStudyBible.com/ Deuteronomy/Intro

What It Says | *A Fresh Presentation of the Covenant*

The entire Bible is the story of covenant. (We affirm that central focus every time we refer to "Old Testament" and "New Testament"—which really mean "Old Covenant" and "New Covenant.") In Deuteronomy, Moses was led by the Spirit of God to do something new and wonderful to express this covenant: he followed a pattern of international treaties between nations. We know about these treaty forms today, especially from Hittite examples. In this case, the Lord was viewed in the place of a great king; the people were viewed in the place of vassal states.

Deuteronomy therefore contains an introduction to the covenant (1:1–5), historical background (1:6—4:43), covenant requirements (4:44—26:19), and curses and blessings (27:1—30:20). The final four chapters (31—34) are not part of the covenant formula but contain final matters associated with the end of Moses' leadership of Israel.

Almost all of Deuteronomy is a series of sermons by Moses—not always chronological, and sometimes repetitious and overlapping. But overall, the book presents a clear, deeply heartfelt appeal to the new generation of Israelites to agree to acknowledge the Lord as their God, along with instruction in how to do so.

What It Means | *God's Love Restated*

The themes of Deuteronomy are foundational to the entire message of the OT:

- **Covenant:** The Book of Deuteronomy restates God's love for Israel, the history of His provision for them, the benefits or blessings of walking in covenant with God, and the consequences for disobeying the stipulations of the covenant (see the summary in 28:1–68). Christians today live in a New Covenant relationship with God, based on the blood of Christ—a covenant written on the heart rather than on tablets of stone (Jer. 31:33, 34).

- **Choice:** Throughout the history of God's relationship with humanity, choice has been integral. God chose Abraham and His descendants (10:15), and He appeals to Israel to choose Him in return (30:19). God clearly outlines the implications of choosing Him or not so that, to borrow the apostle Paul's words, "[We] are without excuse" (Rom. 1:20).

- **Love:** It is easy to overlook the love that flows through the mechanics of covenant stipulations. Love (both divine and human) is mentioned multiple times in Deuteronomy as the basis and evidence of God's relationship with Israel (7:7–13; 10:12–15; 30:16–20).

- **Faithfulness:** The faithfulness of God and the faithfulness of Moses illustrate the best of divine and human love. God is a God of promises kept (2 Pet. 1:4). Indeed, the promises of God to the patriarchs caused Him to be long-suffering toward Israel and finally bring them to the Promised Land (7:7–9).

What It Means for You | *The Lord in Everyday Life*

If the Israelites were going to be established as Yahweh's faithful people, their relationship with Him had to be more than religious formality reserved for special days on the calendar. God's Word needed to become an integral part of everyday life (6:5–9).

It is really no different for believers today. In the NT, Paul tells us to "pray continually" (1 Thess. 5:17), to "set [our] minds on things above" (Col. 3:2), and to "let the message of Christ dwell among [us] richly" (Col. 3:16). Pondering God's Word is not just for Sundays, a weekly Bible study, or morning devotions. It needs to be part of our thinking and reasoning, part of our conversation, part of our household activities, and part of a thousand decisions large and small that we make every day. God wants to be involved in our daily lives—and the more we include Him, the more we will find those lives truly worth living.

To access Dr. Jeremiah's digital library on Deuteronomy, go to
www.JeremiahStudyBible.com/Deuteronomy/library

DEUTERONOMY

The Command to Leave Horeb

1 These are the words Moses spoke to all Israel in the wilderness east of the Jordan—that is, in the Arabah—opposite Suph, between Paran and Tophel, Laban, Hazeroth and Dizahab. ²(It takes eleven days to go from Horeb to Kadesh Barnea by the Mount Seir road.)

³In the fortieth year, on the first day of the eleventh month, Moses proclaimed to the Israelites all that the LORD had commanded him concerning them. ⁴This was after he had defeated Sihon king of the Amorites, who reigned in Heshbon, and at Edrei had defeated Og king of Bashan, who reigned in Ashtaroth.

⁵East of the Jordan in the territory of Moab, Moses began to expound this law, saying:

⁶The LORD our God said to us at Horeb, "You have stayed long enough at this mountain. ⁷Break camp and advance into the hill country of the Amorites; go to all the neighboring peoples in the Arabah, in the mountains, in the western foothills, in the Negev and along the coast, to the land of the Canaanites and to Lebanon, as far as the great river, the Euphrates. ⁸See, I have given you this land. Go in and take possession of the land the LORD swore he would give to your fathers—to Abraham, Isaac and Jacob—and to their descendants after them."

The Appointment of Leaders

⁹At that time I said to you, "You are too heavy a burden for me to carry alone. ¹⁰The LORD your God has increased your numbers so that today you are as numerous as the stars in the sky. ¹¹May the LORD, the God of your ancestors, increase you a thousand times and bless you as he has promised! ¹²But how can I bear your problems and your burdens and your disputes all by myself? ¹³Choose some wise, understanding and respected men from each of your tribes, and I will set them over you."

¹⁴You answered me, "What you propose to do is good."

¹⁵So I took the leading men of your tribes, wise and respected men, and appointed them to have authority over you—as commanders of thousands, of hundreds, of fifties and of tens and as tribal officials. ¹⁶And I charged your judges at that time, "Hear the disputes between your people and judge fairly, whether the case is between two Israelites or between an Israelite and a foreigner residing among you. ¹⁷Do not show partiality in judging; hear both small and great alike. Do not be afraid of anyone, for judgment belongs to God. Bring me any case too hard for you, and I will hear it." ¹⁸And at that time I told you everything you were to do.

Spies Sent Out

¹⁹Then, as the LORD our God commanded us, we set out from Horeb and went toward the hill country of the Amorites through all that vast and dreadful wilderness that you have seen, and so we reached Kadesh Barnea. ²⁰Then I said to you, "You have reached the hill country of the Amorites, which the LORD our God is giving us. ²¹See, the LORD your God has given you the land. Go up and take possession of it as the LORD, the God of your ancestors, told you. Do not be afraid; do not be discouraged."

²²Then all of you came to me and said, "Let us send men ahead to spy out the land for us and bring back a report about the route we are to take and the towns we will come to."

²³The idea seemed good to me; so I selected twelve of you, one man from each tribe. ²⁴They left and went up into the hill country, and came to the Valley of Eshkol and explored it. ²⁵Taking with them some of the fruit of the land, they brought it down to

---

1:1 | These opening **words Moses spoke to all Israel** form an *inclusio* (a frame) of sorts with the words at the end of the book, "the Israelites . . . did what the LORD had commanded Moses" (34:9). The Lord established a relationship of grace with the people of Israel, using an international treaty format to prepare the world and His people for His salvation plan.
1:2 | The 11-day journey took Israel nearly 40 years to complete because of their disobedience (Num. 13–14). **Horeb** is another name for Mount Sinai (4:10, 15; Ex. 3:1), where God revealed His glory and gave the law.
1:5 | Moses explains the **law** that God had already given them in the Books of Genesis through Numbers. In fact, *Deuteronomy*

means "the second [giving of the] law." Those who heard the "first law" were now dead, so God's law was specifically addressed to the new generation; there would be no excuse for ignorance or disobedience.
1:17 | The call not to **show partiality in judging** is one of many warnings against discrimination in the OT (10:17; 16:19; Lev. 19:15; Prov. 24:23; 28:21). These warnings are reiterated in the NT (Rom. 2:11; James 2:1–13).
1:19–21 | **Do not be afraid; do not be discouraged** recalls encouragement given to the first generation. Fear that dominates a person's life may keep him or her from experiencing God's plan.

us and reported, "It is a good land that the LORD our God is giving us."

Rebellion Against the LORD

²⁶But you were unwilling to go up; you rebelled against the command of the LORD your God. ²⁷You grumbled in your tents and said, "The LORD hates us; so he brought us out of Egypt to deliver us into the hands of the Amorites to destroy us. ²⁸Where can we go? Our brothers have made our hearts melt in fear. They say, 'The people are stronger and taller than we are; the cities are large, with walls up to the sky. We even saw the Anakites there.'"

²⁹Then I said to you, "Do not be terrified; do not be afraid of them. ³⁰The LORD your God, who is going before you, will fight for you, as he did for you in Egypt, before your very eyes, ³¹and in the wilderness. There you saw how the LORD your God carried you, as a father carries his son, all the way you went until you reached this place."

³²In spite of this, you did not trust in the LORD your God, ³³who went ahead of you on your journey, in fire by night and in a cloud by day, to search out places for you to camp and to show you the way you should go.

³⁴When the LORD heard what you said, he was angry and solemnly swore: ³⁵"No one from this evil generation shall see the good land I swore to give your ancestors, ³⁶except Caleb son of Jephunneh. He will see it, and I will give him and his descendants the land he set his feet on, because he followed the LORD wholeheartedly."

³⁷Because of you the LORD became angry with me also and said, "You shall not enter it, either. ³⁸But your assistant, Joshua son of Nun, will enter it. Encourage him, because he will lead Israel to inherit it. ³⁹And the little ones that you said would be taken captive, your children who do not yet know good from bad—they will enter the land. I will give it to them and they will take possession of it. ⁴⁰But as for you, turn around and set out toward the desert along the route to the Red Sea.ᵃ"

⁴¹Then you replied, "We have sinned against the LORD. We will go up and fight, as the LORD our God commanded us." So every one of you put on his weapons, thinking it easy to go up into the hill country.

⁴²But the LORD said to me, "Tell them, 'Do not go up and fight, because I will not be with you. You will be defeated by your enemies.'"

⁴³So I told you, but you would not listen. You rebelled against the LORD's command and in your arrogance you marched up into the hill country. ⁴⁴The Amorites who lived in those hills came out against you; they chased you like a swarm of bees and beat you down from Seir all the way to Hormah. ⁴⁵You came back and wept before the LORD, but he paid no attention to your weeping and turned a deaf ear to you. ⁴⁶And so you stayed in Kadesh many days—all the time you spent there.

Wanderings in the Wilderness

2 Then we turned back and set out toward the wilderness along the route to the Red Sea,ᵃ as the LORD had directed me. For a long time we made our way around the hill country of Seir.

²Then the LORD said to me, ³"You have made your way around this hill country long enough; now turn north. ⁴Give the people these orders: 'You are about to pass through the territory of your relatives the descendants of Esau, who live in Seir. They will be afraid of you, but be very careful. ⁵Do not provoke them to war, for I will not give you any of their land, not even enough to put your foot on. I have given Esau the hill country of Seir as his own. ⁶You are to pay them in silver for the food you eat and the water you drink.'"

⁷The LORD your God has blessed you in all the work of your hands. He has watched

---

ᵃ 40, 1 Or the Sea of Reeds

1:26, 27 | This passage recounts the events described in Numbers 13–14. In failing to go into the Promised Land, the Israelites **rebelled against the command of the LORD** (Ps. 106:24, 25). Since God has given His people everything they need to walk in faith, fear is nothing other than disobedience to Him and His principles. To dwell in fear is to live in sin, and it distorts God's purposes in individual lives.

1:29-33 | The point of the **wilderness** experience was for the Israelites to bond with their Father. After generations of slavery under their tyrannical masters in Egypt, God wanted His children to learn what wondrous things transpire when His people follow Him. Instead, their fear caused them to disbelieve His promises (Heb. 3:9, 10).

1:31 | God had **carried** Israel **as a father carries his son**—leading

their steps, providing food, offering protection, and doing everything possible to nurture a trusting, loving relationship.

1:35 | Disobedience is costly. The adults of the Promised Land era were sentenced to a restless, nomadic life in the desert for nearly 40 years, waiting for the last of the forsaken Exodus **generation** to die (Num. 14:29; Heb. 3:16–19). When the final body was set at rest, the nation could finally claim its true home.

1:37, 38 | The aged Moses preached a final series of sermons to the generation that was entering the Promised Land, poignantly recounting his 40 years of hard service. The Israelites had often discouraged him, so as he introduced his successor, Joshua, Moses said, **Encourage him**. One of the most helpful things a retiring minister or leader can do is appeal to the people to support his or her successor.

There is no grief as deep as that of a parent who loses a child—at any age. But when a child dies at a very young age, how does God view that little one's eternal destiny? Here are three reassuring reasons for believing that all infants and small children who die go straight to heaven.

1. *The character of God.* The fact that He is called "Father" in the Bible (Rom. 8:15) is an initial clue as to how He regards the helpless and innocent among us. God is "compassionate and gracious . . . slow to anger, abounding in love and faithfulness" (Ps. 86:15). He is also "good to all; he has compassion on all he has made" (Ps. 145:9). These traits tell us He would never judge anyone unjustly, such as children who do not yet have the ability to understand the gospel.

Interestingly, when the people of Israel were held accountable for their unbelief going into the Promised Land, their children were not (1:39). Another example is the 120,000 children of Nineveh (Jonah 4:11). Although the Ninevites were a cruel people deserving of judgment, God had mercy on the city because of the large number of children "who [could not] tell their right hand from their left." God's justice accounts for those not able to believe.

In Ezekiel 16:20, 21 God refers to children as His, and in Jeremiah 2:34 and 19:4, He refers to them as "innocent." Yes, children are born into sin just like everyone else, but their sins are not willful and premeditated.

2. *The condition for salvation.* Small children do not have the ability to understand that an affirmative response to the gospel is the condition for salvation. They do not know what they must do to be saved (Acts 16:30, 31). Before a child knows how to choose between good and evil, he or she is protected from judgment for sin by the blood of the Lord. If one cannot reasonably accept or reject the payment for sin made by Christ, that person is accepted by God. Since the condition for salvation is accepting the gospel, the inability to do so spares one the judgment for not having done so.

3. *The compassion of the Savior.* Jesus' love for little children is seen on more than one occasion in the Gospels. Indeed, the references to Jesus' interaction with children include the adjective "little," as if to highlight His tender compassion toward little ones (Matt. 19:13, 14; Mark 10:13, 14). In Luke 18:15–17, the reference is to infants or babies who are brought to Him.

Perhaps the most meaningful reference is Matthew 18:14, where Jesus says, "In the same way your Father in heaven is not willing that any of these little ones should perish." It could not be more clear: Jesus is not willing for little ones (Grk. *micros*) to be lost.

In 2 Samuel 12, the story of David's child provides additional compelling evidence. When David committed adultery with Bathsheba, she became pregnant with his child. He then had her husband killed.

After the child was born, God sent the prophet Nathan to confront David about his sins. As part of God's judgment, Nathan told David that the child born to Bathsheba would be taken away in death. The child became ill, and David fasted and prayed for the baby to live. But on the seventh day, the infant died. David then washed and anointed himself and went into the temple to worship the Lord. When asked why David was no longer fasting and mourning, David's reply was, "Now that he is dead, why should I go on fasting? Can I bring him back again? I will go to him, but he will not return to me" (2 Sam. 12:23).

In other words, David was confident that he would see his child again. David believed he was going to heaven when he died, and that is where he expected to see his son. Even though the idea of heaven was not as fully understood theologically in the OT as in the NT, David still believed that he and his son would be reunited in the place of God's blessing where believers go after death.

David understood then what we now know to be true: small children and infants go to be with the Lord when they die.

For Further Reading: Job 1:5; Ps. 62:5–8; 73:23–26; Matt. 19:14, 15; 2 Cor. 5:1, 6–8

over your journey through this vast wilderness. These forty years the LORD your God has been with you, and you have not lacked anything.

[8]So we went on past our relatives the descendants of Esau, who live in Seir. We turned from the Arabah road, which comes up from Elath and Ezion Geber, and traveled along the desert road of Moab.

[9]Then the LORD said to me, "Do not harass the Moabites or provoke them to war, for I will not give you any part of their land. I have given Ar to the descendants of Lot as a possession."

[10](The Emites used to live there—a people strong and numerous, and as tall as the Anakites. [11]Like the Anakites, they too were considered Rephaites, but the Moabites called them Emites. [12]Horites used to live in Seir, but the descendants of Esau drove them out. They destroyed the Horites from before them and settled in their place, just as Israel did in the land the LORD gave them as their possession.)

[13]And the LORD said, "Now get up and cross the Zered Valley." So we crossed the valley.

[14]Thirty-eight years passed from the time we left Kadesh Barnea until we crossed the Zered Valley. By then, that entire generation of fighting men had perished from the camp, as the LORD had sworn to them. [15]The LORD's hand was against them until he had completely eliminated them from the camp.

[16]Now when the last of these fighting men among the people had died, [17]the LORD said to me, [18]"Today you are to pass by the region of Moab at Ar. [19]When you come to the Ammonites, do not harass them or provoke them to war, for I will not give you possession of any land belonging to the Ammonites. I have given it as a possession to the descendants of Lot."

[20](That too was considered a land of the Rephaites, who used to live there; but the Ammonites called them Zamzummites. [21]They were a people strong and numerous, and as tall as the Anakites. The LORD destroyed them from before the Ammonites, who drove them out and settled in their place. [22]The LORD had done the same for the descendants of Esau, who lived in Seir, when he destroyed the Horites from before them. They drove them out and have lived in their place to this day. [23]And as for the Avvites who lived in villages as far as Gaza, the Caphtorites coming out from Caphtor[a] destroyed them and settled in their place.)

Defeat of Sihon King of Heshbon

[24]"Set out now and cross the Arnon Gorge. See, I have given into your hand Sihon the Amorite, king of Heshbon, and his country. Begin to take possession of it and engage him in battle. [25]This very day I will begin to put the terror and fear of you on all the nations under heaven. They will hear reports of you and will tremble and be in anguish because of you."

[26]From the Desert of Kedemoth I sent messengers to Sihon king of Heshbon offering peace and saying, [27]"Let us pass through your country. We will stay on the main road; we will not turn aside to the right or to the left. [28]Sell us food to eat and water to drink for their price in silver. Only let us pass through on foot— [29]as the descendants of Esau, who live in Seir, and the Moabites, who live in Ar, did for us—until we cross the Jordan into the land the LORD our God is giving us." [30]But Sihon king of Heshbon refused to let us pass through. For the LORD your God had made his spirit stubborn and his heart obstinate in order to give him into your hands, as he has now done.

[31]The LORD said to me, "See, I have begun to deliver Sihon and his country over to you. Now begin to conquer and possess his land."

[32]When Sihon and all his army came out to meet us in battle at Jahaz, [33]the LORD our God delivered him over to us and we struck him down, together with his sons and his whole army. [34]At that time we took all his towns and completely destroyed[b] them— men, women and children. We left no survivors. [35]But the livestock and the plunder from the towns we had captured we carried off for ourselves. [36]From Aroer on the rim of the Arnon Gorge, and from the town in the gorge, even as far as Gilead, not one town was too strong for us. The LORD our

---

[a] 23 That is, Crete   [b] 34 The Hebrew term refers to the irrevocable giving over of things or persons to the LORD, often by totally destroying them.

2:8–23 | The **Moabites** and **Ammonites** were peoples descended from Lot (Gen. 19:30–38). The Hebrew people were not to **harass** or **provoke them** because the Lord had reserved land for them. This was similar to the instructions the Israelites were given about Edom, the descendants of Esau (2:1–7; 23:6–8; Num. 20:14–21). Yahweh's promises to other peoples continued to be important, even when His primary focus was on the Israelites.

2:24–3:11 | These descriptions of the defeats of **Sihon king of Heshbon** and **Og king of Bashan** recount the events first described in Numbers 21:21–35. Both victories were from the hand of God (2:33; 3:3). Og was of **the last of the Rephaites**, the giant people who caused Israel's spies to fear going into Canaan (Ps. 136:16–22).

God gave us all of them. [37] But in accordance with the command of the LORD our God, you did not encroach on any of the land of the Ammonites, neither the land along the course of the Jabbok nor that around the towns in the hills.

Defeat of Og King of Bashan

3 Next we turned and went up along the road toward Bashan, and Og king of Bashan with his whole army marched out to meet us in battle at Edrei. [2] The LORD said to me, "Do not be afraid of him, for I have delivered him into your hands, along with his whole army and his land. Do to him what you did to Sihon king of the Amorites, who reigned in Heshbon."

[3] So the LORD our God also gave into our hands Og king of Bashan and all his army. We struck them down, leaving no survivors. [4] At that time we took all his cities. There was not one of the sixty cities that we did not take from them — the whole region of Argob, Og's kingdom in Bashan. [5] All these cities were fortified with high walls and with gates and bars, and there were also a great many unwalled villages. [6] We completely destroyed[a] them, as we had done with Sihon king of Heshbon, destroying[a] every city — men, women and children. [7] But all the livestock and the plunder from their cities we carried off for ourselves.

[8] So at that time we took from these two kings of the Amorites the territory east of the Jordan, from the Arnon Gorge as far as Mount Hermon. [9] (Hermon is called Sirion by the Sidonians; the Amorites call it Senir.) [10] We took all the towns on the plateau, and all Gilead, and all Bashan as far as Salekah and Edrei, towns of Og's kingdom in Bashan. [11] (Og king of Bashan was the last of the Rephaites. His bed was decorated with iron and was more than nine cubits long and four cubits wide.[b] It is still in Rabbah of the Ammonites.)

Division of the Land

[12] Of the land that we took over at that time, I gave the Reubenites and the Gadites the territory north of Aroer by the Arnon Gorge, including half the hill country of Gilead, together with its towns. [13] The rest of Gilead and also all of Bashan, the kingdom of Og, I gave to the half-tribe of Manasseh.

(The whole region of Argob in Bashan used to be known as a land of the Rephaites. [14] Jair, a descendant of Manasseh, took the whole region of Argob as far as the border of the Geshurites and the Maakathites; it was named after him, so that to this day Bashan is called Havvoth Jair.[c]) [15] And I gave Gilead to Makir. [16] But to the Reubenites and the Gadites I gave the territory extending from Gilead down to the Arnon Gorge (the middle of the gorge being the border) and out to the Jabbok River, which is the border of the Ammonites. [17] Its western border was the Jordan in the Arabah, from Kinnereth to the Sea of the Arabah (that is, the Dead Sea), below the slopes of Pisgah.

[18] I commanded you at that time: "The LORD your God has given you this land to take possession of it. But all your able-bodied men, armed for battle, must cross over ahead of the other Israelites. [19] However, your wives, your children and your livestock (I know you have much livestock) may stay in the towns I have given you, [20] until the LORD gives rest to your fellow Israelites as he has to you, and they too have taken over the land that the LORD your God is giving them across the Jordan. After that, each of you may go back to the possession I have given you."

Moses Forbidden to Cross the Jordan

[21] At that time I commanded Joshua: "You have seen with your own eyes all that the LORD your God has done to these two kings. The LORD will do the same to all the kingdoms over there where you are going. [22] Do not be afraid of them; the LORD your God himself will fight for you."

[23] At that time I pleaded with the LORD: [24] "Sovereign LORD, you have begun to show to your servant your greatness and your strong hand. For what god is there in heaven or on earth who can do the deeds and mighty works you do? [25] Let me go over and see the good land beyond the Jordan — that fine hill country and Lebanon." [26] But because of you the LORD was angry with me and would not listen to me. "That is enough," the LORD said. "Do not speak to me anymore about this matter. [27] Go up to

---

[a] 6 The Hebrew term refers to the irrevocable giving over of things or persons to the LORD, often by totally destroying them.   [b] 11 That is, about 14 feet long and 6 feet wide or about 4 meters long and 1.8 meters wide   [c] 14 Or called the settlements of Jair

---

3:12–22 | Numbers 32:1–42 and 34:13–15 describe the gift and terms of the land east of the Jordan for the **Reubenites** and **Gadites** and **the half-tribe of Manasseh**.
3:23–29 | Moses had been forbidden to go into the Promised Land

because of his actions in the Desert of Zin (1:37; Num. 20:2–13; 27:14), but he made one final request to **go over and see the good land**. Although this request was not granted, Yahweh did allow Moses to **look at the land** from the **top of Pisgah** (32:48–52; 34:1–4).

the top of Pisgah and look west and north and south and east. Look at the land with your own eyes, since you are not going to cross this Jordan. [28]But commission Joshua, and encourage and strengthen him, for he will lead this people across and will cause them to inherit the land that you will see." [29]So we stayed in the valley near Beth Peor.

Obedience Commanded

4 Now, Israel, hear the decrees and laws I am about to teach you. Follow them so that you may live and may go in and take possession of the land the LORD, the God of your ancestors, is giving you. [2]Do not add to what I command you and do not subtract from it, but keep the commands of the LORD your God that I give you.

[3]You saw with your own eyes what the LORD did at Baal Peor. The LORD your God destroyed from among you everyone who followed the Baal of Peor, [4]but all of you who held fast to the LORD your God are still alive today.

[5]See, I have taught you decrees and laws as the LORD my God commanded me, so that you may follow them in the land you are entering to take possession of it. [6]Observe them carefully, for this will show your wisdom and understanding to the nations, who will hear about all these decrees and say, "Surely this great nation is a wise and understanding people." [7]What other nation is so great as to have their gods near them the way the LORD our God is near us whenever we pray to him? [8]And what other nation is so great as to have such righteous decrees and laws as this body of laws I am setting before you today?

[9]Only be careful, and watch yourselves closely so that you do not forget the things your eyes have seen or let them fade from your heart as long as you live. Teach them to your children and to their children after them. [10]Remember the day you stood before the LORD your God at Horeb, when he said to me, "Assemble the people before me to hear my words so that they may learn to revere me as long as they live in the land and may teach them to their children." [11]You came near and stood at the foot of the mountain while it blazed with fire to the very heavens, with black clouds and deep darkness. [12]Then the LORD spoke to you out of the fire. You heard the sound of words but saw no form; there was only a voice. [13]He declared to you his covenant, the Ten Commandments, which he commanded you to follow and then wrote them on two stone tablets. [14]And the LORD directed me at that time to teach you the decrees and laws you are to follow in the land that you are crossing the Jordan to possess.

Idolatry Forbidden

[15]You saw no form of any kind the day the LORD spoke to you at Horeb out of the fire. Therefore watch yourselves very carefully, [16]so that you do not become corrupt and make for yourselves an idol, an image of any shape, whether formed like a man or a woman, [17]or like any animal on earth or any bird that flies in the air, [18]or like any creature that moves along the ground or any fish in the waters below. [19]And when you look up to the sky and see the sun, the moon and the stars—all the heavenly array—do not be enticed into bowing down to them and worshiping things the LORD your God has apportioned to all the nations under heaven. [20]But as for you, the LORD took you and brought you out of the iron-smelting furnace, out of Egypt, to be the people of his inheritance, as you now are.

[21]The LORD was angry with me because of you, and he solemnly swore that I would not cross the Jordan and enter the good land the LORD your God is giving you as your inheritance. [22]I will die in this land; I will not cross the Jordan; but you are about to cross over and take possession of that good land. [23]Be careful not to forget the covenant of the LORD your God that he made with you; do not make for yourselves an idol in the form of anything the LORD your God has forbidden. [24]For the LORD your God is a consuming fire, a jealous God.

[25]After you have had children and grandchildren and have lived in the land a long time—if you then become corrupt and make any kind of idol, doing evil in the eyes of the LORD your God and arousing his

---

4:2 | Do not add . . . do not subtract establishes that God's Word is sacred and not to be tampered with (Josh. 1:7; Rev. 22:18, 19). **4:7, 8 |** The Israelites were a special people because (1) no other nation had **God** so **near** that they could **pray to him** for any reason, and (2) no other nation had **such righteous decrees and laws** (2 Sam. 7:23). To be able to draw near to God in prayer and to study His righteous decrees in Scripture is one of His richest blessings.

4:15 | Moses carefully reminded the people that when the Lord's presence came with fire and thunder on Mount Sinai, they saw **no form** (Isa. 40:18). That no one can see God is a teaching that runs through Scripture (Ex. 19:19–21; 33:20, 23; 1 Kgs. 19:11–13; John 1:18; 6:46; Col. 1:15; 1 Tim. 6:16). **4:24 |** Yahweh is also **a consuming fire, a jealous God** (Ex. 34:14; Heb. 12:29). His jealousy is protective of His singularity as God and God alone; His fire is judgment against all idolatry.

anger, [26]I call the heavens and the earth as witnesses against you this day that you will quickly perish from the land that you are crossing the Jordan to possess. You will not live there long but will certainly be destroyed. [27]The LORD will scatter you among the peoples, and only a few of you will survive among the nations to which the LORD will drive you. [28]There you will worship man-made gods of wood and stone, which cannot see or hear or eat or smell. [29]But if from there you seek the LORD your God, you will find him if you seek him with all your heart and with all your soul. [30]When you are in distress and all these things have happened to you, then in later days you will return to the LORD your God and obey him. [31]For the LORD your God is a merciful God; he will not abandon or destroy you or forget the covenant with your ancestors, which he confirmed to them by oath.

The LORD Is God

[32]Ask now about the former days, long before your time, from the day God created human beings on the earth; ask from one end of the heavens to the other. Has anything so great as this ever happened, or has anything like it ever been heard of? [33]Has any other people heard the voice of God[a] speaking out of fire, as you have, and lived? [34]Has any god ever tried to take for himself one nation out of another nation, by testings, by signs and wonders, by war, by a mighty hand and an outstretched arm, or by great and awesome deeds, like all the things the LORD your God did for you in Egypt before your very eyes?

[35]You were shown these things so that you might know that the LORD is God; besides him there is no other. [36]From heaven he made you hear his voice to discipline you. On earth he showed you his great fire, and you heard his words from out of the fire. [37]Because he loved your ancestors and chose their descendants after them, he brought you out of Egypt by his Presence and his great strength, [38]to drive out before you nations greater and stronger than you and to bring you into their land to give it to you for your inheritance, as it is today.

[39]Acknowledge and take to heart this day that the LORD is God in heaven above and on the earth below. There is no other. [40]Keep his decrees and commands, which I am giving you today, so that it may go well with you and your children after you and that you may live long in the land the LORD your God gives you for all time.

Cities of Refuge

[41]Then Moses set aside three cities east of the Jordan, [42]to which anyone who had killed a person could flee if they had unintentionally killed a neighbor without malice aforethought. They could flee into one of these cities and save their life. [43]The cities were these: Bezer in the wilderness plateau, for the Reubenites; Ramoth in Gilead, for the Gadites; and Golan in Bashan, for the Manassites.

Introduction to the Law

[44]This is the law Moses set before the Israelites. [45]These are the stipulations, decrees and laws Moses gave them when they came out of Egypt [46]and were in the valley near Beth Peor east of the Jordan, in the land of Sihon king of the Amorites, who reigned in Heshbon and was defeated by Moses and the Israelites as they came out of Egypt. [47]They took possession of his land and the land of Og king of Bashan, the two Amorite kings east of the Jordan. [48]This land extended from Aroer on the rim of the Arnon Gorge to Mount Sirion[b] (that is, Hermon), [49]and included all the Arabah east of the Jordan, as far as the Dead Sea,[c] below the slopes of Pisgah.

The Ten Commandments

5 Moses summoned all Israel and said: Hear, Israel, the decrees and laws I declare in your hearing today. Learn them and be sure to follow them. [2]The LORD our God made a covenant with us at Horeb. [3]It was not with our ancestors[d] that the LORD made this covenant, but with us, with all of us who are alive here today. [4]The LORD spoke to you face to face out of the fire on the mountain. [5](At that time I stood between the LORD and you to declare to you the word of the LORD, because you were afraid of the fire and did not go up the mountain.) And he said:

---

[a] 33 Or of a god   [b] 48 Syriac (see also 3:9); Hebrew Siyon   [c] 49 Hebrew the Sea of the Arabah   [d] 3 Or not only with our parents

---

The Frailty Rule • 5:12–15

The fourth commandment—the Frailty Rule—is a fascinating one. By the time of Jesus' ministry on earth, Jewish leaders had compiled a list of 1,521 things a person could not do on the Sabbath. This was their way of expanding on God's fourth commandment. In this, they turned the Sabbath into a burden instead of a blessing.

The word *sabbath* means "rest." The Jews were to work hard for six days and rest on the seventh. Shortly after Jesus' ascension to heaven, the followers of Christ moved the meeting day of the church to the first day of the week—the day after the Sabbath, which was the seventh day. In our terms, the Sabbath was on Saturday (and still is for observant Jews), and the Lord's Day—the day of the resurrection of Christ—was on the day we now know as Sunday (Acts 20:7). So the day of rest and worship for Christians has traditionally been on Sunday, to honor the resurrection, rather than on Saturday, the Jewish Sabbath.

The fourth commandment does not bind believers to treat Sunday as a "Christian Sabbath," but the principle of taking one day out of seven to rest (Gen. 2:2) was established "in the beginning" and still has relevance today. Unfortunately, Christians have been widely influenced by the non-Christian approach to Sunday, which is to treat it like any other day of the week. There are no rules about what a person can and cannot do on Sunday. It is a day to enjoy as a gift from God—rest, refreshment, service, worship—a day unlike any other in the week.

6 "I am the Lord your God, who brought you out of Egypt, out of the land of slavery.

7 "You shall have no other gods before[a] me.

8 "You shall not make for yourself an image in the form of anything in heaven above or on the earth beneath or in the waters below. 9 You shall not bow down to them or worship them; for I, the Lord your God, am a jealous God, punishing the children for the sin of the parents to the third and fourth generation of those who hate me, 10 but showing love to a thousand generations of those who love me and keep my commandments.

11 "You shall not misuse the name of the Lord your God, for the Lord will not hold anyone guiltless who misuses his name.

12 "Observe the Sabbath day by keeping it holy, as the Lord your God has commanded you. 13 Six days you shall labor and do all your work, 14 but the seventh day is a sabbath to the Lord your God. On it you shall not do any work, neither you, nor your son or daughter, nor your male or female servant, nor your ox, your donkey or any of your animals, nor any foreigner residing in your towns, so that your male and female servants may rest, as you do. 15 Remember that you were slaves in Egypt and that the Lord your God brought you out of there with a mighty hand and an outstretched arm. Therefore the Lord your God has commanded you to observe the Sabbath day.

16 "Honor your father and your mother, as the Lord your God has commanded you, so that you may live long and that it may go well with you in the land the Lord your God is giving you.

17 "You shall not murder.

18 "You shall not commit adultery.

19 "You shall not steal.

20 "You shall not give false testimony against your neighbor.

21 "You shall not covet your neighbor's wife. You shall not set your desire on your neighbor's house or land, his male or female servant, his ox or donkey, or anything that belongs to your neighbor."

22 These are the commandments the Lord proclaimed in a loud voice to your whole assembly there on the mountain from out of the fire, the cloud and the deep darkness; and he added nothing more. Then he wrote them on two stone tablets and gave them to me.

---

[a] 7 Or *besides*

5:6–21 | The Ten Commandments fall into two categories: the first four speak to humanity's relationship with God; the last six give instructions for relationships with others (Ex. 20:1–17). The commands to love God and to love others summarize the entire Ten Commandments and reflect His holy character (Matt. 22:37–40).

5:16 | Families who heed this command not only honor the Lord, but they also strengthen society, producing good citizens and leaders. A rewarding proposition for children is also offered: **honor** your parents, and God will honor you with a longer life (Eph. 6:2, 3). The practice of honor is respect.

²³When you heard the voice out of the darkness, while the mountain was ablaze with fire, all the leaders of your tribes and your elders came to me. ²⁴And you said, "The LORD our God has shown us his glory and his majesty, and we have heard his voice from the fire. Today we have seen that a person can live even if God speaks with them. ²⁵But now, why should we die? This great fire will consume us, and we will die if we hear the voice of the LORD our God any longer. ²⁶For what mortal has ever heard the voice of the living God speaking out of fire, as we have, and survived? ²⁷Go near and listen to all that the LORD our God says. Then tell us whatever the LORD our God tells you. We will listen and obey."

²⁸The LORD heard you when you spoke to me, and the LORD said to me, "I have heard what this people said to you. Everything they said was good. ²⁹Oh, that their hearts would be inclined to fear me and keep all my commands always, so that it might go well with them and their children forever!

³⁰"Go, tell them to return to their tents. ³¹But you stay here with me so that I may give you all the commands, decrees and laws you are to teach them to follow in the land I am giving them to possess."

³²So be careful to do what the LORD your God has commanded you; do not turn aside to the right or to the left. ³³Walk in obedience to all that the LORD your God has commanded you, so that you may live and prosper and prolong your days in the land that you will possess.

Love the LORD Your God

6 These are the commands, decrees and laws the LORD your God directed me to teach you to observe in the land that you are crossing the Jordan to possess, ²so that you, your children and their children after them may fear the LORD your God as long as you live by keeping all his decrees and commands that I give you, and so that you may enjoy long life. ³Hear, Israel, and be careful to obey so that it may go well with

Tough Questions | How can love be commanded? • 6:4–9

"Love the LORD your God" is a command. One might wonder how love can be commanded. The reason is that love in Hebrew is not confined to feelings; the term *heart* centers on the intellect, sensibilities, and will. So when God commands that His people love Him, it means to decide to cleave to Him—and Him alone.

The command includes *soul*, which here is a synonym for heart—the true essence of a person. *Strength* translates a phrase that means "Give it all you have!" Parents were instructed to focus their principal teachings of Torah in all aspects of life. In addition, as a wonderful symbol, a few verses from Deuteronomy 6 and 11 were to be written on a small scroll and then placed in two small leather boxes. One would be tied on a person's forehead and the other wrapped around one hand. The word for this is *phylactery*. Similar "boxes" for these Scriptures were placed at doorposts and on gates and are still used today.

you and that you may increase greatly in a land flowing with milk and honey, just as the LORD, the God of your ancestors, promised you.

⁴Hear, O Israel: The LORD our God, the LORD is one.ᵃ ⁵Love the LORD your God with all your heart and with all your soul and with all your strength. ⁶These commandments that I give you today are to be on your hearts. ⁷Impress them on your children. Talk about them when you sit at home and when you walk along the road, when you lie down and when you get up. ⁸Tie them as symbols on your hands and bind them on your foreheads. ⁹Write them on the doorframes of your houses and on your gates.

¹⁰When the LORD your God brings you into the land he swore to your fathers, to Abraham, Isaac and Jacob, to give you—a land with large, flourishing cities you did not build, ¹¹houses filled with all kinds of good things you did not provide, wells you did not dig, and vineyards and olive groves you did

---

ᵃ 4 Or *The LORD our God is one LORD*; or *The LORD is our God, the LORD is one*; or *The LORD is our God, the LORD alone*

5:23-27 | God is so holy that the Israelites thought that even hearing His **voice** could mean their death (Ex. 20:18, 19).
5:28-33 | The response of the people in this moment was so right before the Lord that Yahweh wistfully expressed sadness that they would not always respond in this manner (32:29).
6:1-3 | All the words of the Lord—**the commands, decrees and laws**—are His gracious gifts to His people (Ps. 119), designed for their protection and for their communion with Him.
6:4-9 | This passage is at the heart of the Hebrew faith and is called the *Shema*, from the Hebrew word meaning "to hear."

The *Shema* is the "creed of Israel" (Ps. 119:11).
6:5 | When Jesus was asked, "Which is the greatest commandment in the Law?" (Matt. 22:36), He did not quote the first of the Ten Commandments; He quoted this verse.
6:10-15 | The great concern of God was that when His chosen ones entered the land, they would absorb the culture of the Canaanites. Therefore, He communicated to them the importance of preparing their hearts. On the other hand, the **cities**, **houses**, **wells**, **vineyards**, and **olive groves** that were in the land were for the people to enjoy, even though they had not built, planted, or tended any of them (Josh. 24:13).

ESSENTIALS
of the Christian Faith

Loving God
Deuteronomy 6:4, 5

The commandments, statutes, and judgments the Lord gave to Moses in the late 15th century BC presented a challenge to later Jewish scholars, who decided to organize and number them. In the 12th century AD, the great scholar Maimonides categorized all the laws he discerned in Torah (the first five books of the Bible) into 613 distinct items. At the time of Jesus, scholars had already begun these discussions; they had in mind a great many laws when they asked Jesus their question concerning "the greatest commandment."

It was no surprise, then, that when the religious leaders wanted to discredit Jesus in the eyes of His followers, they tested Him in His knowledge of the Law. A Pharisee publicly challenged Him: "'Teacher, which is the greatest commandment in the Law?' Jesus replied, 'Love the Lord your God with all your heart and with all your soul and with all your mind.' This is the first and greatest commandment" (Matt. 22:36–38).

Now, this particular Pharisee might have thought that the greatest commandment would be the first in the list of 10 given to Moses—or at least one of the 10. After all, when the Ten Commandments were given to the children of Israel at Mount Sinai, they had just left a polytheistic land (Egypt) and were promised to inherit another (Canaan). The very first commandment addressed this problem: "You shall have no other gods before me" (Ex. 20:3). Israel needed to learn that their God, Yahweh, was the one true God. He was "jealous" for His own glory (Ex. 20:5) for the Israelites' sake, that they would not become entrapped by images of wood and stone in Canaan.

The generation that received the Law died in the wilderness, so Moses retaught the laws to the generation that would inherit Canaan. As the people stood on the banks of the Jordan River, about to cross into the Promised Land, Moses repeated the Ten Commandments (5:6–21). Yahweh then gave Israel the basic summation of biblical faith: "Hear, O Israel: The LORD our God, the LORD is one [better, "the LORD alone"]. Love the LORD your God with all your heart and with all your soul and with all your strength" (6:4, 5).

The translation "the LORD alone" is preferred here because the people of Israel never had a problem with the question: "Is God one or many?" What troubled them in their early history was the question: "Is there one God or are there many?"

Deuteronomy 6:4 introduces the central biblical texts used in Jewish synagogue worship liturgy, then and now. Known as the *"Shema` Yisrael"* ("Hear, O Israel"), it reaffirms the monotheistic core of Judaism. The next verse (6:5) is what Jesus quoted in answer to the Pharisee's question. The greatest commandment, Jesus said, is to love God with all that we have and are: heart, soul, mind, strength, time, talent, treasure, dreams, gifts, and abilities. When we love God that way, we live a life of worship.

Worship means to ascribe worth to the object worshiped. The Pharisee asked, "Which is the greatest commandment?" Jesus answered with a question (in so many words) of His own: "What is God worth to you? If He is worth all that you are and have, you will love Him with it all. You will become the answer to your own question. To be a lover of God is to be a worshiper of God."

Every part of a human being is to be employed in loving God: thoughts, emotions, energy, and purpose. That is why God created humans. He poured His image into them in order that they might respond in kind. To direct our love toward anything besides God (to love God with *some* instead of *all* that we are) is to fall into the trap of idolatry that the Lord warned the newly freed slaves about.

Are you giving anything to someone or something else that belongs to God? Or does your life confess, "The Lord our God, the Lord alone"?

For Further Reading: Deut. 10:12, 13; Ps. 59:16; Prov. 3:3; Zeph. 3:17; Col. 1:15–20

not plant—then when you eat and are satisfied, [12]be careful that you do not forget the LORD, who brought you out of Egypt, out of the land of slavery.

[13]Fear the LORD your God, serve him only and take your oaths in his name. [14]Do not follow other gods, the gods of the peoples around you; [15]for the LORD your God, who is among you, is a jealous God and his anger will burn against you, and he will destroy you from the face of the land. [16]Do not put the LORD your God to the test as you did at Massah. [17]Be sure to keep the commands of the LORD your God and the stipulations and decrees he has given you. [18]Do what is right and good in the LORD's sight, so that it may go well with you and you may go in and take over the good land the LORD promised on oath to your ancestors, [19]thrusting out all your enemies before you, as the LORD said.

[20]In the future, when your son asks you, "What is the meaning of the stipulations, decrees and laws the LORD our God has commanded you?" [21]tell him: "We were slaves of Pharaoh in Egypt, but the LORD brought us out of Egypt with a mighty hand. [22]Before our eyes the LORD sent signs and wonders—great and terrible—on Egypt and Pharaoh and his whole household. [23]But he brought us out from there to bring us in and give us the land he promised on oath to our ancestors. [24]The LORD commanded us to obey all these decrees and to fear the LORD our God, so that we might always prosper and be kept alive, as is the case today. [25]And if we are careful to obey all this law before the LORD our God, as he has commanded us, that will be our righteousness."

Driving Out the Nations

7 When the LORD your God brings you into the land you are entering to possess and drives out before you many nations—the Hittites, Girgashites, Amorites, Canaanites, Perizzites, Hivites and Jebusites, seven nations larger and stronger than you— [2]and when the LORD your God has delivered them over to you and you have defeated them, then you must destroy them totally.[a] Make no treaty with them, and show them no mercy. [3]Do not intermarry with them. Do not give your daughters to their sons or take their daughters for your sons,

[4]for they will turn your children away from following me to serve other gods, and the LORD's anger will burn against you and will quickly destroy you. [5]This is what you are to do to them: Break down their altars, smash their sacred stones, cut down their Asherah poles[b] and burn their idols in the fire. [6]For you are a people holy to the LORD your God. The LORD your God has chosen you out of all the peoples on the face of the earth to be his people, his treasured possession.

[7]The LORD did not set his affection on you and choose you because you were more numerous than other peoples, for you were the fewest of all peoples. [8]But it was because the LORD loved you and kept the oath he swore to your ancestors that he brought you out with a mighty hand and redeemed you from the land of slavery, from the power of Pharaoh king of Egypt. [9]Know therefore that the LORD your God is God; he is the faithful God, keeping his covenant of love to a thousand generations of those who love him and keep his commandments. [10]But

> those who hate him he will repay to
> their face by destruction;
> he will not be slow to repay to their
> face those who hate him.

[11]Therefore, take care to follow the commands, decrees and laws I give you today.

[12]If you pay attention to these laws and are careful to follow them, then the LORD your God will keep his covenant of love with you, as he swore to your ancestors. [13]He will love you and bless you and increase your numbers. He will bless the fruit of your womb, the crops of your land—your grain, new wine and olive oil—the calves of your herds and the lambs of your flocks in the land he swore to your ancestors to give you. [14]You will be blessed more than any other people; none of your men or women will be childless, nor will any of your livestock be without young. [15]The LORD will keep you free from every disease. He will not inflict on you the horrible diseases you knew in Egypt, but he will inflict them on all who hate you. [16]You must destroy all the peoples

---

[a] 2 The Hebrew term refers to the irrevocable giving over of things or persons to the LORD, often by totally destroying them; also in verse 26.   [b] 5 That is, wooden symbols of the goddess Asherah; here and elsewhere in Deuteronomy

6:16 | Jesus quoted the first portion of this verse (**Do not put the LORD your God to the test**) when Satan tempted Him (Matt. 4:7; Luke 4:12). Humans are the servants of God; for them to presume upon or test God is sin (1 Cor. 10:9).
7:9 | It is true that the punishment for certain sins may have repercussions to the third and fourth generation (Ex. 20:5, 6), yet the Lord keeps His covenant promises for **a thousand generations** to **those who love him and keep his commandments** (Neh. 1:5; Dan. 9:4). By passing one's faith to one's children and their children, a person can impact the world beyond his or her years.

> **For Reflection**
>
> **Living in the Blessings of God • 8:11–14**
>
> God warned the nation of Israel about the dangers of summertime living—the danger of forgetting about God in the good times: "Be careful that you do not forget the LORD your God . . . when you eat and are satisfied, when you build fine houses and settle down, and when your herds and flocks grow large and your silver and gold increase and all you have is multiplied."
>
> The greatest danger in the summer of life is forgetting who is responsible for the good life you enjoy. If you are in one of life's summers right now—a time when things are going well, what evidence in your life shows that you are continuing to walk by faith? Let thanksgiving to God be on your lips for "every good and perfect gift" that has come down from above (James 1:17). It is critical for Christians to stay close and to stay grateful to God in all seasons, but especially in the seasons of prosperity (Phil. 4:12, 13).

the LORD your God gives over to you. Do not look on them with pity and do not serve their gods, for that will be a snare to you.

¹⁷You may say to yourselves, "These nations are stronger than we are. How can we drive them out?" ¹⁸But do not be afraid of them; remember well what the LORD your God did to Pharaoh and to all Egypt. ¹⁹You saw with your own eyes the great trials, the signs and wonders, the mighty hand and outstretched arm, with which the LORD your God brought you out. The LORD your God will do the same to all the peoples you now fear. ²⁰Moreover, the LORD your God will send the hornet among them until even the survivors who hide from you have perished. ²¹Do not be terrified by them, for the LORD your God, who is among you, is a great and awesome God. ²²The LORD your God will drive out those nations before you, little by little. You will not be allowed to eliminate them all at once, or the wild animals will multiply around you. ²³But the LORD your God will deliver them over to you, throwing them into great confusion until they are destroyed. ²⁴He will give their kings into your hand, and you will wipe out their names from under heaven. No one will be able to stand up against you; you will destroy them.

²⁵The images of their gods you are to burn in the fire. Do not covet the silver and gold on them, and do not take it for yourselves, or you will be ensnared by it, for it is detestable to the LORD your God. ²⁶Do not bring a detestable thing into your house or you, like it, will be set apart for destruction. Regard it as vile and utterly detest it, for it is set apart for destruction.

Do Not Forget the LORD

8 Be careful to follow every command I am giving you today, so that you may live and increase and may enter and possess the land the LORD promised on oath to your ancestors. ²Remember how the LORD your God led you all the way in the wilderness these forty years, to humble and test you in order to know what was in your heart, whether or not you would keep his commands. ³He humbled you, causing you to hunger and then feeding you with manna, which neither you nor your ancestors had known, to teach you that man does not live on bread alone but on every word that comes from the mouth of the LORD. ⁴Your clothes did not wear out and your feet did not swell during these forty years. ⁵Know then in your heart that as a man disciplines his son, so the LORD your God disciplines you.

⁶Observe the commands of the LORD your God, walking in obedience to him and revering him. ⁷For the LORD your God is bringing you into a good land—a land with brooks, streams, and deep springs gushing out into the valleys and hills; ⁸a land with wheat and barley, vines and fig trees, pomegranates, olive oil and honey; ⁹a land where bread will not be scarce and you will lack nothing; a land where the rocks are iron and you can dig copper out of the hills.

¹⁰When you have eaten and are satisfied, praise the LORD your God for the good land he has given you. ¹¹Be careful that you do not forget the LORD your God, failing to observe his commands, his laws and his decrees that I am giving you this day. ¹²Otherwise, when you eat and are satisfied, when you build fine houses and settle down, ¹³and when your herds and flocks grow large and your silver and gold increase and all you

---

7:18 | When facing their enemies, Israel was exhorted to **remember well what the LORD their God did to Pharaoh and to all Egypt.** When facing crises, it is wise to recall ways in which God has answered prayer in the past (Ps. 105:5).
8:3 | Jesus quoted these words to the devil in His temptation: man lives **on every word that comes from the mouth of the LORD** (Matt. 4:4).
8:5, 6 | One implication of having God as one's Father is that He **disciplines** His children so that they will walk in His ways (Heb.

12:7). Christian parents must discipline their children for the same reason (Prov. 3:11, 12).
8:6–10 | This is a very important passage on the abundance of the land and its produce. Canaan was **a good land**—well-suited for the agrarian and pastoral lifestyle of the Hebrew people.
8:11–20 | The God who blesses and sustains life was setting before Israel the choice: **forget the LORD your God** and **be destroyed,** or **remember** Him and live (Ps. 119:83, 109, 141, 176).

have is multiplied, [14]then your heart will become proud and you will forget the LORD your God, who brought you out of Egypt, out of the land of slavery. [15]He led you through the vast and dreadful wilderness, that thirsty and waterless land, with its venomous snakes and scorpions. He brought you water out of hard rock. [16]He gave you manna to eat in the wilderness, something your ancestors had never known, to humble and test you so that in the end it might go well with you. [17]You may say to yourself, "My power and the strength of my hands have produced this wealth for me." [18]But remember the LORD your God, for it is he who gives you the ability to produce wealth, and so confirms his covenant, which he swore to your ancestors, as it is today.

[19]If you ever forget the LORD your God and follow other gods and worship and bow down to them, I testify against you today that you will surely be destroyed. [20]Like the nations the LORD destroyed before you, so you will be destroyed for not obeying the LORD your God.

Not Because of Israel's Righteousness

9 Hear, Israel: You are now about to cross the Jordan to go in and dispossess nations greater and stronger than you, with large cities that have walls up to the sky. [2]The people are strong and tall—Anakites! You know about them and have heard it said: "Who can stand up against the Anakites?" [3]But be assured today that the LORD your God is the one who goes across ahead of you like a devouring fire. He will destroy them; he will subdue them before you. And you will drive them out and annihilate them quickly, as the LORD has promised you.

[4]After the LORD your God has driven them out before you, do not say to yourself, "The LORD has brought me here to take possession of this land because of my righteousness." No, it is on account of the wickedness of these nations that the LORD is going to drive them out before you. [5]It is not because of your righteousness or your integrity that you are going in to take possession of their land; but on account of the wickedness of these nations, the LORD your God will drive them out before you, to accomplish what he swore to your fathers, to

Abraham, Isaac and Jacob. [6]Understand, then, that it is not because of your righteousness that the LORD your God is giving you this good land to possess, for you are a stiff-necked people.

The Golden Calf

[7]Remember this and never forget how you aroused the anger of the LORD your God in the wilderness. From the day you left Egypt until you arrived here, you have been rebellious against the LORD. [8]At Horeb you aroused the LORD's wrath so that he was angry enough to destroy you. [9]When I went up on the mountain to receive the tablets of stone, the tablets of the covenant that the LORD had made with you, I stayed on the mountain forty days and forty nights; I ate no bread and drank no water. [10]The LORD gave me two stone tablets inscribed by the finger of God. On them were all the commandments the LORD proclaimed to you on the mountain out of the fire, on the day of the assembly.

[11]At the end of the forty days and forty nights, the LORD gave me the two stone tablets, the tablets of the covenant. [12]Then the LORD told me, "Go down from here at once, because your people whom you brought out of Egypt have become corrupt. They have turned away quickly from what I commanded them and have made an idol for themselves."

[13]And the LORD said to me, "I have seen this people, and they are a stiff-necked people indeed! [14]Let me alone, so that I may destroy them and blot out their name from under heaven. And I will make you into a nation stronger and more numerous than they."

[15]So I turned and went down from the mountain while it was ablaze with fire. And the two tablets of the covenant were in my hands. [16]When I looked, I saw that you had sinned against the LORD your God; you had made for yourselves an idol cast in the shape of a calf. You had turned aside quickly from the way that the LORD had commanded you. [17]So I took the two tablets and threw them out of my hands, breaking them to pieces before your eyes.

[18]Then once again I fell prostrate before the LORD for forty days and forty nights; I

8:17, 18 | Here, Moses warns against remembering the Lord when times are bad and forgetting Him when times are good. His people **remember** Him through thankfulness and generosity in His name (1 Cor. 16:2).
9:4–6 | God's choice of Israel had nothing to do with her

righteousness or her size (Rom. 11:6); she was the least (7:7), and she was made up of a **stiff-necked people**. The two stated reasons that the Lord brought the Israelites into the land were the **wickedness of** the **nations** and the oath God **swore to** their **fathers**.

ate no bread and drank no water, because of all the sin you had committed, doing what was evil in the LORD's sight and so arousing his anger. ¹⁹I feared the anger and wrath of the LORD, for he was angry enough with you to destroy you. But again the LORD listened to me. ²⁰And the LORD was angry enough with Aaron to destroy him, but at that time I prayed for Aaron too. ²¹Also I took that sinful thing of yours, the calf you had made, and burned it in the fire. Then I crushed it and ground it to powder as fine as dust and threw the dust into a stream that flowed down the mountain.

²²You also made the LORD angry at Taberah, at Massah and at Kibroth Hattaavah.

²³And when the LORD sent you out from Kadesh Barnea, he said, "Go up and take possession of the land I have given you." But you rebelled against the command of the LORD your God. You did not trust him or obey him. ²⁴You have been rebellious against the LORD ever since I have known you.

²⁵I lay prostrate before the LORD those forty days and forty nights because the LORD had said he would destroy you. ²⁶I prayed to the LORD and said, "Sovereign LORD, do not destroy your people, your own inheritance that you redeemed by your great power and brought out of Egypt with a mighty hand. ²⁷Remember your servants Abraham, Isaac and Jacob. Overlook the stubbornness of this people, their wickedness and their sin. ²⁸Otherwise, the country from which you brought us will say, 'Because the LORD was not able to take them into the land he had promised them, and because he hated them, he brought them out to put them to death in the wilderness.' ²⁹But they are your people, your inheritance that you brought out by your great power and your outstretched arm."

Tablets Like the First Ones

10 At that time the LORD said to me, "Chisel out two stone tablets like the first ones and come up to me on the mountain. Also make a wooden ark.ᵃ ²I will write on the tablets the words that were on the first tablets, which you broke. Then you are to put them in the ark."

³So I made the ark out of acacia wood and chiseled out two stone tablets like the first ones, and I went up on the mountain with the two tablets in my hands. ⁴The LORD wrote on these tablets what he had written before, the Ten Commandments he had proclaimed to you on the mountain, out of the fire, on the day of the assembly. And the LORD gave them to me. ⁵Then I came back down the mountain and put the tablets in the ark I had made, as the LORD commanded me, and they are there now.

⁶(The Israelites traveled from the wells of Bene Jaakan to Moserah. There Aaron died and was buried, and Eleazar his son succeeded him as priest. ⁷From there they traveled to Gudgodah and on to Jotbathah, a land with streams of water. ⁸At that time the LORD set apart the tribe of Levi to carry the ark of the covenant of the LORD, to stand before the LORD to minister and to pronounce blessings in his name, as they still do today. ⁹That is why the Levites have no share or inheritance among their fellow Israelites; the LORD is their inheritance, as the LORD your God told them.)

¹⁰Now I had stayed on the mountain forty days and forty nights, as I did the first time, and the LORD listened to me at this time also. It was not his will to destroy you. ¹¹"Go," the LORD said to me, "and lead the people on their way, so that they may enter and possess the land I swore to their ancestors to give them."

Fear the LORD

¹²And now, Israel, what does the LORD your God ask of you but to fear the LORD your God, to walk in obedience to him, to love him, to serve the LORD your God with all your heart and with all your soul, ¹³and to observe the LORD's commands and decrees that I am giving you today for your own good?

¹⁴To the LORD your God belong the heavens, even the highest heavens, the earth and everything in it. ¹⁵Yet the LORD set his affection on your ancestors and loved them, and he chose you, their descendants,

---

ᵃ 1 That is, a chest

9:22–24 | Moses catalogs the places where the Israelites had been disobedient to the Lord, from the golden calf at Horeb (Ex. 32:1–10) to the disastrous decisions at Kadesh Barnea (Num. 13–14). He summarizes with these sad words: **You have been rebellious against the LORD ever since I have known you** (Ps. 106:24, 25). Centuries later, the Lord passed over these early examples of rebellion in the words of a forgiving lover: "I remember the devotion of your youth, how as a bride you loved me" (Jer. 2:2).

10:12–22 | This section clarifies the essence of Torah, Yahweh's law for His people. It is commonly alleged that the OT law was something negative—altogether focused on externals rather than the more important issues of the spirit and a poor attempt at achieving salvation through works. But God's amazing grace was evident in OT times, too, as these verses reveal. This is the passage that Micah pointed to when he said, "He has shown you, O mortal, what is good" (Micah 6:8). The words **circumcise your hearts** are repeated in Romans 2:29.

For Reflection

The Goodness of God's Rules • 10:13

James Hatch, beloved professor at Columbia International University, once opened class by leading students in the chorus "God Is So Good." After several stanzas like "He cares for me" and "I love Him so," Hatch added one of his own: "He gives me rules, He gives me rules, He gives me rules. He's so good to me." The students were surprised, but Hatch was right. God has given us His rules for our good; and when we obey them, we're healthier, happier, and holier. Consider the command in Ephesians 4:32 to "be kind and compassionate to one another, forgiving each other." Carrying resentment in our hearts can be like a little pocket of poison that drains our personalities and sours our spirits. But being kind and pleasant can lighten our burdens and brighten our days—not to mention what it does for others. The Creator knows how we function best, and He is an expert on the care of the soul. Obedience not only glorifies Him, it blesses our lives. He gives us rules; He is so good to us.

above all the nations—as it is today. ¹⁶Circumcise your hearts, therefore, and do not be stiff-necked any longer. ¹⁷For the LORD your God is God of gods and Lord of lords, the great God, mighty and awesome, who shows no partiality and accepts no bribes. ¹⁸He defends the cause of the fatherless and the widow, and loves the foreigner residing among you, giving them food and clothing. ¹⁹And you are to love those who are foreigners, for you yourselves were foreigners in Egypt. ²⁰Fear the LORD your God and serve him. Hold fast to him and take your oaths in his name. ²¹He is the one you praise; he is your God, who performed for you those great and awesome wonders you saw with your own eyes. ²²Your ancestors who went down into Egypt were seventy in all, and now the LORD your God has made you as numerous as the stars in the sky.

Love and Obey the LORD

11 Love the LORD your God and keep his requirements, his decrees, his laws and his commands always. ²Remember today that your children were not the ones who saw and experienced the discipline of the LORD your God: his majesty, his mighty hand, his outstretched arm; ³the signs he performed and the things he did in the heart of Egypt, both to Pharaoh king of Egypt and to his whole country; ⁴what he did to the Egyptian army, to its horses and chariots, how he overwhelmed them with the waters of the Red Sea*ᵃ* as they were pursuing you, and how the LORD brought lasting ruin on them. ⁵It was not your children who saw what he did for you in the wilderness until you arrived at this place, ⁶and what he did to Dathan and Abiram, sons of Eliab the Reubenite, when the earth opened its mouth right in the middle of all Israel and swallowed them up with their households, their tents and every living thing that belonged to them. ⁷But it was your own eyes that saw all these great things the LORD has done.

⁸Observe therefore all the commands I am giving you today, so that you may have the strength to go in and take over the land that you are crossing the Jordan to possess, ⁹and so that you may live long in the land the LORD swore to your ancestors to give to them and their descendants, a land flowing with milk and honey. ¹⁰The land you are entering to take over is not like the land of Egypt, from which you have come, where you planted your seed and irrigated it by foot as in a vegetable garden. ¹¹But the land you are crossing the Jordan to take possession of is a land of mountains and valleys that drinks rain from heaven. ¹²It is a land the LORD your God cares for; the eyes of the LORD your God are continually on it from the beginning of the year to its end.

¹³So if you faithfully obey the commands I am giving you today—to love the LORD your God and to serve him with all your heart and with all your soul— ¹⁴then I will send rain on your land in its season, both autumn and

---

ᵃ 4 Or the Sea of Reeds

11:1-7 | The people's firsthand knowledge of what the Lord had done for them in Egypt, in the wilderness, and in destroying **Dathan and Abiram** for their rebellion (Num. 16; Ps. 106:16–18) should have caused them to **love the LORD** and to **keep . . . his commands always**.

11:8-12 | The most obvious and impressive difference between the lands of Canaan and Egypt was in the source of water. **Egypt** was extremely productive for two reasons: (1) The normal flow of the Nile River delivered sufficient water for the daily needs of its populace and for foot-powered irrigation. (2) The Nile's floods renewed the soil and minerals every year. On the other hand, **the land** of Canaan

(which they would cross over **the Jordan to possess**) **drinks rain from heaven** (Lev. 26:4).

11:13-17 | Although Yahweh's promise was, **I will send rain on your land**, all was conditioned on the people's obedience and dedication to the Lord. If the people turned their hearts from the Lord, He might well **shut up the heavens**.

11:14 | The rain actually comes in three seasons (using a modern Western calendar): the **autumn** rain describes the intermittent showers from mid-October through November; the heavier rain comes in December and January; the **spring** rains entail the intermittent showers from February through mid-March (Joel 2:23).

fyi

The Euphrates • 11:24

The Euphrates is one of the great rivers in the world. It flows from the mountains of western Turkey through Syria and continues right through the heart of Iraq, not far from Baghdad. It eventually unites with the Tigris and finally empties into the Persian Gulf. The entirety of the Euphrates River flows through Muslim territory today. In Genesis 15 and Deuteronomy 11, the Lord specified that the Euphrates would be the easternmost border of the Promised Land—a border and a barrier between Israel and her enemies.

spring rains, so that you may gather in your grain, new wine and olive oil. [15] I will provide grass in the fields for your cattle, and you will eat and be satisfied.

[16] Be careful, or you will be enticed to turn away and worship other gods and bow down to them. [17] Then the LORD's anger will burn against you, and he will shut up the heavens so that it will not rain and the ground will yield no produce, and you will soon perish from the good land the LORD is giving you. [18] Fix these words of mine in your hearts and minds; tie them as symbols on your hands and bind them on your foreheads. [19] Teach them to your children, talking about them when you sit at home and when you walk along the road, when you lie down and when you get up. [20] Write them on the doorframes of your houses and on your gates, [21] so that your days and the days of your children may be many in the land the LORD swore to give your ancestors, as many as the days that the heavens are above the earth.

[22] If you carefully observe all these commands I am giving you to follow—to love the LORD your God, to walk in obedience to him and to hold fast to him— [23] then the LORD will drive out all these nations before you, and you will dispossess nations larger and stronger than you. [24] Every place where you set your foot will be yours: Your territory will extend from the desert to Lebanon, and from the Euphrates River to the Mediterranean Sea. [25] No one will be able to stand against you. The LORD your God, as he promised you, will put the terror and fear of you on the whole land, wherever you go.

[26] See, I am setting before you today a blessing and a curse— [27] the blessing if you obey the commands of the LORD your God that I am giving you today; [28] the curse if you disobey the commands of the LORD your God and turn from the way that I command you today by following other gods, which you have not known. [29] When the LORD your God has brought you into the land you are entering to possess, you are to proclaim on Mount Gerizim the blessings, and on Mount Ebal the curses. [30] As you know, these mountains are across the Jordan, westward, toward the setting sun, near the great trees of Moreh, in the territory of those Canaanites living in the Arabah in the vicinity of Gilgal. [31] You are about to cross the Jordan to enter and take possession of the land the LORD your God is giving you. When you have taken it over and are living there, [32] be sure that you obey all the decrees and laws I am setting before you today.

The One Place of Worship

12 These are the decrees and laws you must be careful to follow in the land that the LORD, the God of your ancestors, has given you to possess—as long as you live in the land. [2] Destroy completely all the places on the high mountains, on the hills and under every spreading tree, where the nations you are dispossessing worship their gods. [3] Break down their altars, smash their sacred stones and burn their Asherah poles in the fire; cut down the idols of their gods and wipe out their names from those places.

[4] You must not worship the LORD your God in their way. [5] But you are to seek the place the LORD your God will choose from among all your tribes to put his Name there for his dwelling. To that place you must go; [6] there bring your burnt offerings and sacrifices, your tithes and special gifts, what you have vowed to give and your freewill offerings, and the firstborn of your herds and flocks. [7] There, in the presence of the LORD your God, you and your families shall eat and shall rejoice in everything you have put your hand to, because the LORD your God has blessed you.

11:18-21 | These demands regarding obedience and applied teaching in children's lives repeat the demands in 6:4–9. Not only was repetition an effective means of teaching in the Hebrew Bible, but very important instructions were often delivered in twos for emphasis.
11:26-32 | The Lord instructed Moses to set up a special ceremony on **Mount Gerizim** and **Mount Ebal** to memorialize **a blessing and**

a curse. The mountains are **across the Jordan**, in the Promised Land, so Moses would not be there (26–28; Josh. 8:30–35). This section forms a fitting conclusion to this part of Moses' speech.
12:1-13 | The Israelites were commanded to **destroy** the pagan places of worship to prevent the temptation of idolatry and to preserve the uniqueness of their worship (see note on 12:29–31).

⁸You are not to do as we do here today, everyone doing as they see fit, ⁹since you have not yet reached the resting place and the inheritance the LORD your God is giving you. ¹⁰But you will cross the Jordan and settle in the land the LORD your God is giving you as an inheritance, and he will give you rest from all your enemies around you so that you will live in safety. ¹¹Then to the place the LORD your God will choose as a dwelling for his Name—there you are to bring everything I command you: your burnt offerings and sacrifices, your tithes and special gifts, and all the choice possessions you have vowed to the LORD. ¹²And there rejoice before the LORD your God—you, your sons and daughters, your male and female servants, and the Levites from your towns who have no allotment or inheritance of their own. ¹³Be careful not to sacrifice your burnt offerings anywhere you please. ¹⁴Offer them only at the place the LORD will choose in one of your tribes, and there observe everything I command you.

¹⁵Nevertheless, you may slaughter your animals in any of your towns and eat as much of the meat as you want, as if it were gazelle or deer, according to the blessing the LORD your God gives you. Both the ceremonially unclean and the clean may eat it. ¹⁶But you must not eat the blood; pour it out on the ground like water. ¹⁷You must not eat in your own towns the tithe of your grain and new wine and olive oil, or the firstborn of your herds and flocks, or whatever you have vowed to give, or your freewill offerings or special gifts. ¹⁸Instead, you are to eat them in the presence of the LORD your God at the place the LORD your God will choose—you, your sons and daughters, your male and female servants, and the Levites from your towns—and you are to rejoice before the LORD your God in everything you put your hand to. ¹⁹Be careful not to neglect the Levites as long as you live in your land.

²⁰When the LORD your God has enlarged your territory as he promised you, and you crave meat and say, "I would like some meat," then you may eat as much of it as you want. ²¹If the place where the LORD your God chooses to put his Name is too far away from you, you may slaughter animals from the herds and flocks the LORD has given you, as I have commanded you, and in your own towns you may eat as much of them as you want. ²²Eat them as you would gazelle or deer. Both the ceremonially unclean and the clean may eat. ²³But be sure you do not eat the blood, because the blood is the life, and you must not eat the life with the meat. ²⁴You must not eat the blood; pour it out on the ground like water. ²⁵Do not eat it, so that it may go well with you and your children after you, because you will be doing what is right in the eyes of the LORD.

²⁶But take your consecrated things and whatever you have vowed to give, and go to the place the LORD will choose. ²⁷Present your burnt offerings on the altar of the LORD your God, both the meat and the blood. The blood of your sacrifices must be poured beside the altar of the LORD your God, but you may eat the meat. ²⁸Be careful to obey all these regulations I am giving you, so that it may always go well with you and your children after you, because you will be doing what is good and right in the eyes of the LORD your God.

²⁹The LORD your God will cut off before you the nations you are about to invade and dispossess. But when you have driven them out and settled in their land, ³⁰and after they have been destroyed before you, be careful not to be ensnared by inquiring about their gods, saying, "How do these nations serve their gods? We will do the same." ³¹You must not worship the LORD your God in their way, because in worshiping their gods, they do all kinds of detestable things the LORD hates. They even burn their sons and daughters in the fire as sacrifices to their gods.

³²See that you do all I command you; do not add to it or take away from it.ᵃ

Worshiping Other Gods

13ᵇ If a prophet, or one who foretells by dreams, appears among you and announces to you a sign or wonder, ²and if the sign or wonder spoken of takes place, and the prophet says, "Let us follow other gods" (gods you have not known) "and let us

---

ᵃ 32 In Hebrew texts this verse (12:32) is numbered 13:1.   ᵇ In Hebrew texts 13:1-18 is numbered 13:2-19.

12:14–28 | While the pagan nations in the land of Canaan had many places where they served their gods and offered sacrifices, the Israelites were to have one place—**the place the LORD will choose**—to offer their sacrifices. The Israelites could **slaughter** animals and eat **meat** within their towns, but the prohibition against eating **blood** was valid in all places (Gen. 9:4; Lev. 17:11; Acts 15:20).

12:29–31 | The Hebrew people were not to emulate the religious patterns of the nations they were dispossessing. One of the most repugnant actions of the Canaanites was burning **their sons and daughters in the fire as sacrifices to their gods** (Lev. 18:21; 20:2–5).

13:1–5 | Here is a strong warning concerning a false **prophet** or a **dreamer**. The usual mark of a prophet would be the fulfillment of what was predicted (18:22). However, if the message was one of apostasy, then any accompanying **sign or wonder** should be dismissed. Under Torah, anyone deceiving God's people was to **be put to death**.

worship them," ³you must not listen to the words of that prophet or dreamer. The LORD your God is testing you to find out whether you love him with all your heart and with all your soul. ⁴It is the LORD your God you must follow, and him you must revere. Keep his commands and obey him; serve him and hold fast to him. ⁵That prophet or dreamer must be put to death for inciting rebellion against the LORD your God, who brought you out of Egypt and redeemed you from the land of slavery. That prophet or dreamer tried to turn you from the way the LORD your God commanded you to follow. You must purge the evil from among you.

⁶If your very own brother, or your son or daughter, or the wife you love, or your closest friend secretly entices you, saying, "Let us go and worship other gods" (gods that neither you nor your ancestors have known, ⁷gods of the peoples around you, whether near or far, from one end of the land to the other), ⁸do not yield to them or listen to them. Show them no pity. Do not spare them or shield them. ⁹You must certainly put them to death. Your hand must be the first in putting them to death, and then the hands of all the people. ¹⁰Stone them to death, because they tried to turn you away from the LORD your God, who brought you out of Egypt, out of the land of slavery. ¹¹Then all Israel will hear and be afraid, and no one among you will do such an evil thing again.

¹²If you hear it said about one of the towns the LORD your God is giving you to live in ¹³that troublemakers have arisen among you and have led the people of their town astray, saying, "Let us go and worship other gods" (gods you have not known), ¹⁴then you must inquire, probe and investigate it thoroughly. And if it is true and it has been proved that this detestable thing has been done among you, ¹⁵you must certainly put to the sword all who live in that town. You must destroy it completely,ᵃ both its people and its livestock. ¹⁶You are to gather all the plunder of the town into the middle of the public square and completely burn the town and all its plunder as a whole burnt offering to the LORD your God. That town is to

remain a ruin forever, never to be rebuilt, ¹⁷and none of the condemned thingsᵃ are to be found in your hands. Then the LORD will turn from his fierce anger, will show you mercy, and will have compassion on you. He will increase your numbers, as he promised on oath to your ancestors — ¹⁸because you obey the LORD your God by keeping all his commands that I am giving you today and doing what is right in his eyes.

Clean and Unclean Food

14 You are the children of the LORD your God. Do not cut yourselves or shave the front of your heads for the dead, ²for you are a people holy to the LORD your God. Out of all the peoples on the face of the earth, the LORD has chosen you to be his treasured possession.

³Do not eat any detestable thing. ⁴These are the animals you may eat: the ox, the sheep, the goat, ⁵the deer, the gazelle, the roe deer, the wild goat, the ibex, the antelope and the mountain sheep.ᵇ ⁶You may eat any animal that has a divided hoof and that chews the cud. ⁷However, of those that chew the cud or that have a divided hoof you may not eat the camel, the rabbit or the hyrax. Although they chew the cud, they do not have a divided hoof; they are ceremonially unclean for you. ⁸The pig is also unclean; although it has a divided hoof, it does not chew the cud. You are not to eat their meat or touch their carcasses.

⁹Of all the creatures living in the water, you may eat any that has fins and scales. ¹⁰But anything that does not have fins and scales you may not eat; for you it is unclean.

¹¹You may eat any clean bird. ¹²But these you may not eat: the eagle, the vulture, the black vulture, ¹³the red kite, the black kite, any kind of falcon, ¹⁴any kind of raven, ¹⁵the horned owl, the screech owl, the gull, any kind of hawk, ¹⁶the little owl, the great owl, the white owl, ¹⁷the desert owl, the osprey, the cormorant, ¹⁸the stork, any kind of heron, the hoopoe and the bat.

ᵃ 15, 17 The Hebrew term refers to the irrevocable giving over of things or persons to the LORD, often by totally destroying them.   ᵇ 5 The precise identification of some of the birds and animals in this chapter is uncertain.

13:6–18 | The seduction to worship **other gods** would come from many sources; the most distressing would be from beloved family members, even one's **wife**. Strict punishments were given to those who advocated idolatry. A person who influenced others to **worship other gods** was to be stoned, and that person's death should cause people to **be afraid** and follow God. Similarly, if a town sent people out to other towns advocating other gods, the whole **town** was to be destroyed (Josh. 6:24).

14:1, 2 | The prohibitions against cutting one's self and shaving

the front of the heads for the dead were both likely rooted in pagan customs and therefore unacceptable expressions of mourning for a chosen people who were living for God alone.

14:3–20 | The principal passage on the **animals** the Israelites could **eat** is Leviticus 11. Since Deuteronomy restates the Torah for the second generation, these dietary issues are presented again. All the laws of distinction (clothing, the work week, and diet) had one purpose—to set apart Israel from its neighbors: "Be holy" (Lev. 11:45).

[19] All flying insects are unclean to you; do not eat them. [20] But any winged creature that is clean you may eat.

[21] Do not eat anything you find already dead. You may give it to the foreigner residing in any of your towns, and they may eat it, or you may sell it to any other foreigner. But you are a people holy to the LORD your God.

Do not cook a young goat in its mother's milk.

Tithes

[22] Be sure to set aside a tenth of all that your fields produce each year. [23] Eat the tithe of your grain, new wine and olive oil, and the firstborn of your herds and flocks in the presence of the LORD your God at the place he will choose as a dwelling for his Name, so that you may learn to revere the LORD your God always. [24] But if that place is too distant and you have been blessed by the LORD your God and cannot carry your tithe (because the place where the LORD will choose to put his Name is so far away), [25] then exchange your tithe for silver, and take the silver with you and go to the place the LORD your God will choose. [26] Use the silver to buy whatever you like: cattle, sheep, wine or other fermented drink, or anything you wish. Then you and your household shall eat there in the presence of the LORD your God and rejoice. [27] And do not neglect the Levites living in your towns, for they have no allotment or inheritance of their own.

[28] At the end of every three years, bring all the tithes of that year's produce and store it in your towns, [29] so that the Levites (who have no allotment or inheritance of their own) and the foreigners, the fatherless and the widows who live in your towns may come and eat and be satisfied, and so that the LORD your God may bless you in all the work of your hands.

The Year for Canceling Debts

15 At the end of every seven years you must cancel debts. [2] This is how it is to be done: Every creditor shall cancel any

loan they have made to a fellow Israelite. They shall not require payment from anyone among their own people, because the LORD's time for canceling debts has been proclaimed. [3] You may require payment from a foreigner, but you must cancel any debt your fellow Israelite owes you. [4] However, there need be no poor people among you, for in the land the LORD your God is giving you to possess as your inheritance, he will richly bless you, [5] if only you fully obey the LORD your God and are careful to follow all these commands I am giving you today. [6] For the LORD your God will bless you as he has promised, and you will lend to many nations but will borrow from none. You will rule over many nations but none will rule over you.

[7] If anyone is poor among your fellow Israelites in any of the towns of the land the LORD your God is giving you, do not be hardhearted or tightfisted toward them. [8] Rather, be openhanded and freely lend them whatever they need. [9] Be careful not to harbor this wicked thought: "The seventh year, the year for canceling debts, is near," so that you do not show ill will toward the needy among your fellow Israelites and give them nothing. They may then appeal to the LORD against you, and you will be found guilty of sin. [10] Give generously to them and do so without a grudging heart; then because of this the LORD your God will bless you in all

---

14:21 | The prohibition against eating anything they found **already dead** was probably intended to prevent defilement from consuming blood. Cooking **a young goat in its mother's milk** (Ex. 23:19; 34:26) was a grotesque, inhumane act. Sacrifice of animals is not pleasant in any setting, but excesses like those of the Canaanites were strictly prohibited.

14:23 | Part of Israel's sacred worship included the enjoyment of their festivals and offerings with the Lord (7:7).

14:28, 29 | Torah prescribed three tithes (for the first two, see Lev. 27:30–32; Num. 18:21–32). This third tithe, the benevolence tithe, was collected **every three years** for **the foreigners, the fatherless and the widows**. The Torah demanded that the poor be cared for by God's people, a point echoed in James 1:27. Jesus went so far as

to equate His followers' treatment of the disadvantaged with their treatment of Him (Matt. 25:35–40).

15:6 | A wealthy nation should be known for lending instead of borrowing (28:12; Prov. 22:7). To **borrow** is to forfeit financial and relational power, making the borrower more vulnerable to ruin and to sins such as greed and envy.

15:7–11 | Being **openhanded** signifies the open heart of generosity (Prov. 31:20). In a fallen world, the plight of the **poor** is an ongoing reality that will ultimately be corrected in the Messiah's millennial reign, but for now, it is up to believers to address the reality of poverty (Mark 14:7; Gal. 2:10). God's law presented generosity to the poor as an accepted responsibility; it was not an option (14:29; 15:1–6; 24:12, 13, 19).

your work and in everything you put your hand to. [11]There will always be poor people in the land. Therefore I command you to be openhanded toward your fellow Israelites who are poor and needy in your land.

Freeing Servants

[12]If any of your people—Hebrew men or women—sell themselves to you and serve you six years, in the seventh year you must let them go free. [13]And when you release them, do not send them away empty-handed. [14]Supply them liberally from your flock, your threshing floor and your winepress. Give to them as the LORD your God has blessed you. [15]Remember that you were slaves in Egypt and the LORD your God redeemed you. That is why I give you this command today.

[16]But if your servant says to you, "I do not want to leave you," because he loves you and your family and is well off with you, [17]then take an awl and push it through his earlobe into the door, and he will become your servant for life. Do the same for your female servant.

[18]Do not consider it a hardship to set your servant free, because their service to you these six years has been worth twice as much as that of a hired hand. And the LORD your God will bless you in everything you do.

The Firstborn Animals

[19]Set apart for the LORD your God every firstborn male of your herds and flocks. Do not put the firstborn of your cows to work, and do not shear the firstborn of your sheep. [20]Each year you and your family are to eat them in the presence of the LORD your God at the place he will choose. [21]If an animal has a defect, is lame or blind, or has any serious flaw, you must not sacrifice it to the LORD your God. [22]You are to eat it in your own towns. Both the ceremonially unclean and the clean may eat it, as if it were gazelle or deer. [23]But you must not eat the blood; pour it out on the ground like water.

The Passover

16 Observe the month of Aviv and celebrate the Passover of the LORD your God, because in the month of Aviv he brought you out of Egypt by night. [2]Sacrifice as the Passover to the LORD your God an animal from your flock or herd at the place the LORD will choose as a dwelling for his Name. [3]Do not eat it with bread made with yeast, but for seven days eat unleavened bread, the bread of affliction, because you left Egypt in haste—so that all the days of your life you may remember the time of your departure from Egypt. [4]Let no yeast be found in your possession in all your land for seven days. Do not let any of the meat you sacrifice on the evening of the first day remain until morning.

[5]You must not sacrifice the Passover in any town the LORD your God gives you [6]except in the place he will choose as a dwelling for his Name. There you must sacrifice the Passover in the evening, when the sun goes down, on the anniversary[a] of your departure from Egypt. [7]Roast it and eat it at the place the LORD your God will choose. Then in the morning return to your tents. [8]For six days eat unleavened bread and on the seventh day hold an assembly to the LORD your God and do no work.

The Festival of Weeks

[9]Count off seven weeks from the time you begin to put the sickle to the standing grain. [10]Then celebrate the Festival of Weeks to the LORD your God by giving a freewill offering in proportion to the blessings the LORD your God has given you. [11]And rejoice before the LORD your God at the place he will choose as a dwelling for his Name—you, your sons and daughters, your male and female servants, the Levites in your towns, and the foreigners, the fatherless and the widows living among you. [12]Remember that you were slaves in Egypt, and follow carefully these decrees.

The Festival of Tabernacles

[13]Celebrate the Festival of Tabernacles for seven days after you have gathered the produce of your threshing floor and your winepress. [14]Be joyful at your festival—you, your sons and daughters, your male and female

---

[a] 6 Or *down, at the time of day*

16:1–17 | For more on the **Passover, Festival of Weeks, Festival of Tabernacles,** and other Hebrew celebrations, see Leviticus 23 and Numbers 28–29.
16:10, 17 | The principle of proportionate return—every person should give as he or she is able, as **the LORD your God has blessed you** (2 Cor. 8:12)—was embodied in the Festival of Weeks and the Festival of Tabernacles as individuals brought a **freewill offering**.
16:11, 14 | Celebrations of thanksgiving were not to be observed alone; the Israelites were to gather with their own families at these festivals and also reach out to **the Levites . . . the foreigners, the fatherless and the widows** who lived within their borders so that all could rejoice in what the Lord had done.

servants, and the Levites, the foreigners, the fatherless and the widows who live in your towns. [15]For seven days celebrate the festival to the LORD your God at the place the LORD will choose. For the LORD your God will bless you in all your harvest and in all the work of your hands, and your joy will be complete.

[16]Three times a year all your men must appear before the LORD your God at the place he will choose: at the Festival of Unleavened Bread, the Festival of Weeks and the Festival of Tabernacles. No one should appear before the LORD empty-handed: [17]Each of you must bring a gift in proportion to the way the LORD your God has blessed you.

Judges

[18]Appoint judges and officials for each of your tribes in every town the LORD your God is giving you, and they shall judge the people fairly. [19]Do not pervert justice or show partiality. Do not accept a bribe, for a bribe blinds the eyes of the wise and twists the words of the innocent. [20]Follow justice and justice alone, so that you may live and possess the land the LORD your God is giving you.

Worshiping Other Gods

[21]Do not set up any wooden Asherah pole beside the altar you build to the LORD your God, [22]and do not erect a sacred stone, for these the LORD your God hates.

17 Do not sacrifice to the LORD your God an ox or a sheep that has any defect or flaw in it, for that would be detestable to him. [2]If a man or woman living among you in one of the towns the LORD gives you is found doing evil in the eyes of the LORD your God in violation of his covenant, [3]and contrary to my command has worshiped other gods, bowing down to them or to the sun or the moon or the stars in the sky, [4]and this has been brought to your attention, then you must investigate it thoroughly. If it is true and it has been proved that this detestable thing has been done in Israel, [5]take the man or woman who has done this evil deed

to your city gate and stone that person to death. [6]On the testimony of two or three witnesses a person is to be put to death, but no one is to be put to death on the testimony of only one witness. [7]The hands of the witnesses must be the first in putting that person to death, and then the hands of all the people. You must purge the evil from among you.

Law Courts

[8]If cases come before your courts that are too difficult for you to judge—whether bloodshed, lawsuits or assaults—take them to the place the LORD your God will choose. [9]Go to the Levitical priests and to the judge who is in office at that time. Inquire of them and they will give you the verdict. [10]You must act according to the decisions they give you at the place the LORD will choose. Be careful to do everything they instruct you to do. [11]Act according to whatever they teach you and the decisions they give you. Do not turn aside from what they tell you, to the right or to the left. [12]Anyone who shows contempt for the judge or for the priest who stands ministering there to the LORD your God is to be put to death. You must purge the evil from Israel. [13]All the people will hear and be afraid, and will not be contemptuous again.

The King

[14]When you enter the land the LORD your God is giving you and have taken possession of it and settled in it, and you say, "Let us set a king over us like all the nations around us," [15]be sure to appoint over you a king the LORD your God chooses. He must be from among your fellow Israelites. Do not place a foreigner over you, one who is not an Israelite. [16]The king, moreover, must not acquire great numbers of horses for himself or make the people return to Egypt to get more of them, for the LORD has told you, "You are not to go back that way again." [17]He must not take many wives, or his heart will be led astray. He must not accumulate large amounts of silver and gold.

17:1 | The Hebrew word rendered **detestable** describes utter revulsion—that which may cause stomachache and vomiting.

17:2–5 | Anyone who **worshiped other gods** deserved capital punishment because the person's act threatened Israel's very existence. Worshiping the **sun or the moon or the stars** was forbidden (4:19) because it honored creation rather than their loving Creator.

17:6, 7 | Execution could take place only after the accused was proven guilty by a thorough investigation and the word of **two or three witnesses** (19:15), who would be **the first** in the execution of the guilty party. If a single **witness** lied, no one would be

able to prove or disprove it (Num. 35:30; Matt. 18:16; John 8:17; Heb. 10:28).

17:14–20 | God provided principles for kings for the time when Israel would become a monarchy (1 Sam. 10:19). His law allowed for the normal blessings that would accrue to **a king**, but He had specifically warned against personally motivated accumulation of riches. Solomon's lust for more and more wealth led him to flagrantly disobey the Lord's prohibitions against accumulating large **numbers of horses** or **many wives** or **large amounts of silver and gold** (1 Kgs. 4:26; Eccl. 5–6).

Historically Speaking
The Tribe of Levi • 18:1–8

Each family within the tribe of Levi originally had different responsibilities regarding the tabernacle (Num. 3—4). The Kohathites were divided into two: (1) descendants of Aaron and (2) those who did not directly descend from his firstborn son (Josh. 21:4, 5). Only descendants of Aaron's firstborn son were allowed to serve as priests (Num. 3:10). The rest of the tribe was designated as Levites. So actual priests were a minority in the tribe of Levi (2 Chron. 31:4).

[18] When he takes the throne of his kingdom, he is to write for himself on a scroll a copy of this law, taken from that of the Levitical priests. [19] It is to be with him, and he is to read it all the days of his life so that he may learn to revere the LORD his God and follow carefully all the words of this law and these decrees [20] and not consider himself better than his fellow Israelites and turn from the law to the right or to the left. Then he and his descendants will reign a long time over his kingdom in Israel.

Offerings for Priests and Levites

18 The Levitical priests—indeed, the whole tribe of Levi—are to have no allotment or inheritance with Israel. They shall live on the food offerings presented to the LORD, for that is their inheritance. [2] They shall have no inheritance among their fellow Israelites; the LORD is their inheritance, as he promised them.

[3] This is the share due the priests from the people who sacrifice a bull or a sheep: the shoulder, the internal organs and the meat from the head. [4] You are to give them the firstfruits of your grain, new wine and olive oil, and the first wool from the shearing of your sheep, [5] for the LORD your God has chosen them and their descendants out of all your tribes to stand and minister in the LORD's name always.

[6] If a Levite moves from one of your towns anywhere in Israel where he is living, and comes in all earnestness to the place the LORD will choose, [7] he may minister in the name of the LORD his God like all his fellow Levites who serve there in the presence of the LORD. [8] He is to share equally in their benefits, even though he has received money from the sale of family possessions.

Occult Practices

[9] When you enter the land the LORD your God is giving you, do not learn to imitate the detestable ways of the nations there. [10] Let no one be found among you who sacrifices their son or daughter in the fire, who practices divination or sorcery, interprets omens, engages in witchcraft, [11] or casts spells, or who is a medium or spiritist or who consults the dead. [12] Anyone who does these things is detestable to the LORD; because of these same detestable practices the LORD your God will drive out those nations before you. [13] You must be blameless before the LORD your God.

The Prophet

[14] The nations you will dispossess listen to those who practice sorcery or divination. But as for you, the LORD your God has not permitted you to do so. [15] The LORD your God will raise up for you a prophet like me from among you, from your fellow Israelites. You must listen to him. [16] For this is what you asked of the LORD your God at Horeb on the day of the assembly when you said, "Let us not hear the voice of the LORD our God nor see this great fire anymore, or we will die." [17] The LORD said to me: "What they say is good. [18] I will raise up for them a prophet like you from among their fellow Israelites, and I will put my words in his mouth. He will tell them everything I command him. [19] I myself will call to account anyone who does not listen to my words that the prophet speaks in my name. [20] But a prophet who presumes to speak in my name anything I have not commanded, or a prophet who speaks in the name of other gods, is to be put to death." [21] You may say to yourselves, "How can we know when a message has not been

---

17:18–20 | In the days of the kings, people did not have personal copies of the Scriptures. Instead, they would listen to the priests read Scripture. Here, however, God says that a king should **write for himself on a scroll a copy of this law** and then **read it** every day so that he will **not consider himself better than his fellow Israelites**. God wants believers to know, understand, and apply His Word (Acts 17:10–11; 1 Pet. 2:5).
18:1–8 | Three families made up the **tribe of Levi**: the Gershonites, the Kohathites, and the Merarites.
18:9–14 | The Canaanites—heavily involved in the occult—practiced **witchcraft**, interpreted **omens**, consulted **the dead**, and

practiced **divination** and **sorcery**, in addition to child sacrifice. The Israelites were moving into a dark land and needed to be careful to destroy the people and so avoid their wickedness.
18:15–18 | **The LORD your God will raise up for you a prophet like me** speaks of the coming of the Lord (Matt. 21:11; Luke 1:76; Acts 3:22). There are three standard prophetic offices of the Coming One—Prophet, Priest, and King—along with two more expectations: the Sage and the Suffering Servant. Each of these five ideals was a subject of intense interest in the century before the coming of Christ—texts in the Dead Sea Scrolls show how lively the issues were.

spoken by the LORD?" [22] If what a prophet proclaims in the name of the LORD does not take place or come true, that is a message the LORD has not spoken. That prophet has spoken presumptuously, so do not be alarmed.

Cities of Refuge

19 When the LORD your God has destroyed the nations whose land he is giving you, and when you have driven them out and settled in their towns and houses, [2] then set aside for yourselves three cities in the land the LORD your God is giving you to possess. [3] Determine the distances involved and divide into three parts the land the LORD your God is giving you as an inheritance, so that a person who kills someone may flee for refuge to one of these cities.

[4] This is the rule concerning anyone who kills a person and flees there for safety—anyone who kills a neighbor unintentionally, without malice aforethought. [5] For instance, a man may go into the forest with his neighbor to cut wood, and as he swings his ax to fell a tree, the head may fly off and hit his neighbor and kill him. That man may flee to one of these cities and save his life. [6] Otherwise, the avenger of blood might pursue him in a rage, overtake him if the distance is too great, and kill him even though he is not deserving of death, since he did it to his neighbor without malice aforethought. [7] This is why I command you to set aside for yourselves three cities.

[8] If the LORD your God enlarges your territory, as he promised on oath to your ancestors, and gives you the whole land he promised them, [9] because you carefully follow all these laws I command you today—to love the LORD your God and to walk always in obedience to him—then you are to set aside three more cities. [10] Do this so that innocent blood will not be shed in your land, which the LORD your God is giving you as your inheritance, and so that you will not be guilty of bloodshed.

[11] But if out of hate someone lies in wait, assaults and kills a neighbor, and then flees to one of these cities, [12] the killer shall be sent for by the town elders, be brought back from the city, and be handed over to the avenger of blood to die. [13] Show no pity. You must purge from Israel the guilt of shedding innocent blood, so that it may go well with you.

[14] Do not move your neighbor's boundary stone set up by your predecessors in the inheritance you receive in the land the LORD your God is giving you to possess.

Witnesses

[15] One witness is not enough to convict anyone accused of any crime or offense they may have committed. A matter must be established by the testimony of two or three witnesses.

[16] If a malicious witness takes the stand to accuse someone of a crime, [17] the two people involved in the dispute must stand in the presence of the LORD before the priests and the judges who are in office at the time. [18] The judges must make a thorough investigation, and if the witness proves to be a liar, giving false testimony against a fellow Israelite, [19] then do to the false witness as that witness intended to do to the other party. You must purge the evil from among you. [20] The rest of the people will hear of this and be afraid, and never again will such an evil thing be done among you. [21] Show no pity: life for life, eye for eye, tooth for tooth, hand for hand, foot for foot.

Going to War

20 When you go to war against your enemies and see horses and chariots and an army greater than yours, do not be

---

18:20 | When a **prophet** made a prediction in the name of the Lord that did not come true, the prophet was **put to death**. The failure of the prophecy demonstrated the vacuous nature of the "prophet's" credentials (Jer. 2:8; 14:14, 15; 29:9). Even today, Christians should avoid making predictions about the future because the Bible says, "No one knows" (Matt. 24:34–44). If God's people focus on mysteries they were never intended to unravel, they will neglect the Master's ongoing work in this day and time. Those Satan cannot dissuade, he will distract.

19:1–10 | God commanded the Israelites to set up **cities** where they could be safe from the **avenger**—the person appointed by the family of one who had been slain. These cities were spread out so no one would be more than a day's journey from one (Num. 35:9–28; Josh. 20:1–9).

19:14 | **Do not move your neighbor's boundary stone** is the type of law that was found in numerous law codes in the ancient Near

East (Prov. 22:28; Hosea 5:10). Despite their distinctiveness from pagan neighbors, Israel shared certain "standard values," rooted in ancient times.

19:15–19 | With **two or three witnesses**, the judgment in a matter would be **established** (17:6; John 8:17; 1 Tim. 5:19; Heb. 10:28). This principle also applies in church discipline (Matt. 18:16). A further provision against false testimony was that those who lied would face the same punishment that the falsely accused person had faced.

19:21 | The Latin legal phrase *lex talionis*—law of retaliation or retribution—is based on the OT teaching in this verse: **life for life, eye for eye, tooth for tooth, hand for hand, foot for foot** (Ex. 21:23–25; Lev. 24:17–20). That the punishment should fit the crime was a rule for judges, and a major point of it was to limit retribution. Punishment for a crime should not go beyond the amount of the victim's loss. Jesus expounded on this law in Matthew 5:38, 39.

afraid of them, because the LORD your God, who brought you up out of Egypt, will be with you. ²When you are about to go into battle, the priest shall come forward and address the army. ³He shall say: "Hear, Israel: Today you are going into battle against your enemies. Do not be fainthearted or afraid; do not panic or be terrified by them. ⁴For the LORD your God is the one who goes with you to fight for you against your enemies to give you victory."

⁵The officers shall say to the army: "Has anyone built a new house and not yet begun to live in it? Let him go home, or he may die in battle and someone else may begin to live in it. ⁶Has anyone planted a vineyard and not begun to enjoy it? Let him go home, or he may die in battle and someone else enjoy it. ⁷Has anyone become pledged to a woman and not married her? Let him go home, or he may die in battle and someone else marry her." ⁸Then the officers shall add, "Is anyone afraid or fainthearted? Let him go home so that his fellow soldiers will not become disheartened too." ⁹When the officers have finished speaking to the army, they shall appoint commanders over it.

¹⁰When you march up to attack a city, make its people an offer of peace. ¹¹If they accept and open their gates, all the people in it shall be subject to forced labor and shall work for you. ¹²If they refuse to make peace and they engage you in battle, lay siege to that city. ¹³When the LORD your God delivers it into your hand, put to the sword all the men in it. ¹⁴As for the women, the children, the livestock and everything else in the city, you may take these as plunder for yourselves. And you may use the plunder the LORD your God gives you from your enemies. ¹⁵This is how you are to treat all the cities that are at a distance from you and do not belong to the nations nearby.

¹⁶However, in the cities of the nations the LORD your God is giving you as an inheritance, do not leave alive anything that breathes. ¹⁷Completely destroy[a] them—the Hittites, Amorites, Canaanites, Perizzites, Hivites and Jebusites—as the LORD your God has commanded you. ¹⁸Otherwise, they will teach you to follow all the detestable things they do in worshiping their gods, and you will sin against the LORD your God.

¹⁹When you lay siege to a city for a long time, fighting against it to capture it, do not destroy its trees by putting an ax to them, because you can eat their fruit. Do not cut them down. Are the trees people, that you should besiege them?[b] ²⁰However, you may cut down trees that you know are not fruit trees and use them to build siege works until the city at war with you falls.

Atonement for an Unsolved Murder

21 If someone is found slain, lying in a field in the land the LORD your God is giving you to possess, and it is not known who the killer was, ²your elders and judges shall go out and measure the distance from the body to the neighboring towns. ³Then the elders of the town nearest the body shall take a heifer that has never been worked and has never worn a yoke ⁴and lead it down to a valley that has not been plowed or planted and where there is a flowing stream. There in the valley they are to break the heifer's neck. ⁵The Levitical priests shall step forward, for the LORD your God has chosen them to minister and to pronounce blessings in the name of the LORD and to decide all cases of dispute and assault. ⁶Then all the elders of the town nearest the body shall wash their hands over the heifer whose neck was broken in the valley, ⁷and they shall declare: "Our hands did not shed this blood, nor did our eyes see it done. ⁸Accept this atonement for your people Israel, whom you have redeemed, LORD, and do not hold your people guilty of the blood of an innocent person." Then the bloodshed will be atoned for, ⁹and you will have purged from yourselves the guilt of shedding innocent blood, since you have done what is right in the eyes of the LORD.

Marrying a Captive Woman

¹⁰When you go to war against your enemies and the LORD your God delivers them into your hands and you take captives, ¹¹if you notice among the captives a beautiful

---

[a] 17 The Hebrew term refers to the irrevocable giving over of things or persons to the LORD, often by totally destroying them.   [b] 19 Or down to use in the siege, for the fruit trees are for the benefit of people.

20:1-4 | The chariot was the tank of the ancient Near East. To **see horses and chariots** would be most disheartening for the Hebrews going into battle; they needed to know they had greater strength on their side than all the chariots of the world! God had already shown Himself faithful in bringing the nation **out of Egypt**; His presence would be with them when they were confronted by threatening armies (Ex. 15:3; Josh. 11:6). **20:10-18** | The Israelites were told they should **completely destroy**

the Canaanite cities because of their wickedness, but they were initially to offer **peace** for cities outside of Canaan (Num. 31:7; Josh. 8:2; 2 Sam. 10:19). **21:1-9** | This is a law about an unsolved murder. To **break the heifer's neck** symbolized that the crime deserved capital punishment. The **elders** of the town near the victim were to **wash their hands over the heifer**, symbolizing their innocence in the matter.

woman and are attracted to her, you may take her as your wife. ¹²Bring her into your home and have her shave her head, trim her nails ¹³and put aside the clothes she was wearing when captured. After she has lived in your house and mourned her father and mother for a full month, then you may go to her and be her husband and she shall be your wife. ¹⁴If you are not pleased with her, let her go wherever she wishes. You must not sell her or treat her as a slave, since you have dishonored her.

The Right of the Firstborn

¹⁵If a man has two wives, and he loves one but not the other, and both bear him sons but the firstborn is the son of the wife he does not love, ¹⁶when he wills his property to his sons, he must not give the rights of the firstborn to the son of the wife he loves in preference to his actual firstborn, the son of the wife he does not love. ¹⁷He must acknowledge the son of his unloved wife as the firstborn by giving him a double share of all he has. That son is the first sign of his father's strength. The right of the firstborn belongs to him.

A Rebellious Son

¹⁸If someone has a stubborn and rebellious son who does not obey his father and mother and will not listen to them when they discipline him, ¹⁹his father and mother shall take hold of him and bring him to the elders at the gate of his town. ²⁰They shall say to the elders, "This son of ours is stubborn and rebellious. He will not obey us. He is a glutton and a drunkard." ²¹Then all the men of his town are to stone him to death. You must purge the evil from among you. All Israel will hear of it and be afraid.

Various Laws

²²If someone guilty of a capital offense is put to death and their body is exposed on a pole, ²³you must not leave the body hanging on the pole overnight. Be sure to bury it that same day, because anyone who is hung on a pole is under God's curse. You must not desecrate the land the LORD your God is giving you as an inheritance.

22 If you see your fellow Israelite's ox or sheep straying, do not ignore it but be sure to take it back to its owner. ²If they do not live near you or if you do not know who owns it, take it home with you and keep it until they come looking for it. Then give it back. ³Do the same if you find their donkey or cloak or anything else they have lost. Do not ignore it.

⁴If you see your fellow Israelite's donkey or ox fallen on the road, do not ignore it. Help the owner get it to its feet.

⁵A woman must not wear men's clothing, nor a man wear women's clothing, for the LORD your God detests anyone who does this.

⁶If you come across a bird's nest beside the road, either in a tree or on the ground, and the mother is sitting on the young or on the eggs, do not take the mother with the young. ⁷You may take the young, but be sure to let the mother go, so that it may go well with you and you may have a long life.

⁸When you build a new house, make a parapet around your roof so that you may not bring the guilt of bloodshed on your house if someone falls from the roof.

⁹Do not plant two kinds of seed in your vineyard; if you do, not only the crops you plant but also the fruit of the vineyard will be defiled.ᵃ

¹⁰Do not plow with an ox and a donkey yoked together.

¹¹Do not wear clothes of wool and linen woven together.

¹²Make tassels on the four corners of the cloak you wear.

ᵃ 9 Or be forfeited to the sanctuary

21:10-14 | To become a part of Yahweh's covenant community, a woman had to make a complete break with her former culture—symbolized by shaving her **head**, trimming her **nails**, changing her **clothes**, and mourning for her parents (Ps. 45:10).

21:15–17 | In the case of a man with **two wives**, the standard policy for the rights of the **actual firstborn** son was to be maintained, irrespective of the level of affection the husband had for one wife over the other (Num. 18:15).

21:22, 23 | A **capital offense** was punishable by being **exposed on a pole**, but that was after the offender had already been executed. The pole was not the instrument of execution, but hanging from one was a gesture of shame before the community, to show that the condemned had fallen under God's curse (judgment for sin). Paul refers to this in Galatians 3:13.

21:23 | An unburied corpse was a reproach to God and caused the land to be defiled. In the arid regions in OT times, a person was buried the very day they died. Even the worst of criminals was afforded a burial with some dignity.

22:1–4 | Laws about things such as caring for a **fellow Israelite's ox** reinforced concepts of community responsibility—a part of loving one's "neighbor" (Lev. 19:17, 18).

22:5 | Men and women were commanded not to **wear** the **clothing** of the opposite sex.

22:9–11 | These prohibitions against planting **two kinds of seed** together, yoking together **an ox and a donkey** for plowing, and mixing **wool and linen** were a part of the Laws of Distinction—just like the dietary laws and the workweek (Shabbat) laws. In all that they did, the Israelites had to follow separate standards because they were the Lord's people.

Historically Speaking — Jewish Betrothal Customs • 22:23, 24

Although the Hebrew betrothal (or espousal) corresponds to our modern period of engagement, betrothal was much more permanent than our arrangement. It was marked by a gift or dowry for the father of the bride, along with other gifts for relatives of the bride. The "writings of betrothal" included obligations and agreements such as the amount of the dowry. From the moment of engagement, everyone treated the woman as though she were already married. This was taken so seriously that if a woman's prospective husband died during this time, she was considered a widow, and any breach of faithfulness was considered adultery. After a betrothal, up to 10 or 12 months could pass before the wedding feast, which itself might last a week.

Marriage Violations

[13] If a man takes a wife and, after sleeping with her, dislikes her [14] and slanders her and gives her a bad name, saying, "I married this woman, but when I approached her, I did not find proof of her virginity," [15] then the young woman's father and mother shall bring to the town elders at the gate proof that she was a virgin. [16] Her father will say to the elders, "I gave my daughter in marriage to this man, but he dislikes her. [17] Now he has slandered her and said, 'I did not find your daughter to be a virgin.' But here is the proof of my daughter's virginity." Then her parents shall display the cloth before the elders of the town, [18] and the elders shall take the man and punish him. [19] They shall fine him a hundred shekels[a] of silver and give them to the young woman's father, because this man has given an Israelite virgin a bad name. She shall continue to be his wife; he must not divorce her as long as he lives.

[20] If, however, the charge is true and no proof of the young woman's virginity can be found, [21] she shall be brought to the door of her father's house and there the men of her town shall stone her to death. She has done an outrageous thing in Israel by being promiscuous while still in her father's house. You must purge the evil from among you.

[22] If a man is found sleeping with another man's wife, both the man who slept with her and the woman must die. You must purge the evil from Israel.

[23] If a man happens to meet in a town a virgin pledged to be married and he sleeps with her, [24] you shall take both of them to the gate of that town and stone them to death—the young woman because she was in a town and did not scream for help, and the man because he violated another man's wife. You must purge the evil from among you.

[25] But if out in the country a man happens to meet a young woman pledged to be married and rapes her, only the man who has done this shall die. [26] Do nothing to the woman; she has committed no sin deserving death. This case is like that of someone who attacks and murders a neighbor, [27] for the man found the young woman out in the country, and though the betrothed woman screamed, there was no one to rescue her.

[28] If a man happens to meet a virgin who is not pledged to be married and rapes her and they are discovered, [29] he shall pay her father fifty shekels[b] of silver. He must marry the young woman, for he has violated her. He can never divorce her as long as he lives.

[30] A man is not to marry his father's wife; he must not dishonor his father's bed.[c]

Exclusion From the Assembly

23[d] No one who has been emasculated by crushing or cutting may enter the assembly of the LORD.

[2] No one born of a forbidden marriage[e] nor any of their descendants may enter the assembly of the LORD, not even in the tenth generation.

[3] No Ammonite or Moabite or any of their descendants may enter the assembly of the LORD, not even in the tenth generation. [4] For they did not come to meet you with bread and water on your way when you came out of Egypt, and they hired Balaam son of Beor from Pethor in Aram Naharaim[f] to pronounce a curse on you. [5] However, the LORD your God would not listen to Balaam but turned the curse into a blessing for you, because the LORD your God loves you. [6] Do not seek a treaty of friendship with them as long as you live.

[7] Do not despise an Edomite, for the Edomites are related to you. Do not despise an Egyptian, because you resided as foreigners in their country. [8] The third generation of

---

a 19 That is, about 2 1/2 pounds or about 1.2 kilograms   b 29 That is, about 1 1/4 pounds or about 575 grams   c 30 In Hebrew texts this verse (22:30) is numbered 23:1.   d In Hebrew texts 23:1-25 is numbered 23:2-26.   e 2 Or one of illegitimate birth   f 4 That is, Northwest Mesopotamia

---

22:23, 24 | Because Joseph was engaged to Mary when he discovered she was pregnant (Matt. 1:18, 19), he would have been justified in making a public issue out of her apparent infidelity, according to Torah (Lev. 19:20–22). The law said to **stone . . . to death** both the woman and the man who violated her.

> ## Tough Questions
> ### Who was excluded from the assembly of the Lord? • 23:1–8
>
> The "assembly of the LORD" referred to the people of Israel, who made up the congregation of Yahweh's people (5:22; 9:10; 18:16). Those outside the congregation could be people of faith but were excluded from full participation in its religious life, analogous to one who is "unclean." King Uzziah was considered ritually unclean for the final 17 years of his life (2 Chron. 26), even though he was the reigning monarch!
>
> The exclusion of eunuchs ("one who has been emasculated") marks a clear ban against sexual mutilation in Israel. The exclusion of a person of illegitimate birth reinforced the integrity of the family, something of huge importance in biblical times. Two people groups were excluded as well: the Ammonite and the Moabite (Num. 22–24, 25, 31). On the other hand, friendliness was extended to the Edomite and the Egyptian. For the Ammonite and the Moabite to be excluded from full participation in the assembly of Israel is based on the infamous story of Balak and Balaam (Num. 22—25; 31).
>
> Here is the amazing thing: these people groups are mentioned here *because some would become faithful followers of Yahweh*, such as Ruth the Moabite (see the Book of Ruth), and the people of Israel needed to know how to receive them as fellow believers!

children born to them may enter the assembly of the LORD.

Uncleanness in the Camp

⁹When you are encamped against your enemies, keep away from everything impure. ¹⁰If one of your men is unclean because of a nocturnal emission, he is to go outside the camp and stay there. ¹¹But as evening approaches he is to wash himself, and at sunset he may return to the camp.

¹²Designate a place outside the camp where you can go to relieve yourself. ¹³As part of your equipment have something to dig with, and when you relieve yourself, dig a hole and cover up your excrement. ¹⁴For the LORD your God moves about in your camp to protect you and to deliver your enemies to you. Your camp must be holy, so that he will not see among you anything indecent and turn away from you.

Miscellaneous Laws

¹⁵If a slave has taken refuge with you, do not hand them over to their master. ¹⁶Let them live among you wherever they like and in whatever town they choose. Do not oppress them.

¹⁷No Israelite man or woman is to become a shrine prostitute. ¹⁸You must not bring the earnings of a female prostitute or of a male prostitute[a] into the house of the LORD your God to pay any vow, because the LORD your God detests them both.

¹⁹Do not charge a fellow Israelite interest, whether on money or food or anything else that may earn interest. ²⁰You may charge a foreigner interest, but not a fellow Israelite, so that the LORD your God may bless you in everything you put your hand to in the land you are entering to possess.

²¹If you make a vow to the LORD your God, do not be slow to pay it, for the LORD your God will certainly demand it of you and you will be guilty of sin. ²²But if you refrain from making a vow, you will not be guilty. ²³Whatever your lips utter you must be sure to do, because you made your vow freely to the LORD your God with your own mouth.

²⁴If you enter your neighbor's vineyard, you may eat all the grapes you want, but do not put any in your basket. ²⁵If you enter your neighbor's grainfield, you may pick kernels with your hands, but you must not put a sickle to their standing grain.

24 If a man marries a woman who becomes displeasing to him because he finds something indecent about her, and he writes her a certificate of divorce, gives it to her and sends her from his house, ²and if after she leaves his house she becomes the wife of another man, ³and her second

---

a 18 Hebrew *of a dog*

---

husband dislikes her and writes her a certificate of divorce, gives it to her and sends her from his house, or if he dies, [4]then her first husband, who divorced her, is not allowed to marry her again after she has been defiled. That would be detestable in the eyes of the LORD. Do not bring sin upon the land the LORD your God is giving you as an inheritance.

[5]If a man has recently married, he must not be sent to war or have any other duty laid on him. For one year he is to be free to stay at home and bring happiness to the wife he has married.

[6]Do not take a pair of millstones — not even the upper one — as security for a debt, because that would be taking a person's livelihood as security.

[7]If someone is caught kidnapping a fellow Israelite and treating or selling them as a slave, the kidnapper must die. You must purge the evil from among you.

[8]In cases of defiling skin diseases,[a] be very careful to do exactly as the Levitical priests instruct you. You must follow carefully what I have commanded them. [9]Remember what the LORD your God did to Miriam along the way after you came out of Egypt.

[10]When you make a loan of any kind to your neighbor, do not go into their house to get what is offered to you as a pledge. [11]Stay outside and let the neighbor to whom you are making the loan bring the pledge out to you. [12]If the neighbor is poor, do not go to sleep with their pledge in your possession. [13]Return their cloak by sunset so that your neighbor may sleep in it. Then they will thank you, and it will be regarded as a righteous act in the sight of the LORD your God.

[14]Do not take advantage of a hired worker who is poor and needy, whether that worker is a fellow Israelite or a foreigner residing in one of your towns. [15]Pay them their wages each day before sunset, because they are poor and are counting on it. Otherwise they may cry to the LORD against you, and you will be guilty of sin.

[16]Parents are not to be put to death for their children, nor children put to death for their parents; each will die for their own sin.

[17]Do not deprive the foreigner or the fatherless of justice, or take the cloak of the widow as a pledge. [18]Remember that you were slaves in Egypt and the LORD your God redeemed you from there. That is why I command you to do this.

[19]When you are harvesting in your field and you overlook a sheaf, do not go back to get it. Leave it for the foreigner, the fatherless and the widow, so that the LORD your God may bless you in all the work of your hands. [20]When you beat the olives from your trees, do not go over the branches a second time. Leave what remains for the foreigner, the fatherless and the widow. [21]When you harvest the grapes in your vineyard, do not go over the vines again. Leave what remains for the foreigner, the fatherless and the widow. [22]Remember that you were slaves in Egypt. That is why I command you to do this.

25 When people have a dispute, they are to take it to court and the judges will decide the case, acquitting the innocent and condemning the guilty. [2]If the guilty person deserves to be beaten, the judge shall make them lie down and have them flogged in his presence with the number of lashes the crime deserves, [3]but the judge must not impose more than forty lashes. If the guilty party is flogged more than that, your fellow Israelite will be degraded in your eyes.

[4]Do not muzzle an ox while it is treading out the grain.

[5]If brothers are living together and one of them dies without a son, his widow must not marry outside the family. Her husband's brother shall take her and marry her and fulfill the duty of a brother-in-law to her. [6]The first son she bears shall carry on the name of the dead brother so that his name will not be blotted out from Israel.

[7]However, if a man does not want to marry his brother's wife, she shall go to the elders at the town gate and say, "My husband's brother refuses to carry on his brother's name in Israel. He will not fulfill

---

[a] 8 The Hebrew word for *defiling skin diseases*, traditionally translated "leprosy," was used for various diseases affecting the skin.

24:8 | The **priests** had responsibility for controlling **defiling skin diseases**. They functioned as a sort of center for disease control (Lev. 13–14).
24:14, 15 | The behavior condemned here is exactly what happens today when people pursue wealth but disdain honest labor in favor of ruthless power. The practice of paying wages late or bilking the worker of his wages, and thus getting rich at the laborer's expense, was also common in those times (15:7, 8; Lev. 19:13).

24:19–22 | This law to leave some crops for the **foreigner, the fatherless and the widow** (Lev. 23:22) kept the needy from having to beg and allowed them to still work for their food. The Lord's commands to care for the poor are tied to 10:18, 19.
25:5–10 | The law of family redemption was shared by numerous cultures in the ancient Near East. Yahweh, who is rich in mercy, included it as a gift to hurting people (Gen. 38:9; Matt. 22:2; Mark 12:19; Luke 20:28). When a young woman lost her husband, her future was bleak at best.

the duty of a brother-in-law to me." [8]Then the elders of his town shall summon him and talk to him. If he persists in saying, "I do not want to marry her," [9]his brother's widow shall go up to him in the presence of the elders, take off one of his sandals, spit in his face and say, "This is what is done to the man who will not build up his brother's family line." [10]That man's line shall be known in Israel as The Family of the Unsandaled.

[11]If two men are fighting and the wife of one of them comes to rescue her husband from his assailant, and she reaches out and seizes him by his private parts, [12]you shall cut off her hand. Show her no pity.

[13]Do not have two differing weights in your bag — one heavy, one light. [14]Do not have two differing measures in your house — one large, one small. [15]You must have accurate and honest weights and measures, so that you may live long in the land the LORD your God is giving you. [16]For the LORD your God detests anyone who does these things, anyone who deals dishonestly.

[17]Remember what the Amalekites did to you along the way when you came out of Egypt. [18]When you were weary and worn out, they met you on your journey and attacked all who were lagging behind; they had no fear of God. [19]When the LORD your God gives you rest from all the enemies around you in the land he is giving you to possess as an inheritance, you shall blot out the name of Amalek from under heaven. Do not forget!

Firstfruits and Tithes

26 When you have entered the land the LORD your God is giving you as an inheritance and have taken possession of it and settled in it, [2]take some of the firstfruits of all that you produce from the soil of the land the LORD your God is giving you and put them in a basket. Then go to the place the LORD your God will choose as a dwelling for his Name [3]and say to the priest in office at the time, "I declare today to the LORD your God that I have come to the land the LORD swore to our ancestors to give us." [4]The priest shall take the basket from your

fyi **Israel's Bitter Enemy • 25:17–19**

In the days of Moses and Joshua, the Amalekites attacked the unarmed, unprepared Israelites as they passed through the Sinai desert (Ex. 17:14). The Lord told Israel to remember this atrocity and blot out every remembrance of them under heaven. Years later, it was in a battle with the Amalekites that Saul sinned against the command of Yahweh and spared King Agag's life (1 Sam. 15). David defeated the Amalekites (2 Sam. 1:1), but they were not completely wiped out until the days of Hezekiah, 300 years later (1 Chron. 4:41–43).

hands and set it down in front of the altar of the LORD your God. [5]Then you shall declare before the LORD your God: "My father was a wandering Aramean, and he went down into Egypt with a few people and lived there and became a great nation, powerful and numerous. [6]But the Egyptians mistreated us and made us suffer, subjecting us to harsh labor. [7]Then we cried out to the LORD, the God of our ancestors, and the LORD heard our voice and saw our misery, toil and oppression. [8]So the LORD brought us out of Egypt with a mighty hand and an outstretched arm, with great terror and with signs and wonders. [9]He brought us to this place and gave us this land, a land flowing with milk and honey; [10]and now I bring the firstfruits of the soil that you, LORD, have given me." Place the basket before the LORD your God and bow down before him. [11]Then you and the Levites and the foreigners residing among you shall rejoice in all the good things the LORD your God has given to you and your household.

[12]When you have finished setting aside a tenth of all your produce in the third year, the year of the tithe, you shall give it to the Levite, the foreigner, the fatherless and the widow, so that they may eat in your towns and be satisfied. [13]Then say to the LORD your God: "I have removed from my house the sacred portion and have given it to the Levite, the foreigner, the fatherless and the widow, according to all you commanded. I have not turned aside from your commands nor have I forgotten any of them.

25:17-19 | Amalek was the grandson of Esau, and the **Amalekites** were bitter enemies of Israel.
26:1-3 | Yahweh commanded His people to make a special **firstfruits** offering in gratitude for the Lord's faithfulness to His word. With their gifts, the people were to say, **I have come to the land the LORD swore to our ancestors to give us.** To give the first **of all that** they produced **from the soil of the land** was an act of faith because no one

knew how much more would be harvested (Ex. 22:29; Num. 18:13).
26:5 | The **Aramean** referred to here is Jacob. Jacob and his family were all from near Harran in ancient Aram (Gen. 12:1–3; 24:1–10; Josh. 24:1–3). Famine marked the perilous early years of **wandering** that Jacob's family experienced in Canaan, which prompted the journey to Egypt. There the small family became **a great nation, powerful and numerous.**

fyi   The Land of Milk and Honey • 26:6–11

The words in this passage are cited almost verbatim in the Passover *Haggadah*, the libretto for the celebration of the Passover. These are the great works of Yahweh—He brought His people "out of Egypt" and "to this place," to "a land flowing with milk and honey." This description of Canaan occurs numerous times in the Books of Torah (6:3; 11:9; 26:15; 27:3; 31:20; Ex. 3:8, 17; 13:5; 33:3; Num. 14:8; 16:13, 14).

Milk speaks of flocks and herds; the land will support the sheep and goats of the people. In Bible times, milk was associated not with dairy cows but with dairy goats. Managed beehives were not kept in biblical times, but the people would have discovered the hives—and the honey—within Canaan.

All in all, the phrase "a land flowing with milk and honey" meant that Canaan would be able to support the people of Israel with adequate habitat for grazing sheep and goats as well as arable land on which to raise crops and plant orchards.

¹⁴I have not eaten any of the sacred portion while I was in mourning, nor have I removed any of it while I was unclean, nor have I offered any of it to the dead. I have obeyed the LORD my God; I have done everything you commanded me. ¹⁵Look down from heaven, your holy dwelling place, and bless your people Israel and the land you have given us as you promised on oath to our ancestors, a land flowing with milk and honey."

Follow the LORD's Commands

¹⁶The LORD your God commands you this day to follow these decrees and laws; carefully observe them with all your heart and with all your soul. ¹⁷You have declared this day that the LORD is your God and that you will walk in obedience to him, that you will keep his decrees, commands and laws— that you will listen to him. ¹⁸And the LORD has declared this day that you are his people, his treasured possession as he promised, and that you are to keep all his commands. ¹⁹He has declared that he will set you in praise, fame and honor high above all the nations he has made and that you will be a people holy to the LORD your God, as he promised.

The Altar on Mount Ebal

27 Moses and the elders of Israel commanded the people: "Keep all these commands that I give you today. ²When you have crossed the Jordan into the land the LORD your God is giving you, set up some large stones and coat them with plaster. ³Write on them all the words of this law when you have crossed over to enter the land the LORD your God is giving you, a land flowing with milk and honey, just as the LORD, the God of your ancestors, promised you. ⁴And when you have crossed the Jordan, set up these stones on Mount Ebal, as I command you today, and coat them with plaster. ⁵Build there an altar to the LORD your God, an altar of stones. Do not use any iron tool on them. ⁶Build the altar of the LORD your God with fieldstones and offer burnt offerings on it to the LORD your God. ⁷Sacrifice fellowship offerings there, eating them and rejoicing in the presence of the LORD your God. ⁸And you shall write very clearly all the words of this law on these stones you have set up."

Curses From Mount Ebal

⁹Then Moses and the Levitical priests said to all Israel, "Be silent, Israel, and listen! You have now become the people of the LORD your God. ¹⁰Obey the LORD your God and follow his commands and decrees that I give you today."

¹¹On the same day Moses commanded the people:

¹²When you have crossed the Jordan, these tribes shall stand on Mount Gerizim to bless the people: Simeon, Levi, Judah, Issachar, Joseph and Benjamin. ¹³And these tribes shall stand on Mount Ebal to

---

26:16–19 | God obligated Himself to be Israel's God and to make her **his treasured possession**, exalted **high above all the nations** (28:1; Ex. 19:5; Mal. 3:17); her responsibility was to **keep his . . . commands**. Generations of Israelites forfeited this right through disobedience and rebellion, but the Lord would raise up a generation of faithful Israelites, **a people holy to the LORD**, who would enjoy His grace in a golden age of blessing (Isa. 60–62): the Millennium. **27:1–8** | It was a practice in Egypt to **set up . . . large stones and coat them with plaster** then write laws on them. The phrase **all the words of this law** refers to the Book of Deuteronomy as a whole. These written stones would commemorate the faithfulness of

the LORD, the God of Israel's **ancestors** (1:11, 21; 4:1; 6:3; 12:1; 27:3). The stones were to be **set up . . . on Mount Ebal**, at the base of which lay the city of Shechem, the place where the Lord first appeared to Abraham and where Abraham built his first altar to the Lord (Gen. 12:6, 7).
27:11–13 | Moses divided the 12 tribes in half and had them stand respectively on **Mount Gerizim** and **Mount Ebal**. Those on Gerizim read the blessings of the law, and those on Ebal read the curses. These two mountains are in such proximity that they form an acoustical environment perfect for a communal reading such as this (11:29).

Tough Questions

Are Christians, like the people of Israel, promised to prosper if they obey and cursed if they do not? • 27:1—28:14

Deuteronomy 27 and 28 present a long list of curses on those who disbelieve and disobey God's Word and a long list of blessings for those who trust and obey. Jesus echoed this when He talked about the wise and the foolish builders (Matt. 7:24–27). In the terms of the treaty the Lord brought to Israel, the Hebrew people were promised that everything they did would be blessed and multiplied. They would never need to borrow from anyone—if they kept God's laws (28:1–14).

Promises such as these are not repeated in the NT. God has vowed to bless His children, but under the New Covenant, blessings are more spiritual than physical (Eph. 1:3). So NT believers are told that while they may experience a life of sacrifice and persecution, they will have the grace to be content with food and clothing alone (1 Tim. 6:8) and the grace to give away to others what they have been given (2 Cor. 8:9–14). Yet in addition to the grace to give, God will grace His beloved with the ability to enjoy His good and perfect gifts (1 Tim. 6:17).

To live a good life with bad doctrine is difficult. When we understand what the Bible says, we can live out the level of godliness our heavenly Father expects and experience the spiritual blessings of salvation, peace, victory, comfort, and strength for daily needs, even in troubled times.

pronounce curses: Reuben, Gad, Asher, Zebulun, Dan and Naphtali.

¹⁴ The Levites shall recite to all the people of Israel in a loud voice:

¹⁵ "Cursed is anyone who makes an idol—a thing detestable to the LORD, the work of skilled hands—and sets it up in secret."

Then all the people shall say, "Amen!"

¹⁶ "Cursed is anyone who dishonors their father or mother."

Then all the people shall say, "Amen!"

¹⁷ "Cursed is anyone who moves their neighbor's boundary stone."

Then all the people shall say, "Amen!"

¹⁸ "Cursed is anyone who leads the blind astray on the road."

Then all the people shall say, "Amen!"

¹⁹ "Cursed is anyone who withholds justice from the foreigner, the fatherless or the widow."

Then all the people shall say, "Amen!"

²⁰ "Cursed is anyone who sleeps with his father's wife, for he dishonors his father's bed."

Then all the people shall say, "Amen!"

²¹ "Cursed is anyone who has sexual relations with any animal."

Then all the people shall say, "Amen!"

²² "Cursed is anyone who sleeps with his sister, the daughter of his father or the daughter of his mother."

Then all the people shall say, "Amen!"

²³ "Cursed is anyone who sleeps with his mother-in-law."

Then all the people shall say, "Amen!"

²⁴ "Cursed is anyone who kills their neighbor secretly."

Then all the people shall say, "Amen!"

²⁵ "Cursed is anyone who accepts a bribe to kill an innocent person."

Then all the people shall say, "Amen!"

²⁶ "Cursed is anyone who does not uphold the words of this law by carrying them out."

Then all the people shall say, "Amen!"

Blessings for Obedience

28 If you fully obey the LORD your God and carefully follow all his commands I give you today, the LORD your God will set you high above all the nations on earth. ² All these blessings will come on you and

---

27:12, 13 | The meaning of this moment was visually reinforced by the location. **Mount Gerizim** is usually green with the growth of plants—trees and grasses. **Mount Ebal** typically looks barren. To read the blessings from the green mountain and cursings from the barren hillside would have deeply impressed upon the people that everyone has the opportunity to choose between life and death—and they should choose life.

27:14–26 | Note that the people of Israel needed to **say "Amen!"** to the 12 curses, but there is no record that the

same was true of the blessings. Affirming blessings is easy; God wanted His people to agree with the curses so that the seriousness of sin's consequences would register in their hearts (Dan. 9:11).

28:1 | Being shown the ways of righteousness and then choosing those ways would set Israel apart from **all the nations on earth** (Ex. 15:26). Israel's responsibility was to magnify the character of God as a light to the Gentiles (Isa. 49:6). God always intended for salvation to extend to the ends of the earth.

accompany you if you obey the Lord your God:

³You will be blessed in the city and blessed in the country.
⁴The fruit of your womb will be blessed, and the crops of your land and the young of your livestock—the calves of your herds and the lambs of your flocks.
⁵Your basket and your kneading trough will be blessed.
⁶You will be blessed when you come in and blessed when you go out.

⁷The Lord will grant that the enemies who rise up against you will be defeated before you. They will come at you from one direction but flee from you in seven.
⁸The Lord will send a blessing on your barns and on everything you put your hand to. The Lord your God will bless you in the land he is giving you.
⁹The Lord will establish you as his holy people, as he promised you on oath, if you keep the commands of the Lord your God and walk in obedience to him. ¹⁰Then all the peoples on earth will see that you are called by the name of the Lord, and they will fear you. ¹¹The Lord will grant you abundant prosperity—in the fruit of your womb, the young of your livestock and the crops of your ground—in the land he swore to your ancestors to give you.
¹²The Lord will open the heavens, the storehouse of his bounty, to send rain on your land in season and to bless all the work of your hands. You will lend to many nations but will borrow from none. ¹³The Lord will make you the head, not the tail. If you pay attention to the commands of the Lord your God that I give you this day and carefully follow them, you will always be at the top, never at the bottom. ¹⁴Do not turn aside from any of the commands I give you today, to the right or to the left, following other gods and serving them.

Curses for Disobedience

¹⁵However, if you do not obey the Lord your God and do not carefully follow all his commands and decrees I am giving you today, all these curses will come on you and overtake you:

¹⁶You will be cursed in the city and cursed in the country.
¹⁷Your basket and your kneading trough will be cursed.
¹⁸The fruit of your womb will be cursed, and the crops of your land, and the calves of your herds and the lambs of your flocks.
¹⁹You will be cursed when you come in and cursed when you go out.

²⁰The Lord will send on you curses, confusion and rebuke in everything you put your hand to, until you are destroyed and come to sudden ruin because of the evil you have done in forsaking him.ᵃ ²¹The Lord will plague you with diseases until he has destroyed you from the land you are entering to possess. ²²The Lord will strike you with wasting disease, with fever and inflammation, with scorching heat and drought, with blight and mildew, which will plague you until you perish. ²³The sky over your head will be bronze, the ground beneath you iron. ²⁴The Lord will turn the rain of your country into dust and powder; it will come down from the skies until you are destroyed.
²⁵The Lord will cause you to be defeated before your enemies. You will come at them from one direction but flee from them in seven, and you will become a thing of horror to all the kingdoms on earth. ²⁶Your carcasses will be food for all the birds and the wild animals, and there will be no one to frighten them away. ²⁷The Lord will afflict you with the boils of Egypt and with tumors, festering sores and the itch, from which you cannot be cured. ²⁸The Lord will afflict you with madness, blindness and confusion of mind. ²⁹At midday you will grope about like a blind person in the dark. You will be unsuccessful in everything you do; day after day you will be oppressed and robbed, with no one to rescue you.

ᵃ 20 Hebrew me

28:2–14 | Israel would experience blessings in three areas if they would **keep the commands of the Lord . . . and walk in obedience to him:** (1) military success and financial prosperity; (2) prosperity in farming and family life; (3) as a testimony to **all the peoples on earth.**
28:15–19 | The pattern of these verses (**However . . . cursed**) is to prophesy the negatives of the positive blessings of 28:2–14. All that was promised for good in the first list now becomes a

threat in the second list (Josh. 23:15; Mal. 2:2).
28:20 | Setting aside God's revelation is like a fog that rolls in from the ocean and silently overtakes a fishing village: **confusion** gradually occupies every corner of a person's life, producing arbitrary decisions and pointless actions (Isa. 65:14).
28:27–42 | One penalty for disobedience was that the plagues God visited upon Egypt would be visited upon Israel (28:59–61), including the painful **boils** (28:21; Ex. 9:9), **the dark**, and **locusts.**

30 You will be pledged to be married to a woman, but another will take her and rape her. You will build a house, but you will not live in it. You will plant a vineyard, but you will not even begin to enjoy its fruit. 31 Your ox will be slaughtered before your eyes, but you will eat none of it. Your donkey will be forcibly taken from you and will not be returned. Your sheep will be given to your enemies, and no one will rescue them. 32 Your sons and daughters will be given to another nation, and you will wear out your eyes watching for them day after day, powerless to lift a hand. 33 A people that you do not know will eat what your land and labor produce, and you will have nothing but cruel oppression all your days. 34 The sights you see will drive you mad. 35 The LORD will afflict your knees and legs with painful boils that cannot be cured, spreading from the soles of your feet to the top of your head.

36 The LORD will drive you and the king you set over you to a nation unknown to you or your ancestors. There you will worship other gods, gods of wood and stone. 37 You will become a thing of horror, a byword and an object of ridicule among all the peoples where the LORD will drive you.

38 You will sow much seed in the field but you will harvest little, because locusts will devour it. 39 You will plant vineyards and cultivate them but you will not drink the wine or gather the grapes, because worms will eat them. 40 You will have olive trees throughout your country but you will not use the oil, because the olives will drop off. 41 You will have sons and daughters but you will not keep them, because they will go into captivity. 42 Swarms of locusts will take over all your trees and the crops of your land.

43 The foreigners who reside among you will rise above you higher and higher, but you will sink lower and lower. 44 They will lend to you, but you will not lend to them. They will be the head, but you will be the tail.

45 All these curses will come on you. They will pursue you and overtake you until you are destroyed, because you did not obey the LORD your God and observe the commands and decrees he gave you. 46 They will be a sign and a wonder to you and your

descendants forever. 47 Because you did not serve the LORD your God joyfully and gladly in the time of prosperity, 48 therefore in hunger and thirst, in nakedness and dire poverty, you will serve the enemies the LORD sends against you. He will put an iron yoke on your neck until he has destroyed you.

49 The LORD will bring a nation against you from far away, from the ends of the earth, like an eagle swooping down, a nation whose language you will not understand, 50 a fierce-looking nation without respect for the old or pity for the young. 51 They will devour the young of your livestock and the crops of your land until you are destroyed. They will leave you no grain, new wine or olive oil, nor any calves of your herds or lambs of your flocks until you are ruined. 52 They will lay siege to all the cities throughout your land until the high fortified walls in which you trust fall down. They will besiege all the cities throughout the land the LORD your God is giving you.

53 Because of the suffering your enemy will inflict on you during the siege, you will eat the fruit of the womb, the flesh of the sons and daughters the LORD your God has given you. 54 Even the most gentle and sensitive man among you will have no compassion on his own brother or the wife he loves or his surviving children, 55 and he will not give to one of them any of the flesh of his children that he is eating. It will be all he has left because of the suffering your enemy will inflict on you during the siege of all your cities. 56 The most gentle and sensitive woman among you—so sensitive and gentle that she would not venture to touch the ground with the sole of her foot—will begrudge the husband she loves and her own son or daughter 57 the afterbirth from her womb and the children she bears. For in her dire need she intends to eat them secretly because of the suffering your enemy will inflict on you during the siege of your cities.

58 If you do not carefully follow all the words of this law, which are written in this book, and do not revere this glorious and awesome name—the LORD your God—59 the LORD will send fearful plagues on you and your descendants, harsh and prolonged

---

28:36, 37 | The horrors of God's judgments in these curses are unrelenting, with "typical blessings" being inverted with absurd results. Instead of leaving a pagan nation like Egypt for the freedom to worship Yahweh in a new land, the Israelites would be taken captive to an unknown nation so thoroughly pagan that they would be a thing of horror and an object of ridicule to the people there. 28:43, 44 | God protected the Israelites from the disasters that fell on Egypt. The reverse would be true in this judgment, for foreigners would profit at Israel's expense, becoming the leader (head; 28:13). 28:47–68 | The two worst curses would be that of a future siege when the LORD will bring a nation against Israel from far away (28:49–57) and that of the Lord's threat to scatter Israel among all nations (28:58–68). The attacking nation would be like an eagle swooping down—powerful, brutal, destructive, merciless, and thorough.

Historically Speaking
The Displaced Jew •
28:64

In the classic musical *Fiddler on the Roof*, the poor Jewish milkman Tevye is burdened with poverty and is trying to maintain traditions while coping with oppression from the Jew-hating Russians. At one point, he cries out to God, "I know, I know, we are Your chosen people. But, once in a while, can't You choose someone else?"

Tevye is a picture of the quintessential displaced Jew—one of many who are on the "flow chart" of Jewish people between "then" and "tomorrow." Tevye's lifetime preceded the founding of the state of Israel. Moses foretold that the land of Israel would be conquered and carried into slavery. As it turned out, the first conquest was by Assyria (722 BC), the second by Babylon (586 BC), and the third by Rome (AD 70). It was also prophesied that the Jews would one day return to their homeland, the land of Israel. The culmination of this return was Israel's proclamation of statehood in May 1948 (Isa. 11:11–16; Jer. 25:11; Hosea 3:4, 5; Luke 21:23, 24).

disasters, and severe and lingering illnesses. 60 He will bring on you all the diseases of Egypt that you dreaded, and they will cling to you. 61 The LORD will also bring on you every kind of sickness and disaster not recorded in this Book of the Law, until you are destroyed. 62 You who were as numerous as the stars in the sky will be left but few in number, because you did not obey the LORD your God. 63 Just as it pleased the LORD to make you prosper and increase in number, so it will please him to ruin and destroy you. You will be uprooted from the land you are entering to possess.

64 Then the LORD will scatter you among all nations, from one end of the earth to the other. There you will worship other gods— gods of wood and stone, which neither you nor your ancestors have known. 65 Among those nations you will find no repose, no resting place for the sole of your foot. There the LORD will give you an anxious mind, eyes weary with longing, and a despairing heart. 66 You will live in constant suspense, filled with dread both night and day, never sure of your life. 67 In the morning you will say, "If only it were evening!" and in the evening,

"If only it were morning!" —because of the terror that will fill your hearts and the sights that your eyes will see. 68 The LORD will send you back in ships to Egypt on a journey I said you should never make again. There you will offer yourselves for sale to your enemies as male and female slaves, but no one will buy you.

Renewal of the Covenant

29 *a* These are the terms of the covenant the LORD commanded Moses to make with the Israelites in Moab, in addition to the covenant he had made with them at Horeb.

2 Moses summoned all the Israelites and said to them:

Your eyes have seen all that the LORD did in Egypt to Pharaoh, to all his officials and to all his land. 3 With your own eyes you saw those great trials, those signs and great wonders. 4 But to this day the LORD has not given you a mind that understands or eyes that see or ears that hear. 5 Yet the LORD says, "During the forty years that I led you through the wilderness, your clothes did not wear out, nor did the sandals on your feet. 6 You ate no bread and drank no wine or other fermented drink. I did this so that you might know that I am the LORD your God."

7 When you reached this place, Sihon king of Heshbon and Og king of Bashan came out to fight against us, but we defeated them. 8 We took their land and gave it as an inheritance to the Reubenites, the Gadites and the half-tribe of Manasseh.

9 Carefully follow the terms of this covenant, so that you may prosper in everything you do. 10 All of you are standing today in the presence of the LORD your God—your leaders and chief men, your elders and officials, and all the other men of Israel, 11 together with your children and your wives, and the foreigners living in your camps who chop your wood and carry your water. 12 You are standing here in order to enter into a covenant with the LORD your God, a covenant the LORD is making with you this day and sealing with an oath, 13 to confirm you this

---

a In Hebrew texts 29:1 is numbered 28:69, and 29:2-29 is numbered 29:1-28.

28:58–68 | Israel's dual role of strength and light was dependent on one thing: adherence to the laws of God. Failure to **revere** the Lord's **glorious and awesome name** and manifest His character on the earth in this way would result in the loss of both blessings. Sadly, this happened to the nation multiple times (Dan. 9:12). **29:2–9** | Not everything taken in with physical eyes and ears is also perceived by the heart (Ezek. 12:2; Matt. 13:9). This is why

some people can "study" the Word of God but not **see** the Word of God. The Lord is the One who gives spiritual sight (Acts 28:26, 27; Rom. 11:8; Eph. 4:18). **29:10–13** | The words **all of you are standing today** imply a formal ceremony. The stress is on the present, meaning that the Israelites were recommitting themselves to the Mosaic Covenant, not to a new covenant.